D0443548

PUBLIC ADMINISTRATION
The People's Business

PUBLIC ADMINISTRATION
The People's Business

J. D. Williams

University of Utah

LITTLE, BROWN AND COMPANY

Boston
Toronto

Library of Congress Catalog Card No. 79-87607

First Printing

Published simultaneously in Canada
by Little, Brown & Company (Canada) Limited

Printed in the United States of America

Acknowledgments

The author gratefully acknowledges permission to reprint and reproduce material from the following sources.

Texts:

Robert E. Cushman, excerpts from letter to J. D. Williams (December 2, 1948). Reprinted by permission of Robert F. Cushman.

David Halberstam, *The Best and the Brightest,* pp. 61–62, 157, 209, 348–349, 353. Copyright © 1969, 1971, 1972 by David Halberstam. Reprinted by permission of Random House, Inc.

Robert Townsend, *Up the Organization,* pp. 91, 116, 142. Copyright © 1970 by Robert Townsend. Reprinted by permission of Alfred A. Knopf, Inc. and Michael Joseph Ltd.

The Washington Post (October 1, 1978), pp. A1 and A16. © 1978 The Washington Post. Reprinted by permission.

Photographs:

Part I: Arthur Grace, Stock, Boston.
Part II: The Picture Cube, Terry McKoy.
Part III: Nicholas Sapieha, Stock, Boston.
Part IV: Owen Franken, Stock, Boston.
Part V: John Hey, Stock, Boston.

To Bea Williams and Little, Brown
who waited far longer than
any wife or publisher
should have to wait.

Preface

Two underlying assumptions pervade this book: first, that there is as much drama and significance in the administrative process as in the legislative and judicial processes of government; and second, that the best answer to lifeless governmental bureaucracies lies in giving life and meaning to the human beings who make or break them.

This text was born of the desire to capture for students the intrinsic excitement and importance of public administration: consider the mayor who realizes he is no longer in charge when his sanitation workers are on strike; the land management division chief who has run a tight ship internally but now finds himself beleaguered by ranchers, miners, timbermen, bikers, and backpackers who dog him at every turn; and leaders who never run out of challenges, from a collapsed economy to runaway inflation and from the Nikita Khrushchevs to the oil barons of OPEC.

Episodes like these permeate what I have to say about informal organization, leadership, the manager's political role, public relations and budgeting, and highlight the analysis in each chapter.

The other strong emphasis in the book is the humanistic view of administration which is unabashedly advanced here. Governments are *human* entities doing good or bad things to their own *employees* and to the *people* they are supposed to serve. Part I asserts the primacy of *people* in administration, analyzes their needs and prescribes a management style that strives for continuing reciprocation between human needs and agency needs. I make a bold attempt to suggest some principles of formal organization and ways to employ informal organization. Part II, the Tasks of Management, gives a behavioral view of leadership; concrete suggestions for the management of agency politics; and alternative approaches to decision making, coordination within the bureaucracy, communication, and reorganization. Part III, Fiscal Aspects of Management, compares four approaches to budgeting — from object to zero-base budgets. Part IV, Personnel Administration, discusses the tensions among patronage demands, merit systems, and collective bargaining and the significant injection of the judiciary into public personnel administration. In the concluding part, Administrative Ethics, the ethical dilemmas confronting people in government are canvassed, and suggestions made for cloning the ethical public servant.

Acknowledgments

This book would never have been written without the early encouragement and guidance of Dean Oakley Gordon, University of Utah psychologist, the consistent help of Dr. Frank Shaw, and the moral support of Curtis Spencer of the U.S. Civil Service Commission's regional training staff in Denver. The early subsidies provided by Dr. Louis Goodman made it possible to have the first chapters typed and were much appreciated.

I'm constantly reminded of my dependence upon the magnificent staff at the Marriott Library of the University of Utah — millionaires, all of them, if they were paid by the request! A partial list has to include the reference librarians Mary Jane Hair, Eloise McQuown, and Chezuki Ishimatsu; and the documents librarians Frieda McCoy, Pam Horan, Val O'Reilly, and Ron Bitton.

One of the greatest debts of gratitude is owed the principal typist of the book, Terrie D. Buhler. So much more than a master of the keyboard, Terrie has been a constant nudger and source of inspiration. Other valued helpers with the manuscript have been Margaret Mackay, Jessie Diamond, Marjorie Coulam, Karen Donahue, Jeannette Hanson, Carla Francis, and Michelle Hugie, along with others.

I've been fortunate to have a truly distinguished panel of critics carve me up. Not much is left after George Frederickson, Robert Golembiewski, George Graham, Paul Katz (of the Office of Personnel Management), Paul Van Riper, Wallace Sayre, Allen Schick, Lloyd Short, Albert Somit, and Frank Sorauf have finished. It would have been a much better book if I could have satisfied all of them.

Improvements over the early drafts are largely due to the penetrating review by Professor Dennis Dresang of the University of Wisconsin. Would that every author might have a critic as careful and insightful as he.

I hope that somewhere the editors I have known at Little, Brown, Donald R. Hammonds, John H. Andrews, Richard L. Boyer, Gregory T. Franklin, and Will Ethridge earn the reward their patience deserves.

In the final stages of the project have appeared two new angels at Little, Brown — book editor Cynthia Chapin and copyeditor Frank Kirk. I simply refuse to tell all they've done to make this book publishable . . . other than to say thanks.

Some special appreciation must also be extended to Christine Breen of the College Division and Philip Howrigan, field representative for Little, Brown, who provided so much encouragement and push.

May I also acknowledge the contributions Wendell Lawther has made in the teacher's manual.

Two people must be singled out for the godfather and godmother roles at this christening — Little, Brown's senior editor in the West, Milton H. Johnson, Jr., and my author-wife, Barbara (Bea) Williams. Milt caught the early vision of the book, and never let it die in my own eyes. Bea, while finishing thirty-five children's books in the interim, found time to provide the requisite prod for me to keep going. To Milt and Bea, my inadequate but unremitting thanks.

To the Student

I feel a sense of both appreciation and responsibility for the triangular partnership we now enter — learner, teacher, and author. How keenly I want this book to hold up its end of the deal — to sustain your interest, be accurate, and be stimulating enough to lead many of you into careers in the public service.

Public Administration was started in an era when much of the writing in public administration had to be conceived in dullsville. Frankly, I never could understand why the publications in this field had to be "ether in print." That sad fact provided the impetus for the question that initiated this book: "J.D., can you write a college text in public administration that will catch both the vitality of the field and the interest of students who come to study it?"

There is no denying that lots of dreary things go on in government, as in any bureaucracy: getting out social security checks, sorting the mail, making entries in the ledgers at the city courts office, and filing state tax returns. But that's not where the action is.

In this text, you will see some of the drama in the constructive things agencies can do to make people whole and productive, the promising alternatives that exist to old-fashioned authoritarian leadership, the fine art of managing agency politics, how budgets can be put together to clarify choices for administrators, what governments are doing with affirmative action to become the model employers in this country, and how to clone the ethical public servant. In addition, you will see public administration at its worst: how New York craft unions veto the state legislature on minority hiring, the endless ways bureaucracies make people sick, the sending of a suicide note by the FBI to Martin Luther King, and the failure of an Illinois Department of Mine Safety to prevent the explosion of the Centralia Mine which killed 111 miners.

The excitement in public administration lies there, in the clash between public interest and self interest, and I mean to capture it and share it with you in as stimulating a way as I can.

Public administration is fundamentally the business of people — the people who work in the public sector and need to be turned on to their callings, and the people they serve who deserve responsive and responsible government.

The central bias of the book, then, is humanism. People are primary for me, and thus the early emphasis in chapters 2 and 6 on what makes them tick, and how conflicts between agency needs and employee needs can be reciprocally resolved.

So, frankly, not only do I want to attract you to the public service, but also I would give anything to influence the kind of manager you become — one who will recognize that your most priceless asset is the men and women who work with you, and who acts toward them with full recognition that administration is the people's business.

J. D. Williams

Contents

Part IV
PERSONNEL ADMINISTRATION

Chapter 15
Patronage, Merit, or Muscle?   **395**

Chapter 16
What's a Person Worth These Days?   **423**

Part I
PEOPLE AND THE ORGANIZATION

Chapter 1
Public Administration: The People's Business

FROM CANDIDATE TO PUBLIC OFFICE

It is late November of an all-important election year. No small reason for its importance was your victory three weeks ago in the contest for the governorship of the state. Seven weeks from now you will be taking the oath of office and assuming the burdens of office.

The administration now coming to an end has had hardening of the arteries for the last five of its twelve years in office. Sitting contentedly on his motto that "The tax rate is the measure of statesmanship," the outgoing governor watched the first teachers' strike in the history of the state take place, a steady decline in manufacturing jobs outside the defense industries, and the buildup of a $100 million backlog in critically needed state buildings.

With a Churchillian sense of knowing exactly what needs to be done, you're anxious to get on with it. And with a comfortable majority of your party controlling the incoming legislature, you are darned sure of your chances to change the direction and the tone of state affairs. "The direction and tone of state affairs," you say to yourself. "In what direction? With what kind of tone? I ran in the hope of accomplishing five things." And you list them:

1. Engineer the first overhaul of state government — its departments and bureaus — in thirty years.

2. Within four years, save at least eight hundred lives per year on our highways.

3. Reduce our welfare rolls by thirty thousand people through retraining and job creation.

4. Lift the state from thirty-fifth to thirtieth in per capita income within five years.

5. Effect enough savings in state operations to provide a net tax reduction of 10 percent within two and a half years.

Now the dreams have come home to roost — you won! After inauguration day in January, will you be able to make any of those things happen?

Sizing Up Your Own (Executive) Branch

Can we bring the state agencies around to our point of view?   The outgoing administration instituted a merit system two years ago and "covered in" all their officeholders, from state budget director down to surveying crews in the highway department. You wonder how you are going to get any loyalty or enthusiasm out of those holdovers.

A phone call further disturbs the already marred reverie on the pleasures of power. It's the state party chairman who helped elect you: "Governor, we now have two hundred formal requests for jobs from your campaign supporters, including twenty of first-magnitude importance from big contributors and state senators. How soon are you going to give us the guidelines on how many, and what kinds of jobs will be available for patronage? And by the way, Guv, there's a guy here who says he's from AFSCME — some kind of a union — who wants to talk to you about organizing state agencies. What'll I tell him?"

Before Christmas, you've got to come up with nominees for the fifteen department head posts, men and women who will come as close as possible to meeting four tests: (a) they share your basic philosophy; (b) they know a good bit about the programs they'll be administering; (c) they know a lot about the art of administration; and (d) their respective appointments will be well received by the voters, key legislators, important interest groups, and the media. Intuitively you know that these top appointments are your best hope of pulling the state agencies together in support of your goals.

Can we ignite state employees?   Some 91 percent of them sit secure in their jobs, protected against easy dismissal by the state merit system. Yet you know that not one of your five goals has a chance of accomplishment if lethargy dominates state government. How are you going to set a fire under these twenty thousand employees? How are you going to turn their jobs into crusades?

You haven't arrived at this important point in your career entirely unprepared for those kinds of challenges. Your mind runs back to some long hours spent studying industrial psychologist Abraham Maslow on how to generate self-actualized employees; to time well spent on management professor Frederick

Herzberg and the galvanizing effect on workers of job design, advancement, recognition, responsibility, and autonomy.

A quiet resolve takes shape in your mind: We're going to build those kinds of motivators into the management of every state department. Further, we're going to give management by objectives (MBO) a full ride in this new administration. Then we'll see if MBO can provide any kind of boost to motivation through sharing goal setting, granting to subordinates the autonomy and resources to do the job, tracking the results, and rewarding them when they succeed.

In the battle against lethargic civil servants, you've got all kinds of instruments with which to recharge their batteries.

Sizing Up the Legislature

Pulling your own branch together and giving it a sense of verve are not your only worries. You're up to your ears in politics in this gubernatorial job, and politics will require especially sensitive handling.

The state legislature will be one of your chief concerns, given its lawmaking, appropriating, investigating, and criticizing capabilities. If you blow it here, you won't get the authority to reorganize the executive branch (goal 1) or the funds for highway improvements and more state police (goal 2). The lawmakers can make life miserable for you.

But governors don't stand helpless in this kind of executive-legislative tug-of-war. After all, didn't someone call it the checks and *balances* system? You've got some pretty impressive balancers to call on: judicious use of your major appointments to state posts to win allies in the legislature; the design of a legislative program that advances your goals and takes into account the particular desires of major legislative leaders; development of warm personal relationships with those leaders; superb communication in keeping them informed; and the generation of responsiveness to legislative requests up and down state government.

The Courts and Corrections

The courts seem somewhat further removed from your daily worries than the legislature, but you know there are some troubles there too. A vacancy in the state supreme court is coming, and it will be one of your most important appointments — it has the potential of making one lawyer delighted and fifteen others furious. The modernization of the courts under the state court administrator seems worthy of your full support.

But the state's corrections system is in deep trouble. The recidivism rate at the state prison is about 60 percent — "We're doing darn little correcting," you muse. The prisoner population is now 13 percent beyond the capacity of the state's penal institutions; neighborhoods have become increasingly resistant to halfway houses; and last year the crime rate increased by 6 percent. The scariest thing is that no one seems to have answers for these problems.

To add some personal misery to it all, there are five men on death row awaiting execution. If you don't intervene, they will be the first criminals put to death in your state since the U.S. Supreme Court reauthorized capital punishment a number of years ago. That dilemma is one you didn't ask for when you ran for office.

THE FIRST SIX MONTHS: TWO SCENARIOS

The Crises Come

Inauguration day has come and gone; the contemplations and musings are behind you. Now the people's business is squarely on your shoulders: Can you make it happen? A series of setbacks begins to make you wonder:

A natural gas shortage develops, causing a fair amount of hardship in your state.

Inadequate snowfall indicates a drought next summer, requiring water rationing.

The president compounds the misery by vetoing three water projects for your state.

The legislature approved only 3 percent raises for state employees, and the state employees' association has called for the first strike against the state in its history.

In the midst of all of this, you realize you're being piecemealed to death by speaking engagements, leaving little time for the direction of state affairs.

Two rival scenarios suggest how it might all turn out.

Head-Under-Water Scenario

You blow it with the legislature. Three committee chairmen are alienated by portions of your legislative package and fight you all through the session. Cost-of-living increases are not provided for state employees, and a painful strike breaks out.

The state water commissioner you appointed failed to deliver. The water shortage turns out to be worse than expected because there are no contingency plans.

Heating bills begin to rise precipitously, and the rate hearings before the public service commission become more and more ugly.

As if all that were not enough, the newspapers begin to have at you with editorials and cartoons, leaving you apoplectic.

Or it might turn out this way:

Walk-on-Water Scenario

You developed the fine art of compromise with the legislature, agreed with their tax limitation proposals, and as quid pro quo you got reorganization authority, adequate funds for highway redesign, and cost-of-living increases for state employees.

Your appointee to the public service commission took hold, effectively challenged the utilities' rate hikes, and won plaudits from consumer groups for your administration.

Chemists at the state university made a major breakthrough in discovering a way to burn smokeless coal, worth $1 billion to the state's economy and millions in tax revenues.

Holding separate monthly briefing sessions with the major newspapers and television stations worked a miracle in improving your press image. You called it "sharing the facts"; your critics preferred to call it "managing the news."

Eight days of heavy rain in May significantly altered the water picture. (Your only sadness was in not finding a way to take credit for it!)

Finally, an able staff brought your speaking engagements and appointment schedule under control, leaving you more time for planning, motivating, and coordinating state government around your five-point program.

Seeing you there, walking on water during your first six months in office, Machiavelli would say some of it was simply *fortuna* — good luck. But you would be right in replying, *necessita* — sound administration to meet the necessities of office. You made things happen.

THE SCOPE OF ADMINISTRATION

Your handling of the governorship during those first six months in office points up the three core activities of administration: accomplishing goals, maintaining organizational vitality, and defending your agency in its external environment.[1]

What also begins to emerge from the experience is a picture of what public administration is all about: *the management of scarce resources to accomplish the goals of public policy.*

But what we have not yet seen is the vastness of the stage on which public management takes place in this country. In 1978, for example, there were:

81,000 units of government (federal, state, and local)

15.4 million government employees (15 percent of the labor force)

$651 billion government expenditures (31 percent of the GNP)

On that stage, a lot of humdrum activities take place. Millions of social security checks are printed and mailed each month; entries are made in army personnel folders; the mail is sorted; and wage-and-hour reports are filed with the

Labor Department. The state auditor's staff feeds monthly expenditures of state agencies into the computer; the Welfare Department processes twenty thousand requests for food stamps; the city courts office records the progress of each criminal and civil case in old ledger books; and sanitation crews pick up the garbage. ·

In addition to these routine aspects of the people's business, there are matters of dramatic importance to be dealt with by public servants. A polluting steel mill is shut down by the Environmental Protection Agency (EPA) during a temperature inversion; a woman doctor with the Food and Drug Administration (FDA) removes thalidomide from the American market, protecting newborns from horrible deformities; two federal employees land on the moon; a state personnel official hammers away until women and minorities begin to have an equal chance at obtaining meaningful employment; and a group of local officials get a reservoir and aqueduct built that will guarantee a metropolitan area adequate water for the next fifty years.

Protecting the environment, providing recreation, challenging monopolies, harmonizing labor-management relations, safeguarding the public health, educating the young, and aiding the old — all these things happen because public administrators and their co-workers make them happen.

Thus, your coming to the study of public administration and, it is hoped, to its practice, are matters of real importance to the public good.

THE PUBLIC AND THE PRIVATE SECTORS[2]

Soon you'll be making up your mind on the career choices available to you: law, insurance, real estate, marketing, manufacturing, and so on, in the private sector; or city manager, aide to the mayor, affirmative action officer for the state highway department, budget officer for the public service commission, investigator for the Environmental Protection Agency, or legislative liaison officer for Housing and Urban Development (HUD) in the public sector.

When making that choice, you need to know some of the similarities and differences between the public and the private sector. To see the contrasts, hop back into the governor's chair for a moment and compare your situation with that of your brother, who is the president of a small manufacturing firm. (In case we forget, he earns $60,000 a year and you earn $45,000, but the state provides you with the governor's mansion and a car.)

Similarities Between the Public and the Private Sectors

Both you and your brother head bureaucracies; that is, organizations with an authoritative allocation of duties to regularly staffed positions.

Both of your organizations deliver goods and services. His firm makes and ships electronic components. Your department of wildlife resources stocks streams with fish; the health department conducts an immunization program against measles; the highway department completes the last section of the interstate highway; and the state's technical colleges turn out three thousand technicians every year to meet the needs of an expanding economy.

Your brother's company does not have a merit system, but he, like you, needs good people and needs to know how to motivate them. Human beings work for both enterprises and will be equally demoralized by meaningless jobs, isolation, and boredom. (The absence of a merit system in the electronics company, by the way, gives your brother a much freer hand with personnel than you enjoy.)

Both sectors are subject to federal law, perhaps his in a more direct way than yours. His company must respect the minimum wage and maximum hours law and file regular reports thereunder, the Taft-Hartley Act in regard to collective bargaining, the equal employment opportunity (EEO) provisions of the 1964 Civil Rights Act, and the regulations of the Office of Safety and Health Administration (OSHA), among other requirements.

On your part, the state must comply with the EEO provisions, with the Environmental Protection Act, with the strings attached to federal grants-in-aid (e.g., submitting highway plans for review if built with federal dollars), and with the due process and equal protection requirements of the Fourteenth Amendment, among many others.

In differing degrees, to be sure, you are both involved in politics — your brother for insurance' sake, you because you can't (and wouldn't!) escape it. Your brother contributes heavily to a Republican state senator who chairs the senate committee on labor and business. (For three sessions, that senator has beaten down labor's attempt to get rid of the state's right-to-work, or open-shop, law.) Your brother also contributes to the manufacturers' association, his chief lobbying arm. Moreover, he periodically badgers one of the state's U.S. senators to fight any increase in social security taxes or the federal minimum wage.

In your case, you are immersed in politics — surrounded by the legislature, pressure groups, party barons, voters, and the media — all of whom want to tell you how to conduct the people's business. The difference between your brother and you in this respect, however, is enormous: Failure on his part in political management won't ruin him — but it will you.

Where Public and Private Sectors Differ

While this involves a value judgment on our part, we believe the biggest difference between public and private enterprise lies in the widely differing scope and significance of the missions in the two areas. Granted that the scope and significance of General Motors, the local power company, the private hospital serving your city, the dairy, and many other companies and institutions are very great, they probably are among the exceptions rather than the rule in the world of private enterprise. Your brother's firm, for example, sells electronic parts to eighty-five regular customers who could buy from two or three other intrastate rivals or could make their purchases from out-of-state companies.

As governor, your mission is nothing less than what has come down to us from ancient Rome in these three Latin phrases:

Pro bono publico — for the public good

Salus populi suprema lex esto — let the welfare of the people be the supreme law

Res publica — commonweal, the business of the state

Resting on your shoulders are some awesome responsibilities. You need to provide the leadership to assure the children of your state high-quality education. The health and safety of the people must be protected against dangerous highways, unsafe dams and mines, and air and water pollution. Consumer welfare is dependent upon vigorous state regulatory bodies for protection against price gouging by public utilities. Nothing in the private sector could approach the scope of these activities.

Some other differences between the public and private sector are of a lesser order of importance, yet they are significant. Public administration is subject to greater scrutiny than private — by federal and state auditors, the legislature, the media, the citizenry, the other major political party, and the courts.

Public administrators are dependent upon highly political bodies, the senate and the house, for both authority and funds. Those assemblies are unlike any corporate board of directors to be found.

While government and private enterprise both try to control each other (with corporate power enjoying an incredible success record[3]), in a showdown the sovereign power can make its will felt against corporate giants such as U.S. Steel, Firestone, and the Ford Motor Company. A polluting steel mill can be lawfully shut down; thousands of Ford Pintos can be ordered recalled to correct dangerous gas tanks; and hundreds of thousands of Firestone 500s can be ordered replaced by safer tires.

Meanwhile, back in the executive suite, corporate directors have far greater discretion in handling funds and personnel than do their counterparts in government. Part of the reason for this difference is a governmental phenomenon unknown to the private manager: central staff agencies like the U.S. Office of Management and Budget (OMB) and the Office of Personnel Management (OPM), which significantly impact on an agency director's prerogatives.

The political activities of civil servants, in most jurisdictions, are much more narrowly circumscribed than are those of private employees. So also is the right to strike, which is widely illegal in government (although increasingly engaged in), but is legal in the private sector.

There also is a wide array of occupations peculiar to the public sector that mark off part of the government's work from that of the world of business: astronauts, correctional officers, customs inspectors, bomber pilots, and many, many more.

Finally, in a broader arena once again, as governor you have to help maintain a political system that permits wide citizen participation, government by consent, and orderly change. That responsibility exceeds by many light-years anything your brother in the private sector will ever know.

That political system must also provide justice under law, both for law-abiding citizens and for those accused of crime. In the end, your job is to secure and enhance life, liberty, and property for all of the people of your state. That is why public administration is the people's business, just possibly the most important business around.

A LOOK FORWARD

The public administration course you're taking, this book, and the disciplines they represent are designed to prepare you to handle *res publica*.

The flow of subjects in this book, as in any book, reflects the author's sense of what is important. For me, people come first — thus the title of the book, and thus Chapter 2 on what makes individuals and groups tick. Way ahead of organization charts, PERT diagrams, and job classifications come people, any agency's most priceless asset; and so we begin with them.

Then we turn to aspects of formal organization — the bureaucracy — and the informal organizations that permeate and shape all the formal ones we live under.

In Chapter 6, one of the most critical chapters in the book, we examine the impact of bureaucracy upon people, diagnose a troublesome disease called bureaupathology, and then prescribe ways to find a harmonic mean between organizations and their staffs.

Our concern then turns to the tasks of managers and what they have to do well in order to make things happen in government — lead, manage politics, decide, coordinate, communicate, and handle change.

Then come the critical responsibilities in the fiscal area: budgeting, getting appropriations through the legislative body, and administering the postappropriation controls (accounting and auditing).

Next to last, we examine personnel management in some depth: patronage versus merit, collective bargaining, job classification and salary administration, and recruitment and selection.

In the final chapter on the ethics of management, we raise some of the most difficult questions of all concerning the calling of the public servant: What kinds of means are appropriate to secure what kinds of ends, how to cope with private gain at the public's expense, and how to define the public interest and then motivate people in government to pursue it.

Through it all we admit to an attempted turn-on — of you — to the people's business: public administration.

KEY CONCEPTS

pro bono publico   res publica
salus populi supreme lex

DISCUSSION QUESTIONS

1. In what sense does a governor "manage" a state? Use the chapter illustration to point out gubernatorial management qualities.
2. Compare the head under water scenario with the walk on water scenario. To what extent is a governor *not* able to influence his scenario?
3. Compare and contrast the private and the public sectors. In what ways are they alike? In what ways do they differ?

PROJECT

Select five to ten of your fellow students. Ask them if they plan to pursue careers in the public or the private sector. Analyze their reasons for preferring one or the other.

Notes

1. Chris Argyris, *Integrating the Individual and the Organization* (New York: Wiley, 1964), pp. 315–318.
2. We have drawn on Robert C. Fried, *Performance in American Bureaucracy* (Boston: Little, Brown, 1976), pp. 38–39; Ada R. Kimsey, "Civil Service and the Nation's Progress," *Civil Service Journal* (Jan.–Mar. 1977) 16:21–25; and U.S. Civil Service Commission, *The Federal Career Service at Your Service* (Washington, D.C.: Government Printing Office, 1977), p. 3, for these comparisons.
3. See in particular C. Wright Mills, *The Power Elite* (New York: Oxford University Press, 1956), and G. William Domhoff, *Who Rules America?* (Englewood Cliffs, N.J.: Prentice-Hall, 1967).

Chapter 2
Management Begins with People

THE DISCOVERY OF THE PEOPLE IN MANAGEMENT

A former chief of naval operations, angered by the hardening of the organizational arteries by a tough secretary of defense, ran up the "I quit" flag, with these words written on it:

> I reject the modern fallacy that theories or computers or economics or numbers of weapons win wars. Alone, they do not. . . . Man is the key to success or failure . . . man, his wits and his will.[1]

And women, and their wits and will!

People are the key to government. They are the reason for the existence of the city parks department, the state division of family services, U.S. Department of Education, and all other government agencies as well. And on the delivery end, it is also *people* who give life and direction to government. In brief, P G P = people govern people.

The beginning point, then, for the study of public administration cannot be bureaus, structures, organization charts, or budgets: It has to be *people;* management begins with them.

There Have Been Some Costly Detours

By no means has the focus in management always been on people. Although the Sophists in ancient Greece asserted that "Man is the measure of all things," and Alexander Pope reminded an eighteenth-century world that "The proper study of mankind is man," (for "man" read "man and woman") students of administration somehow lost sight of the people in organizations while fixing on other targets: output, efficiency, and profits.

An American prototype for the latter approach was Frederick W. Taylor, the late-nineteenth-century founder of scientific management.[2] Called upon by industries to increase their productivity, Taylor developed a system for discovering "a science for every job" (*job,* not people) and a pay system that would really motivate workers to produce.

Taylor's key assumptions about people now seem deeply insulting: (a) The chief thing people want from their jobs is money, and (b) people are basically simpletons who require strict guidance in order to perform well:

> All of us are grown-up children, and it is equally true that the average workman will work with the greatest satisfaction . . . when he is given each day a definite task which he is to perform in a given time, and which constitutes a proper day's work for a good workman.[3]

Two replies are worth noting. One was George Bernard Shaw's in *Pygmalion:* "The difference between the flower girl and the duchess is not how the flower girl acts, but how she is treated." Regard workers as grown-up children and every workplace becomes a kindergarten.

The other reply came just five years after Taylor had written the insult, this time from John Dewey, who was about forty years ahead of his time:

> Much is said about scientific management of work. It is a narrow view which restricts the science which secures efficiency of operation to *movements of muscles.* The chief opportunity for science is the discovery of *the relations of a man to his work* — including his relations to others who take part — which will enlist his intelligent interest in what he is doing [emphasis added].[4]

But in that day, efficiency was king, and Taylor was the crown prince. The management concepts he and his followers laid down became a kind of dogma for many decades:

Work is a drudgery, an unpleasant necessity that is external to life.

Economic motives make people produce; they work for money, period.

Workers should perform narrowly defined tasks in ways laid down by management.

They should operate under close supervision of multiple foremen in a hierarchically controlled system.

Management should do the thinking, workers the doing.

Management should focus on output goals (production and profits), not on the needs of the workers.

Person-to-person competition should be encouraged and informal work groups and unions discouraged.

Theory X, 1870 Style

On New Year's Day, 1870, the president of the P.W. Madsen Furniture Company of Salt Lake City posted its new code of employee conduct:

Store will open at 7 A.M. and close at 8 P.M., except Saturdays when it closes at 9 P.M. This is in effect the year around. This store will remain closed each Sabbath.

Duties of Employees: Sweep floors, dust furniture, shelves, and show cases; remember, "Cleanliness is next to Godliness." Trim wicks, fill maps, clean chimneys. Make your pens carefully (but you may whittle the quills to suit your individual taste). Open windows for fresh air. Each clerk shall bring in a bucket of water and a scuttle of coal for the day's business.

An employee who smokes Spanish cigars, uses liquor in any form, gets shaved at the barber shop, or frequents pool halls or public dance halls will give his employer every reason to suspect his integrity, worthy intentions, and all-around honesty.

Each employee is expected to pay his tithing to the Church; that is, 10 percent of his annual income. No matter what your income might be, you should not contribute less than twenty-five dollars per year to the Church. Each employee will attend Sunday Sacrament Meeting and adequate time will be given to attend Fast Meeting on Thursday. Also you are expected to attend your Sunday School.

Men employees will be given one evening off each week for courting purposes, and two evenings each week if they go regularly to Church and attend to Church duties. After any employee has spent his thirteen hours at labor in the store, he should spend his leisure time in reading good books and contemplating the glories and building up the Kingdom of God.

P. W. Madsen, President and Manager

In time, that management philosophy came to be dubbed Theory X,[5] and its foundations have been sorely shaken by modern-day behavioral science. (The concern for productivity, however, has remained, but with answers being sought in some interesting new directions.)

The Hawthorne Experiments

The great breakthrough in the discovery of how people function in a work situation came in 1927–1932 through experimental studies conducted at the Western Electric Company's Hawthorne plant in Chicago.[6] Although the research ultimately became highly complex, the basic experiment can be put simply. Five women employed to assemble telephone relays were pulled off the regular assembly line and placed in a segregated room where observers carefully recorded changes in production of this guinea pig group as working conditions were altered. Workroom illumination,[7] number and length of rest periods, and length of the workday and workweek were varied under controlled conditions. To the surprise of the observation team, with a few exceptions, the productivity of the five team members seemed to rise (in contrast to that of the control group on the main assembly line) regardless of the direction or nature of the changes.

It was clear that physical surroundings and work hours were not the central influences underlying the behavior of the five women in the relay assembly test room. Instead, their discovery by management as persons apart from the anonymous workers on the assembly line, their opportunity to function as a small primary group, and the psychological payoffs that came from being the steady objects of attention in the experiment served to transform the women and their job attitudes. *Human beings, with their feelings and their associations,* apparently were the critical elements in job performance.[8]

Clearly, people are unique and are of fundamental importance, regardless of the institutional setting.

A Second Breakthrough: Abraham Maslow's Self-actualizing People

The road back from Taylorism and the formal organization school of administration (which we will look at in Chapter 3) to the reemphasis on people received a second major advance in 1943 when a young clinical psychologist, Abraham Maslow, published a theoretical paper in the *Psychological Review* on human needs as motivators.[9] That article and his books that followed it provided the underpinning for a new approach to management in America.[10] The central axioms of Maslow's new approach are depicted in Figure 2.1 and are summarized in the following list:

1.   Most of us, regardless of culture, have a set of needs that tends to arise *after lower ones have been satisfied.*

2.   People will fulfill their needs conjunctively if possible, disjunctively if they must (e.g., resort to racial prejudice to establish their own self-esteem).

3.   People will reach the self-actualization (or growth level) only where: (a) their lower-level needs have been met; (b) they are challenged to create; and (c) they enjoy the freedom to do so.

In greater detail, the basic driving needs, Maslow thought, are the physical ones: food, sex, elimination, and so forth. Then arise concerns for physical safety, job security, and provision for old age. Third is the individual's group need, the need to be loved and accepted by significant others. Fourth is the yearning to see oneself as a worthy and admirable person. And fifth, there is the innate striving for self-actualization, to create and to maximize one's talents.

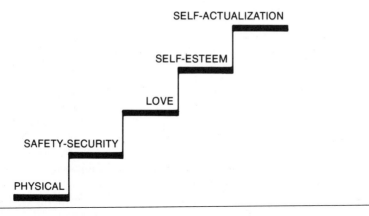

FIGURE 2.1   HUMAN NEEDS ACCORDING TO MASLOW

The four lower-level needs are the demanding (prepotent) ones. Maslow believed that until each one is relatively satisfied, a person will not strive very hard for the next level of need. "Man does live by bread alone when there is no bread," he observed; or, as an old Indian saying goes, "Allah himself wouldn't dare to appear before a starving Indian except as a loaf of bread."[11] When a person is reasonably well fed, secure, loved, and confident, he or she then has the physical and psychic wherewithal to begin to create, self-direct, and accomplish under his or her own power.

Maslow admitted that the priority order among the five need levels may not always hold true as outlined. A soldier in battle, without regard for personal safety, may be so actualized as to perform acts of great heroism. There are also upward mobile people, empire builders who, rising on the backs of their associates, seem to put self-esteem far ahead of any need for the love and admiration of their peers. But Maslow believed that in general, even across cultural lines, most people would climb the need ladder in the manner described.

Frustration of the basic needs can be expected to produce compensatory acts and sometimes sick behavior. The teenager who is rejected by his father may compensate for his low self-esteem (which has been shattered by withdrawal of his father's affection) by expressions of racial prejudice to prove to himself that he is better than some others in society. The dope user, starved for drugs at the physical-need level, engages in theft. The brilliant young sociologist, whose opinions have never been sought by her section chief, writes letters to the editor, has dreams of grandeur, and hates her boss. But what about those individuals whose lower-level needs are met and who therefore move upward rather than outward on Maslow's chart?

The search for self-actualizing people   Who are they? What do they look like? Their portrait, as drawn by Maslow, shows these self-actualizers to be comfort-

---

The Epitaph of a Bureaucrat, Truman Era

An old New Dealer, departing from government service:

> There isn't any fun [in] working for the government anymore. No inspiration. No one to demand you do the impossible, and giving you the confidence that you can. No bold adventures.

Tris Coffin, *Missouri Compromise* (Boston: Little, Brown, 1947), p. 64.

---

able with reality (not escapist), intrigued by the unknown (unspooked), capable of self-examination without guilt, unpeeved, possessed of great spontaneity and individuality, strivers for perfection, philosophically broad, serene in the face of disappointments, comfortable alone or with others (their love need having already been fulfilled), alive and responsive, strongly committed to human brotherhood, deeply democratic, teachable, not orthodox in religion, inventive and creative, reasonable, and thoroughly healthy human beings.[12]

John Gardner has vividly described the feeling of self-actualization:

> What could be more satisfying than to be engaged in work in which every capacity or talent one may have is needed, every lesson one may have learned is used, every value one cares about is furthered.[13]

When that spirit evaporates, something very vital has gone out of life, and out of performance as well.[14] When the bold adventures disappear and the preconditions for self-actualization are unmet, a different kind of person begins to emerge: one that is aloof and cold, stuffy, ruthless, thoughtless, and *self*-oriented (he is still looking for self-esteem) rather than task-oriented.[15] It is clear that people like these are not the stuff that effective work forces are made of. Consequently, *a first task of management would seem to be that of creating the conditions that give rise to self-actualizing individuals who are strongly committed to agency goals.* (We hasten to add that channeling the energies of these self-actualizers toward agency goals may be no easy task.)

The Herzberg Motivation-Hygiene Theory

A more recent formulation of motivation theory, yet still rooted in human needs, has been advanced by Frederick Herzberg.[16] He contends that we experience two levels of need: *hygiene needs* (to remove dissatisfiers), whose fulfillment reduces discomfort and displeasure; and *motivating needs* (the satisfiers), whose fulfillment produces self-actualized people and job satisfaction (Figure 2.2).

The central contribution Herzberg's writings have made to motivation theory is to focus attention on *the job itself,* on the intrinsic factors in employment

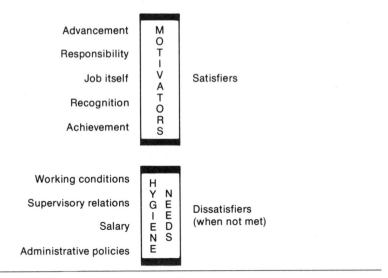

FIGURE 2.2   THE MOTIVATION-HYGIENE THEORY OF FREDERICK HERZBERG

From F. Herzberg, et al., *The Motivation to Work,* p. 73. Copyright © 1959 John Wiley & Sons. Reprinted by permission of John Wiley & Sons, Inc.

rather than the extrinsic factors, such as the supervisor's smile, carpets on the floor, or better magazines in the men's room. Improving surroundings and developing harmonious relations among co-workers and supervisors may generate some euphoria, but what really produces high-level morale and productivity is doing a job worth doing — to repeat John Gardner, where "every capacity or talent one may have is needed."[17] From the days of the Gospel of Matthew down to Frederick Herzberg, losing oneself in a great cause is still the shortest road to finding oneself.

Some Other Ways of Looking at People on the Job

Before turning to the major criticisms of the motivation theories we have been exploring, some note should be taken of three other ways observers have looked at people.

Karl Marx developed the concept of *economic man.* Since the material conditions of life are what really count (economic determinism), people can be changed (or motivated) only by the radical transformation of the economic system they work within: the shift from capitalism — working for someone else — to socialism — working for "ourselves."[18]

It is interesting to note how easily economic man could leapfrog from the Marxists to capitalists like Frederick Taylor in the same century. Recall that Taylor's motivational theory was exclusively economic: pay workers enough and in the right way, and you'll get them to overcome the drudgery of work and really produce.

Jeremy Bentham, before Marx, developed a different calculus for measuring humankind: the utility theory that people are *pleasure seekers* and *pain avoiders*.[19]

In time, the pleasure-pain theory reappeared in the twentieth century as the *reward-seeking person* of B. F. Skinner.[20] Suggesting that behavior is a function of its consequences, Skinner developed an approach to behavior modification that relied on positive rewards to reinforce desired behavior. Both Bentham and Skinner, it seems, would endorse managerial use of incentives of a wide type to stimulate workers' productivity. And Skinner would look to the day when the "aversive techniques" of discipline would no longer be required.

All three theories have something useful to say about human behavior. The materialism and pleasure seeking in us cannot be denied. (Many would subscribe to the old saw that "Money may not be the most important thing in life, but it's way ahead of whatever comes second.")

But people are not only what they eat. They also need security; they hunger for good vibes from people they care about; they will put up with lots of economic denial for a medical or a law degree. As psychiatrist Harry Levinson so cogently put it, "Any view of humans' responding to a stick behind and a carrot in front suggests a jackass in between"[21] — and that is no way to view the men and women who make a government stop — or go.

The Maslow Critics at Bat

The Galileos, Harveys, Einsteins, and Keyneses of this world drew critics much as armies draw massage parlors. So too did Abraham Maslow. In 1943, he saw the criticism coming.

> The present theory, then, must be considered to be a suggested program or framework for future research, and must stand or fall, not so much on facts available or evidence presented, as upon researches yet to be done, researches suggested perhaps by the questions raised in this paper.[22]

The questions and criticisms came for over two decades — almost as if evaluating Maslow had become a full employment program for industrial sociologists and psychologists:

1. There is little if any empirical support for either the Maslow hierarchy or the Herzberg two-factor theory.[23]

Two central features of Maslow's theory have not stood up well under field testing: (a) that there even is a five-level hierarchy of needs, and (b) that satisfaction of one need level removes that need as a motivator and then (and only then) gives rise to a driving desire to satisfy the next higher need.

Let's face it, Maslow was simply wrong on the "disappearing need" feature of his theory. Nowhere was that more plainly evident than in the palpably incorrect statement in his 1943 article that "The perfectly healthy, normal, fortunate man has no sex needs or hunger needs, or needs for safety, or for love, or for prestige, or self-esteem, except in stray moments of quickly passing threat." Ridiculous! Even the most self-actualized among us need meals three times a day and sex about — how often would you say?

There is reason to question whether full gratification of a need *ever* occurs for very many of us. As one critic observed, acquiring a Scirocco only sets in motion the yearning for a Porsche (and so on up the automobile ladder). To add insult to injury, two researchers found evidence suggesting that the pull of a need is the strongest when there is thorough satisfaction of the need.[24] (Common sense would contradict that finding, however. One doesn't have much desire for food after a Thanksgiving meal, or for immediate sex after a satisfying *entente cordiale.*)

In eight field studies reviewed by M. A. Wahba and L. G. Bridwell, there was no confirmation for the five-level ladder; only modest support for the two-level clustering of Herzberg; and some confirmation of self-actualization as a separate, identifiable need. Contradicting Maslow, some field studies among managers and professionals found that *security* and *self-actualization* were the least satisfied, while the love need was the best satisfied. (Maslow would have found it unlikely that the love need mattered among people who felt insecure.)*

2. Maslow downplayed the impact of culture in the determination both of needs and of how they are to be satisfied; and he really led himself astray by assuming that the five basic needs are instinctoid — that is, with us at birth.[25]

Culture clearly makes a difference:

Self-actualization for the Hopi Indian is not defined in personal terms at all but in tribal survival and at-oneness (the love need).

Fulfillment in totalitarian cultures is to be part of the movement, a loyal follower of the Fuehrer.

Salvation for the Christian heretics of the third and fourth centuries A.D. was to be achieved only by denying physical needs (asceticism), not by satisfying them.

Whatever part of the clay of human needs may have come with us at birth the hands of culture have clearly shaped into myriad forms around the world; and administrators who ignore cultural differences while treating everyone alike are likely to find themselves trying to put the broken clay back together again.

3. Furthermore, job satisfaction will be heavily influenced by such factors as worker IQs, personalities (think of the different routes pursued by extrovert and introvert), the technology employed (handcraft, assembly line, automation), and a host of other factors quite different from the unduly restrictive list of Maslow's five inborn needs.

---

* We will return to the rebuttals in the next section.

4. Self-actualized workers, dancing to their own drummers, would be relatively uncontrollable. An organization full of them might approximate chaos much more closely than an orderly attack on the agency's goals.

5. The manager's world includes many workers who are not, and may never be, self-actualized. Robert Presthus's view is that the typical agency will be staffed by an array of people: the upward mobiles (those who are highly actualized), the indifferents (those who are turned off by work), and the ambivalents (those who blow hot and cold).[26]

Many employees are going to get their kicks off the job, not on, and supervisors will have to accept less than full motivation as a fact of life, adopting a leadership style that may be more authoritarian than would be appropriate for a fully self-actualized work force.

The summary judgment of the critics against Maslow's formulation of human needs was expressed by F. K. Gibson and C. E. Teasley in this way:

> In view of the lack of empirical evidence to support the humanistic model, one wonders how it maintains support. There does indeed seem to be an almost metaphysical attraction to the Maslow hierarchy and to the various spin-off theories that comprise the humanistic model. The impact of the model is discernible in practically every form of organization from complex bureaucracies to small intimate groups such as the family. And those who support the thesis may well be right. But our review indicates that for now *faith rather than empirical evidence* must be used to support the concept [emphasis added].[27]

In Defense of Maslow and Herzberg

If the critics need a shot of faith before works, so be it. What kind of an agency would it be where the merit system (see Chapter 15) took care of security needs, where there was honest-to-goodness love among the staff, where everyone's self-esteem was regularly and deservedly fed, and where supervisors challenged you to do the impossible and gave you the confidence to bring it off? What would that be like?

Or turn the argument around. After the debunkers have listed a dozen reasons for doubting the human needs theory, are they prepared to argue that workers (and the human race) would be better off if *deprived* of security, love, self-esteem, and the chance to grow? Acts of faith may be a whole lot more beneficial for humankind than short-nosed empiricism.

But the Maslow defenders are fully prepared to wrestle the critics on the *empirical mat* as well. Let's take an old classic to begin with, C. R. Walker and R. H. Guest's 1952 study of workers on the automobile assembly line.[28] The researchers focused at one point on the lack of socializing opportunities on the main line and the presence of those opportunities among some off-the-line workers who could function as a team. The higher esprit de corps prevailing among the latter group clearly confirmed both Maslow's love need and the benefit Herzberg pointed to when the dissatisfier of isolation is removed.

Second, the searchers for empirical verification cannot ignore the seventeen separate studies completed during the 1950s which are summarized in the verification chapter (7) of Herzberg's 1966 book, *Work and the Nature of Man*. In all of them, among different populations of workers, confirmation was found for the differentiation of hygiene needs and motivators.

Another study from that period by Robert Kahn of manufacturing workers revealed striking support for Maslow's supposition about increased deprivation at the upper need levels. Kahn asked workers what they liked most about their jobs; the results recorded are given in Figure 2.3. However substantiating they may be, the data provide a discouraging picture of the work force Kahn was measuring. Six out of ten workers were groveling at the security level; about a third were plateauing at the love level; and only one fourth were turned on in their employment by the opportunities to grow.

New confirmation of upper-level need deprivation was provided in the early 1970s by Harold L. Sheppard and N. Q. Herrick. They found that among both managers and union representatives, "full recognition of their achievements" was the number one need; blue-collar workers put "full utilization of skills" first and *improvements in their pay last.*[29] (The highly important role money plays as a motivator will be discussed in Chapter 16.) Those data underscored the dramatic change in much of the labor protest of the 1970s, which often was against crummy work rather than against crummy pay.[30]

A penetrating portrayal of the motivational problems confronting the contemporary labor force appeared in 1973 in the U.S. Department of Health, Edu-

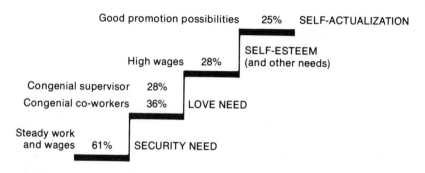

Note: The figures add up to more than 100 percent because of multiple responses.

FIGURE 2.3   JOB SATISFIERS OF MANUFACTURING WORKERS (1958)

From Robert L. Kahn, "Human Relations on the Shop Floor" in E. M. Hugh-Jones, ed., *Human Relations and Modern Management* (Amsterdam: North-Holland Publishing Company, 1958). Reprinted by permission of the author.

cation and Welfare (HEW) task force report *Work in America*.[31] Among the statistics reported were those of a University of Michigan survey indicating that only 43 percent of the white-collar workers studied would choose their present job a second time, and only 24 percent of the blue-collar workers would do the same.

Further evidence of worker alienation appeared in answer to the question, "What would you do with two extra hours a day?" Although two out of three college professors would use the extra time at work, only one out of twenty nonprofessionals would do so.[32] The gap between self-actualization and what most jobs apparently provide is very real.

The proffered explanation for worker alienation provided interesting confirmation of the Maslow-Herzberg theories. The authors of *Work in America* found three kinds of "cancer" eating away at workers: powerlessness, meaninglessness, and isolation.* Powerlessness and meaninglessness are clearly intrinsic aspects of the job, which when corrected are primary motivators for Herzberg, and they relate to critical elements of self-actualization for Maslow. Over and over again, *Work in America* sounds the same theme: the road to an effective work force in America is through "variety, autonomy, and meaningful responsibility," a long-standing theme of Maslow and Herzberg.

* They included a fourth factor of "self-estrangement," but its key components seem to be two of the others — meaningless (boring) work and isolation from co-workers.

Before attempting some kind of a synthesis of proponents' and critics' views about human needs in the workplace, we need to advance one final argument for the Maslow view in the face of the empiricists' challenge. Maslow makes *great normative sense: what a person can become, he or she must become.* If appropriate management styles can be found in the public sector to liberate the best that is in those who work for government, a monumental step will have been taken.

One of Maslow's chief exemplars, Chris Argyris, put it this way:

> The normative view should be based upon the desired potentialities of man. Man should be studied in terms of what he is capable of, not only how he actually behaves. Then we should take the best examples we have of human beings striving to achieve these qualities and study them and their environment in order to produce generalizations that help us to understand and increase the behavior that is preferred.

> Thus Maslow would take the behavior that is characteristic of rare, peak experiences and make them values toward which to aspire. If one replies that such behavior is rarely observed, Maslow would agree and then ask for the systematic research to tell us how to make the behavior more frequent.[33]

Resolution of the Debate and a New Formulation of Human Needs

Maslow's critics score heavily on two points: his indifference to the influence of culture, and his ladder arrangement of how our needs arise (higher ones appearing only after lower ones have been satisfied).

The reply to the cultural objection is in part the normative answer developed above. Wouldn't *all of us,* regardless of culture, be healthier individuals if impediments to our development (such as the authoritarian systems of Theory X) could be removed, allowing for our liberation and growth?

The other part of the answer is the continuing challenge to public administrators to take the cultural diversity of their work force and mold it sufficiently to accomplish the goals of public policy while preserving the distinctiveness of the human mosaic. Remember, "divided we stand and united we fall."

As to the second objection, the Maslow ladder, the time has long since come to bow to the critics and admit that: (a) we are peppered by a wide range of needs; (b) they are rarely, if ever, permanently satisfied; (c) yet there is still some truth in Maslow's assertion that there are preconditions for most of us to reach a stage of creativity and sustained growth. (For the writer of college texts, for example, the "loaf of bread, a jug of wine, and thou" turns out to be some peace of mind, a little time, and a quiet desk somewhere.) It seems to me that the needs of most of us can best be portrayed in the fashion represented in Figure 2.4 (place yourself in the center of the circle).

We accept Herzberg's view that the lower needs (shown in the bottom half of the circle) are more bedrock than they are launching pad for self-actualization. The arrows suggest that all the needs are there virtually all of the time and that some success in satisfying them will provide us with the wherewithal to become what we can become.

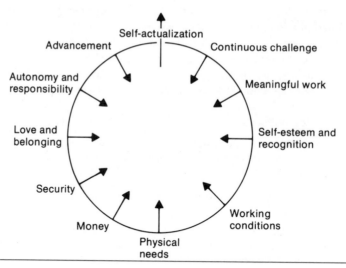

FIGURE 2.4   THE HUMAN NEEDS CIRCLE

Seeing that those needs are met on a continuing basis and that freedom for self-actualization is preserved seems to me to be the most important internal responsibility of managers in the public sector.

Understanding what makes individuals tick is the first step; the second is equally important — understanding human groups. As Aristotle said a long time ago, people are by nature gregarious beings; their natural habitat is life with others.[34] If we are to understand at all clearly why individuals in organizations behave the way they do, then we must get a handle on the ways human groups so significantly influence the behavior of their members.

HUMAN GROUPS — THE NATURAL SOIL OF ADMINISTRATION

Early in our own century, a precursor of the latter-day behavioralists, Arthur Bentley, laid the groundwork:

> The raw material [of government] . . . is never found in one man by himself; it cannot even be stated by adding man to man. It must be taken as it comes in many men together. It is a "relation" between men, but not in the sense that the individual men are given to us first, and the relation erected between them. The "relation," i.e., the action, is the given phenomenon, the raw material, the action of men with or upon each other. We know men only as participants in such activity.[35]

Although for thirty years after Bentley, management theory concentrated on organizational structure,[36] research ultimately followed him in looking behind the structures to the human groups that vitalize — or ruin — all institutions.

Typology of Work Groups

A perceptive director of a state health department could rather easily distinguish four different kinds of groups affecting the lives of her staff ("group" meaning a set of human beings with regular interaction who recognize a degree of association and/or of interdependence). She would first note the *formal group*, the de jure structure of the health department and its subdivisions. Titles, distinctions, rules, prerogatives, and sanctions are all institutionally (formally) defined for this group of personnel.

Second, she could perceive the *informal groups:* the dynamic work groups, the cliques among the workers, formed largely on friendship lines. They have no officers, but they have significant others; they have no manuals, but they have unwritten codes; they have no authorized powers, but they confer benefits and impose penalties on their members.

Third, she might note some *highly institutionalized allied groups* such as the employee union (with officers, dues, bylaws, etc.), the health department employee council, and others almost as formally bureaucratized as the department itself.

Fourth, the director could discern some *informal allied groups* such as the bowling league and the backpackers club, which further expand the associational contacts of her employees.

Beyond identifying these four group types, the director must understand the character of group life and its impact upon people. She needs to see how groups possess their own internal structure (significant others, leaders, followers), belief systems, behavior norms, and sanctions for noncompliance; and how all of these facets of group life vitally affect the way employees perform.[37]

Look at some possible scenarios within a single state agency:

The work groups in the budget and finance office, divided a dozen different ways, are hardly groups at all.

Conversely, the staff in environmental protection exhibits high-level integration, mutual support, and recognition.

The epidemiologists, instead of fighting germs, spend most of their time in defensive maneuvers against their division head.

The senior nursing staff is polarized around two nonspeaking rivals.

Clearly, some of these enclaves of humanity have themselves sufficiently together to function well, while others spend more time jousting with each other than promoting public health. In the budget and finance office, we would expect a lot of deficits in the love and belonging needs of the employees; in environmental protection, many payoffs for both the security and the love needs.

Group Properties

Some of the principal properties or characteristics of groups that group members and supervisors need to be aware of are:

autonomy (from the control of others)

control (or lack thereof) over their members' conduct

flexibility versus rigidity of group processes

pleasant versus unpleasant climate of group life

joint commitment to group life

readiness to integrate new members versus the "tight little island" syndrome

stratification into influence levels and differentiated roles

unity versus disunity

the flow of communications among group members[38]

(Take a minute and note how closely many of these group properties relate to the human needs circle portrayal in Figure 2.4.)

To enhance individual member belongingness and self-actualization and to strengthen the problem-solving capabilities of work groups (other things being equal), the generally desired features from the preceding list would include work group autonomy, no excessive control over group members, flexibility, pleasant atmosphere, solid commitment to the group, openness to new members, minimal stratification, unity, and free-flowing communication. Wise supervisors will work overtime on these fundamental aspects of life within the agency, knowing how much of our behavior is shaped by the groups in which we have found membership.

Group Influences on Human Behavior[39]

Roles and norms   One of the factors that strongly influence behavior is the calculation we all sometimes engage in: "What kind of conduct on my part will get these people to like me?" This is *role taking,* and "these people" are the significant others who loom large in anyone's immediate circle. Role taking then leads to *role playing* as we act out in a way we hope will gain the approval of others around us. In Figure 2.5, you find yourself as a new employee in the diagnostic section of the health department. The need to be accepted in these new surroundings is almost overwhelming, and so you start looking for cues on how to behave, who counts, who the office jerk is, and so forth. Having sent out feelers in the direction of the significant others, you get some tentative answers (office *norms,* suggesting the smart *roles* for you to play). In the pursuit of acceptance, you often then proceed to play those roles, observable in on-the-

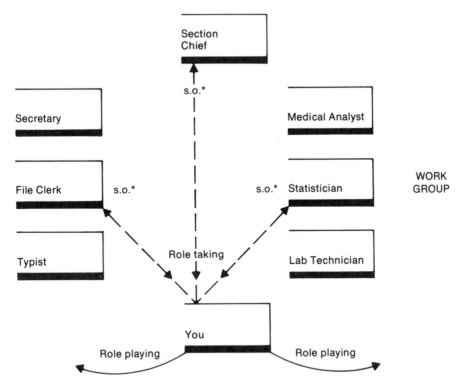

* The abbreviation s.o. = significant other, a person who, for official or personal reasons, looms large in the eyes of a fellow worker.

  — — ➔ feelers sent out for behavior cues.

  ———➔ roles played on the job.

FIGURE 2.5 PRIMARY GROUP AND ROLE DEFINITION

job behavior, and sometimes off the job as well.* Clearly, primary groups — those with close, regular interaction — are tremendously influential in defining approved and unapproved behavior.

In defining those kinds of behavior, groups perform one of their most important functions — norm setting. Tamotsu Shibutani contends that some group-determined norms are essentially universal *in all groups,* from the Girl Scouts to the Mafia:

> Since cooperation of some sort takes place in all groups, there are certain norms governing interpersonal relations that are found almost everywhere. . . . Loyalty is

* We once observed a young secretary buying a black nightgown, who said to the clerk, "The guys at the office really love black." (Her job description must have been a beaut!)

apparently prized everywhere. . . . A sense of decency and fair play is also valued in most groups. . . . Sincerity is another attribute that is prized, even among the cynical who are sure that there are not many sincere people left in the world. . . . It is easy to see why such norms are so widespread: the survival of groups depends upon the participants' retaining some measure of faith in one another. . . . Morality is not the exclusive property of the self-righteous and the respectable. It becomes an essential ingredient of human life.[40]

In the office, the norms readily appear: when to come to work, how long a coffee break is, what is prudent to feed back to the boss, and if it is safe to excel.

At this point, a new worry arises for the manager: how much congruence there is between agency norms and work group norms as to a day's work, complying with leave regulations, handling confidential information about clients, and the like. Congruence is the soil from which cooperative action grows; incongruence between agency and group standards spells trouble.

In a second phase of the Hawthorne Plant study (known as the Bank Wiring Room), the informal work group resented management's production standards and arrived at their own definition of a day's work.[41]

A reorganization of the copy-pulling section of the U.S. Patent Office ran into difficulty in trying to increase the number of patents pulled to eight hundred per day in the face of the work group standard that three hundred constituted a full day's work.[42]

The constitutional norm for the presidency is to "preserve, protect and defend the Constitution of the United States." But in Richard Nixon's presidency, the natural work group of the president and his advisers, John D. Ehrlichman, H. R. Haldeman, and John Dean, substituted some other norms:

Haldeman to Nixon: "The way to contain any meaningful investigation of the Watergate break-in is to have the CIA tell the FBI, 'Stay the hell out of this. . . .' "

Nixon: "Right, fine. . . . Play it tough. That's the way they play it and that's the way we are going to play it. . . ."

Dean: "I have begun to keep notes on a lot of people who are emerging as less than our friends . . . and we shouldn't forget the way some of them have treated us."

Nixon: "I want the most comprehensive notes on all those who tried to do us in. . . . They were doing this quite deliberately and they are asking for it and they are going to get it. . . ."

Dean: "What an exciting prospect."[43]

Group Sanctions

Because these human groups within an agency may seem amorphous and often changing, one should never conclude that they are the jellyfish of administration that can safely be ignored. On the contrary, they possess highly effective sanctions to bring and keep their members in line: warm acceptance and praise; ridicule; the silent treatment; ostracism; and on occasion, physical abuse (such as may occur between strikers and strikebreakers during a protracted labor dispute). Once again, the Nixon transcripts are revealing:

> Praise as an enforcer of group norms:
> *Nixon to John Dean:* "But the way you have handled all this seems to me has been very skillful, putting your fingers in the leaks that have sprung here and sprung there. . . . We are all in it together."

> Praise and pass the buck:
> *Nixon:* "Tell him [Attorney General Richard G. Kleindienst] we have to get things worked out. We have to work together on this thing. I would build him up. . . . But let's remember this [the forced entry and bugging of the Democratic party national head-quarters] was not done by the White House. This was done by the Committee to Re-elect [me], and *Mitchell was the chairman, correct?"* [emphasis added].[44]

All of this seems to stress what groups may negatively do. But it is equally important to see the healthy things they are capable of doing.

Satisfaction of Human Needs Through Group Membership

The rise of labor unions in American history attests to a simple fact: there is *security* in numbers. Surrounded by allies in a natural work group, employees establish their first and most fundamental refuge against the winds of chance in an agency. "Dealing with *all of us*" puts a bargaining session with management on an entirely different plane from that of "dealing with me alone."

Second, acceptance in a natural work group is ipso facto a contribution to the love need, the gregarious drive, in people. And if group life on the job is really meaningful, it may provide the kind of psychic payoff that a person gets nowhere else (thus demonstrating the error of the early scientific management writers who saw work as something *external* to life). There is an impressive amount of research that documents the benefits to both participants and their organizations when people who like each other are able to work on tasks together.[45] Apparently, supervisors who fear cliques should take a second look.

Moreover, groups can build self-esteem. The plaudits and encouragement people receive from significant others may be among the major supports enabling them to see themselves as whole, thus providing some of the psychological underpinnings for self-actualization.

Clearly, then, the quality of group life is of critical importance in the success or failure of all that an agency undertakes to do.

A PLEA FOR MANAGEMENT TO BEGIN WITH PEOPLE

The raw materials of government are human beings. And they are *not* automatons, driven simplistically by a single urge in life — to make money. Nor is work external to life; rather, it is deeply intertwined in a person's whole search for necessities, for security, for affection, and for self.

That kind of search has constituted the principal inquiry of this chapter. Turning away from the earlier mechanistic view of workers, we have waded deeply into the theories of Abraham Maslow, Frederick Herzberg, and their critics. In the light of all the subsequent research, Maslow's ladder of inborn needs requires substantial modification — and one has been offered here.

But a Maslow act of faith and an overriding value judgment still strike us as valid in public administration today. Management ought steadily to enable people to become what they can become, to boost employees toward self-actualization. Agencies with vision and a problem-solving capability must have employees who can dream — and solve problems.

When we add up the postulates about individual needs and the characteristics of group life discussed here, a management philosophy begins to emerge that is in sharp contrast to the philosophy of scientific management (and Theory X). Douglas McGregor labeled the new approach Theory Y.[46] We suggest the following as its key features:

Human needs must be met before an agency's output needs can be effectively met.

Psychological (or ego) needs (love, self-esteem, autonomy, and growth) are as important as economic needs.

Associational needs demand a healthy group structure within an agency.

The steadfast goal of management ought to be the generation of self-actualizing people.

Self-actualization requires some other needs to be met, continuous challenge, and the freedom to grow.

People, whatever their job titles may be, from janitor to department head, are capable of great things.

We find ourselves with organization theorist Victor Thompson, looking forward to the day when administration will be firmly predicated on the recognition and interdependence of all:

Such mutual recognition, in time, will depend upon the achievement of status and function for all. Then men will become adults; and the grown-up kindergartens through which we now conduct our affairs will pass unregretted from the scene.[47]

SUMMARY

The first useful lesson in public administration is the primacy of people. When handled well, they bring agencies alive and make things happen; when misunderstood and treated badly, they can turn their agencies into battlegrounds or hollow shells.

For decades in this century, we have proceeded along detours in trying to understand what makes the worker tick. Frederick Taylor's scientific management school painted employees as "grown-up children," requiring only strict guidance and economic rewards to become highly productive. That approach fathered a management school later dubbed Theory X, exponent of authoritarian leadership style and narrow jobs that could be quickly mastered.

Then came the breakthrough, the rediscovery of the *total person,* in the Hawthorne research studies of the Harvard Business School, 1927–1932, for the Western Electric Company. As a result, Homo economicus had to make room for people with deep social and psychological needs, including meaningful group life and recognition.

Through the research of scholars like Abraham Maslow, Rensis Likert, Robert Kahn, Frederick Herzberg, Chris Argyris, and many others, a new approach to management called Theory Y began to take shape after 1950. It stressed the importance of life at work to satisfy a whole range of human needs — security, acceptance, recognition, and growth — if people were to approach their full potential.

Critics have found significant flaws in both the empirical base and some of the logic of Theory Y. Clearly, its prescriptions do not fit all management situations. But its central precepts — a whole view of the human personality, the need to make work worthwhile, and the potential that lies in self-actualized human beings — have left an indelible mark on management science in the United States.

The men and women who make government function or falter cannot be viewed as isolates; group life is still the natural habitat for most of us. Managers need to understand that, and recognize both the nature of work groups and their potential impact, for good or ill, on their agencies. Groups define roles and set and enforce norms, though not always those the agency hopes for. In addition, human groups can do much to meet the security, belongingness, and esteem needs of individuals, and thus significantly strengthen the human fabric of the organization.

The starting point, then, in our study of public administration is, as Alexander Pope recognized so long ago, the people of the organization. Conducting the people's business is preeminently the *business of people.*

But there is more, of course, for even self-actualized people, alone, do not make a government. Chapter 3 suggests why.

KEY CONCEPTS

Frederick Taylor
Theory X
Hawthorne experiments
Abraham Maslow

self-actualization
motivation-hygiene theory
economic man
reward-seeking person

upward mobiles   work groups
indifferents   role taking versus role playing
ambivalents   group-determined norms
human needs circle   Theory Y

DISCUSSION QUESTIONS

1. In what ways can you support the philosophy underlying scientific man-
    agement? For what types of jobs might it be the most appropriate?
2. Critique Maslow's needs hierarchy. What is the most significant evidence
    supporting its inapplicability? If Maslow is incorrect, what are the impli-
    cations for "management beginning with people?"
3. Identify similarities in the ideas of Maslow, Herzberg, and MacGregor. To
    what extent is their source the same as that which produced the unex-
    pected results found at the Hawthorne plant?

PROJECTS

1. Choose ten jobs or positions. For each, identify how far up the needs
    hierarchy a person filling that position is *most likely* to go. Make sure you
    have chosen at least one position for each of the five levels.
2. Choose a group in which you have been a member. Write a short
    paragraph discussing each of the nine characteristics on page 28 with
    reference to your group.
3. List as many group norms and sanctions as you can. Choose one and
    suggest why that norm or sanction exists.

Notes

1. "McNamara's Human Problem," *Life,* Sept. 20, 1963, p. 4.
2. Frederick W. Taylor, *Scientific Management* (New York: Harper & Row, 1911, 1947).
3. Taylor, *Scientific Management,* p. 120.
4. John Dewey, *Democracy and Education* (New York: Macmillan, 1916, 1961), p. 85.
5. The typology of Theory X and Theory Y was provided in 1960 by Douglas McGregor in
    The Human Side of Enterprise (New York: McGraw-Hill, 1960), pp. 33ff.
6. The findings were reported in Elton Mayo, *Human Problems of an Industrial Civiliza-
    tion* (New York: Viking, 1933, 1960); T. N. Whitehead, *The Industrial Worker* (Cam-
    bridge, Mass.: Harvard University Press, 1938); and F. J. Roethlisberger and W. J.
    Dickson, *Management and the Worker* (Cambridge, Mass.: Harvard University Press,
    1942).
7. Previously studied at the same plant.
8. See especially Chapter 25 in Roethlisberger and Dickson, *Management and the
    Worker.* The application of modern statistical techniques to the Hawthorne data has
    led some authors to reject the humanistic conclusions advanced here and by the early

interpreters — Mayo, Roethlisberger, and Dickson. R. H. Franke and J. D. Kaul are convinced, for example, that the assertion of managerial discipline (in replacing two of the original five workers), the onset of the Great Depression (and consequent fear of job loss), and the introduction of rest periods explain most of the gain in productivity of the five relay assembly workers, rather than the social and psychological payoffs they received as part of the experiment. See Franke and Kaul, "The Hawthorne Experiments: First Statistical Interpretation," *American Sociological Review* (Oct. 1978), 43:623–643.

9. Abraham Maslow, "A Theory of Human Motivation," *Psychological Review* (1943), 50:370–396.

10. Among Maslow's important precursors were Arthur Bentley, Elton Mayo, Mary Parker Follett, and Chester Barnard.

11. Maslow's theories were set forth in *Motivation and Personality* (New York: Harper & Row, 1954) and *Eupsychian Management* (Homewood, Ill.: Irwin, 1965).

12. Maslow, *Motivation and Personality,* chap. 12, and *Eupsychian Management,* pp. 5–10. A number of scholars have suggested techniques for measuring self-actualization: Lyman Porter, *Managerial Attitudes and Performance* (Homewood, Ill.: Irwin, 1968); Chris Argyris, *Understanding Organizational Behavior* (Homewood, Ill.: Dorsey, 1960), chap. 4; and a quicker method by Charles Bonjean and Gary Vance, "A Short Form Measure of Self-Actualization," *Journal of Applied Behavioral Science* (July–Sept. 1968), 4:299–312.

13. John Gardner, "The Luckiest People," *Civil Service Journal* (April–June 1967), 7:7.

14. Chris Argyris said it so well in "We Must Make Work Worthwhile," *Life* May 5, 1967, pp. 56–68.

15. Maslow, *Motivation and Personality,* p. 228.

16. Frederick Herzberg, *Work and the Nature of Man* (Cleveland: World, 1966).

17. For other views of the satisfaction-performance controversy, see Charles N. Greene, "The Satisfaction-Performance Controversy" *Business Horizons* (Oct. 1972), 15:31–41; Robert Dubin et al., *Leadership and Productivity* (San Francisco, Chandler, 1965), pp. 25–26; and David Kuhn et al., "Does Job Performance Affect Employee Satisfaction?" *Personnel Journal* (June 1971), 50:455–459ff. The Kuhn study found higher correlations between satisfaction of the lower Maslow needs and productivity than between self-actualization and productivity.

18. Karl Marx, *Critique of Political Economy* and the *Communist Manifesto* in *Karl Marx and Frederick Engels: Selected Works* (Moscow: Progress Publishers, 1969), pp. 502–506.

19. Jeremy Bentham, *An Introduction to the Principles of Morals and Legislation* (New York: Macmillan, 1789, 1948), chap. 1.

20. B. F. Skinner, *Beyond Freedom and Dignity* (New York: Bantam, 1972), chaps. 2 and 5.

21. Harry Levinson, "Asinine Attitudes toward Motivation," *Harvard Business Review* (Jan.–Feb. 1973), 51:70–76.

22. Maslow, "Theory of Human Motivation," p. 371.

23. Two excellent surveys of Maslow and Herzberg critics will be our primary sources here: F. K. Gibson and C. E. Teasley, "The Humanistic Model of Organizational Motivation: A Review of Research Support," *Public Administration Review* (Jan.–Feb. 1973), 33:89–96, and M. A. Wahba and L. G. Bridwell, "Maslow Reconsidered: A Review of Research on the Need Hierarchy Theory," Proceedings of the 33d Annual Meeting of the Academy of Management (1973), pp. 514–520, reprinted in K. N. Wexley and G. A. Yukl, *Organizational Behavior and Industrial Psychology* (New York: Oxford University Press, 1975), pp. 5–11.

24. D. Hale and K. Nougaim, "An Examination of Maslow's Need Hierarchy in an Organi-

zational Setting," *Organizational Behavior and Human Performance* (Feb. 1968), 3:12–35.

25. H. G. Wilcox, "Hierarchy, Human Nature, and the Participative Panacea," *Public Administration Review* (Jan.–Feb. 1969) 29:53–63.

26. Robert Presthus, *The Organizational Society* (New York: St. Martin's Press, 1978), chaps. 6–8.

27. Gibson and Teasley, "The Humanistic Model of Organizational Motivation," p. 94.

28. C. R. Walker and R. H. Guest, "The Man on the Assembly Line," *Harvard Business Review* (May–June 1952), 30:71–83.

29. Harold L. Sheppard and N. Q. Herrick, *Where Have All the Robots Gone?* (New York: Free Press, 1972), pp. 181–184.

30. For a contemporary magazine description of the problem, see "The Job Blahs: Who Wants to Work?" *Newsweek*, March 26, 1973, pp. 79–89. For a statistical portrayal of frustration by age group, see the study undertaken by the Upjohn Institute for Employment Research for the Department of Health, Education, and Welfare, *Work in America* (Cambridge, Mass.: M.I.T. Press, 1973), p. 45. For further empirical support of Herzberg, see Charles N. Weaver, "What Workers Want from Their Jobs," *Personnel* (May–June 1976), 54:48–54.

31. Department of Health, Education and Welfare, *Work in America*, pp. 1–28.

32. Department of Health, Education and Welfare, *Work in America*, pp. 15–16.

33. Chris Argyris (in his monumental debate with organization theorist Herbert Simon), "Some Limits of Rational Man Organizational Theory," *Public Administration Review* (May–June 1973), 33:265.

34. Aristotle, *Politics* (New York: Random House, 1943). Book I, chap. 2.

35. Arthur F. Bentley, *The Process of Government* (Chicago: University of Chicago Press, 1908), p. 176.

36. There were notable exceptions: the Hawthorne studies noted earlier, followed by Mary Parker Follett, who carefully probed interpersonal relations during the 1930s. See the collection of her papers, *Dynamic Administration* (New York: Harper, 1942), edited by Metcalf and Urwick. Chester Barnard pioneered in the analysis of informal organizations in *Functions of the Executive* (Cambridge, Mass.: Harvard University Press, 1938).

37. Tamotsu Shibutani, *Society and Personality* (Englewood Cliffs, N.J.: Prentice-Hall, 1961), pp. 410, 412, and 426.

38. Suggested by J. K. Hemphill and C. M. Westie, "The Measurement of Group Dimensions," *Journal of Psychology* (Apr. 1950), 29: 325–342.

39. See, generally, B. L. Hinton and H. J. Reitz, *Groups and Organizations* (Belmont, Calif.: Wadsworth, 1971).

40. Shibutani, *Society and Personality,* pp. 392–393, 465.

41. Roethlisberger and Dickson, *Management and the Worker,* pp. 409–423, 517–521ff.

42. Harold Stein, *Public Administration and Policy Development* (New York: Harcourt, Brace, 1952), p. 11; and Robert Golembiewski, *Behavior and Organization* (Chicago: Rand McNally, 1962), pp. 39–46, 166–184.

43. The Watergate transcripts.

44. The Watergate transcripts.

45. See the section on task performance in A. J. and B. E. Lott, "Group Cohesiveness as Interpersonal Attraction: Consequences of Liking," *Psychological Bulletin* (Oct. 1965), 64:259–302.

46. McGregor, *The Human Side of Enterprise,* pp. 45ff.

47. Victor Thompson, *Modern Organization* (New York: Knopf, 1961), p. 197.

Chapter 3
The Structural Side of Administration

WHY BUREAUCRACY?

Unorganized people, however self-actualized, do not make a government! Defective cars do not get tested and recalled by informal groups; a heroin ring is not broken up by a couple of public-spirited citizens; and while a mob may delay the construction of a nuclear power plant, no unorganized collectivity of individuals could carry out a balanced energy policy. No, we organize for the reason that Max Weber, the German sociologist, pointed out a long time ago: There really is no other way to get a complex job accomplished.[1]

Suppose, for example, that your campus is incensed over the governor's dismissal of your university president. Hungering for a cause, a group of you decide that a march on the state capitol, fifty miles away, must be undertaken. The *unorganized* approach would be to find the campus Pied Piper who could sound the signal to "March!" and hope everyone would march. Without any organization, within a day these pooped-out protestors would make the thirteenth-century Children's Crusade look like a paradigm of efficiency by comparison.

Knowing this, the agents provocateurs of the march would organize down to the last box lunch to assure its success. They would pay special attention to the following factors:

Allocation of functions: route determination, fund raising, legal clearances, commissary provisions, sleeping arrangements, medical care, communications on the line of march, drafting the petition, speech writing, preparing the press releases, and so on.

Staffing: selecting the students who have both the heart and the feet for this grind.

Delegation of authority: assigning functions to trusted lieutenants.

Directing and supervising: getting the march under way, reviewing how all phases of the organization are functioning, and adjusting the march as conditions warrant.

On paper, those functions might quickly take the shape of that hallmark feature of all bureaucracies, the organization chart (see Figure 3.1).

In its best sense, then, bureaucracy is a plan of action, a road map of who is to do what to accomplish the goals of public policy. It is inconceivable that we could curb pollution, build highways, provide health insurance, or educate the disadvantaged young without it.

In this chapter we are going to view formal organizations through the eyes of some major administrative theorists, historical and modern; decipher some different ways of looking at bureaucracy and the purposes it serves; get a picture of the large difference it makes how we organize work; and then try to extract a

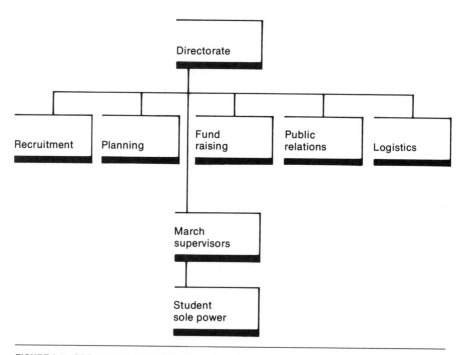

FIGURE 3.1 ORGANIZING A MARCH ON THE CAPITOL

set of principles of formal organization that research findings would seem to justify. We begin with the great defender of formal organization, Max Weber, whose major writings appeared early in the twentieth century.

Max Weber (1864–1920)

The superiority of the formally organized way of doing a job over any other approach (e.g., "get some volunteers to pitch in") could be simply demonstrated, Weber thought, in the efficiency with which bureaucracy accomplishes its tasks. From the clear delineation of duties, he argued, come specialization and avoidance of overlap and duplication. From record keeping and knowledge of precedents (the files) comes a developing expertise that builds on success and avoids past mistakes.

The regularization of services means speed, predictability, unambiguity, and impartiality. As a case in point, you have a piece of private property and want it rezoned as commercial property. A corner of Weber's bureaucracy called the office of planning and zoning, complete with rules and precedents, gives you a quick, predictable, clear-cut, and impartial answer (assuming that you don't control the city commissioner who oversees that office).

Weber contended that placing related services in a planned hierarchy with strict subordination assures unity, reduces friction, and cuts costs:

> The decisive reason for the advance of bureaucratic organization has always been its technical superiority over any other form of organization. The fully developed bureaucratic mechanism compares with other organizations exactly as does the machine with the non-mechanical modes of production.[2]

That must be quite a different picture from the stereotype of bureaucracy you may have held for a long time — that it is tied up in red tape, inflexible, ponderous, stifling, slow, and very costly. But remember two ways in which Weber stacked the deck. He was pitting the organized approach against "the collegiate, honorific, and avocational" disorganized forms of administration; and like Plato he portrayed an *ideal*, in this case an ideal bureaucracy, in order to isolate its features.

By 1909, the German bureaucracy had apparently disenchanted Weber:

> Imagine the consequences of that comprehensive bureaucratization and rationalization which already today we see approaching. . . . By [rational calculation], the performance of each individual worker is mathematically measured;* each man becomes a little cog in the machine; and, aware of this, his own preoccupation is whether he can become a bigger cog. . . . This passion for bureaucracy is enough to drive one to despair.[3]

---

* Probably one of Frederick Taylor's time-and-motion monitors, standing with stopwatch in hand over some hapless worker.

One of Weber's lasting contributions to the study of bureaucracy lay in the distinction he drew between two kinds of rationality — formal and substantive. In bureaucratic terms, *formal rationality* concerns the logical subdivision of a problem into all its component parts (flywheels turn gears that turn drive shafts; small offices turn sections that turn divisions and bureaus) with no guarantee that the problem will be solved. *Substantive rationality* clearly relates means to ends and, without undue concentration on the intervening apparatus, focuses on getting the job done.[4] The two concepts can be readily contrasted:

> A Ralph Nader task force in 1971 indicated that fifteen years, seven laws, and $3 billion after the federal water pollution clean-up program had begun, not a single major waterway had been cleared up — bureaucratic wheels were spinning quite rationally but going nowhere.

> A supply sergeant, substantively rational, sees an overloaded truck inside a warehouse and lets a little air out of the tires so the truck can make it through the door.

The distinction is worth remembering. When we look at agency organization charts later on, the formal rationality will be obvious — bureaucracy quartered and subdivided. But will anyone remember why the organization was set up to begin with and what it is supposed to accomplish — or not to accomplish? We have, for example, a Federal Bureau of Investigation (FBI) that is not supposed to urge black leaders to commit suicide, a post office that is not supposed to impose mail covers (to determine with whom you are corresponding), and a Central Intelligence Agency (CIA) that is not supposed to help "plumbers" burgle a psychiatrist's office.

The Marxists[5]

If Max Weber is the archdeacon of bureaucracy, the Marxists are among its chief critics when out of office and among its heaviest-handed practitioners when in office. The state is the weapon of the ruling class, Karl Marx and Friedrich Engels wrote, and the bureaucracy is the instrument through which the ruling class holds sway. Evidence of that occurs all the time in American public administration.

> A chemical engineer from the state's major polluter becomes executive officer of the state's air conservation committee.

> The president is forced to withdraw the nomination of a trucking executive to a major energy conservation post.

> The president of the Rockefeller Foundation becomes President Jimmy Carter's secretary of defense.

> A senior partner of the one of the biggest investment banking houses is appointed secretary of the treasury.[6]

But let it be added that the ruling class in communist states also quickly co-opts the bureaucracy, as Yugoslav protestors like Milovan Djilas and Czech protestors like Ludvik Vaculik have made clear.[7]

Within bureaucracies, a whole series of insults alienates workers; for example, their surplus value is expropriated by the owners (employees are not paid anywhere near the value of what they produce), and the workers are told daily how little they count through such devices as managerial titles and perquisites (which a century later Victor Thompson would call "dramaturgy"[8]).

The Marxist view of bureaucracy, then, is one of class representation, exploitation, and alienation. Like the capitalist stage itself, bureaucracy must go. In the final stage of communism, what will be left of formal organization? The state will wither away, and government will be reduced to the administration of things.[9] Nicos Mouzelis summarizes the Marxist end to bureaucracy in this way:

> The end of the division of labour marks the end of alienation and the beginning of an era of individual freedom. It is only in such a society that a really democratic administration can exist. The administrative tasks, simplified and demystified, will be the concern of everybody. There will be no more monopoly of the administrative positions. The worker, citizen of a true democracy, will be at the same time elected and elector, administered and administrator. It is only by this kind of "auto-administration" that the "public" authority returns finally to its true basis and the state "withers away."[10]

I've always wondered, though, about the Marxist way of preparing people for freedom by putting them through a couple of generations of dictatorship. As Lord Thomas Macaulay wisely observed a century ago, "If men are to wait for liberty 'till they become wise and good in slavery, they may indeed wait forever."[11] In the meantime, communist bureaucracies plod along in Russia, China, Cuba, and elsewhere without a hint of withering away.

Robert Michels (1876–1936)

At about the same time Max Weber was having second thoughts about the virtues of bureaucracy, Robert Michels was providing new, empirical reasons for being concerned. In a long and careful study of German trade unions and socialist parties, Michels undertook to measure what happens to participation and decision making in organizations that are highly democratic at the outset.

He propounded the "iron law of oligarchy" to summarize his findings. Organizations typically experience a drift of power toward the top, with fewer and fewer members making more and more of the decisions for the entire organization. Eventually, democracy succumbs to oligarchy.[12]

There are many ways in which we structure agencies that make government highly subject to Michels's law: pyramid-shaped organizations that point to the top, the notion of downward-flowing authority, and the security-seeking strategy many employees pursue of "don't rock the boat." As we saw in Chapter 2, the iron law of oligarchy increases the powerlessness of workers, undercuts their autonomy, and thwarts their attempts at self-actualization.

Taking Care of the Inner Circle, Soviet-Style

. . . Brezhnev and some 255,000 of the Communist Party bigwigs are on the receiving end of extensive fringe benefits.

Brezhnev and others like him not only receive an extra month's pay as a bonus; they are entitled to country dachas, town apartments, superior medical care, state transportation, holiday facilities near Yalta, and a monthly allotment of 16–32 "gold rubles" which permits them to buy foreign goods in the *valuta* shops generally restricted to tourists, diplomats, and other holders of hard currency.

In the Soviet Union's so-called classless society, there is indeed a highly privileged class, whose members are secure so long as they conform.

Parade Magazine, May 18, 1975.

The Classical School of the 1930s — Gulick, Urwick, and Others

For the school of thought that dominated public administration in the 1930s, *structure was the thing.* The bible of the period was the collection *Papers on the Science of Administration,* edited in 1937 by one of the twentieth-century greats in American public administration, Luther Gulick, and his British colleague, Lyndall Urwick. The spirit of the classical school was expressed by one of their contributors, James Mooney:

> Organization, and the sound application of its principles, must always remain a potent force in determining industrial destiny. Organization concerns procedure, and the attainment of any human group objective must ever depend, in great measure, on efficient forms and procedure. . . . Without such efficient procedure, all human group effort becomes relatively futile. It is in these facts, I believe, that we may see clearly the importance of these principles of organization.[13]

What emerged from the classical school was a set of principles of organization that were intended to guide administrators in clustering, directing, and coordinating governmental functions. Prominent among the principles were:

Unity of command: each subordinate should have only one superior.

Authority and the scalar principle: the power to issue commands flows downward and should be commensurate with responsibility at each layer of the organization.

Span of control: "no human brain should attempt to supervise directly more than five, or at the most six, other individuals whose work is interrelated."[14]

Line and staff: there should be separate provision for doing operations (the line) and planning (the staff).[15]

As we shall see, some of the principles did not stand the test of time; others continue to influence how we organize governmental agencies to this day. It is worth noting that in the midst of all the structural guidance in the 1937 *Papers,* on closer glance one observes three harbingers of a yet to come public administration that begins with people: "The Effects of the Social Environment" by the Hawthorne plant researchers; Mary Parker Follett's, "On the Illusion of Final Authority," an argument for shared control between management and workers; and V. A. Graicunas's examination of relationships in organizations.

Behavioralists of the Post–World War II Era

Following World War II, Herbert Simon began to turn public administration around on one level, while Abraham Maslow was doing it on another (see Chapter 2). In 1946, Simon published an iconoclastic piece in the *Public Administration Review,* "The Proverbs of Administration."[16] He pointed out the ambiguities and contradictions in the Gulick-Urwick principles of a decade before and called for a research effort to provide an empirical foundation for some substantiated principles of administration. Then in 1950, with coauthors Donald Smithburg and Victor Thompson, Simon published a pioneering text, *Public Administration,* which laid the groundwork for a new behavioral approach to organization.[17]

What these writers and their contemporaries (or coauthors) like James G. March[18] and James D. Thompson[19] principally questioned about the structuralists of the 1930s was the underlying premise that organizations could be laid out and administered in any fully rational way. We all operate within a "bounded rationality" — within unknowables, internal forces and external developments that may be beyond the control of management. That fact of life requires systems that are much more open, more adaptable, living in flux with their environments.[20] Those systems then help produce one of the key marks of healthy organizations, a homeostatic quality (like a thermostat) that enables an organization to move back toward equilibrium after a disturbance.[21]

For James Thompson, the purpose of administration is to narrow the uncertainties so that constructive action can be taken. He suggests a certainty-uncertainty continuum as one guide in the shaping of formal organizations. Those that face highly uncertain environments (e.g., an infantry company) must be decentralized to permit maximum adaptability.[22]

For Herbert Simon, organizations are, first and foremost, decision-making networks. Their ability to generate and then analyze information flows constitutes their primary attack upon the strictures imposed by bounded rationality.[23] But the limitations on knowledge are never fully removed, requiring agencies in their decision making to accept partial solutions (satisfice) rather than to pursue illusory perfect solutions (maximize or optimize).[24]

Although Simon's views on information-responsive, decision-making organizations place him as an architect of the open-systems school, other views he has espoused about organizations place him much closer to the structuralists he once criticized so vehemently. His basic answer to bounded rationality seems really to be to bind together otherwise unbounded individuals in formal organizations where roles may be prescribed, information computer-analyzed, and decisions imposed on all as a way of generating coordinated action.[25]

Thus, the issue is joined between the contemporary structuralists of the Simon school and the humanist school of Abraham Maslow, Chris Argyris, Rensis Likert, and others. Hear Simon first:

> Maslow and Argyris paint a heroic and romantic picture of Man, a picture of an inexhaustibly creative creature who only needs to be given a blank wall of infinite size in order to paint on it an unimaginably beautiful picture.* All the evidence from the fine arts suggests that unlimited freedom is not the best condition for human creativity. . . . Man creates best when he operates in an environment whose constraints are commensurate with the capacities of his bounded rationality. . . . If now, in search of self-actualization, we eliminate those organizational forms, or redesign them to de-emphasize the use of formal authority, will the society remain sufficiently productive to allow opportunity for self-actualization? My own answer to this question is pessimistic, but I would like to have much better evidence than I now have on which to decide such a crucial issue.
>
> In the organizational world that I observe, there is much less need for power, and consequently much less alienation than in Argyris's world. I see a social system making use of hierarchical organizations to reach a high level of productivity, and to produce a large quantity of freedom in the form of leisure. I see creative people using that leisure for all sorts of self-actualization.[26]

Argyris was repelled by Simon's rationalized system in which administrators lay down the organization's goals, plan the procedures, set the standards, train the employees, and initiate most of the communications (all suggestive of Theory X management). Argyris was convinced that such managerial usurpation would stifle the members of an organization, producing entropy, a social disease of bureaucracies that suggests grinding to a halt, and would weaken decision making through the failure to tap employees' ideas.

> One of the consequences of [Simon's] limited view of man is that those employees who may value growth (this includes an increasing proportion of our youth) will not find a hospitable environment in such an organization. An individual oriented toward growth would have great difficulty in obtaining any of the inducements identified by Simon . . . except such inducements as money, power, control. The self-actualizing individual would tend to view these factors, at best, as hygiene factors which, as Herzberg suggests, do not motivate; they just reduce dissatisfaction. (This indicates that deficiency-oriented individuals can exist in an organization that encourages self-actualization but the reverse is not the case.) . . .[27]
>
> Thus we begin to see how a Simon-pure . . . organization is not so pure. It would tend to exclude self-actualizers.[28]

---

* A palpably incorrect statement. See Chapter 2 for the preconditions for self-actualization.

Argyris then developed his case for organizations that take people's feelings into account and contribute to an atmosphere of trust, openness, and commitment. Those are the organizations that give birth to self-actualizers.

The Futurists

Concluding this review of schools of thought on organizations, we need to look at those who seem to view bureaucracy through binoculars (although I'm not sure from which end) and predict its radical transformation — or its sure demise.

The face of change in the post-1950 world — TV, nuclear power, satellites, the civil rights revolution, grass everywhere, the revolution in morals — made turbulence the only constant and books about the future surefire winners in the present.[29] Alvin Toffler's *Future Shock* was one such book; its message for bureaucrats was simple enough: set up "councils on the future" (the old staff principle, really) and govern change, or change will govern you.[30]

Even before Toffler, another observer, funeral sermon in hand, began predicting the coming death of bureaucracy. In a series of articles and books, Warren Bennis began to turn Max Weber over, exposing the ills of bureaucracy:

It stultifies human beings, communications, and innovation.

It thrives on groupthink.

It fails to resolve conflict and to provide due process.

It is hopelessly outdated in a technological age.[31]

Apparently, except for the most routine kinds of work (getting out social security checks, etc.), Bennis saw government moving toward highly democratic organizations, with the predominant form made up of adaptive, flexible, problem-centered temporary task forces functioning more as effective mergers of technical skills and less as rank differentiators.

Then, like Weber a half century earlier, Bennis came to a point of disillusionment while trying to apply his democratic-adaptive theory of administration as president of the University of Cincinnati during the anti-Vietnam War period:

I am not quite as optimistic as I was seven years ago about some of my assumptions. I am less confident that . . . "democracy [in administration] is inevitable." But I am more convinced that our future depends upon making it so.

A year's trials as President of a large university make me even more certain that a viable managerial strategy does not lie in consensus. In caring, surely; in civility, definitely; in comity, especially — but not in consensus. . . . We can adequately deal with our crises only through managers who can devise strategies that will carry us "beyond bureaucracy" into control of our own evolution.[32]

The inherent contradiction in that final sentence ("managers" — "but our own evolution") suggests how foggy Bennis's binoculars had become.

Some who have disagreed with Bennis's portrayal of a dying bureaucracy have simply taken umbrage at what they regard as runaway liberalism; they see bureaucracy and hierarchy as appropriate instruments of coordination and control in our lives.[33] Others, such as William D. Scott and Terence R. Mitchell, see a number of possible futures for bureaucracy:

> the constitutional organization, with emphasis on due process to protect all members of the organization
>
> the federal organization, close to Bennis's, involving task forces and self-coordination by professionals
>
> the totalitarian organization, involving thoroughgoing control and behavior modification of employees by the managerial cadres[34]

The one thing that is certain about the future is that it's coming. Contra Bennis, bureaucracies, for good or ill, will not only be a part of it but will have a fair amount to say about the quality of life we can expect in that next time frame. Self-interest, and our caring about the life our kids will experience, both demand that we develop as much understanding as we can on how to assemble the biggest Tinkertoy of all, the hundred thousand or so governments we live under in this country.

BUREAUCRACY'S MANY FACES: BASICS OF STRUCTURE AND FUNCTION

Plan of Attack

At the beginning of the chapter, we talked about putting together a march on the state capitol. From that project on up to a nationwide effort to eliminate Legionnaires' disease or to remove slums, a *plan of attack* is a prerequisite to success. That is what organizational design is initially all about.

How are functions grouped? This is the first question to be answered. The Bennis answer, as we have seen, is to assemble the necessary technical specialties together in flexible task forces, built around the major components of an agency's mission, in environmental protection, let's say: (a) pollution prevention and (b) environmental restoration — air, land, and water.

The classical school suggested five bases for bringing functions together:[35]

1. *Major-purpose organizations:* organizations are set up, such as a defense department or a natural resources conservation agency, which bring under one administrative roof all the component services required to achieve the program goals.

2. *Organization according to process:* in this type of organization, func-
    tions are clustered according to specialized skills — the office of legal
    counsel, the electronic data processing division, the intelligence division
    of the police department, and the construction division of the state high-
    way department, for example.

3. *Organization according to place:* here the organization strives for either
    geographic specialization (such as the police precinct in a high-density
    crime area so the cops can learn the hangouts and habits of the under-
    world) or for location economics (the neighborhood fire station with its
    short run to fires). Examples include regional offices of the Federal
    Reserve System and the U.S. Office of Personnel Management, the
    "country desks" of the State Department; and, in a large sense, state
    and city governments rendering a multitude of services in their defined
    areas.[36]

4. *Organization according to thing:* the object of this type of organization
    is to provide rather technical specialization around identifiable objects
    such as a bureau of animal husbandry or plant quarantine in an agricul-
    ture department, the Locomotive Inspection Division of the Interstate
    Commerce Commission, and commodity divisions (such as steel, cop-
    per, aluminum, and textiles) of a wartime regulatory agency.

5. *Clientele organizations:* typically, this kind of organization grows out of
    political pressures (e.g., veterans) or the intrinsic complexities associ-
    ated with an identifiable group of people that generate tailored-made
    agencies to cope with such groups; for example, the Veterans Adminis-
    tration; the Women's Bureau; the Children's Bureau; the Bureau of
    Indian Affairs; and, at the local level, such units as the division of pupil
    personnel in a board of education and a youth bureau in a police depart-
    ment.

Expanding on the clientele concept, Peter Blau and W. Richard Scott developed
a classification of organizations in terms of who receives the benefit (cui
bono?): mutual benefit associations, such as labor unions; business concerns
for the owners; service organizations, such as social work agencies; and commonweal units, serving society as a whole, such as a street department.[37]

On a number of grounds, the five bases advanced by the classical school for
grouping functions have been widely criticized.[38] As an attempt at categorizing,
they suffer the major flaws of ambiguity and overlap. For example, is the U.S.
Department of Agriculture's major purpose organization (food and fiber production for the nation), process (agronomy), or clientele (food lovers, the American
Farm Bureau Federation, and so on)? Is the Soil Conservation Service a purpose, a process, or a thing organization? Is a police department's major purpose protection (public safety) or process (criminology)?

Second, critic Simon charged that there is no science of public administration to tell why one base should be preferred over another. He took as an

example the dilemma facing a county board of health of whether to organize nursing services according to place (regional health offices) or according to process (nursing specialties such as school health, communicable disease, venereal disease, and care of shut-ins).

That dilemma is in part resolvable if the board of health can make up its collective mind about the *administrative goal* it is most interested in (in contrast to the *program goal* of protecting public health). There are at least four possible administrative goals: quality, quantity, speed, and economy of operations.[39]

Although economy (how to do the job the cheapest) is an omnipresent consideration in government, it may not always be the dominant administrative goal. For example, the *cheapest* way to teach reading might be to fire all the first-grade teachers except the best one and then put that one before the cameras to teach reading via home television. The potential savings on salaries and classrooms blow one's mind.

But two problems arise. Some children would never learn how to read (Weber's "substantive rationality" test), and thousands of mothers would go nuts having their six-year-olds at home twelve months a year. So quality considerations (learning rates) and clientele pressures both dictate a more expensive approach to first-grade education.

Applying the administrative goals analysis to a couple of functions of county government, we might find the following: Fire protection would emphasize speed of operations, forcing a decentralized location pattern for fire stations; recording property deeds must achieve quality standards of accuracy and also handle a sizable volume of demand, which suggests the possibility of introducing random-access computers into this slowest of manual operations in county government.

Notice how the analysis could help resolve the board of health's dilemma. If the board of health must operate nursing services as cheaply as possible (with economy as the administrative goal), then it would assign nursing generalists to regional centers. With relatively short distances to travel (see Figure 3.2), these nurses would deal with all kinds of medical problems in their territory. Or, under the assumption of a larger operating budget, the board of health might well insist on *quality* as the only acceptable goal for nursing services. This decision would then suggest organization according to process, the nurses being assigned in terms of their medical specialties (e.g., school health nurses and communicable disease nurses).

Of the five bases of organization suggested by Gulick, major purpose has certainly had the most advocates. Three lines of reasoning suggest why. First, legislative and citizen review is greatly aided by concentrating rather than scattering the functions of government. If recreation services are poorly handled in your city, how much easier it is to pinpoint responsibility if there is a unified major-purpose recreation department at city hall.

Second, the major-purpose arrangement greatly strengthens the hand of the

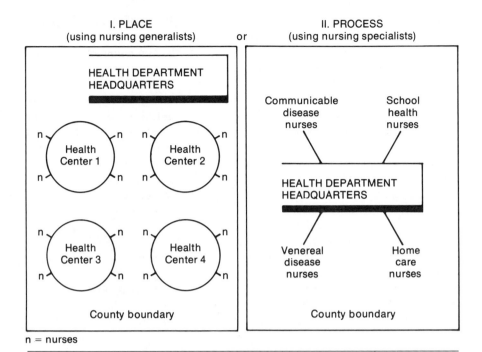

FIGURE 3.2   PLACE VERSUS PROCESS ORGANIZATION OF COUNTY NURSING SERVICES

administrator in providing essentially all the support services necessary to do the job assigned to the agency. Contrast the hamstrung position of the Indian commissioner (directing a clientele agency) who may have to depend on independent agencies for on-the-reservation road and facilities construction and for health care of his clientele, with the more enviable head of a major-purpose department. In the latter case, the agency head has a whole array of required services under his control — purchasing, fiscal, personnel, construction, and legal services — in addition to the line units that carry out the agency's authorized functions. In short, the major-purpose arrangement helps to fulfill that old administrative maxim alluded to earlier: "authority commensurate with responsibility."

Third, a case can be made on human relations and productivity grounds for extending the major-purpose format down to very low levels inside government agencies, where the traditional practice has been to define lower-unit missions narrowly in terms not of major purpose but rather of process, place, thing, or clientele.[40] Major purpose contributes to job enlargement;* and job enlarge-

---

* Either through increased responsibility or through additional duties.

ment enhances self-esteem and invites self-actualization and greater productivity. Being able to relate to end items and to the major reasons for the existence of an agency is one of the best antidotes there is for the syndrome of "I'm a little cog in a big wheel, and I don't know where we're going."

Providing for planning and support   In addition to laying down a sensible way to pull functions together and to determine the administrative goal, the plan of action ought to provide another structural element that has stood the test of time since Elihu Root, as secretary of war, developed the army general staff idea in 1903: provision for *line units* to carry out the major programs of an agency, *staff units* to think through where the agency is going, and *auxiliary* (support) *services* to make life easier for the line units. The intricacies that underlie this administrative trinity are the pièce de résistance of the next chapter, but this much ought to be said here: "Where there is no vision, line operations perish" — or at least wallow around. Writers since March and Simon have pointed to Gresham's law of planning: "Routine activities drive out the nonroutine."[41] That means simply that binocular vision gets thoroughly fogged up when administrators can see nothing but the minutiae of day-to-day operations. The antidote to Gresham's law of planning lies in formal organization: Peel off some analytical types who get a real charge out of future shock and set them up as a staff unit to plan ahead.

Further, we can ease the lives of line people by providing auxiliary units to do the inside jobs required across-the-board by all line units: recruiting, classifying, and training personnel; obtaining equipment and supplies; providing computer services; and many other jobs. To repeat, formal organization is the clue to those gains — pulling away from line organizations some staff people with the time to plan, and auxiliary units with the knowhow to provide the line with people, money, and material, if not with tender loving care.

Formal Organization as a Coordinator of Action[42]

This second face of bureaucracy is intended to provide a regular means for assuring that the left hand knows what the right hand is doing. In the city courts office, how do you prevent the civil deputies and criminal deputies from scheduling too many cases for the judges to hear next Monday? You adjust the formal organization to include a court coordinator to whom both sets of deputies must report. How do you prevent the CIA in a foreign country from subsidizing a rival political party and undercutting the established government that our embassy is supporting? You adjust the formal organization and make the CIA mission chief a deputy of the ambassador, subject to the latter's program and fiscal controls (and then hope that it works!).

The classical writers called this concept the *unity of command;* every deputy should regularly receive directions from only one superior. It communicated the hope of keeping a tight rein on the organization, the way a quarterback pulls the parts together. But countervailing considerations have weakened the principle over time. First, section and division heads of line units feel not only the hot breath of their direct superiors but also the cold stares of fiscal, personnel, purchasing, and legal officers in the technical or service bureaus (see Figure 3.3).

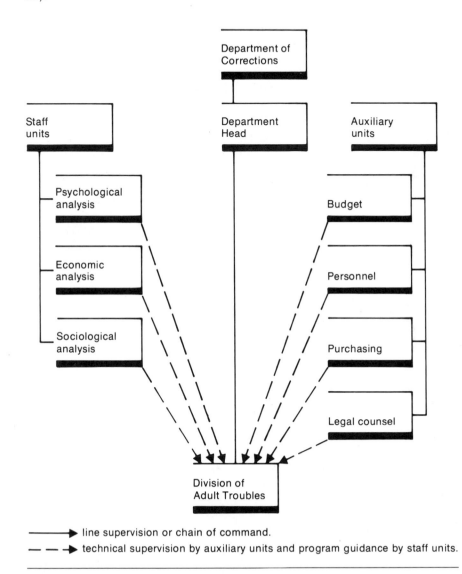

FIGURE 3.3   SACRIFICING UNITY OF COMMAND TO TECHNICAL SUPERVISION

Second, because of the harmful effects of powerlessness in the ranks (as we saw in Chapter 2), there is a good deal less advocacy today for a power monopoly in the executive suite, which Max Weber and others called "monocratic."

Today the unity-of-command principle would be phrased differently. Decision-making channels should be well recognized and understood throughout an organization and yet be sufficiently open to permit the introduction of new ideas and feedback. Identifying the decision-making channels for all to see helps establish the legitimacy of decisions that are made and, like unity of command of old, helps avoid confusion about who ought to be making what kinds of decisions.

The dissents of two contemporary writers even to this phraseology are worthy of note. Victor Thompson makes an impressive plea for achieving the unity goal not through command arrangements but through a widely shared sense of interdependence among the agency's personnel.[43] Chris Argyris would lay stress not on command functions but on the qualities of leadership that generate openness and commitment to the life of an agency.[44]

Another principle from the classical school designed to secure coordination of activities was that of *span of control*. Stated in a simple, believable way, it says that there are limits to the number of functions or subordinates one person can effectively supervise.

The variables that may influence the effective supervisory limits for any given person in an organization include:

the supervisor's personal capability, quickness, and skill in managing time

the dissimilarity and complexity of functions supervised

the skill of the subordinates (requiring great or little supervision)

the quality of the communication system

the physical nature of the work area as it may affect visibility

supervision from others

In an empirical study of those factors in sixty-seven manufacturing companies, John Udell found that only two were significantly correlated with the breadth or narrowness of the spans of control he observed: dissimilarity of functions with narrow spans and additional supervision from others with broad spans.[45]

But common sense would suggest that geographical dispersion of some kinds of workers would influence the supervisory limits of a front-line supervisor. Notice, for example, how the span of control changes for the gang boss of a railroad track-laying crew when they stop working on a straightaway section and begin working around a promontory, where the boss can see only half the crew at one time.

The significance of the span-of-control principle lies in the organizational headaches that result when it is flagrantly ignored. In an extreme case, presuming a too narrow supervisory capability can lead to that administrative oddity known as the "one-over-one-over-one" organization (Figure 3.4). A valuable case study by Philip Foss on the California highway patrol demonstrated the serious consequences internal communications suffer when narrow spans of control result in the kind of layering depicted in Figure 3.4.[46]

In the other direction lies the overburdened city manager with a span of control that is mind-boggling (Figure 3.5). The sign on that manager's desk would be simple enough. Instead of "The buck stops here," it would be "This job is out of control."

There are behavioral considerations of great import in formally laying out spans of control. They relate to the questions of autonomy we encountered in the last chapter, the desire of so many workers to control their own jobs. For years, Robert Golembiewski has led the fight for *flat organizations* with broad spans of control, complementing his other recommendations for major-purpose structuring at low levels within agencies and generous delegations of authority.[47]

A dissenter on that score was Martin Patchen, who found evidence in a narrow study (a single company with seven hundred employees) that close supervision of a low-level task was compatible with high performance. (We are

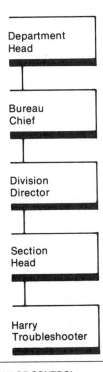

FIGURE 3.4   TOO NARROW A SPAN OF CONTROL

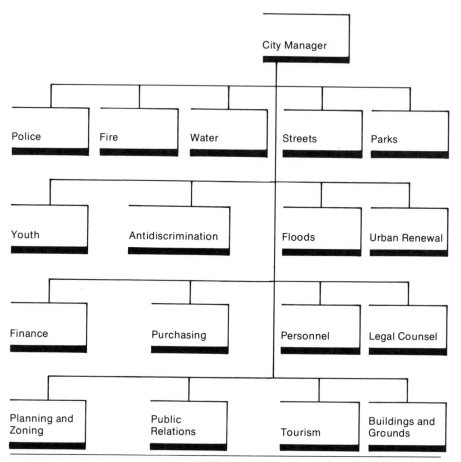

FIGURE 3.5   TOO BROAD A SPAN OF CONTROL

assuming a one-to-one relationship between close supervision and narrow span of control.) Patchen suggested that improved productivity was possible where the supervisor came through as a team member, fought for the group's interest on the upper levels, and was in a position to administer praise and blame on the basis of intimate knowledge of worker performance.[48]

A third contribution formal organization can make to coordination of action is a thoughtful *design that avoids duplication.* Duplication means the identical treatment of the same units by more than one government agency. For example, the FBI and the CIA (and possibly other agencies) keep their earphones to the wall checking out the same radical student groups. A meat-packing plant is visited by federal and state inspectors. Without coordinating machinery, two major universities in the same state lay plans for duplicate medical schools, law schools, and dental schools (although, to be fair, if the enrollment demand is there, duplication will not take place, given the different student bodies).

A sure way to build duplication into government operations is to utilize more than one base of organization for the major departments. The classic example is the duplication of services between the Veterans Administration (VA) and the Department of Health, Education and Welfare (HEW) — clientele and major-purpose organizations, respectively. With HEW serving the general populace and the VA the veterans' sector, both agencies are involved in the following:

manpower training

family services

mental health

medical services

aid to the disadvantaged

vocational education

student financial aid

social insurance

Were it not for the political muscle wielded by veterans' organizations that gives the VA a kind of sacred cow status, all the duplicated functions listed here could be transferred to HEW with some savings. Higher costs are likely to occur as long as major-purpose and clientele agencies continue to operate in highly similar fields.

Although formal organization cannot carry the full load of coordination (Chapter 10 tells why), proper design and allocation of functions can lighten that load. Differentiating missions; avoiding geographical overlap; and, so far as possible, not mixing clientele and thing organizations with major-purpose organizations can help minimize (but not by itself prevent) duplication in government.

A fourth way in which the formal structure can help pull things together and generate action is the contribution it can make to *decision making.* By bringing within ready access of the decision maker the line, staff, and auxiliary units that have significant pieces of the puzzle to be solved, proper organizational structure can help solve the puzzle.[49] This job is impossible. In his role as economic stabilizer, the president needs leverage not only over *fiscal policy,* which he enjoys through the Office of Management and Budget, the Treasury Department, and line agencies, but over *monetary policy,* vested in an independent body, the Federal Reserve Board. He also needs leverage over some key areas of *administered price:* natural gas, electric power, air and rail rates, telephone charges, and the like, a fair part of which rests in the hands of the boards that direct the highly separate independent regulatory commissions like the Civil Aeronautics Board (CAB), the Interstate Commerce Commission (ICC), and the

Federal Communications Commission (FCC). Clearly, the president's decision-making capability in economic stabilization is not equal to his responsibility under the Employment Act of 1946, which called for coordination of federal economic programs to promote maximum employment, production, and purchasing power.

Organization as the Embodiment of Power and Influence

That preceding problem points up organization as a *network of authority.* For the scientific management and unity-of-command people, it was an unambiguous network in which authority, defined as *the power to issue commands,* belonged to those on top and flowed downward (see Figure 3.6). But over time, there were enough experiences to bring the monocratic model into serious question: FBI directors like J. Edgar Hoover, whom no attorney general or president from Calvin Coolidge through Richard Nixon could control; an Army Corps of Engineers with so much political clout on Capitol Hill (sustained by private water and power users) that army secretaries must have come to believe

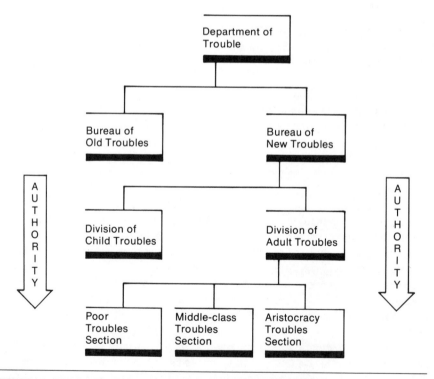

FIGURE 3.6   THE OLDER VIEW OF AUTHORITY FLOWING DOWNWARD THROUGH THE SCALAR PROCESS

What a Great Feeling It Is to Be in Charge

The musings of Winston Churchill on May 11, 1940, after George VI had invited him to become Prime Minister after the fall of Norway in World War II:

> . . . As I went to bed at about 3 A.M., I was conscious of a profound sense of relief. At last I had the authority to give directions over the whole scene. I felt as if I were walking with Destiny, and that all my past life had been but a preparation for this hour and for this trial.
>
> In my long political experience I had held most of the great offices of state, but I readily admit that the post which had now fallen to me was the one I like the best. Power for the sake of lording it over fellow creatures or adding to personal pomp is rightly judged base. But power in a national crisis, when a man believes he knows what orders should be given, is a blessing.

Winston Churchill, *The Gathering Storm* (Boston: Houghton Mifflin, 1948), p. 667 and *Their Finest Hour* (Boston: Houghton Mifflin, 1949), p. 15.

that sovereignty itself was reflected in the stars on the shoulder of the chief engineer.

A young Woodrow Wilson in 1898 may have been one of the first men in modern times to distinguish de jure authority (defined by tradition or law as resting with kings and parliaments) from de facto authority (who is really in command around here?). What he wrote concerning the body politic as a whole still has application for administrators trying to manage government agencies:

> The measure of the Czar's sovereignty is the habit of his people; and not their habit only, but their humor also, and the humor of his officials. His concessions to the restless spirit of his army, to the prejudices of his court, to the temper of the mass of his subjects, his means of keeping this side of assassination or revolution, nicely mark the boundaries of his sovereignty.
>
> Sovereignty, therefore, as ideally conceived in legal theory, nowhere actually exists. The sovereignty which does exist is something much more vital; though, like most living things, much less easily conceived. It is the will of an organized independent community, whether that will speak in acquiescence merely, or in active creation of the forces and conditions of politics. The kings or parliaments who serve as its vehicles utter it, but they do not possess it. Sovereignty resides in the community.[50]

Two decades later, Max Weber would turn to the same question at the administrator's level:

> When and for what purposes, within what limits, or possibly under what special conditions [will] the members of the corporate groups . . . submit to the authority of the

governor? Furthermore, under what circumstances does the governor have at his disposal the administrative staff, as well as the corporate power of the group when issuing orders?[51]

Weber's own answer was that subordinates will normally obey supervisory authority out of respect for their chief's *traditional position* (e.g., the hereditary monarchy); the legitimacy provided by *law* ("The executive power shall be vested in the President of the United States"); the mystique (*charisma*) by which he or she holds them emotionally (e.g., Joan of Arc, Mahatma Gandhi, Adolf Hitler, or Martin Luther King); or the *rational calculation* that the leader is worth following (your supplier of bread, your wife or husband, your whatever).[52]

In the 1930s, a manager turned scholar named Chester Barnard picked up on the Wilson and Weber leads and proceeded to turn the conventional view of authority ("the power to issue commands") upside down: *authority is the power to grant or withhold obedience.*[53] Authority, like Wilson's de facto sovereignty, must therefore rest with employees rather than with decision makers. The organization chart just turned around!

But let's face it, Barnard's view, except at the margin of disobedience (or mutiny!*), is an exaggeration. It does not describe the authority-obedience pattern that prevails most of the time (a point Barnard himself was careful to point out). Obedience to higher authority will normally be granted out of fear of unemployment (resulting from dismissal for ignoring orders); fear of other managerial sanctions (pay cuts, suspensions, etc.); strong commitment to an agency and its mission; admiration for superiors; group norms of compliance; and cultural patterns of respect for authority, among other factors.

But if Barnard's idea was an exaggeration, he also had a point to make of enormous importance. Like the span of control, there are outer limits to the obedience of workers ("You're pushin' me too far!"). Barnard labeled the territory the "zone of indifference,"[54] with boundaries as suggested in Figure 3.7. Asking workers to violate agency goals or their own ethics, or making impossible physical demands on them, can propel workers right out of their zone of indifference and compliance into a posture of disobedience and resistance. For example, an IRS employee discloses Richard Nixon's underpayment of taxes; air traffic controllers engage in a sickout to protest long hours and low pay; blacks in the Library of Congress become hostile because of unequal opportunities for promotion; and so forth.

There are two important lessons here for administrators to grasp. One is to develop a management style that regularly measures employee sentiments, solicits their views, and respects the tensile strength of their morale and physical makeup — much as an experienced guitarist knows so well the pressure her strings can bear.[55] The second is to realize that the formal organization chart is

---

* That business of mutiny revives memories of a favorite *New Yorker* cartoon of years ago: Above the shark-infested water, the blindfolded ship captain is walking the plank. "My first mistake," he said, "was letting them vote."

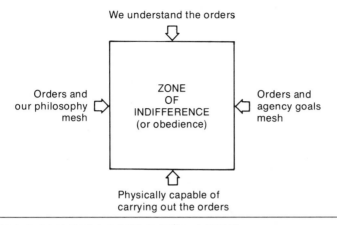

FIGURE 3.7   THE LIMITS TO OUR OBEDIENCE A LA BARNARD

From Chester Barnard, *Functions of the Executive* (Cambridge, Mass.: Harvard University Press, 1946), pp. 167–171. Adapted by permission.

occasionally a bad map of where authority lies in an agency. Some schema for showing a shared relationship would come closer to reality.

In addition to the command-obedience dimension, there is another way in which formal structures reflect power and influence — the *elevation* of important functions and the *demotion* of others. One of the most graphic examples in American administration was the elevation in 1940 of the U.S. Bureau of the Budget (BOB) from low-level bureau status in the Treasury Department to its vaunted position in the new Executive Office of the President.[56]

That move was a signal to all executive agencies that Franklin Roosevelt meant to have a *presidential* budget and a means to shape up administration policy through Budget Bureau clearance procedures. (The physical move from the Treasury Department to offices in the Old State Department Building a hundred yards away from the west wing of the White House further underscored the leap in power and influence the bureau had made.)

At the state level, a governor may demote the merit system to a position under the director of administrative services, or he may bring the state personnel director into the governor's immediate circle. To give a state planning office adequate leverage with old-line state agencies, the governor adds the planning director to his personal staff as well. To emphasize urban renewal, a mayor may lift the redevelopment agency from its hiding place under the municipal building board and relocate it as a part of his office.

The organizational politics suggested here were the subject of one of Charlie Chaplin's funniest satires decades ago: Adolf Hitler inviting Mussolini into a room with two barber's chairs in which the dictators vied for (vertical) supremacy.

All of these examples suggest that "up" equals "more power." But remember the old administrative maxim of "up and out," an often used technique to demote by promoting. Roosevelt shanghaied Henry Wallace to China; Nixon "elevated" David Kennedy of Illinois to the rank of ambassador-at-large and got rid of him as treasury secretary; and he also boosted Robert Finch, his ineffectual HEW secretary, to a White House office, where he was never heard from again.

What the organization charts portray as static, then, is in many agencies of government really an ongoing struggle for power.[57] Like the dictators in the barber's chairs, divisions and bureaus rise and fall as their administrators play the game of realpolitik (see Chapter 8) and as the agencies adapt, or fail to adapt, to the changing forces of politics and community values. Political forces brought environmental agencies to the fore during the 1970s, while the CIA and the FBI were losing their halos. In the organizational structure, power and influence become incarnate.

Organization as a Reflection of Community Values and Political Forces

More fundamental than a plan of attack, an action coordinator, or the scarred emblem of an internal power struggle, formal organization may be a mirror of the surrounding community and its politics — sometimes foggy, sometimes cracked (and therefore in danger), but nevertheless a mirror. That fact of life about bureaucracies takes us to what earlier scholars called the *ecology of administration,*[58] and what writers of late call the *interface* between the agency and its surrounding world.

Ask yourself what impact the following environmental changes have had on agencies of government:

widespread private ownership of motorcycles and snowmobiles on the Forest Service and Bureau of Land Management (BLM)

an energy shortage on the mineral leasing of BLM, on the Bureau of Mines, or on the Oil and Gas Division of the Department of Interior

citizen-band radios on the state highway patrol

teenage use of drugs on school officials and the police

the sexual revolution of the 1960s and 1970s on university housing officials (and segregated dorms with restricted visitation hours)

the civil rights revolution and women's liberation

To put the matter more painfully, what are the likely consequences for the organizations in question that fail to adapt to these kinds of changes?

a county court office that continues record keeping by hand long after the computer revolution

a major state agency that goes along lily-white and male long after the civil rights revolution and women's liberation a police department resorting regularly to third-degree methods long after the Supreme Court in *Miranda* v. *Arizona* had carefully defined "custodial rights"

In the face of environmental changes, agencies may find: (a) subunits without a useful function (perhaps the CAB's rate bureau after a period of deregulation); (b) a need for new units (the ORV Division for Off-the-Road Vehicles in the Bureau of Land Management; the Department of Energy); or (c) staffs and budgets that must be reallocated to meet the changed circumstances (beefing up the drug control unit at the expense of older units in the sheriff's department). "The times change, and we must change with them," says an old Latin motto, or we're dead — and that saying seems to apply fully to organizations.

Managing the interface between organization and environment thus becomes a major responsibility of administrators. Talcott Parsons listed adaptation of the one to the other as the first functional requirement of organizations.[59] And Chris Argyris spoke of maintaining the agency in its external environment as one of the core activities of managers.[60]

Among the authors who have made some useful suggestions on interface management are Paul Lawrence and Jay Lorsch.[61] From their industrial consulting, they concluded that one of the most important dynamics in the interface relationship is the certainty or uncertainty that characterizes the agency's external environment. A steady state "out there" (as might confront the city streets department or automobile licensing division), other things being equal, might best be addressed through a simple organizational structure, traditional rules, and task-oriented leadership. But an unsteady environment (like those confronting the policy-planning people in the State Department or a school district initiating integration and busing) could best be coped with through an adaptable organization, flatter in shape, a superior communications system, and a more person-oriented leadership.

Lawrence and Lorsch provided another example of environmental impact on structure in focusing on two different kinds of situations confronting field offices: Parsons's universalism versus particularism. If the field offices of a large agency such as the Social Security Administration are looking at essentially identical problems everywhere, centralized rule making might well be appropriate; but if variety characterizes field office climate, then decentralization of the structure is strongly suggested.

In time, community forces seem to be almost irresistible in effecting organizational change. A city with a strong business orientation and an effective chamber of commerce quickly sees the appearance of business-promotion agencies in state or municipal government. The federal independent regulatory commissions gradually get swallowed up by their own clientele groups. A consumer movement gives rise to consumer protection agencies in state and local governments.

On occasion, the ineluctable pressure of community values may bring on a lamentable administrative phenomenon that Robert Merton called *goal displacement*.[62] A metropolis gets riled up about welfare cheaters and social workers spend their time policing the system rather than rendering aid. The Internal Revenue Service (IRS) succumbs to the pressure of the wealthy and begins to enforce the tax laws inequitably against low-income earners.[63] A New York State requirement for nondiscriminatory hiring on state construction projects is widely flouted by the white construction unions.[64] The CIA, responding to copper company pressure, is diverted from intelligence gathering and contributes to the overthrow of a Marxist regime in Chile.[65] It's tragic, but in such circumstances community pressures have led to pathological administration.

The Pyramid Face of Bureaucracy

One final facet of bureaucracy, a nearly universal one, now looms up: the pyramid shape of most agencies, determined by the narrow spans of control of top administrators and the broader ones below, as shown in Figure 3.8.

There are exceptions, of course; for example, the flat-topped organizations that are headed by boards or commissions. These collegial types of organization, rather than having the single-head, pyramid structure, may be employed to give formal representation to important interest groups, to permit bipartisan direction of an agency, to diffuse power, or to provide a kind of collective thick skin as a buffer against outside pressures. But the use of boards rather than single administrators is also the source of tremendous headaches, as the governor of any of the fifty states will testify.

HOW WE ORGANIZE MAKES A DIFFERENCE

The conventional wisdom since Alexander Pope has always been: "For forms of government, let fools contest; / Whate'er is best administered is best." But that kind of bureaucratic agnosticism will not wash any longer. Structure makes a difference in administration, just as the way a house is planned affects the quality of the life of its occupants.

Heavily layered organizations (the scalar principle run riot) impede communications.[66] Mixing up the bases of major units of government (clientele and place mixed in with major purpose) invites duplication. Tight adherence to the unity of command, narrow spans of control, endless rule making, and highly specific job descriptions may all seem formally rational, but they are substantively irrational. As Robert Golembiewski has pointed out, frequently their net effect is to reduce rather than to enlarge jobs at all levels except the top, diminish the front-line supervisor's power, and increase alienation in the ranks — all nicely calculated to lower agency performance.[67]

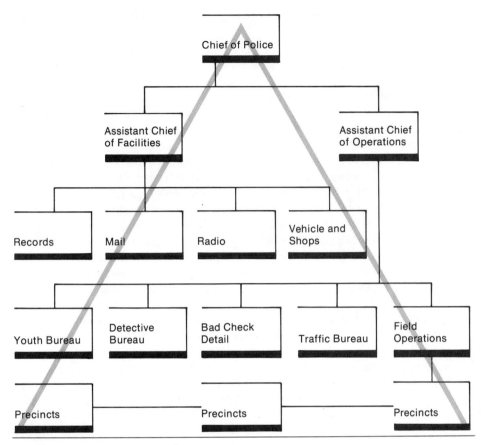

FIGURE 3.8 THE PYRAMID-SHAPED AGENCY

Over two decades ago, James Worthy said it in a manner that does credit to his name:

Our studies have shown that employee morale and operating efficiency are closely related to the degree the organization is integrated. Integration is not necessarily achieved, however, when the organization meets the requirements of machine-logic. As a matter of fact, what may appear to be logical from a purely technical standpoint may run directly counter to the personal and social demands of employees. We have seen a number of organizations which have a logical technology, division of labor, and hierarchy of control but which are badly disorganized from the standpoint of the actual working relationships of the people involved. Such organizations are well-integrated only on paper. In actual fact, they are irritating and frustrating from the standpoint of employees, and inefficient, troublesome, and costly from the standpoint of management.[68]

In badly designed organizations, such critically important functions as budgeting can be buried for years, as we have seen; whole-problem management can be weakened by locating one natural resource agency, the Forest Service, in a separate department (Agriculture) from the other natural resource agencies (in Interior). Too much independence can weaken executive responsibility (the Federal Reserve Board and monetary policy). Too little independence may result in agency subservience to terrible executive machinations (CIA cooperation with the White House in the burgling of Dr. Ellsberg's psychiatrist's office).[69]

Organization makes a difference; and when organizations become huge, they can make a huge difference. Long ago that wise jurist Louis Brandeis warned against the "curse of bigness."[70] But the New Deal and its successors tried to make "big" synonymous with "better." Nationwide unemployment seemed to demand such agencies as the Works Progress Administration (WPA), the Federal Emergency Relief Administration (FERA), and the Civilian Conservation Corps (CCC). Defeating Hitler seemed to demand everything from giant price- and rent-control agencies to the vastly expanded U.S. armed forces.

But as Brandeis warned, bigness increasingly became a curse. All sorts of dysfunctions arose to spoil the symmetry and efficiency of Weber's bureaucratic model. Big agencies could be inflexible (J. Edgar Hoover's FBI never quite understood the civil rights movement); they could substitute means for ends (Vietnam: "We must destroy the city in order to save it"); and they could ultimately become instruments of repression, from the loyalty-security program of Truman's day to the plumbers and "Enemies List" of Nixon's day. (How questionable means gradually overtook the lofty ends of big government has probably been most tellingly recounted in Charles Reich's chapter on "The Anatomy of the Corporate State" in *The Greening of America*.)[71]

In organization theory today we are vitally concerned not only with the earlier questions of how bureaucracies treat others but also with how they treat, and cope with, themselves. Can structure help counteract the forces of *entropy* (the loss of energy) in an agency, facilitate *conflict resolution,* and make it easier to return the organization to *equilibrium* after it is disturbed? Answers to those questions are beginning to appear in cybernetics, which stresses the monitoring and feedback functions of healthy organizations, and in organizational development (OD), which strives to counteract the smothering effects of formal structures with the regenerating effects of group problem solving in organizations built on trust and openness.[72]

One final consequence of structure — the threat to morale in putting it all down on an organization chart — is a bit surprising. As we noted earlier, organizations are arrays of power and influence; that means of course that organization charts are, to some degree, maps of who count and who do not. In *Up the Organization*, Robert Townsend made very clear what it is like to be down on the organization chart:

They have uses: for the annual salary review; for educating investors on how the organization works and who does what. But draw them in pencil. Never formalize, print, and circulate them. Good organizations are living bodies that grow new muscles to meet challenges. A chart demoralizes people. Nobody thinks of himself as *below* other people. And in a good company he isn't. Yet on paper there it is. If you have to circulate something, use a loose-leaf table of organization (like a magazine masthead) instead of a diagram with the people in little boxes. Use alphabetical order by name and by function wherever possible.

In the best organizations people see themselves working in a circle as if around one table. One of the positions is designated chief executive officer, because somebody has to make all those tactical decisions that enable an organization to keep working. In this circular organization, leadership passes from one to another depending on the particular task being attacked, without any hang-ups.

This is as it should be. In the hierarchical organization, it is difficult to imagine leadership anywhere but at the top of the various pyramids. And it's hard to visualize the leader of a small pyramid becoming temporarily the leader of a group of larger pyramid-leaders which includes the chief executive officer.

The traditional organization chart has one dead giveaway. Any dotted line indicates a troublemaker and/or a seriously troubled relationship. It also generally means that an unsatisfactory compromise has been worked out and the direct solution has been avoided.[73]

SOME PRINCIPLES OF
ORGANIZATION

What, then, is the state of the art in designing organizations in the public sector? Thirty years ago Herbert Simon lampooned the principles of the classical school as "the *proverbs* of administration."[74] He found their bases of organization ambiguous, their guidelines contradictory, and their research foundation woefully inadequate. Maybe we are entitled to one laugh, then, in his discovery twenty-five years later that there is some merit in the span-of-control concept, which he disguises here as "attention management":

> Not only must the size of decision problems handled by organizations be reduced
> to manageable proportions by factorization, but the number of decisions to
> be processed must be limited by applying good principles of attention
> management.[75]

My own judgment is that intervening research and experience have carried us far beyond that earlier stage when some scholars found organization theory to be essentially bankrupt. I think we have come to recognize that there are some principles of organization — not immutable verities, to be sure — but some operational guidelines that can contribute to improved conduct of public affairs. Consider these as a start:

Principles of Formal Organization

1. The organizational structure should clearly contribute to the accomplishment of an agency's mission ("substantive rationality" concept).

2. Organizations ought to be structured in a way that will help meet human needs, not frustrate them.

3. In addition to the program goal of an agency, organizational structure will be influenced by the administrative goal — the quality, quantity, speed, or economy of operations.

4. The overall structure of government (i.e., major departments and agencies), while always reflecting political forces, ought to afford the legislative branch and the citizenry the opportunity to appraise whole programs (e.g., national defense, conservation) rather than widely disjointed chunks of programs.

5. The structure should afford administrators and employees, so far as possible, the whole view of a mission rather than bits and pieces.

6. The structure should be free of duplicating and overlapping areas of responsibility and should contribute to the coordination of effort.

7. Decision-making channels in an agency need to be recognized and yet be open enough for the introduction of new ideas and for the critical analysis of proposals from many sides.

8. Authority is neither a fixed quantum in an organization nor the sole monopoly of agency heads.

9. There are limits to the supervisory capability (span of control) of all administrators.

10. Segregating line, staff, and auxiliary services in an organization, while inviting some conflict, may contribute to economy of operations and greatly enhance both top managerial control and advance planning.

11. There must be appropriate congruence between agency structure and the external environment.

Those concepts may help resolve some structural questions, but not all. They may suggest to the design pilot where the airport is, but he must land the particular plane he's flying. Mouzelis is worth noting on that point:

> The important question of structural design is not seen anymore as a problem of finding a set of valid principles which would tell one how to draw the most efficient organization chart. Rather, structural design is seen as a particular decision-making problem. As in every other decisional situation, there are many alternatives (i.e., many possible design schemes) from which the decision-maker should choose the one which would meet in a satisfactory way certain specifications imposed by the major problems and goals of the organization. Thus the problem of design depends entirely on the kind of problems and goals an organization would like to pursue.[76]

SUMMARY

We moved from the humanity of administration in Chapter 2 to the structures of administration in this chapter, agreeing quickly with Max Weber that unorganized people do not constitute a government for very long, ever. Effectively accomplishing any complex task always seems to require some allocation of functions, staffing for their performance, delegation of authority, and direction and supervision. In these four ingredients are the rudiments of formal organization.

We put on some pairs of glasses for viewing bureaucracy, from Max Weber, its greatest defender, to the Marxists, among its staunchest critics. The work of the classical school (Gulick and Urwick of the 1930s) was reviewed, as well as that of the structuralists and humanists of the post–World War II period. The premature death notices for bureaucracy posted by Warren Bennis and others were noted — and rejected.

Formal organization reveals many different faces to the observer and the world: a plan of attack, a coordinator of action, a reflection of power and influence, a mirror of community social and political values, and almost everywhere a pyramid shape. Canvassed here were the concepts, some old, some new, of base of organization, span of control, unity of command, administrative goal analysis, and the debate over where authority lies in an organization.

How we structure governmental functions and group individuals together significantly influence an agency's success or failure. With no real delegation of authority and with Mickey Mouse job descriptions, the agency can easily afflict workers with the pox noted in Chapter 2: powerlessness, meaninglessness, and isolation. Conversely, careful design can minimize the likelihood of duplication and overlap.

The growth of government organizations encounters its own point of diminishing returns — resulting in red tape, jumbled communications, means replacing ends, skewed ethics, and an overpowering impact on citizen and employee alike.

At the end, we suggested a set of principles to be weighed in organizational design. Some tie back to classical concepts, but as revised by modern research; others stress the need for substantively relating organizational parts to agency mission; still others grow out of behavioral research and call for organizational arrangements that will enable people to work effectively together and contribute to their needs for belonging and achievement.

Therein lies the ultimate dilemma about bureaucracy: Is it a means to coordinate human effort or an instrument to stifle human endeavor? Victor Ferkiss expressed this issue especially well:

> Man's destiny lies in continuing to exploit this "openness," rather than entering into a symbiotic relationship with the inorganic machine that, while it might bring immediate increments of power, would inhibit his development by chaining him to a system of

lesser potentialities. . . . *Man must stand above his physical technologies if he is to avoid their becoming his shell and the principle of their organization his anthill* [emphasis added].[77]

In Chapter 4, we turn to the administrative trinity briefly noted in this chapter: the segregation of functions into line, staff, and auxiliary units.

KEY CONCEPTS

Max Weber	unity of command
formal rationality	span of control
substantive rationality	flat organizations
iron law of oligarchy	de jure versus de facto authority
satisfice	zone of indifference
Herbert Simon	goal displacement
administrative goals	entropy
Gresham's law of planning	

DISCUSSION QUESTIONS

1. Why is bureaucracy needed? Incorporate the views of Weber and Marx into your answer.

2. Discuss the four principles of the classical school. On what grounds can they be criticized?

3. Discuss the five bases suggested by the classical school for bringing organizational functions together. How well would they aid an organizer in planning the attack?

4. How could a manager have a great deal of authority but very little power?

5. Discuss the ways in which an emphasis on formal structure can aid the workings of an organization.

PROJECT

Choose an organization, preferably a governmental agency. Pick one to three of the organizational principles found on pp. 65–66. Interview selected personnel from that organization to determine how well it is following these principles.

Notes

1. As to why bureaucracy, see Herbert Simon in the introduction to *Administrative Behavior* (New York: Free Press, 1976), pp. xv–xvii; and Charles Perrow, *Complex Organizations* (Glenview, Ill.: Scott, Foresman, 1972), chap. 1.

2. Hans Gerth and C. Wright Mills, eds., *From Max Weber: Essays in Sociology* (New York: Oxford University Press, 1958), pp. 214–216.

3. Quoted in J. P. Mayer, *Max Weber and German Politics* (London: Faber & Faber, 1944), pp. 126–127.

4. Max Weber, *Wirtschaft und Gesellschaft,* translated by Talcott Parsons and A. M. Henderson (New York: Oxford University Press, 1947), pp. 184ff; and Max Rubenstein, *Max Weber on Law in Economy and Society* (New York: Simon & Schuster, 1967), chap. 8.

5. We follow here the useful summary of Nicos Mouzelis, *Organization and Bureaucracy* (Chicago: Aldine, 1973), pp. 8–15.

6. See William L. Morrow, *Public Administration: Politics and the Political System* (New York: Random House, 1975), chap. 4, on private interest penetration of government agencies. For a portrait of the co-option process in glaring color, see the studies by G. William Domhoff, *Fat Cats and Democrats* (Englewood Cliffs, N.J.: Prentice-Hall, 1972), and *The Higher Circles* (New York: Random House, 1970).

7. Milovan Djilas, *The New Class* (New York: Praeger, 1957) and Ludvik Vaculik, "Two Thousand Words: A Declaration for Democratization," Czechoslovakia, June 27, 1968, and republished in Alvin Z. Rubinstein and Garold W. Thumm, *The Challenge of Politics,* 3d ed. (Englewood Cliffs, N.J.: Prentice-Hall, 1970), pp. 132–135.

8. Victor Thompson, *Modern Organization* (New York: Knopf, 1961), chap. 7.

9. See the *Communist Manifesto;* Friedrich Engels, "Socialism: Utopian and Scientific," in Arthur P. Mendel, ed., *Essential Works of Marxism* (New York: Bantam Books, 1961), pp. 78–79; and Lenin, "State and Revolution," in Mendel, pp. 139, 173, 182–183.

10. Mouzelis, *Organization and Bureaucracy,* p. 11.

11. Lord Thomas Macaulay, quoted in Herman Finer, *Road to Reaction* (Boston: Little, Brown, 1945), p. viii.

12. Robert Michels, *Political Parties* (New York: Free Press, 1911, 1962), Part VI. For the kind of structural and other properties which may help an organization resist Michels's law, see the study by Seymour M. Lipset, M. A. Trow, and J. S. Coleman, "International Typographical Union," *Union Democracy* (Glencoe, Ill.: Free Press, 1956).

13. Luther Gulick and Lyndall Urwick, *Papers on the Science of Administration* (New York: Institute of Public Administration, 1957), p. 98.

14. Gulick and Urwick, *Papers on the Science of Administration,* p. 52.

15. Gulick and Urwick, *Papers on the Science of Administration,* pp. 49–88.

16. *Public Administration Review* (Winter 1946), 6:53–67.

17. *Public Administration* (New York: Knopf, 1950).

18. James G. March and Herbert Simon, *Organizations* (New York: Wiley, 1958).

19. James D. Thompson, *Organizations in Action* (New York: McGraw-Hill, 1967).

20. Thompson, *Organizations in Action,* pp. 159–160.

21. Thompson, *Organizations in Action,* p. 7.

22. Thompson, *Organizations in Action,* pp. 160–161.

23. Simon, *Administrative Behavior,* pp. 240–244.

24. Simon, *Administrative Behavior,* pp. xxviii–xxxi.

25. See the commentary on this aspect of Simon's thinking in Charles Perrow, *Complex Organizations,* pp. 156–157.

26. The Simon-Argyris debate took place in the pages of the *Public Administration Review* during 1973. These opening paragraphs (with some reordering) are from Herbert Simon, "Applying Information Technology to Organization Design," *Public Adminis-*

tration Review (May–June 1973), 33:351, 352. This highly important exchange continued on through the Sept.–Oct. 1973 issue of the *Public Administration Review,* pp. 346–357 and 484–485.

27. Chris Argyris, "Some Limits of Rational Man Organizational Theory," *Public Administration Review* (May–June 1973) 33:255.

28. Argyris, "Some Limits of Rational Man Organizational Theory," p. 261.

29. See the symposium edited by Dwight Waldo, "Organizations for the Future," in the *Public Administration Review* (July–Aug. 1973) 33:299–335.

30. Alvin Toffler, *Future Shock* (New York: Random House, 1970), pp. 358–359.

31. Warren Bennis, *Beyond Bureaucracy* (New York: McGraw-Hill, 1973), p. 6.

32. Bennis, *Beyond Bureaucracy,* p. ix.

33. H. G. Wilcox, "Hierarchy, Human Nature and the Participative Panacea," *Public Administration Review* (Jan.–Feb. 1969) 29:53–64.

34. William G. Scott and T. R. Mitchell, *Organization Theory: A Structural and Behavioral Analysis* (Homewood, Ill.: Irwin, 1972), pp. 378–387.

35. Gulick and Urwick, "Notes on the Theory of Organization," in *Papers on the Science of Administration,* pp. 15–30.

36. See an early classic on place organizations, James W. Fesler, *Area and Administration* (University, Ala.: University of Alabama Press, 1940).

37. Peter Blau and W. Richard Scott, *Formal Organizations* (San Francisco: Chandler, 1962), chap. 2.

38. Herbert Simon, "Proverbs of Administration," *Public Administration Review* (Winter 1946) 6:58–71.

39. Perhaps first clearly set forth in U.S. Bureau of the Budget, *Production Planning and Control in Office Operations* (Washington, D.C.: Government Printing Office, 1949), pp. 18–19.

40. See especially Robert Golembiewski, "Specialist or Generalist: Structure as a Crucial Factor," *Public Administration Review* (1965) 25:135–141.

41. Mouzelis, *Organization and Bureaucracy,* p. 212, n. 38.

42. Coordination is treated at length in Chapter 10.

43. Victor Thompson, *Modern Organization,* chap. 9.

44. Chris Argyris, *Intervention Theory and Method* (Reading, Mass.: Addison-Wesley, 1970), pp. 36–45.

45. John Udell, "An Empirical Test of Hypotheses Relating to Span of Control," *Administrative Science Quarterly* (Dec. 1967) 12:420–439.

46. Philip Foss, "Reorganization and Reassignment in the California Highway Patrol," in Frederick C. Mosher, ed., *Governmental Reorganizations* (Indianapolis: Bobbs-Merrill, 1967), pp. 185–213.

47. Robert Golembiewski, "Civil Service and Managing Work: Some Unintended Consequences," *American Political Science Review* (Dec. 1962) 56:961–973.

48. Martin Patchen, "Supervisory Methods and Group Performance Norms," *Administrative Science Quarterly* (Dec. 1962) 7:275–290, particularly pp. 287–289.

49. Mouzelis, *Organization and Bureaucracy,* p. 134.

50. Woodrow Wilson, *The State* (Boston: Heath, 1898), pp. 600–601.

51. Max Weber, *Basic Concepts in Sociology* (New York: Citadel, 1913, 1962), p. 112. Or see Amitai Etzioni, ed., *Complex Organizations* (New York: Holt, 1961), pp. 4–14.

52. Weber, *Basic Concepts in Sociology,* p. 81.

53. Chester Barnard, *Functions of the Executive* (Cambridge, Mass.: Harvard University Press, 1938), p. 163.

54. Barnard, *Functions of the Executive,* pp. 167–171; and Simon, *Administrative Behavior,* chaps. 6–7.

55. Rensis Likert, *The Human Organization* (New York: McGraw-Hill, 1967), chaps. 8 and 9.

56. Reorganization Plan No. 1 of 1940.

57. See Melville Dalton, *Men Who Manage* (New York: Wiley, 1959).

58. John Gaus, "The Ecology of Public Administration," reprinted in Richard J. Stillman, *Public Administration: Concepts and Cases* (Boston: Houghton Mifflin, 1976), pp. 62–67.

59. Talcott Parsons, *Sociological Theory and Modern Society* (New York: Free Press, 1967), pp. 198, 202–204.

60. Chris Argyris, *Integrating the Individual and the Organization* (New York: Wiley, 1964), pp. 120–124, 315–322.

61. Paul R. Lawrence and Jay W. Lorsch, *Developing Organizations: Diagnosis and Action* (Reading, Mass.: Addison-Wesley, 1969), chap. 3.

62. Robert K. Merton, *Social Theory and Social Structure* (Glencoe, Ill.: Free Press, 1957), pp. 253–254.

63. Louise Brown, "The IRS: Taxation with Misrepresentation," *The Progressive* (Oct. 1973), 37:27–31.

64. Theodore Becker and V. D. Murray (eds.), *Government Lawlessness in America* (New York: Oxford University Press, 1971), pp. 231–238.

65. U.S. Senate, Select Committee to Study Governmental Operations (Intelligence Activities), *Covert Action in Chile,* 1963–73 (a staff report) (94th Cong., 1st Sess., Dec. 18, 1975).

66. Blau and Scott, *Formal Organizations,* pp. 121–128.

67. Golembiewski, "Civil Service and Managing Work."

68. James C. Worthy, "Organizational Structure and Employee Morale," *American Sociological Review* (April 1950) 15:169–179.

69. Testimony of General Robert E. Cushman, former CIA deputy director, on the request of White House aide John Ehrlichman for CIA assistance to E. Howard Hunt in the break-in of Dr. Fielding's office, U.S. Senate Select Committee on Presidential Campaign Activities (1972), *Hearings* (93d Cong., 2d Sess.), Book 8:3290ff.

70. Louis Brandeis, *The Curse of Bigness* (New York: Viking, 1937).

71. Charles Reich, *The Greening of America* (New York: Random House, 1971) chap. 5.

72. See Chapter 12 for a full discussion of organizational development.

73. Robert Townsend, *Up the Organization* (New York: Knopf, 1970), p. 116.

74. Simon, "Proverbs of Administration."

75. Herbert Simon, "Applying Information Technology to Organization Design," *Public Administration Review* (May–June 1973) 33:270.

76. Mouzelis, *Organization and Bureaucracy,* p. 134.

77. Victor Ferkiss, *Technological Man* (New York: Braziller, 1969), p. 255.

Chapter 4
The Administrative Trinity: Line, Staff, and Auxiliary

SEGREGATE THE FUNCTIONS

Visit a city-manager town having five or six thousand people and do a role analysis on the manager. You will find he is the jack-of-all-trades. Then contrast that integrated administrative setup with the complex segregation of functions around the governor of your state (see Figures 4.1 and 4.2).

In the more complex state setting, these kinds of tasks are clear: There are those that serve the major purposes of government and look beyond the government to its outside clientele (*line* functions); and there are those that support line operations, operating across-the-board inside government rather than looking outside. The latter were traditionally called staff services until Leonard D. White wisely suggested a closer role definition of "staff."[1] He suggested that the term "staff" be reserved to describe the functions or offices of government engaged primarily in planning, research, and advice, and that the term "auxiliary" be used to denote those offices which provide the support (or housekeeping) services and controls required by line operations. Auxiliary units may issue orders to, and sometimes veto, line officers, thus constituting dual supervision; but staff units prototypically do not order line units to do anything.

The three different kinds of operations are clearly depicted in a simplified organization chart of the U.S. State Department (Figure 4.3). Here, the line functions are primarily those of overseas representation of the United States and the conduct of diplomatic relations; but the line reaches from the president of the United States through the secretary of state and on to the consul general in Madrid. Staff includes the economic and political analysis divisions and the

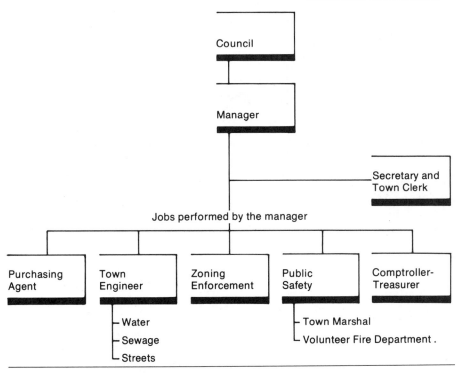

FIGURE 4.1   FUNCTIONAL INTEGRATION UNDER A SMALL-TOWN MANAGER

policy-planning staff, among other groups. Auxiliary embraces the personnel, fiscal, and other units of the department.

The Case for Segregation of the Trinity

In Chapter 3 we argued for the major-purpose arrangement of governmental functions, providing a department head with all the essential administrative tools for accomplishing his assigned mission. Now we are about to argue that below him in his department, and to some degree even above him at the government-wide level, certain kinds of support services should be peeled away from line operators and segregated into units of their own. Why?

There are four overriding reasons to segregate staff and auxiliary services:

1. To relieve line operators of some headaches extraneous to their main responsibility   The function of the sheriff's department is law enforcement, not test design; the sheriff will leave that to the county merit system. The county welfare department does not collect taxes to fund its budget; the county assessor does it for the welfare department. Every state agency need not hire a

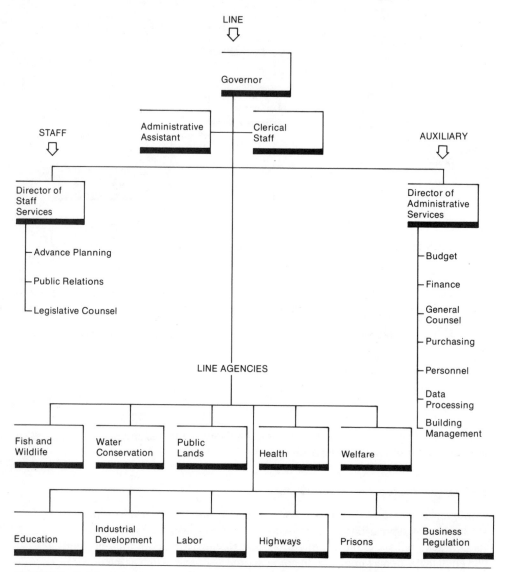

FIGURE 4.2   FUNCTIONAL SEGREGATION IN STATE GOVERNMENT

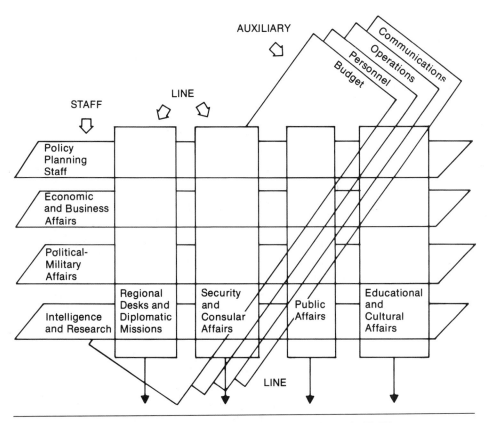

FIGURE 4.3   LINE, STAFF, AND AUXILIARY SERVICES IN THE DEPARTMENT OF STATE

From Henry Wriston, "Secretary and Management of the Department," p. 100 in Don K. Price, ed., *The Secretary of State.* © 1960 by The American Assembly, Columbia University. Adapted by permission of The American Assembly.

purchasing agent and have a shelfful of manuals; the state purchasing office will serve them all.

But there are dissents on this point. Avis car leasing executive Robert Townsend blithely suggested that the whole purchasing department be fired.

> They cost ten dollars in zeal for every dollar they save through purchasing acumen. And that doesn't count the massive unrecorded disasters they cause. Let's say somebody has persuaded a young Edison or Steinmetz to go to work for General Conglobulation, Inc. By the time he's found out that there's no way to get that $900 desk calculator through the purchasing department he's lost all respect for General Conglobulation. ("They'd hire Einstein and then turn down his requisition for a blackboard.")

> So let's be sensible. Fire the whole purchasing department. The company will benefit from having each department dealing in the free market outside instead of being victimized by internal socialism. And don't underestimate the morale value of letting young people "waste" some money. If you must, have a one-man "buying department" . . . for those who want help in the purchasing area and ask for it.[2]

It is a funny exaggeration, but from our point of view, Townsend is just plain wrong. To decentralize final purchasing authority once again to every line department would be an intolerable invitation to vendors' taking advantage of untrained buyers, high-cost procurement (in place of quantity discounts), and grave risks of corruption (kickbacks, etc.) on a wide scale. Sadly enough, however, we must admit that the scandals in the central purchaser of the federal government, the General Services Administration (GSA), in 1978, strongly suggest that the only corruption greater than decentralized corruption is centralized corruption!

There are other dissents worth noting. Line operators would give us a lot of static about what is "extraneous to their main responsibility." They would certainly not regard the hiring of their key personnel as extraneous (and would be quite prepared to "go to the mat" with the personnel office in order to hire whom they want without the latter's interference). And as we'll see shortly, the director of the state highway department isn't enamored at all of the idea of the state purchasing agent's telling the director what kind of heavy earth-moving equipment he ought to buy.

2. To save money by centralizing some common services   The examples of this economy argument are legion. Imagine every state agency sending its own recruiters to every business college in the state for secretaries rather than a state personnel office recruiting for all of them. Consider the costs of letting every county department have its own $100,000 computer rather than having the county electronic data processing division serve them all. Or note the hard fact of life that leads to centralized purchasing: a city buys its gasoline in large quantities at 85 cents a gallon, while some closely associated but independent special-purpose districts buy limited quantities at 98 cents a gallon. So the economic pressures build up to segregate some aspects of personnel, record keeping, and purchasing, among other functions, away from line agencies and centralize them in government-wide service units.

3. To provide top management with a means of getting some things done uniformly throughout all agencies   The U.S. Office of Personnel Management polices agency compliance with a presidential directive for equal employment opportunity for all races.[3] The governor relies on his state personnel director to enforce a forty-hour workweek in all agencies. As directed by the mayor, the city controller will pay only those bills that show a valid purchase order and a signature of a receiving officer. In these activities, auxiliary officers play the role of "eyes and ears of the king" for the chief executive — a role not entirely compatible with the first role of auxiliary units discussed above — that of *serving* line agencies.

4. To see to it that the job of advance planning gets done   One of the most important arguments for segregation is this one, which underlies the *staff* role.

"Mayor, Are You Sure Centralized Purchasing Is Worth the Price?

While professor of political science at Wesleyan University, Stephen K. Bailey was also the mayor of Middleton, Connecticut. In a delightful spoof, he described learning about the land mines cluttering the terrain of a reform like centralized purchasing:

"Mayor."

"Yes, Joe."

"You asked me the other day about what did you call it, central purchasing or something? Would you spell that out again please?"

"Sure, Joe. It's just this. I figure you in Public Works buy tires, and the Second District Highway buys tires, and the Police buy tires, and the Fire Department buys tires. Instead of each one of you going down to a local filling station and buying retail, why don't you pool your orders and buy wholesale?"

"And go *outside* the city, Mayor?"

"Well, not necessarily. Can't you buy wholesale inside the city?"

"Not if you got to bid. The big distributors in Hartford and New Haven would cream the locals."

"They would?"

"Sure. And what'll the local filling stations say if you start buying out of town?"

"Why, they'll say — they'll say that I'm saving the taxpayers' money. That's what they'll say."

"Oh, Mayor — you slay me. You slay me, Mayor."

Stephen K. Bailey, "A Structured Interaction Pattern for Harpsichord and Kazoo," *Public Administration Review* (Summer 1954) 14:204.

The concern is simply this: if someone is not pulled away from the day-to-day crises of line operations and given enough time and repose to chart the future, planning will always get lost in the shuffle — Gresham's law of planning.

What happens when planning is not done? Imagine the Social Security Administration ignoring aging trends in the population or the fact that payouts are beginning to exceed receipts into its trust fund. Visualize a state university that pays no attention to the number of high school freshmen who will arrive at the college three years later. Consider a community that is oblivious to industrial and residential areas encroaching on each other and fails to reserve rights-of-way for freeways. No, in every case, segregation of the planning function is a prerequisite to a government's being on top of its job the day after tomorrow.

LINE OPERATIONS: SERVING THE MAJOR PURPOSE

To repeat, line activities are those that directly carry out the major purposes of an agency for an outside clientele. Line officers who carry out those activities range all the way from chief executive to cop or foot soldier. For example, when widespread violence breaks out in a major city the line responds. A cop on the beat sounds the alarm; squad cars appear; the mayor notifies the governor; the National Guard moves in; as the crisis mounts, word reaches the top of the federal line, the president, and he sends in more line units, including the 101st Airborne Division.

Notice that any notion of line as lower-lowers and staff as upper-uppers is fallacious. The line is a functional route of increasing authority from rank-and-file operatives at one end to their ultimate directors or chief executives at the other; all are involved in the major purposes of their agency (or government). Mayor, governor, and president are all line officers. To confuse the matter slightly, we should note that even an *auxiliary* agency, such as a civil service commission, has *line* functions: recruiting and testing for its constituent agencies, reviewing their classification decisions, and so on.

At the federal level, line activities are the familiar ones: national defense, foreign relations, outer space exploration, regulation of interstate commerce, aid to states and communities (education, slum clearance, and poverty programs), natural resource management, maintaining nationwide communications, among others.

The line activities of state government run from alcohol regulation to watershed protection. They include the critically important areas of education, highways, administration of the criminal laws and state courts, and the regulation of intrastate commerce (child labor, state minimum wage laws, utility rate regulation), and the like.

Finally, at the county and municipal level, line functions cover the recording of property and zoning, health administration, police and fire protection, parks and recreation, the delivery of drinking water, and the removal of garbage and sewage, among other functions.

STAFF OPERATIONS: POLICY PLANNING AND RESEARCH

Planning, research, and policy advice in behalf of line operations are the key roles that characterize the staff function in government. The importance of that function has already been stressed, but it remains to be underscored.

Long-range planning was one of the permanent legacies of the New Deal to American government. The depression era National Resources Board (1934) and Committee (1935) and the National Resources Planning Board (1939) paved the way for the Office of War Mobilization of World War II, and the National Security Resources Board of 1947, then the Office of Defense Mobilization of the Korean War, and from there to the Office of Civil Defense Mobilization, and on to the Office of Emergency Planning. These vital agencies have been central planning mechanisms at the White House level for seeking answers to this kind of question: What natural resources will be on hand fifteen to twenty years hence to meet the predictable commitments and contingencies the United States will be facing? Getting meaningful answers to such questions and developing sensible mobilization plans for times of national crisis contribute so much to the "science of muddling through" that one day, in some crisis, these staff agencies could mean the difference between national survival and national suicide.

As a case in point, the President's Materials Policy Commission (the Paley Commission), a staff body of the Truman administration, tellingly warned the country in 1952 that there were troubles ahead in our oil situation. They predicted that the United States would be using 5.7 million barrels of motor fuel per day twenty-three years later, in 1975; it turned out to be 6.7 million barrels per day. They forecast a domestic production shortfall in 1975 of 2.5 million barrels for all purposes, only one third as bleak as it turned out to be (7.3 million barrels per day). The Paley Commission said in 1952 that our "greatest problem" was an increasing dependence on Middle East oil and recommended the initiation of conservation in production and use and the establishment of underground stockpiles.[4] As the French would say, that was *prévoyance*, seeing down the road very clearly. And as we would say, it was superb staff work.

But staff agencies can't do much more than warn; it then falls to line officers to institute remedial action. In this instance, it clearly seems that at least three presidents, Eisenhower, Johnson, and Nixon, failed to do so. (From this author's point of view, the appropriate action would have included massive antitrust action against Big Oil as well as imposition of needed conservation measures on gas-guzzling car manufacturers.)

Toward the end of the Great Depression the President's Committee on Administrative Management developed a classical definition of "pure staff" in recommending the creation of administrative assistants for the president:

> The President needs help. His immediate staff assistance is entirely inadequate. He should be given a small number of executive assistants who would be his direct aides in dealing with the managerial agencies and administrative departments of the Government. These assistants, probably not exceeding six in number, would be in addition to his present secretaries, who deal with the public, with the Congress, and with the press and the radio. These aides would have no power to make decisions or issue instructions in their own right. They would not be interposed between the President and the heads of his departments. They would not be assistant presidents in any sense. Their function would be, when any matter was presented to the President for action affecting any part of the administrative work of the Government, to assist him in obtaining quickly and without delay all pertinent information possessed by any of the executive

departments so as to guide him in making his responsible decisions; and then when decisions have been made, to assist him in seeing to it that every administrative department and agency affected is promptly informed. Their effectiveness in assisting the President will, we think, be directly proportional to their ability to discharge their functions with restraint. They would remain in the background, issue no orders, make no decisions, emit no public statements. Men for these positions should be carefully chosen by the President from within and without the Government. They should be men in whom the President has personal confidence and whose character and attitude are such that they would not attempt to exercise power on their own account. They should be possessed of high competence, great physical vigor, and a passion for anonymity. They should be installed in the White House itself, directly accessible to the President.[5]

Notice the stress on confidentiality in the relationship to the president; no power to issue orders; and, in the famous phrase, "a passion for anonymity." President Roosevelt obtained his contingent of anonymous assistants in 1939,[6] a White House staff that would mushroom in the hands of later presidents.[7] In the Nixon administration, the staff assistants would lose their anonymity, as Senator Sam Ervin's Watergate Committee, the House Judiciary (Impeachment) Committee, and reporters like Carl Bernstein and Bob Woodward of the *Washington Post* proceeded to make the names of H. R. Haldeman, John D. Ehrlichman, Charles Colson, and others bad household words.

Perhaps the nonpareil of staff agencies at the national level is the Office of Management and Budget (OMB), historically known as the U.S. Bureau of the Budget. First established by the pioneering Budget and Accounting Act of 1921,[8] this office began life as a bureau in the Treasury Department. Then, as noted earlier, following the vision of a great new role for the bureau conjured up in 1937 by the President's Committee on Administrative Management,[9] the bureau was lifted out of Treasury and into the newly created Executive Office of the President by Reorganization Plan No. 1 of 1940.[10] The name change to OMB came in Nixon's Reorganization Plan No. 2 of 1970.[11]

The OMB has a dual personality (which some line agencies might prefer to spell "duel"). It is *auxiliary* in processing agency money requests and carrying out presidential mandates as to expenditure ceilings. It is *staff* in providing agencies with organization and methods research; in advising the president on expenditure trends and budget allocations; and, through its Legislative Reference Division, in flagging the White House on agency proposals to Congress that "are not in accord with the policy of the President."[12]

Another agency at the federal level that clearly portrays the staff role is the Council of Economic Advisers (CEA). Planning, research, and advice are the statutory tasks of the council under the Employment Act of 1946.[13] The CEA analyzes current economic trends, makes projections of where gross national product is likely to go, and recommends to the president policies that will promote maximum employment, production, and purchasing power.[14]

Staff Agencies in State and Local Government

The staff principle is observable as well at the other end of the federal system. Administrative assistants to governors, mayors, and city managers help ease the burdens of research and speech writing for their chiefs. State and local planning commissions chart developing land use and propose master plans to governing bodies; and planning units in state water boards and city water departments are constantly measuring consumption rates, current and projected, trying to determine how community water needs are going to be met fifteen to twenty years hence.

Must One Give Orders to Be Important?

The classical literature on staff agencies always stressed that staff personnel recommend policies but issue no commands, the command function being left to line officers. The notion raised images about staff people as dilettantes among activists, academicians among decision makers, and steers among bulls. Madame Pompadour may not have been staff, steer or bull, but she had power in the court of Louis XV because she had access to the king's ear, and therein lies the answer to this staff image problem. Staff people attached to kingpins in an organization, where their advice is regularly sought and listened to, are powerful, high-status individuals. Conversely, the line operator who is kicked upstairs to a research post and thereafter is never consulted by anyone may be accurately portrayed as a steer among bulls.

Years ago, O. Glenn Stahl argued persuasively that *power* is not a valid demarcation between line and staff, and that differentiated roles are the only real dividing line. Line looks outward, staff looks inward, and *both* have great influence on the administrative course.[15]

Beware the Staff Drift into Unreality

Part of the lament of line officers against staff people is that the latter no longer "talk *our* language" or are "worried about *our* problems." Although the complaint may simply reflect line arrogance, it may also have some basis in fact. Staff people cannot be like the mushroom cloud after an atomic explosion that breaks away from its stem; they must remain in touch with real problems if their advice to decision makers is going to be sound.

One of the best assurances that staff people retain "legs just long enough to reach the ground" is a policy of rotation — interchanging line and staff personnel at perhaps two-year intervals, with benefits on both sides — providing reexposure of staff people to the real world of the line and ventilating the provincialism of the line people by exposing them to the broader view of the staff. This in fact is the policy in that prototype of all governmental staff agencies, the general staff of the armed forces. Here, commissioned officers are rotated from line posts for service on the general staff for tours of up to three years.

AUXILIARY OPERATIONS: ESSENTIAL SERVICES AND CONTROLS

Like staff units, auxiliary services operate inside rather than outside agencies, rendering support across-the-board to all line operations. But as we have noted, unlike staff offices, which in theory are not to command, auxiliary units do have a power of command over technical aspects of line operations (personnel, budgeting, purchasing, etc.).

At the government-wide level, the auxiliary housekeeping units are agencies like the U.S. Office of Personnel Management, the General Services Administration (building management, etc.), the Treasury Department's IRS (collecting taxes for every agency's budget), and the Office of Management and Budget. Inside a government department, auxiliary offices such as finance, purchasing, personnel, data processing, transportation, and building maintenance provide services to, and controls over, the line units.

The dual role of the auxiliary office cannot be overstressed. On the one hand, it renders services to the line. It recruits and pays their personnel, buys their equipment (often at lower prices than the individual line offices could wangle), processes their records, and provides the janitors to scrub their office floors. But alongside that service role is the auxiliary unit's controller role that spooks the line. The personnel office says competitive exams are to be used in selecting new employees, not unfettered line choice; purchasing requires competitive bidding for acquiring equipment; the office of the general counsel points to the illegality of a proposed line action; and the controller brings a line program to a halt for overexpenditure of a budget allotment. In these ways, the long arm of top management reaches through the auxiliary units to control key aspects of line operations.

One other duality that characterizes auxiliary agencies should be noted (mentioned earlier in regard to the Office of Management and Budget). Some agencies play both auxiliary and staff roles. They may render services or controls for line operations while also performing research and advice for decision makers. Thus, the U.S. Office of Personnel Management provides recruiting, examining, and classification services for government agencies (its auxiliary role) while advising those same agencies on improved techniques and the president on developing needs in federal personnel administration (e.g., for a senior civil service, for group life insurance coverage, for pay raises, and so on). A public relations office at a university may turn out brochures and press releases as an auxiliary service while conducting a public opinion poll for the president and board of regents in its staff role.

CONFLICT WITHIN THE TRINITY

You are a district engineer for the state road commission, with full responsibility to maintain state roads in a four-county area of your state. An interoffice memorandum from the state purchasing agent brings this word: "Your request for an eighty-ton earthmover is denied. Submit request for three vehicles of smaller size, which are more economical to buy and operate." Joy! "This birdbrain pencil pusher who doesn't have to move mountains to build freeways and has never driven anything bigger than a power mower is telling *us* what's economical!"

Or, as director of the Long-Range Forecast Division of the U.S. Weather Bureau, in hiring a senior climatologist from three applicants submitted by the board of civil service examiners, you have passed over a black applicant and recommended a white applicant for appointment. The phone melts in your hand when the personnel office calls, rejecting your nominee and ordering you to prepare papers on the black applicant.[16]

Or finally, you are the secretary of defense, locked in a running battle with the director of OMB over ceilings on defense expenditures. You're given the job of defending this country — he's not — and that budget director couldn't even tell you the cost, let alone the kill capability, of a Minuteman missile.

So goes the ever-recurring warfare between line and auxiliary units, and line and staff units. Line officers have the program responsibilities, are sure they have the technical knowhow, and will get the blame if objectives are not reached. Thus, they are inclined to view intrusions by auxiliary people at best as frustrations, at worst as subversion, of their mission to get a job done.[17]

These tensions have many roots: a cocky attitude on the part of line operators that staff and auxiliary people are long-haired dreamers and meddlers; the duality of roles (services as well as controls) of auxiliary units that may not be harmonious, which raises suspicions as to who is really being served, the line or top management; threats to the line manager's success and survival by controlling his means of operation (people, money, and supplies); time interferences; language barriers; and personality conflicts.

The conflicts can be a real pain; but without being a Pollyanna about them, we ought to note that creative tension can sometimes serve a useful purpose.[18] Personnel needs to jar that lily-white male line unit into affirmative action on EEO; a tough budget director must constantly keep the spending plans of the Pentagon in tow; and a planning group in Interior should always be needling the Oil and Gas Division on whether or not they give a damn about aesthetics when they permit offshore drilling in lagoons like Santa Barbara Harbor. The simple truth is that those kinds of conflict are *healthy*.

But some are not healthy. And for those that constitute fruitless attrition and deadlock, some avoidance strategies and remedies are needed.

Avoiding Fights Among the Trinity

One place to begin is with careful role definition of the mission of each service. This amounts to due notice and warning to a new division head as to the kinds of services and interferences she can expect from auxiliary and staff units. Defining the roles will not eliminate the conflicts but may reduce the temperature somewhat through foreknowledge and understanding.

Second, conflict resolution may be abetted by successfully selling employees on agency goals. As a leadership technique, this involves so thorough a job of inculcating *agency* objectives that division chiefs are willing to put up with some personal dissatisfactions in order to advance the broader agency interest.

Third, excellent communications among the potential disputants may permit a talking through of situations that would engender sharp conflict elsewhere. An arrangement to facilitate that kind of communication is the so-called linking pin, or decision making via ad hoc committees, advocated by Rensis Likert.[19] As a case in point, before an agency would embark on a new performance-rating venture, personnel specialists, line-unit representatives, and employee union spokesmen would be linked up without regard to rank for discussions about the proposed change. The hope is that policy decisions would then have wide authorship, with the involvement of many leading to the commitment of many to go along in support. The linking-pin committees may thus provide a helpful way for line and auxiliary officers to share points of view and nip conflict in the bud.

Some Fights Will Have to Be Settled

Despite good use of the three techniques just discussed and others, some fights among line, staff, and auxiliary personnel are inevitable. When the trinity engage in a fight, who settles it? The answer in organizational theory is clear: the department head to whom the disputants report.

In dealing with line-staff-auxiliary tangles, the department head has available a wide range of moves (which we will more fully canvass in Chapter 10), including: *staff meetings,* sometimes involving the useful technique of having the adversaries argue the issue from their *opponents'* point of view; *compromise* ("We will allow the Concorde to make only ten landings a day, and even those only for a trial period"); *head-knocking* ("I expect every city department to show a 10 percent increase in minority hiring by the end of the fiscal year"); and *canning* some of the dissidents (President Carter: "Secretary Califano, you haven't shown enough enthusiasm for a separate Department of Education, and way too much enthusiasm in turning smokers away from a very important crop in my region of the country — thank you for serving.")

For the long pull, we come full circle to the rotation-in-office idea discussed earlier. Move administrators and future administrators from line assignments to staff and auxiliary posts to give them a problem-solving perspective in advance of the "hour of conflict."

INTEGRATION OF THE TRINITY — WHEN NECESSARY

Now comes the turning of the screw that may tear the threads right off you. After pulling staff and auxiliary functions *away* from the line, we come to a contemporary fact of administrative life that says, on occasion, you may need to pull all three together again. That fact underlies project management, which is increasingly giving rise to *matrix organizations,* characterized by temporary mergers of line, staff, and auxiliary units around concrete projects assigned to an agency.

Consider the National Aeronautics and Space Administration (NASA). Instead of using a single pyramid-shaped agency to conduct all their outer space programs, NASA administrators opted for project teams with fully integrated line, staff, and auxiliary units. The teams were frequently put together by major aeronautical firms in the private sector, under contract to NASA. What resulted (with variations, of course) was a matrix organization that looked something like that shown in Figure 4.4. Support personnel would either be detailed from main-line NASA divisions or supplied by the private contractor. Through the matrix organization, the project managers were assured an interdisciplinary team for getting astronauts to the moon and spaceships to Mars.

The matrix concept implies something more, however, than simply structure, more than the temporary merger of line, staff, and auxiliary units for the accomplishment of a project. It also suggests a style of management, which we will examine in detail in Chapter 6. It is a style involving more openness in decision making, rank based on expertise rather than on status in the parent organization, wide delegation of authority to make decisions, and so on.[20]

Some of the virtues of matrix organizations include giving a project manager all the support he needs to accomplish his mission (line, staff, and auxiliary being under his own thumb), rather quickly acquiring trained personnel from main-line divisions of the parent agency, boosting morale through job rotation to the new projects, and flexibility.

But the matrix approach is not all pluses. In a number of the matrix organizations that Chris Argyris has studied, the spirit of shared problem solving has not taken hold, leadership more appropriate to pyramid-shaped agencies continues to prevail, and individuals detailed to the project are nervous about not making points in their main-line divisions while they are on project assignments.[21]

Given the number of relatively short-lived projects governments undertake, from an experimental corrections center in state government to weapons development in national defense, the project team with the matrix design undoubtedly has a promising future.[22] In historical perspective, it seems to represent

Support personnel drawn from:	Vanguard (unmanned satellites)	Mercury (manned orbital)	Apollo (moon landings)	Mariner and Viking (Mars, Venus, etc.)
Astronautical science				
Budget and finance				
Computer services				
Engineering				
Facilities management				
Legal services				
Medical services				
Personnel				
Public relations				
Purchasing				

FIGURE 4.4   MATRIX ORGANIZATION OF NASA PROJECTS

Newton's law in public administration: "Every action has an equal and opposite reaction" — the reintegration of line, staff, and auxiliary services that the conventional wisdom drove asunder.

SUMMARY

In addition to the features of formal organization discussed in Chapter 3, agencies will frequently reflect the key principle of this chapter: the segregation of line, staff, and auxiliary services. The hope is that separate provision of those services may reduce certain burdens of line operators, make for economies, strengthen top management's control, and assure that long-range planning will not be neglected.

Nevertheless, segregation also sets up conflict situations. Line agency managers especially may feel the encroachment of auxiliary units. To prevent and resolve disputes within the trinity, administrators may explore more precise role definitions, coordination by objectives, improved communications, a host of leadership techniques, and head-knocking.

Furthermore, in the last few decades the appearance of matrix organizations for project management represents an interesting reversal of the segregation of functions described in this chapter. The reassembly of line, staff, and auxiliary units as a project team sounds almost like the fulfillment of the (slightly altered) wedding ceremony — what the manager dreams of joining together, let no man put asunder.

KEY CONCEPTS

staff
auxiliary
line
Office of Management and Budget
matrix organizations
conflict resolution

DISCUSSION QUESTIONS

1. Argue in favor of the segregation of staff and auxiliary services. Then note the arguments against this point of view. Which argument, pro or con, carries the most weight?

2. Of the three parts of the administrative trinity, which is likely to have the most power in an organization?

3. Discuss the reasons why there is likely to be conflict among line, staff, and auxiliary. How can such conflict be settled?

Notes

1. Leonard D. White, a twentieth-century pioneer in both the practice and teaching of public administration, *Introduction to the Study of Public Administration,* 3d ed. (New York: Macmillan, 1948), p. 30.

2. Robert Townsend, *Up the Organization* (New York: Knopf, 1970), p. 142.

3. In an analogous way, the U.S. Commission on Civil Rights published a scathing report on the failures of state and local governments in assuring equality of employment opportunity. See *For All the People . . . By All the People* (Washington, D.C.: Government Printing Office, 1969).

4. President's Materials Policy Commission, *Resources for Freedom* (Washington, D.C.: Government Printing Office, 1952), vol. 3.

5. President's Committee on Administrative Management, *Report with Special Studies* (Washington, D.C.: Government Printing Office, 1937), p. 5.

6. Reorganization Act of 1939, 53 Stat. 565, sec. 301. To lift the veil of anonymity, the first three appointed were William H. McReynolds, James H. Rowe, and Lauchlin Currie.

7. See Thomas E. Cronin, "The Swelling of the Presidency," *Saturday Review of the Society* (Feb. 1973) 1:30–6.

8. 42 Stat. 20 (1921).

9. President's Committee on Administrative Management, *Report,* pp. 16–20.

10. For a contemporary view of that elevation, see Robert Sherwood, *Roosevelt and Hopkins* (New York: Harper, 1948), pp. 209–212. A later history of the bureau was written by Eisenhower's budget director, Percival Brundage, *The Bureau of the Budget* (New York: Praeger, 1970), but the reader should be aware of serious gaps in Brundage's work, such as the absence of any discussion concerning the impoundment of funds controversy.

11. The Nixon alteration of the Bureau of the Budget (one of his many unforgivable acts, from this author's point of view) was reviewed in the *Public Administration Review* (Nov.–Dec. 1970) 30:611–619, and 631–634. See also Allen Schick, "The Budget Bureau that Was," *Law and Contemporary Problems* (Summer 1970), pp. 519–539.

12. See Richard Neustadt, "Presidency and Legislation: The Growth of Central Clearance," *American Political Science Review* (Sept. 1954) 48:641–671.

13. 73 Stat. 315 (1946). See a great book on the birth of the Employment Act by Stephen K. Bailey, *Congress Makes a Law* (New York: Columbia University Press, 1950).

14. A debate over the proper conduct of council roles arose during the first three years of the council's life. Chairman Edwin G. Nourse and the man who succeeded him, Leon Keyserling, differed sharply on whether public appearances by council members, especially before congressional committees, would jeopardize a confidential staff relationship with the president. See Edwin G. Nourse, *Economics in the Public Service* (New York: Harcourt, Brace, 1953), pp. 204–208, 221–222, and 272–308. See also Corinne Silverman, *The President's Economic Advisers,* Interuniversity Case Program No. 48 (University, Ala.: University of Alabama Press, 1959).

15. O. Glenn Stahl, "The Network of Authority," *Public Administration Review* (Winter 1958) 18:ii–iv.

16. For some dramatic accounts of fights over personnel between line officials and merit system boards see Paul Ylvisaker, "The Battle of Blue Earth County," in Harold Stein (ed.), *Public Administration and Policy Development* (New York: Harcourt, Brace, 1952), pp. 89–105; and C. B. and V. A. Earle, *The Promotion of Lem Merrill,* Interuniversity Case Program No. 20 (University, Ala.: University of Alabama Press, 1953).

17. See, for example, the perceptive article by Guy B. Ford, "Why Doesn't Everyone Love the Personnel Man?" *Personnel* (Jan.–Feb. 1963) 40:49–52. In addition, see Victor Thompson, *Modern Organization* (New York: Knopf, 1961), pp. 99–112.

18. See Rensis Likert, *New Patterns of Management* (New York: Macmillan, 1961), p. 117.

19. Rensis Likert, *The Human Organization* (New York: McGraw-Hill, 1967) pp. 163–171.

20. Chris Argyris, "Today's Problems with Tomorrow's Organizations," in Jun and Storm, *Tomorrow's Organizations* (Glenview, Ill: Scott, Foresman, 1973), p. 64.

21. Argyris, "Today's Problems with Tomorrow's Organizations," pp. 63–65.

22. See Lawrence A. Bass, *Management by Task Forces* (Mt. Airy, Md.: Lomond Systems, Inc., 1975).

Chapter 5
Impact of People on Structure: Informal Organization

AUTHORITY IN ORGANIZATION: FORMAL AND INFORMAL

A member of your public administration class wants a summer job in Washington, D.C. She begins her job hunting not with the U.S. Office of Personnel Management but with a request to her congresswoman for some leads and wire pulling.

A mayor is planning on proposing a one-half percent increase in the business license tax to raise more revenue; a phone call from the powerful secretary of the chamber of commerce stops him in his tracks.

The county commission plans to merge planning and zoning with building inspection, giving all three a more political hue; an editorial in the evening paper condemning the reorganization halts the change.

The governor wants to close down the agricultural extension service; but 250 extension agents corral thirty rural state senators' votes and save their jobs.

At the national level, the FBI explored the pathways of informal organization to get around the strictures of the Fifth Amendment's grand jury requirement. Unwilling to disclose their undercover operatives in investigations of suspected Communists, the FBI on occasion simply ran around the judiciary by tipping off congressional investigating committees. In public hearings, without the full guarantees of due process, the House Un-American Activities Committee and Senate Internal Security Committee would then expose the alleged subversives against whom the FBI could not obtain indictments.[1]

On the aircraft carrier *Constellation,* as a navy ship the most self-contained of all government installations, newly recruited blacks, relegated to the poorest jobs and having the least hope of advancement, plan and then carry out a mutiny. Most surprised, apparently, was Capt. John Ward who, while holding forth in "officers' territory," had no idea what the meetings of the black sailors decks below were all about.[2]

Meanwhile at city hall, where a strong mayor and council govern the salary structure, the mayor describes the real world of salary raises for his chauffeur:

"Mayor, we gonna get a raise this year?"

"Gee, Al, I dunno. Depends . . ."

"On what, Mayor?"

"Well, Al, it depends on the chief and on the police commission. And, of course, I don't know what the board of finance will say — or the merit rating board — or the council. And of course, if you fellows get a raise, what will the firemen and the boys in public works say? And the school board? To say nothing of the party."

"Election year, huh, Mayor?"

The mayor then privately concludes: "In Centerville we have no scalar system and damn little POSDCORB."[3]

In all of these situations, one might understandably ask, "Who is in charge around here?" Chances are the answer would not be found on the organization chart, for what we are about to see is that organization charts of the formal structure are frequently normative maps of how organization planners hope duties and authority patterns will turn out, rather than existential maps of how an agency actually operates. The pursuit of how an agency actually operates inevitably leads into the fascinating labyrinths known as *informal organization.*

THE TWO FACES OF EMPLOYMENT SECURITY: A CASE STUDY

With apologies to any real employment security office for any unintended correspondence to the description that follows, our case study begins with the organization chart on the administrator's wall (Figure 5.1). But insiders know that the informal structure of employment security looks very different from that (Figure 5.2).

The administrator (1), an appointee of a discredited former governor, has been aced out of effective control of the agency by Baxter (9), chamber of commerce secretary and the chief power wielder of the local business establishment.

The deputy for operations (2) has suffered the same fate. She alienated the business community by championing passage of a tough consumer protection law.

And the deputy for auxiliary services (3) in employment security has also

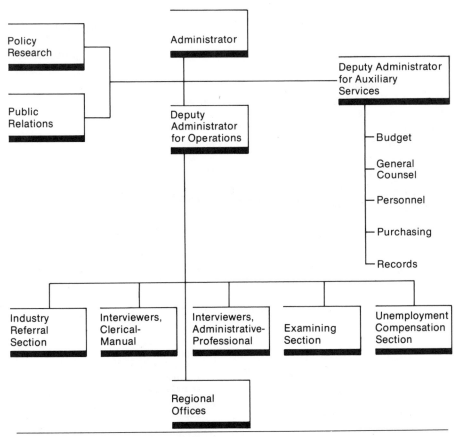

FIGURE 5.1   FORMAL ORGANIZATION OF THE STATE EMPLOYMENT SECURITY OFFICE

been shunted aside for waging a campaign for referring black applicants for job interviews ahead of whites.

The purchasing agent (4) finds himself in the out-group for insisting on competitive bids rather than negotiated contracts, which had antagonized local supply houses.

The legal counsel (5) has been on the chamber of commerce' "most-wanted" list for almost a decade for championing a city manager form of government that would have weakened Baxter's domination of municipal affairs.

The director of policy research (6) is in outer-outer land simply because Baxter does not believe in "all this newfangled research stuff." Rumor is that Baxter consults an astrologer on the tough decisions.

The head of the examinations section (7) has been completely discounted since he recommended the head of the local chapter of the National Organiza-

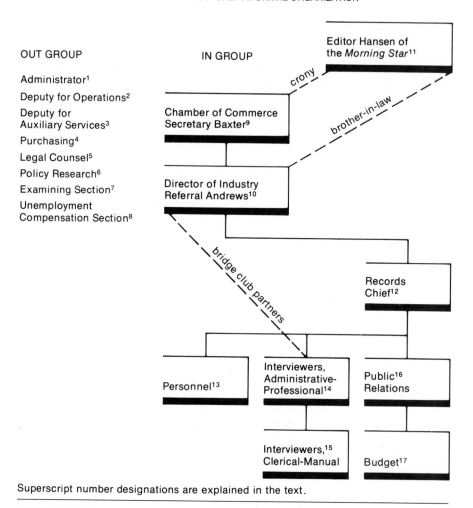

Superscript number designations are explained in the text.

FIGURE 5.2   INFORMAL ORGANIZATION OF THE STATE EMPLOYMENT SECURITY OFFICE

tion for Women (NOW) for the presidency of the state university when it was last vacant.

And the unemployment compensation section (8) was predestined to fall from grace in this business-dominated agency because of the welfare state aura surrounding its work, which Baxter cannot stand.

Baxter's position (9) of being able to call the shots in employment security stems mostly from the solid phalanx of businessmen behind him who refused to give the agency, as originally led, any job referrals. Another source of Baxter's power is his personal association with the other member of the city's duumvirate, Hansen (11), editor of the *Morning Star* newspaper.

Of necessity, Baxter leaves day-to-day operations in employment security in the hands of the director of the industry referral section, Tom Andrews (10). That section maintains close relations with the business community, making Andrews thoroughly persona grata with the local barons. His position vis-à-vis Baxter is strengthened by virtue of the fact that Andrews's wife is Hansen's sister.

Below Andrews, the in-group of employment security consists of six of the original eleven sections of the agency. The records chief (12) is truly a major-domo because she has the goods on everyone. The personnel director (13) is a brother of the state merit system head, through whom he has wangled both strong applicants and many favors for his agency.

The two interviewing sections (14 and 15) are well accepted by Baxter and Andrews because of their key screening role in weeding out unsuitables for the business clientele. But the two sections are in a clearly ranked order, stemming from the higher-status jobs filled by the administrative-professional unit (in con-trast to the clerical-manual jobs of the white-collar unit). Incidentally, an effec-tive medium of coordination exists between the heads of industry referral and the administrative-professional interviewing section — their frequent social contacts through a bridge club to which they both belong.

The public relations director (16) is high status in this agency as a result of a personal friendship with Chamber Secretary Baxter in the Town Athletic Club and the public relations director's long association with advertising firms throughout the city.

Finally, the budget director's (17) influence is considerably bolstered by a decades-old friendship with Andrews (10), going all the way back to their col-lege days together in the Sigma Nu fraternity.

So goes the life of an organization. The organization chart is kaput; status, missions, and lines of authority are all skewed; and new patterns of allegiance and power have replaced the old. Outside pressures and contacts; inside affili-ations and views; old friendships, stigmas, and myths have all combined to make an agency what it is in fact, not fancy. The scenario of course exaggerates the outside pressures, which in real life arise in degrees, all the way from indif-ference to agency affairs on to dominance, as portrayed here. Those external forces are to be contrasted with the power-and-personality factors *within* an agency, which are perhaps even more influential in shaping its informal orga-nization.

THE NATURE OF INFORMAL ORGANIZATION[4]

Chester Barnard contended, and rightly, that formal organizations always gen-erate informal organizations and consequently are always permeated by the latter. The reason is fundamental. Organizations come alive only when people are plugged into the organization chart; as soon as that happens, their lives and interaction patterns begin to shape the agency itself.

Informal organization consists of the actual groupings of human beings in an agency. The key ingredients of that organization include the employees' value systems, their customs and myths, their affiliations and likes and dislikes, and the authority network resulting from all of these. If the informal organization is sharply different from the formal structure, it constitutes the invisible government, the power behind the throne.[5]

Informal organization therefore embraces all the interpersonal relations and alliances that prevail in an agency, from the shifting, dynamic friendship cliques and ad hoc work groups on up to rather institutionalized associations of workers in the agency bowling league and the employee union. All have a part in the informal organization and the life processes of the agency.

In attempting to map out the informal organization of an agency, one strives to convey the *actual* lines of authority, the natural groupings of human beings, and the patterns of obedience that prevail among the work force.[6] Even with the sociologist's sociogram as an aid, such a chart can never be done with final accuracy, because so many of the associations and informal groups are intrinsically dynamic, shifting as issues, moods, and personalities change.

SIGNIFICANCE OF INFORMAL ORGANIZATION

It goes without saying that the administrator lives in a real world and needs to deal with *that* world if he is to enjoy success for very long. That fact of life requires a superb sensing system to recognize not only the reality of informal organization but also what it is currently doing to his agency, where it is tending, and how, in unparanoid fashion, he might possibly work with the informal structure to advance the public good.

Fine-tuning that sensing system, the administrator might perceive that the informal organization in his agency is having these kinds of impacts:

challenging the operating authority of one of his bureau chiefs, almost to the point of dethroning her

bringing strength and vitality to another bureau where congruence has been achieved between the formal and informal organizations

setting production norms in one line division far below the unit's capability, where rate busters are being punished for trying to challenge the informal group's outputs norms[7]

providing multiple communication channels within the agency, some of them usefully supplementing the official lines, others filled with misinformation and "garbage"

giving some people significant recognition and influence whom the formal organization has heretofore ignored generating a pluralistic quality, which for the most part is bringing fresh ideas, diversity of viewpoints, and healthy association into the fabric of agency life

While the astute manager is taking these soundings, the equally smart employee is also taking a close look. She realizes that making it in the agency will require an understanding of what goes on in the real world behind the organization charts. That means, on the employee's part, identifying clearly who has the boss' ear (his secretary, his scientific staff man, his golf companion, his bedroom companion, a newspaper editor, or a political wheel). As a case in point, a friendly word from the secretary to her boss may get a leave application approved ten times as fast as a formal memorandum to him; in administration as in politics, sometimes the shortest distance between two points is a curved line.

On the boss' part, he must strive to have the clearest possible understanding of the significant others in the informal society of his employees, the people they listen to and sometimes blindly follow. These are the natural leaders, and he must have them on his side if he is to keep his work force pulling with him.

Tearing the Organization Apart

Having his people against him instead of with him is by no means an uncommon plight for the administrator. National leaders experience it: King George III (1776), Czar Nicholas II (1917), and President Richard Nixon (1973–1974) are good examples. The mayors of Newark and Detroit (1967) and Memphis (1968 and 1978) also knew it — as did college presidents of Columbia, Wisconsin, SUNY-Buffalo, and the University of California at Berkeley in the anti–Vietnam War period.

A split may develop between the formal hierarchy and the informal organization within government agencies as well, subverting the cooperative base on which bureaucracies must depend for successful operation. The hiatus lies in plain view in school boards at war with teachers' unions; in a hospital that nurses have just struck; or in an army unit that gives only foot-dragging compliance to the orders of its commander.

Reasons for the alienation of the informal organization are, of course, legion. They may stem from specific grievances such as payless paydays, inadequate pay, hostile managers, unsafe working conditions, or policy decisions that run deeply against the grain of the rank and file and their significant others. Or the alienation may be based on long-standing deprivation of human needs (Figure 2.4 of Chapter 2) — especially the feeling that "Nobody knows my name"; "No one ever asks my opinion around here"; or "I'm a lousy pencil pusher with nothing to contribute to this outfit." The historian Crane Brinton spoke of the "flight of the intellectuals" from the regime in power as a precursor to revolution;[8] so too the alienation of employees in any of those ways may be the beginning of real trouble for an administrator. A deeply alienated informal organization is likely to mean that an agency is at war with itself.

Healing the Breach

A fundamental law of survival, as well as securing any prospect for agency success, demands that strife be healed. Administrators who are unable to manage the "old barons" and the "young Turks" of their informal societies are headed for oblivion. In resisting Gen. Douglas MacArthur's insubordination, Harry Truman knew full well what it would mean for the presidency if "five stars came to outweigh forty-eight stars" (in Herblock's classic phrase). Administrators, then, must have some techniques available for healing the breach in their organizations.

At least four techniques are available for welding the formal and informal structures back together. The first is to remove the causes of the alienation, and then hold out the olive branch. The second is conscientiously to woo the informal leaders over to your side (described in the following section). The third is to remove the dissidents — by transfer, by reorganization (out), or by dismissal — if one can do it under civil service laws.

A fourth technique is to weave the informal leaders into formal positions in the organization where the administrator feels that they are in the right or that the replacement would be healthy on other grounds. It is the old trick of "If you can't lick 'em, join 'em." Notice the frequency with which this technique has been used in reaction to civil rights disturbances: blacks are added to police units and the National Guard and are appointed to advisory boards and the like.

POSITIVE USES OF INFORMAL ORGANIZATION[9]

Communication Channel

Communication is the freest in those circles where one feels comfortable and secure and where mutual confidence prevails on all sides. Those conditions are the hallmarks of the natural groups that constitute the agency's informal organization. Consequently, for the administrator, one of the benefits of informal organization is the communication network it provides.

Suppose a division of the state industrial school were considering a workweek change from one week of day shifts, one of night, to a new schedule of two weeks of day shifts and two weeks of night. The division chief realizes that it is imperative to ascertain rank-and-file feelings in the matter before instituting the switch. With the concurrence of his formal deputies, so they will not feel bypassed, the chief calls on three or four key people in the informal structure and raises the question of the workweek shift.

Such Clear Messages from the Informal Organization

Some years ago this love note greeted me at State Campaign Headquarters:

> I came in early this morning to get some songs and the paper out. Just called you at home thinking it was better to discuss this with you, but the note will have to do.
>
> I know this is going to be difficult for you because it is a touchy situation; but I believe that you, as the office manager, will have to take the bull by the horns about the situation here with Mrs. Flynn.*
>
> I have had several calls from the girls, and if Mrs. Flynn is not stopped, you will have no office, except empty desks, or paid help that you will have to bring in to take the place of these wonderful volunteers who are giving literally eight to ten hours and more a day to work for the Party.
>
> I understand enough about human relations to know that Mrs. Flynn needs to feel needed; but I also know what can happen when one personality like her is in the midst of a group of women who will not be *bullied*, and especially *on their own time* —
> I know what can happen to an office.
>
> So someone has got to be strong enough to tell Mrs. Flynn to keep out of everyone else's business here at State Headquarters. We are losing prestige all around just because no one has the courage to tell her to either stay home or to shut up when she is here.
>
> I expect you will have a meeting Monday A.M. and this is the reason for the note. It is very simple, really. Either you have an office where everyone is happy working together, like a family, or you have Mrs. Flynn and empty desks.
>
> > Best,
> > *Name (withheld)*

* Fictitious name.

In no time, this trial balloon has been thoroughly circulated among the employees and either punctured or sent floating back up to the boss. In that way, the significant others of the informal society have been consciously utilized by management for downward communication; in this case, downward to generate a response upward.

The inputs may just as easily originate at low levels in an organization. If the group structure is healthy, creating a climate for employee candor (either griping or suggesting) and for spontaneous upward communication, this communication can provide extremely valuable clues to top management about rank-and-file sentiments.

However, as Raymond Valentine has pointed out, there are some pitfalls in using the informal organization as a network of communication.[10] Leapfrogging downward runs the risk of severely undercutting lieutenants in the line whose subordinates get the word through informal channels before they do. Lateral leapfrogging may result in pockets of information and pockets of ignorance about new developments when everyone's understanding and concurrence are vital.

Maintaining Cohesiveness

The significant others of the informal network can be thought of as linking pins. Workers see their local heroes as influential with management and thus tend to tie closely around those natural leaders. That increasing solidarity behind leaders who are themselves committed to agency goals helps to meet the belonging need and to strengthen cohesiveness throughout the agency.

At the upper end, the smart administrator has long since identified the informal leaders in the work force and goes to extra lengths to win their support; he knows that as these significant others go, so go the natural groups behind them. Telling his secretary that his door is always open to these influentials, calling them in for consultation, feeding them the inside word, granting their requests, and being seen with them at coffee breaks are ways in which the manager can link these kingpins firmly into the life of the agency and thereby build cohesiveness.

Boosting Self-esteem

Feeling wanted (the love need) and feeling a sense of personal worth, it will be recalled from Chapter 2, are psychological stepping-stones to accomplishment and personal growth. But there are a lot of bureaucratic features that militate against fulfillment of these needs.

In particular, the pyramid shape of formal organization can easily produce a dead-end psychosis that undermines all the aspiration that an employee might muster. "Here are all of us grade 7 statisticians, and in this whole regional office there are only two grade 11s and only one grade 15 — hell, there's no place to go but out!"

It is at this sad stage that informal organization begins to look like the Emancipation Proclamation, for through informal organization the opportunities are almost unlimited to supply the love and self-esteem needs and compensate for the frustration imposed by the narrowing of the pyramid structure. The clue is to use informal groups as legitimate adjuncts to the formal organization as a means of meeting employee desires to belong and to feel important.

In the agency portrayed in Figure 5.3, there may be only one GS-15 and one GS-16 (high-level jobs in the federal civil service). But the pyramid has been

INFORMAL GROUPS   FORMAL STRUCTURE   INFORMAL GROUPS

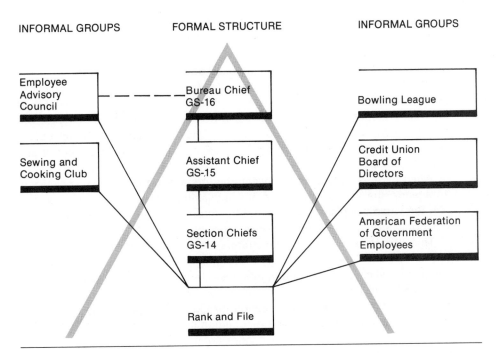

FIGURE 5.3   EXPANDING THE PYRAMID VIA INFORMAL GROUPS

broken open by means of many social groups that have the full endorsement of management: a union, a sewing club, a bowling league, a credit union, and an employee council advisory to the bureau chief. The leaders of these groups are often elected from rank-and-file positions in the agency. Thus, the aspirations of people who may get bottled up in the formal structure because of limited positions topside can in part be compensated for through the opportunities for recognition in the informal structure.

Instead of fearing the appearance of these associations of workers, then, the wise manager reflects on Aristotle's sound observation that people are basically gregarious, and he then goes out to generate such organizations all over the agency lot, knowing the contributions they can make to employee happiness and psychological health, and through these to agency esprit de corps.

SUMMARY

In the world of bureaucracy, there is something that doesn't love an organization chart.

Often with a good deal of planning we lay out an organization, delegate authority, pinpoint responsibility, and provide for information channels — and then add human beings to the mix — and in no time, all the walls, channels, and organization charts begin to come tumbling down.

Perhaps at no other point in public administration do we see the power of people over institutions so clearly demonstrated as we do in the impact of their informal organizations upon the formal structures through which we try to conduct the public's business. Groups, alliances, power shifting to informal leaders in the ranks, norms and myths, and outside influences — all these factors significantly shape the way agencies behave.

When there is congruence between the formal and the informal societies in an agency, the added strength in accomplishing agency goals can be widely felt. But when a schism develops and the informal society begins to challenge the formal structure, administration is in trouble.

Thus, it is imperative for administrators to understand the informal networks that lattice their agencies. With a reasonably clear picture of who speaks to whom and who listens to whom, administrators may begin to utilize informal organization in the highly constructive ways Chester Barnard suggested long ago: expanding honest communication through the grapevine, building cohesiveness, and granting status and recognition to employees in informal organizations who may be stifling in the confines of the agency pyramid.

But when push comes to shove between the formal and informal organizations, administrators risk being vetoed in the ranks if they do nothing. Techniques that may help to heal the fracture include eliminating the causes of employee unrest; wooing the informal leaders; transferring or firing the dissidents (which may be difficult under civil service); or moving them into the formal organization, replacing others who are on their way out anyway.

In short, be wary of formal organization charts; they may be as misleading as they are neat.

KEY CONCEPTS

organization chart   feedback
informal networks   lines of authority

DISCUSSION QUESTIONS

1. Why does an informal organization exist? What is its significance for good management? What barriers may it pose?

2. Discuss the positive uses of the informal organization. Which of these is the most important?

3. How can the informal organization be integrated with the formal one?

Notes

1. See Chapter 18, note 21, for documentation.

2. Henry P. Leifermann, "Mass Mutiny Aboard the U.S.S. Constellation," in Richard J. Stillman, *Public Administration: Concepts and Cases* (Boston: Houghton Mifflin, 1976), pp. 112–119.

3. POSDCORB was the Gulick-Urwick "funny word" to suggest the gamut of administration: planning, organizing, staffing, directing, coordinating, reporting, and budgeting. The colloquy is from that delightful spoof on formal organization by Stephen K. Bailey, "A Structured Interaction Pattern for Harpsichord and Kazoo," *Public Administration Review* (Summer 1954), 14:202.

4. For many years still to come, all who write on informal organization must acknowledge their heavy dependence upon the pioneering treatment of the subject written years ago by Chester I. Barnard (president of New Jersey Bell Telephone Co.). In many ways ahead of its time, his book, *The Functions of the Executive* (Cambridge, Mass.: Harvard University Press) appeared in 1938 while the doctrines of the formal organization school were much in vogue. Chapter 9 of that book, dealing with informal organization, argued that formal organization may not be the most important aspect of administration at all; and Chapter 12 (as noted in Chapter 3 of this text) suggested strikingly new ideas about who holds authority in organizations.

5. Barnard, *Functions of the Executive*, p. 121.

6. For a usable instrument to map the informal organization, see Donald B. Vogel, "Analysis of Informal Organization Patterns," *Public Administration Review* (Sept.– Oct. 1968), 28:431–436.

7. The pioneering study of work group alteration of official production norms was the "bank wiring room" phase of the Hawthorne experiments. See F. J. Roethlisberger and William J. Dickson, *Management and the Worker* (Cambridge, Mass.: Harvard University Press, 1942), chap. 22.

8. Crane Brinton, *The Anatomy of Revolution* (New York: Vintage Books, 1956), pp. 41–52.

9. See Barnard, *Functions of the Executive*, p. 122.

10. Raymond Valentine, "The Pitfalls of Informal Organization," *Management Review* (Jan. 1968) 57:38–46.

Chapter 6
Organization and People: A Search for the Harmonic Mean

BUREAUCRAT TO BUREAUPATH[1]

See yourself for a moment as a mail sorter in the Atlanta Post Office, a nurse with three years' service in San Francisco's Letterman General Hospital, a foot soldier with the Sixth Army, a New York City social worker, or a filing clerk in the Census Bureau. The crowd is lonely, all right, and bigness *is* a curse in your bureaucratic world.[2] As a young GI's first letter home from Vietnam poignantly stated, "Please write soon so I'll know somebody knows I exist."

The pay grade designations such as "Grade II Nurse," "PS-6 Mail Sorter," or "GS-3 Filing Clerk" don't help at all; they seem only to translate the anomie into a numbers game that hastens depersonalization.

If these civil service examples seem far removed, then take a long look at yourself (unless you are fortunate enough to be in a small liberal arts college). You must know the feeling of being an IBM card, of attempting to learn in a 220-person lecture class (where you are simply row 10, seat 7, instead of a human being), and of not being able to find a single professor in your senior year who knows you well enough to write a letter of recommendation for you. So you have experienced the curse of bigness, an inherent disease in bureaucracies. When you add to the sheer problem of size the old style of management (McGregor's Theory X), the crush of the human personalities who work for such an organization is overpowering.

The Clash Between the Agency and Its Workers

Simultaneously, the agency (the army, the FBI, the highway patrol, the city parks department) will strive to achieve its goals while its employees will be working to secure theirs.[3] Depending upon the way administration is conducted and how well the employees are organized, the clash between agency and work force may be sharp and destructive.[4]

The agency will have as its primary concerns carrying out public policy and "staying alive."[5] To illustrate, it will strive to cut costs, which may include dumping employees, in order to meet legislative and auditor pressure. In the name of getting the job done, the agency may squelch dissent, exact compliance with rules and regulations, manipulate employees (promote, transfer, train, ignore, direct, fire), and secure itself externally. "These rules and the corresponding status system," Victor Thompson contends, "are simply incompatible with democratic egalitarianism."[6]

Thompson identifies the features of bureaucracy that are the most dysfunctional to human beings: routinizing work; breaking up large, meaningful goals into bits and pieces small enough for small minds to master; narrowing the skills required in a job; confusing means and ends; impersonally managing; classifying jobs and human beings; resisting change; and cutting employees out of influence by a tight managerial hold on decision making ("monocractic power structures").[7]

In one of his earliest books, Chris Argyris described the conflict between organizational demands and human needs:

> There are some basic incongruencies between the growth trends of a healthy personality and the requirements of the formal organization. If the principles of formal organization are used as ideally defined, employees will tend to work in an environment where (1) they are provided minimal control over their workaday world, (2) they are expected to be passive, dependent, and subordinate, (3) they are expected to have a short time perspective, (4) they are induced to perfect and value the frequent use of a few skin-surface, shallow abilities, and (5) they are expected to produce under conditions leading to psychological failure.
>
> All these characteristics are incongruent to the ones *healthy* human beings are postulated to desire. . . . They are much more congruent with the needs of infants in our culture.[8]

Infants are not the stuff of which healthy agencies are made; adult men and women are. And, although the agencies they work for have needs, these men and women have deep-seated human needs that require fulfillment — needs such as personal growth, self-esteem, mutual support and affection, security, adequate compensation, and so on, as we said in Chapter 2.

Consequently, if agencies hire adults but treat them as children, managers and workers are going to be confronted everywhere by a *clash of the pyramids*

Turning Adults into Infants

From the job diary of a woman college graduate:

> I didn't go to school for four years to type. I'm bored, continuously humiliated. They sent me to Xerox school for three hours. . . . I realize that I sound cocky, but after you've been in the academic world, after you've had your own class [as a student teacher] and made your own plans, and someone tries to teach you to push a button — you get pretty mad. They even gave me a gold-plated plaque to show I've learned how to use the machine.

Joyce Starr, "Adaptation to the Working World," in Health, Education and Welfare, *Work in America* (Cambridge, Mass.: MIT Press, 1973), p. 44.

— the agency pyramid being narrow at the top, broad at the base, with formal authority flowing downward; and the inverted human needs pyramid being narrow at the bottom (physical needs) and broad, probably open-ended, at the top for self-actualization and self-direction, with aspirations flowing upward (see Figure 6.1). Clearly the hierarchical, pyramid structure of formal organizations is directly antithetical to the strivings of human beings who want increased (not narrowed) opportunities for responsibility and authority.

In terms of specific human drives, the agency may have minimal impact on the *physical* needs of its workers (leaving aside such obvious exceptions as military and paramilitary units). At the *security* need level, the wide extension of merit systems in government has greatly reduced the threat of job loss.

But the threatening implications of bureaucracy for the *love* need are plain to see. Hierarchy means that some civil servants are more equal than others. Out of the superior-subordinate relationship may emerge many sentiments — respect, awe, contempt — but rarely love, which far more often is the shared feeling of *equals*.[9] It is tough to love the man who can order you around, grant or withhold promotions and pay raises, and is your chief critic.

As for the superior himself, he may already have climbed the Maslow ladder (see Chapter 2) beyond the love need and thus be indifferent to his deputies' attitudes toward him. Moreover, he is convinced that employees operate in a "zone of indifference,"[10] regularly complying with his orders for reasons having little to do with their love or respect for him.

Bureaucracy erodes the love relationship in other ways as well. The rules and regulations, the code book, the formulas for sick and annual leave are the portrait of a machine, not human beings loving human beings. And the person-to-person competition that sometimes prevails in an office, either in production or in battling for a promotion, is hardly the stuff that interpersonal affection is made of.

The chilliness, aloofness, officiousness, the hierarchical relationships, and

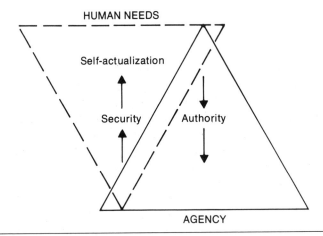

FIGURE 6.1 THE CLASH OF THE PYRAMIDS

the competitiveness that may prevail in bureaucracies all pose serious barriers to one's inevitable yearning to be loved. If deprived at the love need level, then few will make the ascent toward personal achievement (see Chapter 2).

The destructive impact of bureaucracy on *self-esteem* is equally great, and for many of the reasons just discussed. Fresh out of college, you take a job with the Bureau of Reclamation as a GS-5 in the Denver regional office. Almost immediately you get clobbered with the "totem-pole syndrome"* —

GS-15 (1)   GS-9s (20)

GS-14s (2)   GS-7s (24)

GS-13s (7)   GS-5s (32) — You!

GS-12s (10)   GS-2s, 3s, 4s (40)

GS-11s (15)

Instead of thinking, There's room at the top (and a promotion plan to get me there), you get the bureaupathic blues and wonder, Can anyone see me down here? Do I count?

The symbols of rank, while denoting that some people in government count a lot, also say loud and clear that a great many people (those in the lower wastelands of the pyramid) do not count at all. And the symbols of rank are to be seen on all sides.[11] Some agency officials rate having their names on the door; they have private secretaries and the title, grade, and pay to go along with their high status; some shoulders bear stars, eagles, oak leaves, or bars; and some public servants merit a salute. What is forgotten is the impact of all this

* The number of positions at each grade level is hypothetical.

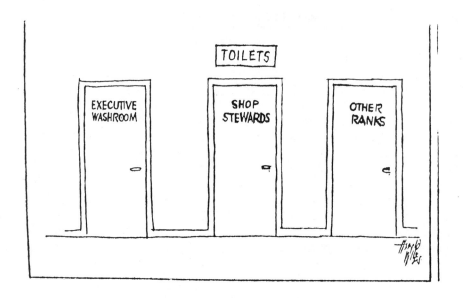

Personnel Management (February 1977) 9:44; published by permission of Mercury House Publications, Ltd., London, England.

"statusing" on the self-esteem of corporals, GS-3s, and grade 4s who enjoy none of the symbols. Reminiscent of the Jew in Shakespeare's *Merchant of Venice,* one can hear the alienated employee saying, "Am I not also a person who needs recognition and praise and some evidence that I count around here?"

Beyond the status symbols, other features of bureaucracy may undermine self-esteem. Close supervision plainly indicates a lack of a superior's confidence in her deputy's ability to function properly. And modern-day application of the Frederick Taylor prescription that management should do the thinking, workers the doing, transforms workers into robots and tools.[12]

If bureaucracy has that kind of undermining effect on the love and self-esteem needs, it pulls employees away from, rather than propelling them toward, *self-actualization.* Too often, job descriptions hem in personnel rather than lift them to creativity (see Chapter 16).[13] Unimaginative superiors who have no vision make it hard for their younger associates to dream dreams. Fearful chiefs will neither take risks nor delegate authority so that others might. Rarely will they demand the impossible of their deputies. As a result, only a small part of workers' skills are used, probably little of their rational and creative powers.[14]

The tragedy is that bureaucracy, which Max Weber saw as a finely tuned mechanism to get a job done, has many *built-in features* that hinder people from getting the job done. Clearly we need to understand some of the unintended consequences of bureaucratic organization.[15]

Bureaupathic Response

One of the central axioms of human behavior is that one way or another *people will satisfy their needs* — hopefully in a conjunctive fashion if conditions permit, disjunctively if they do not. Given the barriers in bureaucracy to human need fulfillment that we have just reviewed, administrators must anticipate some bureaupathic behavior — because the organization will actually make some workers sick.[16]

Because of the greater impediments to self-esteem and actualization among the ranks, the incidence of bureaupathology is undoubtedly greater at the lower levels than in the upper echelons.[17] As the *Civil Service Journal* once observed:

> People in high places who know they're good are motivated to everyday excellence by the recognition they have already achieved. But the vast bulk of Federal employees are not in high places, and need recognition. They do want special credit for the things they do that are above and beyond their daily job requirements.[18]

What are the signs of the bureaupathic syndrome? Among them are worker frustration, alienation (and its concomitants, noncommitment and disloyalty to the agency), boredom, poor workmanship, goofing off, absenteeism, interpersonal hostilities, high turnover, insubordination, and sabotage. These symptoms also constitute ways in which individuals can get even with the system that has ignored them. Whereas employee behavior of this sort is disjunctive from the point of view of the agency, it may be thoroughly conjunctive and integrative from the point of view of the employee.

In addition to these kinds of compensatory acts, which clearly undermine an agency, Argyris suggests that employees have at least two other courses of action available. One is "schizophy": employees separate their own and the agency's worlds, satisfy their personal needs elsewhere, and simply accept their bimonthly paychecks for their on-the-job burdens; in taking the other course, employees defend themselves and strive to change the system through unions and collective bargaining.[19]

Taking Employees' Temperature

How many administrators have almost no inkling of staff sickness within their agencies can never be known, but the number must be very high. The reason for that conclusion lies in the overconcentration of managers on the *output indicators* (costs, production, etc.) and the indifference of many to what Rensis Likert has appropriately called the *intervening variables.* Employees need to have their attitudinal temperatures taken long before falling output confirms the sickness.

Likert dramatically makes the case for a new set of measurements by pointing out that *in the short run,* authoritarian, Simon Legree leadership can achieve production spurts. Then the hotshot manager with his flashy output totals is promoted, leaving his successor with an organization whose human fabric has

Measuring ALL the Costs

The costs of the way we manage enterprises in this country

> are not fully tallied in the annual reports of our corporations and bureaucracies; they are the costs of such job-related pathologies as political alienation, violent aggression against others, alcoholism and drug abuse, mental depression, an assortment of physical illnesses, inadequate performance in schools, and a larger number of welfare families than there need be. These costs are borne by the citizen and by society; they must be included in any systematic accounting of the costs and benefits of work in America.

Health, Education and Welfare, *Work in America* (Cambridge, Mass.: MIT Press, 1973), p. 28.

been torn apart. What a tragedy that top management did not look beyond the quotas being met to see the long-run havoc the hotshot was creating.[20]

Likert's appropriate rejoinder, and seriously meant, was that the value of the functioning human group that had been destroyed should be charged off against the increasing productivity as an incurred cost.[21] So the plea is made to measure *all* of bureaucracy's costs — not just hours and wages, materials, rent, interest charges, depreciation, and the like; and not just output figures such as quotas achieved, sales, profits, or cost/benefit ratios, narrowly conceived. Beyond all these, managers must develop a new set of measuring devices to keep watch on such intervening variables as:

continuity of work in the absence of a supervisor

employee attitudes toward high producers and supervisors

turnover (the quit rate among employees)

interpersonal, intragroup, and intergroup feelings

absenteeism

quality of work performed

incidents subject to disciplinary action

feelings of unreasonable pressure

Through the use of carefully designed attitude tests and improved accounting techniques, data and trends on all these variables can be secured that will make management much better informed on what is happening to their human assets.[22]

Assuming that management cares when there is evidence that bureaupathology is seriously afflicting their staff, what options are open to them? About the same options as were open to Louis XVI and Marie Antoinette before the Bastille fell: (a) Do nothing ("Let them eat cake"); (b) tighten up for the impending agency-employee conflict; (c) relax here and there in hope of an uneasy coexistence; or (d) make some fundamental changes in both structure and management style in the direction of reciprocation between people and organization.

Organization watchers can see this kind of managerial choosing going on at regular intervals. In deciding between organizational needs and human needs, such as at budget time when push comes to shove, the mayor and city council will typically opt for (b) — grant the employees a token pay raise, not increase taxes, and then hold on while the employee unions volley and thunder.

Of the four options, numbers (a) through (c) are as imprudent and hopeless as the course Louis XVI chose; the fourth alone has promise. Psychiatrist Harry Levinson lays the groundwork: conflict between people and organization is *not* inevitable.[23] To the contrary, *they need each other,* and therein lies the basis for reciprocation between organizational and human needs. The employing agency gives a person a livelihood and a sense of involvement in a major undertaking and reinforces personal defenses (in such obvious ways as regular income, health insurance, and so on). In turn, the employees *are* the agency, bringing to it ideas and labor and carrying out its mission. This reciprocity, Levinson argues, may be totally healthy for both people and organization and for society as well. We emphatically agree.

THE SEARCH FOR THE HARMONIC MEAN BETWEEN AGENCY AND EMPLOYEES

As we begin our search for structural arrangements and management styles that will best reciprocate agency and worker needs, a caveat is in order. There is no universally applicable approach in public administration because of the wide differences in people's needs, talents, and cultural settings. As cases in point, recall that the great democrat Jean Jacques Rousseau could justify temporary *dictatorships* under certain circumstances.[24] Today, what might work with social workers might flop in a Job Corps camp; and scientists at the Johnson Space Center would require a vastly different approach than the guards in the maximum security wing at the state prison.

Among the variables that will materially affect the right managerial mix are the age and maturity of administrators and clients, available skills, complexity of work, time pressures, and resources available. Counterbalanced against those variables are the basic needs of people everywhere for physical well-being, security, love, self-esteem, and growth. They provide some uniformities around which administrative models can be constructed, always leaving room for modifications dictated by the factors noted earlier that are not constant.[25]

Given both the variables and the uniformities, can we find a managerial philosophy that has a fair chance of reducing human being-agency conflict and enhancing the self-actualization and the commitment of those who work for government?

We strongly think so, and it is a managerial philosophy that begins with people, with their human needs and aspirations, treats them with trust and openness, regularly seeks their ideas, and continually challenges the best that is in them. McGregor called it Theory Y, participative management (in Rensis Likert's phraseology, System 4).

The Theory Y Approach

Theory Y rests on a set of assumptions and values that can be clearly set forth:

1. Human needs must be met before the agency's production needs can be efficiently met over time (see Figure 2.4).

2. Psychological needs are as important to worker performance as economic needs (and contra Maslow, few of these needs ever really evaporate after being met).

3. People are gregarious, and thus group life ought to be encouraged and not bucked.

4. People are capable of great things.

5. We need to make work worthwhile.[26]

6. We need to build organizations that are full of trust, openness, and commitment.

That philosophy starts with research as old as Aristotle's (the associational needs of people); builds on the clinical and industrial psychology of Abraham Maslow and his followers; finds validation in the empirical studies of Likert, Argyris, and Herzberg; asserts some self-evident truths (that people respond better when doing meaningful things and when performing them in a work atmosphere that generates communication and confidence); and finally, asserts a pound of faith, a la George Bernard Shaw and John Gardner, that people are capable of far more than managers have traditionally assumed.

How is that philosophy translated into organizational design and management practice? The major prescriptions of Theory Y for a harmonic mean between agency and human needs go somewhat as follows:

1. *Major-purpose organization as the basic pattern throughout the agency.* So far as possible, divisions, sections, and offices (as subunits of agencies and their bureaus) should be built around end items of administration, whole units of work programs rather than badly fractionated parts. A youth bureau of a police department meets the prescription; a copy-pulling section of the Patent Office does not.

The hope is that when employees see their personal impact on end items of administration (their reason for employment), their involvement, commitment,

---

Work: More Than the Protestant Ethic?

Albert Camus:

> Without work, all life goes rotten. But when work is soulless, life stifles and dies.

---

and contribution will increase. The concept suggests at least two things that are not immediately obvious: (a) organization according to process (or technical specialty, as is described in Chapter 3) may be particularly prone to cause impaired motivation of workers; and (b) organizational design must meet something more than on-paper tests of efficiency; we need to know what their impact will be on employees.

2. *The job itself must be made meaningful.* That postulate will always stand as Frederick Herzberg's lasting contribution to management theory, although many before and after him have written important things about "job enlargement."[27]

Instead of moving in the scientific management direction of little jobs that little minds can master, Theory Y urges that jobs be designed to lift people to self-actualization. Mickey Mouse jobs, after all, tend to produce mousy people; demanding jobs force people to grow.

Job enlargement takes on a number of forms in the private and public sectors: (a) a *variety* of duties instead of unifunctional jobs (e.g., firemen with county recreation scheduling to do during slow hours at the station house); (b) *increased responsibility* (planning and controlling as well as doing; production workers responsible for inspecting and signing off on their own work); (c) *greater autonomy* (working with less supervision); and (d) *job improvement* (such as the suggestion systems at Lincoln Electric or the federally subsidized incentive awards program).

We should note that *job rotation* is different. Instead of building variety into a person's primary position, management at least attempts to take some steps toward attaining that same goal by shifting a worker among a number of posts (maybe all of them boring). In a city courts office, for example, time modules may be used so that a worker spends part of the day at the front counter, a few hours taking incoming calls, and then some time preparing criminal actions for the computer center.[28]

Herzberg makes a distinction between *horizontal* job enlargement (adding more duties, rotating assignments) and *vertical* job enrichment (more autonomy and responsibility for one's work). He questions the efficacy of the former approach as a motivator while strongly commending the latter.[29]

Some private sector experiments in job enlargement have taken these forms:

In the stock transfer department of Bankers Trust in New York City, five separate typing and review operations were combined into one. Some $300,000 in savings accrued in the first year as a result of improved worker interest and reduction of the supervisory force.[30]

At Texas Instruments, maintenance crews were completely turning over every three months, and the facilities were unkempt. Nineteen janitorial teams were formed, with the authority to plan, schedule, and carry out their own work. The turnover dropped from 100 to 9.8 percent, and the cleanliness scores rose from 65 to 85 percent of standard.[31]

At the General Foods plant at Topeka, Kansas, production teams selected new team members, chose their own foremen, rated the performance of co-workers, set production schedules, and were paid according to the number of tasks they had mastered in the plant. Absenteeism fell below 1 percent and productivity was about 25 percent higher than at a more traditionally organized sister plant in Illinois.[32]

And at Travelers Insurance Company in Hartford, Connecticut, the keypunch operation was altered to enable the operators to see a whole job through to completion and to work regularly for the same clients. In the first year productivity rose 26 percent and absenteeism declined 24 percent.[33]

One of our favorite examples of job enlargement is the experiment in *planned understaffing* at a branch bank described by Chris Argyris. Tellers were not increased as volume increased, and the branch manager authorized and encouraged tellers to help wherever they were needed. In consequence, employees who had previously seen themselves as pigeons in narrow pigeon-holes marked "Bonds and Collections," "Savings Accounts," "Checking Accounts," and the like now found they could operate across all the customer windows. They bailed each other out as work ebbed and flowed. They discovered a new sense of interdependence, helpfulness, and rewarding interaction. The results in terms of productivity and the intervening variables (morale, commitment, and so on) were remarkable.[34]

The job enlargement movement has had equally important applications in the public sector as well:

The Ohio department of highways conducted an experiment in crew determination of work schedules, which clearly revealed improvements in morale as employee participation increased.[35]

The city manager of Scottsdale, Arizona, introduced self-evaluation into his city's performance-rating system, set up linking-pin committees for the analysis of municipal problems, initiated job rotation, and opened the municipal intern program to any city employee with a college degree.[36]

A personnel clerk making entries on leave records is made responsible for reviewing the accuracy of the work.

Drafters of letters now sign off for their chief in their own name.

The researcher in the Congressional Research Service of the Library of Congress is encouraged to visit a senator's office for direct talks on a major project the senator has asked the CRS to prepare.

The city auditor's staff moves from bookkeeping to program evaluation.

If job enlargement is to be accomplished successfully and provide a meaningful step toward self-actualization, some other things must be at work in the agency. Top management needs to believe in it; employees and their unions need to understand and want it; a climate of openness for bold ideas on job redesign must exist; education and training must be available; job descriptions must themselves invite growth; and job enrichment, as Harold L. Sheppard and N. Q. Herrick have said, "must be a way of life" in the agency.[37] (Reservations about job enlargement will be analyzed below.)

3. *Broadened spans of control.* Management should move increasingly to more generous delegations of authority and looser supervision.

The intended consequences include reducing those costs that are associated with extra executive levels (when spans of control are narrow), freeing up agency communications by eliminating some executive levels, greatly enhancing the self-esteem of workers who are complimented by the greater trust being shown in them, and building self-actualization by giving employees increased freedom to innovate.

Broader spans of control are not synonymous with laissez-faire leadership (see Chapter 7). They do not suggest that administrators wash their hands of their deputies' work. What the proposal does call for is more concentration on results and less dictation of means, by weekly review rather than daily oversight, for example. If some take advantage of the looser supervision, they must be dealt with — by challenge, training, and/or discipline to get them going, growing, or departing.

4. *Encouragement of natural work groups and associated employee organizations and winning their loyalty to agency goals.* Likert states the issue clearly:

> Management will make full use of the potential capacities of its human resources only when each person in an organization is a member of one or more effectively functioning work groups that have a high degree of group loyalty, effective skills of interaction, and high performance goals.[38]

People need to belong, they need the security and affection of others, and they need to avoid the anonymity that too often prevails in impersonal bureaucracies — all of which means they need a place in a harmonious work group on the job.

Instead of panicking at the first evidence that cliques are appearing among their workers, managers should maintain an agency atmosphere hospitable to the formation of such groups. Within reason, providing agency time and facilities for activities both of dynamic work groups and for associated organizations such as an agency bowling league is one concrete way of building that kind of atmosphere.

Beyond the generation of a healthy group structure, managers must also concern themselves with the closely related matter of *group loyalty to the agency*. Groups, from the agency's point of view, may be either conjunctive or disjunctive; it is up to the manager to get more of the "con" and less of the "dis."

Three of the best routes open to a manager in influencing group loyalties are the atmosphere she generates about group existence to begin with; her willingness to deal with employees in groups rather than exclusively on an individual basis; and, highly important, her skill in identifying and wooing the significant others in each group. These front-line leaders become critical linking pins through which the administrator ties groups and the formal organization together.[39] For these kingpin linking pins, she maintains an open-door policy, seeks them out, asks advice, shares confidences, and rewards appropriately. When the administrator has these informal leaders on her side, she is essentially assured of also having their followers with her.

5. *A significant employee voice in agency affairs.*[40] One of the most hopeful concepts for enhancing both self-actualization and loyalty is the principle that *involvement leads to commitment*. The concept underlies the whole genius of democracy — the willingness of people to go along with a majority even when they themselves are on the losing side, so long as they have an equal chance to be involved in the electoral process.

So it is in administration. When employees are meaningfully involved in matters affecting them and also have the right to contribute ideas on broader agency matters, a degree of commitment builds up even though employee views on a given question might not prevail.

The urgent cry for black power that emerged during the 1950s and 1960s was rooted in a sound principle: people must have a voice in the conditions affecting them. That applies to civil servants as well as to WASPs, blacks, schoolteachers, or the Longshoremen's and Warehousemen's Union.

The contribution employee involvement in decision making makes to self-actualization is as fundamental as it is obvious: "They think I've got enough brains to help organize the work in our shop." Thus involved, a worker is elevated from the slot that confines him to the calculator, the typewriter, statistical tables, or lab reports to the status of creative person; this is the point where employee and agency begin to come alive.

Consider the consequences of one experiment at the Weston Manufacturing Company, a Pennsylvania clothing firm. Before reorganization, design people (in a staff role) laid out the patterns, and seamstresses and other production workers turned out the pajamas. With the acquisition of Weston by Harwood Manufacturing, the new managers began to involve the production workers in designing the garments they were to make, keeping the specialists on tap for consultation only. It was a mind-blowing experience for fabric cutters and sewing machine operators, and the intervening variables recorded the change. Absenteeism fell from 17 to 4 percent, and employee turnover dropped from 18 to 6 percent. The output variables responded in kind, with improvements in both quality and quantity.[41]

Turning to employees for their suggestions and criticisms also builds self-actualization by helping to fulfill two other levels of need, love and self-esteem. "They cared enough to ask me." "I think they're going to adopt my suggestion about giving poor kids a head start on their education through summer kindergartens." We may not all be upward mobiles, but being king for a day is an exhilarating brush with royalty for anyone.

There is, of course, another payoff for the agency that opens up communication channels to its employees: the increased flow of useful ideas. One hires specialists for the expert ideas they can generate; but why assume a monopoly of brains on their part? As the Harwood Company discovered, there are brains in the ranks as well — a great reservoir that management is foolish not to tap. When you employ a person, do you hire hands only, or mind as well? Then use the *whole person.*

Once committed to such a philosophy, how can an agency actually achieve the employee participation we are talking about? The old stereotyped suggestion box does not even begin to provide an answer.

An important beginning is found in the organizational and work flow designs themselves. A pure separation of line and staff implies that the brains are with the staff specialists; that arrangement institutionally squelches creativity in the line. The Harwood reorganization, as we have noted, suggests another approach, which invites production workers to be imaginative.

Next is the frequent use of employee discussion groups *on agency time* to review operations, to brainstorm, and to make new plans. However, some caveats are in order. First, someone in management must be listening to the suggestions coming from those work groups, for the day has long since passed when getting the staff together as an idle ritual will win any adherents for very long.

Second, and closely related, Theory Y demands that *meaningful* decisions about group life must be delegated if any real benefit is to accrue to both employees and their agencies. Some years ago, Maxine Bucklow undertook a comprehensive review of attempts around the world to involve workers in decision making. What counted in the successful experiments was the delegation to the workers of *important matters* about the work and mission of their group, enough to generate the feeling of responsible autonomy.[42] (We ought to recall from Chapter 2 how critically important that feeling of autonomy is in the lives of creative productive people.)

A third method for assuring employee involvement is the widespread use of

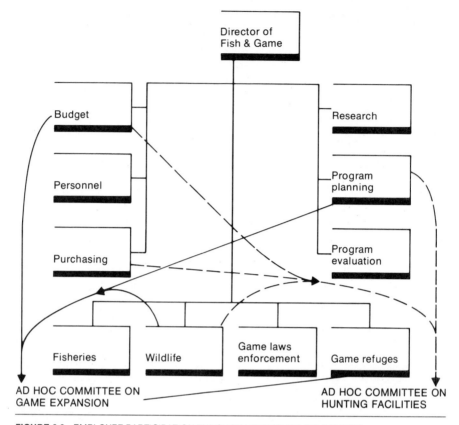

FIGURE 6.2 EMPLOYEE PARTICIPATION THROUGH LINKING-PIN COMMITTEES

·From Rensis Likert, *New Patterns of Management*, pp. 105–106. Copyright © 1961 by McGraw-Hill Book Company, Inc. Reprinted by permission of McGraw-Hill Book Company.

interdepartmental and interlevel committees for problem solving.[43] Part of the value of such committees lies in bridging hierarchical levels. so that GS-7s may exchange ideas with GS-14s in committee sessions where they both sit (with self-esteem payoffs for the GS-7s). In addition. these ad hoc committees may bring together line. staff. and auxiliary people where the chances for broadening viewpoints are great and the chances for remaining provincial are very few (see Figure 6.2).

Likert's linking-pin committees are clearly seen in this fish and game department. where the ad hoc committee on game expansion draws a diversified group together with overlapping expertise and the sister committee to improve hunting facilities proceeds in a similar fashion.

A fourth approach to participative management has been the appointment of employee representatives to managerial policy boards (e.g.. the occasional appointment of a faculty member or student body president to a university's board of regents). But the risk of institutional tokenism is very great in this arrangement. as cartoonist Ned Riddle has pointed out. Manipulative behavior in these appointments will no longer wash. Employees should go on policy boards only when managers are convinced that they have something to offer and are willing to open executive ears to hear them.

Some have turned to union representation as a possible way to draw employees more meaningfully into agency decision making. But the Tennessee Valley Authority experience with that arrangement was revealing. Rank-and-file workers still did not feel any real sense of involvement. Arthur Thompson reported that:

> TVA's policy of indirect participation through unions fails to allow substantial numbers of employees sufficient opportunity to express their ideas or use their own initiative, creativity, and judgment in performing their jobs.[44]

MR. TWEEDY   By Ned Riddle

"We need a new perspective, gentlemen, so I've invited to our meeting an employee who doesn't have, nor will ever have, a piece of the action."

Whatever techniques are used, Theory Y calls for the discovery of significant and fruitful ways to involve employees in decision making about their jobs.

6. *A democratic leadership style.* The posture administrators strike vis-à-vis their employees is probably the major determinant of whether employees are going to be robots or contributors. What we shall see more fully in Chapter 7 is a case for leaders in the government hierarchy who (a) share decision making with employees because these leaders earnestly believe they can tap better ideas that way, and also earnestly believe that involvement leads to commitment; (b) place greater emphasis on their workers than on output, perhaps intuitively understanding that self-actualizers are made, not born; and (c) still demonstrate that they are not patsies, that they have standards of excellence to which they intend to hold their organizations.

In three brief words, the democratic leader *listens builds* and *challenges.* In three equally brief words, the democratic leader does not *dictate, placate,* or *abdicate.* Rensis Likert has put the contrast into sharp focus:

> It is essential that the group method of decision making and supervision not be confused with committees which never reach decisions or with the "wishy-washy," "common denominator" of committees about which the supervisor can say, "Well, the group made this decision, and I couldn't do anything about it."
>
> Quite the contrary! The group method of supervision holds the superior fully responsible for the quality of all decisions and for their implementation. He is responsible for building his subordinates into a group which makes the best decisions and carries them out well. The superior is accountable for all decisions, for their execution, and for the results.[45]

An old State Department yarn provides a case in point. On his first day as secretary of state (in the 1945 era), Edward Stettinius, Jr. polled a policy conference and said, "The consensus here seems to favor such-and-such a policy, and that will be my decision." As they left the room, Undersecretary Dean Acheson commented to his new chief, "I know you were striving for a favorable first impression here today, Mr. Secretary, but in the State Department, we *weigh* heads, we don't *count* them."

Democratic leadership is not plebiscitary leadership, but it is consulting, draw-them-out, weighing leadership. With the right employees and technology, that can make a lot of difference in bridging the gap between agency and human needs.

7. *Generating a sense of "mission impossible" throughout the ranks.* Self-actualization, it will be recalled, depends not only on other needs being regularly met but also on the constant invitation one feels on the job to solve, innovate, and excel. Autonomous workers will get the needed pressure from the work itself (e.g., at the Jet Propulsion Laboratory in California in designing an automated chemistry lab for the Mars lander to detect life on that planet).

Workers who have less glamorous assignments are likely to get their sense of challenge primarily from their chiefs, who demand that you do the impossible and give you the confidence that you can.

The empirical evidence for that belief has been provided in the continuing studies of the Survey Research Center at Michigan, which show that employees with high production goals are usually associated with superiors who have and transmit those same kinds of goals.[46]

8. *Utilize a range of payoffs to satisfy the basic needs of workers.* The argument of Chapter 2 is that self-actualization begins to take hold when the basic needs of people have been met (a decent rate of pay, to name a fundamental one), when the social needs of love and belonging are being constructively met, when the job itself is challenging, and when the worker enjoys the autonomy to begin acting creatively in meeting the challenge.

That analysis begins to suggest that a whole range of payoffs is available to supervisors: incentive pay for work beyond the call of duty, a variety of signals a supervisor employs to tell her staff how much she cares, the communications that develop self-esteem, and revised job descriptions that transform drones into responsible and creative human beings operating at their highest potential.

Argyris offers a telling example of how a training effort markedly enhanced worker self-esteem.[47] In searching for engineers, the Polaroid Corporation decided to look inward instead of going outside to the high-priced job market. They proceeded to give their workers with less than a high school education the equivalent of college engineering training. What counted was the clear evidence to the workers that the company saw their inherent worth and then brought it forth.

9. *Create a reasonable hope for advancement.* Robert Presthus has suggested that we are not all upward mobiles; but we surmise that given a meaningful choice more workers than not would opt for getting out of ruts for some more money and responsibility.[48] Support for that belief emerges particularly in Frederick Herzberg's search for motivators. Advancement, he found, is one of the most potent motivators of them all.

Herzberg's findings clearly suggest that one of the most meaningful things an agency can do to promote a harmonic mean with its staff is to lay out career ladders and promotion plans and then *live by them.* The best encouragement to self-actualizers lies in that kind of assurance, that there is room for them upstairs.

Taken together, these nine foregoing recommendations constitute much of Theory Y's response to the clash between agency and human needs. It builds on Harry Levinson's belief mentioned earlier in the chapter, in reciprocation between the two needs. It asserts that agencies greatly increase their chances for success as they design challenging jobs, grant workers increased autonomy and responsibility, generate group work, involve employees in decision making, meet employee needs, and provide opportunity for growth.

Ask yourself: Would an agency that came close to doing those things be worth working for or not?

A CRITICAL VIEW OF THEORY Y

There are scholars and managers aplenty who say that the Theory Y approach is all dreamsville — and more.

Hear Herbert Wilcox: "Embracing the participative belief as an ideology requires an act of faith. . . . An organization based on . . . trust, openness and valid communication is yet to be seen."[49] The statement is an exaggeration, of course (given the successes of the city manager in Scottsdale, Arizona; Disney Productions; Harwood Manufacturing; and many others), but it expresses the large doubts many hold concerning Theory Y.

Here are some of the most telling arguments against this theory:[50]

1. Managers who may have worked hard and stood in line for years to attain power aren't about to share decision making with their employees.

2. If they did, their superiors would want to know right now if they've gone soft — "Not capable of making your own decisions, eh?"

3. There is a notorious scatter of power in government (budget controls this, personnel that, the GAO this, and the attorney general that). With so many vetoes floating around, employee decision making doesn't have a chance.

4. Contra Maslow and Herzberg, not all employees are looking for self-actualization and more responsibility. Many workers just want to do their own job and leave the driving to the administrator.[51]

5. Theory Y errs in downplaying the enormous importance of economic rewards to most workers.[52]

6. Involving employees in decision making is an invitation to opposition and contention in the ranks.

7. There isn't time to have employees sit around in staff meetings wrestling with policy when the clientele are begging to be served.

8. Using employee representatives on management councils won't do; they are co-opted too easily.

9. Further, participative management is basically manipulative — using consensus-building techniques to win employee support for the course management has already decided on.

10. There may be reason to question whether or not participation in decision making really leads to extra effort in carrying out the decisions.

11. Hierarchy is not the great evil Theory Y suggests. It provides an orderly ladder for the upward mobiles to climb toward increasing responsibility and authority.

12. The quality of group decisions may be considerably below that of decisions suggested by gifted staff people and bright people in the chain of command.

13. The case for agency democracy defeats democracy in the political system at large, for if the employees are calling the shots within agencies, then members of Congress and the president are not.

14. Theory Y is blatantly utopian and attempts to fly in all kinds of weather, regardless of worker skills and personality, the job to be done, and the technology employed.

H. R. Kaplan and Curt Tausky summarize the indictment of Theory Y in this way:

> There is an unmistakable ideological air about [it] . . . which we believe has led to a distorted conception of employees' motivation and desire for control in organizations. Filled with exuberance to usher in a new society founded upon challenging work and participatory democracy, they consider the hierarchical structure of organizations repugnant. Clinging to a belief in the desire for men to be creative and autonomous, they label pathological the preoccupation of large segments of the contemporary labor force with material rewards. Yet, the variability and choice they claim to be basic in man and essential ingredients of a "better" society are somehow ignored in their attempts to encapsulate all workers under a single motivational scheme based upon an ideologically-laden conception of man's personality.[53]

What kinds of evidence do the critics of Theory Y point to?[54] For one, they note the collapse of one of the best-known Theory Y experiments during the 1960s at a California electronics firm, Nonlinear Systems.[55] Second, there are some signs of entropy in the General Foods' application at Topeka, Kansas, a model effort of the 1970s.[56]

In terms of public sector evidence, there are the doubts raised by Frederick Mosher's review of twelve governmental reorganization case studies.[57] His specific purpose was to test the "participation hypothesis" that administrative change could be brought off more successfully if the employees to be affected had some voice in the reorganizations.

At one point in his review chapter, Mosher pointedly says that "The cases in this volume do not support the participation hypothesis."[58] But a closer reading finds some interesting admissions. Some of the reorganizations involving employee input were successful (as were some of those with little or no involvement). But it is of further interest that *none* of the reorganizations with employee participation were failures; two that did not involve employees were. Mosher then concedes this:

> It appears that there is some support for a more limited statement of the general [participation] hypothesis. Where there was substantial employee participation in

implementation, there was less employee resistance. And the greatest resistance occurred in those cases in which there was no employee participation at all.[59]

Mosher's reservations may well be compared with Floyd Mann's analysis of a company that contracted with Michigan's Survey Research Center in undertaking a program of planned change involving extensive employee input and feedback. Looking back, Mann reported:

> In general, the greatest change occurred where the survey results were discussed in both the departmental organizational units *and* the first-line organizational units. The greater the involvement of all members of the organization through their organizational families — the department heads, the first-line supervisors, *and* the employees — the greater the change [emphasis in original].[60]

Troubles with Job Enlargement

Making work more meaningful has been a phase of Theory Y with many pitfalls and a bevy of opponents.

Consider, for example, the IRS experiment at its data center in Detroit in the late 1960s.[61] With experimental and control groups and before-and-after measurements all provided for, the study focused on GS-4 and GS-5 clerks engaged in examining and verifying corporate tax returns, plus the more experienced GS-6s. The experiment ran for six months.

The job enlargement techniques included the following:

self-review of work

direct feedback from verifiers to clerks who had goofed (eliminating two supervisory levels)

rotation of clerks between examining and verifying

appointment of some of the sharper clerks as industry specialists

holding of weekly problem-solving sessions during the experiment

The overall results were mixed. Among the lower-level employees, production did rise and errors dropped (vis-à-vis the control group), but there was no improvement in worker attitudes (as measured by questionnaire). Among the GS-6s, the production rate among the job-enlarged was poorer than that of the control group; error rates and attitudes were unchanged.

Interpreters of these mixed results have suggested what may have gone wrong. First, some lower-level needs (Herzberg's hygiene needs) had not been provided for prior to job enlargement, so that the experiment may have run aground on a coral reef of existing gripes; second, the women in these low-level grades had little job commitment to this tedious review of corporate tax returns; third, jobs were not enlarged significantly enough to matter.

Job enlargement advocates would not accept the validity of the first two explanations. The whole thrust of Herzberg's motivation theory is to change people's job attitudes and behavior by addressing head-on the absence of *motivators* (the job itself, the chance to achieve and be recognized, etc.). The third explanation for the lack of success seems more important: job enlargement that doesn't enlarge neither enlarges nor motivates.

What seems equally important in the modest results were two critical factors not touched upon by the analysts of the data: (a) reminiscent of the failures of the imposed Patent Office reorganization in 1946, this IRS experiment was apparently not undertaken with any meaningful employee consultation or concurrence; (b) analysts should remember that experiments of this sort usually experience the "Likert lag" — a delay of perhaps a year before the changes fully take hold and alter people's behavior and feelings.

Rather than being the panacea that all workers rush to, job enlargement generates a lot of resistance. Workers often prefer staying in ruts to getting out of them; union officials may balk, contending that job enlargement means more work for the same pay; and supervisors may feel threatened as they watch subordinates' duties grow, getting ready to absorb the supervisors' own empires like some kind of expanding amoebas in a science fiction movie.[62]

Labor's Questions About Theory Y

It is clear that participative schemes will not be welcomed by all segments of the labor movement.

The left wing of that movement regards Theory Y as tokenism of the worst sort, that it amounts to management's going through the motions of consulting the workers while retaining all the decision-making authority. As British union leader Ernie Roberts says:

> Copartnership schemes offer an illusory sense of security and involvement to workers; they are an attempt on the part of the employer to show that the lions are prepared to lie down with the trade-union lamb — providing the lamb gives an understanding not to eat the lion.[63]

The worry is expressed that unions are intended victims when management begins to involve workers, sans union leaders, in discussions about working conditions. Participative management is no substitute, Roberts contends, for union-conducted collective bargaining. For him, the only thing worth having is *worker control* of enterprise within a socialist economy.

But under socialism there is also evidence of workers feeling left out. In 1950 Yugoslavia began to decentralize its socialist system in the direction of syndicalism; that is, worker control of individual enterprises. The typical pattern was a workers' council in each enterprise (elected by the workers) and an executive committee of the council called the management board, consisting of the top managers appointed by the workers' councils.

Here, then, on paper, was the ultimate in participation: workers' representatives hiring the managers. In the late 1960s, studies were undertaken to determine the perceived influence of the various power wielders in Yugoslav enterprises.[64] Following George Orwell's *Animal Farm* right down to a pig's eye, the studies found that top management possessed the dominant influence, and the workers' council came second. All the power centers in efficient companies showed higher perceived influence than those in less efficient companies.

In addition, there was a substantial gap in the influence workers felt they had and what they wished to exercise (desire greatly exceeding possession). Author Veljko Rus concludes:

> From the point of view of the worker, we must remember that the early days of self-management gave him the dream that influence would be equalized. Workers are more realistic today. But it is still not clear whether the loss of this dream has been healthy or has resulted in greater frustration. . . .

> Although self-government may have changed the pattern of influence exerted, the distribution of influence received remains unchanged. Thus top management remains the dominant group; it exerts influence without being subject to satisfactory control.[65]

To which George Orwell would probably reply: "Whichever pigs occupy the executive suite, that's where the power lies."[66]

In February 1970, the journal *Industrial Relations* published a thoughtful cross-cultural symposium on participative management. Much of the evidence was discouraging to the devotees of Theory Y. For example, as we noted earlier, many participation schemes in other countries simply resulted in co-optation of the workers' representatives who sit with management. Milton Derber painted the large picture as follows:

> At the level of practice, the dominant note once again is uncertainty rather than a clear progression toward either success or failure. Neither the Scanlon Plan in the U.S. nor the Glacier Metals experiment in England has generated many followers. Joint consultation schemes appear generally to have declined in number. In Israel Koor experiments in joint management at the plant level have frittered away. Participation has not even been seriously tried in Australia. Reports from Yugoslavia and Germany, where participation programs have been most fully developed, raise questions about the impact of participation on the productivity and efficiency of the enterprises involved, as well as the degree of involvement of workers.

> On the other hand, there are some positive currents. The spread of collective bargaining to the local level in England and other European countries, the rising interest in productivity bargaining, the absorption of joint consultation committees by unions — all point in the direction of *more* worker participation in management, although the model may be one of bargaining rather than integration.[67]

CONTINGENCY THEORY: THEORY Y IS NOT FOR EVERYONE

Researchers John Morse and Jay Lorsch have published field research that suggests that we'd better pay attention to the nature of the work to be performed and the staff characteristics at an installation before choosing a management style, X or Y, a priori.[68]

They contrasted the results of rival management styles in two research laboratories (one under Theory X, one under Theory Y) and in two manufacturing plants (again, one X and the other Y). Summarizing briefly, Morse and Lorsch found that the Theory X manufacturing plant outproduced the Theory Y plant, whereas the Theory Y research lab outproduced the Theory X lab.

Those results then led the team to formulate their *contingency theory:* (a) there is no universally preferred management style; and (b) management style should fit the tasks to be done and the characteristics of the workers.

In some instances, those considerations would clearly call for a more controlled and formalized organization than Theory Y would ever endorse. Where the work is open-ended problem solving and the staff is composed of intellectuals, Theory Y makes better sense as a means of liberating self-motivated people to do their jobs. But manufacturing operations are better handled, the authors contend, under more authoritarian conditions where procedures are laid out and workers are closely supervised.

There is no quarrel with their point about Theory Y in research labs. But in apposition to their acceptance of Theory X in manufacturing, we must resurrect what was said earlier in this chapter about the Theory Y experiments in such manufacturing companies as General Foods, Polaroid, and Harwood. Contra Morse and Lorsch, those experiments testified loud and clear as to the production and morale benefits of job enlargement, work group autonomy, and employee involvement in decision making.

Just to single out the results at the pajama firm of Harwood (with a technology somewhat similar to Morse and Lorsch's container plants, i.e., assembly line), we should recall that within about a year of the transition from Theory X management to Theory Y, the following occurred at Harwood:

A 17 percent profit replaced the 15 percent loss of the year before.

A production rate of 11 percent below standard rose to 14 percent above.

The turnover rate of production workers fell in two years from 18 to 6 percent.

The absenteeism rate was cut by two thirds.

The defect rate fell 39 percent.[69]

Rebuttals aside, we have to acknowledge the value of the contingency theory's main point: No one management style will fit every contingency. There are no managerial panaceas.

But in searching for a management style that has the greatest chance of generating a harmonic mean between an agency and its people, I lean toward a managerial posture that attempts to accomplish the following:

employ (and use) the *whole* person we have hired

challenge the best that is in the employees

get their ideas and feelings about our joint enterprise

indicate in concrete ways that we care about them as fellow human beings

In that philosophy lies the best hope. I am convinced, of curing bureaupathology, of bridging the gap between the agency and its workers, and of tapping not only the talent but the spirit of all who work for it.

SUMMARY

Our concern in this chapter has been dual. Is there an inevitable clash between bureaucracy and employees? Or, to the contrary, is there any hope for a harmonic mean?

Government agencies have needs to fulfill; so do their employees. Out of conflicting ways of meeting those needs have come undermined agencies and bureaupathic people. But clash is not inevitable; there is also ground for believing that reciprocation is possible where agency and staff can benefit each other. The beginning point is careful measurement of the intervening variables to determine what is happening to the human beings on whom the agency so heavily depends for its success.

Having looked in Chapter 2 and also here at the roots of bureaupathology, we have attempted to lay out the philosophy and principal features of Theory Y, or participative management, as a promising answer to the people versus agency conflict. Among others, these nine postulates suggest the approach:

1.   major-purpose organization at all levels
2.   meaningful job assignments
3.   broadened spans of control
4.   encouragement of natural work groups and winning their loyalty to agency goals
5.   significant employee voice in agency affairs
6.   a democratic leadership style
7.   demanding the impossible of everyone in the agency
8.   satisfying a whole range of employee needs
9.   providing the hope of advancement

The objections to Theory Y have also been reviewed: supervisors who won't delegate, employees who won't grow, the scatter of power, the lack of time for employee decision making, the abdication of responsibility, and the recognition of the need to fit the managerial style to the contingencies of technology and characteristics of the work force, among other objections.

There is no universally applicable managerial style. But we all tilt a bit in life, and this author believes in reducing agency-people conflict by drawing a circle to bring them in, rather than shutting them out, and by making work worthwhile. As Abraham Maslow so tellingly stated, "The proper management of the work lives of human beings, of the way they earn their living, can improve them and improve the world, and in this sense be a utopian or revolutionary technique."[70]

KEY CONCEPTS

clash of the pyramids
bureaupathic syndrome
intervening variables
Theory Y
job enlargement
job rotation
planned understaffing

linking-pin committees
"Likert lag"
worker control
contingency theory
totem pole syndrome
participative management

DISCUSSION QUESTIONS

1. Bureaucracy seems to have a tendency to undermine human needs. Identify some of the ways in which this tendency can be observed.

2. In searching for the harmonic mean, what are some of the variables that must be examined?

3. Discuss the major prescriptions of Theory Y that contribute to the harmonic mean. Which is the most significant?

4. Compare the arguments that support job enlargement with those that point to its unworkability. Which set of arguments do you think carries more weight?

5. For what reasons might a participative management program fail?

PROJECT

Choose an organization that has a job enlargement or a participative management program. Interview at least three members: a manager, a union officer (if there is a union), and a lower level employee. Attempt to unearth difficulties with the program. Be attentive to different points of view among the members interviewed. Your report should analyze the program examined.

Notes

1. "Bureaupath" is Victor Thompson's apt phrase for the employee who is suffering "organization sickness." See *Modern Organization* (New York: Knopf, 1961), pp. 23–24 and chap. 8.

2. The terms, respectively, are from David Riesman, *The Lonely Crowd* (New Haven, Conn.: Yale University Press, 1950) and Louis Brandeis, *The Curse of Bigness* (New York: Viking, 1934).

3. Thompson, *Modern Organization*. pp. 81, 92–100 and chap. 8.

4. As case in point, see Ray Marshall and Arvil Van Adams, "The Garbagemen's Strike that Led to Dr. Martin Luther King's Assassination," in Richard J. Stillman, *Public Administration: Concepts and Cases* (Boston: Houghton Mifflin, 1976), pp. 86–100.

5. See Chris Argyris, *Integrating the Individual and the Organization* (New York: Wiley, 1964), p. 123.

6. Thompson, *Modern Organization*. p. 64. The built-in authoritarian nature of old-style administration received frank recognition in a U.S. Civil Service Commission pamphlet, *Leadership and Supervision*. some years ago: "It is doubtful that formal work organizations can be anything but authoritarian, in that goals are set by management and a hierarchy exists through which decisions and orders from the top are transmitted downward. Organizations are authoritarian by structure and need. . . ." (Personnel Management Series No. 9, Washington, D.C.: Government Printing Office, 1955), p. 18.

7. Thompson, *Modern Organization*. pp. 14–20 and 25–27.

8. Chris Argyris, *Personality and Organization* (New York: Harper & Row, 1957), p. 66.

9. There are, of course, major exceptions to the generalization. Love between parents and child is one. For another, there certainly are administrators with deep compassion and love for their staffs. The author himself was one of the beneficiaries years ago of such an administrator in Dr. Ernest S. Griffith, director of the Legislative Reference Service, Library of Congress.

10. The phrase is Chester Barnard's, from *Functions of the Executive* (Cambridge, Mass.: Harvard University Press, 1938), p. 167.

11. See Thompson's perceptive treatment of "dramaturgy" in *Modern Organization*. chap. 7.

12. Out of a dim past still echo the words of Immanuel Kant, "Treat every man as an end, and no man simply as a means." *Fundamental Principles of the Metaphysics of Morals* (Indianapolis: Bobbs-Merrill, 1949), p. 46.

13. As Thompson says, "The microdivision of work, by making the goal of activity invisible, deprived work of any meaning for the individual. He was no longer engaged in a "worthwhile" task. He became alienated from his work, and at the same time this work lost its social identity." *Modern Organization*. p. 53.

14. See Argyris, *Integrating the Individual and the Organization*. chap. 3.

15. See Chris Argyris, *Understanding Organizational Behavior* (Homewood, Ill.: Dorsey, 1960), pp. 13–18.

16. Thompson denotes a number of causes of bureaupathology: the hiatus between specialists and the chain-of-command generalists, insecurities at many levels in an organization which generate "bureaupaths," and the immaturity of clients which turn them into "bureautics"; see *Modern Organization*. p. 177. Thompson errs in his attribution of the bureaupathology of employees to the single factor of insecurity; the Maslow thesis of general need deprivation seems far more encompassing and sound.

17. Argyris, *Integrating the Individual and the Organization*. pp. 37–42. See also Porter and Lawler, "Properties of Organization Structure in Relation to Job Attitudes and Job Behavior," reprinted in L. L. Cumings and W. E. Scott, *Readings in Organizational Behavior and Human Performance* (Homewood, Ill.: Irwin, 1969) pp. 406–407.

18. Philip Sanders, "The Awards Story," *Civil Service Journal* (April-June 1967), 7:26. The article goes on to relate the Federal Incentive Awards program to the need of lower-rung employees for recognition.

19. Argyris, *Integrating the Individual and the Organization*. p. 93.

20. Rensis Likert, *The Human Organization* (New York: McGraw-Hill, 1967), pp. 81–91, 114. Likert indicates that at the end of the experiment the organization was in a state of unstable equilibrium. Increasing turnover of personnel, developing "hostility toward high producers and toward supervision, decreased confidence and trust in management" — all clearly pointed to a group of human beings coming unglued. Over the long pull, they would bring production down.

21. Likert, *The Human Organization*, chap. 6. Even more biting was Maslow's recommendation to find a way to tax organizations which make their employees more paranoid and less capable of living in a democratic society. *Eupsychian Management* (Homewood, Ill.: Irwin, 1965), p. 59.

22. Likert correctly warns: "The measurement of these variables is a complex process and requires a high level of scientific competence. It cannot be done by an untrained person." *New Patterns of Management* (New York: Macmillan, 1961), p. 196. According to a 1977 survey, Rensis Likert's plea for rigorous human asset accounting had not significantly dented corporate record keeping or the accounting profession. The "indigestible lump" for accountants has been putting a current monetary value on intangible assets — the human beings of an enterprise. See J. B. Paperman and D. D. Martin, "Human Resource Accounting: A Managerial Tool?" *Personnel* (Mar.–Apr. 1977) 54:41–50. Nevertheless, there are some payoffs in store for those who are willing to undertake the Likert measurements. See P. H. Mirvis and E. E. Lawler, "Measuring the Financial Impact of Employee Attitudes," *Journal of Applied Psychology* (Feb. 1977), 62:1–8.

23. Harry Levinson, "Reciprocation: The Relationship between Man and Organization," *Administrative Science Quarterly* (March, 1965), 9:370–90.

24. Jean Jacques Rousseau, *Social Contract* (Baltimore, Md.: Penguin Books, 1975), Book IV, chap. 6.

25. Theory Y's assumption of uniform needs is disputed by many critics. See H. R. Kaplan and Curt Tausky, "Humanism in Organizations: A Critical Appraisal," *Public Administration Review* (Mar.–Apr. 1977), 37:176–177, and the research cited by these authors.

26. See "The Job Blahs: Who Wants to Work?" *Newsweek* March 26, 1973, pp. 79–89; and Chris Argyris, "We Must Make Work Worthwhile," *Life* May 5, 1967, pp. 56–68.

27. See, for example, Robert N. Ford, *Motivation through the Work Itself* (New York: American Management Association, 1969); Fred Foulkes, *Creating More Meaningful Work* (New York: American Management Association, 1969); and Peter Schoderbeck and W. E. Reif, *Job Enlargement* (Ann Arbor, Mich.: University of Michigan Press, 1969); and Department of Health, Education and Welfare, *Work in America* (Cambridge, Mass.: M.I.T. Press, 1973).

28. For a description of Polaroid Corporation's "Pathfinder" program of job rotation, see Harold L. Sheppard and N. Q. Herrick, *Where Have All the Robots Gone* (New York: Free Press, 1972), p. 172.

29. See Frederick Herzberg, "One More Time: How Do You Motivate Employees?" *Harvard Business Review* (Jan.–Feb. 1968) 46:58–62.

30. W. W. Detteback and Philip Kraft, "Organization Change through Job Enrichment," *Training and Development Journal* (Aug. 1971) 25:2–6.

31. Harold Rush, *Job Design for Motivation* (New York: Conference Board, 1971), pp. 39–49.

32. "The Job Blahs," *Newsweek*, p. 84. Reaffirmation for Harry Levinson's reciprocity came from the Topeka manager, Ed Dilworth: ". . . work can be organized for both business needs and people needs, and it pays off both ways."

33. "The Job Blahs," *Newsweek*, pp. 88–89.

34. Argyris, "Make Work Worthwhile," p. 63.

35. Reed M. Powell and John L. Schlachter, "Participative Management: A Panacea?" *Academy of Management Journal* (June 1971) 14:165–173.

36. William Donaldson, "Tapping Municipal Employees' Creative Talents," *Civil Service Journal* (Jan.–March 1971), pp. 16–17.

37. Harold L. Sheppard and N. Q. Herrick, *Where Have All the Robots Gone,* p. 176.

38. Likert, *New Patterns of Management,* p. 104.

39. Likert, *The Human Organization,* pp. 160–162. See also Chapter 5, page 98, in this work.

40. See the special symposium "Collaboration in Work Settings," in the *Journal of Applied Behavioral Science* (July–Sept. 1977) 13, no. 3.

41. See Alfred J. Marrow et al., *Management by Participation* (New York: Harper and Row, 1967) for the case history of the Harwood experiment.

42. Maxine Bucklow, "A New Role for the Work Group," *Administrative Science Quarterly* (June 1966) 11:59–78.

43. Likert, *The Human Organization.* chap. 10; and R. E. Walton and J. M. Dutton, "The Management of Interdepartmental Conflict: A Model and Review," *Administrative Science Quarterly* (March 1969) 14:73–84.

44. Arthur A. Thompson, "Employee Participation in Decision Making: The TVA Experience," *Public Personnel Review* (April 1967) 28:85.

45. Likert, *Human Organization.* p. 51.

46. Likert, *Human Organization.* pp. 59–63.

47. Argyris, "Make Work Worthwhile," p. 60.

48. Robert Presthus, *The Organizational Society* (New York: St. Martin's Press, 1978), chap. 6.

49. H. G. Wilcox, "Hierarchy, Human Nature and the Participative Panacea," *Public Administration Review* (Jan.–Feb. 1969) 29:53–63.

50. We have run together for this "indictment" of Theory Y the criticisms of a number of authors. Among them are Milton Derber, Robert Dubin, Frederick C. Mosher, Herbert G. Wilcox, Mahmoud A. Wahba and Lawrence G. Bridwell, and H. Roy Kaplan and Curt Tausky. Their works are cited in the bibliography.

51. See H. Roy Kaplan and Curt Tausky, "Humanism," *Public Administration Review* (March–April 1977) 37:171–180.

52. Kaplan and Tausky, "Humanism," p. 177.

53. Kaplan and Tausky, "Humanism," p. 177.

54. See the research literature marshaled by Kaplan and Tausky in "Humanism," pp. 178–180.

55. "Where Being Nice to Workers Didn't Work," *Business Week,* Jan. 20, 1973, pp. 98ff.

56. "Stonewalling Plant Democracy," *Business Week* March 28, 1977, pp. 78–82; and R. E. Walton, "Work Innovations at Topeka: After Six Years," *Journal of Applied Behavioral Science* (June–Sept. 1977) 13:422–433.

57. Frederick C. Mosher, *Governmental Reorganization* (Indianapolis: Bobbs-Merrill, 1967).

58. Mosher, *Governmental Reorganization.* p. 534.

59. Mosher, *Governmental Reorganization.* p. 526.

60. Floyd C. Mann, "Studying and Creating Change," as reprinted in Robert Sutermeister, *People and Productivity* (New York: McGraw-Hill, 1969), p. 273.

61. Harold Rush, "The 'Work Itself' Experiment," in *Job Design for Motivation* (New York: Conference Board, 1971), pp. 46–54.

62. Schoderbeck and Reif, *Job Enlargement*, pp. 43, 55.

63. Ernie Roberts, *Workers' Control* (London: Allen and Unwin, 1973), p. 23. For a survey of union nervousness about participative management, see Joseph Mire, "European Workers' Participation in Management," *Monthly Labor Review* (Feb. 1973) 96:10.

64. Veljko Rus, "Influence Structure in Yugoslav Enterprise," *Industrial Relations* (Feb. 1970) 9:148–160.

65. Rus, "Influence Structure in Yugoslav Enterprise," p. 160.

66. For a view of these Yugoslav developments as seen through a British socialist's eyes, see Ernie Roberts, *Workers' Control*. pp. 269–271.

67. Milton Derber, "Crosscurrents in Workers Participation," *Industrial Relations* (Feb. 1970) 9:136.

68. John Morse and Jay Lorsch, "Beyond Theory Y," *Harvard Business Review* (May–June, 1970), pp. 61–68.

69. Marrow et al., *Management by Participation*. chap. 12.

70. Maslow, *Eupsychian Management*. p. 1.

Part II
TASKS OF
MANAGEMENT

Chapter 7
Administrative Leadership

THE IMPACT OF LEADERSHIP

Try imagining the history of the United States minus an Abraham Lincoln, a Franklin D. Roosevelt, or a Martin Luther King, Jr. Restructure the twentieth century without Nikolai Lenin and Joseph Stalin, Adolf Hitler, Winston Churchill, Mahatma Gandhi, and Mao Tse-tung. What have you got?

At a lower level, measure the impact, for good or ill, of a J. Edgar Hoover on the FBI, a William D. Ruckelshaus on the Environmental Protection Agency, or a Robert R. Gilruth on NASA's outer space program.

In an earlier time, where would Notre Dame football have been without a Knute Rockne or the New York Jets, in a later age, without a Joe Namath? Or find a university campus not seriously scarred by the student violence of the 1960s and there perceive a dean of students whose vision of student rights, whose persuasive powers and gentle hand of mediation engineered change with peace through a hectic decade and kept a university intact. When one reflects on the influence of people like these, one can appreciate why the first question of the person who perceives the need for building an ark must be, "Do you know a Noah?"

Leaders are crucial in government, from chief executives through department and division heads on down to the critically important level of front-line supervisors.[1] When performing well, leaders give vision and tone to their agencies; they build people, and they transform pieces into programs; the Tennessee

What Makes a Leader?

There are a lot of definitions of leadership:

"Leadership is the capacity and will to rally men and women to a common purpose" — Field Marshal Montgomery

"Leadership is the consistent ability to influence people in desired ways" — Robert Golembiewski

"Leadership is a kind of work done to meet the needs of a social situation" — Philip Selznick

"Leadership is the exercise of authority in the making of decisions" — Robert Dubin

"Leadership is the ability to provide those functions required for successful group action" — Weldon Moffitt

"Leadership is the process of influencing group activities toward goal setting and goal achievement" — Ralph Stogdill

"A leader is best when people barely know that he exists" — Witter Bynner

Valley is reclaimed. Hitler is defeated. Western Europe is reconstructed, southern blacks at last receive their franchise, poor kids get a summer head start on an education, and a young president's dream becomes a reality when two Americans take a "leap for mankind" on the cratered surface of the moon. Leadership is critical — but what is it?

THE NATURE OF LEADERSHIP

For our purposes, a leader in a public administration setting is *one who can generate effective individual and group action to accomplish agency goals.* What it takes to fulfill that role will be defined not by the leaders themselves nor even primarily by the personal talents they bring to the job; rather, the requisites for success will be defined by individual employees, their work groups, the tasks to be performed, and the resources and time available to do the job. This formulation suggests that leadership is some function of the work *situation* rather than some combination of some universal traits that spells success in any managerial climate. Management consultant Peter Drucker has argued:

I soon learned there is no "effective [executive] personality." The effective executives I have seen differ widely in their temperaments and abilities, in what they do and how they do it, in their personalities, their knowledge, their interests — in fact in almost everything that distinguishes human beings. All they have in common is the ability to get the right things done.[2]

And as that early precursor of modern-day political science, Arthur Bentley, wrote in 1908:

Leadership is not an affair of the individual leader. It is fundamentally an affair of the group. Pomp and circumstance are but details. Leadership by an individual leader is not even a typical form. It is only a minor form; or what comes to the same thing, leadership can most often be given an individual statement only from certain minor and incidental points of view. The great phenomena of leadership are phenomena of groups differentiated for the purpose of leading other groups. One specialized group leads certain other groups in a special phase of their activity. Within it are the phenomena of individual leadership in various grades. . . .

This is not to say that there is no difference between man and man in the capacity for leadership. Nothing is more evident than that there is in fact just such a difference. Some adult men, just as one finds them, will fit certain group needs of leadership, and others will fit other group needs; some will answer best at one time, others at another; some perhaps will not do at all as leaders in any group activities which we are apt to have under investigation.[3]

Let it quickly be added and emphasized that the intellectual, emotional, social, and ethical skills (traits) the leader does possess will be tremendously relevant in determining success in meeting the situational demands that confront him. It is not a tabula rasa relationship where the group exists and the leader is some kind of spineless chameleon that takes on the color the work group imposes on him; to the contrary, the unfolding relationship between group and leader is clearly an interactionist one in which there is *joint* influence and *mutual* development. This author surmises, for example, that the impact of Dr. Martin Luther King, Jr., on the movement for black civil rights was far greater than the impact of his organization, the Southern Christian Leadership Conference, was on him.

To grasp the *situational* nature of leadership, consider for a moment the different kinds of leaders the following circumstances would seem to demand:

creating and leading a Ralph Nader public interest research group to challenge the utilities in your state

formulating a new welfare plan for presentation to Congress

responding to an enemy encirclement of your infantry company in the battlefield

providing emergency relief and protection after a hurricane in Mississippi or a ruptured dam in Idaho

running a job locator service in the state department of employment security

Clearly, the leadership styles required by those situations would range from the most consultative, democratic leader types to tough, fast-acting authoritarian types. The work situation is primary.

The principle can also be seen in how leaders perform in different work situations, sometimes rising high, then falling flat as they perform in different areas. For example, contrast the extraordinary record of Lyndon B. Johnson in leading the U.S. Senate during the 1950s with his tragic failure in the presidency. One of his predecessors experienced that record in reverse. Harry Truman was an average senator, a pipsqueak of a vice-president, but a tiger in the White House.

The analysis suggests that instead of beginning with heroes, we should begin with a worm's-eye view of leaders — and that is through the eyes of groups who have some need to be led.[4]

GROUP NEEDS REQUIRING LEADERSHIP

In a pioneering study of group needs published in 1966,[5] David G. Bowers and Stanley E. Seashore suggested that to be successful, all work groups require: (a) support for individual needs; (b) interaction help to smooth out human relations; (c) goal emphasis; and (d) work facilitation, the selection of means, planning the procedures, and so on.[6] The question that remained to be answered, of course, was the degree to which these four needs could be provided by the work groups themselves and which ones clearly required a leader.

Our own preference is the analysis developed shortly after World War II by Kenneth Benne and Paul Sheats for the first National Training Laboratory in Group Development.[7] First of all, the authors suggested, every work group has *task roles* to be taken care of (defining problems, determining goals, selecting means); second, it has to fulfill *maintenance roles* (to enable human beings to function harmoniously together).[8] The Benne and Sheats analysis is represented in outline form in Table 7.1.

TABLE 7.1 NATIONAL TRAINING LABORATORY FORMULATION OF GROUP NEEDS

All work groups must provide for:

1. *Task Roles*
   a. goal setting
   b. means selection

2. *Maintenance Roles*
   a. extending support for worker needs (a la Maslow)
   b. representing workers before management
   c. improving interpersonal relations, developing cohesiveness and resolving conflicts

Data from Kenneth Benne and Paul Sheats, "Functional Roles of Group Members," *Journal of Social Issues* (Spring 1948) 4:41–49.

The President Attends to Some Task Needs

On April 21, 1961, nine days after Soviet cosmonaut Gagarin's startling space venture, President John F. Kennedy began some goal setting:

> We have to consider whether there is any program now, regardless of its cost, which offers us hope of being pioneers in a space project. . . . If we can get to the moon before the Russians, we should.

Leonard Mandlebaum, "Apollo: How the United States Planned to Go to the Moon," *Science* (1969) 163:649–653.

Task Roles

Goal setting   In government, the major goals of work groups are determined by public policy; the job of leadership is to insure that those policies are in fact transmitted to the agency's work units. The opportunity for leadership here calls for more than being simply a conveyor belt between Congress and the president and one's agency; it calls for capturing the imagination and commitment of employees so that one's agency is set in motion to accomplish the goals of public policy.

Making goals come alive for workers is surely one of the great opportunities and challenges for people in leadership posts in government. As we have seen in earlier chapters, having a clear view of what their job is all about and being able to relate their work to significant purposes are critical in people's search for self-actualization. "Where there is no vision, the people perish," says an Old Testament text. It is the job of the leader to see to it that all of her associates catch the vision of that part of the public good that is entrusted to them.

In this era of substantial delegation of authority to executive agencies, it may be only very broad goals that are imposed from above on a division of some department, thus leaving the operating agency considerable room in defining subgoals, priorities, and program planning. In those areas a strong case can be made for shared goal setting (i.e., involving the rank and file).

First, the administrator doesn't know it all and needs the assistance of her staff; second, the smart administrator will long since have learned that involvement leads to commitment, and so she consults with her staff with an eye to the cohesion that may accrue; third, she understands how her employees develop when challenged and thus confers frequently with them before making up her mind.

Means selection   Although some goal setting will have to be handled in government on an authoritarian basis (via congressional or presidential mandate), a substantial part of means selection ought to be left in the hands of the work units. (We exclude those obvious exceptions where Congress has specified the means; e.g., monetary and fiscal tools to control inflation instead of price-and-wage control, decontrol of gasoline prices instead of rationing, and storage of surplus agricultural commodities instead of direct income payments to farmers). The entire analysis presented in Chapters 2 and 6 and the experience of firms like Harwood and General Foods, among many other organizations, strongly support the proposition that leaders should delegate the authority to work groups to develop their own procedures rather than play God themselves by imposing detailed operations manuals on all their units.

Maintenance Roles

As we have argued before, the provision of individual needs and the preservation of healthy group life among workers cannot be taken for granted; beyond that, the satisfaction of both is an absolute prerequisite for successful administration over the long run. Therefore, in addition to the task roles that need to be fulfilled, there are maintenance needs to be taken care of: to build human beings, to fight their battles with management, and to improve the quality of group life (strengthening interpersonal relations, building cohesiveness, and resolving conflicts). *The job of the leader is not, by any means, to do all of these things personally;* but it is his responsibility to make certain that these maintenance activities are performed. The kind of contribution he himself may make may be administrative and indirect rather than personal and direct.

Consider the director of the state highway patrol in your state. He may have within his organization seven hundred highway patrolmen. The kinds of contributions the director may make to their maintenance needs might be as follows. He establishes a training course for front-line supervisors where they will be exposed to the human need analysis and receive training in human relations, in part so that they can in turn enhance the growth of the patrolmen under them. He fights for salary increases and the budget allocations to finance them. He instructs his personnel assistant and personal secretary to be his eyes and ears so that critical events in the lives of his staff do not go unnoticed (he expresses condolences when deaths affect his staff, sends congratulatory notes for significant achievements, and presents awards for service beyond the call of duty), and he trains his deputies to act in like fashion.

At some point during the course of his own training this state highway patrol director has heard that the influence supervisors have on their workers is related to their influence with higher levels of management in behalf of those workers.[9] Realizing this, the director strengthens his deputies' linking-pin role by going to great lengths to respond favorably to the requests and suggestions they present to him for his action.

At the level of improving interpersonal relations, the director authorizes training programs that will bring his patrolmen together, develops an agency mystique (analogous to that of the Forest Service, for example), and is prepared to move vigorously when dissidents appear in the ranks and threaten the group life of his agency. Through it all, he knows that most of the maintenance work in preserving the human fabric of his agency will have to be done by significant others in the work groups themselves and by the front-line supervisors, not by him from the head office.

By Way of Emphasis

Let it be stressed again from the foregoing analysis that while work groups *universally* have both task and maintenance needs, those needs do not constitute an agenda for leaders alone. It will come as some shock to the omnicompetent, overpowering leader how quickly he can generate employee resentment as a result of his own rushing in where angels fear to tread. The administrator would be well advised to memorize a maxim of John Stuart Mill's, that the whole purpose of government is to make people more self-governing — not to usurp the business of life from those who are perfectly capable of tending to that business themselves.[10]

The portrait of the successful leader that begins to emerge, then, is that of *one who can enable the organizations* being led to define goals, achieve them, see that personal needs are met, develop interpersonal relations, and build cohesiveness. Enabling the organization rather than unilaterally doing these things himself is the nub of the matter. Happily, there are a number of styles for a leader to choose from for those acts of enabling.

STYLES OF LEADERSHIP

Autocratic, Democratic, and Laissez-faire Leadership

Students of leadership going a long way back have identified three types of leadership: authoritarian, democratic, and laissez-faire. Figure 7.1 compares

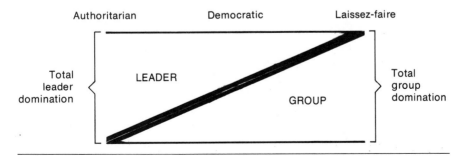

FIGURE 7.1   CALLING THE SHOTS UNDER THREE LEADERSHIP STYLES

From Robert Tannenbaum, Weschler, and Massarik, *Leadership and Organization*, p. 69. Copyright © 1961 by McGraw-Hill Book Company, Inc. Adapted by permission of McGraw-Hill Book Company.

Different as Night and Day

A student of ours some years ago provided a vivid contrast between the authoritarian and democratic leaders he had encountered on a summer job:

> Last summer I was employed at Geneva Steel. Every two weeks we had a new foreman, supervising six of us working on brick salvage. One foreman stood watching us constantly. In case one of us stopped to take a breath he would shout, "Get to work. You have two hands — I want two bricks." We were not allowed to talk to each other. We even tried to avoid looking at him or greeting him. When he left for a few minutes, we stopped working or did an inadequate job. There was no possibility to communicate with him and we resented his presence.

> The second foreman was just like one of us. We joked together and when we worked hard he let us have a half hour of rest. If another boss happened to come by and tell us something, he used to tell him to leave us alone. We were ready to do anything for him; we even started propaganda for him. Our performance was almost perfect.

them graphically in terms of the leader's and the group's decision making and influence. As indicated, the authoritarian leader tries totally to dominate his organization. His attitude toward his employees echoes Tennyson's paean to bravery in "The Charge of the Light Brigade": "Theirs not to make reply, / Theirs not to reason why,/Theirs but to do and die." This kind of leader assumes both the task roles and the maintenance roles, makes the work assignments, lays down the time schedules, encourages uniform procedures, criticizes poor workmanship, and by tone of voice and iron hand makes it unmistakably clear who is boss.

The democratic style indicates a leader who involves her workers significantly in means selection (a task role) and in group maintenance activities; where feasible and appropriate, consults with them in regard to objectives and long-range plans; is a builder of people rather than robots; knows that she does not know it all and that her employees know a great deal; and is strongly committed to the proposition that management begins with people. Let there be no misunderstanding about her. The democratic leader leads but rarely dictates; consults, listens, and persuades but rarely commands; sees to it that issues are faced and resolved, not dodged; and makes perfectly clear that, along with her concern for the human beings who work with her, she also has production standards against which she will measure the whole organization's performance.[11]

Why not continue — go all the way to the right in the box in Figure 7.1 to the laissez-faire position where the group calls all the shots?

The laissez-faire style is a kind of anarchistic pattern in administration where all the task and maintenance roles fall upon the work groups themselves. The spirit of this system seems to be, "Do your own thing and we'll hope for the best." Perhaps the most common locale for the laissez-faire style is the recreational friendship group where the performance of task and maintenance roles seems to be passed around on a highly informal basis (e.g., the bridge club, five doctors who ski together on Thursday afternoons, the ten-couple theater group); initiators, energizers, tension reducers, and expediters can appear anywhere in the group.

A laissez-faire pattern in government would seem as out of place as a McDonald's hamburger looming up in the TV lenses of the Mars lander. That style would immediately flunk the responsibility test of "Who's in charge in this unit?" In addition, there has been wide agreement since Kurt Lewin's studies at Iowa State in the 1930s of boys assembling face masks that laissez-faire generates the worst productivity of the three styles (a kind of collective goofing off).[12]

Boss or Friend — or Both?

There are still other important ways to cut the leadership pie. The management science people at Ohio State, for example, years ago developed a two-dimensional leadership framework (see Figure 7.2).[13] The vertical scale measures leader behavior that *initiates structure* (I S) — helping to define goals, select means, and plan work processes. The upper end suggests authoritarian conduct; the opposite end, laissez-faire. The horizontal scale measures leader *consideration* (C) for workers: improving interpersonal relations, giving support,

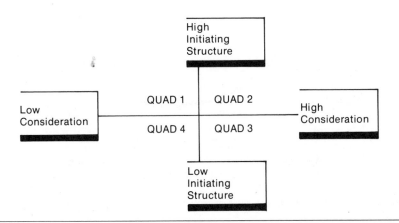

FIGURE 7.2 THE OHIO STATE LEADERSHIP CONFIGURATION

From Edwin A. Fleishman, et al., *Leadership and Supervision in Industry*. Copyright © 1955 by Bureau of Educational Research, Ohio State University. Reprinted by permission.

and the like. The right end of the scale suggests considerate leader behavior, moving toward hostility at the left end.[14]

The quad 1 leader is a veritable Simon Legree, cracking the whip and smirking with each lash. Quad 2 leaders approach the Rensis Likert ideal: leading on the one hand and stroking on the other, attending appropriately to the group's task needs and thoughtfully ministering to the maintenance needs. The quad 3 leader is a first-class patsy, loving everyone and leading no one. And the quad 4 leader is nobody's favorite: he lets everything go and then falls apart when everything goes wrong.

As might be expected, the Ohio State surveys of *supervisors'* opinions called for much higher levels of I S behavior than those desired in the workers' surveys. But did the research produce any data supporting one quadrant over another?

1. *Managers* gave higher marks to foremen who are high on initiating structure and somewhat low in consideration.

2. But these rather aloof authoritarians supervised crews that exhibited the highest rates of absenteeism, accidents, grievances, and turnovers (the intervening variables going soft as the workers retaliate).

3. However, considerate foremen can safely initiate more structure without alienating their workers.[15]

Then some agnosticism crept into the findings: the possibility of "diminishing returns" (along a curvilinear scale) when some critical point is reached in increasing consideration too far and decreasing the foreman's rule (see Figure 7.3. Without suggesting any actual magnitudes, Figure 7.3 compresses relationships between I S and C behavior on the one hand and the turnover and griev-

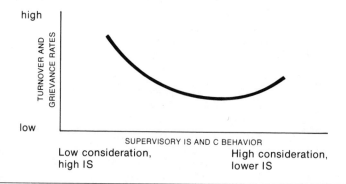

SUPERVISORY IS AND C BEHAVIOR

Low consideration,   High consideration,
high IS   lower IS

FIGURE 7.3   CURVILINEAR RELATIONSHIP BETWEEN I S AND C VALUES AND THE INTERVENING VARIABLES

From Fleishman and Harris, "Patterns of Leadership Behavior Related to Employee Grievances and Turnover," *Personnel Psychology*, vol. 15 (1962), pp. 45–53. Adapted by permission.

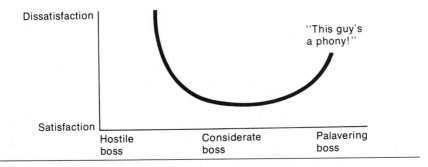

FIGURE 7.4   TOO MUCH OF A GOOD THING MAY BE A BAD THING

ance rates on the other. These two sets of relationships are represented by Ohio State researchers in separate graphs.) Figure 7.4 renders the curvilinear concept in perhaps a simpler way and warns us that diminishing returns in the form of rising worker resentment await the supervisor who is too sweet, too considerate. "I smell a manipulator" would be the standard reaction.

Second-generation researchers at Ohio State seem to have bought a contingency theory in applying their I S and C schema.[16] Among the factors in the work situation that need to be taken into account are top management's attitudes (can democrats survive on the first floor when kings preside on the third?), what kind of influence the immediate supervisor wields upstairs, intrinsic job satisfaction, time pressures, and task certainty or uncertainty.

What this more recent review suggests is something like this:

1.   Time pressures make higher degrees of initiating structure more tolerable.

2.   Where jobs are intrinsically satisfying, workers want the leash strings in their own hands and balk at alterations in I S and C.

3.   In cases of task certainty, high consideration contributes to worker satisfaction.

Overall, the researchers conclude that the more workers depend on their leader's providing needed services, the healthier the impact on worker satisfaction and performance of higher supervisory initiating structure and considerate behavior. To some degree, then, every front-line supervisor is left with the ancient Greek's search for the golden mean — balancing the right amount of initiating structure with the right amount of consideration.

The Managerial Grid

In the early 1960s, Robert Blake and Jane Mouton developed a managerial grid to help measure a leader's progress toward that point, the 9,9 combination where the managerial statesman brings people and production concerns into perfect balance.[18] Blake and Mouton admitted that conditions might prevail that would call for some other leader posture but concluded that "to the degree operating requirements permit, 9,9 is the more mature managerial style."[19]

Fiedler's Contingency Model

Within a year of the Blake and Mouton study, Fred Fiedler began publishing the results of his extensive field research on effective leadership styles.[20] Similar in one sense to the Ohio State configuration, Fiedler begins with a measurement of task-oriented versus person-oriented leader behavior.

Then he examines three critical dimensions of the work situation: (a) leader-member relations (high trust, low trust, etc.); (b) the nature of the task (open- or close-ended); and (c) the power position of the leader.* (He regards the nature of the relationship between leader and subordinates as of prime importance in determining the appropriate leadership style.)

In pulling the situation variables together,† Fiedler suggests that highly favorable work situations (well-liked leader, structured tasks, and adequate power in the leader) and highly unfavorable work situations (poor relationships with the work group, unstructured tasks, and a weak power position) *both* call for leader emphasis on controlling tasks and performance (low LPC score or high I S score). In work situations of intermediate favorableness — those composed of good relationships, unstructured problems, some weak supervisory power — the leader should veer toward the consideration side of the scale (high LPC scores) and away from heavy initiating structure. Fiedler states:

> As can be seen from the results of [the] studies, the highly accepted and strongly rejected leaders perform best if they are controlling and managing, while the leaders in the intermediate acceptance range, who are neither rejected nor accepted, perform best if they are permissive and nondirective.[21]

Some of Fiedler's conclusions have been challenged by other research. One thinks particularly of Morse and Lorsch's comparison of leadership styles at two research laboratories.[22] Fiedler suggests that an initiating-structure leader would be called for if leader-member relations are good in this open-ended work situation and if the leader enjoys a strong power position. But Morse and Lorsch found that the *successful* research lab (Stockton, California) had a much looser leader style, a Theory Y atmosphere, in contrast to the *less successful* research lab (Carmel, California), which operated under more Theory X conditions (approximating Fiedler's recommendation).

---

* The Fiedler approach, from my point of view, is excessively complex. He attempts to get at task versus person orientation by measuring the supervisor's attitude toward his least-preferred co-worker (LPC score). If the supervisor exhibits a positive attitude toward the least-preferred co-worker, the supervisor is person-oriented; if he exhibits a negative attitude (low LPC score), he is task-oriented.

† Here are two possibilities: (a) a disliked leader over a structured task with little power, or (b) a well-liked leader over a structured task with great power.

To Fiedler's credit is his clear demonstration of the importance of situational factors such as relationships, tasks, and power in selecting the appropriate leader style.

How to Choose a Leadership Style?[23]

One thing seems certain as we enter the thicket of choosing among authoritarian, democratic, and laissez-faire styles: The right style seems to make a large difference in an organization's performance. A study by N. Z. Medalia measured the leadership preferences of authoritarian and nonauthoritarian personality types among workers. Medalia found that where only 36 percent of the nonauthoritarians expressed hospitable attitudes toward their leaders, 59 percent of the authoritarians accepted theirs. In terms of that sample, correctly identifying the authoritarian personalities of a given set of workers and then providing them with strong leadership could result in a 23 percentage point improvement in group attitudes toward their chiefs.[24]

A study by A. D. Calvin also suggested the kinds of gains in productivity that are possible when leadership style is properly matched with the intelligence of the workers. His findings indicated a 100 percent improvement in the output of workers of comparatively low intelligence under authoritarian leadership in contrast to their output under democratic leadership.[25]

A number of authors have pointed to still another variable that may markedly influence the choice of leadership style — the nature of the task and the technology to perform it. In an early article, for example, Morton Deutsch set up a laboratory situation to test leader-centered versus group-centered teams in solving close-ended (right or wrong) problems and open-ended problems. In both situations, the group-centered teams performed better.[26]

For Robert Dubin, the independent variable that counts most in dictating a leader style is technology — how the work is to be done.[27] He identifies three possibilities: whole-unit technology (e.g., the social worker, the antitrust lawyer, the highway patrolman); assembly-line technology (processing the mails, filling patent orders, publishing the *Congressional Record* at the Government Printing Office); and continuous-flow technology (in the private sector, an oil refinery or fully automated bakery; in government there are few examples, perhaps some phases of a computer center).

Drawing heavily on British scholar Joan Woodard's research, Dubin concludes that worker autonomy and more generalized supervision (the democratic style) are appropriate for whole-unit technologies but that assembly-line and continuous-flow technologies call for more authoritarian leadership (closer supervision, etc.).[28]

A substantial number of experiments with Theory X in manufacturing firms cast some doubt on Dubin's findings: General Foods, Texas Instruments, Sun Oil, Harwood Manufacturing, and others. Each of these companies found significant gains in intervening and output variables as a result of shifting toward more democratic leadership.

What do we know, then, about choosing a style of leadership that will enhance our chances of accomplishing agency goals? In summary, the work situation — group characteristics, task needs, and technology — will heavily influence the kind of leadership style likely to be the most effective. Selection of the right leadership style can make a substantial contribution to worker attitudes and performance. On essentially every measurement, the laissez-faire mode flunks out as a possible leadership approach in government. In work situations of a repetitive character calling for low intelligence and simple steps, the authoritarian style may be the best of the three styles. Where workers with above-average intelligence are wrestling with reasonably complex problems and multiple solutions, the democratic style is much preferred. In terms of the major argument of this book for producing self-actualizing people and truly creative civil servants, the democratic style of leadership has great intrinsic strengths in its favor.

A Systems Approach for Selecting Leaders

As we will see in Chapter 17, modern-day recruitment and selection of personnel begin with a careful analysis of the tasks to be performed and then proceed to the design of selection instruments (tests, review of past experience, interviews, and so on) to determine which applicants have the ability to perform those tasks.

To a certain extent, such reasoning is certainly applicable in choosing division chiefs, section heads, city managers, and the like. There have even been suggestions that tests could be devised to sort out candidates who would be unfit for the presidency. Long ago, Harold Lasswell suggested that tests be used by the national parties to eliminate authoritarian personality types who would be a threat to democratic institutions.[29] More recently, James David Barber has made a similar suggestion to help identify "active-positives" and shun "active-negatives" who might seek the presidency.[30]

Psychologists have been hard at work to develop tests that might validly predict managerial success. The data from these validation studies are not broad enough to afford any general conclusions, but two of them might be noted. John A. Hicks and J. B. Stone found a significant correlation between certain intellectual traits (the theoretical and pedantic traits in the Rorschach scale), activity potential, and human relationships on the one hand with managerial performance and promotability on the other. The authors concluded that:

> It appears from this study that managerial success can be predicted to a significant degree using current testing instruments. Managers in this study represent a wide range of skills and background and have in common only the fact that they are operating as managers in a technical organization.[31]

In the early 1960s, M. E. Spitzer and W. J. McNamara undertook a careful validation study of six tests that might be used in measuring managerial potential. The tests covered IQ, leadership attitudes, occupational preference, personality profiles, supervisory judgments, employment and general biographical background. The investigators found that the tests with the best predictive value of on-the-job managerial performance were the Otis Mental Ability test, which corroborated one element in the Hicks and Stone research, and the Background and Contemporary Data (BCD) form, which provides a kind of whole-person portrayal of an applicant.[32]

The appropriate procedures, then, in leader selection seem to be:

1. Determine, in Benne and Sheats fashion, the task and maintenance roles to be performed, including the open- or close-ended nature of the tasks.

2. Review the technologies involved and the personality types (authoritarian or democratic) and IQ levels of the workers.

3. Determine what kinds of tasks and style will be appropriate for the leader *in this setting.*

4. Lean a bit in the democratic direction with George Bernard Shaw's admonition that how we treat the flower girl strongly influences how she turns out.

5. Find the valid indicators that, hopefully, will compare the talents of those seeking a leadership post.

6. Bring that woman or man on board.

Having reviewed group needs for leaders, alternative styles, and methods of selection, let's conclude the analysis by focusing on a key leadership position in public administration — the presidency.

LEADERSHIP AT THE HIGHEST LEVELS

What the Presidency Demands

A role analysis indicates at least five major things the nation has come to expect of its presidents: he is head of the nation (analogous to the British king), chief executive (the administrator), primary policymaker (the legislative role), overseer of foreign affairs, and political leader (the party role). Against those role expectations, how would you grade Thomas Jefferson, Franklin Pierce, Abraham Lincoln, Woodrow Wilson, Richard Nixon, and Jimmy Carter?

Twice during the last twenty years, panels of American historians have appraised the whole roster of our presidents, and in doing so they have discovered some of the leadership factors they had in common. The 1962 appraisal judged five of our former chief executives to be in the great category, in the

"Your Old Men Shall Dream Dreams, Your Young Men Shall See Visions"

From Franklin D. Roosevelt's second inaugural, March 4, 1937:

> But here is the challenge to our democracy: In this nation I see tens of millions of its citizens — a substantial part of its whole population — who at this very moment are denied the greater part of what the very lowest standards of today call the necessities of life. . . . I see one-third of a nation ill-housed, ill-clad, ill-nourished.
>
> It is not in despair that I paint you that picture. I paint it for you in hope — because the Nation, seeing and understanding the injustice in it, proposes to paint it out. We are determined to make every American citizen the subject of his country's interest and concern; and we will never regard any faithful law-abiding group within our borders as superfluous. The test of our progress is not whether we add more to the abundance of those who have much; it is whether we provide enough for those who have too little.

Inaugural Addresses of the Presidents of the United States (House Document 93-208) (Washington, D.C.: Government Printing Office, 1974), pp. 242–243.

following order: Abraham Lincoln, George Washington, Franklin D. Roosevelt, Woodrow Wilson, and Thomas Jefferson.[33] Of these great ones, only George Washington and Woodrow Wilson were regarded by the historians as really effective administrators; the qualities of greatness in most instances lay elsewhere than in keeping a tidy house. All of the outstanding presidents showed deep concern for the ends of public policy ("Where are we tending?"), and each one had a large view of his country and its destiny. All five were innovators and seemed comfortable with change. And each one seemed to have a sense of history that deepened his perspective of his mission in the White House.

In reviewing the balloting by the panel of historians, Arthur Schlesinger, Sr., the distinguished professor of history at Harvard, suggested these tests of a president:

Did he exhibit a creative approach to the problems of statecraft?

Was he the master or the servant of events?

Did he use the prestige and potentialities of the presidency to advance the public welfare?

Did he effectively staff his key government posts?

Did he properly safeguard the country's interest in relation to the rest of the world?

How significantly did he affect the future destinies of the nation?[34]

To perform the task and maintenance roles the Constitution and our political system have imposed on the executive office, what traits would your ideal president bring to the White House?[35] My list would include seven essentials:

1. *Breadth of vision:* He could dream of a time when the algebra of our national life would in reality become $1 = 1$, to send a Lewis and Clark into the unknown West, to visualize a Union preserved without slavery, to see humankind no longer earthbound.[36]

2. *Personal integrity:* He would be not an angel, but full of cool and courage when the French are badgering us to get involved in a war with England in the 1790s, and when Russian missiles are found in Cuba in 1962, plus having some pretty clear standards of right and wrong.

3. *The ability. when the facts are in. to make decisions:* He could decide whether or not to use the atom bomb to end World War II; to back up the UN in Korea; to use troops to break a picket line around a high school in Little Rock, Arkansas, to let nine black students through.

4. *The art of compromise:* He would know when to give a little in order to get a lot in the name of the public good.

5. *The ability to delegate and to confer status:* He would realize that his is not a one-person government.

6. *Great language skills:* He could strengthen the nation's commitment to its highest goals and deepen the people's confidence that they can reach them.*

7. *A sense of humor:* He could laugh, not because the presidency is a laughing matter, but because a democratic society needs to be reminded of the humanness of its chief executive and because wit is such a superb weapon for presidential self-defense.†

---

* For example, do any of the following do anything for you?

"We hold these truths to be self-evident . . . and . . . we mutually pledge to each other our lives, our fortunes and our sacred honor."

"With malice toward none, with charity for all. . . ."

"We have nothing to fear but fear itself."

"The hand that held the dagger has struck it into the back of its neighbor."

"Let us therefore brace ourselves to our duties, and so bear ourselves that, if the British Empire and its Commonwealths last for a thousand years, men will still say, 'This was their finest hour.' "

"The energy, the faith, the devotion which we bring to this endeavor will light our country and all who serve it — and the glow from that fire can truly light the world . . . here on Earth, God's work must truly be our own."

† There is something delicious about the thought of Franklin D. Roosevelt in an annual address to the Daughters of the American Revolution greeting them as "My fellow immigrants." And somehow history and the moment both seemed to come together through President Jack Kennedy's humor when he welcomed America's Nobel laureates to a White House dinner: "the greatest assemblage of brains in this House since Jefferson had breakfast alone." See Bill Adler (ed.), *The Kennedy Wit* (New York: Bantam, 1964).

The President Sacks the General

Smarting under the administration's restrictions on how he was to fight the Korean War, General Douglas MacArthur wrote a letter of criticism to Representative Joseph W. Martin, the Republican leader of the House of Representatives. President Truman reacted:

> The time had come to draw the line. MacArthur's letter to Congressman Martin showed that the general was not only in disagreement with the policy of the government but was challenging this policy in open insubordination to his Commander in Chief.

A series of meetings with the Secretaries of Defense and State then ensued.

> I was careful not to disclose that I had already reached a decision. . . . I then directed General Bradley to prepare the orders that would relieve General MacArthur of his several commands. . . . Full and vigorous debate on matters of national policy is a vital element in the constitutional system of our free democracy. It is fundamental, however, that military commanders must be governed by the policies and directives issued to them in the manner provided by our laws and Constitution. In time of crisis, the consideration is particularly compelling.

And so, in cartoonist Herblock's elegant phrase, "Forty-eight stars triumphed over five."

Harry S. Truman, *Memoirs* (Garden City, N.Y.: Doubleday, 1956) 2:445–449.

SUMMARY

The leadership function in government is vital, from chief executive to front-line supervisor. No less an opportunity is entrusted to leaders than giving tone and vision to their agencies, building self-actualizing employees, and pulling whole programs together where only pieces lay before.

The heart of the art of leadership is being able to identify what work groups need for success that they cannot efficiently provide for themselves and then fill those gaps. There are basically two kinds of group needs: *task needs* — defining goals and selecting means; and *maintenance needs* — individual problems, group cohesiveness, interpersonal relations, and the like.

How much and what kind of leadership inputs are required to meet such needs will be influenced by group skills, individual talents, the technological complexity of the problems, time allowances, and other vectors. Leadership, then, is situationally defined, not an a priori matter of a bundle of traits that might serve any work group equally well.

In terms of how much voice workers have in handling their task and maintenance needs, leaders may be classified as authoritarian, democratic, or laissez-faire. Research flunks the laissez-faire style on almost every count; suggests conditions when the authoritarian or democratic style would be appropriate; and finds a perplexing curvilinear, or diminishing-returns, relationship between initiating structure, consideration, and how workers respond.

If the older trait approach has any remaining validity, it can stem only from a careful task analysis beforehand of what a leadership post requires. We have attempted that kind of analysis here in a brief look at presidential leadership.

KEY CONCEPTS

leadership
task roles
maintenance roles
authoritarians

democrats
laissez-faire
initiating structure

DISCUSSION QUESTIONS

1. Discuss the nature of leadership, commenting on the various definitions of leadership provided at the beginning of the chapter. To what extent is a good leader the result of a combination of specific traits and to what extent the result of specific situations?

2. What can a leader do to ensure that the task and maintenance needs of her subordinates are fulfilled?

3. Compare and contrast authoritarian, democratic, and laissez-faire leadership styles. What are the advantages of each?

4. Discuss the relationship between initiating structure and consideration values. Is there an optimal combination that would produce an ideal leader?

5. What factors must be taken into consideration when choosing the best leadership style? To what extent would the seven essentials listed for an ideal president hold true for any ideal leader?

PROJECT

Read a biography of a famous leader. Identify the essentials of the task and maintenance roles for the most important position that person has held.

Notes

1. The critical importance of the chief executive officer in the life of an organization was effectively argued by Chris Argyris in "The CEO's Behavior: Key to Organizational

Development," *Harvard Business Review* (Mar.–Apr. 1973) 51:55–64. A central point of the article was the importance of the CEO's actual behavior, not his theories or pieties, but how he treats his deputies, handles feedback, and demands conformity or experimentation from his people.

2. Peter Drucker, *The Effective Executive* (New York: Harper & Row, 1967), pp. 21–22.

3. Arthur Bentley, *The Process of Government* (Chicago: University of Chicago Press, 1908), pp. 223–227.

4. See Sidney Verba, *Small Groups and Political Behavior* (Princeton, N.J.: Princeton University Press, 1961), pp. 117–126.

5. David G. Bowers and Stanley E. Seashore, "Predicting Organization Effectiveness with a Four-factor Theory of Leadership," *Administrative Science Quarterly* (Sept. 1966) 11:238–63.

6. Bowers and Seashore, "Predicting Organization Effectiveness with a Four-factor Theory of Leadership," p. 247.

7. Kenneth Benne and Paul Sheats, "Functional Roles of Group Members," *Journal of Social Issues* (Spring 1948) 4:41–49.

8. Benne and Sheats also mentioned individual roles in their three-factor formulation. Those roles may pose special demands on and for leaders, to be sure, but we have left the matter out of our discussion here, which is concerned with the needs of groups as groups.

9. The empirical study was by Donald Pelz and recorded in "Influence: A Key to Effective Leadership in the First-Line Supervisor," *Personnel* (Nov. 1952) 29:209–217.

10. John Stuart Mill, *Considerations on Representative Government* (New York: Liberal Arts Press, 1958), p. 28.

11. Rensis Likert, *The Human Organization* (New York: McGraw-Hill, 1967) p. 58.

12. See Ronald Lippitt and Ralph White, "Leader Behavior and Member Reaction in Three Social Climates," in D. Cartwright and Alain Zander (eds.), *Group Dynamics* (Evanston, Ill.: Row, Peterson, 1960), pp. 318–335.

13. The original study was reported by Edwin A. Fleishman, E. F. Harris, and H. E. Burtt in *Leadership and Supervision in Industry* (Columbus, Ohio: Ohio State University Press, 1955), and was reprinted in Robert Sutermeister, *People and Productivity* (New York: McGraw-Hill, 1969), pp. 380–395.

14. The complexities of defining and measuring I S and C behavior were reviewed by Chester Schriesheim, Robert House, and Steven Kerr in "Leader Initiating Structure," *Organizational Behavior and Human Performance* (April 1976) 15:297–321; and by H. K. Downey et al., "The Path-Goal Theory of Leadership: A Longitudinal Analysis," *Organizational Behavior and Human Performance* (June 1976) 16:156–176.

15. Sutermeister, *People and Productivity*, pp. 391–395.

16. Steven Kerr et al., "Toward a Contingency Theory of Leadership Based upon the Consideration and Initiation Structure Literature," *Organizational Behavior and Human Performance* (Aug. 1974) 12:62–82.

17. Robert R. Blake and Jane Mouton, *The Managerial Grid* (Houston: Texas Gulf Publishing, 1964).

18. "The 9,9 managerial style" is treated in Chapter 7 of Blake and Mouton, *The Managerial Grid*.

19. Blake and Mouton, *The Managerial Grid*, p. 317.

20. Fred E. Fiedler, "Engineer the Job to Fit the Manager," *Harvard Business Review* (Sept.–Oct. 1965) 43:115–22; and *A Theory of Leadership Effectiveness* (New York: McGraw-Hill, 1967).

21. Fiedler, "Engineer the Job," p. 120.

22. John J. Morse and Jay W. Lorsch, "Beyond Theory Y," *Harvard Business Review* (May–June 1970) 48:63–65.

23. One of Robert Golembiewski's early articles is still enlightening on this dilemma: "Three Styles of Leadership and Their Uses," *Personnel* (July–Aug. 1961) 38:36–7.

24. N. Z. Medalia, "Authoritarianism, Leader Acceptance, and Group Cohesion," *Journal of Abnormal and Social Psychology* (Sept. 1955) 51:207–213.

25. A. D. Calvin et al., "The Effect of Intelligence and Social Atmosphere in Group Problem-Solving Behavior," *Journal of Social Psychology* (Feb. 1957) 45:61–74.

26. Morton Deutsch, "The Effects of Cooperation and Competition upon Group Process," in Cartwright and Zander (eds.), *Group Dynamics: Research and Theory* (New York: Harper & Row, 1968), pp. 319–53.

27. Robert Dubin et al., *Leadership and Productivity* (San Francisco: Chandler, 1965), chap. 1.

28. Dubin, *Leadership and Productivity.* pp. 46–50.

29. Harold Lasswell, *Power and Personality* (New York: Norton, 1948), pp. 186–187.

30. James D. Barber, 2nd. ed., *The Presidential Character* (Englewood Cliffs, N.J.: Prentice-Hall, 1977).

31. John A. Hicks and J. B. Stone, "The Identification of Traits Related to Managerial Success," *Journal of Applied Psychology* (Dec. 1962), 46: 428–32.

32. M. E. Spitzer and W. J. McNamara, "Managerial Selection Study," *Personnel Psychology* (Spring 1964) 17:19–40.

33. Arthur M. Schlesinger, "Our Presidents: A Rating by 75 Historians," *New York Times Magazine* July 29, 1962, pp. 12–13ff. The two failures who cropped up on both the earlier rating as well as in 1962 were Ulysses S. Grant and Warren G. Harding. They will undoubtedly have to move over for a new arrival, the only president ever forced out of office.

34. Quoted in Schlesinger, "Our Presidents: A Rating by 75 Historians," p. 12.

35. For the response of one of our best American historians, see Thomas A. Bailey, *Presidential Greatness* (New York: Appleton-Century-Crofts, 1966).

36. How right John Vieg was in his observation that "The national chief executives who are least well remembered are precisely those who lacked the impulse or the capacity to be imaginative about their office. They tended to look upon their powers in narrowly legal terms or seemed unable to conceive of any higher public service than that of reducing the tax rate." In Fritz Morstein Marx (ed.), *Elements of Public Administration,* 1st ed. (Englewood Cliffs, N.J.: Prentice-Hall, 1946), p. 167.

Chapter 8
Politics and Survival

THE ADMINISTRATOR IN POLITICS[1]

A president announces his opposition to compulsory school busing on the threshold of a national election and garners more votes among the angered mothers of the northern middle class.[2]

A governor decides to ask the legislature to impose tuition on heretofore free schooling in the state's colleges and universities, antagonizing students but winning plaudits from harried taxpayers whose kids have completed their schooling.

A mayor wants to have the Winter Olympics held in his city, which hungers for the tourist dollar, and he is almost flattened by the resulting confrontation between skiers and environmentalists.

A school principal refuses to fire a music teacher who has slurred some unruly black students, and the school board swims helplessly against the riptide of minority rage for two months. And a secretary of agriculture, after making a racist joke, is removed from office.

A Bureau of Land Management range officer sticks to the rule book, curtails grazing on an overworked section of forestland, incurs the wrath of local stockmen, and protects the watershed from a devastating runoff the following spring. The public never hears about his tough stand; and he probably never realizes how deeply it involved him in the politics of administration.

Look at them all — distributing and withholding benefits, touching the raw

The Sagebrush Rebellion: Declaring War on the Bureau of Land Management

In 1979 the western cattlemen declared war on the federal Bureau of Land Management, custodian of 450 million acres of public land in the United States. The strident tone of the rebellion strongly suggested that the survival of some BLM agents, if not the agency itself, might be at stake. Here, a BLM summary of San Juan, Utah, County Commissioner Calvin Black's remarks at a public meeting in southeastern Utah, April 1979:

> We've had enough of you guys telling us what to do. I'm not a violent man, but I'm getting to the point where I'll blow up bridges, ruins, and vehicles.
>
> We're going to start a revolution. We're going to get back our lands. We're going to sabotage your vehicles. You had better start going out in twos and threes because we're going to take care of you BLMers.

A BLM agent asked if the county commissioner were threatening him. "I'm not threatening you, I'm promising you." he was told.

When confronted with the summary of the remarks, Black said he was really only reflecting what others had been saying, but "I did indicate that sometimes I got to feeling that way."

Joseph Bauman, "Cool off the Rhetoric over Environment," *Deseret News* (May 31, 1979), p. 6A.

nerve of race relations, affecting the power structure, altering the use of public resources, butting up against contentious pressure groups — all of these administrators are up to their ears in politics.

A New Kind of Fire for the Forest Service to Fight

Visualize the dilemma this political involvement poses for a very unsuspecting guy, the regional forester of region 1, U.S. Forest Service, in Missoula, Montana. This dedicated civil servant majored in forestry and range management at an agricultural college in Idaho, never took a political science course, entered the Forest Service through competitive examination sixteen years ago; since then he has operated most of the time under the assumption that politics was "someone else's fire to put out."

Then like lightning flashes over the Bitterroot range, politics ignites all around him:

Lumbermen come within an ax blade of getting a bill through Congress telling his agency to increase timber sales regardless of all other (i.e., environmental) considerations.

The timber lobby loses that one but wins another in requiring weekly reports on timber production from the national headquarters of the Forest Service.

Montana conservationists bitterly complain about clear-cutting (leaving wide-open swaths down a mountainside) in the Bitterroot, while ten days later lumber companies tell the forester they must have a permit to clear-cut.

Snowmobilers, bikers, backpackers, drive-and-park picnickers, cattlemen, miners, and woodcutters begin to chop each other up over access to the forests.

The forester decides to get some input via a public meeting and then watches it turn into a free-for-all fistfight.

Although visitor use is rising by 6 percent a year in the national forests, Congress imposes a 5 percent personnel cut and a 10 percent cut in summer positions in the Forest Service.

The forester scratches his head on learning that Congress has reduced Forest Service appropriations by $26 million while increasing the Park Service appropriations, in another department, by $16 million, and he begins to muse about the art of who gets what when.

Through a baptism by fire, this forester discovers he is in politics, and he had learned nothing in Agronomy 320 to help him cope with it.

It would be too much to say that every administrative decision is political. Changing the files from chronological to alphabetical, completing the quarterly report before starting an inventory, requesting an analysis of personnel turnover rates from the personnel office are not. But we are prepared to argue that every public administrator is immersed in a political world, a world that may seem neutral, if not invisible, to him. It is there, nevertheless, regularly supplying (or denying) sustenance, authority, restrictions and demands, periodic brickbats, and occasional praise.

James Anderson's map of that political environment suggests how encompassing it is (Figure 8.1). After some pain, the regional forester has begun to understand a good deal about that map. He almost never hears from the political parties, but he hears from interest groups at least weekly. As for the unorganized citizens out there, he maintains an abiding concern for their long-range good, their need for fiber and food and a place to unwind. One of his political headaches is to balance their rarely spoken needs with the strident demands of very vocal pressure groups who are constantly after him.

What about the inputs rising from the bottom of Anderson's chart? When the so-called oil shortage was triggered by the Organization of Petroleum Exporting Countries (OPEC) in 1973, the economic consequences seemingly were tele-

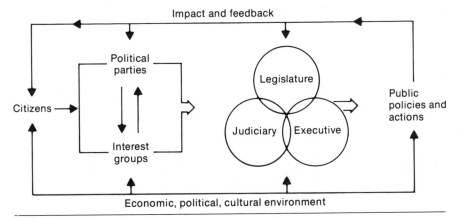

FIGURE 8.1   THE ECOLOGY OF ADMINISTRATION

From James E. Anderson, *Politics and the Economy*, p. 53. Copyright © 1966, Little, Brown and Company (Inc.). Adapted by permission of the author.

graphed to the forester: the cost of laying forest roads and of running timber-cutting and retrieval equipment began to rise astronomically. He could hardly believe that the politics of the Middle East could alter the economics of Montana so quickly.

As to the cultural-economic environment, the forester senses that he is a socialist manager of a public island (the national forest), surrounded by a sea of capitalists. That helps explain a bit more clearly why the private lumber companies so unabashedly press their demands on him.

When Congress begins to alter some of the basic statutes governing Forest Service management, the chief forester is painfully reminded of the legislative politics that so intimately affect his bureau and himself. What he never quite gets used to, however, is the wide array of masks politics can don to haunt him.

The Many Faces of Politics

"My streets superintendent is ticked because his is now the only office without a carpet." ("Politics is the science of who gets what when.") The Chicano ombudsman reports an uproar among his constituents because of police brutality at a La Raza dance last Saturday. ("Politics is the art of living peaceably together.") "The state legislature has once again refused us urban renewal authority to cope with our slums — something about 'The property right shall be inviolate in this state.' " ("Politics is the system whereby ends get defined, and means to accomplish them are obtained.")

The beleaguered mayor recognizes many faces of politics in city hall. Taking a closer look, he might discern at least six: his own world view of what is really important, politics of choice, keeping peace with legislative bodies, executive branch power struggles, clientele demands, and the grubbiest kind of all — in-house politics.

The administrator's world view   At the loftiest end of the political scale, perhaps, is the administrator's view on such fundamental questions as: "What will advance the public interest — a short-run gain or a long-run benefit?" and "Who is entitled to my highest loyalty?"

Notice some responses to those kinds of questions. At one point, Abraham Lincoln was willing to temporize on slavery if such a stand would save the Union. But later he would say, "A house divided against itself cannot stand."

Harry Truman felt it wise to end the Pacific war by means of two atomic bombs, oblivious, it seems, to the Pandora's box he was opening.

A basketball coach puts victory at any price ahead of ethics when he keeps his star forward on the team following the player's arrest and conviction for burglary and grand larceny in the student dorm. (The coach's rationalization revealed an interesting world view: "We can't throw this young man on the ash heap at this stage in his life.")

A Secretary of War Ruminates About Hiroshima and Nagasaki

What was the world view of the Secretary of War who recommended the dropping of the first atom bombs on Japan in August, 1945?

Henry L. Stimson, looking back in 1947:

> As I look back over the five years of my service as Secretary of War, I see too many stern and heart-rending decisions to be willing to pretend that war is anything else than what it is. The face of war is the face of death; death is an inevitable part of every order that a wartime leader gives. The decision to use the atomic bomb was a decision that brought death to over a hundred thousand Japanese. No explanation can change that fact and I do not wish to gloss it over. But this deliberate, premeditated destruction was our least abhorrent choice. The destruction of Hiroshima and Nagasaki put an end to the Japanese war. It stopped the fire raids, and the strangling blockade; it ended the ghastly specter of a clash of great land armies. . . .

> [The bombs] made it wholly clear that we must never have another war. This is the lesson men and leaders everywhere must learn, and I believe that when they learn it they will find a way to lasting peace. There is no other choice.

Henry L. Stimson and McGeorge Bundy, *On Active Service in Peace and War* (New York: Harper & Row, 1947).

Consider one other balancer of values: an IRS employee who decided, in spite of the law, that it was the people's business to know that Richard Nixon was paying almost no federal income taxes and divulged that information to reporters.

What one's world view may initially be is a philosophical concern, but the answer ultimately triggers political behavior.*

The politics of choice   The decision "to allocate X dollars to Activity A instead of Activity B" (in V. O. Key's phraseology) may rest upon careful fact finding and cost/benefit analysis; but more often than not, politics will heavily influence the choice:

"New York gave me 41 electoral votes; California did not — the shipbuilding contract goes to the Brooklyn Navy Yard."

"Texas gets the TFX contract — my home state."

"I voted for Representative Kirwan's 'fishbowl' [an aquarium for the District of Columbia] so he would support reclamation dams on the Snake River."

Choosing, when it means distributing scarce benefits among rival contenders, is deeply political, and administrators have to do it all the time: Ask the city council for more golf courses or for more tennis courts? More school dollars for Central City or for suburbia? Recommend to Congress a cut in corporate taxes or in withholding taxes? It is a *political* hand that holds the razor to cut those slices. (How those choices are made is the subject of the following chapter on decision making.)

Legislative politics   As James Anderson's chart clearly portrays, the nexus between legislature and executive is ultraclose. The legislature gives, and the legislature takes away.

At the end of one session of the legislature, the commissioner of higher education and four university presidents couldn't believe what had happened to them. The lawmakers required that every college student take a course in United States institutions (and provided no additional funds to staff ten sections per quarter of Political Science 110), raised tuition, transferred 7 percent of the higher education budget to vocational education, and imposed a loyalty oath on the teaching staff. Instead of concluding that "We're in politics," these educational administrators probably said, "We're really out of it."

At all levels of government, administrators cast a wary eye at Capitol Hill, hoping that the lawmakers will make the sun rise on their agency and set on someone else's. The administrators' "Agenda of Anxieties" has many entries; obtaining the legislative authorizations and appropriations that are needed,

---

* One might reflect how all of this was revealed in the lives and crises of Louis Glavis (Interior Department), Billy Mitchell (U.S. Army), Daniel Ellsberg (Defense Department), and Elliot Richardson and William Ruckelshaus (Justice Department), many of whom we will revisit in Chapter 18.

escaping a full-fledged investigation, and avoiding a hearing to prove the need for their continued existence under the state's sunset law.

The would-be administrator should take some encouragement from the numerous cases in American history where agency heads have successfully swum in the sea of legislative politics over long periods of time: Army Secretary Robert T. Stevens against the tide of Senator Joseph McCarthy in the 1950s; the National Aeronautics and Space Administration, in obtaining ample appropriations to land men on the moon a year ahead of schedule in 1969; and Allen "Scotty" Campbell, then chairman of Carter's Civil Service Commission, in winning congressional approval of the first major reorganization of the federal government's personnel system since 1883.

Executive branch politics Winning and holding a place in the sun in the executive branch can be as challenging as preserving one's hide with the legislature. One of the reasons is that few chief executives are patsies; they intend to have their will carried out.

So the navy gets the jolt of the 1970s when ex-navy man Jimmy Carter vetoes funds for an additional nuclear carrier.[3] A department of community affairs at the state level, riddled with dissension, gets its comeuppance from an unhappy governor by being merged with the department of development services. And a Dallas mayor, frustrated by the foot-dragging of the city manager, dumps rain on the latter until he resigns, the victim of his own inability to manage executive branch politics.[4]

Administrators' political concerns about their own branch of government also focus on central staff agencies that have a lot to say about budget and personnel allocations. One of the most painful examples of this kind of executive branch politics involved White House and Bureau of the Budget (BOB) pressure on the Interior Department to relent and let the Union Oil Company have a lease for oil exploration in Santa Barbara Harbor. Lyndon Johnson and the BOB's world view was short-range enough. They yearned for $500 million in oil-lease payments to help balance the fiscal 1969 budget. Within a few short months after the lease was granted, Union Oil crews ruptured the thin shell under the harbor, and 3 million gallons of oil surfaced, contaminating the beaches and wildlife in the area. Presidential politics had worn down the far-sighted environmental concerns of a line department.[5]

In similar fashion, presidential politics in the Nixon administration bent the U.S. Civil Service Commission into a position of wholesale violations of the federal merit system from 1969 to 1973.[6] Executive branch politics also takes other forms, such as interagency rivalry. There have been numerous "battles of the Potomac" over time: interservice competition over America's rocketry and outer space programs; the running contest between the old U.S. Civil Service Commission and the Office of Management and Budget over position management (who should control the number of "job slots" each agency in the executive branch is entitled to?); and the often tense relations between the president's national security adviser (in the White House) and the secretary of state.

Those kinds of contest understandably put wary administrators into a posture of agency self-defense and lead many of them to try the karate techniques of realpolitik, which we describe later in this chapter.

Clientele politics This ranges all the way from citizen requests for a four-way stop sign at a dangerous intersection to outright vetoes on agency activities and thoroughgoing co-optation of regulatory agencies by the industries they are supposed to be regulating.

Let's note some examples. Veto behavior was apparent during the Indian occupancy of the offices of the Bureau of Indian Affairs during 1972. (The bureau might have preferred to deal with Sitting Bull.)

The Environmental Protection administrator knew precisely what and who would hit him when he hinted at outlawing the operation of automobiles in Los Angeles — a citizen uproar.

One of the clearest cases in the literature of this kind of clientele politics concerns the frustrated hopes of the New York state legislature of bringing about increased hirings of blacks on state construction projects. The legislature had passed three significant Equal Employment Opportunity (EEO) statutes and maintained five separate enforcement agencies. But essentially it was all for naught. The white construction trade unions kept the blacks out, and none of the five state agencies dared to challenge them.[7]

Then there is a kind of client cannibalism, whereby the regulatees have co-opted the regulators. The pattern stretches from the Interstate Commerce Commission and the old Federal Power Commission at the national level to the utility-regulating bodies in state government. The politics in these cases seems to amount to how *not* to be eaten up.[8]

In-house politics This is the last of the six faces of politics and may be the one the administrator would most like to escape. It can best be described as the art of one-upmanship on your co-workers. The games are nastier versions of Monopoly and others of that kind. The issues are not "Boardwalk" but who gets the larger office with windows; not "Park Place" but who occupies an office in the governor's suite rather than one or two floors down.

Who gets two weeks' official leave for the training course at the management center at Kings Point? Who will get the division chief's job, and who will be passed over? Who has the boss' ear? Must one be a Freemason to advance in the Bureau of Ships? Was Kate Millett's book *Sexual Politics* a manual on how to make it in the office?

Frankly, those are crummy politics: self-serving, acquisitive, sexist, and bigoted. Yet they clearly permeate the pursuit of who gets what and when. One of the saddest features of this sixth face is that the more time the administrator has to spend mediating in-house games, the less time she has for political management in those arenas where the stakes are critical.

COSTS AND BENEFITS OF POLITICS IN ADMINISTRATION

Political Pain

Clearly, there are some costs. William Morrow points to one when he suggests that "there is such a thing as [an administrator] being too responsive."[9] That kind of administrator listens to so many voices that he becomes immobilized.

We had a gracious mayor like that in our town years ago; they told cruel jokes about him: "Mayor, what time is it?" Looking at his watch, the mayor replied, "What time would you like it to be?"

"Mayor, what's your favorite color?" "Plaid," His Honor replied.

Administrators like this, always counting heads and not wanting to break any, too frequently turn out to be of the opinion of the last person they talked to. There is no buck-stopping here, only buck-passing. That is not leadership; it is not administration. It *is* unsuccessful political management.

A second cost of politics in administration is its diversionary effect. It takes you away too long from your program responsibilities to put out political fires. Your staff in region 1 of the Forest Service are desperate for a decision on Weyerhaeuser Lumber Company's request for clear-cutting, but you're away being nice to the Montana congressional delegation.

One thinks of some administrative tragedies that have stemmed from this kind of sidetracking. One was the missed opportunity of the Voice of America (VOA) in February 1953 to stage a propaganda coup with the Czechs because Secretary of State John Foster Dulles was trying to placate Wisconsin Senator Joseph McCarthy. The Voice of America wanted to quote back to the Czechs on the fifth anniversary of the Communist takeover of their country the promises the Communists had made in 1948 and then let the Czech listeners be the judges. But McCarthy had railed against "Communist material being used by the Voice," and Dulles folded.

Clientele politics and legislative politics may require that we scatter our resources to placate many rather than concentrate resources significantly to help a few. Some federal aid programs have failed on that score.

Putting us on the defensive and leading us toward unethical practices must also be chalked up among the costs of inadequately insulating administration from politics. Some CIA directors come to mind in this connection.

A Look at the Benefits

In a democratic society, we always need to be asking of administration: "Is anybody listening?" and "Is someone accountable?" Politics forces those questions to the front burner.

Holding Them Accountable, British-Style

Accountability of the executive to the legislative branch is the essence of the parliamentary system. In all the annals of British government, it may never have been more powerfully demonstrated than in the House of Commons in early May 1940, with the demand for Prime Minister Neville Chamberlain's resignation after the fall of Norway. Winston Churchill's account (paraphrased in part):

Chamberlain was taunted by members on all sides. Said Conservative M. P. Amery, quoting Cromwell's words to the Long Parliament: "You have sat too long here for any good you have been doing. Depart, I say, and let us have done with you. In the name of God, go!"

On the eighth of May, what had started out as a debate on an adjournment motion assumed the character of a vote of censure. Here Mr. Lloyd George, former Conservative Prime Minister, expressed himself sharply to Chamberlain: "It is not a question of who are the Prime Minister's friends. It is a far bigger issue. He has appealed for sacrifice. The nation is prepared for every sacrifice so long as it has leadership, so long as the Government show clearly what they are aiming at, and so long as the nation is confident that those who are leading it are doing their best. . . . I say so solemnly that the Prime Minister should give an example of sacrifice, because there is nothing which can contribute more to victory in this war than that he should sacrifice the seals of office."

Although Chamberlain carried the adjournment vote, it constituted in Churchill's phrase "a violent manifestation of want of confidence in Mr. Chamberlain and his administration," and he then resigned.

Winston Churchill, *The Gathering Storm* (Boston: Houghton Mifflin, 1948), pp. 659–660.

For example, look at two superbly calculated moves of twentieth-century presidents to steal a voting bloc from the opposite party: FDR's advocacy of social security in 1935 to bring the older population from their Republican mooring over to the Democrats, and Richard Nixon's abortive proposals in 1970 for an income maintenance plan that might help woo lower-income groups away from the Democratic party. Whatever their motives may have been, politics forced the two presidents to listen to the complaints of millions of citizens. Some think they needed to be heard.

As to accountability (which we address in Chapter 18), politics can be a tough taskmaster: the congressional investigations of corruption in the Harding and Truman years, Senator Sam Ervin's special committee hearings on Watergate, and ultimately the removal of Richard Nixon from office in 1974 — all these suggest that the political system was providing answers to the question, "Is someone accountable?"

Seen in this light, politics seems to have a lot to do with two fundamental Jeffersonian concepts: the government should be the servant of the people, and it should be removable if it violates its trust.

Neutering Administration

There are many who do not endorse that kind of balancing and who work overtime to take administration away — far away — from politics. Those moves have included some significant developments in American public administration: the council-manager system in city government to provide professional nonpolitical management of urban affairs; the extension of the merit system upward, outward, and downward, followed by the Hatch Acts (1939–1940) to keep civil servants unsullied from partisan politics; and independent regulatory commissions with bipartisan membership.

While I readily admit to much good in some of these experiments, I must dissent from the general proposition that administrators should be removed and insulated from politics. As George Bernard Shaw said, "You can have politics and politicians without democracy, but you cannot have democracy without politics and politicians." Is anybody listening? Is someone accountable?

Letting the Environment Slip Away

One of the great dangers in diminishing the political management role of the administrator is the risk that he will lose his grip on the surrounding world and thereby lose his ability to read the signals it is trying to flash to him (see Figure 8.1).

What happens at that interface between agency and environment when one gets significantly away from the other? The result is an unstable political equilibrium that begs for correction.[10] When Nixon saw the Interior Department suing his oil company campaign contributors for their oil spills and his interior secretary, Walter Hickel, siding with the young in their antiwar protests, he fired Hickel and all the top leadership of the department.

What our illustration and others like it suggest is that the color of administration cannot differ very long from that of the surrounding, dominating environment. What may be fundamentally at stake here is agency, or administrator, survival.

ADMINISTRATIVE SURVIVAL

Alchemy or Good Works?

Staying alive politically demands some chemistry that some administrators possess but not many fully understand. It embraces a kind of intuitive skill to understand the pressures from outside which must be dealt with, and those that can be ignored. It's the ability to read a key congressman's most sensitive points, and then respect them. It is a masterful sense of timing (as we discuss below). When truckers are blockading the highways, protesting speed limits and diesel shortages, or state employees are on strike, you become painfully aware that alchemy has given you the wrong potion.

For other administrators, good works may be the ticket to staying alive. School superintendents who restore racial peace in a city's high schools are retained by an anxious school board. A governor, to the end of his term, holds on to a state budget director whose revenue projections have been uncannily accurate. Delivering the goods in its best sense protected the hides of these successful operators against the countervailing forces of politics that have wounded so many others.

In addition to these approaches, some others can be suggested for the political struggles most administrators face. They include a set of heuristics (operating rules, often intuitively discovered) for managing politicians; agency outputs that influence the environment; and the techniques of realpolitik.

On the Art of Managing Politicians

Rarely is a supportive political environment the result either of chance or of good works alone. Show me that environment, and I will show you an administrator with political savvy.

From the diaries of those administrators who have successfully mastered the political world around them, we can extract heuristics such as these:

When one blustering congressman has you down, others can be found who can render help.

The collective judgment of Congress, or the state legislature, is normally better than that of one of its members.

Keep the congressman informed — he thrives on being in the know.

Respond with speed and accuracy to his information requests.[11]

The red-carpet treatment is welcomed by most politicians.

Notify the congressman when you have summer jobs to fill that are not subject to civil service rules.

When you must lower the boom on one of his constituents, let the congressman know the reasons for the action.

Treat his constituents with kindness and dignity; they are his and your reason for existence.

Give pressure groups a fair hearing; they often know where the shoe pinches.

Bring a number of pressure groups into a citizen advisory board, remembering that involvement may lead to commitment.

In coping with an obnoxious pressure group, feed information to a group on your side and let them carry the fight (the countertrump in realpolitik).

Agency Outputs

Agencies dish out as well as receive from their political environments, a fact that gives an administrator some leverage in altering the environment. The levers include, among others, the regulation, encouragement, and prohibition of activities, and the distribution and withholding of benefits. Within limits, the administrator can play politics with all of these.

An administration that has been bought looks the other way at a corporate merger violating the Clayton Act (1914), tips off favored grain dealers about a lush wheat sale to Russia, raises the support level for dairy products, and refuses to impose tough flammability standards on favored carpet manufacturers who have contributed generously to the president's reelection campaign.

Or a city commission can deny a park permit to a New Left group for a "Festival of Light." The Kansas City elections clerk can refuse permission to the National Movement for the Student Vote to allow roving registrars into the city ("who would only scare up opposition voters").

We can time our news releases to meet the press deadline of the newspaper that believes in us. We can woo support in rural areas of the state by having our road crews extend the tar a foot or two into the adjoining private driveways. And we can mend some fences with minority neighborhoods by recruiting some of their numbers for the police force, fire department, and other agencies.

What we do may have much more impact on our political environment — and on our survival — than *what we say.*

THE ART OF REALPOLITIK

Those Dangerous Woods

Four important pages of advice for the administrator in the *Public Administration Review* a few years ago were prefaced by this observation about "administration in the raw":

Only in pure theory is the *implementation* of governmental policy the sole concern of the administrator. From his point of view, the administrative structure is also the scene of an unending and sometimes desperate battle for personal survival, power, and prestige. In large part, his career depends upon his skill at the game of bureaucratic realpolitik, i.e., his mastery of the administrative version of "who gets what, when, and how" [emphasis added].[12]

Consider, for example, the president of a state university making annual preparation for the who-gets-what struggle at the legislature. The perennial foe was the agricultural college, whose president was a past master in corralling important state legislators by organizing and then serving key groups in their constituencies. But the crisis during this particular year stemmed from a different sector of the woods — an adroit power play by an ambitious president of a church school located in a different community to keep ahead of the state university in a silly "enrollment derby."

Within a day or two of the state university's budget submission to the legislature, President Pontifex of the church school announced that the church would build a junior college in the same community as the state university. The meaning was clear to everyone. The state university's budget requests, based on projections of large freshman and sophomore classes, could now be materially pared down. Those freshmen and sophomores could attend a non-tax-supported institution. As president of the state university, how would you fend off this invasion?

The struggle just described was over funds and students. But there are other targets that invite clash in the administrative woods: *over authority and agency mission* (the air force versus a civilian space agency over outer space exploration during the 1960s); *over personnel* (the competition for physicists and engineers during the same decade); and *over policies* (aid Israel and lose Arab oil?).

At the personal and sometimes petty level, one also may get the feeling that the woods are full of enemies. The struggle to hold on to your job, the campaign to win a promotion, and the hunger for a little personal glory are but a few of the commonplace occurrences in the realpolitik of the civil servant at whatever level. Beyond that, regrettably, realpolitik seems to be the name of the administrative game everywhere, in both public and private enterprise.

Who are the enemies that transform the clean, professional administrative world into a jungle of rapacious infighters? Albert Somit lists the unappreciative superior, the troublesome rival, and the overambitious subordinate. Others include the hostile congressional committee, the unsympathetic Congress, the jaundiced examiners from OMB, the inspector general's detectives, the penny pinchers from the GAO, the hostile editor, and the citizen pressure group that has singled out your agency for attack.

In the face of such lurking dangers, administrators everywhere have developed an array of weapons for personal or agency defense. Together they constitute the armory of realpolitik,

The Overtrump

In a game of bridge, you never worry very much about the king held by your opponent on your left, when the ace is in the dummy's hand across from you. So in administration, access to your boss promises security and reassurance that the heat from your immediate superior will never become unbearable. An OMB director would have a tough time chopping the budget of the Justice Department when the attorney general is a long-time crony of the president.

The Outside Trump

The shortest distance between two points in politics — and administration — may be a curved line. As we saw in Chapter 5, an influence map of an agency has lines running right off the organization chart. Somewhere on those external lines lie the outside trumps that can be used to spur or to checkmate.

Consider an example from private life: the We Stand By You Insurance Company has refused to pay your claim for an internal engine explosion that has wrecked your car. When it is satisfied that your father and brothers are prepared to cancel their insurance policies on their cars and office building with the company, it sees things differently and pays your claim — you have played the outside trump.

As a deputy in the Office of Price Administration (OPA), you are furious that your superiors are knuckling under to the housing lobby in unfreezing rents from wartime rent control. The chain of command is of no use to you. But a well-planted word in the ear of the head of the United Steelworkers of America does the trick: the word goes from an OPA underling to a powerful union leader to the White House and then back to the OPA, and the rent order is killed.

Similar use of the outside trump was evident in the fight over the B-70 bomber. The craft, strongly recommended by the air force, encountered turbulent winds in the upper echelons of the Defense Department — one might even say a destructive downdraft from Secretary of Defense Robert McNamara.

But the air force is not so easily grounded. Information was fed to an outside trump of no mean proportions, Representative Carl Vinson, chairman of the House Armed Services Committee. A merry fight lasting for months then ensued between the secretary of defense and the committee chairman over air force weaponry. But the outside trump failed to carry the day, and the B-70 never joined the air force.

The Countertrump

This weapon requires leverage that can persuade a rival to do your bidding. It was well illustrated to me when a U.S. Civil Service Commission training director asked me a few years ago, "What secretary do you think has the highest job classification in the Denver region?" "Dunno." "A GS-9 with the General Ser-

THE ART OF REALPOLITIK

Slipping a Memo to Jack Anderson

In 1970, International Telephone and Telegraph (ITT) encountered some resistance from the Nixon Justice Department over their proposed acquisition of the nation's fifth largest insurance company, Hartford. ITT's president, Harold Geneen, offered to underwrite the 1972 national convention of the Republican Party in San Diego to the tune of $400,000. Then in February 1972 someone, perhaps in ITT or the Justice Department, leaked an internal memo from ITT's lobbyist, Dita Beard, to newspaper columnist Jack Anderson:

> Other than permitting [Attorney General] John Mitchell, [Lt. Governor of California] Ed Reinecke, Bob Haldeman, and Nixon. . . . no one has known from whom the 400 hundred thousand commitment had come. I am convinced . . . that our noble commitment has gone a long way toward our negotiations on the mergers eventually coming out as Hal [Geneen] wants them. Certainly the President has told Mitchell to see that things are worked out fairly. . . .
>
> I hope, dear Bill, that all of this can be reconciled . . . if all of us in this office remain totally ignorant of any commitment ITT has made to anyone. If it gets too much publicity, you can believe our negotiations with Justice [over Hartford] will wind up shot down. Mitchell is definitely helping us, but it cannot be known.
>
> Please destroy this, huh?

It was an explosive use of the outside trump — but it didn't quite work. The deal struck finally forced ITT to give up five subsidiaries but permitted the acquisition of Hartford to proceed.

Lewis Chester, et al., *Watergate: The Full Inside Story* (New York: Ballantine Books, 1973), chap. 12.

---

vices Administration," he replied. "How so?" I asked. "Because they control our space, we take care of their secretaries." GSA leverage had engineered a comfortable quid pro quo.

The Memorandum as an Offensive and Defensive Weapon

From city hall to the White House, administrators discover early in their careers the utility of the memorandum in fighting their battles for survival. Consider first the case of a city health commissioner, pinched by a tight budget corset, who starts to scratch for additional revenues (or fewer outlays). He hits upon the idea of asking the school board to pick up the tab for the school nurse program, which until now has come out of the health department's budget.

The school board turns him down. This wily administrator, as smart in politics as he is in medicine, turns to the memorandum as his first line of offense.

Writing to the local PTA presidents, the health commissioner reports that the school health program must be sacrificed because of pressing demands upon his budget and the intransigent attitude of the school board.

Within days the PTA membership mounts the ramparts. Letters and resolutions flow into the school offices; the board takes a second look at its coffers and finds the cash for the school health nurses. Here, a memorandum to an outside trump did the trick.

As a defensive weapon, the memorandum may ask questions, request information, give evasive answers, chart blind alleys for an interloper to pursue, or thoroughly stack the deck that is about to be passed to the decision maker. David Halberstam suggests that one of the best and brightest of the Kennedy and Johnson administrations, McGeorge ("Mac") Bundy was a past master at deck-stacking via the memorandum:

> Mac was a terrific memo writer, facile, brief and incisive. It was not, as publication of documents would later prove, exactly something which would make the literary world envious, but to be a good memo writer in government was a very real form of power. Suddenly everyone would be working off Bundy's memos, and thus his memos guided the action, guided what the President would see. For example, friends think that he killed the ill-conceived, ill-fated plan for a multilateral nuclear force, first by determining the crucial bit of evidence, and then by a memo. It was a major policy decision and it was done in typical Bundy fashion. He was against the MLF from the start, it jarred the cleanliness of his mind, and he bided his time as the evidence on the proposal came in; then he dispatched Richard Neustadt of Columbia to make a special investigation, knowing that Neustadt, a specialist in operational procedure, would be appalled by it, which Neustadt was, and thus Bundy summed up the case pro-MLF and anti-MLF, which left the MLF bleeding to death on the floor, speared, as it were, by a memo.[13]

Use of Committees for Delaying, Dodging, and Holding Actions

Many heads may be better than one for policymaking, but they are a whole lot better for policy stifling, especially when the many heads are institutionalized as a committee.

Assignment of a touchy matter to a committee seemingly has everything to commend it: the committee is ordinarily rational, consultative, and deliberative. It may in fact be so dedicated to these processes that it never generates action. Indeed, if all the committees in the world were laid end to end, they would never reach a conclusion — and if they were laid end to end, it might be a good thing.

While ordinarily the go-slow character of a committee is a much-lamented fault, in the art of administrative realpolitik it is perhaps the committee's greatest virtue. Note a possible application.

As deputy base commander of Fort Pershing, you have been directed by army authorities to launch an affirmative action program on the base. As a smart administrator, however, you don't restrict your reading to the official issuances that come down through channels. Both the daily papers and the *Congressional*

Determining the Coefficient of Inefficiency of Any Committee

C. Northcote Parkinson explained algebraically how committees are designed to prevent anything from happening. The formula, he said looks like this:

$$x = \frac{m^{\circ}(a-d)}{y + p\sqrt{b}}$$

Where m = the average number of members actually present; $^{\circ}$ = the number of members influenced by outside pressure groups; a = the average age of the members; d = the distance in centimeters between the two members who are seated farthest from each other; y = the number of years since the cabinet or committee was first formed; p = the patience of the chairman, as measured on the Peabody scale; b = the average blood pressure of the three oldest members, taken shortly before the time of meeting. Then x = the number of members effectively present at the moment when the efficient working of the cabinet or other committee has become manifestly impossible. This is the coefficient of inefficiency, and it is found to lie between 19.9 and 22.4. (The decimals represent partial attendance; those absent for a part of the meeting.)

C. Northcote Parkinson, *Parkinson's Law* (Boston: Houghton Mifflin, 1957), p. 43.

Record you occasionally see have already clued you in on the fact that a significant white backlash is reaching Congress. Furthermore, the tension mounts on your base with the rumor that some of the white soldiers on the base have organized a klavern of the Ku Klux Klan. Nevertheless, as an officer in the chain of command, you have an order to obey. Given this kind of a mine field to walk across, what should you do?

Why, hire a small staff and appoint a committee. They will constitute two entries on your first progress report without committing you or the army base to any line of action. Then, while waiting for the political smoke to clear, the committee can consume months in setting up internal organization, agenda planning, authorizing studies, reviewing drafts, hearing presentations (complete with flip-charts and other visual aids), and formulating alternative lines of action.

Safeguarded by the committee's busywork spread over time, you should be in a position to make a recommendation whenever pressed to do so by your superiors. In the meantime, that much-abused instrument, the committee, has saved you and Fort Pershing from precipitate action and embarrassment (should the "wrong side" win in the political struggle). But note the risks you are running with these delaying tactics: race relations continue to deteriorate, with the possible ultimate embarrassment awaiting you of an outbreak of violence on your post.

Jamming the Works with Red Tape

In Chapter 14, we'll take a look at a presidential device — impounding funds Congress has appropriated — as a means of preventing projects the president disapproves of from starting.

In 1974, Richard Nixon saw lots of handwriting on the wall, some of which, as Congress completed work on the congressional Budget and Impounding Control Act of 1974, told him that his impounding days were over. But, never without tricks, the master of them all in the art of realpolitik found a new way to prevent money from being spent on projects he disliked, such as highways and sewage treatment plants: tie up the agencies' requests for funds in the Office of Management and Budget's red tape.

The results were dramatic. From 1971 to 1974, OMB processing time for construction grants increased from 79 to 348 days. In one instance, OMB red tape reduced spending on a water pollution project over fifteen months to 4 percent of what Congress intended.[14]

The overall curtailment was as dramatic as that which used to be affected by outright impoundments. Within the first year of enactment of the clean water program, only $17.3 million of an authorized $5 billion had been spent. Red tape can tie spenders in knots.

Reorganization as Surgery

A loose-leaf version of red tape most governmental administrators must live with is the civil service rule book. The new administrator taking over an office especially feels the constraining effect of civil service, for she must live with a staff not of her own choosing. All of her future appointments will be largely restricted by the "Rule of Three" to the top three scorers on an examination.[15] Furthermore, she will have almost no power to dismiss unwanted employees.

But there is a sharp knife available to cut through such staff rigidities in the form of *removal by reorganization.* When an office is abolished people and jobs are eliminated, with their tenure and retention rights governing placement elsewhere. After the housecleaning, the function is reestablished under a new organizational name, and the administrator can build from scratch (within the limits of the "Rule of Three," however).

One of the clearest instances of reorganization for such a purpose occurred in Idaho some years ago. Disgruntled by the policies of the public utilities commission, the Idaho legislature abolished the commission one day, thus removing its total staff, and reestablished it on the following day.[16]

In short, reorganization is a sharp enough scalpel to eliminate an unwanted crew en masse.

At the federal level, a Court of Claims case of the early 1960s demonstrates the surgery via reorganization technique at work. In *Keener* v. *U.S.* (decided April 17, 1964), a GS-18 "super grader" charged that a departmental reorganization had been engineered for the specific purpose of removing him. The Court of Claims disagreed, holding that an otherwise lawful reorganization would not be rendered void by a subordinate purpose of removing an unwanted employee. "This secondary consideration was the source which spiced the roast, but added little to its nourishment."[17]

"If You Can't Lick 'Em . . ."

A classic rule of international politics has great applicability in administrative realpolitik as well — "If you can't lick 'em, join 'em." The principle was deftly applied by Adolf Hitler in August 1939. After nursing his Anti-Comintern Pact with Italy and Japan for some three years, he found that Russia not only had not disappeared but was threatening his schemes in Eastern Europe as well. Thus, in that fateful August, the emissary of the Anti-Cominterns journeyed to Moscow to sign an accord with the central Comintern power, the USSR. That pact enabled the Nazis to wield the butcher knife while the Communists held the fork in carving up Poland.[18]

In domestic politics, application of the principle can be seen in Franklin Roosevelt's attempted packing of a hostile Supreme Court in 1937 (until the switch in time of Mr. Justice Roberts saved nine) and in the merger of the AFL with the CIO in 1955.

In an administrative context, joining those you can't lick might be the appropriate tactic to use in dealing with the advent of centralized purchasing in an agency. Rather suddenly, line operators find themselves subjected to the decisions of a central purchasing officer. But all is not lost: they succeed both in establishing a purchasing advisory committee and in having their representatives appointed to the committee (to advise, if not to checkmate, the new purchasing officer).

There was an element of this conquest-through-union principle in an ill-fated recommendation of a 1949 Hoover Commission task force.[19] Having reviewed the long, unsavory competition between the U.S. Army Corps of Engineers (flood control and power generation) and the Interior's Bureau of Reclamation (irrigation and power generation), the Natural Resources Task Force and the parent Hoover Commission recommended merging civil functions of the corps with those of the Bureau of Reclamation. But Congress has never accepted that kind of union for one of its most sacred cows, the Corps of Engineers.

Changing Colors Without Commitment

One of Somit's tactics for administrative self-defense calls for "avoiding a stand on an issue until the winning side emerges, while, at the same time, conveying to all disputants the impression of unwavering loyalty and support."[20]

We don't know the life expectancy of the chameleon or other animals that can adapt their body color to the background, but we surmise that it must exceed, on a comparative basis, that of nonadaptive animals. Now, the chameleon is not known as one of the braver beasts — being perhaps more like Machiavelli's fox than his lion — but its longevity is remarkable.

That may be the ultimate value for many in government service as well. Floating downwind, as this tactic of avoidance calls for, may not be as easy as one might first think. The man who is of the opinion of the last opinion he heard, and is even afraid to express that, is an office leper that everyone shuns. How, then, to avoid taking stands until the victor is in sight without alienating the various sides requires extraordinary skill, a cleverly twisted mouth, and an ingenious vocabulary. Clearly, not everyone is so artful. The danger of playing both ends against the middle lies squarely in being caught there.

David Halberstam suggests that Defense Secretary Robert McNamara was adept at using this technique:

> He did not recommend bombing; he had checked first with the President, and the President was not ready for it. But he did not want to be in conflict with the Chiefs; so he recommended that they go ahead with the planning of what they wanted, concentrating on two particular types of bombing. The first would be a quick strike, to be launched within seventy-two hours, primarily in retaliation for specific guerrilla incidents. The second part was the real bombing program. This, unlike the other, would not be tit for tat; it would be ready to go on thirty days' notice, and it would be a major strike against the North's military and industrial centers. These would be sustained raids, in effect what Rostow had been talking about for more than three years. A real bombing program, the use of the threat of bombing to coerce Ho Chi Minh to de-escalate the war rather than lose his precious industrial base.

> McNamara made these recommendations officially on March 16, after checking how far the President wanted to go on the subject (which was that he wanted the study in the works, that and nothing more; he wanted his options open).[21]

What is called for is a set of superb antennas, good staff work, having all sides prepared, and a clairvoyant sense of timing — and you come up a smiling chameleon.

Timing

The politician's shrewd sense of when to *speak,* when to *listen,* and when to *duck* is equally essential for the administrator's self-defense. As Shakespeare observed so long ago:

> There is a tide in the affairs of men,
> Which, taken at the flood, leads on to fortune;
> Omitted, all the voyage of their life
> Is bound in shallows and in miseries. . . .
> . . . we must take the current when it serves,
> Or lose our ventures.[22]

The administrator can just as easily lose her ventures if she has no sense of timing.

On occasion, the time factor may be as plain as what the clock watchers watch: a deadline fixed by statute, a forthcoming election, or the opening of Congress. Here the administrator doesn't need so much of a sixth sense to foresee a deadline as she needs the somewhat less occult power of how to get ready for it.

Such was the situation confronting the surplus property administrator, W. Stuart Symington, in 1945. In order to break the Aluminum Company of America's leases on government-built plants, he had to act while the plants as a whole were operating below 40 percent of capacity. Alcoa had indicated it would dispose of its lowest-producing plants by August 31, 1946, boosting productivity for the remaining plants above the statutory minimum. Thus, August 31 became a veritable D day for Symington. He did meet the deadline and broke the leases.[23]

November elections can be put to fine administrative use, realpolitik style. Just before the 1958 congressional elections, for example, Eisenhower's Agriculture Department rushed gasoline tax rebate checks to farmers for their off-highway use of farm vehicles. It was a larger operation than that of the old-time ward heeler who handed the voters a buck as they queued up outside the polling place, but the aim was the same.

The Kennedy administration engineered a double take four years later. The administration was able to get two statutes out of Congress, one raising postal salaries just before the 1962 election day, and the other raising postal rates two months after the votes had been counted.

For realpolitik, the implications of timing failures may be as convincing as timing successes. One recalls that great snafu in American foreign policy in May 1960, the U-2 incident. With President Eisenhower slated to go to Paris for a summit conference within a matter of weeks, the CIA, with no sense of either timing or gambler's odds, permitted overflights to continue above Russian territory. In that timing blunder the CIA saw shot down in rapid-fire succession the pilot, his high-flying craft, America's image abroad, Eisenhower's credibility, the summit conference, and the Republican ticket the following November.

It would seem that in the practice of administrative realpolitik *timing* has all the potential of a time bomb.

Invasion

The tactic of invasion is as bold a stroke in administration as it is in warfare. Sometimes merely the fumbling outgrowth of empire building, invasion of the kind contemplated here is a bald power play to fend off rival agencies, capture their programs, or eliminate their support.

Edwin O'Connor graphically describes how New Deal welfare programs invaded a preserve of county and municipal governments in the late 1930s and the 1940s. The net effect was to undercut a principal base of local political machines — welfare handouts.[24]

In the rivalry that prevails among many state institutions of higher learning, invasion becomes almost a stock-in-trade. The agricultural college spoken of earlier in this chapter modestly adopts as its motto, "The *state* is our campus." Its extension agents and home demonstration agents provide many community services, thereby building up goodwill the college can draw on when the rural legislators arrive at the state capitol each year.

Having taken their knocks from their country cousins too long, the state university decides to move, invasion style, into the base of rural support of the agricultural college. It does so, after an intensive struggle, with a wide-ranging community development program that takes state university officials and faculty members all over the state.

Administrative invasion requires many of the same ingredients needed for success in military operations. Strategic planning is essential: "Who is the enemy?" "Where are his defenses the weakest?" "What is the right timing?" Lines of support must be charted. "Will a move on our part into his territory extend beyond the reach of our support in public opinion or the legislature?" "Have we the resources to carry out the invasion successfully?"

Of supreme importance is the *ability to decide* to go ahead. The invasion tactic carries great risks. When the strategic analysis is over, the administrator must artfully combine prudence and daring, the fox and the lion: invasion cannot be executed with halfhearted measures. The boldness required in the decision making, plus the ethical questions involved, largely explain why invasion is among the rarer techniques of administrative realpolitik.

Dirty Tricks

Although Watergate and the 1972 election added the phrase "dirty tricks" to our lexicon, those events certainly did not invent them. I suppose the reason is that one's inhumanity to another goes all the way back to the Garden of Eden.

When administrators are sure they are right, when the stakes are high but the obstacles portend defeat, then a law of strategy takes over in which success conquers ethics:

Presidents Kennedy, Johnson, and Nixon put the FBI on the trail of their congressional critics and then unlawfully distributed the files around the executive branch to discredit congressmen and senators.[25]

The CIA authored a book about China and then arranged to have a CIA agent give it a favorable review in the *New York Times.*

The CIA opened a quarter of a million stateside letters between 1953 and 1973.

The National Security Agency intercepted perhaps a million telegrams going abroad.

The Post Office Department willingly imposed mail covers on citizens at the request of investigative agencies.

But the most inventive genius of them all in the dirty-tricks business must have been J. Edgar Hoover of the FBI. Just look at his record:

Establishing the Cointelpro (Counterintelligence Program) to disrupt left-wing, antiwar student groups and others: sending anonymous letters to the parents of the students to put heat on the "radical brats"; anonymous letters to spouses of the radicals, alleging indiscretions, to destroy marriages; anonymous letters criticizing political positions to get students fired from their jobs; and egging on a Chicago street gang to go after the Black Panthers.*

Authorizing endless burglaries and wiretaps without court orders, in blatant violation of the Fourth Amendment and the Omnibus Crime Act of 1968.

Sending a note to Martin Luther King, Jr., whom Hoover hated, telling him of FBI tapes recording King's trysts with other women and *suggesting suicide* (my nomination for the ugliest trick in the annals of modern American government).[26]

It is tragic and ludicrous that Congress has named the FBI building on Pennsylvania Avenue after this man.

Fertilizing the Grass Roots

Administration can learn an important lesson from ward-level politics in the political arena. Party pros will testify that as many elections are won by year-round work in the precincts, tying the fortunes of the voters to that of the beneficent party, as are won by candidates and issues. The grass roots expresses itself on election day in voting a straight ticket, in gratitude for past favors or in anticipation of future ones.

Smart administrators recognize that. Even though they may be a good step

---

* One can't get out of his mind J. Edgar Hoover's often repeated disclaimer, "We are only an *investigative* agency."

removed from electioneering politics, they are an appendage of the political process and are ultimately dependent upon grass roots support. The hope is that the hand that fertilizes those roots can regularly harvest a crop of support.

The brands of fertilizer are legion. Three months before a state legislature meets, the president of the agricultural college and his chief aides climb aboard the college plane and launch their community tour around the state. At every hamlet the line is the same: "What Old Aggie can do for you."

The secretary of defense appoints a civilian advisory council of three or four hundred opinion molders from every section of the country. At least once a year these VIPs are brought to Washington for briefings on overall U.S. defense posture and on the posture of the Defense Department in particular (kneeling in prayer just before appropriations time).

Air base jets have alienated community support with their noisy flights over residential areas. The base commander applies some fertilizer in the form of permitting his fire trucks, helicopters, and ambulances to respond to mercy calls in the communities adjoining the base. Tours of the base are arranged for the Cub Scouts. Air force officers begin to join civic clubs in the towns ("if you can't lick 'em, join 'em"). A speakers' bureau is established to provide programs for the nearby luncheon meetings of the Rotary and Kiwanis clubs. These examples represent only a few of the fertilizers available to administrators to nurture the grass roots.

Propaganda and Censorship in Public Information Programs

In the art of self-defense, giving your opponent a dimly lit or fictitious image to shoot at may be an effective maneuver. Or opponents may be overawed if you make yourself out to be a giant. In an agency, either defense may be effected through the proper control of information leaving the agency.

The FBI is perhaps the best example of giant building through skillful use of public information programs. From "Gangbusters" in radio days to "I Led Three Lives" to "The FBI" on television, and from scores of books and speeches by J. Edgar Hoover and others, an eager public followed the string of FBI successes against John Dillinger, "Baby Face" Nelson, Ma Barker, the atom spies Julius and Ethel Rosenberg, and a bevy of kidnappers and bank robbers.

Operating in a sensational field with a sensational news sense, for awhile the FBI achieved a kind of untouchable status as the professional cop who could do no wrong. Thus, when Mr. Newbold Morris was hired as a grand inquisitor to investigate the Justice Department in the unhappy closing hours of the Truman administration, the FBI alone of the Justice Department's divisions was exempted from a searching questionnaire. When queried, Morris explained, "The FBI has been in operation thirty years and I have never heard even a breath of scandal involving it. The FBI's integrity is one of the backbones of our security."[27]

Telling It as
It Never Was — Nixon Style

Caught with his tapes down, Richard Nixon pushed the direct lie to its most unblushing limits during 1973–74 as the Watergate scandal unfolded. Here is but one sample of the President's resort to this form of realpolitik:

Nationwide broadcast of President Richard Nixon, August 15, 1973:

On May 22, I stated in very specific terms — and I state again to every one of you listening tonight — these facts: I had no prior knowledge of the Watergate break-in; I neither took part in nor knew about any of the subsequent cover-up activities; I neither authorized nor encouraged subordinates to engage in illegal or improper campaign tactics.

That was and that is the simple truth.

But that integrity got bent in ways that we've seen during the civil rights and antiwar disturbances of the late 1960s and early 1970s. FBI public relations could not save the agency's reputation forever, given what was happening beneath the surface.

Agencies also try to safeguard their positions by what they don't, as well as by what they do, say. When a group of inquiring senators arrives in Thailand to inspect the U.S. foreign aid program, realpolitik's standard operating procedure calls for a guided tour that is really guided.[28] The senators see the fertilizer plant and hospital built with American money but are steered away from native protest meetings, interviews with local critics, and over-fancy billets occupied by "ugly Americans."

In the 1950s, when Senator Joseph McCarthy wanted to probe the army's security files, a vexed President Eisenhower ordered a no-release policy on documents involved in the Army-McCarthy dispute.[29]

A decade later, another senator from a different state (New York Senator Kenneth Keating) functioned as a gadfly on the Kennedy administration's handling of the Cuban missile crisis. As a defense against his attacks, censorship reappeared with a new hue: "news management."

Watergate then produced the ultimate application of realpolitik in news management:[30] (a) Richard Nixon's lies to the American people that John Dean had thoroughly investigated the break-in of Democratic headquarters; (b) then the cover-up, by bribing defendants not to talk and having the CIA tell the FBI to bug off (instead of bugging in, for once), shredding documents, erasing some tapes and withholding others; and (c) finally submitting to the House Judiciary

(Impeachment) Committee an incredibly doctored volume — the White House's transcription of the tapes.[31]

How can we resist the object lesson of this incredible display of realpolitik? He who threw the boomerang got it in the head.

Dying Gracefully

There are times when all of Machiavelli's *fortuna* and *necessita* and all of Somit's realpolitik simply cannot save you. You have become persona non grata to your chief: Defense Secretary Lewis Johnson and price regulator Alan Valentine for Truman, Navy Secretary Korth for Kennedy, John Dean for Nixon, James Schlesinger for Ford, and Califano, Schlesinger, and company for Carter. Or the pressures simply demand your sacrifice — Sherman Adams, Eisenhower's chief of staff, after involvement in charges of influence peddling with the Federal Trade Commission; Walter Jenkins of LBJ's staff after an arrest on charges of homosexuality; and Spiro Agnew after he had become a household word as Richard Nixon's vice-president.

While it may seem a strange twist on the other rules of realpolitik, the guideline here is clear-cut: *die gracefully* — it may assure you a noble resurrection in mortality. The motto is an old one: we shall "live to fight again another day."

The ne plus ultra example of dying gracefully was the resignation of Dean Acheson as undersecretary of the treasury on November 15, 1933.[32] Having been appointed to the post only in the preceding May, Acheson keenly opposed a gold-buying program that President Roosevelt endorsed. Overruled and rebuked, Acheson wrote a warm and courteous letter of resignation to the president, stepping aside to assure the president freedom of choice in managing the nation's financial affairs and thanking him for having given him the chance to serve "in these stirring times."

At a White House swearing-in ceremony of his successor, the uninvited Acheson showed up and went over to thank the president for the opportunity of working with him. Roosevelt pulled Acheson into a seat and said, "I have been awfully angry with you, but you are a real sportsman." The president then promised him a "good letter in answer to yours" (which was never sent, apparently).

Better than a letter was the compliment that came to Acheson through the grapevine a number of years after his dismissal. In the passage of time, another Treasury Department official got the boot; but unlike Acheson, he sat down and wrote a feisty letter to the president. Roosevelt turned it over to his secretary with the instruction, "Return it to him and tell him to ask Dean Acheson how a gentleman resigns."[33]

Sweeter still was Acheson's ultimate resurrection. The same president who fired him in 1933 brought him back into the government as assistant secretary of state in December 1941. From there Acheson moved to undersecretary in 1945, authored the Marshall Plan (under Secretary George C. Marshall), and became Truman's secretary of state, serving from 1949 to 1953.

The moral of the story: if you don't smack your coffin lid down on the boss' fingers, you may come up smelling like a rose.

REALPOLITIK AND THE ETHICAL DILEMMA

In writing *The Prince* in 1513, Niccolò Machiavelli seemed very little concerned with the ethics of his prescriptions. Rather, he seemed to hold up a mirror for his Florentine master's self-look, "What must I do to rule successfully?"[34]

Such has been our concern to this point. Starting from a central fact of administrative life that survival is not assured and is worth fighting for, we have catalogued a number of devices administrators use to defend themselves. Few if any of the techniques would stand up under the applications of traditional ethical precepts ("If he asks for your coat, give him your cloak also"; "Do unto others as you would have them do unto you"). If there is any ethical foundation for the kinds of tactics we've been looking at, it may be found in a kind of means-end rationale, or "reason of agency": "We have the public interest at heart; whatever protects us protects the public interest."

That there may be a case for the ethically right way of conducting administrative life will be examined in Chapter 18, "The Ethics of Management."

SUMMARY

Public administrators are in politics, and despite the added headaches that brings, it is a good thing. Administration is not an island but a part of the whole, drawing from its surrounding environment the sentiments and demands of people, legislative support and oversight, and the watchful eye of the media, among many other political inputs.

Skillful administrators accept the political facts of their job, roll with them, and learn to manage their external portfolios along with their internal ones. Some administrators secure their place in the sun by employing the weaponry of realpolitik; others survive by the quality of service rendered and their mastery of the art of the care and feeding of both politicians and citizenry.

In the face of the tortuous path we've followed here, an old question comes back to haunt us: Would we all be better off if government had turned out as Frank Goodnow perceived it decades ago — politics *and* administration instead of politics *in* administration? Something cleaner, more scientific, more professional? Maybe — and maybe far less humane.

True, managing the politics of the Forest Service adds a new range of headaches to an administrator perhaps ill equipped to handle them. It would be so much easier simply to focus on timber cutting and reforestation. On the other hand, most administrators are not dealing with sissy stuff, with matters that don't count for much. Rather, they are on the razor's edge of controversy, umpiring, allocating, and controlling. In our kind of system, that spells *politics*, as much for the administrative as for the elected branch of government.

The governing charter for administrators is not one whit different from that for legislators. As our Declaration of Independence says, "To secure these rights, governments are instituted among men, deriving their just powers from the consent of the governed." Administrators who ignore that precept soon find themselves either in trouble or out of office. Indifference to the pinching shoe seems to invite the boot!

While at one end politics can so easily drift into favors and influence peddling, at the other end it transmits the deepest aspirations of a free people, reminding the government that it is their servant and not their master. That is why, in our kind of system, it is mandatory that administrators be subject to the forces of politics.

KEY CONCEPTS

ecology of administration
politics of choice
clientele politics
realpolitik

outside trump
counter trump
red tape
removal by reorganization

DISCUSSION QUESTIONS

1. In what different ways can the economic, political, and cultural environments influence the world of the administrator? Which environment is likely to have the most important influence on the administrator's decisions?

2. In what respects is there likely to be "overlapping" between legislative politics and clientele politics?

3. Many public administration theorists in the past have advocated a "neutral" administration, one free from politics. In what ways does politics cause "pain" to the administrator by interfering in the delivery of a service? In what ways is a neutral administration dangerous?

4. Analyze the realpolitik strategies:
    a. which is the most frequently used?
    b. which is the rarest?
    c. which is likely to produce the greatest benefits?
    d. which is the most dangerous?
    e. which is the most complex?
    f. which is your favorite?

Notes

1. As a start, see William L. Morrow, *Public Administration: Politics and the Political System* (New York: Random House, 1975); John R. Rehfuss, *Public Administration as Political Process* (New York: Scribner's, 1973); and Gordon Tullock, *The Politics of Democracy* (Washington, D.C.: Public Affairs Press, 1965).

2. The story of Nixon's tortuous ride on the school bus was carefully recounted by Max Frankel in the *New York Times* March 18, 1972, p. 14.

3. See "Carter Veto" in the *Congressional Quarterly Almanac, 1978* (Washington, D.C.: Congresssional Quarterly, 1979), pp. 336–341.

4. The story is told by Bruce Kovner in "The Resignation of Elgin Crull" in Richard J. Stillman (ed.), *Public Administration: Concepts and Cases* (Boston: Houghton Mifflin, 1976), pp. 222–226.

5. Morrow, *Public Administration,* pp. 68–69.

6. U.S. House of Representatives, Committee on Post Office and Civil Service, *Final Report on Violations and Abuses of Merit Principles in Federal Employment* (94th Congress, 2d Session, 1976) (Washington, D.C.: Government Printing Office, 1976).

7. Adam Walinsky et al., *Official Lawlessness in New York State (1969)* as excerpted in Theodore L. Becker and V. G. Murray, *Government Lawlessness in America* (New York: Oxford University Press, 1971), pp. 231–238.

8. See Murray J. Edelman, "The Administrative System as Symbol," in M. P. Smith (ed.), *American Politics and Public Policy* (New York: Random House, 1973), pp. 178–184.

9. Morrow, *Public Administration,* p. 34.

10. On "interface management," see particularly F. E. Emery and E. L. Trist, "The Causal Texture of Organizational Environments," *Human Relations* (Feb. 1965) 18:21–32; and Paul R. Lawrence and Jay W. Lorsch, "Organization-Environment Interface," in their text, *Developing Organizations: Diagnosis and Action* (Reading, Mass.: Addison-Wesley, 1969). The articles were reprinted in Jong S. Jun and W. B. Storm, *Tomorrow's Organizations* (Glenview, Ill.: Scott, Foresman, 1973), pp. 141–162.

11. As a case in point of how legislators typically react when lied to, see Winifred McCulloch, "The R.E.A. Personnel Report," in Harold Stein (ed.), *Public Administration and Policy Development* (New York: Harcourt, Brace, 1952), pp. 623–632.

12. Albert Somit, "Bureaucratic Realpolitik and Teaching of Administration," *Public Administration Review* (Autumn 1956) 16:292–295. We acknowledge our great debt to Professor Somit for many of the central ideas in this chapter.

13. David Halberstam, *The Best and the Brightest* (New York: Random House, 1972), pp. 61–62. The memorandum was well used by Abraham Lincoln in dealing with some questionable peace negotiations with the Confederates in which the president's critic, Horace Greeley, played a role. The meeting was to take place on the suspension bridge at the town of Niagara Falls, on the U.S.-Canadian border. Lincoln's memo, indicating a yearning for peace and readiness for serious discussion with duly authorized envoys from the Confederacy, left the New York newspaper editor up the falls without a bridge to stand on (should he accuse Lincoln of an unwillingness to negotiate). Carl Sandburg, *The Prairie Years and the War Years* (New York: Harcourt, Brace, 1954), pp. 532–534.

14. *Washington Post,* July 2, 1974, p. A2.

15. See Chapters 15 and 17 of this text.

16. Claude Burtenshaw, "The State: Cooperation or Contest," (Ph.D. diss., University of Utah, 1955), pp. 186–187.

17. As quoted in the *Civil Service Journal* (July–Sept., 1964) 5:10.

18. William L. Shirer, *The Rise and Fall of the Third Reich* (New York: Simon & Schuster, 1960), pp. 540–544.

19. U.S. Commission on the Organization of the Executive Branch of Government (hereinafter cited as I Hoover Commission), Natural Resources Task Force, *Organization and Policy in the Field of Natural Resources* (Washington, D.C.: Government Printing Office, 1949), pp. 28–31; and I Hoover Commission, *Reorganization of the Department of the Interior* (Washington, D.C.: Government Printing Office, 1949), pp. 26–35.

20. Somit, "Bureaucratic Realpolitik," p. 294.

21. Halberstam, *The Best and the Brightest,* p. 353.

22. *Julius Caesar,* Act IV, Scene III.

23. Harold Stein, "The Disposal of the Aluminum Plants," in *Public Administration and Policy Development,* pp. 331–332.

24. Edwin O'Connor, *The Last Hurrah* (Boston: Little, Brown, 1956), pp. 374–375.

25. *Facts-on-File,* March 8, 1975, pp. 139–140 (summarizing the testimony before the House Judiciary Constitutional Rights Subcommittee).

26. *Facts-on-File,* May 8, 1976, p. 330 (summarizing findings of Senator Frank Church's Senate Select Committee on Intelligence Activities of the 94th Congress).

27. Quoted in the editorial "Lèse Majesté," in the *Washington Post,* March 25, 1952.

28. See Thomas S. Loeber, *Foreign Aid: Our Tragic Experiment* (New York: Norton, 1961), pp. 60–61. For a hypothetical case, see Eugene Burdick and William J. Lederer, *The Ugly American* (New York: Norton, 1958), chap. 20.

29. "Eisenhower v. Congress," *U.S. News and World Report,* May 28, 1954, pp. 105–109.

30. The literature on Watergate is extensive, with books by such participants as Nixon, Magruder, Ehrlichman, Haldeman, Dean, E. Howard Hunt. Other perspectives are offered in books by Special Prosecutor Leon Jaworski and Judge John Sirica. We also recommend the *London Times* team book by Lewis Chester et al., *Watergate: The Full Inside Story* (New York: Ballantine Books, 1973); the *New York Times* paperback, *The Watergate Hearings* (New York: Bantam Books, 1973); and Carl Bernstein and Bob Woodward, *All the President's Men* (New York: Warner Books, 1975).

31. The White House version is known as, U.S. President, *Submission of Recorded Presidential Conversations to the Committee on the Judiciary, April 30, 1974* (Washington, D.C.: Government Printing Office, 1974). It should be contrasted with the House Judiciary Committee's version, U.S. House Judiciary Committee, *Transcripts of Eight Recorded Presidential Conversations* (93d Congress, 2d Session) (Washington, D.C.: Government Printing Office, 1974). For an equally painful analogue, see Halberstam's indictment of secrecy and lying in the Kennedy administration, *The Best and the Brightest,* pp. 407–411.

32. As retold in Dean Acheson's *Morning and Noon* (Boston: Houghton Mifflin, 1965), pp. 186–194.

33. Acheson, *Morning and Noon,* p. 194.

34. That the ethical problem may have disturbed him a bit is suggested by his short-hand prescription that "The end justifies the means," *The Prince* (New York: Modern Library, 1940), p. 66.

Chapter 9
Decision Making

CALL IT THE NEXUS

The point where politics and administration become politics in administration is decision making. It is at this juncture that the administrator finds himself testing the waters that surround his agency. He wonders, "Do I have the authority to do it?" and asks, "Can we bring it off?" It is here that he most resembles the legislature, exercising some quantum of quasi-legislative power as he resolves a dilemma, redirects his agency in the face of changed facts, or moves to implement a new mandate given him by Congress or his superiors in the executive branch. Decision making is not the be-all and end-all of administration that some have claimed it is; but when done well, it gives tone and meaning and direction to all other aspects of administration. Perhaps more than any other administrative challenge, it proves the mettle — or the rubber spine — of the administrator. A quick canvas of dilemmas confronting decision makers from presidents on down will suggest why.

We begin with some of the major decisions American presidents have had to make:

For John Adams, support France in the 1790s or ignore our treaty obligations and stay out of Napoleon's wars?

For Lincoln in the fall of 1862, respect "private property" or free the slaves?

For Woodrow Wilson in 1919, return to isolationism or commit America to the League of Nations?

For Franklin Roosevelt, close the banks, build the TVA, confront Adolf Hitler, form the United Nations?

For Harry Truman, drop the atom bomb, begin our involvement in French Indochina, save Berlin, recognize Israel, launch the Marshall Plan, defend South Korea, fire General MacArthur, seize the steel mills?

For John F. Kennedy, use force against Mississippi Governor Ross R. Barnett and compel the Russians to remove missiles from Cuba?

For Lyndon Johnson, the Great Society or a tragic war?

For Richard Nixon, reverse our foreign policy toward China and Russia, impose price-and-wage controls, expose or cover up the Watergate felonies?

For Gerald Ford, drop the speed limit to fifty-five miles per hour and face the truckers' wrath?

For Jimmy Carter, cut taxes to reduce unemployment or balance the budget in the fight against inflation, relinquish the Panama Canal, deregulate gas prices?

Any one of these would be an existentialist's field day; but the record of the American presidency is that any president worthy of his salt is faced with four or five such dilemmas during every term. And nothing so catches the imagination of the American people as when a president acts boldly, marshaling the full power of his office to send Lewis and Clark to the West, men to the moon, or himself to Gettysburg, Versailles, Casablanca, Berlin, Peking, Camp David, or Vienna.

The tensions and stakes surrounding some of the decisions state governors have to make can also be great:

How do I cope with a legitimate protest being staged on the Capitol grounds by families on welfare?

Do I ask for federal troops when Detroit is in flames in a racial conflagration?

Can I approve stiff fines on a nearby copper company — the state's largest private employer, the area's worst polluter, and a major contributor to my campaign chest?

Dare I veto a Sunday closing law in a state whose people are largely of fundamentalist faith?

Can I significantly shift the state's support away from higher education to vocational education?

Do I push for a coal-fired power plant that will create jobs and significantly pollute the air over three national parks?

CALL IT THE NEXUS   **189**

A President Acts

In September 1957 demonstrators around Central High School in Little Rock, Arkansas, disobeyed a U.S. district court order calling for the admission of black students. Governor Orval Faubus placed the Arkansas National Guard around the school, not to protect the black students from the mob but to prevent integration itself. President Dwight Eisenhower then moved, federalizing the Arkansas National Guard and flying in the tough 101st Airborne Division to carry out the court's order. The President said this in his television address on September 24, 1957:

> In that city, under the leadership of demagogic extremists, disorderly mobs have deliberately prevented the carrying out of proper orders from a federal court. Local authorities have not eliminated that violent opposition and, under the law, I yesterday issued a proclamation calling upon the mob to disperse.
>
> This morning the mob again gathered in front of the Central High School of Little Rock, obviously for the purpose of again preventing the carrying out of the court's order relating to the admission of Negro children to that school.
>
> Whenever normal agencies prove inadequate to the task and it becomes necessary for the executive branch of the federal government to use its powers and authority to uphold federal courts, the president's responsibility is inescapable.
>
> In accordance with that responsibility, I have today issued an Executive Order directing the use of troops under federal authority to aid in the execution of federal law at Little Rock, Arkansas. This became necessary when my proclamation of yesterday was not observed, and the obstruction of justice still continues.

Dwight D. Eisenhower, *Public Papers of the Presidents of the United States* (Washington, D.C.: Government Printing Office, 1958), p. 690.

Then look at the decision-making headaches mayors must sustain:

Kiss insularity good-bye and lead the fight for metropolitan government?

Move the widows from their homes and usher in urban renewal?

Take on the city employees union in a fight to achieve racial integration in city hall jobs?

Insist on competitive bids and offend local merchants?[1]

All of the foregoing are chief executive decisions. But we also need to ask what kinds of decisions have to be made by the great barons of bureaucracy, the bureau chiefs:

A police chief wrestles with shifting priorities from victimless crimes to victim crimes (crimes against persons and property in contrast to public drunkenness, prostitution, and homosexuality).

An urban renewal director must decide if, under the prevailing criteria, a neighborhood has so deteriorated as to require demolition.

A state health commissioner looks at atomic radiation levels and wonders if he should order a temporary ban on milk sales.

A state parks director prepares new restrictions on snowmobilers.

The state highway director decides to ignore the environmentalists and straighten the road through a scenic canyon.

An Interior Department solicitor decides to sue the Chevron Oil Company for a major oil spill off the Louisiana coast.

An Antitrust Division chief decides not to prosecute ITT, one of the biggest contributors to the president's reelection campaign.

The commissioner of the Internal Revenue Service wrestles with a White House edict to "put some tax pressure" on twenty "enemies of the President."

Some decisions concern tactics, while others concern the implementation (or misimplementation) of the law, and all are shot through with vital ramifications for private rights and safety, high economic stakes, and agency reputation.

Finally, what kinds of decisions are made at the section and office level?

The typing pool supervisor sets priorities for the typists to follow.

The head of the hematology lab appoints the first black technician.

The chief of the patent copy-pulling section agrees to a reorganization of the unit.

The disbursements officer okays her secretary's time off for a funeral without charging her annual leave.

The city court clerk bucks staff opposition and decides to computerize.

So it goes, the existential moments arising constantly, sometimes on minute matters, sometimes on matters that affect the peace of the world. No wonder some would regard decision making as the essence of administration.

We turn now to the perplexing question: How does the decision maker decide?

VECTOR ANALYSIS

One answer holds that the decision maker decides according to the pressures that surround her and how she is able to manipulate them: that is the essence of vector analysis, or the force-field theory borrowed from physics.

Look at the contrast posed in Figure 9.1 — where will the boat go versus how will the school superintendent resolve the issue of integrating a junior high

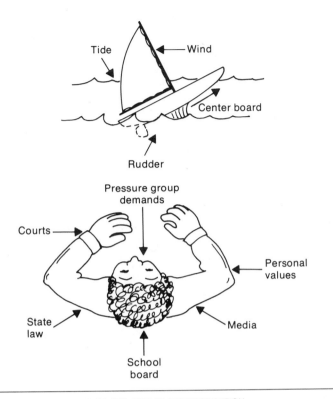

FIGURE 9.1   VECTORS IN PHYSICS AND PUBLIC ADMINISTRATION

school next fall? The frustration, of course, is that the physicist, with his gauges and formulas, can tell you where the boat will go, whereas in the social sciences we are not always even sure which vectors are worth studying.

The pioneering effort in applying vector analysis to the public administrator was James L. McCamy's in 1947,[2] an exploration that still stands as one of the major contributions in the mushrooming literature on decision making. We will stay close to McCamy's formulation in the following pages, using the school superintendent with the integration problem as our case study.[3] First, let us note McCamy's general propositions about the decision-making process.

1. The number of persons and their influence are cumulative as the proposal moves from initial to final stages. Thus, what the staff lawyer wrote in an early memorandum about the court order requiring integration, what the plant and facilities director reported on space at the junior high, and the principal's analysis about how tensions can be overcome in September all build up on the superintendent's desk — and more important, in his mind.

2. There is a lingering influence of early contributors who may have disappeared entirely from the decision-making scene. In our instant case, they could have included the National Association for the Advancement of Colored People (NAACP), Linda Brown of Topeka, Kansas (*Brown* v. *Board of Education,* 1954); Chief Justice Earl Warren; Martin Luther King, Jr.; and some local people who have left their mark on the struggle for $1 = 1$.

3. The number and variety of considerations regarding the policy proposal increase as it moves to higher levels. This observation of McCamy's is illustrated in our present case as shown in Table 9.1.

Now focus closely on the superintendent as we get inside him through McCamy's *personal vectors:*

1. The decision maker's personality, drive or lethargy, love of ruts or getting out of them.[4]	This superintendent values stability and avoiding fights as the highest good in life.
2. Personal prestige considerations.	"This is a helluva quandary for me — be a hero to the district court and the blacks and a bum in everyone else's eyes."
3. Economic security of the decision maker.[5]	"I only have three years until retirement. . . . I couldn't possibly find a job now if I blow this one and get fired. Better drag my feet."
4. His subject matter knowledge and expertise.	"We've never dealt with school integration in the district before — I know there are land mines out there but I don't know where they are."
5. The decision maker's ideological and moral makeup: sense of	"I'm no Abraham Lincoln, predestined to educate blacks with

TABLE 9.1 THE LADDER OF RISING COMPLEXITY

(read up)

Superintendent's level:	What will be the white reaction, the black reaction, the school board's attitude, the media's, the chances of achieving integration smoothly?
Third staff level:	Is the Lincoln Junior High School faculty equipped for the interracial experiment?
Second staff level:	Does the school have space available and is it close enough to black neighborhoods?
Initiatory level:	How can we comply with a court order?

mission, commitment to professional standards versus loyalty to pressure groups.	whites. If God had wanted us to live together, He wouldn't have made us so different."
6. Attitudes toward significant others involved in the issue.	"The judge that ordered racial mixing is imposing a commie plot on us, and my deputies are all dreamers."

Beyond these six vectors are still other personal ones, such as intuition and faith, which have something to do with the way decisions are made. Their chief applicability probably lies in the area of our marital choices, where hunch, urges, and a sense of gamble often drive reason to the wall.

But they clearly play a role in public decision making as well. The facts of continual flooding in the Tennessee and Ohio river valleys would tell Franklin D. Roosevelt and Nebraska Senator George Norris that something had to be done; intuition and faith in their dream of a new government entity, the Tennessee Valley Authority (TVA), told them something could be done.

Intuition about the need for a large air force would provoke Civil Aeronautics Board member Robert H. Hinckley in 1938 to launch the Civilian Pilot Training Program (CPTP) and the "putt-putt" air force of pre–Pearl Harbor days. That foresight and administrative derring-do would produce over fifty thousand pilots waiting for planes when war came in 1941.[6]

While reason, we hope, lies behind almost every major new departure in public policy, there is also a collective act of faith exerted that somehow life will be better for many as a result of integrated schools, Medicare, Head Start, and polio and influenza immunizations. For some, the Apostle Paul expressed what faith is all about: "The substance of things hoped for, the evidence of things not seen."[7] For others, Justice Oliver Wendell Holmes said it best: "Every year, if not every day, we have to wager our salvation upon some prophecy based upon imperfect knowledge."[8] We simply have to take into account such nonrational elements as intuition and faith in any listing of personal vectors.

McCamy then turned his analysis to *expersonal* factors in decision making.

1. The *exogenous* factors, external ones over which the agency has no control but that vitally affect its work.*[9]	The superintendent cannot deny the rising militancy of the black citizenry, nor the whole cultural imperative calling for equality.

* One of the most painful examples in national policymaking concerns the external veto that latent McCarthyism exercised on Democratic decision making about China. David Halberstam recounts that in 1961, George McGhee, in charge of Secretary of State Dean Rusk's think tank, the Policy Planning Council, put the quietus on any discussion of recognizing Communist China. President Kennedy's science adviser, Jerry Wiesner, was put down when he broached the same question, should "the idea that the Administration was even *thinking* of China . . . somehow leak out to the press and arouse the primitives" (the Far Right, exercising an incredibly powerful veto over foreign policymaking). (*The Best and the Brightest*, pp. 102–103, and 120.) But the Right could not put the label of "twenty years of treason" on Communist fighter Richard Nixon when he opened the door to China in February 1972.

2. Research findings and analysis.[10]

The school board staff has resolved in the affirmative all questions about available classroom space, proximity of black students, minimal need for busing, and readiness of the teaching staff to accept integration.

3. Expected reactions of external publics toward possible policy outcomes — from clientele groups, the legislature, higher levels of authority, the media.[11]

"Whites are in the majority in this city and they will resent integration; the school board, city council, and state legislature all reflect that view. I prefer blacklash to backlash."

4. The reputation and security of the agency.

"This is the concern I'm most nervous about — the Court will consign us to purgatory, and then the U.S. Office of Education will send us to hell, with no federal aid to cover the shipping charges. How can I appear at the next superintendents' convention dressed in sackcloth and ashes?"

5. Resources available for implementing the policy.

"Classroom space, teacher training time, getting student leaders committed to integration, buses where we need them, and police if needed to control troublemakers — is it worth it?"

6. Legal factors.[12]

"Do I know the law in this case? I am the Dempsey of *NAACP* v. *Dempsey!* The judge was looking right at me when he issued the order to integrate."

7. Time.[13]

"We cannot be ready by September 5 for the influx of black children at Lincoln Junior High. If that is an immovable deadline, then the answer is no — we will not integrate this fall."

8. Myths and guiding ethical, political, social, or economic principles.[14]

"God never intended white and black kids to be educated together — it could only lead to intermarriage."

Did the CIA Really Think It Would Never Get Caught?

James McCamy thought that calculations about an agency's reputation might deter it from certain unwise moves. The CIA either wasn't worried, or thought its secrecy shield so impregnable that its role in helping to overthrow the freely elected government in Chile, Salvador Allende, 1970–1973 would never be discovered. But the sorry record was uncovered and revealed to all by the U.S. Senate's Select Committee to Study Intelligence Activities:

> What did covert CIA money buy in Chile? It financed activities covering a broad spectrum, from simple propaganda manipulation of the press to large-scale support for Chilean political parties; from public opinion polls to direct attempts to foment a military coup. The scope of "normal" activities of the CIA station in Santiago included placement of station-dictated material in the Chilean media through propaganda assets, direct support of publications, and efforts to oppose communist and left-wing influence in student, peasant, and labor organizations. . . . The CIA attempted, directly, to foment a military coup in Chile.

U.S. Senate Select Committee to Study Governmental Operations with respect to Intelligence Activities (staff report), *Covert Action in Chile, 1963–1973* (Washington, D.C.: Government Printing Office, 1975), pp. 1–2.

Another major vector influencing decision making, suggested in one of McCamy's personal lists (attitude toward others in the organization), is a central atom in modern behavioral research: *the small group*. Note that it is a dynamic thing, not a fixed associational pattern. On the matter of integrating Lincoln Junior High School, the superintendent turns to one group; in handling unionization of teachers, he turns to another; and the membership of either one may be radically changed six months from now.

In addition to the love reasons Maslow suggested for associating with others, we form and join groups for self-interest; we look for those who believe in us and who can help us reach our goals. These people become very important in the lives of most of us. The cues and norms, the rewards and punishments they provide are among the most significant vectors that influence the decisions we make. If you have to know the territory of decision making, the interaction of the small group around the decision maker cannot be overlooked.

At least one other vector of sometimes frightening proportions belongs on that list: the flywheel of tradition, of present policies, committing each new administrator to carry on the policies of her predecessor, cum mistakes.

In our national history, the best example of that phenomenon at its worst was the compounding of errors in Vietnam from Harry Truman to Richard Nixon. David Halberstam graphically portrays the flywheel of precedent in that war:

Lyndon Johnson would also find out the hard way: that the capacity to control a policy involving the military is greatest before the policy is initiated; but once started, no matter how small the initial step, a policy has a life and a thrust of its own, it is an organic thing. More, its thrust and its drive may not be in any way akin to the desires of the President who initiated it. There is always the drive for more, more force, more tactics, wider latitudes for force.[15]

Is There a Predestination Element in Vectors?

One of the major developments in the study of decision making since McCamy's seminal article was published has been the attempt by later scholars to measure the vectors empirically. A roll call would include such names as Richard Dawson, James Robinson, Ira Sharkansky, Thomas Dye, Kenneth Dolbeare, Charles Cnudde, and Donald McCrone, among others. They have come to constitute a new school in political science, *public policy analysis.*

The framework has largely been the general systems theory (with its input-output focus) of David Easton, which is represented in Figure 9.2. The researchers gather data on economic and adult education levels within a state, urbanization and voter participation, among other factors, together with the data on policy outcomes such as school expenditures per child, mean salary levels for teachers, support levels for welfare families, and so on. Employing correlation and multiple regression analysis, they attempt to discover if there are any causal links between the societal inputs and the policy outputs, as the Easton model would suggest.

The research results have been mixed and have caused something of a schism in the public policy school between the structuralists and the economic determinists.[16]

Craig Lundberg found some institutional vectors worth looking at that supplement McCamy's expersonal list: the number of persons and organizational levels involved (similar to McCamy's general propositions about decision making), the amount of information they have available, the number and length of the information channels,[17] and the frequency with which the problem comes up.[18]

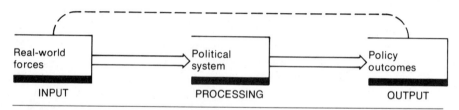

FIGURE 9.2 DETERMINISTIC SYSTEMS THEORY

From David Easton, "An Approach to the Analysis of Political Systems," *World Politics* vol. 9, no. 3 (April 1957). Copyright © 1957 by Princeton University Press. Figure from p. 384, adapted by permission.

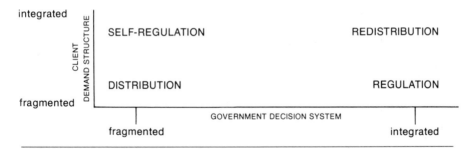

FIGURE 9.3   THE INTEGRATION-DISPERSION VECTORS AND THEIR POLICY OUTCOMES

From Robert Salisbury and John Heinz, "A Theory of Political Analysis and Some Preliminary Applications" in Ira Sharkansky, ed., *Policy Analysis in Political Science* (Chicago: Markham Publishing Company, 1970), p. 24.

Looking both at agency structure and external factors, Robert Salisbury and John Heinz put a different vector to the test: the *integration or dispersion* of the client groups and of the decision-making system.[19] For example, in their terminology, if the power structure of a local community is a close-knit triumvirate and it confronts a five-ring circus sometimes called the commission form of government, you have an integrated demand structure confronting a dispersed decisional system.[20] The authors conclude that that kind of interface will result in self-regulation for the local power structure. The integration-dispersion factors on the two sides of the equation, then, may yield predictable results in government handling of clientele groups (see Figure 9.3).

The terms denoting the dependent variables* in the center of Figure 9.3 suggest the following:

1. *Self-regulation:* the governmental system is so weak that it allows the oil companies to regulate themselves.

2. *Distribution:* a weak government faces a fragmented power structure and hands out pork-barrel favors to keep the rivals happy.

3. *Redistribution:* a tough government deals with a powerful client by redistributing benefits to favor this client (e.g., programs favoring veterans).

4. *Regulation:* a strong government tells fragmented pressure groups exactly where to go (e.g., the wheat farmers).

* The terms "independent" and "dependent variables" are probably old hat to you. (We have already encountered "intervening variables" in Chapter 6.) But a definitional aside at this point may be helpful. The independent variables are those which stand on their own, and whose interaction then produces the dependent variables. For example, at the end of the Ford administration, President Ford and Texas Democrat turned Republican John Connally represented independent variables. Ford's refusal to name Connally as his 1976 running mate probably contributed to a dependent variable, the Republicans' loss of Texas. In our discussion of decision making, we use the terminology of inputs and policy outputs in an analogous way to our use of independent and dependent variables.

These are useful concepts for studying the options that may be open to the decision maker as he compares the troops on both sides of the battlefield.

One of the most dedicated empiricists in the public policy school has been Ira Sharkansky of the University of Wisconsin. His teams have looked for causal relationships among a wide array of societal vectors and the policies state legislatures and school boards were adopting. The findings to date, with a few exceptions, have turned some of the empiricists into hardened agnostics. Hear Ira Sharkansky as he concludes a laborious input-output analysis on Georgia school districts:

> Neither the eight measures of policy nor the three measures of environmental conditions show strong relationships with any of the three output measures. These findings suggest some severe limitations in our model — or in the variables used to measure each of the major concepts. . . . Policy-making is a complex phenomenon that reflects political and economic forces and perhaps many elements that do not lend themselves to readily-quantified district-by-district measurement.[21]

In a companion study designed to measure the vectors that might explain changes in public spending and public services, Sharkansky again came up all hook and no fish: "On the basis of existing data, it is virtually impossible to assess the elements that do influence changes in public services."[22]

Sharkansky's judgment, after assaying all of the research represented in his 1970 anthology, *Policy Analysis in Political Science.* was that "at this point, we can only *list* some forces that shape policy and assess the conditions under which each may be weak or powerful [emphasis added]."[23]

But the economic determinists are not so modest. In suggesting how he has toppled the pluralist temple in political science, Thomas Dye points to the linkage he found between the economic variables of urbanization, industrialization, state per capita income. and education on the one hand, and an array of policy outcomes on the other.

> On the whole, economic resources were more influential in shaping state policies than any of the political variables previously thought to be important in policy determination. Doubtlessly these findings disturbed scholars who felt more comfortable with the reassuring notion of pluralist democracy that "politics counts."[24]

Down that road lies a conclusion that must be appalling to anyone who still believes that we are not what we eat and that we do have some control over our lives — that some combination of economic inputs would predestine a set response by government. If that day ever comes, then the human element in politics is dead and cybernetics has become king. I prefer politicians doing what they can do with the vectors.[25]

If You Can't Measure Them, Are the Vectors Important?

You better believe it! From the administrator's point of view, development of a strategy to reach a desired goal may well begin with counting up the forces we have going for us (my personal aspirations, the law, and the resources available, let's say), and the forces against us (what others will think, risks to the agency, and the short time frame). Then a concrete plan can be laid down for converting or neutralizing the opposing vectors to increase our chances of success.[26]

If the Nixon-Kissinger team in their China planning in the early 1970s had focused only on the predictable, shocked reaction of American conservatives, the attempt at reopening the door to China might never have been made. But adding up the gains (the positive vectors) they could expect from the liberal intellectuals,[27] businessmen anxious to resume the China trade,[28] and the yearning for normalcy in the Far East of many Americans tired of the Vietnam War, Nixon and Kissinger could find plenty of encouragement for engineering the détente with Peking.[29]

Freedom to move, then, the soil from which healthy decision making comes, depends on how accurate a map an administrator has of supportive and opposing forces.

Vector analysis is also of benefit to the student of administration who wants to find out why a given decision was arrived at, over and beyond the often superficial reasons given for public consumption. Why did Truman decide to drop the atomic bomb? Why did Eisenhower send the 101st Airborne Division to Little Rock, Arkansas? Why did Nixon (the free market champion) decide to impose price-and-wage controls? What was behind Ford's decision to pardon Nixon? When the participant-observer can get at the facts, vector analysis will help provide meaningful answers to those kinds of questions.

Let's turn now from the forces that surround the administrator to three major schools of thought on how decision making should proceed: incrementalism (or muddling through), systems analysis (the rational-comprehensive approach), and mixed scanning.

DECISION-MAKING SYSTEMS: THE MAJOR SCHOOLS

Incremental Decision Making

In contrast to the global approach to decision making known as systems analysis, most administrators, it is thought, fly by the seat of the pants more than by the wings of the mind. Incrementalism dolls up that method, suggesting that the commonplace practice is to tackle a problem by inches, not by yards or miles.[30] The incremental sequence looks something like this:

1. Identify the problem.

2. Ask how we have handled it, or similar ones, in the past.

3. Analyze a small number of solutions that on their face are plausible.

4. Choose one that makes some contribution to solving the problem without drastically altering our present processes and institutions.

Incrementalism's first defender, Charles Lindblom, called the method "The Science of Muddling Through."[31] Lindblom argued that administrators are, by and large, practical people; they are problem solvers rather than dreamers. In most cases, they lack both the intellectual capacity and the time to make any wide search for alternative solutions. They will spend little if any time on impractical approaches; they will quickly link ends and means rather than searching for unique, discrete ways of solving their problems; and they will prefer minimal rather than maximal departures from the status quo.

The defenders of incrementalism take confidence not only in the widespread popularity of the method but also in some of its concrete strengths: we are not a society that lives comfortably with wrenching change — the inevitability of gradualness is much easier to take; if the method invites tunnel vision by searching rather narrowly for alternative approaches, some other viewpoints are still possible because of the pluralism that exists among many clientele groups as well as within agencies. The incrementalists contend that there will be no dearth of advocates for other approaches to the problem.

But Lindblom claimed too much when he argued that incremental, or small, changes help us avoid monumental errors. That would be true only if the status quo itself were sound. But the reverse argument that bold steps must be taken can be made if blacks have lived in bondage for three hundred years, if consumer well-being is daily jeopardized by false advertising, and if business as usual in the petroleum industry continues to mean monopoly profits for oil companies and price gouging for automobile owners. At such times, the pain of change is less than the cost of standing still; at such times, "one small step" may *not* represent "a giant leap for mankind."

Systems Analysis (the Rational-Comprehensive Approach)[32]

Assuming that Lindblom is correct in charging many administrators with muddling through (or lazy decision making), it is still desirable, as George Washington said, to "raise a better standard to which the wise and honest can repair." There is nothing so admirable about the status quo and its conventional wisdom, in decision making or anything else, that we need either to exalt or to perpetuate it. Although the rational-comprehensive approach to decision making is complex, it holds some promise of improving the policy process in government.

Systems analysis means the careful definition of goals, the analysis of a wide number of alternatives and their likely effects on the goal and on other vital concerns, and scrupulous provision for monitoring the results of the policy chosen. See systems analysis as rational in defining goals, and in the search for and measurement of alternatives; as comprehensive in the breadth of its search for alternatives and the effort to calculate their impact upon the goal and upon other values of public policy. At the outset, see the need for it the next time you pass a grade school on the wrong side of a fifty-mile-an-hour thoroughfare that separates kids from their school — a monument to muddling through by some school board that held on to an irrelevant piece of property and blithely went ahead with construction without thinking through where the children lived.

The basic cognitive steps of decision making have been laid out in simple fashion by Herbert Simon[33] and are illustrated in the accompanying chart. But the heart of systems analysis lies in a more detailed sequence, which we must now spell out.[34]

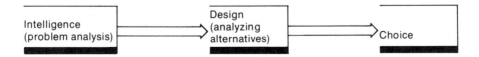

A. *Careful definition of the problem and the goal.* The importance of the opening step cannot be overstressed. If the wrong diagnosis is made, irrelevant goals may be selected and the decision-making process derailed from the outset. Let the tragedy of our involvement in Vietnam ever be a monument in the Cemetery of Horrors to fouled-up decision making as a result of pursuing the wrong goals.

Perhaps the central quality policy analysts need at this first stage is the ability to ask the right questions. Consider these examples:

1. The wrong question being asked by some of the hawks in the 1962 Cuban missile crisis was: How do we get rid of Castro's Communism? The right question was: How do we get rid of the missiles?

2. The wrong questions on Vietnam were: How do we help the French retain their empire (Truman's focus at Potsdam),* and is this a case of Communist expansion calling for an eastward extension of our containment policy? The right question was: Is this a twenty-year revolutionary civil war to get rid of foreign influence and puppet governments so the Vietnamese can enjoy what we won for ourselves in 1781?

3. At a homespun level, note the importance of asking the right question. You drop 30 cents in a Coke machine and it reappears in the coin return. Assuming the machine is broken, you pound it and walk away. Maybe the right question was: "Is someone else's money already in the works?" Pressing the button, you then extract a bottle and ride home free for once.

---

* Halberstam recounts a 1950 mission to French Indochina led by publisher Robert Griffin. Its purpose was to assay communist pressure on the French positions. Finding that pressure intense, Griffin then asked the wrong question, "Do the French need arms aid from us?" and failed to ask the right question, "Is the French position in Southeast Asia proper and defensible?" Consider the tragic consequences of that analytic error! (The quotation is from *The Best and the Brightest*, pp. 335–336.)

Answers to the right questions then begin to suggest policy goals. In systems analysis, the hope is that many goals can be defined with quantitative exactness:

1. We desire to reduce traffic fatalities per million passenger miles by 3 percent in the next two years.

2. We seek to raise Mississippi's per capita income from fiftieth in the nation to at least forty-fifth during the next decade.

3. We intend to put a man on the moon by 1970.

4. We intend to close the gap between median white and black family incomes by 1980.

Probably most problems demanding administrative action partake of a routine character, and a programmed response will solve them: the use of existing formulas (e.g., when inventories run low); reference to the rule book (is the steno eligible for maternity leave?); application of the law (may an extension be granted on this man's tax payment?). Others are sui generis, or unique, and call for the full systems treatment and nonprogrammed responses. Realizing the difference between the two types requires an analysis of the problem as the first step.

B. *Designating the criteria and constraints within which an acceptable solution will lie.* In this step, the analysts and decision makers think through the "metes and bounds" imposed by the nature of the problem they defined in the first step. Some of the limits will relate closely to McCamy's list of personal and expersonal vectors (ethics, legality, attitude of others, resources, and time).

In the Cuban missile crisis of 1962, the criteria and constraints conceivably were these:

1. The missiles will be removed.

2. Removal will be achieved without resulting in a war with Russia.

3. A solution will minimize the possibility of Russian retaliation against us elsewhere in the world (especially Berlin).

4. The American voters will be relatively satisfied.

5. The plan will be in effect within twenty days (when the missiles will be operational).

6. It must be viewed by most observers in the Organization of American States, the UN, and at home as a reasonable, ethical response to the threat posed.

On matters of such magnitude, it can readily be seen that in-house debate over the constraints themselves can be — *and should be* — intense. The pragmatics, ethics, and politics surrounding the issue should all be on the table for examination at this stage. In consequence, decision making on vital issues is likely to be permeated with high drama, deep feelings, and large stakes.

C. *The search for. and measurement of. alternative solutions.* At this stage there should be a premium for a quality of mind we call *heuristic problem solving* — the ability to look at complex situations and discover solutions. This is the sergeant looking at a truck loaded a bit too high inside a warehouse, who then lets air out of the tires so the truck can clear the doorway without being unloaded. This is an Einstein whose equations give him the clue to the enormous power inside the atom. This is the unknown genius who concocts educational subsidies (the GI Bill) as a way for the country to express its gratitude to veterans. This is Charles Curran of the Bureau of the Budget in World War II who dreams up impoundment of funds (or frozen reserves of appropriation acts) to prevent the wasteful expenditure of scarce dollars.[35]

In the whole decision-making sequence, this is when the intuitive geniuses are needed most, conjuring up ways to build a better mousetrap, remove missiles, establish racial peace, calm labor-management relations, and enable the citizens of Los Angeles to say, "On a clear day, we can see the house across the street."

Some suggestions are in order on how to discover these heuristic problem solvers and create an atmosphere encouraging others to think creatively. First, there are some personnel tests that may help spot them. They include the Watson-Glaser Critical Thinking Appraisal,[36] Remote Associates Test,[37] California Psychological Inventory (the Flexibility Scale),[38] and the Torrance Test of Creative Thinking.[39]

Second, managers must create a mood in which people are expected to think and contribute without intimidation. Brainstorming sessions have been designed for that specific purpose; they are characterized by rapid-fire suggestions on a given problem without any evaluations permitted until no other ideas seem to be forthcoming.

Third, concrete incentives for creative thinking should be fully exploited in a positive reinforcement atmosphere.[40]

One of the devices of systems analysis that invites analytical thinking about alternative solutions is the decision-making tree. The tree normally lies on its side, with the trunk representing the goal, the limbs the major program alternatives, and the branches the subprograms. We can illustrate its use in recalling the search for alternatives in the Cuban missile crisis (see Figure 9.4). Seeing it this way can stimulate the search for more alternatives and clarify the interrelationships of possible solutions and the goal.

The search for solutions to some kinds of problems is facilitated by one of the bona fide miracles of our time, the electronic computer. Now far more sophisticated than simply hardware for storage and retrieval, computers can be programmed for certain kinds of heuristic problem solving. That means that it

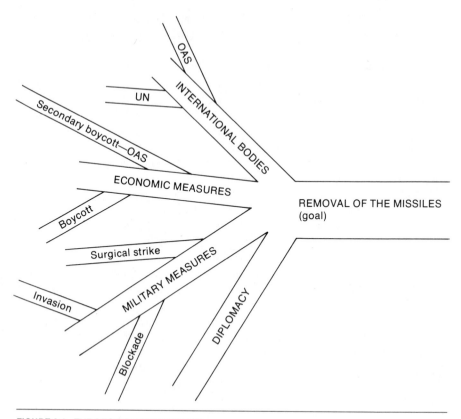

FIGURE 9.4 THE DECISION-MAKING TREE

is possible to state a management problem, lay down the constraints, and have the computer canvass the alternatives to discover which one comes closest to accomplishing the goal it has been instructed to reach.[41]

The spirit of systems analysis calls for a thorough survey of conceivable solutions to the problem at hand, followed by carefully measuring each one against the goal and against the constraints. In our Cuban missile crisis example, this step can be clearly illustrated. Among the alternatives for the removal of the missiles were the following: do nothing; negotiate through regular diplomatic channels; put pressure on Cuba through the Organization of American States (OAS), pressure Russia through the UN; boycott Cuba; institute a sea blockade against Russian ships; conduct "surgical air strikes" on the missile sites; invade Cuba.[42]

A quick reading of those options against the list of constraints noted earlier readily eliminates a number of them:

1. Doing nothing would be unacceptable to an American populace now within reach of the intermediate range ballistic missiles (IRBMs).

2. Invasion would seem to create a high risk of either war with, or retaliation by, Russia.

3. Gentle diplomacy would very likely fail in removing the missiles.

4. A "surgical bombing strike" would make us guilty of an American Pearl Harbor.

Increasingly the discussion among Kennedy's advisers turned to the midway solution of the blockade at sea, coupled with firm diplomacy and presidential ICBM rattling. That mix would indicate to Premier Nikita Khrushchev that we meant business, that no new missiles could be landed in Cuba, and that the pressure was on to remove the ones already in place. Furthermore, it left Kennedy room to escalate to tougher measures if this mix failed.

The decision to institute the blockade illustrates a critical rule about decision making in government, principally identified by Herbert Simon.[43] That rule is: *in most complex situations. the administrator will satisfice* (or suboptimize); that is, he will not strive for a nonexistent perfect solution but rather will accept one that significantly contributes to the goal and meets most of the major constraints.[44]

In the case in question, it was a satisficing answer because the odds seemed acceptable that the missiles would be removed without war and that American voters would approve of the solution. But removal of the missiles was not guaranteed by a stop-and-search procedure on the high seas.

The need for half-a-loaf solutions to tough political problems has been well recognized for a long time. Abraham Lincoln once said:

> There are few things wholly evil or wholly good. Almost everything, especially of government policy, is an inseparable compound of the two, so that our best judgment of the preponderance between them is continually demanded.[45]

One of the original satisficers is the dry-fly trout fisherman. He hopes for an insect hatch on the water that will entice the trout to surface for food, but he hates the bugs flying around. So he waits for the hatch, puts on the insect repellent, swats the bugs, and then does his best to catch fish: that is satisficing (and for thousands, satisfying).

To use the terminology of game theory, most public policy decisions are nonzero sum, which means that the pluses and minuses of any solution do not perfectly balance each other out at zero.[46] (Zero-sum games are illustrated by a two-party race for governor where one party wins, the other loses, and the sum of the two is zero.) Rather, the pluses and minuses of a given decision are complex. For example, you get ready to levy heavy penalties on a nearby polluting steel mill (zero sum as far as cleaning up pollution is concerned), only to realize that the mill may be forced to close, wiping out five thousand jobs and

$13 million in state and local taxes. Such situations frequently require the most delicate balancing on the part of decision makers: the ability to calculate trade-offs among the various constraints and a willingness to live with imperfect solutions that represent at least a net gain on the goal while satisfying the most critical constraints.

One of the characteristic features of systems analysis to help in the selection of alternatives is cost/benefit analysis.[47] Some kinds of government activities are naturals for this approach, with ready-made dollar values as indices of benefit or utility (e.g., the dollar value per acre feet of water for irrigation versus power generation from the Grand Coulee Dam). In other cases, the quantification becomes almost impossible (such as benefits from federal aid for school construction versus federal welfare payments). Quantified or not, the cost/benefit table (Table 9.2) may enable administrators to see interrelationships more clearly, to ask tougher questions, and perhaps to make better decisions.

Table 9.2 looks at five programs for reducing automobile fatalities and subjects each one to three criteria: the success in reducing deaths, the ease of winning compliance and support, and the speed with which each program could be accomplished. The weights and benefits assigned would be determined by the jury method (a panel of experts). These values, and the costs for each program for an imaginary state in the Union, are entirely hypothetical. The goal of cost/benefit analysis is in the right-hand column, where an attempt is made to identify the very costly programs, in terms of benefits received, and the bargain programs. In our example, as in an actual HEW study, a program to encourage the use of seat belts emerges from the comparison smelling like a

TABLE 9.2 COST/BENEFIT TABLE ON PROGRAMS TO REDUCE AUTOMOBILE FATALITIES (hypothetical)

Benefits:	Death-reducing capability	Ease of winning compliance and support	Tooling-up time	Total benefits	1 year costs ($ millions)	Cost/benefit
Weights:	(100)	(40)	(50)	(190)		
Programs						
A. Compulsory drivers' education	15	40	20	75	$ 1	$ 13,333
B. Highway redesign	70	15	10	95	50	526,316
C. More policemen	40	13	35	88	2	22,727
D. Seat belts	80	18	40	138	.1	725
E. Stiffer penalties for law violators	20	5	10	35	.05	1,428

live driver (at $725 per benefit versus $526,316 for a benefit accruing under highway redesign).[48]

We have simplified the presentation to convey the concept of cost/benefit analysis. But don't be misled. No simple determination of values is arrived at by putting numbers on the chart or into the computer, and then presto — having a winner! On any meaningful queston of public policy, the values are hard to come by, the analysis tough, and the decision making painful.

Beyond calculations of costs and possible benefits, collateral considerations also enter into the narrowing of the list of alternatives. Anthony Downs offers some prudent suggestions. Other things being equal, he says, the decision maker will likely prefer solutions that:

Provide "side benefits"

Are relatively simple and easy to comprehend

Involve marginal rather than major adjustments in the bureau's operations or structure, and

Do not depend upon estimations or consideration of highly uncertain variables[49]

Having generated the alternatives, measured them against the goal and constraints, traded off and balanced, and accepted less than a perfect solution, the decision maker has now arrived at the existential moment — deciding.

D. *Deciding.* The preliminaries, the cogitation, the weighing are over. The time has come to put down the Whiskey Rebellion, impose an embargo on England, force South Carolina to respect the tariff of 1828, sign the Emancipation Proclamation, launch the antitrust prosecution of Standard Oil, issue the executive order to start the Works Progress Administration, order the nisei into relocation centers, desegregate the armed forces, pardon Lieutenant Calley, and grant a pardon to Richard Nixon and amnesty to the draft dodgers of the Vietnam War.

In that moment of truth, what's going on in the decision maker's mind and gut? She reviews priorities (what are the ultimate values at stake in this decision?); looks for an existing rule that might get her off the hook; reflects on who is applying pressure and the obligations she may have to them; thinks through what her most trusted advisers and significant others have counseled; calculates the consequences of the decision for her own career and how she's going to feel about herself; applies the wisdom that earned her this hot spot to the likely outcomes of the decision for those most directly affected. Then she stews and then dictates the departmental order. At the end, she is not quite sure if the dominant sensation is existential perspiration or pure exhilaration.

What prepares a person for that moment, what makes a decision maker out of one manager and a coward out of another is hard to say. The roots of the inquiry must certainly go to child psychology and the climate of freedom and

The Anguish of Deciding

October 1962 was a hellish month for President John F. Kennedy. The presence of Russian missiles in Cuba had been confirmed; and the executive committee of the National Security Council had spent thirteen days in wrestling with our possible options to secure the removal of the IRBMs. Kennedy's close adviser, Theodore Sorensen, describes the presidential mood at the decision-making moment:

> Similarly, in our meetings and in his office during those two weeks he was calm and deliberate, his mind clear, his emotions controlled, never brooding, always in command. He retained that composure even when fatigue was overtaking us all. After one meeting during the second week he expressed concern to me that one official had overworked himself to the point of mental and physical exhaustion.
>
> The presidency was never lonelier than when faced with its first nuclear confrontation. John Kennedy never lost sight of what either war or surrender would do to the whole human race. His UN mission was preparing for a negotiated peace and his Joint Chiefs of Staff were preparing for war, and he intended to keep both on rein. He was determined, despite divided counsel and conflicting pressures, to take all necessary action and no unnecessary action. He could not afford to be hasty or hesitant, reckless or afraid. The odds that the Soviets would go all the way to war, he later said, seemed to him then "somewhere between one out of three and even." He spoke on the back porch on that Saturday before his speech not of his possible death but of all the innocent children of the world who had never had a chance or a voice. While at times he interjected humor into our discussions, his mood can best be illustrated by the doodles he scratched on two sheets of his yellow legal pad during one of our meetings shortly after his speech:
>
>> serious . . . serious . . . 16–32 [missiles] within a week . . . 2200 [miles] . . . Khrushchev . . . Soviet submarines . . . submarines . . . submarines . . . blockade . . . Sunday . . . Guantanamo . . . 16–32 . . . Friday morning . . . increases risk . . . need to pursue . . . McCone . . . 1 million men . . . holding the alliance.

Theodore C. Sorensen, *Kennedy* (New York: Harper & Row, 1965), p. 705.

responsibility (or their opposites) in which the young are raised. The inquiry must also come to terms with all that is required to produce self-actualized people (as discussed in Chapter 2).[50]

Suffice it to say that all the preceding steps of systems analysis are designed not to obfuscate and delay, but to clarify and generate this moment of deciding.

E. *The Operations Plan.* The next to final step in systems analysis is preparing the detailed plan for putting the decision into effect. Perhaps less glamorous than the act of deciding, operations planning is nevertheless one of the distinctive contributions of the able administrator, and is as essential to the decision as skis are to skiing.

Three features normally characterize the operations plan: who is to do what (task assignments), using what resources, and in what time frame. Returning to the Cuban missile crisis, we might find the outline of some top-secret Joint Chiefs of Staff planning document to look (in bare detail) like Table 9.3.

The president then fixes responsibility by designating the chairman of the Joint Chiefs of Staff to oversee the operation, requiring him to report to the president on a need-to-know basis through the Situation Room at the White House.

The operations plan thus becomes the antidote to the daydream, "we hope it will happen," by specifying who will make it happen and when. That is administration.

F. *Providing Feedback.* The manager no more assumes that he will get reliable feedback than he assumes decisions will be self-implementing. He gets useful feedback by providing for it in the operations plan.

In the Cuban case, the management information system President Kennedy called for may have looked something like this:

U-2 overflights, twice daily, to photograph the dismantling of the missile sites

CIA spies on the ground to file reports

National Security Agency to intensify its monitoring of all electronic transmissions between Cuba and Russia

naval reports on ship and cargo movements within the blockaded area

daily briefings at 0830 hours of the president and chairman of the Joint Chiefs at the White House for the duration of the blockade, and at other hours on a need-to-know basis

In the civilian sector, the advance planning of feedback is equally essential. We embark on Head Start. Longitudinal data on the learning curves of the children must be gathered and attitude surveys taken among their parents to ascertain levels of satisfaction, problems arising, and so on.

The state's air conservation commission has already had its nostrils burned by phony promises of "we'll clean up" and this time installs monitors to measure pollutants still coming from the copper refinery stacks.[51]

A special unit of the Civil Service Commission is established for the next two years to probe deeply into agency compliance with the commission's Equal Employment Opportunity directives: Are any more minorities being hired than before? Are any more of them being promoted than before?

The design of the appropriate management information system calls for creative minds, as did the steps outlined earlier of generating alternative solutions and writing operations plans. If a decision is worth the sweat of making it, then

TABLE 9.3 OPERATIONS PLAN FOR THE SEA BLOCKADE TO INTERDICT RUSSIAN TRANSPORTS WITH MISSILES FOR CUBA, BEGINNING 22 OCTOBER 1962 AT 0900 HOURS (hypothetical and abbreviated)

Forces	Mission	Logistic support	Command and control
I. Second Fleet	Interdict all Soviet bloc ships entering Atlantic or Caribbean waters within a 1,000 mile radius of Cuba and maintain circular surveillance around Cuba, 15 miles off-shore; interdict any Cuban military aircraft or ships moving beyond that perimeter. a. Stop and search. b. Turn back any ships carrying missiles or missile supports. c. Do not launch any attacks prior to receipt of JCS and CINCLANTFLT clearance.	To be provided by units of the Service Force, Atlantic Fleet; and by shore activities located at Norfolk, Mayport, Charleston, and Guantanamo Naval Base.	Report to CINCLANTFLT and JCS. (Submit situation reports every four hours.)
II. Guantanamo Naval Base	Maintain security and defense of Guantanamo Naval Base. Provide logistic support to CINCLANTFLT and other supporting forces.		JCS via CINCLANTFLT, Second Fleet and Tactical Air Command.
III. Tactical Air Command	Provide supplementary air support to CINCLANTFLT and Second Fleet as directed.	To be provided by Air Force Logistics Command and Continental Air Command.	JCS via CINCLANTFLT and Second Fleet.
IV. Wings 15, 29, and 35 of the Air Force Reserve	To be mustered on 15 October 1962, on station 20 October at Robins Air Force Base, Georgia, for further disposition as directed.	To be provided by Air Force Logistics Command and Continental Air Command.	Report to Commander, Tactical Air Command.

it is worth some expenditure to find out if it is succeeding or failing.[52] That is the final responsibility under systems analysis.

The Pros and Cons of Systems Analysis[53]

It is charged that public administrators rarely have the brains and never the time for the laborious six steps outlined above, that cost/benefit analysis has no applicability to nonquantifiable areas of public policy, and that high-level decision making is far more a matter of political insight and wisdom than it is an act of comprehensive rationality.

Nowhere have those charges been better illustrated than in David Halberstam's indictment of the Vietnam War in *The Best and the Brightest.* In a biting paragraph describing Defense Secretary Robert McNamara, the prime exemplar of systems analysis, Halberstam suggests that:

> He had to come to terms with his constituency, so his attitudes, his love of statistics, his determination to quantify everything, his almost total absence of sense of nuance and feel, were also dominant. (In 1964 Desmond FitzGerald, the number-three man in the CIA, was briefing him every week on Vietnam, and FitzGerald, an old Asia hand, was made uneasy by McNamara's insistence on quantifying everything, of saying it in terms of statistics, infinite statistics. One day after McNamara had asked him at great length for more and more numbers, more information for the data bank, FitzGerald told him bluntly that he thought most of the statistics were meaningless, that it just didn't smell right, that they were all in for a much more difficult time than they thought. McNamara just nodded curtly, and it was the last time he asked FitzGerald to brief him.)[54]

Another basic objection to the rationalistic approach to decision making is whether anyone really uses it. A 1976 empirical study by three Canadians left large doubts on this score.[55] In reviewing eighty-three discrete policy choices in both the public and the private sector, Henry Mintzberg and his colleagues failed to find serious analytic techniques being employed in more than eighteen of the cases: "No study finds that even weightings on goal dimensions are established in advance of making choices; rather, the weights are determined implicitly in the context of making choices.[56]

In case after case the researchers found that only one policy alternative was fully explored. "Screening is used first to reduce a large number of ready-made alternatives to a few feasible ones; evaluation choice is then used to investigate the feasible alternatives and to select a course of action."[57] Clearly, the Canadians were documenting what Herbert Simon once called "bounded rationality" and what Etzioni has labeled "mixed scanning," which we will examine shortly. On the other hand, management literature is replete with applications of systems analysis, from missile system planning to the problems of local government.[58]

At another level, objection is made to the implication in systems analysis that the most important issues in government can be resolved by playing numbers games (whether zero sum or not). This criticism is well founded, we think. The toughest affairs of state are not going to be resolved by computers or mechanical cost/benefit tables for a long time to come. Truly able politicians are still critically important in our kind of a system where we expect experts to be on tap, not on top, and where we expect ultimate decisions to lie with those who have mastered the art of the possible and who must count heads to stay in office. One question needs to be asked, however, in the face of all that: Is that political wisdom aided and abetted, or befogged and undermined, by systematic policy analysis by the deputies a level or two below?

Mixed Scanning

Amitai Etzioni, in looking at the dialectic between incrementalism and systems analysis, finds a synthesis of the two a better way for management to go. He calls it mixed scanning.[59]

This approach to decision making has two basic features: (a) careful analysis of the problem to be resolved; and (b) a scan of the plausible alternative solutions, focusing only on the one most promising for systematic study. (In a nice aside, Etzioni observes that weather controllers are not going to spend much time on how to spawn hurricanes in the desert.)

Try mixed scanning on for size yourself. You're the school superintendent in the district where Lincoln Junior High is located. With two of your high schools now more than 60 percent black, you sense that court-ordered busing is less than two years away. Your problem: What is your best approach to desegregation in this district? Brainstorm ten or twelve alternatives, scan the list for the really promising ones, and then zero in on those, using systematic policy analysis. That is the essence of mixed scanning.

It improves on incrementalism by being far less wedded to how a similar problem was solved last year and in its more creative search for alternatives. It improves on systems analysis in its more realistic assessment of the time available for policy analysis, relinquishing any desire to canvass the universe. Mixed scanning brings the exception principle to decision making and wastes little time on hurricanes for the desert.

IMPLEMENTING THE DECISION

Up to this point our concern has been with how we reach decisions: respond to forces in the field around us, weigh the past, search for alternatives, gauge consequences. We turn now to the closely related matters of who should make decisions and how to track results. Some important answers lie in management by objectives (MBO), operations research (OR), and critical path analysis (CPM) or Program Evaluation and Review Techniques (PERT).

Management by Objectives[60]

With roots going back to World War I, MBO is a managerial system that calls for shared goal setting of concrete objectives, providing deputies with required support, and then tracking and rewarding results.

Early experimenters included Du Pont Chemical and Alfred P. Sloan at General Motors in the 1920s. Luther Gulick and his collaborators in the classical school of administration had useful things to say about goal/task management during the 1930s. In 1938, a pioneering study was published on measuring the results of government programs, *Measuring Municipal Activities.* by Clarence Ridley and Herbert Simon.

In the same year that saw Maslow's pioneering study, *Motivation and Personality.* 1954, Peter Drucker published the first how-to-do-it treatise on MBO, *The Practice of Management.* The genealogy of this idea would be incomplete without the name of George Odiorne, who is to MBO what Rensis Likert is to System 4 management.[61]

The first experiments with MBO in the federal government came in the Department of Health, Education and Welfare after 1969,[62] and it was then extended government-wide by two memorandums of April 18 and 19, 1973, from the Office of Management and Budget. Within two years, MBO was integrated into the regular budget process, with the Office of Management and Budget's A-11 budget circular for fiscal 1977 requiring the submission of MBO targets together with the related funding requests.[63]

That, briefly, is the history of MBO; but now, what is this decision-making and tracking system?

Basic features of MBO[64] Five concepts characterize management by objective. As employee, you would expect your supervisor to:

1. *negotiate* with you some specific goals she's going to hold you to during the next year

2. give you the *resources* to accomplish them

3. grant you the *autonomy* to pursue them

4. insist on progress reports and then tell you how you're doing (*tracking and feedback*)

5. then *reward* you when you succeed

Two critical things about the first step of goal setting are the participative management aspects (you okay the goals after we have discussed them together) and the need for specificity: Not "Improve health care during the next fiscal year in your division of the hospital," but rather "Achieve a 3 percent reduction in the death rate of premature babies."[65]

The second step, providing the resources to achieve the goals, has many implications for both budgeting and personnel management. Note has already been taken of the linkage at the federal level between MBO goals and agency budget requests in the summer of 1975. That suggests what the logical order should be: problem analysis → political analysis → goal determination → funding the agreed-upon lines of endeavor.

On the personnel side, MBO may well demand that some of the strictures of the merit system (see Chapter 15) may have to develop some give. Broader job descriptions (Chapter 16) and greater ease in detailing employees to management by objectives task forces may be required if the unit chief is really going to have a shot at the goals she has negotiated with her superior. Drucker's wise phrase says that "structure follows strategy."[66]

The grant-me-autonomy plea of MBO's step 3 is pure Herzberg, as we recall from Chapter 2. It is this step more than any of the others in MBO that holds promise of generating great personal growth and innovation. Regrettably, it is also the one hardest to come by in most bureaucracies where chiefs really cannot let go of the reins.

Measuring progress (step 4) and providing feedback ordinarily pose no insuperable obstacles.[67] If the negotiated goals meet the specificity requirement, then key indicators and benchmark dates can certainly be laid down.

In terms of reducing the death rate of premature babies by 3 percent, the hospital's chief of pediatrics would want to hear from you, the head of the newborn unit, at two-month intervals for the first six months: What reforms have you introduced? What results have they achieved? If that kind of tracking suggests that you are on target by the end of June, then a quarterly report on October 1 and a final report on December 31 should do.

Feedback and tracking must go hand in hand. As we said in Chapters 6 and 7, the effective superior will both hold her deputies to a standard of excellence (initiating-structure conduct) and will be full of commendation and encouragement as the year unfolds (consideration behavior). The contrast becomes clear when I recall a visit with a former student who had switched her major to art. Her comment was, "Can you imagine what it's like to have been painting for a year and a half and not a single word of encouragement?"

The fifth step, rewarding for success, is no more difficult in the public sector than in the private. Federal supervisors have in their cookie jars awards that include a double jump in an employee's annual pay increase (the "quality step increase"), cash awards ranging up to $25,000, the president's medallion for distinguished civilian service, and the Medal of Honor for military heroes. When linked to the kind of accomplishment MBO is striving for, even Herzberg would agree that money can be a motivator. In a capitalist system, it's a standard way of saying thanks.

An MBO application With solid management training behind him, a new governor takes office and promptly concludes some negotiations with key department heads about goals:

The development director: Within two fiscal years, lift this state from fortieth to thirty-ninth in per capita income.

The health director: Achieve a 4 percent reduction in rheumatic heart disease deaths for each of the next two years.

The corrections director: Bring about a 5 percent reduction in the state's recidivism rate by the end of my term.

The highway director and public safety director: Achieve a 3 percent reduction in automobile traffic fatalities.

The personnel director: Have at least fifty women and blacks and Chicanos of either sex in upper-grade jobs within eighteen months.

The governor asks each one to translate the goal into requests for needed funds, legislation, and personnel; he then promises his support. Benchmark indicators and dates are agreed upon with each deputy. By employing MBO, the governor engineers direction rather than drift.

Some objections to MBO   At the outset, concern exists that MBO in government was the fad of the 1970s, comparable to performance budgeting of the 1950s and the planning-programming-budgeting system (PPBS) of the 1960s.[68] That invites a posture of "Don't take it seriously; it's not long for this world."

There are also concerns about the selection of goals in MBO: (a) Subordinates will proffer easy goals, assuring accomplishment by year's end; (b) the goals will be stated in a vacuous way, without possibility of measurement; (c) it may be dangerous to be explicit about goals when what a beleaguered program needs is a cover-up, not a laser beam.[69]

In addition, there is no guarantee that ample resources and autonomy will follow the agreement on goals. Administration is still the art of the possible, and that often translates as, "Do what you can with what you have."

Furthermore, there is Drucker's sage warning that with all the activity generated by MBO, chiefs and subordinates alike will confuse activity with accomplishment and thus will fail to press for the latter.[70]

Finally, does MBO really have a place in the routine activities of government — getting the mail delivered, processing social security checks, issuing automobile license plates, and so on? What kinds of goals could be negotiated for these areas that would have any specificity and pulling power?

Some hopes remain   Drift is so easy in government. So are violations of employee due process by supervisors who fail to give notice and warning as to the criteria they will use to judge their workers.

MBO strikes at all of that. It charts horizons, with employee help; it maps out landmarks to measure progress; it lets employees know what will be expected of them; and it uses positive reinforcement when those goals are accomplished. Worth a try?

Operations Research (OR)

We will use the term "operations research" to refer to mathematical decision-making techniques at agency levels below that of top policymaking, where goals are already set and the objective is efficient accomplishment of the goals.[71]

Although extending back to the scientific management movement of the nineteenth century, OR stems more immediately from innovations developed by British scientists to solve military problems just prior to World War II. One of the wartime contributions suggests the flavor of OR. Commanders of ponderous aircraft carriers and of more versatile destroyers, confronted with the frightening tactics of the Japanese kamikaze pilots ("I'm going to fly this Zero right down your smokestack"), needed a maneuvering strategy that would minimize hits by the Japanese planes. Navy analysts realized that experience talks and began to gather data on hit/miss records of the aircraft in terms of alternative defensive tactics of the ships. Statistical data provided a clear-cut recommendation: the aircraft carriers should zigzag to the limits of their capability, becoming slightly more difficult to hit; and the destroyers, small and already tough to strike, should steer a straight course in order to improve the stability and accuracy of their antiaircraft batteries.

That example illustrates the heart of OR: quantification and analysis to resolve operational dilemmas such as inventory control, batching, scheduling, assembly-line staffing, paper and product processing, and many other functions.

Techniques employed in OR to answer some of those perennial problems include CPM, or PERT, and the more sophisticated mathematical aids such as queuing theory, linear programming, minimax strategies, models, game theories, and heuristic problem solving.[72] In essentially all phases of OR, the computer is an indispensable partner.[73]

PERT/CPM

Contra the old maxim, Program Evaluation Review Technique, or the critical path method, attempts to find *the longest distance* between two points (starting and completing a project). It seeks two vital objectives: (a) to tell a manager how she can reach her goal sooner; and (b) to provide her with a detailed time schedule to assure completion by the desired date.

PERT employs a network diagram[74] that shows the interrelated production events (those circled in Figure 9.5), required production time, slack time (or float), and important interfaces that indicate which steps must be completed before others can begin.[75] As a case in point, consider how a PERT network might be employed in planning the start-up of a state gas-rationing program.

Operations research analysts have laid the PERT network in Figure 9.5 before the governor midway during the special session of the legislature. The governor is dissatisfied that it will take forty-two days to get rationing started. So informed, the OR staff then focuses on the critical path to see where things might be speeded up. First, they noted the ten-day delay in getting the major functions under way after the agency head's appointment. With some detailing of experienced hands from other state agencies, the analysts felt that public relations (PR) planning, designing the ration books, setting the formulas, and recruiting inspectors could begin within three days, saving a week all along the line (see Figure 9.6).

Then they spotted some unnecessary delays on the critical path itself (the top line). There is no need to delay PR planning six days while the rationing formulas are being determined; some kinds of public information can be planned starting on the sixth day (which would save another six days).

The analysts saw no reason to wait ten days to book TV time for the governor's address on rationing and thus booked it on the seventh day.

An even closer look at the design and printing of the ration books and regulations revealed more standing-around time. The dashed lines after the design of the ration books indicated a seven-day float while the ration books waited for the regulations before going to the printer. "No reason for that," the PERT planners concluded, who then changed the sequence: print the ration books as soon as they are designed while the regulations are being finished and printed. Even at that there will be a two-day float for the ration books (probably a healthy margin for error!).

With these changes, the critical path has been cut from forty-two days to twenty-eight, four weeks instead of six. But what about the bottom line, the recruiting and training of inspectors? That still stands at thirty-nine days. But the planners conclude that rationing can begin a couple of days before enforcement is ready to go, and that leaves the PR function governing the time span for the whole process at twenty-eight days.

Now a refinement is in order: How do we calculate the projected times, remembering Murphy's Law that "If anything can go wrong, it will"? (In this case, for example, we should expect the petroleum dealers of the state and the state's automobile club to take the whole rationing effort into federal court to have the program voided as an improper state restraint on interstate commerce.) A simple formula for calculating the time factors is often employed:

$$\frac{1(\text{Optimistic Time}) + 2(\text{Likely Time}) + 1(\text{Pessimistic Time})}{4} = \text{Predicted Time}$$

Thus, we might figure the recruiting and selection of inspectors according to the formula in this way:

$$\frac{18 \text{ days (OT)} + 2 (22 \text{ days) (LT)} + 24 \text{ days (PT)}}{4}$$

$$\frac{18 + 44 + 24}{4} = \frac{86}{4} = 21.5 \text{ days (Predicted Time)}$$

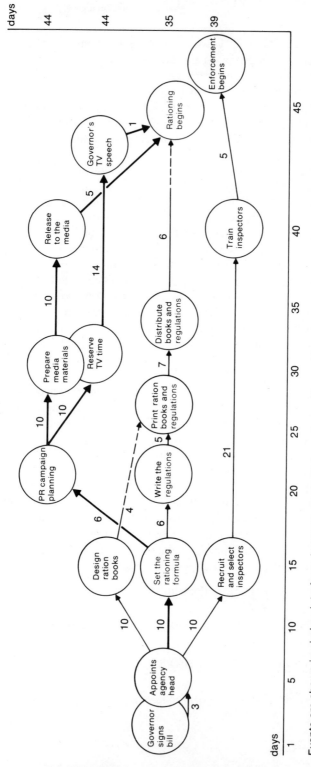

Events are shown in circles; interfaces between sequential events are denoted by arrows; and the estimated time for each event is represented by the number preceding each circle. The bold line represents the critical path; the *longest* distance between start-up and final completion. The total time span for each horizontal sequence of events is shown in the column of days at the far right. The dashed lines indicate slack (or waiting) time.

FIGURE 9.5 PERT FOR A STATE RATIONING PROGRAM

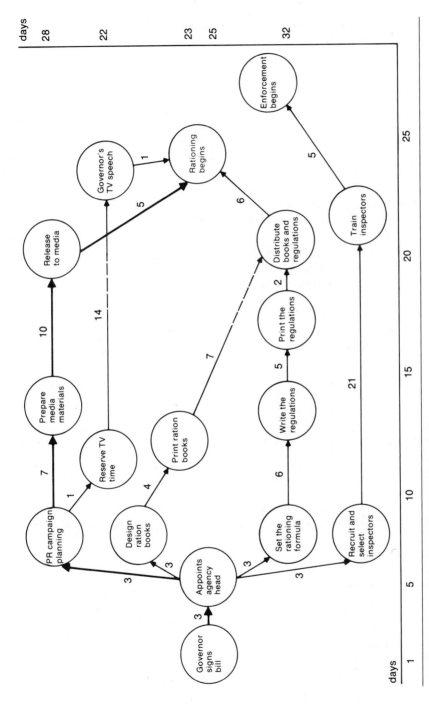

FIGURE 9.6 THE RATIONING PROGRAM AS REDESIGNED

PERT is a remarkably simple management tool, almost a must in properly guiding any project with a number of interrelated events subject to a time deadline. Try it — you'll like it.

SUMMARY

Decision making is a particularly political aspect of the administrator's job. The role makes him part legislator; and fulfilling it will involve him in such typical political activities as supporting, denying, regulating, allocating, and umpiring; and vital stakes hang on the choices he makes.

The decision maker is bombarded with dozens of vectors, some personal, some expersonal, that help shape his policies. Knowing what the forces are and being able to organize and manipulate some of them greatly enhance his freedom to decide.

Although earnest efforts have been made to measure the vectors, perhaps to discover deterministic, predictive relationships between them and policy outcomes, the results have been disappointing (economic determinists to the contrary notwithstanding).

Three contrasting modes of decision making were analyzed: incrementalism (muddling through), systems analysis (rational-comprehensive), and mixed scanning. Though not often fully followed, the steps involved in systems analysis hold out the promise of a more careful search for solutions and their evaluation against both goals and constraints. Even with all the aids now available — computers, cost/benefit tables, and the like — there is still a critical need in high-level posts for rare vintage political wisdom.

Decisions don't execute themselves; they require planned effort and review. It is at this juncture that MBO has been developed to energize those who carry out policies.

We reviewed operations research for lower-level management problems, focusing particularly on PERT networks. The mathematical applications of operations research we leave to advanced texts in quantitative analysis. We turn next to coordination — how to keep the whole enterprise pulled together.

KEY CONCEPTS

ladder of rising complexity	decision-making tree
personal vectors	nonzero sum
expersonal vectors	cost/benefit analysis
deterministic systems theory	mixed scanning
integration-dispersion vectors	management by objectives
incremental decision making	operations research
rational-comprehensive approach	PERT/CPM
heuristic problem solving	

DISCUSSION QUESTIONS

1. Discuss McCamy's personal and expersonal vectors. How would you rank them in terms of their importance to a decision? In what sense can personal vectors "cause" a decision? In what sense are expersonal vectors the major determinants of a decision?

2. Compare incremental decision making with the rational-comprehensive approach. Which of the steps of the latter is the easiest to take? Which works least well in making most decisions?

3. Discuss the procedures that are the essentials of a management by objectives system. Under what conditions would management by objectives be successful? What would be the major barriers to an effective management by objectives system?

PROJECT

Choose a decision that someone employed by the public sector has made. This person can be an elected or appointed official, in a position of leadership or not. Apply vector analysis to the decision, identifying both personal and expersonal vectors. Speculate on those for which you can't obtain complete information.

Notes

1. "Creaming the locals," as Steve Bailey put it in his delightful article on mayoral decision making years ago, "A Structured Interaction Pattern for Harpsichord and Kazoo," *Public Administration Review* (Summer, 1954) 14:202–204.

2. "Analysis of the Process of Decision-Making," *Public Administration Review* (Winter, 1947) 7:41–8.

3. To measure the difference between vector and role analysis, see the highly relevant empirical study by Neal Gross, W. Mason, and A. McEachern, *Explorations in Role Analysis* (New York, Wiley, 1958), a study of the actual behavior of school superintendents.

4. See Saunders and Stanton, "Personality as an Influencing Factor in Decision-Making," *Organizational Behavior and Human Performance* (Apr. 1976) 15:241–257.

5. There is in the literature a classic instance of economic security "making all the difference" in one decision-maker's public record. The case study concerns a wealthy manufacturer, John B. Atkinson, who was hired as the first city manager of Cambridge, Massachusetts. The story records how Atkinson royally thumbed his nose at a hostile city council for seven years, bullying his measures through, safe in the knowledge that any time the council cared to fire him, he had a "better job" to return to. See Frank C. Abbott, "The Cambridge City Manager," in Stein, *Public Administration and Policy Development* (New York: Harcourt, Brace, 1952) pp. 574–620.

6. U.S. Federal Aviation Administration (Patricia Strickland), *The Putt-Putt Air Force* (Washington, D.C.: Government Printing Office, 1970) pp. 1–13.

7. Epistle to Hebrews.

8. *Abrams* v. *U.S.*, U.S.616 (1919), p. 630, with Justice Holmes dissenting.

9. Other examples would include crises in the weather affecting the Department of Agriculture and food production, the aging of the population affecting the Social Security Administration, and China's production of ICBM's affecting our State and Defense Departments, and so on.

10. Notice how the decision-making process in the Cuban missile crisis was affected when the U-2 aerial photos of the launching pads were laid on President Kennedy's desk, confirming the threat. See Theodore Sorensen, *Kennedy* (New York: Harper and Row, 1965), pp. 672–675.

11. The "trial balloon" provides evidence of how sensitive decision makers are about reading the reaction of the media in advance.

12. Of course "the law" is not always preemptive. Harry Truman ignored the Taft-Hartley Act when he seized the steel mills in 1952 (but "the law" won in the ensuing case, *Youngstown Sheet and Tube Co.* v. *Sawyer,* 343 U.S. 579 (1952)). The Nixon Administration ignored the laws restricting the CIA to external surveillance when it obtained CIA help for the burgling of Dr. Daniel Ellsberg's psychiatrist's office in 1971 (and we all know what happened to Richard Nixon when the boomerang flew back).

    A legal factor that severely restricts a governor's budgetary freedom is the ear-marking of certain revenues for specific purposes by the legislature or state constitution (highway funds, fish and game license fees, and so on). The Tax Foundation estimates that 50% of all state expenditures in nearly two-thirds of the states are so earmarked and thus not subject to de novo allocation by the governor and legislature.

13. One of the most graphic case studies portraying the time vector concerns Stuart Symington's midwifing the birth of Reynolds and Kaiser Aluminum during his days as surplus property administrator. The whole effort to end Alcoa's monopoly turned on a certain day by which he had to break Alcoa's leases on government-built aluminum plants. See the story in "The Disposal of the Aluminum Plants," in Stein, *Public Administration and Policy Development,* pp. 314–361, especially pp. 331–332.

14. One decision which apparently was influenced by the raising of an ethical objection was Kennedy's response to the Cuban missiles. The "hawks" in the executive committee (a rump national security council) were urging a "surgical air strike" against the sites. Robert Kennedy then slipped the president a note, "I now know how Tojo felt when he was planning Pearl Harbor." Reported in Robert Kennedy, *Thirteen Days* (New York: Norton, 1971, p. 31. This author applauds someone tough enough to question the morality of a military response we might make.

    But the former Secretary of State, Brahmin Dean Acheson, dismissed Robert Kennedy's moralizing as "puerile" in being "moved by emotional or intuitive responses more than by the trained lawyer's analysis of the dangers threatened and of the relevance to these of the various actions proposed." In addition, Acheson continued, "the charge that we were planning a Pearl Harbor for Cuba seemed to me to obfuscate rather than clarify thought by a thoroughly false and pejorative analogy." "Acheson Says Luck Saved JFK on Cuba," *Washington Post* (Jan. 19, 1969) pp. B1–B4.

    As one reviews the testimony of the denizens of the 1972 Committee for the Re-election of the President — McCord, Barker, Porter, Magruder, and all, one wonders where even a touch of conventional morality entered their thinking as they hatched Watergate, the "dirty tricks," and the cover-up of the whole affair. Then into the immorality play slips not the ghost of Banquo, but the ghost of the old Nazi, Adolf Eichmann, the murderer of the Jews, whose name will forever stand for the ugliest form of the success ethic: "If my leader ordered it, that made it moral." So even Watergate turned out to have its guiding principle.

15. David Halberstam, *The Best and the Brightest* (New York: Random House, 1972), p. 209.

16. One feels the intensity of that division particularly in the writings of a leading economic determinist, Thomas Dye. See his short paperback, *Policy Analysis* (University, Ala.: University of Alabama Press, 1976), pp. 25–35, as case in point.

17. As a case in point, see Phillip O. Foss, "Reorganization and Reassignment in the California Highway Patrol," in Frederick Mosher, *Governmental Reorganizations* (Indianapolis: Bobbs-Merrill, 1967), pp. 187–213, especially p. 195, col. 2.

18. We will distinguish programmed (repetitive) and nonprogrammed (sui generis, or unique) decision making below. Lundberg's research is reported in the reader by William Gore and J. W. Dyson (eds.), *The Making of Decisions* (New York: Free Press, 1964), pp. 17–30.

19. Robert Salisbury and John Heinz, "A Theory of Policy Analysis and Some Preliminary Applications," in Ira Sharkansky (ed.), *Policy Analysis in Political Science* (Chicago: Markham, 1970), pp. 39–60.

20. See, for example, J. D. Williams, *Defeat of Home Rule in Salt Lake City* (New York: Holt, Rinehart and Winston, 1970).

21. Sharkansky, *Policy Analysis in Political Science,* p. 77.

22. Sharkansky, *Policy Analysis in Political Science,* p. 126.

23. Sharkansky, *Policy Analysis in Political Science,* p. 8.

24. Dye, *Policy Analysis,* p. 29.

25. The best rebuttal I know to all forms of predestination, historicism, and the triumph of mechanism over people is still Karl Popper, *The Open Society and Its Enemies* (New York: Harper and Row, 1962), 2 vols.

26. A simple diagram that lines up the rival forces is provided in Chapter 12.

27. The pleasure of the Left over Nixon's China diplomacy can be readily sensed in the *New Republic* editorial, "Breaching the Chinese Wall" (March 10, 1973) 168:7–8.

28. Within a few months of the accords between China and the United States, Boeing Aircraft made a $150 million sale to China.

29. For an insightful look into decision making on the China question, see James C. Thompson, "Dragon under Glass: Time for a New China Policy," *Atlantic Monthly,* Oct. 1967, pp. 55–61, which preceded the Nixon Administration. Writing on the tail of Nixon's 1972 trip to China, Lucian Pye offered additional interpretation in "China and the United States: a New Phase," *Annals* (July 1972) 402:97–106.

30. Maybe the motto of incrementalism should be, "An inch is a cinch, a yard is hard."

31. *Public Administration Review* (Spring 1959) 19:79–88; and Charles Lindblom's monograph, *The Policy-Making Process* (Englewood Cliffs, N.J.: Prentice-Hall, 1968). Another defender has been Aaron Wildavsky, *The Politics of the Budgetary Process,* 3d ed. (Boston: Little, Brown, 1979).

32. As a start, see David Cleland and William King, *Systems Analysis and Project Management* (New York: McGraw-Hill, 1975).

33. Herbert Simon, *The New Science of Management Decision* (New York: Harper and Row, 1960), p. 2.

34. Following Peter Drucker's formulation, "The Effective Decision," *Harvard Business Review* (Jan.–Feb. 1967) 45:92–98.

35. See my case study, *The Impounding of Funds by the Bureau of the Budget,* Interuniversity Case Series No. 28 (University, Ala.: University of Alabama Press, 1955), pp. 9–10.

36. New York: Harcourt, Brace, 1964.

37. Boston: Houghton Mifflin, 1967.

38. Palo Alto, Calif.: Consulting Psychologists Press, 1956.

39. Princeton, N.J.: Personnel Press, 1966.

40. For a discussion of how pay plans may be designed to provide incentives for creativity, see Edward E. Lawler, III, *Motivation in Work Organizations* (Monterey, Calif.:

Brooks/Cole, 1973), chap. 6; and Allan N. Nash and Stephen J. Carroll, *The Management of Compensation* (Monterey, Calif.: Brooks/Cole, 1975), pp. 27–39.

41. One of the pioneering heuristic programs was designed by Rand staffer Fred M. Tonge to solve a problem in proper balancing of assembly line stations. Results were reported in *Summary of a Heuristic Line Balancing Procedure* (Santa Monica, Calif.: Rand Corporation, 1959, P-1799) See also Herbert Simon, *The New Science*, pp. 21–34; and C. L. Hinkle and A. A. Kuehn, "Heuristic Models: Mapping the Maze for Management," *California Management Review* (Fall 1967) 10:59–68.

42. See Max Frankel, "Air Raid on Missile Sites Was Weighed," *New York Times*, Oct. 30, 1962, pp. 1, 3.

43. See *Administrative Behavior* (New York: Free Press, 1976), pp. xxv–xxvi; and March and Simon, *Organizations* (New York: Wiley, 1958), pp. 140–141.

44. By way of contrast, see Louis C. Gawthrop, *Bureaucratic Behavior in the Executive Branch* (New York: Free Press, 1969), chaps. 4 and 5.

45. Source unknown.

46. For a discussion of zero-sum games and their opposite, see David Miller and Martin Starr, *Executive Decisions and Operations Research* (Englewood Cliffs, N.J.: Prentice-Hall, 1969), p. 123.

47. On cost/benefit analysis, see Robert N. Anthony, *Management Control in Nonprofit Organizations* (Homewood, Ill.: Irwin, 1975), pp. 186–203; E. J. Mishan, *Economics for Social Decisions: Elements of Cost/Benefit Analysis* (New York: Praeger, 1973); and Alice Rivlin, *Systematic Thinking for Social Action* (Washington, D.C.: Brookings Institution, 1971), pp. 46–62.

48. The official study is U.S. Department of Health, Education and Welfare, Office of Program Coordination, *Motor Vehicle Injury Prevention Program* (Washington, D.C.: Government Printing Office, 1966).

49. Anthony Downs, *Inside Bureaucracy* (Boston: Little, Brown, 1967), p. 170.

50. For a mind-bending start, see Anders Richter, "The Existentialist Executive," *Public Administration Review* (July–Aug. 1970) 30:415–422.

51. For the kinds of fun and games that politicians can play with smog-monitoring equipment in Mayor Daley's Chicago and U.S. Steel's Birmingham, see Patrick J. Sloyan, "The Day They Shut Down Birmingham," in Richard J. Stillman, *Public Administration: Concepts and Cases* (Boston: Houghton Mifflin, 1976), pp. 50–51 and 54.

52. See Elmer Struening and Marcia Guttentag, *Handbook of Evaluation Research* (Beverly Hills, Calif.: Sage, 1975).

53. Ida R. Hoos, "Systems Techniques for Managing Society: A Critique," *Public Administration Review* (Mar.–Apr. 1973) 33:157–164.

54. Halberstam, *The Best and the Brightest*, pp. 348–349.

55. Henry Mintzberg, et al., "The Structure of 'Unstructured' Decision Processes," *Administrative Science Quarterly* (June 1976) 21:246–275.

56. Mintzberg, "The Structure of 'Unstructured' Decision Processes," p. 258.

57. Mintzberg, "The Structure of 'Unstructured' Decision Processes," p. 257.

58. See T. C. Rowan, "Systems Analysis in Society," *Industrial Research* (Aug. 1966) 8:63–66.

59. Etzioni, "Mixed Scanning: A 'Third' Approach to Decision-Making," *Public Administration Review* (Dec. 1967) 27:385–392.

60. We call your attention to two recent symposia on MBO in government. The first, "Management by Objectives in the Federal Government," edited by Chester Newland in *The Bureaucrat* (1973) vol. 2, no. 4; the second, "Management by Objectives in the Public Sector," edited by Jong Jun in *Public Administration Review* (Jan.–Feb. 1976) 36:1–45 (hereafter cited as the 1976 *Public Administration Review* Symposium).

61. See George Odiorne, *Management by Objectives* (New York: Pitman, 1973).

62. See Rodney Brady, "MBO Goes to Work in the Public Sector," *Harvard Business Review* (Mar.–Apr. 1973) 51:65–74.

63. Chester Newland, "Policy/Program Objectives and Federal Management," *Public Administration Review* (Jan.–Feb. 1976) 36:20–21.

64. George Odiorne, "MBO in State Government," *Public Administration Review* (Jan.–Feb. 1976) 36:28–33.

65. Peter Drucker, "What Results Should You Expect?" *Public Administration Review* (Jan.–Feb. 1976) 36:13 and 16.

66. Drucker, "What Results Should You Expect?" p. 19.

67. See Chester Newland's helpful discussion of productivity measurement, program evaluation, and social indicators in the 1976 *Public Administration Review* Symposium, 31:22–23.

68. See Richard Roe, "Implementation and Evaporation: The Record of MBO," *Public Administration Review* (Jan.–Feb. 1977) 37:64–71; and George West, "Bureaupathology and the Failure of MBO," *Human Resource Management* (Summer 1977) 16:33–40.

69. Frank Sherwood, 1976 *Public Administration Review* Symposium, 36:9.

70. Drucker, "What Results Should You Expect?" p. 13.

71. As a starting point into the literature on OR, see Russell L. Ackoff and Patrick Riveti, *A Manager's Guide to Operations Research* (New York: Wiley, 1963).

72. For a not too complicated introduction to mathematical approaches to decision making, see Charles Wilson and Marcus Alexis, "Basic Frameworks for Decisions," in Gore and Dyson, *The Making of Decisions* (New York: Free Press, 1964), pp. 180–195. For a complete text on the subject, see David Miller and Martin Starr, *Executive Decisions and Operations Research* (Englewood Cliffs, N.J.: Prentice-Hall, 1969).

73. See R. H. Brady, "Computers in Top-Level Decision-Making," *Harvard Business Review* (July–Aug. 1967) 45:67–76.

74. Which bears some resemblance to the *flow process chart* used in organization and methods analysis (see Chapter 12).

75. See Richard Levin and C. A. Kirkpatrick, *Planning and Control with PERT/CPM* (New York: McGraw-Hill, 1966).

Chapter 10
Coordination

BUREAUCRACY: WE DON'T HAVE IT TOGETHER

Any one of you might be called as an expert witness on the lack of coordination in government — the victim knows best!

The general education program at your university calls for three quarters of English, but you can't get a class card for even the first quarter.

The state government makes a big push against pollution but fails to equip its own fleet of cars properly.

The Environmental Protection Agency puts pressure on industries and state governments to clean up the air but finds itself overruled by the White House on deadlines to the automobile industry for nonpolluting cars.

Some of the failure is due to stupidity, some to cupidity, and most of it to poor administration. But this disorganization in government must be counted as the migraine of all headaches in the public sector.

What we want in its place is *coordination* — policies and the execution of policies that work harmoniously toward common goals.

Conflicting Policies

In the depths of the Great Depression, the Agricultural Adjustment Administration (AAA) paid farmers to curtail production, while other units of the Department of Agriculture were helping farmers to be more efficient, and the Bureau of Reclamation, in the Interior Department, was bringing water to new lands for cultivation. That was a case of not wanting our wheat but getting it!

During World War II, the Office of Price Administration (OPA) fought to hold food prices down, while the farm bloc in Congress and the War Food Administration sought higher prices for farmers (110 percent of parity for some commodities) in order to stimulate agricultural production. In this case an old coordinating device was then resorted to: the president fired Chester Davis, known as the "food czar," for his resistance to price and rationing policies developed in OPA.[1]

Early in the postwar period, the next president's left and right hands were out of touch. In 1947, President Truman's Committee on Civil Rights published a pioneering study, *To Secure These Rights.*[2] Chapters 2 and 3 of the report dealt with freedom of conscience and expression and the climate of opinion. But on March 21 of the same year, Truman issued Executive Order 9835, ushering in the government's loyalty-security program with a crunching effect on the climate of opinion that would ultimately stifle foreign service officers like John Paton Davies and John Stewart Service, and nuclear physicist J. Robert Oppenheimer.[3]

Toward the end of the Truman presidency, an all-time classic in policy conflict arose. The Treasury Department hoped to manage the huge World War II debt at low interest rates (2.5 percent on the long terms!), whereas the Federal Reserve Board wanted to unpeg the market for government bonds (which would result in rising interest rates) to control bank reserves and the money supply in coping with the inflation brought on by the Korean War. We return to this case study below. In brief, the question was whether to set interest rates to borrow cheaply or to fight inflation.

Presidents Kennedy and Johnson would launch programs and rhetoric to fight poverty, but they would also divert billions of dollars to moon programs, where there are no poor, and to Vietnam, where some got richer and many more got killed.

President Nixon talked softly about civil rights during 1968 and then nominated two southern conservatives for the Supreme Court (both of whom were defeated in the Senate) and opposed government aid for low-cost housing in suburbia (one road out of the ghetto). The whole so-called southern strategy of the Nixon administration suggested that these were coordinated, rather than uncoordinated, moves against black Americans.

Perhaps nothing portrays the problem of uncoordinated policies more than the mixed-up world of Adm. Morton Ring, vice-chairman of the Defense Department's Munitions Board in the 1950s. Asked by a congressional committee what guidelines he followed in buying material for the armed forces, the admiral cited fourteen. They included the congressional mandates to buy cheap (lowest competitive bidder), buy American, buy in depressed areas, and buy from small businesses. Head bruised but unbowed, the admiral had found a way to stay alive: "If you'd ask me which one I would follow as a purchasing officer, I'd say

To Coordinate Is to Juggle

The ultimate juggler these days is the Bureau of Land Management district manager, who tries to keep airborne all the policies congress has laid down for the management of the public lands.

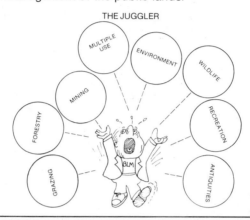

THE JUGGLER

I'd follow the policy on which the pressure is the greatest — and then duck."[4]

Ducking would seem to be a skill every administrator should master, for policy conflicts recognize neither season nor administration. In the first year of the Nixon administration, an assistant attorney general expressed his strong opposition to exempting jointly operated newspapers from the antitrust laws, even though he had to admit that that was no longer administration policy; the Commerce Department now spoke for the White House on this issue and favored the exemption "to aid failing newspapers." The Associated Press reported that Democratic Congressman Emanuel Celler of New York, in his forty-seven years in Congress, "had never before seen a situation in which two executive departments testified on opposite sides of an important matter."[5]

The Unmeshed Gears[6]

Even if Congress had been able to make up its collective mind on the procurement policy for Admiral Ring to follow, his ship might still have come apart because of unmeshed gears below him. Lack of coordination involves not only policy conflicts but also mixed-up work relationships of the executors as well: interpersonal hang-ups, mismatched job assignments, lethargy at some point in the production line, bottlenecks and breakdowns with a hundred causes.

A case in point added intensity to the energy crisis of the 1970s. At a time when the new Department of Energy was pressing the search for power sources other than oil, the Bureau of Land Management in the Department of the Interior was making it tough for mining companies to explore for, and mine, coal on the public domain.[7]

Often, lack of coordination takes the form of inputs not followed by outputs. President after president has complained of the problem while watching directives get lost in the labyrinth below the White House. Consider the laments from three administrations. During World War II, Harry Hopkins, longtime adviser to President Roosevelt, ranted about White House decisions being "vetoed in the ranks":

> Estimates can be made and agreed to by all the top experts and then decisions to go ahead are made by the President and the Prime Minister and all the generals and admirals and air marshals — and then a few months later, somebody asks, "Where are all those landing craft?" or "Whatever became of those medium bombers we promised to China?" and then you start investigating and it takes weeks to find out that the orders have been deliberately stalled on the desk of some lieutenant commander or lieutenant colonel down on Constitution Avenue.[8]

Ten years later, the lost-in-the-labyrinth problem had not changed.

> In the early summer of 1952, before the heat of the campaign, President Truman used to contemplate the problems of the General-become-President should Eisenhower win the forthcoming election. "He'll sit here," Truman would remark (tapping his desk for emphasis), "and he'll say 'Do this! Do that!' and nothing will happen. Poor Ike — it won't be a bit like the Army. He'll find it very frustrating."[9]

For John F. Kennedy, the source of frustration was the State Department. Adviser-historian Arthur Schlesinger, Jr., recounts the problem:

> Other departments provided quick answers to presidential questions and quick action on presidential orders. It was a constant puzzle to Kennedy that the State Department remained so formless and impenetrable. He would say, "Damn it. Bundy and I get more done in one day in the White House than they do in six months in the State Department." Giving State an instruction, he remarked, snapping his fingers with impatience, is like dropping it in the dead-letter box. "They never have any ideas over there," he complained, "never come up with anything new." "The State Department is a bowl of jelly," he told Hugh Sidey of *Time* in the summer of 1961. "It's got all those people over there who are constantly smiling. I think we need to smile less and be tougher."[10]

At the state level, the governor orders a forty-hour workweek in all state agencies. A survey by state personnel two months later still finds three agencies with thirty-eight-hour workweeks — lost in the labyrinth.

In addition to the labyrinth syndrome, there is the familiar problem of the left hand not knowing what the right hand is doing. The examples are legion at all levels of government. A navy supply train filled with tomatoes moves west from St. Louis, headed for a naval base in San Francisco. Somewhere in Nevada it passes an eastbound train loaded with California tomatoes heading for an army base in Colorado. As the trains pass in Reno, a warning light flashes on the console of the train dispatcher that he had never noticed before: SNAFU!

Following the population curve, governments grow like weeds in a metropolitan area. Some four hundred thousand people are served by forty separate units of government, including three independent mosquito abatement districts with authority to spray each other's ponds.[11]

In the public library, the stack and reader division is anxious to put new books into circulation. But their hands are tied by an understaffed cataloging division, which has a three-month backlog of books to process. Little gears hold up big gears.

As a final painful example of unmeshed gears, consider the frustrations of a student body whose increased fees built a beautiful fifteen-thousand-seat special events center. Then the student groups found they could not afford to use their own building because of exorbitant overhead charges imposed on them by the director of athletics, who ran the center.

The Etiology of Coming Unglued

The lack of coordination in government stems from many sources, some deeply imbedded in the nature of politics, others in poor organizational design and in management.

The conflict of ends   A perennial cause of trouble might be labeled government bipolarity — the pursuit of competing or incompatible goals. The examples are numerous — deregulate gas prices to curtail consumption while worsening inflation; promote minority admissions to professional schools and discriminate against whites; switch industry from oil back to coal-fired power and significantly pollute the air once again.

Wanting incompatible things, we start off in our dispersed governmental system to try to get them, hoping that we can reduce unemployment and poverty without generating more inflation. The conflict of ends, if not moderated, predestines lack of coordination.

The conflict of means   On the surface, this conflict is, of course, what uncoordination is all about. One school district raises teacher salaries, and the neighboring district blows its mind. The state health department's air pollution committee allows the local copper company to dump its garbage in the sky, and the same department's division of respiratory health then cannot handle the workload as the asthmatic patients come coughing in.

Thus the means to reach government objectives step on each other, and agencies get out of step.

Faulty organization   A perennial cause of uncoordination is poor structural design from the outset. Mixing up major-purpose and clientele bases of organization (see Chapter 3) is one such way to invite trouble. For example, consider the range of social services offered to the general public by the U.S. Department of Health, Education and Welfare, a major-purpose organization, and the highly similar services extended to veterans only by the Veterans Administration, a clientele organization.

In an earlier era, managing a coordinated foreign policy with a Central American country would be extremely difficult where diplomacy was handled by the State Department, economic aid by an independent Economic Cooperation Administration, military aid by the Defense Department, and commercial and agricultural relations by the Departments of Commerce and Agriculture.

The refusal of a county sheriff and the city police chief in the same metropolitan area to combine their records bureaus means duplication and less effective police work. The underlying cause is the failure to create a metropolitan police force in place of rival law enforcement agencies.

At the office level, the same principle about sound organization holds true. Nothing can discombobulate a secretary so fast as having five people all dump work on her, with competing deadlines and no one to resolve the priorities.

The root of the trouble may sometimes lie as deep as the job classification system itself (see Chapter 16). The failure of line managers and job classifiers to properly relate positions to each other may only invite duplication or conflict later on as employees proceed to carry out their assigned but overlapping roles.

These are the kinds of situations that may demand reorganization to straighten out the basic structural design of positions and agencies if coordination is to be achieved.

Communication breakdowns   The rear wheels of an automobile do their separate things in perfect coordination with each other through a communication link called the differential. Automated bakeries start the right amount of dough through the ovens to match the baked loaves coming out the other end, all coordinated by a cybernetic system where computers monitor machines and keep them synchronized.

However, when coordination requires a simple little thing like human beings talking to each other, it sometimes falls apart. Interpersonal rivalries lead us to clam up so that competitors won't know what we are doing. For example, having failed to sit down and work out a combined approach, the representatives of a university's college of business and its public administration school suddenly find themselves both trying to sell a management training program to a nearby air force base.

The lack of communication may stem from lethargy or the failure to realize that someone else may be interested or affected by what one is doing. For such reasons, counselors in employment security and vocational rehabilitation may fail to get together to place an epileptic whom they have both been guiding.

Race, age, and sex prejudices may impose additional barriers to free-flowing communications between administrators. Differences in status and role between line and staff may also block the sharing of data and plans between the left hand and the right hand.[12]

Whatever the cause, when communication breaks down, administrators get

You Can Make Liars out of People if You Don't Keep Them Informed

Roger Hilsman has graphically recounted from the Eisenhower and Kennedy administrations how lack of coordination (in these cases, the failure to share information) made liars out of administration spokesmen and sorely embarrassed the United States:

> Another, more subtle aspect of secrecy is the way it tends to corrode confidence among different officials and between the government and the public and the press. Adlai Stevenson at the UN was ignorant of the planned invasion of Cuba [1961] and read into the UN record a statement that the planes that had bombed Havana's airfield were "defectors" from the Cuban air forces — not knowing that he was repeating the CIA "cover" story. At the time that the U-2 was shot down [over Russia] in 1960, Lincoln White, the official State Department spokesman, in all innocence flatly and indignantly denied that the United States had flown a spy plane over the Soviet Union. "There was absolutely no — N-O — no deliberate attempt to violate Soviet airspace," White said. "There never has been." And he repeated the CIA "cover" story that what had been shot down was a "weather" plane that had strayed.

Roger Hilsman, *To Move a Nation* (New York: Dell Publishing, 1967), p. 83.

out of phase with each other — duplicating, counteracting, nullifying, and sometimes stabbing the back that lies between.

Inept leadership   A final major contributor to lack of coordination is ineffective leadership; leadership that is unperceiving, unimaginative, or gutless.

Take a football coach in what we assume should be his last game. There is *no conflict of ends.* He wants to rub the other team's noses in the sod. The organization of the team is sound (assignments well laid out, positions all filled, etc.). And communication is excellent. There are spotters with binoculars on top of the press box looking down on the play, relaying their observations to the coach by walkie-talkie. But there is a *conflict of means:* the offensive tackles and blocking backs have quit trying whenever a disliked fullback carries the ball.

At this point, two leadership failures occur: refusing to make the appropriate substitutions, and failing to develop cohesion and team spirit among the players. Since the coach won't correct the situation, his team's offense falls apart.

To put the point the other way around, when other factors threaten to destroy coordination, effective leadership can often cope with the problem. But if the leadership is not there, then unstabilizing developments can take hold unchecked.

A weak mayor watches rival poverty agencies carve each other up. A governor stares out the window while the state public works authority ignores directives from the state manpower council to make jobs available for the disadvantaged. And a president fails to exert the full powers of his office on labor and business to curb the cost-push aspects of inflation. In addition to all the other things that were said in Chapter 7 about leadership, leading means keeping the parts functioning together.

Having assayed some of the root causes of uncoordination, can we root any of them out?

ACHIEVING COORDINATION

Harmonizing Ends and Policies

Let's not kid ourselves, the pursuit of incompatible objectives can be mollified but never eliminated in our kind of political system. Given the influence of pressure groups, the dispersed nature of our governmental structure, and our weak two-party system, there are too many opportunities to start government agencies down uncoordinated paths.

On the congressional side, there are occasional rays of hope for reordering our priorities and then sticking to them. The strong commitment to full employment made in the Employment Act of 1946 was one. The historic civil rights statutes of 1964–1965 constituted a second when human rights were clearly preferred to states' rights or property rights. The defeat of the supersonic transport plane (SST) in the spring of 1971 was another moment when congressmen seemed willing to put their votes where their noses were in the fight against pollution.

But in any long-range view of the Congress, these victories for coordinated attacks on national problems seem episodic. The obstacles are great in the national legislature to any consistent policy planning. The provincialism that may leave a congressman with not much more than a hometown view of the world,[13] the sectionalism, and the lack of party government all strongly militate against coordinated policy planning in Congress toward agreed-upon national goals.[14]

As the Founding Fathers intended, the president is in a better position to take a holistic view of national needs, goals, and policies than any single congressman is. But human weakness in the presidents and the demands of politics may distort executive vision and leave us with conflicting ends. A very bright president wanted to end racial discrimination and poverty in the early 1960s but then invested chunks of our national budget in Southeast Asia and the moon. Thus, even one almost as bright as "Jefferson having breakfast alone" could not spare us from the policy conflicts that permeate our democratic soil.[15] Nevertheless, many presidents have been concerned with long-range planning and coordinated efforts to reach agreed-upon goals. An example was Dwight Eisenhower's chartering of a Commission on National Goals.[16]

Perhaps the best we can hope for in harmonizing ends and policies is to establish clear priorities among goals and pinpoint for decision makers inconsistencies in our choices. In short, we need *policy analysis* of a high order in both the executive and the legislative branches of government.

Provision for such analysis was made a long time ago in the executive branch with the elevation noted earlier of the old Bureau of the Budget from bureau status in the Treasury Department to a level of commanding importance in the new Executive Office of the President in 1939. Coordination efforts through policy analysis got a great boost. The Bureau's Office of Legislative Reference was charged with the analysis of legislative proposals from executive agencies, including those from the independent regulatory commissions — the headless fourth branch of the government — to determine if they were "in accord with the policy of the President." And the budget director's review of agency budget estimates in the late fall of each year became a focal point for coordinating executive branch fiscal policy.

Furthermore, policy analysis for the specific purpose of achieving coordination in economic areas was assigned to the Council of Economic Advisers by the Employment Act of 1946. Section 4(c) of the act read:

> To appraise government programs with a view to determining which contribute to, and which militate against, the employment, production, and purchasing power objectives of the act and to make recommendations to the President with respect to government programs.[17]

Although the council's central staff role has varied over time, its presence must clearly be counted on the asset side of keeping the president apprised of economic goals and the country's progress, or lack thereof, in achieving them.[18]

Policy analysis in the legislative branch has come a long way during this century. The Congressional Research Service of the Library of Congress, with its highly trained staff, is constantly engaged in policy analysis — but rarely for congressional leadership bodies like the party policy committees. The research service performs in response to requests from individual members and separate committees of Congress — and that spells pluralism — perhaps not in the analysis but in what congressmen do with the analysis.

The standing committees of the House and Senate have their separate staffs. The Joint Economic Committee has its gifted economists, but the influence of this committee's findings varies from issue to issue and session to session. The party policy committees have small staffs that undertake policy analysis. But to what end? As Professor Victor Jones cryptically stated years ago, these policy committees can't lead because "there is no Congressional party to be led."[19] All the legislative policy analysis in the world won't change that. The only lasting remedy lies in a fundamental strengthening of the legislative parties and the authority of their leaders, including an end to the seniority rule.

The signal development in Congress in the last twenty years was the creation of the budget analysis staff under a talented economist, Dr. Alice Rivlin, as a result of the Budget and Impoundment Control Act of 1974. For the first time in American history, Congress enjoyed policy analysis on a par with that of the president in fiscal policy.

The chief hope for some harmonizing of means and ends lies, we think, in strengthening the quality of policy analysis in the two elected branches, and through vigorous presidential and congressional leaders who utilize that analysis.

Getting the Gears to Mesh

The first step, as noted above, is getting a *sound organization* to start with. That calls for clear definition of agency mission and minimal overlaps with sister agencies. Moreover, the basic design should provide for coordinating devices to smooth out interagency relationships, adjust missions, and resolve conflicts as agency activities begin to unfold. Let's look briefly at some of the coordinating devices that are available.

One is simply *interagency negotiation.* on an ad hoc or on a continuing basis. A professor of politics wants to share some state legislative internships with three other colleges in the state; coordination is achieved by means of a long-distance conference call with his colleagues at the other universities.

Before the council of governments (COGs) era, mayors of five adjoining communities would have a working lunch at the beginning of each month to resolve problems. The secretary of state and secretary of defense sit down together to resolve critical interagency matters on which the peace of the world might depend.[20]

Continuous interrelationships probably demand regularly established linking pins, the *interagency committees.* The examples are many: the Interagency Advisory Group (IAG) of the U.S. Office of Personnel Management, which brings top personnel administrators together as a communication link between the office and the executive departments; the Federal Executive Associations in major cities of the United States, which bring federal agency managers together on a regular basis;[21] the Advisory Commission on Intergovernmental Relations (ACIR), with representatives from federal, state, and local governments coming together for problem solving; the Interdepartmental Committee on the Status of Women; the Federal Council for Science and Technology; the National Advisory Council on International Monetary and Financial Policies; the New England Action Planning Commission, one of the multilevel interagency regional development bodies in the United States; and by 1977, some 875 other interagency committees.

Their common pattern is to pull heads together, compare plans, share information, and often, through a full- or part-time executive director, attempt to coordinate the activities of the participating agencies.

A third coordinating technique is that of *cross-staffing.* In the present context, this means transferring an administrator from one agency to another in order to harmonize the work of both. President Nixon's appointment of his trusted economic adviser, Dr. Arthur Burns, as chairman of the Federal Reserve Board in 1970 illustrates the technique. Nixon hoped thereby to achieve some coordination of monetary and fiscal policy. But Dr. Burns's independence as chairman of the Fed suggested a principle about cross-staffing: once you let them out of your stable, they often run their own race.

Often the cross-staffing technique seeks to promote coordination by broadening agency viewpoints and breaking down provincialism. As high-level management and budget people are moved out to line agencies, the broad view of the executive office begins to permeate the narrower outlook of the line. In the Department of Defense, military officers are given three-year tours of duty on the Joint Staff (the modern-day version of the general staff) for the same reason, as well as to assure that overall defense planning has continuous inputs from officers with line experience. But one of the negative aspects of a joint staff approach is that the members assigned outside the agency often lose their agency identity and thereafter may be regarded as having joined the enemy. Thus, it is difficult to work them back into the agency routine when they are rotated home.

The hope in cross-staffing is that if the left hand once was the right hand, holding hands becomes much easier thereafter.

A more direct coordinating device is the *central staff* (used here in the military sense as a body with command authority over satellite line agencies). The Joint Chiefs of Staff wield such coordinating authority over the branches of the armed forces in a context rife with rivalry and separatism. But keeping field commanders in line with military policies approved by the president and defense secretary is no easy task. Especially is this so when the Joint Chiefs are trying to corral a five-star Napoleon like Douglas MacArthur during the Korean War.[22]

Central staffs with potent coordinating powers also appear on the civilian side of government. A president orders a $10 billion budget cut in the middle of the fiscal year, and his OMB then excises that amount from the quarterly allotments of money available for agency spending. The president wants to reduce the federal work force by two hundred thousand employees, and OMB then imposes personnel ceilings on the agencies, restricting the number of job slots an agency is authorized to fill.

The president means business about equal employment opportunity in the federal service. The Office of Personnel Management launches a results-oriented, affirmative action program to coordinate the hiring, training, and promotion policies of all federal agencies in line with the EEO objective. But, as a painful reminder that central staffs are not always able to influence intransigent line agencies, the U.S. Commission on Civil Rights reported in 1970 that the EEO effort within federal agencies themselves had been a near failure.[23]

Another familiar coordinating device is the *superagency.* War seems to generate this kind of structure, such as was embodied in the War Production Board (WPB) and Office of War Mobilization and Reconversion (OWMR) of World War II.[24] The WPB was established within a month after Pearl Harbor as a super-agency to allocate scarce resources to defense needs and essential civilian industry. Replacing the market mechanism that would perform these roles under a free market during peacetime, the WPB received requests from industry and governmental agencies, made estimates of available supplies of key metals and petroleum, and then made the allocations.

Theoretically even the War Department was to bow to the decisions of this superagency. But WPB Administrator Donald Nelson allowed his coordinating authority to slip away. He lost ground to the War Department's representative, Gen. Brian H. Somervell; the War Food Administration was created outside Nelson's chain of command to generate agricultural production, the War Man-power Commission to control labor assignments, the Petroleum Administration for War to regulate gas and oil, and the Office of Price Administration (OPA) to control prices. The coordination problems that resulted exceeded Nelson's grasp, requiring the creation of a new superagency over them all — the Office of War Mobilization (OWM).[25]

The OWM had ample authority to tell line agencies what to do, but the coordination philosophy of presidential czar James F. Byrnes was of a softer sort. His mode of operation called for circulation of memorandums for all interested parties to see, then negotiation and resolution. He left a legacy for administrators for a long time to come: "The powerful don't have to roar."

The inflation of the early 1970s generated a new superagency coordinator, the Cost of Living Council, to oversee President Nixon's wage-price freeze in August 1971. Chaired by Treasury Secretary John Connally, the council knocked heads together, told the Defense Department to hold up military pay raises, instructed the governor of Texas to do the same thing with teacher salary increases, and similarly informed the Postal Service regarding pay hikes for postmen.

Nixon also experimented with Jimmy Byrnes-type czars. Following his 1972 reelection, he established five supercoordinators for his second term: H. R. Haldeman for White House management, John Ehrlichman for domestic affairs, Henry Kissinger over foreign affairs, Treasury Secretary George Shultz as economic overseer, and Roy Ash over federal management and budgeting. The Watergate scandal would shortly wash away Ehrlichman and Haldeman; but Shultz would coordinate the work of the Treasury, Commerce, and Labor departments in the difficult years of domestic inflation and the overseas collapse of the dollar.[26]

At the state level, one finds evidence of the superagency approach in handling rivalry and duplication among the institutions of higher learning. The technique employed by some states is the coordinating council or state board of higher education. Through such an agency, budgets can be harmonized, course duplication stopped, missions and specialties made compatible.

One level higher than the superagency is the *top coordinating body* such as the cabinet, the National Security Council (NSC), or Nixon's Domestic Council.[27] In British government, the Cabinet is the brain center of the whole parliamentary system. In our presidential system, the cabinet is an institution whose potential for interdepartmental coordination has never really been reached. But its periodic meetings do afford the president the opportunity of laying down policy directives, asking for reactions, and working out differences in order to see that the gears mesh at the highest level of government.

One senses that the National Security Council has a better coordination record than the cabinet. In the NSC, the interests are more focused, the membership smaller, and the staffing more impressive than in the cabinet.[28] The statutory members, in addition to the president and vice-president, consist only of the secretaries of state and defense. With discussions veiled in secrecy, these few decision makers have maximum opportunity to work out coordinated plans to deal with Cuban troops in Africa, Russian troops in Cuba, or American troops in Pigalle.[29]

Perhaps the least complicated and most direct of all the coordinating devices is *executive intervention*. Two city departments are brawling over control of computer time; the city manager settles the issue. The state highway department and the parks and recreation department are going at each other over a road improvement that will ruin a beautiful fishing stream; the governor plays Zeus. The Joint Chiefs want to bomb Hanoi while the State Department worries about Communist Chinese retaliation; the commander in chief resolves the impasse.

While such intervention may bring coordination, and rapidly, it may also have latent dangers. Does it lessen the desire and capability of subordinates to resolve their own problems? Does it waste the time of the chief executive in putting out fires so that he has none left for fire prevention?

If none of the techniques we have been looking at succeed in getting left and right hands to hold hands, there is one more radical approach available: *combine them via reorganization*.[30] After all, in the market economy, horizontal and vertical mergers among competitors happen all the time (despite the Clayton Act). Why not in government?

> The sheriff and police chief act like feudal barons and will not cooperate — merge them into a metropolitan police force. The city fire department, paying more attention to boundaries than to fires, refuses to handle calls from nearby county locations — merge them into a metropolitan fire department.
>
> Highly independent purchasing agents in the major state departments will not comply with the governor's mandate for competitive bidding — centralize all state purchasing.
>
> There is a piecemeal approach to private group welfare in the federal government, with functions scattered over many departments and agencies — bring

the Children's Bureau and Women's Bureau from Labor and the Veterans Administration all under one roof in HEW.[31]

The only troublesome thing about bringing them all under one roof in a big holding-company-type department is just this: they will still need to be coordinated. Getting them together may take more doing than getting them married.

Case Study of a Failure in Coordination

In 1952, Treasury Secretary John Snyder of the Truman administration would look back on a nine-month fight with the Federal Reserve Board and reflect:

> The Treasury and Federal Reserve felt that everything possible should be done to terminate the unwholesome situation that had developed and to coordinate the debt management responsibility for restraining credit expansion.[32]

What had happened was one of those dramatic ruptures in government when two powerful agencies begin to move in opposite directions. Through a good part of the early post–World War II period, the Federal Reserve's Open Market Committee stood as a ready buyer of government bonds and short-term treasury bills that would be offered on the market. The Fed did so to aid the Treasury in refinancing the enormous national debt and to maintain an atmosphere of credit ease through low interest rates. When the Fed buys bonds, bond prices rise, and the yield rate of interest for these bonds falls, putting downward pressure on interest rates generally.[33] In doing this, the Fed acts like the Commodity Credit Corporation for farmers, who can turn their wheat into money at guaranteed prices. With the Fed supporting the government bond market, banks can, without loss, turn their bonds into cash (actually bank reserves), which will support a five- to- six-fold multiplication of the money supply (depending on bank reserve requirements). That kind of monetization of the debt in a full-employment economy can have serious inflationary effects.

Following the economy's recovery from the 1949 recession, the Fed began to have increasing doubts about feeding the fires of inflation through its support of the government bond market. Then when Korean hostilities broke out in June 1950, the Federal Reserve Board cut the financial knot with the Treasury, deciding to let government bonds find their own level (they would fall) and interest rates rise as a counterinflationary strategy. In August 1950, a $13.5 billion issue of new government bonds found no purchasers (they were now scrounging for higher-interest-paying securities). There must have been near apoplexy in the Treasury Department: the Fed had double-crossed them.[34]

There the antagonists stood — the Treasury faced with refinancing $50 billion of the national debt (earlier issues maturing plus new borrowing to finance the war in Korea), badly needing a stable bond market; and the Federal Reserve Board, anxious to use monetary policy to fight the war-induced inflation, withdrawing its support from the bond market.

The moves that were made to achieve coordination between these two agencies ran almost the full gamut of the techniques we have talked about. There were prolonged interagency negotiations; an interagency committee, the Defense Mobilization Board, created by executive order in January 1951, with the Fed, Treasury, the economic defense agencies, and a number of other departments represented; presidential intervention; and cross-staffing. These last two deserve a close look.

Treasury Secretary John Snyder implied in mid-January 1951 that the Fed was willing to go along with a pegged rate of 2.5 percent for the Treasury's long-term bonds. But the Fed ignored the implication and dropped its support price for the Victory loans in late January. President Truman then called the Fed's Open Market Committee to the White House on January 31. According to the former chairman of the Board of Governors, Marriner Eccles,* this confrontation with the president was a pretty stiff affair. The president lectured them on the responsibilities of the government to protect the savings the American people had invested in their nation's defense. Chairman McCabe did what responding there was to be done; and the Open Market Committee then left, without, according to Eccles, having made any commitment to the president.[35]

Truman then reported to the press that the Fed would support the bond market. Eccles, now just a member of the board, resorted to defensive realpolitik.[36] He called in top financial reporters of the *New York Times* and the *Washington Post* over the weekend and leaked the Fed's side of the story to them. Both papers gave that story page one coverage. With the word out that the Fed's pegging operations were over, confusion returned to the bond market.[37]

Truman asked the board to negotiate with the treasury secretary, and high-level interagency negotiations were resumed.[38] On March 4, 1951, the famous accord was announced, largely on the Fed's terms. The Fed would use some moral suasion on big institutional investors to buy up the next long-term treasury bonds and would help maintain an orderly market for them, but on a "scale down" of prices.[39] Support would no longer be given the short-term bills, forcing banks that needed more reserves to borrow from the Fed rather than sell their treasury bills to the Fed, thus making the Fed's rediscount rate — their interest rate to banks — more effective as a monetary restraint. The two parties agreed to consult more regularly to work out their difficulties.

Perhaps stung by his defeat in this accord, in late March President Truman appointed his assistant secretary of the treasury, William McChesney Martin, to be the new chairman of the Federal Reserve Board in a striking instance of cross-staffing based on the principle of "If you can't lick 'em, join 'em."

But even with his own man holding the gavel at the Fed, Truman did not obtain a board subservient to Treasury policies. The nine-month imbroglio during 1950–1951 gave birth to the Fed's tight money policy, which generated

---

* The Giannini banking family of California had persuaded Truman not to reappoint Eccles as chairman in 1948 in a truly ugly case of pressure-group domination of the chief executive. See Marriner S. Eccles, *Beckoning Frontiers* (New York: Knopf, 1951), pp. 434–456.

rising interest rates for the next two decades. Federal Reserve independence defied coordination by the executive.[40]

We turn now from case study back to the search for a solution to those two remaining causes of uncoordination: faulty communication and leadership.

Communicating to Coordinate

At the outset, we encounter a tough dilemma perhaps first identified by Peter Blau: the carefully rationalized formal organization, with moderately narrow spans of control and a number of supervisory levels in the hierarchy, is precisely the kind that is shot through with barriers to communication.[41] This kind of organization, built to achieve coordination through close supervision and harmonization of the parts, undermines one of the central requisites of a coordinated system — the free flow of ideas, suggestions, and criticism. Blau's point is that we may achieve far closer coordination by simplifying the structure and enhancing communication than by multiplying supervisory levels.[42]

Coordination in its most fundamental sense rests upon shared knowledge of the work others are doing that bears on yours, and on the reduction of what Professor Leonard White once called "administrative distance," the psychological gap between two people who ought to relate to each other but who do not.

Staff openness is the antidote — if it can be achieved. The Walt Disney executives represent the ne plus ultra of such a model, with the assignments bulletin board reporting everyone's current projects and the unbelievable practice of executives going through each other's files to see what they are doing. In this highly actualized staff, there are apparently few threats to individual security.

This kind of openness is achieved through the listening abilities of wise leaders and the techniques of organization development, which we examine in Chapter 12.

The linking pins we discussed in Chapter 6 are basic ways to enhance communication and coordination. Whether they are simply key people in informal groups who are thoroughly integrated in agency life or men and women carefully chosen to provide representation on ad hoc committees where they serve, these significant others can relay ideas, problems, and gripes up and down the chain of command. They are in a unique position to develop that shared knowledge on which coordination rests.

Staff meetings are another way of doing it. In late November, for example, the superintendent of schools brings together his assistant superintendents for pupil personnel, teacher personnel, and facilities; his budget officer; his long-range planner; and others to see where the district stands in the third year of its five-year plan and what adjustments must be made for the new school year starting next September. The superintendent's demeanor in these meetings will be a critically important determinant of whether any meaningful communication takes place or not. If he is seen as Caesar, there may be no communication at all (the amens coming from his yes-men are not to be confused with communication). But if he has an agenda the staff have helped to build, if he has mastered the art of listening, and if he can be satisfied with raising questions and letting others do most of the talking, the superintendent and his associates have a fair chance of finding out about each other's activities and seeing the district as a whole — from which comes coordination!

Take Me to My Leader

Throughout this chapter the impact of strong and weak leaders on the workings of government has been felt. One almost sees them in fictitious contrasts: those who get things to move and those who don't. When we take a closer look, however, we see some, like FDR, who certainly got things to move, but in all directions much of the time, one feels.[43]

There are many opportunities for talented leaders to coordinate their enterprises. Fulfilling them, however, demands that administrators be proactive, not just reactive, on top of their jobs and not submerged in endless detail. An old work of teacher-administrator Marshall Dimock made the point well:

> The executive who analyzes his functions deliberately will find that he has three principal concerns, the importance of which occurs in the following order: First, he must keep the enterprise on an even keel, by which I mean that he must constantly expect the unexpected and be ready to deal with crises whenever and wherever they appear. Second, he must delegate everything that he can to those working under and with him. Third, if the program is going along satisfactorily, he then has the time and nervous energy with which to chart the course that lies ahead, to survey new horizons, and to add to the effectiveness of existing equipment. Some executives, of course, spend all their time on the first function; others are able to master the first two; but the test of the good executive is whether he is able to discharge all three. If he is not, then he is not on top of his job; and it is surprising how many, both in business and in government, are in this unhappy predicament.[44]

The first contribution leadership can make is creating an atmosphere where coordination can take place. The openness in human relations discussed earlier, the shared feelings of people who meaningfully care for each other, the minimizing of bureaucratic posturing and dramaturgy — the tone for all of these can be set in an agency by its leader. The leader is critical in reducing the administrative distance spoken of before.

In fulfilling his task roles, the administrator gives his staff a sense of direction, insuring that agency goals are defined with reasonable precision (unless Congress has demanded that the "Admiral Rings" do absolutely contradictory things!). The administrator will insist that priorities be established among these goals and will make budgetary and personnel decisions to back up those determinations.

To stay on top of the scene, he will require regular feedback from his management information systems on goal accomplishment. "Have the new recreational center, the employment security field office, and the monthly city council meetings held in Central City made any measurable difference in the crime rate,

Keeping Things Fuzzy, FDR-Style

[Franklin D. Roosevelt] evidently felt that both the dignity of his office and the coherence of his administration required that the key decisions be made by him, and not by others before him. . . . Given this conception of the presidency, he deliberately organized — or disorganized — his system of command to insure that important decisions were passed on to the top. His favorite technique was to keep grants of authority incomplete, jurisdictions uncertain, charters overlapping. The result of this competitive theory of administration was often confusion and exasperation on the operating level; but no other method could so reliably insure that in a large bureaucracy, filled with ambitious men eager for power, the decisions, and the power to make them, would remain with the president. This was in part on Roosevelt's side an instinct for self-preservation; in part, too, the temperamental expression of a restless, curious, and untidy personality. Coexistence with disorder was almost the pattern of his life.

Arthur M. Schlesinger, Jr., *The Coming of the New Deal* (Boston: Houghton Mifflin, 1958). pp. 527–528.

unemployment, and alienation among black residents there?'' The city manager will regularly ask such questions.

He builds self-actualizers with a strong commitment to the agency mission and to the public good. While the self-actualized may be headstrong and hard to coordinate, the administrator no longer has to draw maps for them or set fires under them.

He gives considerable attention to the maintenance needs of the organization, especially the quality of interpersonal relations. (How do you like coordinating with someone you can't stand?)

When the situation leaves no other recourse, the effective administrator is prepared to coordinate by deciding issues, resolving disputes, and sometimes knocking heads together.

Coordination, like the population explosion, is everybody's baby in the agency, but the administrator is the "Top Mamma." To lead is, in part, to coordinate.

SUMMARY

Achieving and executing policies that work harmoniously toward common goals is probably the second biggest frustration (after lack of money) of most public administrators.

Policies are difficult to coordinate because of the pluralist nature of our politics, the human tendency to want incompatible things at the same time, and such institutional factors as the separation of powers and American federalism, among other factors.

Execution is hampered by unmeshed gears in agencies that stem from the conflict of means, faulty organization, communication breakdowns, and inept leadership.

The chief hopes for coordinating policies lie in increasing sophistication of policy analysis in both executive and legislative branches, and in rigorous chief executive and departmental leadership.

A number of techniques are available to aid in getting the administrative gears to mesh: interagency negotiation and interagency committees, cross-staffing, powerful central staffs with command authority, superagencies, top-level coordinating devices such as the cabinet or the National Security Council, executive intervention, and merger via reorganization.

Communication and other leadership techniques can help provide both the informational base and the psychological climate that are the prerequisites of effective coordination.

KEY CONCEPTS

labyrinth syndrome
conflict of ends
conflict of means
policy analysis

interagency negotiation
cross-staffing
superagency

DISCUSSION QUESTIONS

1. Identify the various ways by which bureaucratic gears can become unmeshed. Which do you think is the most common? Which is the most significant?

2. Many of the reasons for a lack of coordination are based in poor organization and design rather than in the nature of politics. Discuss these reasons.

3. Assess the effectiveness of policy analysis as a coordinating device. To what extent do you think it can neutralize or overcome the tendencies toward a lack of coordination produced by politics?

4. Of the eight coordinating devices available to smooth out interagency relationships, which do you feel is the most effective? Which is the least effective?

Notes

1. This phase of the "battle of the Potomac" is related in Ray Harvey, ed., *The Politics of This War* (New York: Harper, 1943), ch. 7; and U.S. Bureau of the Budget, *The United States at War* (Washington, D.C.: Government Printing Office, 1946), pp. 399–400.

2. President's Committee on Civil Rights, *To Secure These Rights* (Washington, D.C.: Government Printing Office, 1947).

3. The story of what happened to the two "China hands," Davies and Service, was recounted in *Time* (Aug. 2, 1971) 98:14–15. A feeling for what happened to liberty during that era when we concentrated more on security than on "securing these rights" can be osmosed from Alan Barth, *The Loyalty of Free Men* (New York: Viking, 1951); and Elmer Davis, *But We Were Born Free* (Indianapolis: Bobbs-Merrill, 1954). Even the *administration* of the Truman loyalty-security program ran into coordination troubles. See Alan D. Harper, *The Politics of Loyalty* (Westport, Conn: Greenwood, 1969), pp. 237–240.

4. "Admiral Cites Pressures on Military Buyers," *Washington Post* (Feb. 13, 1952), p. 2.

5. *New York Times* (Sept. 26, 1969), pp. 94:1.

6. For a satire on unmeshed gears in the publishing business, see James Thurber, "File and Forget," *New Yorker* (Jan. 8, 1949) 24:24–28.

7. See Davin Kirschten, "The Coal Industry's Rude Awakening to the Realities of Regulation," *National Journal* (Feb. 3, 1979), pp. 178–182.

8. Robert Sherwood, *Roosevelt and Hopkins* (New York: Harper, 1948), pp. 554–556.

9. Quoted in Richard E. Neustadt, *Presidential Power* (New York: Wiley, 1960), p. 9.

10. Arthur M. Schlesinger, Jr., *A Thousand Days* (Boston: Houghton Mifflin, 1965), p. 406.

11. How to mesh those (potentially) unmeshed gears is neatly illustrated by informal organization at work. The abatement districts had as their managers three graduate students of an eminent biologist at the nearby state university. The old professor kept his protégés in touch (and in line).

12. See pertinent discussions on these barriers to communication in Guy Ford, "Why Doesn't Everyone Love the Personnel Man?" *Personnel* (Jan.–Feb. 1963) 40:49–52.

13. In explaining his pro-Israeli stand on certain Middle East issues during the 1950s, Congressman Wayne Hays (D-Ohio) gave the home-town syndrome classic definition: "I don't have any Egyptians in my district."

14. On these points, see the authoritative judgments of two insiders — Congressman Richard Bolling, *House Out of Order* (New York: Dutton, 1965), ch. 11; and Senator Joseph S. Clark, *Congress: The Sapless Branch* (New York: Harper & Row, 1964), pp. 23–30 and ch. 8.

15. For some of the reasons why, see David Halberstam, *The Best and the Brightest* (New York: Random House, 1972).

16. The Commission's report, *Goals for Americans* (Washington, D.C.: Government Printing Office), appeared in 1960.

17. P.L. 79-304; 60 Stat. 24.

18. For an appraisal of the council's work, see Edward S. Flash, *Economic Advice and Presidential Leadership: The Council of Economic Advisers* (New York: Columbia University Press, 1965).

19. "The Political Framework of a Stabilization Policy," in Max F. Millikan, ed., *Income Stabilization for a Developing Democracy* (New Haven, Conn.: Yale University Press, 1953), p. 605.

20. A painful instance is recounted in Halberstam, *The Best and the Brightest.* p. 308.

21. See U.S. Civil Service Commission, *An Instrument for Progress* (Washington, D.C.: Government Printing Office, 1965).

22. For the various sides to that struggle which led ultimately to President Truman's sacking the General, see Douglas MacArthur, *Reminiscences* (New York: McGraw-Hill, 1964), pp. 341–344, 357–396; and Harry S. Truman, *Memoirs* (Garden City, N.Y.: Doubleday, 1955), vol. 2, pp. 440–450; and the anthology of the statements made by the principals in Theodore Powell, *Democracy in Action* (New York: Macmillan, 1962), pp. 197–210.

23. U.S. Commission on Civil Rights, *Federal Civil Rights Enforcement Effort* (Washington, D.C.: Government Printing Office, 1971).

24. For the historical account of efforts to coordinate the homefront during World War II, see U.S. Bureau of the Budget, *The U.S. at War,* ch. 12.

25. For this history, see John D. Millett, *The Process and Organization of Government Planning* (New York: Columbia University Press, 1947), pp. 97–103, 152–159.

26. Dan Bonafede, "President Nixon's Executive Reorganization Plans Prompt Praise and Criticism," *National Journal* (Mar. 10, 1973), pp. 329–340, at 335.

27. The Domestic Council was created by Reorganization Plan No. 2 (E.O. 11541) in 1970 with Cabinet-level representatives and chief White House aides of the Nixon administration. Its track record was reviewed by Raymond J. Waldman, "The Domestic Council: Innovation in Presidential Government," *Public Administration Review* (May–June, 1976) 36:260–268.

28. Paul Y. Hammond, "The National Security Council as a Device for Interdepartmental Coordination," *American Political Science Review* (Dec., 1960) 54:899–910.

29. For the role of the National Security Council in the 1962 Cuban missile crisis, see Robert Kennedy, *Thirteen Days* (New York: Norton, 1971).

30. For a case study of a governmental reorganization designed to pull disparate operations together, see Frederick C. Mosher, "The Reorganization of the California State Personnel Board," in his *Governmental Reorganizations* (Indianapolis: Bobbs-Merrill, 1967), pp. 397–439.

31. But not without a fight! For the battle over the Children's Bureau, see E. D. Godfrey's study in Frederick C. Mosher, ed., *Governmental Reorganizations.* pp. 149–167.

32. U.S. Congress, Joint Committee on the Economic Report, *Monetary Policy and the Management of the Public Debt* (82d Congress, 2d Session, 1952), p. 74. (Cited hereafter as *Monetary Policy.*)

33. In the summer of 1950, for example, when the Korean War broke out, the interest rate on long-term government bonds was 2½% and on short-term bills, 1.25%.

34. The Treasury's recounting of these painful days will be found in the Joint Committee, *Monetary Policy.* pp. 69–74.

35. Marriner Eccles, *Beckoning Frontiers.* (New York: Knopf, 1951), p. 486.

36. Eccles, *Beckoning Frontiers.* pp. 490–498.

37. In his memoirs, Truman said, "I was taken by surprise when subsequently [the Fed] failed to support the program," Truman, *Memoirs,* vol. 2, pp. 44–45. Eccles regarded that as a lie.

38. See Eccles, *Beckoning Frontiers.* p. 490.

39. Details on the accord will be found in the Joint Committee, *Monetary Policy.* pp. 75–76.

40. The Fed's views on coordination were submitted to their bete noire on Capitol Hill, Congressman Wright Patman, the populist from Texas, and appear in the Joint Committee, *Monetary Policy.* pp. 263–272.

41. Peter Blau and W. R. Scott, *Formal Organizations* (San Francisco: Chandler, 1962), ch. 5.

42. For a dramatic instance of this point, see Philip Foss's study of the reorganization of the California Highway Patrol in Frederick C. Mosher, ed., *Governmental Reorganizations.* pp. 185–213.

43. See Arthur Schlesinger, Jr., "Franklin Roosevelt's Approach to Managing the Executive Branch," in Richard J. Stillman, *Public Administration: Concepts and Cases* (Boston: Houghton Mifflin, 1976), pp. 204–211.

44. Marshall E. Dimock, *The Executive in Action.* (New York: Harper, 1945), pp. 83–84.

Chapter 11
Communication: Inside and Out

IN-HOUSE COMMUNICATION

It is not so much the tyranny of words that haunts the public administrator as it is the snafu of words, of too many words, of too few words, of the wrong words:

You arrive at a meeting, only to find that another person in the office has been designated to take your place — no one had the guts to let you know.

The school superintendent says, "We've got to economize in our supplies account," which the teachers translate as, "Start buying classroom stuff out of our own pockets."

The section chief resorts to a memo when a personal visit, or flowers, or a pat on the back would have been so much better.

An agency representative fails to keep his associates informed on a touchy interagency negotiation and loses a program of vital importance.

Regional headquarters issues a manual on a new insurance plan for the agency, and two months later only half of the field directors and one third of the employees understand the changes.

Clearly, communication can ruin you — or it can save your neck:

A mayor has perfected the fine art of listening and finds solutions to the strained relations between Chicanos and his police force.

I Have a Dream Today

Dr. Martin Luther King at the Lincoln Memorial, August 28, 1963:

> It is obvious today that America has defaulted on this promissory note [to assure equality to all] insofar as her citizens of color are concerned. Instead of honoring this sacred obligation, America has given the Negro people a bad check; a check which has come back marked "insufficient funds." But we refuse to believe that the bank of justice is bankrupt. We refuse to believe that there are insufficient funds in the great vaults of opportunity of this nation. So we have come to cash this check — a check that will give us upon demand the riches of freedom and the security of justice. We have also come to this hallowed spot to remind America of the fierce urgency of now. This is no time to engage in the luxury of cooling off or to take the tranquilizing drug of gradualism. Now is the time to rise from the dark and desolate valley of segregation to the sunlit path of racial justice. Now is the time to lift our nation from the quicksands of racial injustice to the solid rock of brotherhood. Now is the time to make justice the reality for all of God's children.

Broadside Records, *We Shall Overcome* (New York: Broadside Records, 1964).

By the power of his oratory, a British prime minister marshals an island kingdom in 1940 to the defense of the realm and of Western civilization.

A Moses of our time has a dream on the steps of the Lincoln Memorial, his people follow him, the Congress hears, and civil rights legislation pours forth like a mighty stream.

That the transmission of ideas is so portentous of good and yet sometimes so capable of nothing, of confusion, or of evil is perhaps the first shocker of this critical phase of administration we call *communication*.

The Whys of Communication

Both the pathways and the reasons for communication inside an agency are numerous. An agency's communication network reminds one of the paths students lay out on campus: regardless of cement, all of the buildings are interconnected (see Figure 11.1). Messages are sent across those pathways to generate ideas, stimulate action (of both the giving-orders and the motivating kind), report results, share feelings, and correct errors. In very large measure, the success of an agency in achieving its output goals rests upon its success in doing those five things well.[1]

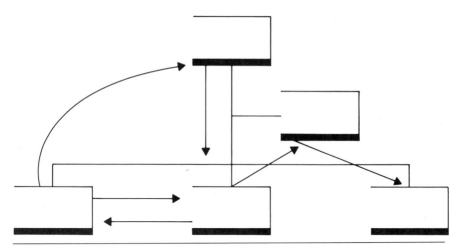

FIGURE 11.1   THE AGENCY COMMUNICATION NETWORK (without blockages)

Is Anybody Understanding?

The essence of communication can be put simply: it is the *sending of a message and having it understood.* There are four key elements:

MESSAGE ⟶ MEDIUM ⟶ RECEPTION AND UNDERSTANDING ⟶ FEEDBACK ⤶

The goal of the whole process — recipient understanding — can be obstructed by "noise," irrelevant data entering the communications channel that may distract and confuse the listener. Moreover, there are other barriers that can frustrate the process. The intended recipient didn't receive the message; she couldn't hear; she couldn't cope with the vocabulary; her understanding became completely skewed by her attitude toward the message sender and by her peers who didn't like the message; and so on. In short, at every point in the communication process trouble may arise to prevent understanding from taking place. We turn therefore to an analysis of all four elements — message, medium, reception and understanding, and feedback — in the pursuit of guidelines that may improve the chances of meaningful communication within government.

The Message

The message of the message arises out of the administrator's analysis of the work situation: deadlines not being met, new priorities for consideration, group maintenance needs requiring inputs, rule changes that need to be explained, to name but a few possible things.

Along with the work situation, the administrator also needs to take a long look at the employees he intends to communicate with. Where they are located, what their mood and potential reaction to the message he has in mind will be, and what their intellectual and language skills are, which so vitally determine what part of the message gets through.

A host of questions arises at this stage of the game: Should the matter be ignored (no message transmitted at all)?* Should the communication be delayed? What tone should be struck in formulating the message? The conventional wisdom on those kinds of questions may sometimes have applicability for the administrator: sometimes things are better left unsaid; never write in anger; a soft answer turns away wrath. The right response is certainly going to be determined, not by a priori prescriptions, but by the realities of the work situation. Whatever the variables are, the target remains the same in all communication — *employee understanding.*

Understanding can be improved if administrators will familiarize themselves with three aspects of communication: the Whorfian-Sapir hypothesis, the abstraction ladder, and gobbledygook.

The Whorfian-Sapir hypothesis The proposition developed by Edward Sapir and Benjamin L. Whorf is basically this: *we see through our vocabularies.*[2] As semanticist S. I. Hayakawa and others have long pointed out, words are maps of the territories of human experience; new words provide new maps, which in turn open up the possibility of new human experiences and broadened understanding. One sees the Whorfian-Sapir hypothesis at work in the early development of Helen Keller, who became blind, deaf, and mute as an infant and who began "to see" by acquiring an understanding of the verbal symbols of objects her eyes could not behold. She began to comprehend water as her teacher wrote "w-a-t-e-r" on the palm of one of her hands while spilling water over the other.[3]

The hypothesis of Whorf and Sapir is also illustrated in the linguistic eyes of Eskimos. It is said that they have over a dozen words for snow, greatly sharpening their comprehension of the white stuff that means nuisance to so many homeowners in more southerly climates. There are Eskimo words for snow with high water content, snow that is suitable for building igloos, snow that will support a man's weight, snow that gives no sound when tracking a seal or polar bear, plus a variety of others.

Whorf and Sapir may be great for the Eskimos, but what do they have to offer

---

* One of the clearest applications of this kind of calculation occurred during the Cuban missile crisis. Khrushchev had sent Kennedy two different communications — one bellicose, one softer. Kennedy ignored the former and responded in kind to the latter, a stratagem that clearly pulled us back from the abyss of war. See Robert Kennedy, *Thirteen Days* (New York: Norton, 1971), pp. 64–69, 71–74, 79–82.

the public administrator? Visualize how our knowledge of public affairs expands as we begin to develop new verbal maps for the problems that governments must cope with: "Cultural bias in written examinations," "generation gap," the "parity ratio in agriculture," the "multiplier" effect of public investments in fiscal policy, "recidivism" in law enforcement, and "self-actualization" in management philosophy. In one sense, administrators may look upon the vocabularies of their anticipated audience as a constraint (you better talk their language!); but the primary significance of the Whorfian-Sapir hypothesis is that vocabularies (more specifically, vocabulary building) may be the means for greatly expanding the conceptual grasp of an agency staff. How many kinds of snow do you know?

The abstraction ladder   The second two propositions mentioned above — the abstraction ladder and gobbledygook — both dramatize the painful fact that we can get lost with words. Our messages may turn out to be very bad maps of the territory we want employees to cover. The semanticist uses the abstraction ladder to suggest how far verbal reports and mental impressions can become separated from what is being described. The abstraction ladder is portrayed in Figure 11.2.

The poverty problem shown in the top block of Figure 11.2 is the entity itself that the poor live with and that government agencies would resolve if they could. The abstraction process begins as analysts start to study the problem and then verbalize their findings; others, further removed, then formulate their impressions and recommendations based on abstractions of abstractions. The final impressions that emerge (the contours of the bottom block) faithfully reflect a few dimensions of the actual poverty problem and badly distort others. How easily bad messages can lead people on bad trips!

One antidote to the abstraction ladder problem is direct involvement of employees in the problems themselves. VISTA workers (Volunteers in Service to America, in the domestic Peace Corps), for example, are sent for their training to Indian reservations, to Puerto Rican sections of New York City, and to other problem areas prior to their assignments in community development. Astronauts practice moon descents in highly realistic earthbound simulators. In each of these instances, one can see employees leapfrogging up the abstraction ladder to experience the real thing.

A second antidote to the problem is the extra caution an administrator exercises in his attempt to transmit understanding about reality to his employees. Third, he may strive to reduce the number of levels through which communications have to pass to reduce the likelihood of distortion. Fourth, the prudent administrator will provide for feedback to ascertain how closely his employees seemed to understand what he was driving at in his communication.

Gobbledygook   Employee understanding is undermined not only by the distances down the abstraction ladder but also by the multiplication of words in

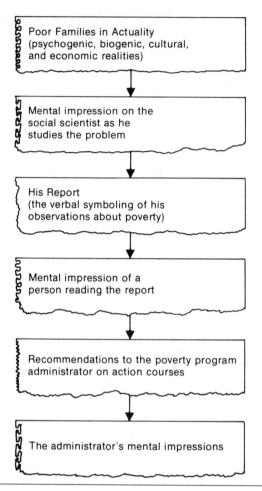

FIGURE 11.2   THE ABSTRACTION LADDER AND THE POVERTY PROBLEM

From S. I. Hayakawa, *Language in Thought and Action*, 2nd ed., p. 169. Copyright 1939, 1940 by S. I. Hayakawa. Copyright 1941, © 1963, 1964 by Harcourt, Brace and World, Inc. Reprinted by permission of Harcourt Brace Jovanovich, Inc. and George Allen & Unwin (Publishers) Ltd.

conveying a message. Not a monopoly of government, this verbal diarrhea is called gobbledygook — using twenty-five words to express a thought where five would do.[4] As Owen Remington has demonstrated, "The redcoats are coming" becomes, under gobbledygook, "This is classified information on a need-to-know basis. British, red-coated, armed, are proceeding in this direction." "I have not yet begun to fight" becomes "Full combat potentials available to me have not been effectuated at this point in time."[5]

In an imaginary rewriting of Lincoln's Gettysburg Address, the Defense

Down the Abstraction Ladder (Alias the Chain of Command)

Colonel to Executive Officer: Tomorrow evening at approximately 2000 hours Haley's comet will be visible in this area, an event which occurs once every 75 years. Have the men fall out in fatigues, and I will explain this rare phenomenon to them. In case of rain, we will not be able to see anything, so assemble the men in the theater and I will show them what they missed.

Executive Officer to Company Commander: By order of the Colonel, tomorrow at 2000 hours, Haley's comet will appear above the battalion area. If it rains, fall the men out in fatigues, then march to the theater where this rare phenomenon will take place, something which occurs every 75 years.

Company Commander to Lieutenant: By order of the Colonel, in fatigues at 2000 hours tomorrow evening, the phenomenal Haley's comet will appear in the theater. In case of rain in the battalion area, the Colonel will give another order, something which occurs once every 75 years.

Lieutenant to Sergeant: Tomorrow at 2000 hours, the Colonel, in fatigues will appear in the theater with Haley's comet, something which happens every 75 years. If it rains, the Colonel will order the comet into the Battalion area.

Sergeant to Squad Leader: If it rains, Haley's comet in its 75th year will appear in the Battalion theater tomorrow at 2000 hours. It will be accompanied by the Colonel in fatigues.

Squad Leader to Squad: When it rains tomorrow at 2000 hours, 75-year old Haley, accompanied by the Colonel, will drive his comet through the Battalion area theater in fatigues.

Source unkown.

Department representative on the "Air Confusing Committee" objected to the phrase "engaged in a great Civil War" —

> since mention of war made many people think of the costs of war and this was, unfortunately, often reflected in military budgets. In its place, Defense suggested "entered upon a period of civil uncertainty involving fairly full mobilization." Defense said that the phrase "all men are created equal" was objectionable to the Air Force but that, in the interests of unification, it would not make an issue of it. There was also objection by Defense to such phrases as "brave men, living and dead," and "honored dead" on the grounds that this unnecessarily called attention to one of the by-products of war to which many people still objected. If the thought must be retained, Defense suggested that the word "casualties" was a better choice than "dead."[6]

Our own favorite examples of gobbledygook appeared in the 1949 and 1950 annual reports of the librarian of Congress (which Senator Harry Flood Byrd of Virginia was unkind enough to call attention to in the *Congressional Record* of August 15, 1951). Page 11 of the 1949 report contained a single sentence of twenty lines of pedantic gobbledygook at its worst. That was followed on page 32 with this eyebrow-raiser, where some unknown writer is describing the form in which people send in reference questions to the Library of Congress:

> Some write in the clumsy characters of children, some in finely shaded Spencerian, some in the legibility produced by keys struck upon inked ribbon against a piece of paper, some in formality, some in familiarity, some in the bewildering idioms of countries left behind, some in hard wrought felicities. Their questionings are conveyed on penny postcards, on lined leaves ripped from notebooks, on flower-decorated paper, or on bond with letterheads handsomely embellished and engraved.[7]

There are at least three antidotes to gobbledygook. One is rigorous self-criticism, involving generous use of the red pencil on your own writing. The second involves training courses in effective writing (for which the O'Hayre manual, cited in note 4, would be a highly useful text). The third would be the employment of a skilled writer on your staff to apply the red pencil if you are unable to perform surgery on your own matchless creations.

While avoiding needless multiplication of words, the message writer in government should observe as well a few "thou shalts" in preparing a communication:

Determine and then designate to whom it applies.

Make it relevant.

Make it interesting.

Say it simply.

Pitch it at the right intelligence level.

Pretest it by trying it on some unsuspecting people who may be available.

Rewrite it.

Issue it.[8]

So much for the conception, or message stage, of communication; we turn next to delivery systems for getting the message across.

Media for Communication

Delivery systems The first remarkable thing about communication channels is the large number of them that are available to the administrator: the raised eyebrow in the staff meeting, the silent treatment for two weeks after the staff meeting, a phone call, face-to-face give-and-take, a pat on the back, a stab in the back, a kick in the right place (not thought to be widely used in government), a notice on the bulletin board, a memo, an official policy issuance (perhaps numbered and prepared for the loose-leaf binder), a letter, a Telelecture,*

---

* Telelecture is a communications system that utilizes both telephone and loudspeaker equipment. The communicator utilizes long-distance telephone. Her listeners hear her via the PA equipment and query her by means of traveling mikes attached to the special telephone gear.

closed-circuit television, word of mouth through the hierarchy, and word of mouth through the grapevine. In addition to these, agency newspapers, employee and union publications, agency monographs, annual reports, and films constitute additional ways of getting a message across.

The live, oral modes of communication possess one distinct advantage: they provide opportunities for interplay between sender and listener. Unless there are hang-ups of some kind that obstruct frankness, these forms of communication provide immediate feedback. The oral modes ordinarily do not provide a written record, which may sometimes be needed. However, with the ready availability of the tape recorder, and the mike that is easily attached to a telephone, today most kinds of oral communication can be transcribed for permanency. Written communications, on the other hand, permit more detailed study and can convey highly technical content.

While the grapevine is usually looked upon with disdain, some research documents its utility to the administrator. Keith Davis reports one study, for example, that found an accuracy rate of 75 to 80 percent for information transmitted via the grapevine.[9] But clearly there are some precautions to be taken when an administrator decides to utilize the network of informal organization for getting the word out (see Chapter 5). One is letting his deputies in the formal organization know what he plans to do so they do not feel that the ground is being cut out from under them. Another is the necessity of knowing the significant others in the informal structure who can play the communication role effectively in their work groups.

Upward communication moving through the grapevine should be encouraged and listened to. In fact, it is the most natural channel for employee sentiments to follow. Although there are always dangers of fact losing out to myth and of problems being inflated to crises, the grapevine should be viewed by the administrator as one of his most valuable instruments for tapping employee attitudes.

Selection considerations   Which mode of communication should you use to tell one of your sections that Congress has just eliminated funding for that unit's further operation, meaning that the entire section will be abandoned on September 30? How should you inform an employee that she is to be dismissed? Which method would you utilize to tell your field directors scattered throughout the United States of a major new program responsibility assigned to your bureau? Which means would be best for sharing the details of a new vacation and sick-leave policy with a staff of fifteen hundred employees?

Clearly, audience and cost factors will influence the choice of medium, as will the central dictum of communications expert, Marshall McLuhan, that *the medium is the message.*[10] How you go about conveying content may fundamentally alter the perceptions of that content by your intended recipients. To notify the members of one of your sections of its imminent demise by means of a cold, written memorandum would tell them something far more than their death penalty; the message that would hit them hard is that you are an unsympathetic, gutless wonder who obviously has neither empathy nor love for his staff. The message of the medium chosen will speak so loudly that its recipients may never hear its real contents. Thus, the McLuhan doctrine poses both an opportunity and a warning about the critical significance of choosing the right medium to use to get your message across.[11]

The kind of audience constraints that influence the selection of medium will include the location of your staff, their mood and likely reaction to the message itself, their likely reaction to the personalized or impersonalized media available, and the intelligence and language skills they possess.

Finally, cost factors may further limit the choices. Telelecture may involve fairly expensive long-distance telephone charges, as well as the cost of the equipment itself. The agency may not own closed-circuit television facilities. At the other end of the scale, a day off for the secretary who has just done a superb piece of work may be a thousand times more effective (in cost/benefit analysis!) than the dictated memorandum of appreciation.

Reception and Understanding

The third phase of communication is the critical one: Is the recipient getting the point? The hoped-for understanding is the result of a complex set of relationships involving the clarity of the message itself; the impact of the medium; and the IQ, language skills, ability to concentrate, and group climate of the recipient. With the obvious possibility that any of those may be out of whack, it is remarkable that communications systems work as well as they do.

Is anybody listening?   One of the great obstacles to understanding is the simple laziness or unwillingness of individuals fully to concentrate and digest the messages directed at them. If the message is unpleasant, the listener may turn away from it to avoid its impress. The message may seem only slightly relevant, and so the listener allows other things to cross her mind. Noise distracts her attention. In addition, there seems to be a considerable disposition on the part of many listeners to *evaluate* the message rather than hear what it has to say. For these and many other reasons, the unwillingness or inability of message recipients to focus on what is sent to them constitutes one of the very weak links in the communication chain.[12]

The ability to listen may also be obstructed by the personal attitudes between sender and receiver. The antiestablishment syndrome on the part of some may pose a substantial barrier in giving an honest hearing to messages from higher levels in the hierarchy. Conversely, the snob syndrome of some executives may make it impossible for them to hear or to understand what subordinates are saying by way of complaints or suggestions for agency improvement.[13]

Can the first sergeant with twenty-five years in the army really act on orders from the second lieutenant just out of a college ROTC program? Can the white interviewer fully perceive without distortion what the black applicant is saying?[14] When the Democrats take over county government after the Republicans have established a merit system, will those covered-in Republican civil servants be able to hear and grasp the new policy directives coming "from their left"?

Those significant others again   Apparently we not only see through our vocabularies (Whorf and Sapir); we may also see through others' eyes more than through our own (Tomatsu Shibutani).

We saw in Chapter 2 how role taking and role playing within a work group provide the norms of personal and group behavior. That same search for recognition and acceptance on the part of nonstatus members of primary groups vitally affects their perception of communications coming from outside the group. "How should I react to a communication?" readily becomes, "How are my significant others reacting whose favor I'm trying to win?" Shibutani puts the point this way:

> What any person experiences of the larger organization is necessarily filtered through the eyes of those with whom he is in immediate contact. The particular ways in which he interprets new policies and events depend to a large extent upon the views of those around him. Thus, each local unit develops a perspective and a set of norms, and the particular standards that arise make a difference in the manner in which official regulations are enforced. Such primary groups, even when the participants are not too intimate, exercise considerable control over the conduct of most of their members.[15]

So in communication as in essentially every other aspect of administration, the significant others of the dynamic work groups turn out to be extremely important in regulating the kind of reception messages get as they come down through the chain of command.

Structural styles   How the chain of command is organized constitutes still another factor influencing communication and understanding. As Winston Churchill once observed, "We shape our institutions and then they shape us." Four organizational shapes and their communication patterns have been dissected by Alex Bavelas [16]:

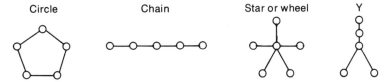

Circle   Chain   Star or wheel   Y

In the circle and chain arrangements each individual has a direct communication link with two other individuals (except those on either end of the chain). The advantage of the circle over the chain as well as over the wheel and Y is that the communications circuit is complete. A message, if blocked in one direction, has the possibility of moving in the reverse direction. Furthermore, an opportunity would exist for checking information that someone thought to be false in a different direction from which the original message came.[17]

In the wheel and Y arrangements, however, with no interplay among the recipients (as postulated in the diagrams), there is total dependence of the listeners on the communicator who stands astride the hierarchy. If he cannot communicate or does so poorly, members of these two types of organizations can suffer severely. A classic illustration of this kind of impairment of communication in an authoritarian climate was Stalin's handling of Soviet military decision making in World War II. Surrounding yourself with yes-men is no way to gauge the tide of battle, but an awfully good way to lose some.[18]

Can I handle bad news?   One final factor that shapes an individual's reception and understanding is the impact of the message on her whole need structure. We surmise, without having the empirical data to prove it, that receptivity and meaningful understanding are positively correlated with good news and negatively correlated with bad news. In a sense, we all have earphones and stand ready to click them off when the message is threatening to our security, our love, or our self-esteem needs.

In the day-to-day life of an agency, all news cannot be good news. Budgets are rarely what we would like them to be; a key deputy has let us down; legal counsel has questioned our authority to proceed; and so on. Thus the framing of the message and the choice of media are all the more critical in counterbalancing content that is naturally upsetting to the person on the receiving end.

When one surveys all the factors that influence receptivity — intelligence and vocabulary levels, ability to listen, noise, attitudes, group climate, structural arrangements, and individual needs — one must conclude that the climate in which messages are received is generally murky. Fortunately, there are two indicators that may tell whether or not the message made its way through that murk: the subsequent actions of the recipients, and their feedback which completes the communications circuitry.

The Feedback Cycle

The great need   Before we begin searching for upward communication in a *governmental* setting, how good is it in your *classroom* and on your *campus*? When you are elated with an especially able professor, does he ever know it? Do you have a tradition on your campus of applause at the conclusion of a course for those who deserve it? Do you have student evaluation of teachers? As an individual, can you express meaningful praise for the professor who has more than repaid your whole tuition by his class alone?

Conversely, what feedback mechanisms are available for those uninspired faculty members who are still lecturing from the faded class notes they took as graduate students fifteen years ago? Can you discuss your disappointment directly with them, or is grade intimidation far too great an obstacle for that kind of reverse communication? Must you pursue an end run to department heads and deans in that perennial and universal problem of coping with academic deadwood? If so, are you willing to play the overtrump (see Chapter 8)? You don't need to look beyond your own campus in order to see the urgent need for feedback and the obstacles that exist everywhere to giving and getting it.

Now look at the need for it in government. Congress goes through the motions of passing the 1965 Voting Rights Act. Whether it was worth the effort can be decided only if there is a flow of reliable data from the registrars who have been assigned to get blacks on the polling books. Has a poverty program aided only the middle class by providing them cushy jobs in the administrative superstructure of the poverty agencies? Or has the effort brought needed help to those whose view of heaven is plaster falling from the ceiling and whose zoo is their own living room where rats chase cockroaches in a nightmare theater? How will a president know the outcome of his gamble on a naval quarantine to force the removal of missiles from Cuba if he does not call for surveillance of Cuba thereafter by using espionage agents on the ground and U-2 overflights? On a more prevalent but less dramatic basis, must an administrator wait until a turnover rate of 40 or 50 percent finally tells her that staff morale has been shot in the head before realizing that she has personnel problems of a gigantic order? *You need feedback to stay in business!*

Any kind of feedback — factual or phony — may be helpful. Remembering that all behavior is purposeful, the administrator can ask what purpose underlies the supplying of incorrect feedback. But the dangers that lurk in erroneous feedback can be seen in White House handling of the Vietnam War in the 1960s. David Halberstam has suggested how grossly erroneous the reports from the field were (e.g., the 1961 report of Gen. Maxwell Taylor and Walter Rostow), thus giving encouragement to Kennedy's escalation of U.S. involvement. Halberstam alleges of another general, Paul Harkins, that:

> [He] began by corrupting the intelligence reports coming in. Up until 1961 they had been reasonably accurate, clear, unclouded by bureaucratic ambition; they had reflected the ambivalence of the American commitment to Diem, and the Diem flaws had been apparent both in CIA and, to a slightly lesser degree, in State reporting. Nolting [a Kennedy observer in Vietnam] would change State's reporting, and to that would now be added the military reporting, forceful, detailed and highly erroneous, representing the new commander's belief that his orders were to make sure things looked well on the surface. In turn the Kennedy Administration would waste precious energies debating whether or not the war was being won, wasting time trying to determine the factual basis on which the decisions were being made, because in effect the Administration had created a situation where it lied to itself.[19]

From observers in the field, through command posts, to the Joint Chiefs of Staff, to adviser Walt Rostow, and then to the president, every level suffered from the good-news syndrome, shaping the communiqués as they went by to meet the anticipated desires of the level above. Well into the war, presidential advisers convinced themselves that pacification was being achieved. The feedback mechanism had failed.

Monitoring operations and correcting errors are two of the major reasons why feedback is so important. At the classroom level, the midterm examination is a feedback device that provides some clues to the professor on whether any concepts he has been talking about are getting through. At the administrative level, getting reliable feedback in police administration tells the chief whether assigning black policemen to black neighborhoods is improving police-citizen relationships or not; and citizen objection to a proposed garbage dump tells the county planners to search further for an acceptable site before the county's goodwill has become completely eroded by a poor decision about its location. What is required for effective monitoring are management information systems (similar to MBO and PERT) that lay down the things to be measured, the target deadlines, and the indices of success.[20]

A third purpose served by keeping feedback channels comfortably open is the generation of new ideas.[21] Hopefully we have long ago agreed that management has no monopoly on creativity and wisdom. Brains are distributed up and down the ranks! The added payoff for having channels open to employee input, of course, is the boost that is given to self-actualization when employees see a meaningful chance to influence policy, and perhaps even the course of events.

Barriers to feedback   There are many obstacles to effective upward communication. To begin with, there are the problems posed by the natural lethargy, reticence, and unwillingness of many workers to look beyond the confines of their immediate job. As we have noted, some people love ruts and do not wish to get out of them.

Then there are the hurdles of the hierarchy itself: the posturing and dramaturgy of the higher-ups creating an ego barrier, which some lower-downs may hesitate to crack; and the role differentiation that some managerial types cling to that they are to do the thinking and subordinates the doing. As Blau and Scott observed:

> The free flow of communication — in the form of criticisms, suggestions, manifestations of respect and expressions of approval furnishing social support — furthers problem-solving. Hierarchical differentiation of status usually impedes the free flow of communication, and for this specific reason such differentiation tends to be detrimental for task performance. If leadership does not block but frees the flow of communication . . . then leadership will further rather than hinder problem-solving.[22]

In addition to the obstacles noted, we would also have to count racial and religious prejudice, invidious sex distinctions, and age differentiation among the factors that lead employees to clam up when they should be feeding back.

Getting feedback   There are four basic conditions for free-flowing upward communication in an agency, conditions within the power of administrators to create. They must (a) earnestly want feedback, (b) provide ways to get it, (c) listen to it, and (d) act on it. Agency atmosphere would seem to be critical. Do the upper echelons on a tight authoritarian ship want compliance and feedback or just compliance? Or rather, is there meaningful solicitation of suggestions from the rank and file? One of the things that can destroy the latter approach is phoniness: asking for suggestions and constructive criticism and then never acting on any of the things the employees bring forth.

Providing for feedback obviously does not mean assuming that feedback will come. But there are a number of ways by which an administrator can generate a flow of ideas from his associates. One is the use of questionnaires to measure employee attitudes.[23] Another is knowing the informal organization and the significant others in the natural work groups. Having identified them, the administrator can keep in close touch with these eyes, ears, and voice of the rank and file. Yet another is maintaining an open-door policy, even if for only part of a day — and getting the word around that the chief is available during those hours for anyone on the staff who needs to see her.

Employee meetings, held during working hours and in agency facilities, create situations where dialogue may take place, grievances may be aired, and suggestions generated.

Regularly held staff meetings can be productive if the climate is right for people to speak up. But if the regional director never stops talking, flusters easily in the face of criticism, or is abusive toward his staff, then the reaction to be anticipated is one of either silent associates or yes-men. If you want feedback, *you've* got to stop talking.[24]

Some have proposed institutionalized employee feedback in the form of an agency ombudsman whose primary responsibility would be the protection of employee rights. To a degree, that role has long been played by counselors in agency personnel offices who are prepared to do battle with line officials when employee rights have been jeopardized. Another way of institutionalizing feedback is through agency recognition of an employee union. Unlike many employees, union officers are not ordinarily known for shyness and reticence. Feedback is their business. At a higher level, the U.S. Civil Service Commission established a complaint office in July 1968, with governmentwide purview.[25]

An uncensored employee newspaper or house organ may provide a vehicle to carry employee views home to management. The editorials and letters to the editor these shop gazettes carry can be far more revealing than the old-time suggestion box. Whether by means of a suggestion box or not, the flow of ideas from employees may be considerably enhanced with a financial carrot authorized by the 1954 Incentive Awards Act.

One final source of feedback that ought not to be overlooked is the exit interview with departing employees. Many of them will feel totally free of intimidation and ready to evaluate their experiences with the agency candidly. The interviewer will want to probe for the areas of satisfaction and dissatisfaction during their employment and for their suggestions on improving management in the agency. But note that there are some dangers. Some employees may be leaving in a rage; an interview with them would detect enormous heat and little light. Others, counting on favorable letters of recommendation from the supervisors they are leaving, will hesitate to say anything critical during the interview lest their job hunting and future be jeopardized. In these latter cases, the exit questionnaire may be a better tool than the interview. Former employees can have a chance to cool off and look at their old agency more dispassionately, and they can answer the form anonymously.[26]

These, then, constitute some of the numerous ways in which administrators may openly solicit regular employee feedback.

Beyond the internal communication network that, it is hoped, links together administrators and employees is another one of equal importance to agency success — communications between the agency and its publics.

COMMUNICATING WITH THE PUBLIC

In the summer of 1978, the voters of California adopted an initiative called Proposition 13 requiring a sharp cutback in the property taxes governments could impose on them. But beyond engineering some local tax relief, Proposition 13 also sent a telegram throughout the country telling government how bad its breath had become.

The subliminal message of the tax revolt began to come through: in the eyes of a lot of Americans, government is a mess. That poor image resulted not only in sharply reduced revenues available to government in the Proposition 13 states in 1978–79 but also in a whole array of difficulties: open hostility toward Bureau of Land Management employees for tough restrictions on mining on public lands, rising distrust of the Nuclear Regulatory Commission for inadequate safety standards in atomic power plants, and mounting suspicion about the administration of welfare programs everywhere. Down that road lie not only inadequate funds to carry out public functions but also citizen resistance to the policies and regulations of governments they no longer respect.

But the public sector isn't constantly knocking on the administrator's head. A small-town city manager gets a constituent's postcard in the morning mail (with the original spelling and punctuation left intact):

> I never seen the cemetary and streets look better.
> I like your new garbageman he turned your can
> over, you don't a fine job with the water infact
> you are doing a nice job, thanks a lot.*
> *Jet*

A carefully prepared and well sold urban renewal program wins a crucial ballot test. A school bond issue is approved. A popular mayor is reelected.

* So far as we know, Jet had never read James Joyce's *Finnegans Wake*.

Something Wrong Besides High Taxes

On October 1, 1978, in the wake of California's Proposition 13, the *Washington Post* published a survey of the things that were bugging people about their government:

While three out of four people in the nationwide survey would endorse severe tax cuts, seven out of eight said they were more concerned with the way tax dollars were being spent than with tax levels themselves.

Eighty percent of the respondents said the federal government employed too many people; and 63 percent said far too many.

Seventy-three percent said they believed that government wastes their tax dollars.

By a 2 to 1 margin, the respondents said that clerks and salespeople in the private sector were more courteous and honest than government employees.

By a 3 to 1 margin, private employees were perceived as harder working and more efficient than civil servants.

Since the popularity index of some administrators may be like a roller coaster ride — from hero to bum in one fiscal year — an agency's public relations clearly cannot be taken for granted. As Chris Argyris has observed, stabilizing the external environment is one of the manager's most critical tasks.[27] The management of agency public relations is essential in stabilizing that environment.

The Compelling Reasons for Government Public Relations

First, in a democratic society, the people have a *right to know* what their government is up to. Like many rights, this one needs constant reassertion. From city councils through school boards to the National Security Council, there is a great penchant for arriving at decisions in secret and then role playing thereafter with the press present.

Jefferson said correctly: "If a nation expects to be ignorant and free, in a state of civilization, it expects what never was and never will be"; and: "Whenever the people are well informed, they can be trusted with their own government."[28] Whereas the media have the primary responsibility for informing the people, substantial inputs on public affairs come from government officials: statistics on the crime rate, changes in the wholesale price index and unemployment, costs of veterans' benefits, and impact on learning rates of such educational projects as Headstart, Upward Bound, and the like.

A second reason for agency dissemination of news is to *convey information* that is essential for either their constituents' compliance or benefit. For example, the poverty agency or Agriculture Department must set forth eligibility requirements for food stamps. The Veterans Administration needs to publicize the medical services available to veterans. The surgeon general caps the work of his research teams by launching an aggressive campaign against tobacco. (Even car bumper stickers have gotten into the act: "Smoking cures cancer.") The county recreation department publicizes its summer program for kids.

Third, agencies engage in PR to *build support* for their programs. The National Guard in one state appoints a wing of honorary colonels (who also happen to be the eagles of the state's power structure). The governor judiciously appoints representatives of all the key minority groups to his commission on human rights. The Defense Department empanels citizen advisory councils from around the country. The State Department brings in fifty professors of international relations for briefings. The secretary of state carries on diplomatic relations with the elite of the Washington press corps at the Burning Tree Country Club on Sunday afternoons. From civilian colonels to nine irons, sage administrators will employ all the tools of the trade to win support for their agencies.

The support-building face of government PR can also be seen in the use of media. The sign on the golf course construction site never reads "Built with taxes for taxpayers"; but rather, "Golf course expansion, under the direction of Joe Niblick, Parks Commissioner." From there we go to the police department's annual report, the State Department's white paper on arms for the Middle East, and a president's televised defense of his Middle East policies. In each instance, the Holy Grail being sought is public endorsement and backing.

Public relations is also available as a *defensive weapon* against attacks. When Henry Cabot Lodge, Sr., and a group of isolationist senators railed against the Covenant of the League of Nations, Woodrow Wilson began a whistle-stop tour around the country to defend his postwar diplomacy. And when a latter-day group of senators begin to fire salvos against Jimmy Carter for giving away our national security to the Russians in a SALT treaty, the president tried to pull the fuse with a dramatic PR defensive move — he authorized a start-up on the MX missile (which calmed some nerves and rattled some others).

At the local level, agencies also come under attack, and then find some defensive weaponry in PR. In one city we know of, a reactionary mayor unleashed a hurricane of criticism against a community development program of a nearby town. He labeled it "a part of the '1313' conspiracy of social scientists to impose city manager dictatorship, metropolitan government, and urban renewal on unsuspecting voters who would lose their vote to a government by experts." After regaining his cool, the harassed community development director in the nearby town canvassed his options — silence, quiet explanation, take the offense, line up allies, and others.[29] He chose quiet explanation before a town meeting, received a vote of confidence, and the development program carried on.

A fifth reason for government PR concerns the *feedback phase* rather than the output phase of public relations. Agencies need to know how constituents are being affected by their efforts, what unmet needs exist, and what creative ideas clientele groups are generating the agency might pursue. In a surprising democratic aside, that apostle of princely sovereignty, Thomas Hobbes, wrote:

> The best counsel in those things that concern not other nations but only the ease and benefit [of] the subjects . . . is to be taken from the general informations and complaints of the people of each province, who are best acquainted with their own wants and ought, therefore, when they demand nothing in derogation of the essential rights of sovereignty, to be diligently taken notice of.[30]

Consider the school board as a case in point. Blissfully assuming that all is well in race relations, the board is shocked by the black community's demand for the dismissal of a white high school teacher who had rebuked five unruly black students outside his door by saying, "You niggers had better behave in the halls." The board is brought up short at a meeting with the black parents as the latter group tell of seven- and eight-year-olds being expelled from school for the most trivial offenses. Then heat gives way to light as the black spokesmen begin to outline their demands for school reform (ungraded classes, smaller classes, guaranteed graduation, and so on). What a tragedy that regular methods for generating and getting that kind of feedback had not been provided decades earlier.

Nature of Government Public Relations

The term "public relations" is not a synonym for publicity. Eleanor Ruhl expressed the matter succinctly in algebraic form: $P + R = PR$. Here, the P stands not for publicity but for *performance,* and the R for reporting.[31] The formula immediately suggests that agencies with high performance and great public exposure may need little reporting to generate favorable attitudes outside. Examples would be the city street department, cemetery, or public parks. No amount of publicity — reporting — could counteract potholes that rip your tires apart, weeds that bury the dead, and litter so deep the kids can't swing.

Conversely, agencies with distasteful jobs to perform or little natural exposure may have to give more attention than some others to the reporting of their good works in order to maintain their place in the sun of public (and appropriators') affection.[32] Principal case in point is the police department. Much of its contact with specific citizens is bad news: one is pinched for speeding; another is detained for disorderly conduct; someone else is arrested for wife beating. And the local newspapers can have such fun with copper-whopper headlines:

"Takes Police Ambulance 30 Minutes to Reach Traffic Accident Across Street from Station"; "Beer Arrests at Baseball Park Skyrocket — So Do Unsolved Safe Crackings"; "Police Brutality Triggers Ghetto Uprising."

But there is a broad laity of citizens who need to know something of the crime rate and, more important, something of the *solution* rate. Blacks might feel some confidence to find out, by deeds as well as words, that cops are arresting dope pushers in black neighborhoods instead of receiving kickbacks from them. Police bad news is obvious; police good news has to be told: P + R = PR.

Ruhl's formula, in the sequence she suggests, also stresses that performance must precede reporting. We don't want police bulletins to report an upsurge in narcotic arrests when everything is status quo ante the press release. The distance between P + R in the formula is now called credibility gap. Such a gap contributed to the embarrassment of one president in 1960 (the U-2 incident with Russia), and the fall of two later ones, in 1968 and in August 1974.

You ought to be the expert on this subject. Look at your own university. How much effort and money do the university's administrators expend telling students, parents, and taxpayers what a great job they are doing? On the other side, what kind of treatment do *you* receive from the registrar's office, the departmental receptionist, your professor when appealing an exam score, or in getting an appointment to see her? Is it performance or reporting that constitutes the heart of healthy public relations?

Thus, it becomes impossible to speak of the *public relations function;* to the contrary, public relations management is a multiplicity of things. Press releases and press conferences are a part of it. Public tours through agency facilities are another. Transferring a telephone operator with a voice like soggy oatmeal to a quiet job is a third. Counseling decision makers on the public impact of alternative A versus alternative B is a fourth. How clientele are treated by the receptionist, traffic cop, forest ranger, and census taker is an all-important fifth.

Managing Public Relations

Maintaining the public image of an agency is a *continuing* responsibility of management, not an episodic one. If it were the latter, a police department might be able to handle the hostile reaction of a crowd to an episode of police brutality. But if a solid foundation for agency-clientele cooperation has not been laid, all the press releases and PR techniques in the world will be of little use.

Management's job, then, is twofold: (a) to build a reservoir of goodwill with all publics, and (b) to establish healthy relationships with the media. Contributing to these ends over the long pull are high-level performance of agency functions, getting and listening to feedback, honesty in reporting, minimal resort to secrecy and censorship, availability to and cooperation with reporters, and judicious distribution of news patronage — timing of releases to benefit the

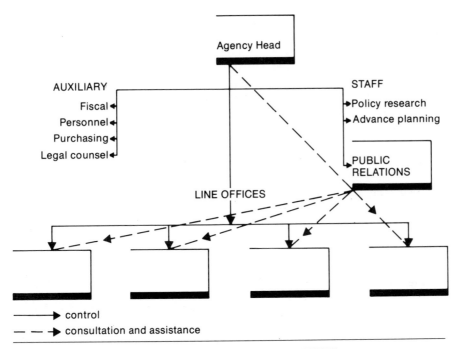

FIGURE 11.3   PUBLIC RELATIONS IN THE ADMINISTRATIVE FRAMEWORK

morning and evening dailies on some alternating schedule, distribution of paid advertising, fair play in subscriptions, and so on.

Segments of the PR job may be delegated, but not responsibility for agency tone and image. The commissioner of reclamation cannot say to his public information officer, "You take the PR ball and run with it; I'm going to concentrate on engineering." Rome burned while Nero played with his slide rule, remember.

The PR office under the agency head has at least three important jobs to do: give counsel on the PR dimensions of all major agency decisions; supply information to the media; and obtain data on clientele attitudes toward the agency, through their own research or through contracted arrangements with polling organizations (see Figure 11.3).

Consider the counseling role. Looking at the Cuban missile crisis of 1962, the outsider would assume that the public relations consideration must have vetoed any possibility of a do-nothing policy. Detroiters, along with millions of other Americans, would have been incensed if our government had left them within range of Castro's IRBMs. Whether or not a public relations adviser is present, the public relations concern is omnipresent.

At the municipal level, the mayor and city council would want the best estimates they could obtain on the likely receptivity to the first urban renewal project in the community. The PR people ought to help supply that information.

One other aspect of managing the PR function might conceivably fall in the hands of the personnel people and their training staff. That is getting across the message of "PR at all levels." The point is well illustrated by a sign on the full-length mirror in the salesmen's dressing room of a men's clothing store: "Do your clothes sell ours?"

As examples, contrast the public relations sense of two police officers, from the same department, doing their thing two blocks apart the same morning. Cop A, with keen regret and real courtesy, gives you a ticket for making an illegal U-turn. Cop B has parked his motorcycle astride an available parking space while he hands out parking tickets for cars parked by expired meters.

Every employee with any public contact — from switchboard operator to receptionist to agent in the field — helps to build or damage the agency's image.* Most need some training on how to build.

A Public Relations Sequence

Let's assume that a PR problem of serious proportions is jeopardizing our agency; for example, the increasing reputation of the university as a "hotbed for revolutionaries and acid heads." Evidence mounts that the image is hurting us in reduced state appropriations, in student recruitment, and in alumni support. What should be done? Applying the decision-making scheme suggested in Chapter 9, the college heads might proceed as follows:

1. *Careful definition of the problem:* find out whether there is in fact a pattern of lawlessness among the students, or rather community misinformation on the issue and lack of understanding on what differentiates a university from a seminary.

2. *Intelligence phase:* conduct an empirical study of community attitudes to establish what our public profile really is (door-to-door sampling, mailing lists of alumni, interviews with community influentials, etc.).

3. *Determining the constraints:* identify those factors that will limit our efforts to improve the university's image — time, funds, attitude of newspaper editors and TV operators, cooperativeness or intransigence of the student body, and so on.

4. *Canvasing all the alternatives:* rectify any actual on-campus conditions that have given rise to the tarnished image; utilize students for person-

---

* One thinks of a group of air force mechanics flown to an American air base in Morocco to repair fighter aircraft. After making them airworthy, the mechanics then proceed to "shoot the planes down" by photographing veiled women, engaging in public drunkenness, and eating with their left hands (a cultural taboo in the Middle East) — contributing to a rising tide of anti-Americanism and cancellation of the lease for that air base.

to-person contacts, statements by regents and top-level university administrators, mailing pieces, woo the media, and the like.

5. *Decision making:* weigh each of the alternatives, and their mixes, against the objective and the constraints; find what combination of techniques will reach our minimum expectation of a change in public attitudes toward the university at least cost.

6. *Program planning:* translate the decision making into a concrete plan, with missions assigned to the university president, public relations staff, the dean of students office, the academic heads, and the student leaders.

7. *Pretesting:* stage a dry run of any planned techniques or PR materials on a control group to uncover the bugs and measure the effects.

8. *Provision for feedback:* specify precisely how the monitoring of the program is to take place (spot interviews, newspaper content analysis, hostile mail count, etc.); schedule a review session for adjusting the program in the light of the feedback.

In some such way, an agency might rationally analyze an external threat and devise an appropriate response to enhance its public relations.

SUMMARY

Communication in an agency is like the nervous system in the body. From brain to extremities and back again pass the vital signals that generate action, coordination, and correction. For an agency, the free flow of understandable ideas is an indispensable condition for its success and survival.

Communication is sending a message and having it received and understood. The key elements are message, medium, reception and understanding, and feedback.

Analyzing the audience, noting that we see through our vocabularies (the Whorfian-Sapir hypothesis), and getting lost with words (the abstraction ladder and gobbledygook problems) must be taken into account along with subject matter in message preparation.

In selecting the communication media. the administrator must remember McLuhan's point that the medium is the message, realize that there are cost differences among the alternative modes of communicating, and weigh the possible audience reactions to the various modes.

The objective of the whole communication process is understanding. The recipients' levels of intelligence, vocabulary skills, concentration ability, and group climate will vitally affect what comes through. That people tend to see through group eyes and ears makes the role of informal group leaders, the significant others, especially critical in the communications network of an agency.

Agency circuitry without the return wiring (feedback) will either fizzle or explode. Top brass need the word on program accomplishments, rank-and-file ideas and problems, and public reactions. Feedback that is factual and frank does not simply happen. Hierarchy, fear, group climate, and supervisory attitude may create blocks in the circuitry. The administrator must go to extra lengths to provide for return data.

Government communication is external as well as internal. The people's right to know and the agency's need to build popular support and defend itself from attack underscore the importance of effective public relations.

Public relations begins not with publicity but with performance. While the responsibility for agency PR cannot really be delegated, essentially everyone in an agency has a piece of the action. Until the message of public relations at all levels thoroughly sinks in, there will be gaping holes in the agency's communication armor.

KEY CONCEPT

message
medium
reception and understanding
feedback

gobbledygook
circle, chain, star, Y
exit questionnaire

DISCUSSION QUESTIONS

1. What is the Whorfian-Sapir hypothesis? Of what importance is it to the administrator? If the message communicated is misunderstood, how could knowledge of the W-S hypothesis help to clear up communication problems?

2. To what extent do you agree with McLuhan that the medium is the message for the administrator? Which medium is the best? Which the worst?

3. Discuss the four organizational shapes and their communication patterns. Is the best organizational shape for communication purposes also the best in terms of organizational effectiveness?

4. Why is feedback so important? What are the major barriers to feedback and how can they be overcome?

5. Discuss the reasons why government should have a public relations function.

PROJECT

Choose a local, state or federal agency. Through interviews, phone calls, or letters, learn all you can about the public relations efforts of that agency. Obtain any printed information that may be distributed by the agency. Analyze the agency effort in terms of its success. Do some agencies deliberately avoid PR?

Notes

1. The critical importance of communication in a complex job such as moving an agency from the East coast across the country to southern Arizona was effectively shown in "How to Move a Staff 2400 Miles by Use of PR Techniques," *Public Relations Journal* (Nov., 1968) 24:12–14.

2. Edward Sapir, *Selected Writings* (Berkeley, Calif.: University of California Press, 1949), p. 10; Benjamin L. Whorf, *Language, Thought and Reality* (New York: Wiley, 1956), pp. 27 and 214.

3. Helen Keller, *The Story of My Life* (New York: Doubleday, 1954).

4. See John O'Hayre, *Gobbledygook Has Gotta Go* (Washington, D.C.: Government Printing Office, 1966), pp. 37–42; and A. J. Tresidder, "On Gobbledygook," *Military Review* (Apr., 1974), pp. 16–24.

5. "Famous Quotations from History Translated into Officialese," *Army Digest* (May, 1967).

6. This rewriting of the Gettysburg Address appeared in mimeograph form in the early 1950s under the title "Air Confusing Committee," author unknown.

7. From the 1949 *Annual Report of the Librarian of Congress,* p. 32, as reproduced in the *Congressional Record,* vol. 97, Part 14, p. A5157.

8. For a technical treatment of the subject, see Dean C. Barnlund, *Interpersonal Communication* (Boston: Houghton Mifflin, 1968).

9. Keith Davis, *Human Relations at Work* (New York: McGraw-Hill, 1962), p. 248.

10. Marshall McLuhan, *Understanding Media: The Extensions of Man* (New York: McGraw-Hill, 1964), and other works.

11. The McLuhan thesis, in a bit more detail, is that the communication medium, by affecting our physical responses and social interaction, is a fundamental influence on our behavior. Prior to the printing press communication was aural, forcing people into closer groups for hearing purposes. The introduction of printing then stressed visual communication, calling for individual effort rather than group effort and stimulating rational, categorizing kinds of mental activity.

    The appearance of telephone, radio, and television reasserted the importance of aural communication. To McLuhan, TV is primarily aural and tactile (that is, communication which can be felt), and not primarily visual. This is perhaps the chief paradox in McLuhan's writings and the most severely challenged by his critics. McLuhan contends that TV is a tactile medium in that viewers tend to fill in the depth behind the two-dimensional screen and thus get involved personally, with the resultant feeling that they are surrounded by the medium.

12. Carl R. Rogers and F. J. Roethlisberger, "Barriers and Gateways to Communication," *Harvard Business Review* (July–Aug., 1952) 30:47, 52. See also A. W. Farrant, "Boss, Are You Listening?" *Supervision* (Sept., 1976) 38:9.

13. For discussion of the impact of status differences on the communication process see Blau and Scott, *Formal Organizations* (San Francisco: Chandler, 1962), pp. 121–134.

14. Vernon R. Taylor, "You Just Can't Get Through to Whitey," *Public Personnel Review* (Oct. 1969) 30:199–204.

15. Tomatsu Shibutani, *Society and Personality* (Englewood Cliffs, N.J.: Prentice-Hall, 1961), p. 407.

16. Alex Bavelas, "Communication Patterns in Task-Oriented Groups," in Daniel Lerner and Harold Lasswell, eds., *The Policy Sciences* (Stanford, Calif.: Stanford University Press, 1951), ch. 10; or Bavelas and Dermott Barrett, "An Experimental Approach to Organizational Communication," *Personnel* (Mar. 1951) 27:366–371.

17. For some efficiency measurements of the alternative arrangements, see Harold J. Leavitt, *Managerial Psychology* (Chicago: University of Chicago Press, 1972), pp. 189–198.

18. See Nikita Khrushchev's denunciation of Stalin (on this and other points), *New York Times* (June 5, 1956), pp. 13, 15, 16.

19. David Halberstam, *The Best and the Brightest* (New York: Random House, 1972), p. 157.

20. A management information system for the U.S. State Department to measure staffing, utilization, and intervening variables (like absenteeism, turnover, etc.) is described by A. C. Hyde and Jay Shafritz, in "HRIS: Introduction to Tomorrow's System for Managing Human Resources," *Public Personnel Management* (Mar.–Apr. 1977) 6:70–77.

21. For an outstanding example in private enterprise, see the accomplishments of the Lincoln Electric Company. There the most significant part of one's paycheck consists of incentive payments for innovative suggestions about his own job. See James F. Lincoln, *Lincoln's Incentive System* (New York: McGraw-Hill, 1946).

22. Blau and Scott, *Formal Organizations*. p. 125; and see also p. 131 for a number of examples of what happens when upward communication begins to freeze up.

23. See a useful form for soliciting employee feedback about a state personnel system in J. J. Marsh, "Personnel Employees' Perceptions of a State Merit System," *Public Personnel Management* (Mar.-Apr. 1977) 6:93–97.

24. See Rensis Likert, *The Human Organization* (New York: McGraw-Hill, 1967), p. 110.

25. See Irving Kator, "When Federal Employees Complain," *Civil Service Journal* (Jan.–Mar. 1969) 9:16–19.

26. See Julius Yourman, "Following up on Your Terminations," *Personnel* (July–Aug. 1965) 42:51–55.

27. The others' being maintaining the internal system and accomplishing agency goals. Chris Argyris, *Integrating the Individual and the Organization* (New York: Wiley, 1964), pp. 120–123.

28. Jefferson, letters to Col. Yancey, 1816, and Dr. Price, 1789, respectively, in Saul Padover, ed., *Thomas Jefferson on Democracy* (New York: Mentor Books, 1954), pp. 149, 160.

29. For a fascinating example of an attempt to use realpolitik (suppression of hostile news stories about an agency) as a defense, see "The Regional Director and the Press," in Harold Stein, *Public Administration and Policy Development* (New York: Harcourt, Brace, 1952), pp. 739–745.

30. Thomas Hobbes, *Leviathan* (New York: Liberal Arts Press, 1958), pp. 275–276.

31. Eleanor Ruhl, *Public Relations for Government Employees* (Chicago: Civil Service Assembly, 1952), p. 1.

32. An old text reminds us: "Neither do men light a candle, and put it under a bushel, but on a candlestick; and it giveth light unto all that are in the house." And a phrase in the next verse is worth remembering: ". . . that they may see your good works. . . ." (Gospel of St. Matthew.)

Chapter 12
Government Reorganization and Agency Renewal

GOVERNMENT BY COMMITTEE?

In the seedtime of government reform early in the twentieth century, the New York Bureau of Municipal Research found mismanagement in New York City government everywhere, some of it chargeable to faulty organization and some not:

hospitals, without scales on their delivery docks, paying for hundredweights of ice that weighed eighty pounds

contracts being let to political favorites for under $1,000 so the amounts would look small and the plums could be passed around

severe irregularities in working hours

the maintenance of 301 city telephones in private homes (293 of them not even listed as city phones)

city advertising in seventy papers, which when cut down to five saved the city $410,000

fire department horses going the rounds of favored blacksmith shops without regard to the condition of shoes, as a kind of crummy subsidy to the anvil beaters

Seventy years later, the horses were gone, the techniques remarkably similar, and the stakes a whole lot larger:

In the interagency motor pools of the General Services Administration (GSA), eighty-five thousand cars were covered during the 1970s by individual credit cards that permitted the cars to make the rounds of gas stations like the horses and blacksmiths of an earlier day, with these kinds of tricks: (a) charges for fifty gallons of gas for cars that held only twenty, the overcharge being used as a payment for service on the GSA employees' private automobiles; (b) charges for four and five car washes per day and two sets of tires in a month for the same car, again as payoffs to the favored service stations for service to privately owned vehicles of GSA employees.

In the Public Buildings Division of the GSA, anyone with authority could authorize a private contractor to undertake repair work in a public building, with the GSA official then receiving a kickback by certifying completion of the work, whether it had been done or not. (In a way, it seems kinder than making horse hooves take unnecessary punishment!)*

In the 1970s nine federal departments and twenty independent agencies handled education matters.

Seven departments and eight independent agencies were concerned with health.

Four agencies in two departments were involved in the management of public lands.

Recreation management was scattered throughout six different agencies in three federal departments.

Seven agencies provided assistance for water and sewer systems.[1]

Nor are state and local governments immune to the headaches of faulty organization:

A governor struggles with the consequences of the long ballot; he is outvoted on the state apportionment board by the secretary of state and attorney general of the opposite party.

A governor sizes up his impossible span of control over sixty state agencies that report to him.

Three mosquito abatement districts in one county spray each other's ponds.

Three talented people are bored in Mickey Mouse jobs that two of them could easily handle.

An agency begins to succumb to a bureaucratic disease called entropy, its life system starving for some new ideas.

Inviting corruption, generating delays, frustrating its employees, and increasing the costs of government, faulty organization has been a constant concern in public administration. To see how governments respond, first we are going

---

* A 1978 estimate suggested that waste, negligence, and fraud within the GSA were costing the taxpayers over $150 million (United Press International dispatch, August 7, 1978).

to sketch the historical background of the reorganization movement and then we will probe rather deeply into both *macro*reorganization, which involves governmentwide restructuring, and then into *micro*reorganization, which involves restructuring within an agency.

Inputs from Scientific Management

In America, the spirit of becoming analytical about work methods and organization came initially from a group of industrial engineers in the private sector, led by Frederick W. Taylor toward the end of the nineteenth century. Coming in the wake of the 1873 depression and then flowering during the first two decades of the twentieth century, these men — Taylor, Henry L. Gantt, Carl Barth, Horace Hathaway, Sanford E. Thompson, Frank B. Gilbreth, Harry Emerson, and others — developed the principles of *scientific management* that encouraged entrepreneurs, drove labor up the wall[2] and left a legacy of both good and ill for public and private administration for years to come.[3]

These men were concerned about low-level production and nonmotivating modes of pay (including straight-time and even piecework, where employees held back lest management cut the piece rate). Their maxim was to develop *a science for every job,* primarily through time-and-motion studies, to determine what a worker could produce per day when working at full tilt and without wasted motions. After determining that quantity of output, the industrial engineers could then establish a basic rate of pay for a normal day's work as the baseline in a new differential piece rate (or task-bonus system). If workers achieved the predetermined level of output, they would receive the basic piece rate; if they produced more than the standard, they could receive a bonus rate per piece.

The inquiry led not only to slide rules and early slow-motion pictures of work processes but to shop management and organization as well. What ultimately emerged was a set of principles. whose carryover into public administration is shown in Table 12.1.

Much of that legacy was useful in that it inspired an empirical approach to organization and management and suggested many concepts that are still followed (such as line-staff-auxiliary segregation, discussed in Chapter 4, and job classification and other personnel techniques to be reviewed in Chapters 16 and 17).

But the debit side is a heavy one for scientific management to bear. By elevating time-and-motion study to a pinnacle of supreme importance, the Taylor school diverted researchers' attention for thirty years from the central truth that management begins with people. In 1916, John Dewey, in addition to the labor protestors, tried to sound the warning:

Much is said about scientific management of work. It is a narrow view which restricts the science which secures efficiency of operation to movements of the muscles. The chief opportunity for science is the discovery of the relations of a man to his work —

TABLE 12.1 PRINCIPLES OF SCIENTIFIC MANAGEMENT AND THEIR PUBLIC ADMINISTRATION ANALOGUES

Scientific management principles	Public administration analogues
1. Development of a science for every job	Organization and methods (O&M) analysis and job classification
2. Segregation of roles — management to do the thinking, workers the doing	The staff-line distinction
3. Imposition of eight functional foremen to oversee different aspects of the workers' conduct	The specialization of auxiliary services (finance, personnel, purchasing, legal counsel) to check on the line
4. The task-bonus system	Cash awards (the federal Incentive Awards Act of 1954)
5. Scientific recruitment and training of workers	Merit system recruitment and selection, followed by performance ratings and training
6. Standardization of tools and machines	Standardization and central purchasing
7. Use of routing and scheduling	Flow process charts, PERT, etc.
8. Cost systems	Cost accounting and performance budgeting
9. Encouragement of individual competition rather than group effort	Theory X

including his relations to others who take part — which will enlist his intelligent interest in what he is doing. Efficiency in production often demands division of labor. But it is reduced to a mechanical routine unless workers see the technical, intellectual, and social relationships involved in what they do, and engage in their work because of the motivation furnished by such perceptions. The tendency to reduce such things as efficiency of activity and scientific management to purely technical externals is evidence of the one-sided stimulation of thought given to those in control of industry — those who supply its aims. Because of their lack of all-round and well-balanced social interest, there is not sufficient stimulus for attention to the human factors and relationships in industry.[4]

Within ten years, the Hawthorne studies would begin at Western Electric, rediscovering what the scientific managers should never have overlooked, the human beings of any organization's work force.

In its heyday, however, scientific management gave a spur not only to in-house reforms but also to a public demand for reform as well. The Ralph Nader of that day, Louis Brandeis, opposed a railroad request for a rate hike before the Interstate Commerce Commission (ICC) with the argument that the railroads should institute scientific management before any increase was granted to them.[5]

With corruption and mismanagement rampant in the public sector, reform mounted into a tidal wave in American history known as the Progressive era. It was the period of the muckrakers — Lincoln Steffens, Jacob Riis, Teddy Roosevelt, and others going after government; Ida Tarbell, Upton Sinclair, and others going after industry. During that period reform movements and pressure groups appeared on a wide front: the National Municipal League in 1894, the New York Bureau of Municipal Research in 1906, and in 1916 the Institute for Government Research, forerunner of the Brookings Institution, to watchdog the national government.

Interestingly enough, some of the tidal waves were real, like the one that hit Galveston, Texas. in 1900. That wave washed away a weak mayoral government system when a group of five businessmen were called in to run the city in the wake of the flooding and established the new commission form of government at the municipal level.

On its heels another approach to city government came in 1908 in Staunton, West Virginia, when the city council hired the first city manager in American history and thereby launched the council-manager plan. Centralized purchasing and improved fiscal management would shortly appear at the municipal level.

The reform spirit began to affect state governments as well. Short ballots were introduced to fill by appointment many positions that had formerly been filled by election, thus integrating authority around the governor. (Illinois voters accepted the new approach in their 1917 constitutional revision.) A legislative reference bureau, strengthening the lawmaking process, was established in Wisconsin in 1901.

Primary elections began to transfer the nominating power away from party conventions to the voters, who by 1913 would also be directly electing senators and by 1920 would look up from their ballots to find women at the polls. The initiative, the referendum, and the recall would appear in a number of states, strengthening the hand of the electorate vis-à-vis their public officials in state and local government.

Nor was the federal government immune to the reform movement. Congressional committees began chipping away at the executive branch in the late 1890s; presidential commissions carried on the work of reorganization during the regimes of Theodore Roosevelt and William H. Taft; and the Woodrow Wilson presidency would see important new establishments created in the Federal Reserve Board and Federal Trade Commission. By 1921, a national budget system was finally developed. The Progressive era was a bold and exciting time in American history.[6]

Against the backdrop of scientific management and the Progressive era, we turn now to some of the highlights of reorganization efforts at the federal level.

MACROREORGANIZATION OF THE FEDERAL GOVERNMENT[7]

An Overview

Since many of the earliest attempts at reorganization from the administration of Grover Cleveland down through the 1920s seem almost like ancient history, we can survey some of the milestones most readily in table form (see Table 12.2).

TABLE 12.2 MAJOR REORGANIZATION EFFORTS IN THE FEDERAL GOVERNMENT, 1887–1973

Name	Years	Membership	Focus	Highlights
1. Senate Select Committee on methods of business in the executive depts. (Cockrell committee)[a]	1887–1889	5 senators	Executive procedures and red tape	
2. Joint Commission on Executive Departments, organization (Dockery-Cockrell Commission)[a]	1893–1895	3 senators 3 representatives	Efficiency and economy in the executive branch and financial management	Dockery Act created the controller of the treasury to preaudit expenditures; accounting reforms
3. Committee on Department Methods (Keep committee)[b]	1905–1909	Bureau chiefs and subcabinet officials	Organization and methods analysis	Agencies should appoint O&M inspector; government needs a classification and salary plan and a retirement system; records management
4. President's Commission on Economy and Efficiency (Taft Commission)	1910–1913	Six distinguished experts appointed	Financial operations. paperwork management. etc.	Recommended a national budget, increased use of office machines. new filing techniques
5. Bureau of Efficiency (informally reported to Senator Reed Smoot)	1913–1934	Created by act of Congress first as a division within the Civil Service Commission, later made independent	O&M analysis and personnel studies	Supervised performance-rating system; investigated personnel needs of agencies; pushed for laborsaving devices; standardization of supplies and personnel classification system
6. Joint Committee on the Reorganization of the Administrative Branch of the Government (Brown committee)	1920–1924	3 senators, 3 representatives, 1 by the president	Macroreorganization	Create a Dept. of National Defense, reorganize Treasury, create Dept. of Education and Welfare, attach administrative functions of independent agencies to the regular departments

[a] Vincent J. Browne. *The Control of the Public Budget* (Washington, D.C.: Public Affairs Press, 1949), pp. 59–60.

[b] Harold Pinkett, "The Keep Commission. 1905–1909: A Roosevelt Effort for Administrative Reform," *Journal of American History* (September 1965) 52:297–312.

TABLE 12.2 MAJOR REORGANIZATION EFFORTS IN THE FEDERAL GOVERNMENT, 1887–1973

Name	Years	Membership	Focus	Highlights
7. President's Committee on Administrative Management (Brownlow committee or the PCAM)	1936–1937	3 appointed by the president	Overburdened presidency, weak auxiliary services, dispersed authority	Provide assistance to president, management and planning role for Bureau of the Budget, restrict GAO to auditing, expand the merit system, integrate independent agencies within departments, and divide regulatory commission functions
8. Senate Select Committee to Investigate the Executive Agencies of the Government (Byrd committee)	1936–1937	5 senators	Overlap, duplication, economy, and efficiency	Disagreed with some of the PCAM integration recommendations; recommended large holding-company-type departments, with bureau autonomy
9. Division of Administrative Management, Bureau of the Budget	1939–1952	Civil servants of BOB	O&M studies, technical aid to line agencies	Elevated organization and methods analysis to the highest level since the days of the Bureau of Efficiency
10. First Commission on Organization of the Executive Branch of the Government (first Hoover Commission)	1947–1949	4 Senate appointees, 4 House appointees, 4 presidential appointees (6 from government, 6 from private life, with an even number of Republicans and Democrats)	Macrostudy to eliminate duplication, unnecessary functions, and to achieve economy and efficiency	Reduce number of agencies outside the departments by ⅔, performance budgeting, strengthen departmental secretaries (vis-à-vis their bureaus)
11. President's Advisory Committee on Management	1949–1952	12 appointed by the president	Executive development and management practices	President needs permanent reorganization authority; agencies need continuing management improvement programs

TABLE 12.2 MAJOR REORGANIZATION EFFORTS IN THE FEDERAL GOVERNMENT, 1887–1973 (continued)

Name	Years	Membership	Focus	Highlights
12. Second Commission on Organization of the Executive Branch of the Government (second Hoover Commission)	1953–1955	Similar to first Hoover Commission (with 7 Republicans and 5 Democrats)	Same as first Hoover Commission plus eliminating government functions that compete with private enterprise	Accrual accounting and cost-based budgeting; diminished federal role in water and power generation; sell federal business-type enterprises that compete with private firms
13. President's Advisory Committee on Government Organization (Rockefeller committee)	1953	3 appointed by the president	Macrostudies of executive branch efficiency	
14. Special Assistant for Regulatory Agencies (James M. Landis study)	1960–1961	Presidential appointee	Independent regulatory commissions	Strengthen hand of commission chairmen, permit delegation of authority within the commissions, discretionary review of lower-level decisions; White House office to oversee the regulatory agencies
15. President's Advisory Council on Executive Organization (Ash committee)	1969	6 presidential appointees	Executive Office of the President	Set up a Domestic Council and change BOB to Office of Management and Budget
16. President Richard Nixon's proposals to cut departments from 11 to 9 by creating four new super departments	1971–1972	Ash committee and OMB staff	Major-purpose consolidation and president's span of control	Proposal called for large departments on community development, human resources, natural resources, and economic development (plus State, Defense, Justice, Treasury, and Agriculture departments)

A number of things are worth observing about the compressed history of federal reorganization shown in Table 12.2. One is the diverse origins and research formats of the studies. In the list we find: (a) congressional committees (like those of Dockery, Brown, and Byrd); (b) presidential advisory teams (like the PCAM and the Ash committee),[8] (c) mixed commissions — legislative, executive, private citizen groups like the first and second Hoover Commissions); (d) civil servant teams (the Keep committee); and (e) permanent bureau studies (such as those of the Bureau of Efficiency and the Division of Administrative Management). The employment of independent consulting firms to conduct the fact-finding studies (like the Brookings Institution in the 1937 Byrd committee study; Booz, Allen, Hamilton for many state reorganizations) should also be noted.

Another aspect of the history is how prescient some of the reorganization reports have been. Our own favorite on that score was the Brown committee's work during Warren Harding's administration. Vindicated by the test of time — in some cases over a quarter of a century later — that joint committee made these kinds of recommendations. a la 1923:

merger of the armed forces into a Department of National Defense (achieved in 1947)

transfer of the nonmilitary functions of the War Department (e.g., Corps of Engineers) to civilian departments (reasserted by the first Hoover Commission and again in the 1970s)

shift of the nonfiscal functions of the Treasury Department elsewhere (the Coast Guard was moved to the Department of Transportation in 1965)

establishment of a Department of Education and Welfare (Eisenhower brought HEW into being in 1953)

transfer of administrative work of the independent commissions and agencies to the regular departments, leaving only the quasi-judicial functions apart (the very plan of the PCAM in 1937, with partial fulfillment in the Civil Aeronautics Authority reorganization in 1940)

giving the Bureau of the Budget in the Treasury Department independent status (Reorganization Plan No. 1 of 1939)

It was the kind of track record that would lead the British Fabians to give three cheers for the inevitability of gradualness.

There are also, thank goodness, some touches of humor in the record:

a "daring recommendation" of the Brown committee to change the name of the Post Office Department to the Department of Communications[9]

the action of Congress in 1945 changing the Board on Geographical Names to become the Board on Geographic Names the turndown on Kennedy's effort in 1962 to create a Department of Urban Affairs and Housing, followed by the creation of the Department of Housing and Urban Development (HUD) three years later during the Johnson administration[10]

the storm-tossed history of the Weather Bureau — first located in the War Department, then moved to Agriculture, and then to Commerce

the matching peregrinations of the Bureau of the Mines from the Department of Interior to the Commerce Department and back to Interior again

The 1930s and the Shape of Things to Come

With the United States deep in the Great Depression and with a Congress not yet comfortable with unbalanced budgets, economy in the national government became the watchword in 1932. Four months before the presidential election, Congress passed the Economy Act on June 30,[11] which established a reorganization pattern that we have followed ever since: the presidential reorganization plan, subject to a legislative veto (note that this reversed the traditional order of the Congress legislating and the president vetoing). The statute conferred no power to abolish functions, only that of reorganizing, and significantly, without time limit (although this unusual grant was restricted nine months later to two years). Presidential proposals would go into effect sixty days after presentation to Congress unless vetoed by a negative resolution passed in one house. Later reorganization statutes would institute a two-house veto, making it more difficult to kill a reorganization plan.

The size of the federal bureaucracy became an issue in the Hoover-Roosevelt election that fall, evoking some famous campaign oratory from candidate Franklin D. Roosevelt — at Pittsburgh, October 19, 1932: "Before any man enters my Cabinet he must pledge . . . complete cooperation with me looking to economy and reorganization in his department."[12] At Brooklyn, New York, November 4, 1932:

> The people of America demand a reduction of Federal expenditure. It can be accomplished not only by reducing the expenditures of existing departments, but it can be done by abolishing many useless commissions, bureaus, and functions, and it can be done by consolidating many activities of the government.[13]

Trounced at the polls, the lame duck Herbert Hoover attempted a midnight reorganization of the federal establishment before going out of office. In December 1932, he submitted to Congress reorganization plans involving fifty-eight agencies. The common threads running through his proposals were single-head (rather than board-type) agencies, organized around major purpose, with quasi-legislative and judicial roles to be left to boards and commissions.[14]

The House of Representatives was already in Democratic control, and Representative William Bankhead gave the clue to the party's feelings:

The Republican President is going out of power. The people of America by their mandate have placed the responsibility of executing this reform, if it shall prove a reform, in the hands of the incoming executive, and upon a large view of the whole situation from a broad political aspect it seems to me that inasmuch as the incoming President is to be charged with the results of these efforts at consolidation, and they are to be effectuated by men under his control and direction, it seems to me to be a fair proposition that if he is to be held answerable for the results of the effort that all of the agencies and instrumentalities to achieve it should be placed in his hands. I do not think this is a narrow political consideration.[15]

Representative Adolf Sabath then offered a few famous last words:

I feel that the Democratic Party will bring about consolidation at the proper time with economy and efficiency. I know that the incoming President of the Democratic Party will eliminate all useless commissions, boards, and thousands of useless offices that have been created during the present Republican administration. Now, as to President Hoover's doing large things. President Hoover has done large things. We never before witnessed a deficit of two or three billion dollars in a single year.[16]

Those sentiments prevailed as the Democratic majority in the House (under the one-house veto) proceeded to kill all of Hoover's plans in the name of not tying the incoming president's hands.

But Hoover, like Antony with Cleopatra, proved to be one of the great sports of ancient times. On his last day in office he signed into law a new reorganization act that would authorize Franklin Roosevelt to submit reorganization plans for two years, including proposals to abolish agencies outright, subject to a two-house veto.[17]

Arriving in office, Roosevelt put policy initiatives ahead of reorganization as he ushered in the hundred days whirlwind. Then, just as his historic Congress was about to adjourn, he apologetically sent up his reorganization proposals on June 10, 1933.[18] The reorganization plans embraced in that executive order included transferring control over the apportionment of funds from agency heads to the Bureau of the Budget (see Chapter 14), centralizing procurement in the Treasury Department, consolidating functions in the National Park Service, shifting solicitors from the Justice Department to the various agencies, and abolishing a number of other agencies. As it had since March, Congress went along.

The decade of the 1930s ended with a flurry of presidential and congressional reorganization activity. Emboldened by the proposals of his Committee on Administrative Management,[19] Roosevelt asked for and received new authority in the Reorganization Act of 1939,[20] essentially identical to the 1933 provisions except for the exemption of twenty-one agencies from any reorganization.[21]

Roosevelt quickly put the authority to use, translating a number of the PCAM's recommendations into the five plans he submitted in 1939 and 1940, all of which were approved by Congress (the two-house veto provision saved Plan No. 4, which was disapproved in the House but sustained in the Senate). Roosevelt created the Executive Office of the President, bringing to it an important

---

The Presidency Is in Need of Help

In transmitting the report of his Committee on Administrative Management, Franklin D. Roosevelt said this:

> The Committee has not spared me; they say, what has been common knowledge for 20 years, that the President cannot adequately handle his responsibilities; that he is overworked; that it is humanly impossible, under the system which we have, for him fully to carry out his constitutional duty as Chief Executive, because he is overwhelmed with minor details and needless contacts arising directly from the bad organization and equipment of the Government. I can testify to this. With my predecessors who have said the same thing over and over again, I plead guilty.

President's Committee on Administrative Management, *Administrative Management in the Government of the United States* (Washington, D.C.: Government Printing Office, 1937), p. ii.

---

new member, the Bureau of the Budget; created three large new subcabinet agencies (Federal Security, Federal Works, and the Federal Loan Agency); and peeled off the administrative functions of the Civil Aeronautics Authority, transferring them to the new Civil Aeronautics Administration in the Department of Commerce, while leaving the rule-making and adjudicating powers with the Civil Aeronautics Board.

On this last point we need to digress for a moment to relate some administrative history never published before. A number of years ago, we persuaded Robert E. Cushman, a constitutional law scholar, to relate the background of the PCAM's recommendations to split up the independent regulatory commissions,[22] the "headless fourth branch of the government," which regulate banking, labor relations, communications, power rates, and trade practices, among others.*

Professor Cushman replied that the study of the independent commissions, which he had conducted, was the only one President Roosevelt had specifically requested the Brownlow committee to undertake.

> [FDR] had developed a grudge against the Interstate Commerce Commission because the Commission had refused to be governed by an executive order which he had issued applying to the executive agencies generally, and he was reported to be rather sore about it.[23]

Cushman was frustrated at not being able to discuss tentative ideas with commission members but went ahead with the proposal of splitting up some of

---

* Recall that the Supreme Court's decision in *Rathbun* v. *U.S.* 295 US 622 (1935), which underscored the federal trade commissioners' independence from the president's removal power, had been handed down the year before the creation of the PCAM.

the newer regulatory bodies into two halves: rule making and adjudicating to be under collegial bodies independent of the president, and administrative roles to be integrated into presidential agencies. "None of us had any intention or desire at that time to propose its application to any of the long established independent commissions."

Luther Gulick, the distinguished public administrator on the three-man PCAM, later reported to Cushman what transpired when the committee presented its recommendations to President Roosevelt following the November 1936 election:

> When he came to the independent commission item on his list, the proposal was essentially this: That Congress should in the future exercise very great restraint in setting up additional independent commissions. The President, who had up to this time been very greatly pleased with all of the committee's proposals, turned to Brownlow and said, somewhat sharply, "Is this all that you fellows have got to propose with regard to these commissions?" Brownlow said that it was, but that the committee had had a man studying the whole problem, and that he had prepared a memorandum setting out an alternative plan for dealing with the commissions which the committee was disposed to publish as a tentative and experimental approach to the problem. The President then said, "I would like to know about it," and Brownlow had to explain the substance of my proposal. When the President had heard it, he immediately said, "I like that very much. We will adopt that as part of the proposals of the committee, and furthermore, we will propose it as a method of dealing with all the existing regulatory commissions." Brownlow protested that it would be inexpedient to bring out so drastic a proposal which would be regarded as an attack upon the independence of the old-line commissions and called the President's attention to the fact that 1937 was the fiftieth anniversary of the creation of the Interstate Commerce Commission. The President's answer was, "You may leave the matter of expediency to me."

Professor Cushman then wrote:

> I found myself for the next two years going around like a sheep in wolf's clothing, trying to explain to a lot of people how this new idea would be applied concretely to any one of the existing regulatory agencies. . . .

> I suppose the plain truth is that our attention was mainly focused upon the problem of the so-called merger of administrative and quasi-judicial functions in such an agency as the Federal Trade Commission. We had much less sharply in mind the problems presented by an agency which was exercising quasi-legislative powers.

Thus, a new chapter is added to the continuing legend of Franklin D. Roosevelt, in this case "how to get even via reorganization."[24] But a review of the whole New Deal period suggests much broader purposes in FDR's organizational moves: (a) to provide the agencies to carry out vastly expanded functions of government (the National Recovery Administration [NRA], the Federal Emergency Relief Administration [FERA], the National Labor Relations Board [NLRB], etc.); (b) solve intraagency conflict by giving both sets of disputants a home of their own (e.g., the creation of the Resettlement Administration, predecessor to the Farm Security Administration, for the left-wingers from the old

Agricultural Adjustment Administration [AAA]. which continued on under conservative control); (c) to strengthen *presidential* management of the executive branch (creation of the Executive Office of the President); (d) to begin long-range resource planning (the National Resources Committee); and (e) to provide a full employment program for deserving Democrats (through the creation of the alphabet-soup agencies "without regard to civil service rules").

The Second Coming of Herbert Hoover

In one of those rare moments of the mid-twentieth century. the Republicans captured both houses of Congress in 1946. Since Congress had already gotten the mote out of its own eye earlier that year in the *congressional* Reorganization Act. the Republican majority decided the time had come to get the beam out of the president's eye. Thus, in July 1947. Senator Henry Cabot Lodge, Jr., and Representative Clarence Brown put through P.L. 80-162. without a dissenting vote in either house, creating the first Commission on Organization of the Executive Branch of the Government.[25]

Consider the politics of the situation. The first Republican Congress since 1930 (the Eightieth) confronted a Democratic president. Harry Truman; a presidential election year was coming up the following year; and the New Deal and World War II had produced a swollen bureaucracy with vastly increased functions. Undoubtedly with those facts in mind. the sponsors of the 1947 legislation chose an interesting kind of tripartite. bipartisan commission to conduct the study: the president. the Speaker of the House. and president pro tempore of the Senate (the last two being Republicans) would each appoint four members — two from their own branch, two from private life — and their appointees would have to include two Republicans and two Democrats. President Truman appointed two impressive officers from his branch. James Forrestal of the Defense Department and Dean Acheson of the State Department; Speaker Martin appointed the former president of the United States. Herbert Hoover; and Senate President Arthur H. Vandenberg appointed Ambassador Joseph P. Kennedy and political scientist James K. Pollock. among other appointees. As the law required. the twelve were evenly divided in terms of party affiliation. But on philosophical grounds there were perhaps seven conservatives and five liberals. Understandably. the new commissioners chose former President Herbert Hoover to be their chairman.

The statute laid down five goals for the commission to pursue:
1. Find ways to cut costs of government (the economy goal).
2. Eliminate duplication and overlap.
3. Consolidate similar functions.
4. Abolish unnecessary functions.
5. Define and limit executive branch activities.[26]

To get at those goals and understand the existing organization of the executive branch. the commission utilized twenty-four task forces composed of prestigious citizens, who in turn hired the necessary research help. Some turned outside the government — to the Brookings Institution for the transportation study, to the Council of State Governments for federal-state relations, to Price-Waterhouse and Company on government lending; other task forces utilized government agencies, as did Natural Resources in its contract with the Legislative Reference Service of the Library of Congress (later called Congressional Research Service).

Probably the most important decision as to research strategy made by the first Hoover Commission was to avoid questions of policy, the deep philosophical issues as to the roles the government should or should not be undertaking.[27] It was an important tactical move, given the fact that different parties controlled the executive and Congress. It represented a rather successful exception to the rule that politics and administration cannot be separated. With few deviations, the first Hoover Commission went after structure and outdated processes and avoided forays into the much murkier ground of what the essential and nonessential functions of government are.

The dominant themes in the recommendations of the first Hoover Commission were integrating independent agencies into larger departments according to major purpose; strengthening the hand of departmental secretaries vis-à-vis their bureau chiefs; adopting performance budgeting; restricting the General Accounting Office to the postaudit and having them perform it onsite instead of through wasteful shipment of millions of vouchers to GAO centers; giving the Commerce Department responsibility for transportation instead of creating a new Department of Transportation; and elevating the Federal Security Agency into a Department of Health, Education and Welfare.[28]

It has been estimated that 72 percent, or 196, of the first commission's 273 recommendations were adopted, 111 by administrative action and 85 by legislative action.[29] Judged by this kind of batting average, and the early accomplishment of some of its most important recommendations — the performance budget, reducing the president's span of control, delegation of preaudit responsibilities from the GAO to the line departments, and so on — this 1947–1949 reorganization effort was an enormous success. But in the judgment of some Republicans, the first Hoover Commission was not successful enough.

Hoover Rides Again, 1953–1955

With Dwight Eisenhower in the saddle and the Republicans riding high in the Eighty-third Congress it seemed like a once-in-a-half-century opportunity to corral the New Deal bureaucracy and thin out the herd. No matter that the dust had not even gathered on the 1949 reports of the first commission; the Republican Congress went ahead in 1953 and created a new one, but it was cleverly different this time: they would drop the bipartisan requirement and broaden the assignment for the second commission, authorizing it to wade into policy matters and search out government functions that competed with private enterprise.[30] In short, while Republicans controlled the Congress and the presidency, they were going to *undo the New Deal.*[31]

Thus, Herbert Hoover came riding out of retirement for the second time, to chair the second Hoover Commission, with seven Republicans and five Democrats among the twelve commissioners, but more important, with at least nine conservatives and only three liberals on board (a pretty good working majority in any league).

The commission did not disappoint its framers. With a vengeance, its recommendations went after government programs that competed with private enterprise and neatly overlooked government activities that aided big business. Thus, Army PXs and parcel post were slated to be scrapped, but not heavily subsidized fourth-class mail rates for magazine publishers; crop loans, housing loans, Rural Electrification Administration (REA) loans and the like were to be axed, but there was not a word about government subsidies to large manufacturers, banks, air and ship operators, and the like. As Commissioner Chet Holifield said in protest:

> The Commission made no systematic study on the whole subject of subsidies, nor does it recommend their elimination in all fields. The ones complained of in this report appear to be . . . those which bring wide-spread benefits to the whole population.[32]

On the management side, the second commission stressed structural integration less and interdepartmental committees or executive offices more for coordination than did the first commission; for example, there was no recommendation to move the civil functions of the Corps of Engineers to the Bureau of Reclamation in the Department of the Interior. The second Hoover Commission wanted to centralize rather than decentralize legal services. It seemed to favor dismemberment of foreign aid, assigning chunks of the program to the Departments of Agriculture and Commerce. The commission recommended accrual accounting rather than cash flow accounting for federal fiscal management.[33]

When it came to implementation, Eisenhower was still president, but a Democratic Congress, with no zest for repealing the New Deal, looked down at him from the other end of Pennsylvania Avenue from 1955 to the end of his term. The statistics are dramatic: whereas all ten of Eisenhower's reorganization plans were sustained by the Republican Eighty-third Congress (1953–1954), he lost both of his proposals in 1956, got plans through in both 1957 and 1958, and lost his only proposal in 1959.[34]

Overall, the second commission saw roughly 64 percent of its 314 recommendations put into effect,[35] but the government stayed in the housing business, the crop-supporting business, and would soon expand its efforts to help young people get an education, buy homes, and so on.

Two lessons must be learned from the experience of the politically oriented second Hoover Commission:

1. Don't expect reorganization bodies to accomplish what Congress itself has never been able to do (i.e., alter the whole direction of government backward).

2. Don't count your reorganization plans until they hatch, because a different Congress may conclude that you laid an egg.

The Kennedy-Johnson Era

The two and a half years of the Kennedy presidency are remembered not for dramatic reorganization moves but rather for headline events like the Bay of Pigs (a crowning failure), the removal of the Russian missiles from Cuba (success), the launching of the Peace Corps, and the embarkation of the war corps (for the stepped-up U.S. involvement in Southeast Asia).

Kennedy's batting average in getting 60 percent of his reorganization measures past Congress was a good deal better than his general legislative record of only 23 percent in 1963, but it was a bit poorer than the 77 percent average earned by five presidents on reorganization proposals from 1939 to 1965.

Johnson's percentage even fell below Kennedy's during his first year in office, to 50 percent, but it rose dramatically to 88 percent in 1965.[36] Among Johnson's coups were two new departments: Housing and Urban Development, and Transportation, in 1965. But his proposed merger of the Commerce and Labor Departments in 1967 met opposition from both business and the unions and came up ragweed instead of roses.

Reorganization, Nixon Style

Shortly after his inauguration, Richard Nixon appointed the Advisory Council on Executive Reorganization under the chairmanship of Litton executive Roy Ash. A third of a century after the Brownlow committee, the council under Ash sounded some old familiar tunes: strengthen the presidency and integrate the executive branch.[37]

Nixon moved rapidly, proposing in his 1970 reorganization plans: (a) the creation of a new White House office, the Domestic Council, for policy analysis on "what we should be doing"; (b) beefing up the Bureau of the Budget (dressed in new garb as the Office of Management and Budget) into something approaching a domestic general staff (in the military sense) to tell agencies "how to do it"; and (c) creating the Environmental Protection Agency.[38]

The Post Office Department lost its cabinet status and departmental form when it became the U.S. Postal Service in 1971, a federal business enterprise. Another Nixon initiative forced common regional boundaries on the field operations of all federal agencies.

Then in his January 1971 State of the Union message, Nixon announced his corker: keeping five departments (State, Defense, Justice, Treasury, and Agriculture), and then merging the remaining six into four giant, major-purpose establishments, the Departments of Community Development, Human Resources, Natural Resources, and Economic Affairs.[39] With no action in the first session of the Ninety-second Congress, Nixon pushed the reforms again in his 1972 annual message and once more on March 29, 1972.[40] The only one of the four to make any progress was the proposed Department of Community Development. Favorably reported by the House Government Operations Committee, the bill, H.R. 92-6962, died on the Union Calendar (agenda of the House) without floor action in December 1972.

In the meantime, Nixon had piled up his sweeping electoral victory in November 1972. Like a Franklin Roosevelt fresh from the 1936 election ("as Maine goes, so goes Vermont") all ready to pack the Court, Nixon dumped essentially all his first cabinet members and their subcabinet assistants and replaced them with a coterie of men personally dedicated to him.[41] In filling the key slots in December and January, he announced that he was effectuating a part of his "giant four department" plan by *presidential assignment.* not subject to congressional veto. Treasury Secretary George P. Shultz would also serve as a presidential assistant for economic policy coordination, overseeing the related work of the Departments of Labor, Commerce, Transportation, Agriculture, and State (foreign economic policies). In similar fashion, Nixon designated HEW Secretary Casper W. Weinberger over human resources, Agriculture Secretary Earl L. Butz over natural resources, and James T. Lynn of HUD over community development.

Nixon sent two reorganization plans to the Congress just before the April 1 expiration of his reorganization authority. One transferred some staff functions, including those of the Office of Emergency Preparedness, to old line agencies; the other combined federal drug enforcement activities in a new unit of the Justice Department. Both plans were adopted. The 1949 reorganization authority then lapsed. Then Watergate happened, flooding away Nixon's last ounce of credibility, and Congress declined to renew the Reorganization Act until Jimmy Carter's presidency in 1977.

The New Broom from Georgia

Jimmy Carter rode into office with the promise of sweeping out of the bureaucracy old faces, red tape, and inefficient ways of doing things. His Democratic Congress promptly gave him reorganization authority in April 1977 (P.L. 95-17), subject to a one-house veto.

Four months later, the Ninety-fifth Congress gave him his first substantive victory in the reorganization field by creating (in P.L. 95-91) the new Department of Energy (DOE). Although DOE's track record during the next few years in reducing the energy crisis was a great disappointment, on paper the new department seemed to represent a sensible consolidation of heretofore disparate agencies in the energy field.

Carter's plan to bring together the federal government's equal employment enforcement activities was sustained by Congress. Then came one of the most important legislative victories of his administration, the Civil Service Reform Act of 1978 (Reorganization Plan No. 2 of 1978 and P.L. 95-454, which we discuss in Chapters 15–17). He also succeeded in pulling together a number of disaster agencies (not disastrous!) under the umbrella of the new Federal Emergency Management Agency.

During 1978, Carter's reorganization staff in OMB prepared blueprints for large-scale reorganizations in the fields of economic and community development (e.g., shifting some agencies from the Commerce Department to HUD), natural resources (moving the Forest Service from the Department of Agriculture back to its old mooring in the Interior Department), food and nutrition, and trade. Each new proposal generated a flock of opponents, which resulted in an increasing reluctance of the Carter White House to promote any of the OMB plans. One adviser said, "Ride on your laurels of reorganizing the civil service for awhile before picking any more fights."[42]

The Targets of All That Reorganizing?

In terms of age and continuity, the four horsemen of the reorganization apocalypse have been and will likely continue to be *economy. efficiency.* and an end to *duplication* and *overlap.*[43] In one way or another, every act of Congress authorizing the study of government has conjured up that galloping foursome.[44]

The Nixon message of March 1971 offered a whole catalogue of reasons for reorganizing the executive branch:[45] (a) it is impossible to pinpoint responsibility when functions are irrationally dispersed; (b) if missions are too narrow, agencies begin to espouse a parochial view; (c) policy analysis demands the consideration of wide alternatives that only large agencies normally encompass; (d) where everyone is in charge, no one really is, and important considerations of public policy slip between the cracks; (e) scattered responsibilities mean that higher authorities are called on too frequently to arbitrate disputes, resulting in increasing centralization of authority;[46] (f) federal disorganization makes life very tough for state and local administrators who would prefer one-stop shopping when they come to Washington; (g) unorganized government is not responsive government — getting results is like pushing on a string: nothing moves; and (h) organizing around process and clientele is a bits-and-pieces approach, when what we need is a structure built around the large purposes of government (what we do to human beings, to natural resources, to our communities, and to the economy. Nixon was saying). Nixon had at least two other goals in mind as well: to reorganize some functions out of existence (the Office of Economic Opportunity, for one) and to channel more responsibilities and funds to state and local governments under his policy of the New Federalism.

In Harvey Mansfield's thoughtful look at thirty years of federal reorganizing, he suggests some additional reasons for grasping scalpel and sutures to deal with the bureaucracy:[47] A shift in policy does require a new organizational format (foreign aid in 1948 might have been smothered in the State Department — thus the creation of the independent Economic Cooperation Administration); related activities need to be brought together under one roof (e.g., HEW and HUD); a function can be upgraded by moving it higher on the organization chart (the Bureau of the Budget, 1939, 1970); sometimes you can keep them down on the farm by burying them on the organization chart (the three armed forces under the Defense Department, 1947, 1949); functions can be reorganized out of existence (the National Resources Planning Board, abolished in 1943; the Office of Economic Opportunity, 1972–1973); programs can come alive by providing them with strong administrators (FERA and Harry Hopkins, nuclear submarines and Adm. Hyman Rickover); technological change may force a reshuffling (the Nuclear Regulatory Commission and NASA); controversy can be pushed away from the chief executive (OWMR overseeing the "battle of the Potomac" in World War II); he can be aided through better staff services (the beefed-up Executive Office of the President), through a narrower span of control (the first Hoover Commission's integration moves), and through a strengthened unity of command ("bring the independent commissions under my thumb"); departmental management can be enhanced by transferring final decision making from bureau chiefs to the department secretary; and functions can be protected by encasing them in a strong agency (the Forest Service in the Agriculture Department rather than with the Interior Department during the troubled years of the Taft administration).

Even after considering these long lists, there are still additional reasons for macroreorganization:[48] (a) to meet the thrust of an agitated clientele (create an advisory board as a buffer);[49] (b) to counteract entropy (join the sluggish agency to a going concern for transfusion purposes); and (c) in the face of one agency's failure, give the responsibility to someone else (transfer civil rights enforcement from Commerce to the Justice Department). Any and all of these may create the pressure to reorganize — immediately generating the questions of whose toes will get stepped on and whether the plans will succeed.

The Politics of Reorganization[50]

What was said about the politics of administration in Chapter 8 has to be doubled and squared when it comes to reorganizing the government — politics permeates the whole scene:

Supporters of the incoming president (FDR) didn't want to see his hands tied, and so they defeated all of outgoing President Hoover's reorganization plans.

The rivers and harbors lobby didn't want the sacred cow position of the Corps of Engineers diminished, and so they won exemption after exemption for the corps from reorganization plans.

Nixon wanted to pull the shade down on the aura of the Kennedy-Shriver domestic Peace Corps and proceeded to reorganize it under the new name of ACTION, which never caught fire.

A governor, sick and tired of the corruption that permeates the state liquor control agency, places the agency under a new liquor control commission, one echelon further away.

A mayor doesn't want the heat of collective bargaining searing the city council directly and therefore creates the city board on labor-management relations.

Reorganization is political because it can so vitally affect the stature of an agency (the state personnel director who now reports to the governor instead of to the director of administrative services); its improved span of control (the clustering of federal energy agencies in the new Department of Energy, 1977); its budgetary clout (HEW's versus its predecessor's, the Federal Security Agency); and its competitive position versus its rivals (Nixon's Domestic Council or Ford's Economic Policy Board[51]).

The political significance of reorganization is further demonstrated by the frenzied activity of pressure groups when their pet agency is being put on the block — of the airline companies when Ford hinted deregulation of that industry, diminishing the role of the Civil Aeronautics Board; of veterans whenever a reorganizer casts a glance toward the VA; of lumber interests whenever a Hoover Commission begins to talk about shifting the Forest Service from Agriculture back to Interior where it belongs (the *public* land agency); of the housing lobby that killed Kennedy's proposal for a cabinet-level department and then, having wangled enough changes from Johnson, supported the latter's plan for HUD.

In planning organizational moves, presidents cast wary eyes toward the pressure groups that may aid — or kill — the contemplated changes. For example, Harry Truman planned to shift the U.S. Employment Service from the broad Federal Security Agency to the Department of Labor where it would enjoy strong union support. But a Republican Congress, not anxious for annual bouts with organized labor coming to bat for the Employment Service, said no.[52]

Nixon's proposed reorganization of federal drug enforcement in Plan No. 2 of 1973 ran into stiff objections from the American Federation of Government Employees (AFGE). This powerful union balked at the contemplated transfer of narcotics agents from the Justice Department, which they represented, to the Customs Service in the Treasury Department, which they did not represent. The union dictated the compromise.[53]

Then there is the matter of the balance of power in politics. As we noted earlier in this chapter, when the Eightieth Republican Congress faced a Democratic president in 1947, proponents of a reorganization study were forced to write a restrained statute for the first Hoover Commission. Then when the Republicans controlled both branches six years later, they authorized the second Hoover Commission to get even with Hoover's departed nemesis, Franklin Roosevelt. But in 1954 power shifted once more. By the time the second commission started to recommend dismantling the New Deal, it was faced with the newly returned Democratic Eighty-fourth Congress: that was like a worn-out pitcher facing the Yankees' Murderers' Row, led by the Texas Twins — Sam Rayburn in the House and Lyndon Johnson in the Senate. At that point, the second commission's earned run average got clobbered.

As with all other significant moves in administration, politics will define the metes and bounds within which reorganization can take place.

The Macroreorganization Track Record

One should not conclude from the omnipresence of politics in these matters that nothing is accomplished. A master politician like FDR uses politics to help accomplish his goals — to scratch enough backs, feed enough districts, and sufficiently mold public opinion until he gets his relief agencies, Civil Aeronautics Authority, War Production Board, and United Nations Organization.

Taken as a whole, the record of federal reorganization includes some impressive things:

shaping a bureaucracy to carry the country through the Great Depression and then win the war against the Axis powers

the steady strengthening of the president's staff services from the PCAM on down

bringing the armed forces under one tent during 1947–1949

dramatically reducing nonaligned agencies after the first Hoover Commission

modernizing the federal merit system under the new Office of Personnel Management

creating the necessary agencies to cope with contemporary challenges — the U.S. Civil Rights Commission; the Environmental Protection Agency; NASA; the Departments of Transportation, Housing and Urban Development, and Energy, and others[54]

Harvey Mansfield summarized the period since the PCAM report in this way:

Departmental jurisdictions have been clarified and rationalized and their central staff and managerial capacities enormously strengthened. The General Accounting Office retains its autonomy in fiscal administration but is no longer an obstruction. The Civil Service Commission's leadership has been reoriented to more positive goals, the coverage of the system extended, and its terms greatly improved. The independent regulatory commissions are probably somewhat more responsive to broader policy goals and contexts; at any rate they matter less, relatively and collectively. Three new departments, HEW, HUD, and Transportation, leave less room for orphan activities or for conglomerate catch-alls like the Treasury of old.[55]

But like a good love story, macroreorganization has no ending. If it stops, we're dead, for as was said in Rome long ago, "The times change, and we must change with them."

The same is equally true of what goes on inside agencies where the day-to-day work of government is carried on: in one agency, there are harmonious relationships and goal accomplishment; in another, human beings are snarled in red tape and snarling at each other. Thus, organizational renewal is as crucial on that scale as on a governmentwide scale.

MICROREORGANIZATION WITHIN GOVERNMENTAL ORGANIZATIONS

Signs of Trouble

"We are a dispirited bunch — people draggin' in late, bitchin' if we have to work overtime, leavin' the place a mess, barking at each other, ignoring clients standing at the service counter."

"The turnover rate has shot sky high, and so has absenteeism. There is a lot of equipment breakage and disappearance of supplies."

"We've got a bunch of new women in the Copy Pulling Section, just arrived from the dismantled war agencies, and they're getting paid more than the old timers. Everybody's complaining about the two-and-a-half acres we have to cover chasing dusty patents. Some days we're busy — other days just sittin' around; and it makes no sense because other women doing the same work aren't busy when we are. I guess it's no wonder we've got a three-months' backlog; and with patent requests coming in at the rate of 20,000 a day, you ought to see what 500,000 unfilled orders look like in an office as small as ours."[56]

An administrator has a production quota of 850 old age and survivor's insurance applications to process monthly. "We're doing 700, and I know we could do more." He recognizes the *failure to achieve goals.*

"The problem in our department is a *failure to manage tensions* — between the young Turks and the old barons, between technical specialists and the line managers.[57] I'm afraid Carl Sandburg would call it 'the war years.' "

"In our Placement Bureau, we are still matching jobs up with applicants by hand. And there sits the University's computer just waiting to be asked. We're afraid of *technological change.*"

"I think our whole approach to budget review is wrong — Fiscal Division, Estimates Division, Administrative Management. No one around here *can see the whole picture* on international affairs, national defense, health and welfare, and economic growth."

"Troubles are coming here in Civil Service. The Organization and Methods

(O&M) team wants us to scrap our process units — recruitment, testing, rating, and training — and shift to a clientele basis, with jacks-of-all-trades serving the public safety agencies, the education offices, and the general government group. I'm not sure we can cope with *the external pressure, or with change.*"

From these diary entries of civil servants we get a feeling for the signs of trouble within an organization, signs that would lead any manager worthy of her post to probe deeper. The probe is likely to reveal a variety of troubles. There may be relatively simple faults in office procedures, or tougher problems in the way both the work and the agency have been organized. The technology may be sadly out of date. Or there may be a weakening of the whole social fabric that has heretofore held the work groups together and given them both cama-raderie and a loyalty to the agency. But this much is clear: there are problems, and they must be handled.

Making the Diagnosis

Let's assume that you've been brought in as the organization consultant for our agency. Here are some pointers to bear in mind during your fact-finding.

How you handle us — and yourself — will be crucial   While gathering the facts about what's right and wrong in our shop, please allay fears, soften resis-tance, build confidence as you proceed. You can contribute to those ends by exhibiting attitudes that stress that you've come to help, not to hinder or em-barrass; that your mind will work objectively, your mannerisms empathetically; that you'll give us the facts as you perceive them without value judgments (nonevaluative feedback); that together we can build a sound relationship as we solve this problem.[58]

Don't let the formal structure bedazzle you   Human beings live, love, accom-plish, and louse each other up; organization charts merely decorate walls. If we are going to improve an organization, we must understand its living system (the thing we called informal organization in Chapter 5), which may differ vastly from the map drawn by the O&M people.[59]

Can the organization chart tell you anything?   The chart is partly a normative rendition, partly an existential rendition of superior-subordinate relationships in the agency and in lines of authority, responsibility, and reporting. One of the delightful aspects of the analyst's job is to get employees in the know to draw their *operational* version of the chart (as we attempted with "Employment Se-curity" in Chapter 5). It is the differences between the two sets that can provide useful clues to explore.

Some of the questions to be asked of the formal structure grow out of the

principles advanced in Chapter 3: organization units built around large purposes, appropriate provision for staff and auxiliary services, evidence of overlapping jurisdictions, excessive supervisory spans, and a base of organization
appropriate to the agency's goal (of quality, economy, or speed of operations).
Robert Golembiewski would be watching for signs on the chart of tall (hiss-
and-boo), rather than flat (applaud-and-cheer) organizations.[60]

Keep one eye on history Steep yourself in previous studies of the agency,
attitude surveys others may have taken, exit interviews, legislative hearings and
reports, and any other documents that may help fill in the background (but
remember what Thomas Jefferson said: "The Earth belongs always to the living
generation").

See the place (and be seen) Accompanied by one or two of the most significant of our significant others (see Chapter 2), make a *reconnaissance* of the
principal work areas of the office. What do you see — crowded desks, high
noise level, clutter, but signs of *healthy interaction* and *live-wire people* or
disorder and *dispirit?*

Being seen with those significant others of the employee work force can take
a little of the "foreigner" out of you. "A friend of Ted's can't be an enemy."

Statistics tell something Thanks to a previous survey, the agency now keeps
gauges on the intervening variables as well as on the output variables. So data
are available on absenteeism, turnover, levels of commitment and loyalty, critical incidents, and the like. They'll provide important insights into the living
system you are trying to understand.

Output figures may be obtained in various ways. Reports issued or cases
concluded may be numbered seriatim, making the work count very easy. Pa-
trons served may be toted up by means of an electronic counter at the entry
door. The hand count may sometimes be required. Of course what you are
ultimately looking for are trends, differing production rates from identical work
groups, and fluctuations in work load and/or output, which may suggest faulty
staff balancing or scheduling, among other possible explanations.

"Would you mind answering a question or two?" Interviewing is both an
important and a risky fact-finding tool. But the time will probably come when
interviewing (desk audits) will become indispensable.[61]

Respondents must be put at ease; as we said earlier, they need to be assured
that you are friend, not foe. Skill in asking factual rather than emotionally loaded
questions must be developed (but note that some facts may be emotionally
explosive with some people; e.g., "How many cases do you review each day?"
when the case worker you are interviewing is far below the office average). And,

while showing empathy, you must be able to distinguish baloney from bully straight. Where note taking during the interview seems to spook the respondent, you should summarize the conversation immediately after it is over. (Sometimes problems of accuracy in critical interviews can be resolved by allowing the employee to edit your write-up.)

"It takes only twenty minutes to fill out"   Questionnaires are often useful fact-finding and attitude-measuring devices. They assure us at least of standardized presentation, which of course does not guarantee uniform understanding; of the chance to cover a fairly large number of employees, who may be spatially some distance apart; and of the possibility of automatic data processing of the responses, depending on format and the questions asked.

Some of the key rules about questionnaire design include: determining what it is you want to know (stressing the *living system* first, operational details second); framing questions clearly; precoding answers, where possible, to speed up subsequent computer inputs; and (where appropriate) the clear designation of respondent, unit, deadline, return address, and so on.

The questionnaire must be tested before use. Insightful people who know English as well as something about measurements should have a chance to red-pencil your creation first. Then comes the field test, trying it out on a representative sample of employees in order to discover bugs in the instrument (e.g., vague questions, inadequate space for replies, etc.)

"The files face the wrong way"   You may find the need for some charts and diagrams in figuring out relationships, procedures, and snafus. The first is the *layout chart*. which is a bird's-eye view of the office. It locates the key work centers (e.g., desks, files, work bench, supply cabinet) and traces the physical movement of people and work units (letters, reports, lab samples, IRS audits, and so on) among the centers. In essence, the layout chart is employed to help you find the shortest distance between two points (whereas the PERT diagram discussed in Chapter 9 focused on the longest distance from start to finish) — files facing the secretary instead of the executive, how to shorten the two and a half acres that had to be traveled by the copy pullers in the Patent Office, and so on.

"Baby, you are supernumerary"   A bit more complex is the *work distribution chart*. which is illustrated in Figure 12.1. The figure is a composite of the task lists of each member of the unit. When put together, they yield a tabular picture of office activities and priorities (the total hours spent each week), distribution effort, and the job mix of each employee.

Note what the analyst could discern from the work distribution chart of the "plumbers unit," a White House intelligence group during the Nixon administration:

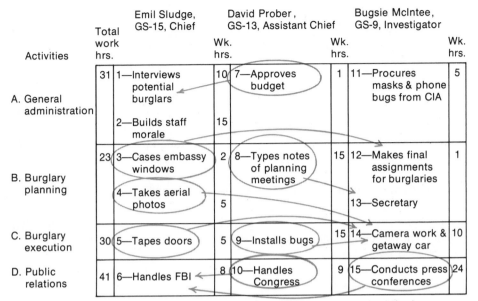

Activities	Total work hrs.	Emil Sludge, GS-15, Chief	Wk. hrs.	David Prober, GS-13, Assistant Chief	Wk. hrs.	Bugsie McIntee, GS-9, Investigator	Wk. hrs.
A. General administration	31	1—Interviews potential burglars 2—Builds staff morale	10 15	7—Approves budget	1	11—Procures masks & phone bugs from CIA	5
B. Burglary planning	23	3—Cases embassy windows 4—Takes aerial photos	2 5	8—Types notes of planning meetings	15	12—Makes final assignments for burglaries 13—Secretary	1
C. Burglary execution	30	5—Tapes doors	5	9—Installs bugs	15	14—Camera work & getaway car	10
D. Public relations	41	6—Handles FBI	8	10—Handles Congress	9	15—Conducts press conferences	24

Note: The circled duties should be reassigned as the arrows indicate; this shift of duties suggests that the position of Mr. Prober, the GS-13, can be eliminated.

FIGURE 12.1 WORK DISTRIBUTION CHART FOR THE WHITE HOUSE PLUMBERS' UNIT (bobtailed version)

As to Chief Sludge

Task (1) is below the level of a GS-15.

(2) Does plumber morale need 15 hours per week?

(3) & (4) These are tricky but do they demand the chief?

(5) This would indicate quite a few break-ins a week; the two hours allocated to casing the joints wouldn't be enough.

As to GS-13 Prober

(7) Budget approval belongs to the chief.

(8) Stupid to have a GS-13 typing minutes (clearly a paranoid security syndrome)

(9) Installing bugs beneath his dignity, if not in his job classification.

(10) Congressional relations too sensitive for the assistant chief.

↑

THIS POSITION SHOULD
BE ABOLISHED

As to GS-9 McIntee

(12) The junior man does not make final assignments.

(13) If only around for ten hours, that means the assistant chief has no getaway car for five hours of bugging time.

(14) When the unit's work is so sensitive, even a diplomat like this GS-9 could not answer questions for half the week without blowing the lid.

The questions to be asked of the completed work distribution chart include: (a) Is there misdirected effort (such as public relations receiving forty-one hours per week)? (b) Are skills being properly used (employees operating above or below their expected levels)? (c) Is there a proper distribution of duties — anyone with a boring, single-track job? Anyone with too many duties to perform?

In the case at hand, answers to those questions would strongly suggest that all of the assistant chief's assignments should be given to others, as the arrows suggest, and his job abolished. (Therein lie the utility and the threat of this particular O&M chart. Also consider the exasperation the chart generates when employees are asked to account for their forty hours of work each week.)

"Why does that form cross my desk three times?" One of the best of the O&M instruments is the *flow process chart.* Briefly stated, it symbolically represents the life history of any work unit (a VD case, a TV license, a summons, etc.) moving through the shop, with time spent and distance traveled. Figure 12.2 shows what a flow process chart looks like.

The symbols on the chart are as follows (with the appropriate one opposite each step being penciled in):

○ operation (the action steps that count)

○ sometimes ▷ transportation (moving things around)

△ storage (sitting in the in-basket, files, waiting for action)

☐ inspection (proofread yet? did the finance office sign off? legally sound?)

The O&M analyst would quickly spot these kinds of things for questioning (the numbers refer to step numbers in column four of the figure):

(4) Why couldn't the master register be at the file clerk's desk rather than 120 feet away?

Are the two registers (2) and (6) both necessary?

(15) Why not use a form letter (saving three steps)?

(19) Why the two-hour delay before the typist can do her thing?

(31) (37) (42) Must this certification be read three times, twice by the same man?

(45) Could this four-hour delay be cut down?

The questions to be asked of a completed flow process chart should include: Why is this step necessary? Where should it be performed? What is the right sequence for this step? Who should do the job? How should this job be done?[62]

The final step in process charting is drawing up a revised one, with new routing, sequences, and use of equipment all being shown with the savings in steps, time, and distances.

By way of review, then, a whole array of fact-finding devices is available for organizational analysis: organization charts, past surveys, reconnaissance, work load and performance data, interviews, questionnaires, layout chart, and the work distribution and flow process charts, among others. In passing, note how many of these can be used by employees for *self-analysis*.

Getting the facts is one thing; deciding how to employ them is another question.

Strategies for Change[63]

Basically two things are likely to be involved in reorganizing agency life: structural change and behavioral change.[64] In the former, for example, we might be broadening spans of control by eliminating one supervisory level or going to automation. With behavioral change, we have a different kind of agenda, including lifting the level of employee consciousness about agency mission, opening up communications, harmonizing some ragged interpersonal relations, changing attitudes toward high producers and new employees, and lifting employees to self-actualization.

There seem to be three basic approaches to the management of change: fiat, persuasion, and self-renewal (or OD, organization development).[65] They clearly fall from one pole to another on Likert's spectrum of Systems 1 through 4.

Change by Fiat

Far and away the most frequent kind of change is that which the boss asks for or directs: "Ms. Hawthorn is being transferred from the typing pool to the economics section"; "Forget about carbon copies and use the copier instead"; "Begin microfilming the civil court records — we've run out of shelf space."

The method can claim quickness and decisiveness and build the image of an authoritarian leader who means to dominate all the task roles of his agency. But change by fiat also runs the risk of seeing the reform scuttled in the ranks (as Chester Barnard warned with his definition of authority as the "power to grant or withhold obedience," noted in Chapter 3).

Change by fiat is risky for other reasons as well. Since management does not have a monopoly of knowledge about what goes on in the agency, these reforms may be based on poor information, resulting in half-baked solutions. Further-

WORK SIMPLIFICATION PROGRAM PROCESS CHART

PROCESS CHARTED Certification Procedure UNIT Certification

DATE October 15, _____ DIVISION, BRANCH, ETC. Field

In Feet	Time in Minutes	Operation	Transport	Storage	Inspector	Step No.	DESCRIPTION OF EACH STEP (SHOW WHAT IS DONE—WHO DOES IT)
		○	O▲	□		1	Incoming case at master register desk
		●	O△	□		2	Case entered in master register
	10	○	O▲	□		3	In outgoing basket
120		○	●△	□		4	To file clerk
	20	○	O▲	□		5	In incoming basket
		●	O△	□		6	Case entered in file room register
		●	O△	□		7	File searched for previous action
		●	O△	□		8	File pulled and attached to case
		●	O△	□		9	Charge-out slip made on file
	40	○	O▲	□		10	In outgoing basket
180		○	●△	□		11	To clerk A
	120	○	O▲	□		12	In incoming basket
		○	O△	■		13	Case checked against file for change of address
120		○	●△	□		14	To correspondence clerk
		●	O△	□		15	Acknowledgment dictated
10		○	●△	□		16	To stenographer's desk
		●	O△	□		17	Acknowledgment A
60		○	●△	□		18	To student of recommendations prepared
	130	○	O▲	□		19	To typist
		○	O△	□		28	Statement typed
50		○	●△	□		29	To case editor
	60	○	O▲	□		30	In incoming basket
		○	O△	■		31	Statement checked for form
130		○	●△	□		32	To section chief
	120	○	O▲	□		33	In incoming basket
		●	O△	□		34	Draft revised for conformance to policy
130		○	●△	□		35	To case editor
	120	○	O▲	□		36	In incoming basket
		○	O△	■		37	Statement checked for form
50		○	●△	□		38	To typist
		●	O△	□		39	Final draft of statement typed
60		○	●△	□		40	To analyst
	20	○	O▲	□		41	In incoming basket
		○	O△	■		42	Reads
	40	○	O▲	□		43	In outgoing basket
90		○	●△	□		44	To section chief
	240	○	O▲	□		45	In incoming basket
		●	O△	□		46	Reviewed and signed
1105	985	13	14 14		5		TOTAL

more, the agency may pay dearly in the intervening variables in imposing changes on people they have not consulted.

Change by Persuasion

The empirical-rational method of Robert Chin and Kenneth Benne suggests that change can take place when workers are convinced by a presentation of facts that a change is in order. For example, the data supporting a prepaid medical insurance plan make it look better to them than private payment of health care.

The charting of fluctuating work load statistics through two parallel pipelines convinces the engineering staff that the pipelines should be merged. An excursion by city court workers to the Blue Cross–Blue Shield customer service desk with its playback of insureds' records on desk-top computer screens quickly convinces the court personnel to computerize and give up hand tallying cases.

Contrary to change by fiat, change by persuasion is complimentary to workers. It recognizes their ability to see a better way of organizing the work once the facts are in. But the primary initiative in this approach to change still rests with management.

Change Through Self-renewal — The Organization Development Approach

Organization development (OD) was generated about 1957, in the same decade that saw the birth of Maslow's and Herzberg's motivation theories and Drucker's theory of management by objectives. The product of behavioral scientists, OD's approach to organizational change was that of continuous self-renewal within agencies.[66]

We define OD as a change system that involves employees significantly in both problem analysis and the generation of solutions in a climate of trust and openness where change becomes the status quo.

The underlying philosophy is simple:

1. Employees are capable of diagnosing problems they live with and suggesting solutions.
2. The climate must be right to elicit their suggestions.[67]
3. Implementation of reforms will be smoother if employees are involved at the analysis stage.
4. The best remedy for entropy is continuous self-renewal.

FIGURE 12.2   FLOW PROCESS CHART (bobtailed)

From U.S. Bureau of the Budget, *Supervisor's Guide to the Process Chart* (Washington, D.C.: Government Printing Office, 1953), p. 4.

The first two items listed are not self-fulfilling prophecies; they need to be tended to. Managers build a capability for self-analysis by doing the following: meeting the security, love, and self-esteem needs of workers; sharing information with them; involving them in the reorganization process; challenging them; and rewarding useful innovations they suggest.

Furthermore, OD requires a great amount of attention to such maintenance activities as team building and harmonizing interpersonal relations.[68] A variety of techniques to do these things have been explored, including T-groups (sensitivity training),[69] and transactional analysis (TA).[70] Their common goal is to reduce defensiveness, promote adult kinds of behavior, and generate a willingness to confront rather than dodge problems.

The most important contribution to the kind of climate that can sustain continuous change must be provided by management. Managers must deeply value employee ideas, solicit them, and then listen. Victor Thompson said it best, we think:

> The innovative organization will allow the diversity of inputs needed for the creative generation of ideas. Long periods of pre-entry, professional training, and wide diffusion of ideas within the organization, including a wide diffusion of problems and suggested solutions, will provide the variety and richness of experience required. Included should be a wide diffusion of uncertainty so that the whole organization is stimulated to search, rather than just a few professional researchers. Involving larger parts of the organization in the search process also increases chances of acceptance and implementation. This wide diffusion, in turn, will depend upon ease and freedom of communication and a low level of parochialism.[71]

The point bears repeating: a climate ripe for an OD undertaking will provide solid evidence to all of trust, openness, commitment, and challenge.

The OD Sequence[72]

1. An individual or a group in the agency makes sure that an existing or upcoming problem is recognized by management. A rap session with employees is conducted, and they indicate their support for the next steps (see Figure 12.3 for an illustration of the sequence).

2. An employee task force is assigned to begin some systems analysis (problem identification, data gathering, exploring alternatives). Often an outside consultant is now brought on board, not to design solutions, but to aid and abet the self-analysis that is proceeding.

3. The findings and alternatives are fed back to the work group for joint discussion. Now two important things take place: the generation of ideas and reactions on what should be done; and the slow building of "involvement leading to commitment." Then follows a recommendation to the unit chief.

4. The decision to go ahead, which still belongs to that designated officer, now is made with the knowledge that the staff supports the decision.

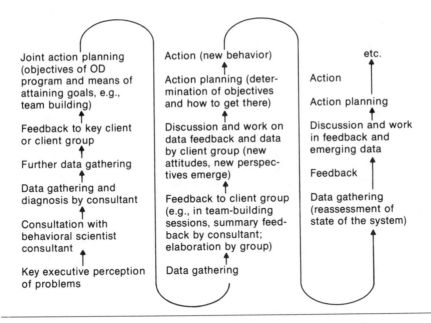

FIGURE 12.3 AN ACTION RESEARCH MODEL FOR ORGANIZATION DEVELOPMENT

Reprinted from Wendell French, "Organization Development," *California Management Review*, vol. 12, no. 2, p. 26, only by permission of the Regents. © 1969 by the Regents of the University of California.

5. Implementation planning begins and calls into use a problem solver (see Table 12.3). With employee involvement, assignments are made and a timetable is agreed to.

6. Then we plan for feedback, get it, review it, and effect changes as required.

TABLE 12.3 THE OD PROBLEM SOLVER (for a city court decision to computerize)

Decision: to computerize our records

OBSTACLES	ASSETS
1. Getting the funds for the software from the city commission	1a. Enlist the court administrator to lobby with the city commission; or
	1b. Obtain a start-up grant from the law enforcement assistance administration
2. Convincing a nervous chief judge as to computer reliability and fail-safe capacity	2. Get travel funds for the judge to see the computerized court records in Anchorage, Alaska (the empirical-rational approach)
3. Training the staff	3. Court administrator will approve compensatory time for off-hours training

That is why we refer to OD as "planned change." Its legacy is not only a creative response to the instant problem; it is also a problem-solving capability for the next ones. Continuous change has become the status quo.

Some Pluses in the Track Record of Microreorganization

Agencies don't walk down the road of microreorganization for the exercise or to make employees feel better. They do so in pursuit of cost savings, better service, and employee growth, among other goals.

The record is replete with accomplishments (and of course with many failures):

In the first Patent Office reorganization, involving work counts, flow process charts, and shifts from parallel to serial organization, the three-month backlog was eliminated, copy-pulling rates rose 100 percent, and the staff was reduced 20 percent while the work load was rising 25 percent.

Thanks to computerization, the cost of issuing government paychecks was cut by more than two thirds during the late 1950s.

A merger of two Treasury Department disbursing offices in the major centers of New York and Philadelphia generated $189,000 in annual savings.

An automatic microfilm retrieving system for social security claims saved $70,000 annually.

A new social security technique for stuffing check envelopes saved $550,000 per year.[73]

Some Obstacles to Be Overcome[74]

Pit microreorganization against the Maslow need ladder and then see why many employees are spooked at the first suggestion of internal change. If reorganization portends the elimination of jobs, employees are sent tumbling down the ladder in panic to Maslow's first and second need levels: "Will my job be eliminated? Then how am I to feed my kids?"

If reorganization is going to mean reassignment of personnel, then what happens to work groups and the ways in which love needs are currently being met? For healthy individuals, life on the job is so much more than performing duties, accumulating leave, and getting paid; it also means new friends, sustainment, symbiosis — "And if the O&M people contemplate jerking all that apart, they are going to get me where I live. Those birds aren't going to shatter the things that make this place so much more than a job for me; they will just O&M me into quitting."

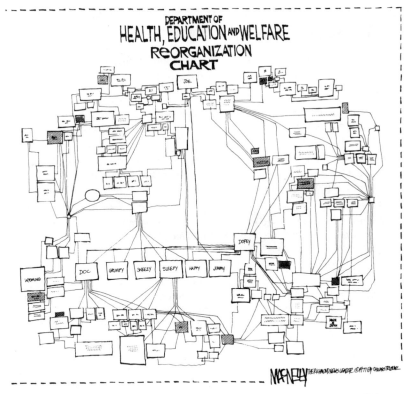

The *Richmond News Leader;* Copyright © 1977 by the Chicago Tribune. Reprinted by permission of the Chicago Tribune-New York News Syndicate.

What about the higher levels of the Maslow ladder? Will reorganization diminish an employee's responsibilities and prestige? If it does, it may kill his self-esteem. In the name of work simplification and a science for every job, will reorganization so reduce his duties that a moron could perform them? Such changes will harm more than help, for they will destroy self-actualization.

Threatening every level of individual need, reorganization looks like some kind of multiheaded antipersonnel weapon. Sensing that, defensive employees can quash the best-laid plans of the O&M staff. The second phase of the Haw-thorne study (the Bank Wiring Room) demonstrated the power informal groups possess to resist change (see Chapter 2). Further documentation came in the unhappy cycle of events that occurred in the U.S. Patent Office after World War II. The 1946 reorganization of the copy-pulling section came unglued through the failure of management to win employee support for the changes being made. Two years later that section had to be rereorganized, with broader supervisory spans of control, job variety and rotation, more opportunity for worker decision making, and improved training and promotion possibilities.[75]

O&M and the Ninth Symphony

An unknown source some years ago provided an organization and methods analysis of the National Symphony's rendition of Beethoven's Ninth Symphony:

> For considerable periods the four oboe players had nothing to do. The numbers should be reduced and the work spread more evenly over the whole of the concert, thus eliminating peaks of activity.

> All the twelve first violins were playing identical notes. This seems unnecessary duplication. The staff of this section should be drastically cut; if a large volume of sound is required, it could be obtained by means of electronic amplifier apparatus.

> Much effort was absorbed in the playing of demi-semi-quavers. This seems an excessive refinement. It is recommended that all notes should be rounded up to the nearest semi-quaver. If this were done, it would be possible to use trainees and lower grade operatives more extensively.

> There seems to be too much repetition of some musical passages. Scores should be drastically pruned. No useful purpose is served by repeating on the horns a passage which has been handled by the strings. It is estimated that if all redundant passages were eliminated, the whole concert time could be reduced to 20 minutes, and there would be no need for an interval.

> The conductor agrees generally with these recommendations, but expresses the opinion that there might be some falling-off in box office receipts. In that unlikely event, it should be possible to close sections of the auditorium entirely, with a consequential saving of overhead expenses — lighting, attendants, etc.

> If the worst came to the worst, the whole thing could be abandoned, and the public could go to some other hall instead.

Overcoming Resistance to Change[76]

Generating a climate hospitable to reorganization cannot begin when the signs of trouble first appear, for by definition one is *already in trouble* at that point. When O&M experts appear on the scene under those circumstances, employee antennas are twitching nervously, interviewers get the cold shoulder, and questionnaires produce negative responses, sometimes even panic.

Thus the generation of a supportive atmosphere and a widely shared problem-solving capability is so vitally important. In saying that, we are back once again in Chapter 6, pursuing all the leads provided by Theory Y, meeting the Maslow needs, developing a healthy group structure, and *regularly* involving employees in problem-solving discussions.[77]

Innovations thrive when there is time to think, when there are resources to experiment with, and when there is goodwill on the part of managers and co-workers, as Victor Thompson has reminded us.[78] Information sharing and colleagues whose brains serve as resonant sounding boards for each other's ideas are also critical.

Managers can help shape such a climate. As we noted earlier, executives at Walt Disney list projects on a current assignments board and roam freely through each other's domains. Innovators can be sent to retreats and conferences to absorb and reflect. The Supreme Court, for example, takes a February recess and a long summer vacation to provide just that kind of repose.

Innovation is fostered by decentralized decision making, based on the notion of more heads equals more ideas, and by rotation and rhythm in the agency's cycle. Illustrating what he called "periodicity," Herbert Shepard referred to a combat company that employed Theory Y during the planning of an attack — with privates to colonels chipping in their ideas — and then reverted to Theory X during the execution of the plan. The rotation of military people to the general staff described in Chapter 4 is another kind of periodicity that can broaden viewpoints and liberate new ideas.

Competition may even be employed to foster innovation. If resources will allow, set two project teams in motion to find a solution to an agency problem. That was the technique employed during World War II by the secret atomic bomb project, the Manhattan Engineering District, at Los Alamos, New Mexico; Hanford, Washington; Oak Ridge, Tennessee; and the Universities of California, Chicago, and Columbia. Enrico Fermi's team won that race in successfully controlling atomic fission in the squash court beneath the University of Chicago stadium.[79]

What seems of uppermost importance is the agency's receptivity to and nurturing of risk takers and self-actualizers. The contrast emerges in our twentieth-century military history. Gen. William Mitchell was court-martialed in 1924 for advocating an air force, while Adm. Hyman Rickover was virtually knighted during the 1950s for pioneering the nuclear submarine.

The problem-solving capability of agencies would be greatly enhanced if they could live by the old folk wisdom that it is better to try and fail than never to try at all. In brief, there need to be Brownie points for risk takers.

Those kinds of innovators are going to come from the ranks of self-actualized people in an agency. Shepard described them as possessing great creative energy, trust in others, psychological security, and organizing skill.[80] The self-actualizer, Shepard goes on to say,

> is his own man rather than the organization's man; his behavior and sense of self-worth are not blindly determined by the organization's reward and punishment system (either in the form of submission to it or rebellion against it); if he cannot transform his situation into one in which he and others can be both autonomous and interdependent, he feels free to fight it or to leave it.

> Such men are rare because the institutions of our society do not provide the conditions under which many persons are able to grow to this degree of human maturity. The

innovation-producing organization must aim to provide an environment in which this kind of growth can occur. This means a climate in which members can view one another as resources rather than competitive threats or judges; a climate of openness and mutual support in which differences can be confronted and worked through, and in which feedback on performance is a mutual responsibility among members so that all can learn to contribute more. Such an environment is difficult to provide, since it is at variance with traditional management doctrine.[81]

That conventional doctrine, we should remember, questions any approach to change other than fiat.

Doubts About Employee Participation in Reorganization

In 1967, political scientist Frederick C. Mosher, of the University of California at Berkeley, published his important casebook, *Government Reorganizations*, with a view to testing the "participation hypothesis" that employee involvement in reorganizations facilitates change. Mosher's conclusion was to the contrary: "The cases in this volume do not support the participation hypothesis."[82]

In place of the openness and access to information we have been advocating, Mosher found that the preliminary discussions about an impending reorganization,

and even the fact that the subject was being discussed, were usually a closely guarded secret among a very few officials in the immediate circle of the principal executive. Likewise, where a survey was authorized by a legislative body, the initial talks were confined to a small circle. Secrecy was apparently aimed to prevent unrest, rumor, and sometimes the mobilization of opposition.[83]

The reply, of course, is: Will employees feel any better five months later about a fait accompli that affects their lives?

Mosher properly pointed out that some employees have little interest in reorganization so long as their paychecks are undisturbed. They either operate in a zone of indifference on such matters or, a la Chester Barnard, they "delegate upward" to agency heads the unquestioned right to restructure the place.

A close look at the cases in the collection, however, leaves some large doubts as to Mosher's negative findings on Theory Y. Of the twelve case studies, there was no employee participation in three of the reorganizations, slight to moderate in six, and moderate to substantial in three.[84] Most of the involvement came during the implementation stage, with little at the initiatory or decision-making stages. But it is Mosher's admissions that are of most interest:

Reorganizations that are "imposed upon the organizations from above or outside, which include all of those by private consultant groups . . . usually met substantial opposition within the agencies concerned; and by and large were least successful."[85]

Some participation of persons whose behaviors are to be modified is almost by definition essential in implementing phases of reorganization.[86]

Where participation occurred, employee resistance was lowered; where employee resistance was the greatest, there had been no participation at all.[87]

Apparently participation makes a whale of a difference!

Of equal import, so does reorganization make a difference: changing the structure and processes of government to enable agencies to cope with the new challenges people and environment may impose.

SUMMARY

Given the vagaries of politics, passing time, and people, our governmental institutions may sometimes look strange when created and become funnier by the decade. High cost, low efficiency, overlapping, and duplication translate into more taxes and sometimes fewer services. Goals go unfulfilled; technology changes; new demands are laid on government. The erosion of existing institutions caused by all those winds and streams forces us to reform — or pay the consequences.

Consequently, reorganization has been a recurring if not a continuous aspect of American public administration. Since 1887, executive departments have been brought under the microscope of congressional committees, presidential panels, special commissions, and private scrutiny in every decade.

And change has come, on the macroscale by legislative enactment and presidential reorganization plans; on the microscale through organization development (OD), organization and methods analysis (O&M), and other forms of internal improvement.

Macroreorganization is bounded, like all of public administration, by what politics will permit; microreorganization, by what employees can tolerate. So those who enter the thicket of restructuring government agencies must do so with one eye cocked toward politicians and another toward employees. Ultimately, these two groups determine whether the best-laid plans are of mice or men.

KEY CONCEPTS

principles of scientific management
reform movement
Brown Committee
The Economy Act
(Presidential) Committee on
   Administrative Management

the first Hoover Commission
The Ash Council
layout chart
work distribution chart
flow process chart
organization development

DISCUSSION QUESTIONS

1. Compare the various presidential reorganization efforts since Hoover. What similarities are present? To what extent did the personality of the president play a significant role in introducing successful reforms?

2. Discuss the most important reasons for macroreorganization. To what extent do they accomplish the four major goals of reorganization?

3. Identify the procedures you must follow in order to discover organizational troubles and their solution. In doing so, prepare a list of do's and don'ts.

4. Discuss the philosophy underlying organizational development. To what degree is it an extension of Maslow, Herzberg, and Theory Y?

5. Discuss the possible obstacles that must be overcome before organization development (OD) would be successful. Would some organizations be more receptive than others to OD? Why?

Notes

1. U.S. President, *Executive Reorganization* (House Doc. 92-75) (Washington, D.C.: Government Printing Office, 1971), pp. 3–4.

2. For the labor protests, see two early congressional reports by the House Labor Committee, *Taylor System of Shop Management* (House Report. 62-52) (Washington, D.C.: Government Printing Office, 1911); and *Taylor and Other Systems of Shop Management* (House Report. 62-403) (Washington, D.C.: Government Printing Office, 1913).

3. The history was recounted in Horace Drury, *Scientific Management* (New York: Columbia University Press, 1915).

4. John Dewey, *Democracy and Education* (New York: Macmillan, 1916, 1961), p. 85.

5. See Drury, *Scientific Management*. p. 16.

6. For starters read Richard Hofstadter, *The Progressive Movement. 1900–1915* (Englewood Cliffs, N.J.: Prentice-Hall, 1963); Arthur Link, *Woodrow Wilson and the Progressive Era* (New York: Harper, 1954); and the *Autobiography of Lincoln Steffens* (New York: Harcourt, Brace, 1931).

7. The principal source book on the history of Federal reorganization is the U.S. Legislative Reference Service, *A Compilation of Basic Information on the Reorganization of the Executive Branch of the Government of the United States. 1912–1947* (Washington, D.C.: Legislative Reference Service, 1947), hereafter cited as *LRS Compilation*. The title of the *Compilation* is unfortunately misleading, since events back to 1887 are in fact covered. The historical chart on p. 1301 is especially helpful.

8. Harvey Mansfield has observed that study bodies appointed exclusively by the president have "the advantages of confidentiality in getting advice and preparing reorganization proposals. . . . The appointment of a mixed public commission is likely to be read as a sign of weakness or irresolution on his part." "Federal Executive Reorganization: Thirty Years of Experience," *Public Administration Review* (July–Aug. 1969) 29:335.

9. Although poking fun is not entirely fair, for the Joint Committee was envisioning new responsibilities for telephone, telegraph, and wireless, in addition to carrying the mails.

10. The housing lobby had come around in the interim.

11. 47 Stat. 413.

12. *LRS Compilation,* p. 1224.

13. *LRS Compilation,* p. 1225.

14. *LRS Compilation,* pp. 602–634.

15. *Congressional Record* (January 19, 1933) 76:2104.

16. *Congressional Record* (January 19, 1933), 76:2105.

17. 47 Stat. 1517.

18. Executive Order 6166.

19. See U.S. President's Committee on Administrative Management, *Report with Special Studies* (Washington, D.C.: Government Printing Office, 1937).

20. 53 Stat. 56.

21. Mansfield contends that the innovative feature of this 1939 act was the modification of House and Senate rules governing consideration of resolutions disapproving reorganization plans. "Federal Executive Reorganization," p. 337.

22. President's Committee on Administrative Management, *Report,* p. 41.

23. This and the following passages are from a personal letter to the author from Professor Cushman, then at Cornell University, dated December 2, 1948.

24. For a larger view of the era, see Richard Polenberg, *Reorganizing Roosevelt's Government* (Cambridge, Mass.: Harvard University Press, 1966).

25. 61 Stat. 246.

26. Provision 5 may have been the acorn from which the mighty oak of subsection 5 in the second Hoover Commission grew — to get rid of government functions which compete with private enterprise.

27. See especially the first Hoover Commission's *Concluding Report* (Washington, D.C.: Government Printing Office, 1949), p. 2.

28. See either the commission's *Concluding Report* or Dudley Ball, *Summary of the Recommendations of the (I) Hoover Commission* (Washington, D.C.: Legislative Reference Service, 1950, mimeo).

    Where Harry Truman failed in his effort to carry out this last-named proposal (at a time when FSA Administrator Oscar Ewing and socialized medicine were the scarecrows of the day), Dwight Eisenhower brought the giant Health, Education, and Welfare Department into being by Reorganization Plan No. 1 of 1953, with a favorable vote in both chambers of his Republican Eighty-third Congress.

29. Citizens' Committee for the Hoover Report, *Reorganization News* (Washington, D.C.: Citizens' Committee, October, 1958). See also U.S. House Committee on Government Operations, *Summary of the Objectives, Operations, and Results of the Commissions on Organization of the Executive Branch of the Government* (committee print) (Washington, D.C.: Government Printing Office, 1963), pp. 6 and 28–31. Hereafter cited as Government Operations *Summary.*

30. P.L. 83-108; 67 Stat. 142; sections 1 (5) and 3. See also Government Operations *Summary,* pp. 10–12, for a treatment of the differences in the enabling acts of the two commissions.

31. Note the contrast between Hoover's own words in 1948: "Major functions of the government are determinable as needed by the Congress. It is not our function to say whether it should exist or not, but it is our function to see if we cannot make it work better," and in 1955: "We are trying to strengthen the philosophical foundations of our country." Quoted in William R. Divine, "The Second Hoover Commission Reports," *Public Administration Review* (Autumn 1955) 15:263–269. Hoover's own views after the second round were expressed in "Government Is Too Big," *U.S. News and World Report* (August 5, 1955) 39:48–52.

32. As quoted in W. V. Eckardt, "The Hoover Reports," *New Leader* (July 11, 1955) 38:3–6.

33. Since the second Hoover Commission published no summary volume, see William Divine, "The Second Hoover Commission Reports," for commission highlights.

34. From the historical data in Mansfield, "Federal Executive Reorganization," p. 340.

35. Government Operations *Summary*, p. 14. Going back to 1945, the House Government Operations Committee in 1963 found the greatest period of presidential reorganization activity followed the first Hoover Commission. "There has been no comparable submission of Presidential reorganization plans based on the recommendations of the second Commission . . . in 1955." House Government Operations Committee, *Reorganization by Plan and by Statute* (committee print) (Washington, D.C.: Government Printing Office, 1963), p. 2.

36. Data from Mansfield, "Federal Executive Reorganization," p. 339.

37. See Richard P. Nathan, *The Plot That Failed: Nixon and the Administrative Presidency* (New York: Wiley, 1975), pp. 86–89.

38. See Stephen Hess, *Organizing the Presidency* (Washington, D.C.: Brookings Institution, 1976), pp. 131–133.

39. Nixon's original proposal would have swallowed up the Department of Agriculture, but he changed his mind in November 1971.

40. See House Documents 92-75 and 92-273. The rationale and details of the proposed mergers were set forth in U.S. Office of Management and Budget, *Papers Relating to the President's Departmental Reorganization Program* (Washington, D.C.: Government Printing Office, 1972). See also Nathan, *The Plot That Failed,* pp. 68–69.

41. See Nathan, *The Plot That Failed,* pp. 63–68, and Hess, *Organizing the Presidency,* pp. 134–139.

42. Rochelle L. Stanfield, "The Best Laid Reorganization Plans Sometimes Go Astray," *National Journal* (Jan. 20, 1979) 11:84–89.

43. Of course, one man's economy is another man's extravagance. We especially like one paragraph in Teddy Roosevelt's fifth annual message to Congress in December 1905: "Yet in speaking of economy, I must in nowise be understood as advocating the false economy which is in the end the worst extravagance. To cut down on the Navy, for instance, would be a crime against the nation. To fail to push forward all work on the Panama Canal would be as great a folly." *LRS Compilation,* p. 1206.

44. In the 1949 Reorganization Act, the basic law on the subject from Truman to Ford, these goals were laid down in addition to the traditional four: promote better execution of the laws, group functions according to major purpose, and consolidate those with similar functions. 63 Stat. 203, section 2.

45. House Document 92-75, pp. 4–8.

46. This was a bit specious, of course, in the context of Nixon's proposals for four very centralized czars in the super-departments described earlier.

47. Mansfield, "Federal Executive Reorganization," pp. 333–334.

48. Following some perceptive observations by Louis Gawthrop, *Bureaucratic Behavior in the Executive Branch* (New York: Free Press, 1969), chap. 7.

49. See Thomas R. Wolanin, *Presidential Advisory Commissions* (Madison, Wis.: University of Wisconsin Press, 1975).

50. For a perceptive treatment, see I. M. Destler, *Presidents, Bureaucrats, and Foreign Policy* (Princeton, N.J.: Princeton University Press, 1972), pp. 40–46 and elsewhere.

51. "Elite Committee Forms Economic Policy," *Congressional Quarterly Weekly Report* (Feb. 28, 1976), 34:475–476.

52. One of the many useful observations in Weldon Barton's "Administrative Reorgani-

zation by Presidential Plan," *Rocky Mountain Social Science Journal* (Apr. 1970) 7:120–123.

53. See House Government Operations Committee, *Hearings on Amending Reorganization Plan 2 of 1973* (93d Cong., 1st Sess.) (Washington, D.C.: Government Printing Office, 1973).

54. The reorganization plans from 1945 through 1964 are reviewed in the Congressional Quarterly, *Congress and the Nation* (Washington, D.C.: Congressional Quarterly, 1965), pp. 1458–1470. For congressional initiatives in reorganization, 1945–1962, see House Committee on Government Operations, *Reorganization by Plan and by Statute*, pp. 3–27; and the box score on reorganization plans from 1939 to 1970 can be found in Senate Report 92–485, p. 17.

55. Mansfield, "Federal Executive Reorganization," p. 341.

56. Abstracted from one of the all-time classic case studies in microreorganization by Arch Dotson, "Production Planning in the Patent Office," in Harold Stein, ed., *Public Administration and Policy Development* (New York: Harcourt, Brace, 1952), pp. 1–13.

57. See Frederick Mosher's penetrating analysis of "Organizations as a System of Tensions," in his *Government Reorganizations* (Indianapolis: Bobbs-Merrill, 1967), pp. 487–492.

58. Some of the "thou shalts" of Chris Argyris, *Understanding Organizational Behavior* (Homewood, Ill.: Dorsey, 1960), pp. 31–38.

59. Argyris, *Intervention Theory and Method.* (Reading, Mass.: Addison-Wesley, 1970) pp. 78–81.

60. Robert Golembiewski, *Behavior and Organization* (Chicago: Rand, McNally, 1962), pp. 198–205.

61. See Argyris, *Understanding Organizational Behavior.* ch. 2.

62. U.S. Bureau of the Budget, *Supervisor's Guide to the Process Chart* (Washington, D.C.: Government Printing Office, 1953), pp. 5–6.

63. We especially commend Chapter 6 and Part 4 of Jun and Storm, *Tomorrow's Organizations* (Glenview, Ill.: Scott, Foresman, 1973), for their excellent treatment of organizational change.

64. Jun and Storm, *Tomorrow's Organizations.* p. 299.

65. Robert Chin and Kenneth Benne dolled up the three approaches to organizational change in fancier clothing: "Power-coercive, empirical-rational, and normative-reeducative." See their "General Strategies for Effecting Changes in Human Systems," in Jun and Storm, *Tomorrow's Organizations.* pp. 310–330.

66. Among principal works in the field are Ronald Lippitt, et al., *The Dynamics of Planned Change* (New York: Harcourt, Brace, 1958); Warren Bennis, *Organization Development* (Reading, Mass.: Addison Wesley, 1969); Chris Argyris, *Intervention Theory and Method* (1970); and Robert Golembiewski, *Approaches to Planned Change* (New York: Marcel Dekker, 1979), 2 vols.

67. That it can be done has been convincingly demonstrated at the Lincoln Electric Company. See James F. Lincoln, *Incentive Management* (Cleveland, Ohio: Lincoln Electric Co., 1951).

68. Jun and Storm, *Tomorrow's Organizations.* p. 391.

69. Jun and Storm, *Tomorrow's Organizations.* pp. 322–323, 387–388; see also Golembiewski, *Renewing Organizations* (Itasca, Ill.: Peacock, 1972), Part II; and Golembiewski and Blumberg, *Sensitivity Training and the Laboratory Approach* (Itasca, Ill.: Peacock, 1973).

70. Thomas A. Harris, *I'm O.K., You're O.K.* (New York: Harper & Row, 1969); Eric Berne, *Games People Play* (New York: Grove, 1964).

71. Victor Thompson, "Bureaucracy and Innovation," in Jun and Storm, *Tomorrow's Organizations*, pp. 172–173.

72. We are especially indebted to the excellent article by Wendell French, "Organization Development: Objectives, Assumptions and Strategies," in Jun and Storm, *Tomorrow's Organizations*, pp. 379–393.

73. U.S. Joint Financial Management Improvement Program, *Annual Report* (Washington, D.C.: Government Printing Office, 1971), p. 29.

74. See David Mechanic, "The Power to Resist Change Among Low-Ranking Personnel," *Personnel Administration* (July–Aug. 1963) 26:5–11.

75. The Patent Office story is probably the most graphic one in the literature of O&M's scoring short-run gains, followed by serious setbacks. The "before" part of the story is related in Stein, *Public Administration and Policy Development;* the "after" phase by Robert Golembiewski in *Behavior and Organization*, particularly Chapter 9.

76. We particularly call your attention to Herbert A. Shepard, "Innovation-Resisting and Innovation-Producing Organizations," in Jun and Storm, *Tomorrow's Organizations*, pp. 179–186.

77. For the superiority of group discussion over lecture in effecting attitude change, see Kurt Lewin in Cartwright and Zander, eds., *Group Dynamics* (Evanston, Ill.: Row, Peterson, 1960), pp. 280–301.

78. Thompson, "Bureaucracy and Innovation," p. 172.

79. See Herbert Feis, *The Atomic Bomb and the End of World War II* (Princeton, N.J.: Princeton University Press, 1966).

80. Shepard, "Innovation-Resisting," p. 184.

81. Shepard, "Innovation-Resisting," pp. 184–185.

82. Mosher, *Government Reorganizations*, pp. 526 and 534–535.

83. Mosher, *Government Reorganizations*, p. 504.

84. Mosher, *Government Reorganizations*, p. 524.

85. Mosher, *Government Reorganizations*, p. 514.

86. Mosher, *Government Reorganizations*, p. 523.

87. Mosher, *Government Reorganizations*, p. 526.

Part III
FISCAL ASPECTS OF MANAGEMENT

Chapter 13
Budgeting

BUDGETING: TAXING AND SPENDING

It is a rugged forest we now walk into, cluttered with program trees, crosswalks, impoundments, discounting, decision packages, program memorandums (PMs) and a dozen other concepts that all make budgeting look plenty formidable. These woods may be dark and deep, but if you have money to keep, you'd better press on.

Your taxes tell you that, and so do the statistics. All levels of government consumed only 10 percent of the gross national product in 1929, 21 percent just before the Korean War, and 31 percent midway in the Carter administration. If you imagine a family of six sitting down to eat everything this country now produces, two of the members are government (with its state and local component consuming 13 percent of the total pie and the Feds about 18 percent).*

In 1929, governments spent $86 per capita in this country; in 1978, $3,100. Even in constant dollars the comparison is dramatic — from $414 per person in

---

* The figures for governmental expenditures are drawn from the national income and product accounts in the *Economic Report of the President* (Washington, D.C.: Government Printing Office, 1979). They have been adjusted to eliminate double counting of federal grants-in-aid to the states. The percentages are much larger than those in the gross national product tables that utilize final purchases of goods and services rather than total outlays by government. Note also the discrepancy between the 18 percent federal share and the calculation by the Carter administration that federal outlays in 1978 constituted 22 percent of gross national product. The difference lies primarily in the exclusion of federal grants-in-aid from our federal figures.

1929 to $2,000 in 1978 — five times the governmental activity that prevailed before the Great Depression.[1]

The federal government is now spending about $500 billion a year and carries a continuing debt approaching $900 billion; in sixty fiscal years since 1920, it has run into the red forty-three times and has not seen a budgetary surplus in its administrative budget since 1960! Compounding the problem, Congress now controls less than one quarter of the budget, with interest on the national debt and commitments to the elderly, the sick, veterans, and other groups making up the rest.

If all that fails to impress you, then notice the value preferences that are revealed in budget making. In his proposed budget for fiscal year 1980, Jimmy Carter recommended an $11 billion increase in defense spending, a $600 million decrease in social security payments, and a decrease in urban programs designed to provide municipal jobs for the unemployed through funds made available by the Comprehensive Employment and Training Act (CETA, 1973) and by decreasing the number of families eligible for housing subsidies. While Carter was recommending a 3 percent real increase for national defense above the projected rate of inflation, his recommendations for social programs fell below the rate of inflation in almost every instance and thus constituted the likelihood of a real cutback in the level of social services. A Bill Mauldin cartoon portrays the preferences pretty clearly.[2]

Carter's 1980 budget revealed how far he had moved from his 1976 campaign promise to reduce defense spending. Projecting a highly conservative estimate of 7.4 percent inflation during late 1979–1980, his budget recommended a 10 percent increase ($10.8 billion) for the Defense Department and only a 7.7 percent increase in total federal spending (or $38 billion over fiscal 1979). The budget contemplated a $29 billion deficit, down from the $37 billion deficit projected for fiscal 1979 (see Chapter 14).[3]

THE GREAT PURPOSES OF BUDGETING: THE LARGE VIEW

In essence, public budgeting is financial planning by government, allocating dollars to achieve the goals of public policy.

The main steps in the annual sequence we will examine later in detail are these: formulation of broad policy by the chief executive, estimating spending needs by line agencies, preparation of the budget by an executive staff, legislative review and appropriation, and agency spending and final audit. The budget process involves, then, both the executive and the legislative branch, with the executive proposing, the legislature disposing, and only occasional involvement of the judiciary.*

---

* As witness the sudden flurry of court cases in response to Richard Nixon's impounding of funds and attempted dismemberment of the Office of Economic Opportunity, the poverty agency, during 1972–1973.

Courtesy of the Chicago Sun-Times, copyright © 1973. Reproduced by courtesy of Will-Jo Associates, Inc., and Bill Mauldin.

Close twins to budgeting are public finance and taxation, which offer guidelines to the question of where the money is to come from. We must leave these critical matters to other authors and concentrate on the purposes to be served by budgeting; the major approaches and types of budgets; a model system for preparing the federal budget; and finally, the politics of the budgetary process.

In Chapter 14, congressional handling of the budget and postappropriation practices and controls will be reviewed.

Governments engage in systematic budgeting for some or all of four reasons: (a) to influence economic conditions through their taxes and spending (the *fiscal policy* concern), (b) to *manage* programs and measure efficiency, (c) to *plan* and shape the future, and (d) to achieve *accountability*.

The Budget as an Instrument of Fiscal Policy[4]

Some feeling for the economic significance of government budgets at all levels can be osmosed from the gross national product equation:[5]

Y	=	C	+	I	+	G	±	E
(total $ value of goods and services produced)		(consumer purchases)		(business investment in plant & equipment)		(government outlays for goods and services)		(net exports)
1978 values:	$2.1 trillion =	$1.3 trillion +		$345 billion +		$434 billion −		$12 billion

The $434 billion of the gross national product that all levels of government were consuming in the fall of 1978 constituted 21 percent of the total purchases of goods and services, remember. Basically, all fiscal policy is saying is that when government's direct share of the GNP is that big, government budgets have an enormous impact on the status of the country's economy.*

Add to the direct expenditures by governments the many levers the federal government has on personal consumption (withholding tax rates and excise taxes) and on investment (corporate taxes, depletion allowances, amortization rules, subsidies, etc.), and you begin to sense the potent instruments the government wields, wisely or foolishly, to promote full employment, redistribute incomes, or foment inflation, among other things. In recognition of that fact, at the end of World War II Congress permanently committed the federal government in the Employment Act of 1946 to use its budgets and other instruments of national policy to promote maximum employment, production, and purchasing power.[6]

An episode in American economic history three years later dramatized in a convincing way the economic potential of federal fiscal policy. The United States suffered its first postwar recession in 1949. But in 1948 Congress had significantly reduced income tax rates. As the recession hit, business investments (*I* in the GNP equation) dropped by $10 billion, with a potentially greater

---

* Caveat: please observe that we do not have one budget for G, but rather budgets for all the eighty-one thousand independent units of government in this country. Note also that they do not all dance to the same fiscal policy tune. American federalism and a coordinated fiscal policy are not exactly bedmates! Third, please note the footnote on the first page of this chapter explaining the different ways of computing the government's share of the GNP.

diminution in the GNP itself because of the multiplier effect. Wages and salaries dipped $900 million. But the lower tax rates and the rise of unemployment compensation rather miraculously sustained consumption (C in the equation), which actually rose by $3.2 billion during the recession. The great swing factor was the shift in the federal government's cash budget from a $7.9 billion surplus in 1948 to a $2.1 billion deficit in 1949, a net change of $10 billion, which meant that the federal government was injecting that much more into the economy than it was taking out. This exactly counterbalanced the $10 billion slippage in business investment. With the federal budget providing most of the counter-cyclical punch, the GNP declined only $1 billion instead of more than $10 billion in the wake of the falling investment rate. Federal fiscal policy, whether planned or accidental, had saved the day.

The evidence of the attention given to fiscal policy concerns (i.e., conditions of the economy) in federal budget making over the past three decades is unmistakable. As long ago as January 1942, the U.S. Bureau of the Budget began to include in the annual budget document what later came to be called the *cash budget,* measuring total cash receipts from the public (e.g., general fund taxes and the large revenues coming into the social security trust fund) and total cash outlays to the public (general government expenditures plus social security payments, etc.).[7] The cash budget was a much better instrument for measuring the government's economic impact than the traditional *administrative budget* of the regular departments of government, now called the federal funds budget, which ignored the billions of dollars flowing annually into and out of the trust funds, dollars that could not be overlooked if one were interested in the economic consequences of federal finances (see Table 13.1).

Later on a new refinement was introduced, the *national income accounts budget,* which many economists regarded as the best measure yet of the economic implications of the national budget. It worked in part on an accrual rather than on a cash basis, and it ignored federal credit operations but did include trust fund activities.[8]

The Joint Economic Committee of the Congress published an important study in 1963, whose title suggests its relevance to our present concern, *The Federal Budget as an Economic Document.*[9] The committee recommended, among other things, that the "full employment budget theory," advocated in the 1962 *Economic Report of the President,* be adopted. That theory called for government expenditures at the level of tax revenues that would come in if we were at full employment; below full employment would mean operating at a deficit, because the suggested rule would peg expenditures to a hoped-for higher level of revenues not currently being realized. Thus, it would provide some pump priming to reach full employment, a kind of self-fulfilling prophecy first advocated by the Committee for Economic Development.[10] The full employment budget concept was adopted by the Nixon administration in January 1971 in presenting the 1972 budget.[11]

TABLE 13.1   BUDGET TOTALS BY FUND GROUP (in billions of dollars)

	1978 estimate	1979 estimate	1980 requests
Budget receipts:			
Federal funds	$270.5	$306.1	$332.8
Trust funds	168.0	189.5	212.2
Interfund transactions	−36.5	−39.6	−42.5
Total budget receipts	402.0	456.0	502.6
Budget outlays:			
Federal funds	332.0	361.3	381.8
Trust funds	155.3	171.7	192.2
Interfund transactions	−36.5	−39.6	−42.5
Total budget outlays	450.8	493.4	531.6
Budget surplus or deficit (−):			
Federal funds	−61.5	−55.2	−49.0
Trust funds	12.7	17.8	20.0
Total budget deficit (−):	−48.8	−37.4	−29.0
Memorandum:			
Outlays, off-budget federal entities[a]	−10.3	−12.0	−12.0
Total deficit including off-budget federal entities	−59.1	−49.4	−41.0

Source: *U.S. Budget in Brief, 1980* (Washington, D.C.: Government Printing Office, 1979), p. 71.

[a] Off-budget federal entities have no receipts. Virtually all off-budget outlays would be classified as federal funds outlays if they were restored to the budget.

Another reform had been recommended in October 1967 by the President's Commission on Budget Concepts, a proposal to merge the federal funds budget with the essence of the cash budget. This *unified budget* would thus bring together the usual surpluses in the trust funds and the normal deficits in the federal funds budget.

Two consequences of the unified budget were obvious. It would make deficit-financing presidents look better because their deficits would be swallowed up or minimized by trust fund surpluses; and it would be a truer measure of the economic impact of the federal budget, the real cash flows of all federal taxes and expenditures. The budgets since January 1968 (for fiscal 1969) have all followed the unified budget format.

Measuring the economic impact of the budget has become an increasingly important part of the congressional process since the establishment of the budget committees in the House and Senate under the Congressional Budget and Impoundment Control Act of 1974. As evidence, note their hearings: *The Federal Budget and Inflation* (1974), *Economic Impact of the Federal Budget* (1975), and the *Fiscal Year 1977 Budget and the Economy* (1976), among others.

A look at President Carter's proposed budget for fiscal 1979 reveals the kinds of economic calculations that now underlie budget making. Prepared in the late fall 1977, when unemployment averaged 6.5 percent and inflation was approaching 10 percent a year, the budget needed, if possible, to contribute to a real growth rate in GNP of at least 5 percent without generating further inflation, meeting essential needs for government services, moving toward a balanced budget by fiscal 1981, and providing tax relief in the face of the sharp rise in social security taxes and the explosive tax revolt of 1977–1978.

The Carter administration's response to those competing demands was a proposed budget of $500.2 billion in outlays, an 8 percent increase above fiscal 1978 (6 percentage points for inflation and only 2 percentage points for program expansion); $439.6 billion in revenues after a proposed tax cut of $25 billion, with a resulting deficit of $60.6 billion, a fraction smaller than the preceding fiscal year's.* The hope was that that fiscal combination would generate a 4.75 percent growth rate, which if sustained for three years would produce a balanced budget in 1981. For the short run, his fiscal 1979 proposals left most of the hoped-for expansion of the economy to the nonfederal sector.[12]

One thing that this history demonstrates is that the economics of John Maynard Keynes and his disciples have injected into federal budgeting a deep concern for fiscal policy. While our track record of adopting budgets with the right fiscal policy has been less than impressive — since good fiscal policy does not always make good politics — what a travesty it would be if we ignored the economic effects flowing from the government's share of the GNP.

The Budget as a Tool of Management[13]

If your cash has been cut back by your parents in the last three or four years, you know full well the power of the purse.

With the purse strings (and a little cooperation from Congress), a president can strangle programs he dislikes or use them as arteries to transfuse new life into enterprises he approves of. Harry Truman could hold down air force expansion to forty-eight air groups in 1949 and open up the Marshall Plan pipeline to Europe. Eisenhower could decree a "no new starts" reclamation slowdown but find enough funds for gunboat diplomacy in Guatemala and Lebanon. Lyndon Johnson could turn on a hundred spigots to pour billions of dollars into his Great Society programs: federal aid to education, the antipoverty campaign, and the like. And Richard Nixon, emboldened by losing only one state and the District of Columbia in 1972, could unveil a conservative switch in his January 1973 budget, cutting back the Johnson programs while channeling more funds to defense and business interests.

What is illustrated in all of these examples is one of the single most important

---

* Please note the differences between these *proposed* figures for fiscal 1979 (as of January 1978) and the one year later *estimates* for fiscal 1979, which appeared in *U.S. Budget in Brief* (as shown in Table 13.1).

managerial uses of budgeting: *program control.* Table 13.2 provides us with some feeling for Jimmy Carter's program priorities in his budget proposals for fiscal 1980.

Money may just be the most powerful scepter a manager holds, superior to personnel controls, to the power to issue orders, and to the right to demand reports. Money talks — and in our kind of culture everybody understands.

Assume, for example, that a tough police chief has considerable say over the internal allocation of departmental funds. (In technical terms, this would mean that the city commission had given him a lump sum budget for law enforcement, leaving the program allocations to the chief.) Convinced that the youth bureau has been picking fly specks out of the pepper, the chief reduces funds amounting to two positions. A youth bureau lieutenant wakes up very fast.

TABLE 13.2   BUDGET OUTLAYS BY FUNCTION, 1978–1980 ($ billions)

Outlays by function	1978 (act.)	1979 (est.)	1980 (est.)
National defense	105.2	114.5	125.8
International affairs	5.9	7.3	8.2
General science, space, and technology	4.7	5.2	5.5
Energy	5.9	8.6	7.9
Natural resources and environment	10.9	11.2	11.5
Agriculture	7.7	6.2	4.3
Commerce and housing credit	3.3	3.0	3.4
Transportation	15.4	17.4	17.6
Community and regional development	11.0	9.1	7.3
Education, training, employment, and social services	26.5	30.7	30.2
Health	43.7	49.1	53.4
Income security:			
Social security	92.2	102.3	115.2
Other	54.0	56.5	63.9
Total income security	146.2	158.9	179.1
Veterans benefits and services	19.0	20.3	20.5
Administration of justice	3.8	4.4	4.4
General government	3.8	4.4	4.4
General purpose fiscal assistance	9.6	8.9	8.8
Interest	44.0	52.8	57.0
Allowances	—	—	1.4
Undistributed offsetting receipts	−15.8	−18.7	−19.0
Total budget outlays	450.8	493.4	531.6

Source: *U.S. Budget in Brief, 1980* (Washington, D.C.: Government Printing Office, 1979), p. 73.

A governor gets fed up with higher education: the professors are always out campaigning for his opponents; the university administrators double-cross his budgets by raising tuition fees; and he can't get reliable accounting reports from the university's fiscal officers. The governor cuts them all back to size by persuading the legislature to expand vocational education through cutbacks in higher education.

The budget serves another great need of managers in addition to program control as a *measure of efficiency*. It turns, in part, on a gift from the accounting profession, *cost accounting*. Consider the following:

A VA hospital administrator sees more than inflation when an operations report shows a cost picture this year of $10,000 per bed in contrast to $8,000 last year.

A street superintendent is elated when his fiscal officer reports that a new piece of equipment will cut the cost of repairing a mile of street from $35,000 to $30,000 this year.

A Department of Transportation official scratches his head when his deputies offer some evidence that a $900 million national seat-belt program will probably reduce traffic fatalities by as much as a $2 billion effort to redesign federal highways.

Managers who are on top of their jobs in the public sector, like those in the private, are concerned about the kinds of outputs they are getting for the inputs being applied ($E = O/I$, remember). And cost accounting and performance budgets can provide useful data on the efficiency curves in their agencies. In short, the budget is the manager's tool par excellence.

The Budget as a Planning Instrument

Organizational goals for which there is no financing are pie in the sky. The only kind of planning worth doing demands attainable goals, programs to reach them that have been well thought through, and the resource base to sustain them. The critical element in that resource base is the financial capability to make them work.

As a case in point, the commissioner of reclamation in the Interior Department has his staff undertake a two-year study on the need for additional water (for irrigation, culinary, and recreation purposes) in the western states that will be occasioned by a population growth of 2 million in the next decade. There are potential dam sites available; the engineering studies look good; and the economic feasibility analysis indicates recovery of costs through the regular reclamation formulas.

However, after the proposal has cleared the Interior Department and reaches the Office of Management and Budget, the budget analysts begin to raise some additional questions:

"What interest rate have you used to discount the resources you will be taking out of the private sector" (an opportunity cost that public investment should be charged with)?

"The cost/benefit comparisons are terrible; in terms of measurable economic benefits, it would be cheaper for the government to give all the direct beneficiaries in the affected states $50 a head per year than to build the dams."

"There has been no consideration of alternatives such as tapping water surplus areas in Washington, Oregon, and Canada and importing the water into the lower western states — 'We want cost/benefit comparisons on *all* plausible alternatives.'"

Thus, the budget review generates a whole new array of concerns that are absolutely requisite to intelligent planning; and it raises not only these kinds of concerns but some others as well, because the budget process also provides the right moment to ask some of the global questions that demand answers if we are to know "where we are tending": What are the implications of the Defense Department's procurement budget for balanced deterrence vis-à-vis the Soviet Union and the People's Republic of China and prospects for prudent disarmament?[14] What kinds of funds should be made available to the Park and Forest Services to assure the nation of adequate recreational retreats by 1985? In the face of diminishing gasoline supplies, would funds be better spent on research to produce a smokeless use of coal, a vast energy source, or on subsidies for solar heat installations in private homes? To raise the level of analysis to address these kinds of concerns has been one of the chief hopes of the Joint Economic Committee in Congress in its annual hearings on national priorities and the budgetary process.[15]

When those kinds of planning dilemmas are resolved, then agency budgets can be prepared to deal with such questions as how much to ask from Congress, what the availability is in existing budgetary authority, what the cash needs per time period will be, and so on. To do these things well was the hope of the planning-programming-budgeting system (PPBS) of the 1960s.

Clearly, planning and budgeting must walk hand in hand, and that implies a great deal about the kinds of relationships and communication that should prevail between the fiscal people and the planners at every level of government.

Then there is a fourth purpose in budgeting — to guarantee responsiveness to the legislative will and honesty in the spending of taxpayers' money.

The Budget as an Instrument of Accountability

A good budget will answer the questions chief executives, legislators, and taxpayers want answered: "Who is going to spend how much money on what programs and when?" The budget document is a blueprint of proposed expenditures; the appropriation act (which we will look at in Chapter 14) makes some changes, reflecting the legislative will. Then a cluster of postappropriation controls is brought to bear to assure accountability: agency accounts, obligated funds, monthly cash balances, the preaudit, and the postaudit. The budget and these associated controls become the means for carrying out the compromises between the executive and the legislative branches and providing some assurance of payments by authorized officers for approved projects to appropriate suppliers and at the proper rates. That is how we try to achieve accountability.

It should be clear from the foregoing discussion that the budget itself must serve many masters. It must have the right fiscal impact on the economy, answer the needs of managers and planners, provide accountability, and still meet the test of political acceptability. That frustrating fact is one of the first painful lessons a new president has to absorb. In his 1976 campaign candidate Jimmy Carter boldly promised to reduce defense expenditures, unemployment, and the rate of inflation, and to balance the federal budget by 1981. But not long after taking office, President Jimmy Carter agreed with our NATO allies to a rise in real defense expenditures of 3 percent per annum (above the inflation rate); found that his $60 billion annual deficits were contributing to inflation without having much impact on unemployment; and was forced by the tax protest movement of 1977–1978 (e.g., Proposition 13) to propose further tax reductions in the election year of 1978 with the budget already unbalanced, contributing further to inflation, which zoomed back up over 12 percent during the first half of 1979.[16] The peanut vendor should have been a juggler!

Without the tool of a national budget, some of these dilemmas might be swept under the White House carpet; yet the problems wouldn't go away. No matter how painful the dilemmas are, all observers would agree that it's a good thing we ultimately achieved a national budget system. But it didn't come overnight.

DEVELOPMENT OF MODERN GOVERNMENTAL BUDGETING

From the Civil War through World War I, there was no executive budget in the national government. Agencies simply put together their asking figures, went to the corresponding legislative committees,[17] and wangled what appropriations they could get.[18]

Since (except in wartime) the size of the federal budget in that long period was as minuscule as the Democratic vote in Vermont, fiscal policy could not have suffered much. But certainly there was little chance for any kind of coordinated analysis of government programs beyond what the Congress as a whole could provide, since the president had no opportunity to compare one agency with another.

In 1910 a reorganization body, the Taft Commission on Economy and Efficiency, came on the scene and made recommendations that made eminently good sense. Before the Taft Commission's work was done in 1913, the commission would call for the creation of a true executive budget that would include functional categories over and beyond the traditional listing of personal services and things to be bought.[19] President Woodrow Wilson endorsed the proposal in his annual message to Congress in 1919, but he then vetoed the first bill Congress sent him in 1920, opposing the independence of the legislative auditor the law would create. The philosopher-king president then retired from office without ever enjoying the fiscal reins over his branch that only an executive budget could have provided.[20]

Congress reenacted the law, the historic Budget and Accounting Act of 1921, which President Warren Harding signed.[21] It created a new bureau in the Treasury Department, the U.S. Bureau of the Budget, to receive agency estimates and prepare the president's budget. In addition, the statute established the General Accounting Office (GAO) in the legislative branch as the independent auditor of executive accounts. The president would appoint its head, the controller general of the United States, for a fifteen-year term; he would be removable only by joint resolution of the Congress. From then until almost 1950, the GAO would drive presidents up the wall, exercising not only the postaudit review but the preaudit as well — passing in advance on the legality of proposed expenditures — a function presidents always claimed was an executive, not a legislative prerogative.

With the appointment in 1921 of an old Treasury hand, Charles G. Dawes, as first director of the Bureau of the Budget, a major new era in federal financial management was to begin, presidential budget making.[22] Some of the milestones in U.S. budgetary history are listed in Table 13.3.

To illuminate the peaks and valleys of some of the budgetary history outlined in Table 13.3, we strongly commend to your reading one of those insightful pieces of research that brighten our field every fifteen years or so, Allen Schick's "The Road to PPB: The Stages of Budget Reform."[23]

Schick sees three major purposes and dominating themes in budgeting since 1921 (the dates are only suggestive of the periods):

1. *Controlling expenditures:* use of object classification budgeting, 1921–1939.

2. *Managing agencies:* establishment of new roles for the Budget Bureau, activity budgets and performance budgeting, 1939–1961.

3. *Planning:* introduction of the planning-programming-budgeting system, 1961–1971; management by objectives; zero-base budgeting, and so on.

Now let's come to grips with these different budget systems.

A Quickie Contrast of Budget Styles

You're the city manager for the moment. Figure out what you would like to know about the operation of the city parks department both this year and next, a determination that will probably turn on whether you have a control, management, or planning orientation; then decide which of the budget formats shown in Table 13.4 comes the closest to providing you with that information.

The *object classification* focuses on things to be bought, not on activities to be financed or goals to be accomplished. As city manager you will note that the parks people plan a building program next year (02), but you have no idea if they have gone overboard for arts and crafts at the expense of baseball and tennis; the object budget does not tell you that.

The *performance budget* is laid out by activity, so the city manager can see at a glance where the priorities lie. But even more distinctive is the unit-costing feature of the performance budget. Here work load and work accomplishment data are gathered, to be divided into the costs of financing the respective activities. In the present case, the city manager sees tennis (07) receiving two-thirds more dollars than programs for little kids (the arts and crafts, 06) and wonders if that is the right balance. The manager is concerned about a 12 percent rise in the cost per acre of park care (05) when he knows that inflation explains only half of the increase.

If he has only the performance budget before him, the city manager no longer knows how many light bulbs and gallons of gasoline the parks department wants to buy, but he knows a lot more about outputs.

With *PPBS* the city manager learns some new things about the parks department: (a) the program budget now gives him the constituent elements (subprograms) that lie behind the activity structure of the performance budget; (b) he now knows not only the costs but benefits, the ultimate goal in mind, after all, to his park users, and on a comparative basis among programs; and (c) with the expanded time horizon, he can get a feel of where the parks department may be five years from now. The city manager will wonder long and hard about keeping the band concerts where benefits don't even equal costs (.48/1), in a recreational mix where tennis is delivering 2.8/1 and arts and crafts 2.5/1 benefits to cost.

In a *zero-base budgeting* format (the Jimmy Carter innovation in Georgia and Washington), the parks department budget would look quite different from the three preceding ones. Each recreational program would be broken down into decision packages, containing different levels of activity. The levels of activity would range from package 1, below the current year's operation (thus the term "zero base"), on up to an expansive (and expensive!) level if funds should be available. The tennis manager, for example, would then rank her decision packages (see Table 13.5), as would her superiors during the review process: the parks director, the city manager, and the city council. In the case at hand, the

TABLE 13.3 HIGHLIGHTS IN THE HISTORY OF U.S. BUDGETING

1789	Establishment of the U.S. Treasury Department
1796	House Ways and Means Committee and Senate Finance Committee established to handle both taxation and appropriations
1865–1867	Appropriations committees are split away from the taxing committees in both houses
1885	Appropriations committees lose their exclusive jurisdiction over funding to other standing committees
1894	Dockery Act creates the Treasury's controller and lays out accounting and auditing procedures
1904–1906	Congress instructs agency heads to apportion funds over full fiscal year in the Anti-Deficiency Acts (a basis for later impoundings)
1909	Appropriations cross the $1 billion mark for the first time
1912	Taft Commission on Economy and Efficiency recommends an executive budget to replace uncoordinated departmental requests
1920	Appropriations committees regain sole jurisdiction over funding
1921	Budget and Accounting Act creates the U.S. Bureau of the Budget and General Accounting Office; Budget Bureau initiates object classification budgeting
1933	Apportionment authority transferred to Budget Bureau
1937	President's Committee on Administrative Management recommends the creation of an Executive Office of the President and a new managerial focus in executive budgeting
1939	Reorganization Plan No. 1 moves the Budget Bureau out of the Treasury Department to become the central unit in the Executive Office of the President
1941	The Budget Bureau recommends impounding of appropriated funds to control unwanted projects (in contrast to former impoundments to effect savings)
1942	The budget document begins to report cash receipts from, and payments to, the public, aiding fiscal policy analysis
1946	Congress adopts the concept of a legislative budget ceiling in the Legislative Reorganization Act
1948	The Budget Bureau imposes agency ceilings for the first time
1948	The General Accounting Office, Budget Bureau, and Treasury begin the joint program for improving accounting in the federal government, leading to delegation of preaudit controls from the GAO to line agencies

tennis manager wants the city to serve an ace by adopting package 5. City manager, what kinds of information do you want from the budget?

We turn now from this quickie contrast of budgetary types portrayed in Tables 13.4 and 13.5 to an in-depth look at the object, performance, program, PPBS, incremental, zero-base, and capital budgets.

The Object Classification Budget — A Shopping List

An object classification budget, historically the most widely used and we surmise still the most popular among the cities, tells you relative amounts of the

1949	The three-year experiment in legislative budget ceilings comes to an end
1949	The first Hoover Commission calls for performance and program (activity) budgeting
1950	Budget and Accounting Procedures Act authorizes the performance budget and accounting reforms
1950	Congress makes a one-year attempt at an omnibus appropriation act and approves impounding of funds
1950	Performance budget adopted at the federal level with an activity budget in addition to the object classification data
1955–1960	Rand Corporation studies on program budgeting lay the groundwork for planning-programming-budgeting system (PPBS)
1956	Congress endorses program budgeting and accrual accounting
1961	Defense Department under Secretary Robert McNamara adopts the planning-programming-budgeting system
1963	National income accounts budget is added to the budget document to strengthen economic analysis
1965	President Johnson extends PPBS governmentwide
1968	Cash and administrative budgets merged into the unified budget by the Johnson administration
1970	A new Legislative Reorganization Act calls for cost/benefit studies by the GAO, five-year price tags on new legislation, and revised presidential estimates on revenues and expenditures (an updated budget) by June 1 each year
1970	Bureau of the Budget becomes the Office of Management and Budget under the Nixon administration
1971	OMB quietly deemphasizes PPBS
1971	Nixon adopts the full employment budget concept
1972–1973	Nixon impoundments generate hostile legislative and court reactions
1974	Congressional Budget and Impoundment Control Act is passed, re-creating the legislative budget and the Congressional Budget Office; provides a congressional veto over executive impoundments
1975	MBO replaces PPBS in federal budgeting
1977	Jimmy Carter introduces zero-base budgeting at the federal level

things the parks department intends to buy, that is, what the priorities are on their shopping list. It also provides incremental data on next year's increases. There is no information about the objectives of the parks department — the programs administered or the people served.

The object budget serves the control purpose only. In the sample budget we looked at in Table 13.4, the city manager might veto the buying of a new striping machine for the tennis courts and fancy lawn edgers and additional lawn mowers for the maintenance crews, a $4,000 increase in 04. But the object budget gives him no feel whatsoever for what the parks department is doing to satisfy the people's recreational needs.

TABLE 13.4 ALTERNATIVE PRESENTATIONS OF THE CITY PARKS DEPARTMENT BUDGET

Object Classification			Performance Budget[b]		
	CY[a]	BY[a]		CY	BY
01. Heat , power, and water	$25,700	$27,000	01. Administration	$71,000	$75,000
			Cost per park user	2.40	2.50
02. New construction	5,000	75,000	02. Band concerts	28,000	30,000
03. Office supplies	4,500	5,000	Cost per concert	1,180	1,250
04. Park equipment	76,000	80,000	03. Baseball program	72,000	75,000
05. Personnel	228,000	240,000	Cost per game	48	52
06. Rent	5,000	5,000	04. Horseshoe program	9,500	10,000
07. Transportation	17,000	18,000	Cost per game	.85	.90
	$361,200	$450,000	05. Park care	95,000	100,000
			Cost per acre	850	1,000
			06. Summer arts and crafts	57,000	60,000
			Cost per child hour	5.50	5.86
			07. Tennis program	28,700	100,000
			Cost per court hour	2.25	2.81
				$361,200	$450,000

[a] CY = current fiscal year (an estimate always).
BY = budget year, or next fiscal year.

[b] The performance ratios under each program are based on park user statistics (not shown here), divided into the current year estimates and next year's requests.

Congress has resisted the omission of the object data from the federal budget in its yearning to control the details of administration (which we will return to in Chapter 14). And so OMB's annual circular A-11 instructing agencies on how to prepare their estimates still lays out a section for objects of expenditures (personnel, travel, transportation of persons and things, rent, utilities, supplies, equipment, etc.). There is a final justification for such figures in the fact that Treasury Department spending accounts are still kept by object.

TABLE 13.4 (CONTINUED)

PLANNING-PROGRAMMING-BUDGETING SYSTEM (subprogram details omitted)

PPBS

	B/Cᶜ	BY	Five-Year projectionᵈ
01. See 05 (below)			

02. Band concerts
    Operations
    Promotion
	$ .48/1	$30,000	$38,288

03. Baseball program
    Little League promotion and
      supervision
    Lot construction
    Lot maintenance
	1.06/1	75,000	95,721

04. Horseshoe program
    Contest management
    Pit maintenance and improvement
	1.7/1	10,000	12,762

05. Park care and administration
    General administration
    Gardens
    Lawns
    New acquisitions
	.34/1	175,000	223,349

06. Summer arts and crafts
    Art
    Ceramics
    Games
	2.5/1	60,000	76,576

07. Tennis program
    Construction
    Instruction
    Maintenance
	2.8/1	100,000	127,628

		$450,000	$574,324

ᶜ The benefit/cost ratios. The benefits are based on $2 an hour to obtain entertainment in the private sector (movie prices as prototype), multiplied by park user statistics. These dollar benefits are divided by the program budget for next year to yield B/C.

ᵈ Compounded for inflation.

The Performance Budget — Measuring Efficiency

What the performance budget attempts to answer for the manager is the question "How are we doing?" in terms of work units, or units of accomplishment, which are not to be confused with ultimate benefits as measured in PPBS.

The performance budget is laid out in terms of activities, not of objects. (The reformers of the first Hoover Commission referred to the new format as a program budget. In time, the terminology became clouded, with "program budget" gradually assuming a much more ambitious meaning as PPBS began to surface.)[24]

TABLE 13.5 DECISION PACKAGES FOR THE 1980 TENNIS PROGRAM (Zero-Base Budgeting)

Decision packages	Estimated cost	What it would buy	Consequences of each package
(read up)			
Pkg. 5	$100,000	Build courts in remaining subdivisions; light all courts; handle 140,000 user hours; summer instruction and tournaments	All neighborhoods now have lighted double courts; summer instruction available; tournaments; some reduction of juvenile delinquency; boost to sporting goods businesses
Pkg. 4	$75,000	Could build another 2 courts and conduct a summer tournament	One subdivision now without courts
Pkg. 3	$50,000	Could build 2 new courts ($20,000) and light 2; 3,000 more hours' playing time available	Two subdivisions still without courts; no tournaments
Pkg. 2	$28,700	Could light 1 more court; 12,700 hours of user time available	Reduce waiting time slightly; no tournaments; still no expansion into 3 subdivisions
(current year)			
Pkg. 1	$25,000	Nets and upkeep on the present 7 city courts, providing 11,000 hours' play over 5 months	No tournaments; only 1 month of instruction; no new courts lighted; 3 subdivisions unserved

The computations of the number of work units accomplished, often divided into the man-hours employed or the cost of each activity, constituted the heart of performance budgeting.[25] Thus, the police department is reporting on detective hours per crimes solved, the state road commission on cost per mile of new highway construction, the Veterans Administration on costs per hospital bed, and so on. It was in these features that the management benefits loomed large: one could see whether the activity mix made sense and look for changes in output that needed further probing.

The push for the performance budget at the federal level came from the first Hoover Commission in 1949.[26] The commission's condemnation of sole reliance on object classification data was a quiet tribute to the Taft Commission, which had registered the same complaint almost forty years earlier. The Budget and Accounting Procedures Act of 1950 authorized the performance budget format,[27] and it was generally applied throughout the federal government in the budget for 1951.

Although the McNamara reforms involving PPBS would take the spotlight away from it in the 1960s, performance budgeting has never really died. The A-11 circulars of OMB continued to tell federal agencies at budget preparation time that:

Quantified performance indicators in the form of effectiveness measures, qualitative measures, service measures, work measurement, unit costs, and productivity indexes should be used to the maximum extent practicable to supplement narrative justifications.[28]

The data requested appear in special analyses of federal programs in the fields of education, manpower, health, income security, civil rights, and crime reduction. In these tables annexed to the budget document itself, figures on people served, morbidity and mortality statistics, social security beneficiaries, and so on are all shown alongside dollar outlays.[29] But it is interesting to note that the budget analyses do not in every case provide the cost per unit or services per unit figures with multiple year comparisons.

Looking back on the transition period, Allen Schick has observed:

PPB came on the scene before the aims of a previous reform — performance budgeting — had been realized. One of the chief purposes of performance budgeting was the use of work and cost measures in the preparation and execution of the budget. . . . With only a few exceptions, performance budgeting failed in reaching these objectives. Consequently, when PPB arrived, most agencies lacked adequate work and cost reporting systems.[30]

Thus, the coming of a planning emphasis in federal budgeting demanded a better fact base than then existed and the refinement of another feature of performance budgeting, the activity structure, into full-fledged *program budgeting*.

Program Budgeting — Activities with a Purpose

The transitional step from performance budgeting as a tool of management to PPBS as a tool of planning was the evolvement of program budgeting. Beginning with the helpful foundation of *activities* in the performance budget in the 1950s, systems analysts in the Rand Corporation and elsewhere began to sharpen the concept of "how well we are performing activities now" into a tool for determining "what are we trying to accomplish and how."[31] In making that leap, budgeting moved from an emphasis on managing the present to planning the future.

The decision tree discussed in Chapter 9 provided the analytical breakthrough for program budgeting. Applying it to our recreation budget, the program tree might look something like that shown in Figure 13.1. The program tree attempts to lay out for quick visualization and then for deeper analysis everything the city plans to do to fulfill one area of responsibility; for example, recreation. The limbs denote the major subprograms; the branches, the program elements. As soon as adequate cost data per element, persons served (ultimate beneficiaries), and benefit calculations become available, the budget analysts, the city manager, and the city councilmen will be prepared to make some intelligent decisions on the whole recreational mix and the trade-offs that

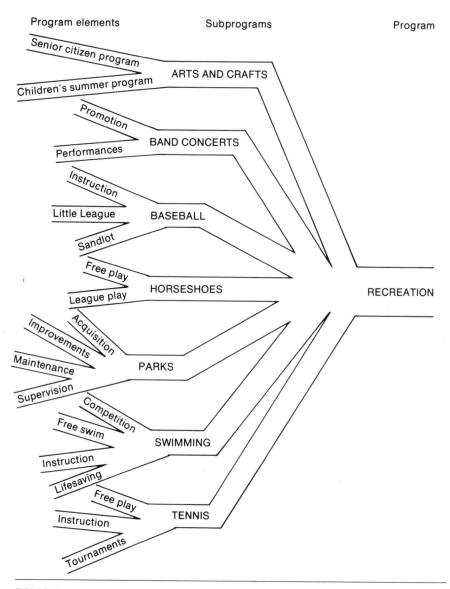

Program elements   Subprograms   Program

Senior citizen program

Children's summer program

ARTS AND CRAFTS

Promotion

Performances

BAND CONCERTS

Instruction

Little League

BASEBALL

Sandlot

Free play

League play

HORSESHOES

Improvements

Acquisition

Maintenance

Supervision

PARKS

Competition

Free swim

Instruction

Lifesaving

SWIMMING

Free play

Instruction

TENNIS

Tournaments

RECREATION

FIGURE 13.1 THE PROGRAM TREE IN BUDGETING

ought to be made: too much being spent on kids' programs with resulting indifference to adult needs; too much effort going into competitive activities (tournaments and the like) and too little allowed for free time for tennis, swimming, sandlot baseball, and so on.

When properly done, program budgets will be laid out with goals to be accomplished clearly specified; quantification supplied, where relevant and possible; agency end products defined; programs and elements spelled out; and agency or office lines ignored where necessary to present a holistic program view.[32]

In keeping with these prescriptions, a state public safety department might propose a program memorandum to the state budget director that will look like that shown in Table 13.6. Note the quantification of the goal, one hundred additional lives to be saved; the major subprogram components, changes in the law, in law enforcement, in highway design, and in driver and car performance; and the specificity of most of the program elements. These are the hallmarks of program budgeting. With the coming of systematic ways (primarily cost/benefit analysis) to compare the program elements and to project costs over a five-year future, we were ready to move from the threshold of program budgeting into full-fledged PPBS.

Planning-Programming-Budgeting System (PPBS)

Birth of the system   PPBS probably took budget management to the outer limits (the critics would say "beyond") of the *rational* allocation of resources

---

TABLE 13.6   A PROGRAM TO CUT TRAFFIC FATALITIES 10% NEXT YEAR (100 lives saved) (budget data omitted here)

A. Changes in the law
   1. Closing taverns at 11:30 P.M. instead of 1:00 A.M.
   2. Increasing the penalty for drunk driving convictions
   3. Lowering the alcohol content definition of legally drunk
B. Changes in law enforcement
   1. A 10% expansion in highway patrolmen
   2. Permission to use patrol cars for private use by highway patrolmen (so as to increase the frequency of their appearance in normal traffic)
C. Changes in highway design
   1. Installation of protector devices on 200 miles of state highways next fiscal year
   2. Elimination of the five most dangerous grade crossings (train tracks crossing roads on the same level) next fiscal year
   3. New lighting and regulatory devices at the 15 intersections with the highest accident rates in the state during the next fiscal year
D. Changes in driver and car performance
   1. Mandatory requirement for seat belt usage
   2. Promotions program for seat belt usage
   3. A 20% increase in surveillance of service stations performing annual vehicle safety inspections

---

among governmental activities. In a word, PPBS was systems analysis in budgeting: goals, constraints, measuring alternatives, deciding, and evaluating. PPBS called for:

1. *A planning phase:* the specification of goals to be reached over a five-year time frame, not tied to last year's approach.
2. *A programming phase:* the spelling out of alternatives and their analysis through cost/benefit studies.
3. *A budgeting phase:* development of the financial plan for the program mix selected.

PPBS asked government agencies to explain clearly the methods used in choosing objectives, the alternatives considered to attain those objectives and their relative benefits and costs, the effectiveness of present and proposed programs, and the constraints that limit the choices.[33]

Allen Schick summed up the high promise of PPBS:

> If PPB were successfully implemented, it would have an impact on the conflict-resolving capabilities of the budget process. PPB would escalate conflict by pushing for greater consistency in program objectives (recent budgets, for example, have spent money to promote tobacco growing and to discourage tobacco smoking); it would seek more explicit understandings on program purposes (all that the budget now requires is agreement on dollars and activities); it would advocate the termination of some low-yield programs (nowadays it is hard to excise anything from the budget); it would expand the range of alternatives the budget process considers (generally, the only alternative now considered is the one advocated by the agency). Probably its most significant effect would result from the unveiling of some of the costs and benefits of Federal programs, thereby arming historically weak budget claimants with greater capability to alter the outcomes. In sum, PPB would take some of the comfort out of the incrementalism that now dominates budgeting.[34]

PPBS was a budget system not wedded to last year's figures and thus incorporated what Jimmy Carter would later popularize — zero-base budgeting.[35] Instead of last year plus 5 percent, PPBS set out the options with great clarity and made choices in terms of hard facts rather than of precedent or intuition. PPBS did indeed mean to be rational and comprehensive.

The pioneering effort in program budgeting may well have occurred in Wisconsin in 1959, the same state that gave the Union the legislative reference bureau idea fifty years earlier. PPBS then came to the federal government with Robert McNamara and his systems analysts from the Rand Corporation and elsewhere — Roland McKean, Charles Hitch, Alain Enthoven, and others, in 1961. It was a fortuitous testing ground for PPBS, where costs could be ascertained and hard outputs such as weapons had measurable effects (benefits?) to a greater degree than in soft-goods agencies such as education and labor.[36] By the time Lyndon Johnson directed other federal agencies in 1965 to adopt PPBS, the new system was making some inroads at the state and local government level.[37]

Features of PPBS[38]   The major components of the planning-programming-budgeting system were: (a) goal analysis, (b) identification of alternative ways to accomplish the goal (the program tree), (c) five-year cost projections, (d) cost/benefit analysis of the alternative programs, and (e) the decision as to the final mix to be funded.[39] The first two elements have been discussed; we now need to look at cost/benefit analysis.[40]

Think through the dilemmas program planners have to live with: the Cruise missile, submarine-borne missiles, ICBMs, B-1 bombers, neutron bombs, and the like; family assistance plans versus manpower training and job placement; income supports or price supports for farmers, and so on.

Cost/benefit analysis is designed to help make those choices by requiring every program element to prove its worth against alternative ways of reaching a common goal. On the cost side, an effort is made to properly allocate the research and development, investment and operating costs, and opportunity costs through the discounting procedure — and to do so with projections over a five-year period.[41]

Opportunity costs and discounting may be the most foreign of these cost concepts. A word of explanation is in order. The old maxim, "One in the hand is worth two in the bush," is a kind of heuristic about life that we prefer the here and now to the less certain future.

Budgetary analysis is not immune to those preferences and is often faced in the evaluation of high-cost public investments with the question of whether or not future benefits are really worth going after today. The procedure involved is called *discounting.* a way of looking at future costs and benefits and reducing them to a common denominator for comparison — *the present.*

Economists sometimes take a different perspective in explaining discounting. If tax revenues are going to be invested in a public works project, the returns should equal what the same resources could have earned in the private sector. That is the opportunity cost to be charged against the public investment for foregoing private utilization.

Choosing the discount rate is still a subject of great controversy.[42] One school of thought suggests that the discount rate should be the net interest rate the government must pay to borrow money for its projects. Another argues for the private rate of interest the funds could earn in the private sector with comparable risk.

For the basic discounting procedure, a set of present value tables (found in standard finance and accounting textbooks) is needed which tell you for various years into the future and for different discounting rates the present value of a dollar that is due at the end of n years. Its companion table tells the present value of a dollar that is received annually for *n* years into the future, at different discounting rates.

The basic formula underlying the tables is the division of compound interest into a dollar (representing costs or revenues):

$$\frac{\text{Annual Revenues or Costs}}{(1 + r)^n} = \begin{array}{l}\text{today's discounted value}\\\text{of a sum } n \text{ years hence}\end{array}$$

Where r = the discount rate and n = number of years until that cost or revenue is realized (or happens).

Assume construction of a toll bridge, estimated at $20 million. In terms of discounted values, will it be a worthwhile venture from a cost/benefit point of view if annual operating costs will be $12 million for twenty-five years and annual revenues will be $14 million for the same period? With a 10 percent discounting rate, we would make the comparison as follows:

There will be net revenues each year of $14 million − $12 million = $2 million, lasting for 25 years, a net revenue stream of $50 million.

When discounted at 10 percent back to the present, the $2 million in net annual revenues turns out to be:

$9.077   (table value for 25 years at 10%)
× $2m
$18.154m benefits discounted to the present

The cost/benefit ratio thus looks unfavorable: $18.1 million in benefits and $20 million in invested capital, or a ratio of 0.91 to 1.

But at 5 percent the proposal would look attractive:

$14.09   (table value for 25 years at 5 percent)
× $2m
$28.188m benefits: $20 million in invested capital or a ratio of 1.4 to 1

Calculating benefits is, in many instances, a tougher proposition than allocating costs.[43] The benefit of an acre-foot of irrigation water provided by a Bureau of Reclamation dam can be calculated in a straightforward way, according to the going water rate. But what is the benefit of a life saved in a seat-belt program, of an additional tennis court, or of a new procedure for treating schizophrenia?

The cost/benefit comparison is obviously made easier when numerical values can be attributed to benefits (dollars, or "utils," for utilities); but as the examples suggest, the quantities may be hard to come by. We stretch quantification almost beyond reasonableness when, for example, we evaluate a life saved according to the future earnings the average person of that age will generate until retirement (as the Bible says, "Is not life more than meat and raiment?").

In the sample budget we began with, recreation benefits were computed almost in an opportunity cost sense: What does it take to buy an hour's entertainment in the private sector? While the possibilities boggle one's mind, we used a movie cost of $2 an hour as a way of attributing a monetary value to an hour of tennis or baseball in a free public facility.

The benefit/cost table that underlies that budget illustrates the quantification of benefits in a soft-goods agency (see Table 13.7). In a budget squeeze, the parks superintendent would look closely at the $30,000 going into band concerts, where the benefit/cost ratio is less than 0.5 to 1. (He can't do much with the item of park care, unless there are cost reductions he might make; the parks must be maintained as a support for all the other park-located services.)

An instance of *nonquantifiable* benefits was suggested by David Novick's analysis of rival weapons systems in a hard-goods department, Defense (see Table 13.8). It may on occasion not be too risky to ask a panel of experts to put *numerical* values on the kind of qualitative judgments suggested in Table 13.8. Where such a jury method is defensible, the imputed values (utils) lead directly to the arithmetic calculation of cost/benefit ratios.

The final step in PPBS was selecting and budgeting the program mix. Note that the cheapest or the best cost/benefit program may not always be the way to go, for the simple reason that by itself the program cannot accomplish the goal or may even flunk important constraints. For a far-out example, can you imagine a state highway safety bureau investing all its money in a seat-belt program (which looked very good on B/C) and ignoring street lighting, protective devices, and highway patrolmen? That suggests the necessity of a *program mix*. A useful thing about PPBS, when working well, was the clear indication it gave of the relative worth of each element going into the mix. But a recurring problem was how tough, and sometimes unreliable, benefit/cost analysis turned out to

TABLE 13.7 BENEFIT/COST ANALYSIS OF RECREATION PROGRAM ELEMENTS

	Benefits[a]	Costs	B/C
Band concerts 12 concerts, 600 average attendance = 7,200 user hours × $2[a]	$14,400	$30,000	.48/1
Baseball 39,750 player hours × $2	79,500	75,000	1.06/1
Horseshoes 8,500 user hours × $2	17,000	10,000	1.7/1
Park care 29,750 user hours × $2	59,500	175,000	.34/1
Summer arts and crafts 75,000 user hours × $2	150,000	60,000	2.5/1
Tennis 140,000 user hours × $2	280,000	100,000	2.8/1

[a] Benefits were computed on the basis of $2 per hour for a movie in the private sector.

TABLE 13.8   BENEFIT ANALYSIS WITHOUT QUANTIFICATION — WEAPONRY

	Invulnerable to:			Useful for:	
	Enemy ICBMs	Enemy ABMs	Air defense	Hitting known target	Show of force
Long endurance aircraft	yes	no	no	yes	yes
Minuteman ICBMs	yes	no	yes	fairly	yes
Polaris (submarine-fired)	yes	fairly	yes	fairly	yes

Source: Adapted from David Novick, in *Program Budgeting*, p. 116. © 1965, 1967 by the RAND Corporation. Adapted by permission of Harvard University Press.

be. It demands comprehensive records and analytical minds, and one or both may come in short supply.[44]

The criticisms   The bold, almost utopian reform of federal budgeting lasted just a decade at the national level, 1961–1971. What led to its demise, and what did it leave behind of any use?

The critics and historians of the experiment — Aaron Wildavsky, Frederick Mosher, Allen Schick, and others — have offered numerous explanations.[45]

The preparation of the program memorandums (PMs) and program and financial plans (PFPs) was plain damn tedious; in a word, backbreaking.*

PPBS might provide a basis for choosing between tennis courts and baseball diamonds or between two systems for supplying the Vietnam War, but it couldn't make any contribution to the really significant budgetary questions of how much money should be allocated for defense, how much for welfare, and how much for community development.[46]

The internal organization of the Budget Bureau denied the importance of the reform; the PPBS staff unit was not integrated with the program bureaus that called the shots on agency estimates.

The system was unbelievably complex, and this very complexity got in the way of hard-hitting policy analysis.[47]

Asking agencies even to think in terms of zero-year budgeting (i.e., to pretend they are starting from scratch) was a chimera at worst and at best contradictory to PPBS's other notion of five-year budgeting.

In many instances, benefit calculation was gamesmanship at its worst.

The analytical demands ran counter to a more dominant, built-in demand: "We gotta get the budget out!"

---

* Illustrating the part of Parkinson's Law that suggests that "people make work for each other without regard to final output."

PPBS impressed the White House less and less, which then assigned program evaluation under Nixon to the Domestic Council while leaving budgeting with OMB.

PPBS tried to pour new, heady wine into old bottles, and budget analysts found it bitter alongside the gentler draft of "last year plus 5 percent."

Thus full-blown PPBS at the federal level slipped away in the late spring of 1971, dying in T. S. Eliot fashion, not with a bang but a whimper, as OMB director George Shultz let go of it without benediction or epitaph.[48] Yet like Alice's vanished cat, the smile lingered on. The PFPs became PFSs (program and financing schedules); the PMs became PAPs (program and performance memorandums); and Congress statutorily endorsed five-year cost projections and instructed the GAO to monitor programs via cost/benefit analysis in 1970.[49] Two other PPB features would reappear in 1977 with the coming of zero-base budgeting: the search for program alternatives (in zero-based budgeting's decision packages) and three-year time projections.

PPBS's real legacy lay in its demonstration of the importance of systematic analysis in budgeting: What ends do we want? Do we really know the best means to attain them? Consider one horrible story as evidence of what happens when the systems approach is ignored. The North Carolina legislature had called for a 100 percent expansion in medical school enrollments but failed to provide adequately for building the extra facilities to handle this doubling of the student body. The governor then asked for a state coroner who was to be housed on the eighth floor of the new but unbuilt medical school facility, forgetting to request funds for the bottom seven floors. The legislature approved his request, then realized there was a floating eighth floor and proceeded to provide additional funds for the bottom seven. Call it a finesse if you want; it had the earmarks of a colossal goof.[50]

Incremental Budgeting[51]

The conventional wisdom is to allow agencies to build their budgets each year step-by-step, with no sudden leaps into the future that would offend vested interests and shock the legislative appropriations committees: go incrementally, the current year plus a percentage increase for inflation, and then haggle for funds to do a better job or take on new roles.[52]

The Utah budget system is illustrative. The governor announces a budgetary policy of x percent increase over the current year's appropriations for all agencies — the *standard budget.* Agencies may include in their estimates a request for a *work load increase* to finance unavoidable new responsibilities (more families on welfare, more students entering college, etc.). Third, they may try to justify an *expansion budget* to allow them to do new things. In the budget review stage, the governor and his aides take a fresh look at new revenue

---

Why Incremental Budgeting Survives

Aaron Wildavsky describes the staying power of incremental budgeting in this way:

> Traditional budgeting makes calculations easy precisely because it is not comprehensive. History provides a strong base on which to rest a case. The present is made part of the past, which may be known, instead of the future, which cannot be comprehended. Choices that might cause conflict are fragmented so that not all difficulties need be faced at one time. Because it is neutral in regard to policy, traditional budgeting is compatible with a variety of policies, all of which can be converted into line items. Traditional budgeting lasts, then, because it is simpler, easier, less stressful, and more flexible than modern alternatives like ZBB and PPB.

Aaron Wildavksy, *The Politics of the Budgetary Process*, 3rd ed., (Boston: Little, Brown, 1979), p. 221.

---

projections and legislative prospects, the total asking figures in all three budgets, the priorities as they strike the governor, and the intensity of the tax protest movement versus clientele demands for more state programs. In the normal case, the governor then proceeds to veto essentially all expansion budgets (except for such burning new issues as air pollution) and most of the requests for work load increases, thus leaving state agencies with "this year plus 5 percent" to cover civil service grade escalation and cost-of-living changes.

Widely used, and probably the most popular of all, incrementalism has the virtues of simplicity, predictability, and minimizing sharp conflicts over radically changed shares, which in any case rarely occur in this kind of budgeting.[53] Furthermore, there is little strain on analytic thought. Incrementalism implies: "We have already found the answer, and 5 percent more will make it that much better."

But all that is a worn-out tire: plans miss; programs lose their zip; new ideas come along; better solutions have been overlooked — yet most of that goes unrealized with incremental budgeting. The base (this year) is sacrosanct — we don't have to examine its premises, or really even its consequences — current year plus 5 percent equals wisdom, and why strain the cerebrum? So a Gresham's law of budgeting prevails in which precedent drives out analysis in allocating scarce tax dollars to public programs.

Zero-Base Budgeting (ZBB)

Like a Hegelian dialectic, the thesis of incrementalism found its antithesis in a new approach to financial management called zero-base budgeting. The reform was pioneered at Texas Instruments in 1969 following the prescriptions of Peter A. Pyhrr.[54]

The term "zero base" was intended as a direct challenge to incrementalism, implicitly suggesting that there is nothing sacrosanct about the current fiscal year as a base for next year's estimates. Thus, the array of decision packages in a zero-base presentation must begin with a level of operations *below* this year's. The purpose of that is to assure that decision makers will have the option of either cutting back the scale of a program or eliminating it — but with the consequences fully spelled out in the budget prospectus.

The fundamentals of ZBB are these:[55]

the identification of the appropriate units of government that administer discrete programs

the specification of individual programs that can be ranked by level of effort and funding (the critical *decision packages*)

the arrangement of the decision packages in a priority order (as in Table 13.5), with a spelling out of what can be accomplished at each level and what the major consequences will be if a given level is not funded

A unit manager recommends to her department head her priority listing of the decision packages to be included in the budget. The department head and his budget staff then undertake the critical analysis of competing decision packages coming up from the divisions below them. Cost/benefit analysis is implied but is not necessarily used with the rigor of that key step in PPBS. The senior staff of the department then puts together the department's asking budget, which is a bit like pushing a shopping cart through the supermarket: DP 5 (for decision package) for tennis, DP 3 for swimming, DP 3 for softball, DP 4 for crafts, and DP 0 (no funding this year) for horseshoes.

In like fashion, the city manager puts together the citywide budget, with a good data base to guide his inclusions and exclusions. He knows, for example, that dropping down one decision package (or level) in the fire department will mean one less fire station and a rise in the city's insurance class from 4 to 5 (with a resulting rise in insurance premiums). Including the top decision package in the park department's budget will provide a significant new playground in a Chicano neighborhood, providing recreation, reducing alienation, and possibly securing thirty-five hundred votes for the incumbent city councilor for that area.

Zero-base budgeting began to receive a lot of attention with the rise of Jimmy Carter's political star. As governor of Georgia, Carter introduced ZBB in January 1972 and became its strong advocate. On one occasion he pointed out how computerization of eleven thousand decision packages had revealed that seven different state agencies were providing services to deaf children.[56] He also utilized ZBB in fiscal 1975 in effecting a $57 million cutback in state programs. But it should be noted that instead of simply "dropping the line" on the priority rankings of the agencies' decision packages, as ZBB theory would imply, Carter asked the departments for new packages to guide his cuts. One budget officer then made a telling observation: "The priority ranking of our decision packages when we expect 140% funding simply is not the same as when we expect 115% funding."[57]

That begins to suggest some of the fun and games that can be played both with the decision packages themselves and with how they are ranked (e.g., listing an obviously critical program among lower-priority packages, forcing the hand of the budget makers to fund more projects).[58]

A 1975 survey of Georgia's ZBB system indicated some gains but a great deal of dissatisfaction. Only two out of thirteen department heads indicated that ZBB had led to a reallocation of resources within their units (and those two were unable to provide specifics). The other eleven reported no shifting of dollars, strongly suggesting that zero-base budgeting was having almost zero influence in Georgia.[59] On the other hand, there was more significant involvement of first-line supervisors in budget preparation under the new system and better information for budgetary decisions than under the former incremental approach.[60]

Jimmy Carter brought ZBB with him to Washington and in April 1977 instructed agencies to prepare their fiscal 1979 requests in a decision package format. Carter's fiscal 1980 budget document, presented to Congress in January 1979, suggested expanded use of, and continued satisfaction with, the new reform.[61]

ZBB weaknesses[62] In time, a number of shortcomings in ZBB began to emerge. First, more personnel hours were spent up and down the line in preparing and analyzing the decision packages. In incremental budgeting, executives focus primarily on the significant marginal changes from the previous year rather than rethinking all the facets and options in an agency's operations — the exception principle again.

Second, ZBB makes some sense when a government is offering services to its clientele and can do so at various service levels (e.g., the number of tennis courts, of OSHA inspections, of EPA monitoring stations). But a fair part of the federal budget is dominated by indirect programs, contractual obligations, and statutory formulas that prevent or impair analysis by level of activity (e.g., interest on the national debt, federal welfare payments under the supplementary security income program, federal grants to the states, etc.).

Third, ZBB ordinarily appeared in one-year dress rather than in a multiyear time frame, and no prudent budget maker wants to agree on planting little acorns now if he knows he can't water the mighty oaks a couple of years from now (crop subsidies, Medicare, and social security are glaring cases in point).[63]

To correct the myopia, the Congressional Budget Office has been providing Congress with five-year cost projections and has included such projections as a nonbinding part of the first congressional budget resolution during April and May. In similar fashion, in January 1978 President Carter directed the federal agencies to provide three-year projections of their fiscal requests, thus giving the federal budget a multiyear planning format reminiscent of the five-year planning horizons of PPB.[64]

One budget format we have not yet discussed is the epitome of long-range planning, the capital budget. Like the others we've reviewed, it poses some dilemmas.

Capital Budgeting

A much-debated concept in fiscal management is that of the capital budget: segregating costs and revenues of long-term public *investments* (dams, parks, toll roads, bridges, etc.) from the costs of *operating* the government.[65]

The arguments can be briefly stated. The advocates of capital budgeting contend that the segregated capital budget is a way of insuring that the future will not be starved at the table of present needs and that long-lived assets will be paid for, through borrowing, by many years of beneficiaries rather by than today's taxpayers alone.[66]

The countervailing arguments plead instead for a unified (or unitary) budget that gives legislators and others the true picture of budget balance, whether surplus or deficit. To pretend that the budget is balanced when a separate capital budget calls for $25 million in borrowing is misleading, these observers say. Furthermore, in PPBS theory, every program must be tested against its rivals, which demands proper allocation of investment costs and discounting as well as operating costs.[67]

A MODEL BUDGETING SYSTEM FOR THE FEDERAL GOVERNMENT

At the outset of this chapter, we reviewed the major purposes of budgeting: fiscal policy, management, planning, and accountability. Their interplay can be illustrated in the design of a model budget system for the federal government (see Figure 13.2).[68]

Fiscal policy concerns are provided for through: (a) the two long-range forecasts of the Council of Economic Advisers (one in March before agency ceilings are determined, one in November before the president makes final decisions on the size of the budget); and (b) the imposition of agency ceilings to carry out the president's decisions on the desired total size of the budget.[69]

Agency opportunities during the summer to elicit decision packages and budget requests from their subdivisions and to collect performance data all aid

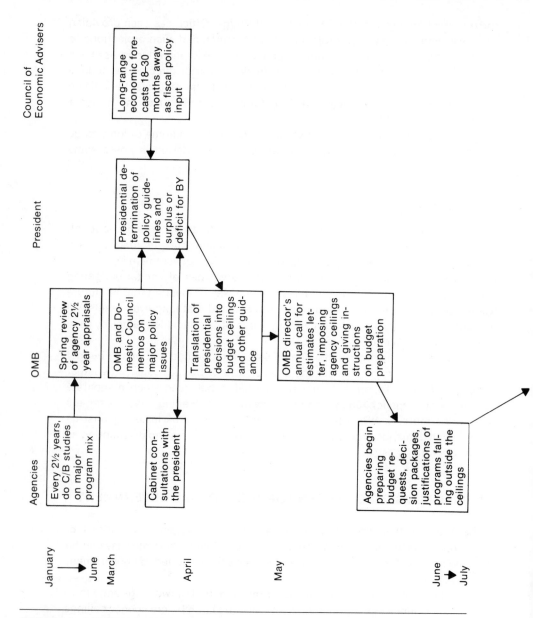

FIGURE 13.2 A FEDERAL BUDGETING MODEL

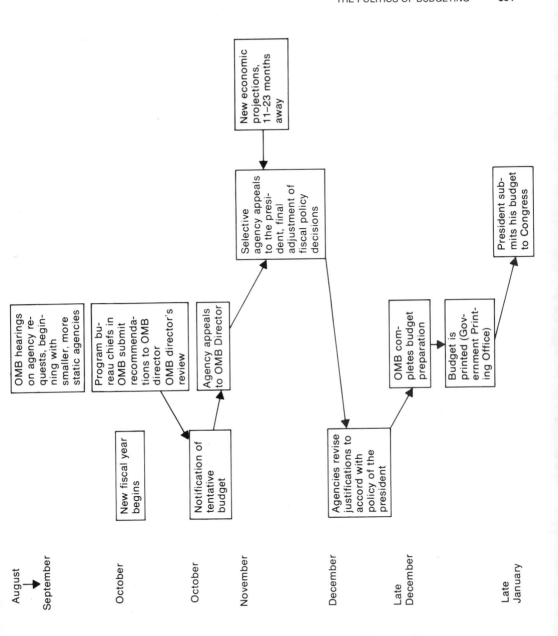

August
→ September

October

October

November

December

Late
December

Late
January

OMB hearings on agency requests, beginning with smaller, more static agencies

Program bureau chiefs in OMB submit recommendations to OMB director OMB director's review

New fiscal year begins

Notification of tentative budget

Agency appeals to OMB Director

New economic projections, 11–23 months away

Selective agency appeals to the president, final adjustment of fiscal policy decisions

Agencies revise justifications to accord with policy of the president

OMB completes budget preparation

Budget is printed (Government Printing Office)

President submits his budget to Congress

management. While it is sometimes painful, being brought to book to answer for their management practices before the early fall hearings of the OMB examiners is a healthy experience for agency heads.

The planning purpose will be served by what the model offers as a compromise to zero-base budgeting, the two-and-a-half year program review (with a five-year planning horizon). Analytical studies of the PPBS type will be undertaken at the beginning of the five-year cycle and again halfway through. Cost/benefit studies will be required; program trees will be analyzed; and goal accomplishment will be carefully reviewed.

Only part of the accountability side of budgeting is revealed in Figure 13.2 — the program reviews at the agency level, the OMB, and the White House. What is not shown are the checks to be discussed in Chapter 14: congressional scrutiny, agency and Treasury Department accounting systems, the preaudit and postaudit, and so on.

THE POLITICS OF BUDGETING[70]

It's hard to think of anything except power with as much political potential as money. It creates jobs, bails out the unemployed, props up failing industries (like Chrysler and the railroads), builds parks and highways, sustains farm prices, shifts voting blocs from one party to another (blacks working for the WPA who left Lincoln's party in 1934 for Roosevelt's), and conveys enormous regional benefits (defense contracts in California and Texas).

In its largest brushstrokes, the budget might properly be regarded first as a political portrait and second as a financial plan with management overtones. Look at the politics of budgeting in state and local governments:[71]

A governor deletes from his budget requests funding for abortions at public expense.

A New York governor holds up on state aid to New York City until it "cuts the fat from the city budget."

A governor is looked upon as a revolutionary when he proposes borrowing $65 million for a state building program.

A wealthy neighborhood is ignored in the building of tennis courts.

A poor neighborhood has no park or playground.

A teacher strike erupts when the legislature appropriates a 4 percent salary increase after prices have risen 11 percent.

Like a powerful whirlpool, budget making draws in pressure groups who hunger for government dollars (wheat farmers, aircraft manufacturers, road builders), agencies vying for scarce funds, and presidents who fully understand the political benefits that can flow if the budget is handled wisely.

You Pinch Them and You'll Hear from Them

In late October, 1978, word leaked out to mayors and interest groups that Carter's Office of Management and Budget was proposing cutbacks in public housing and countercyclical employment funds in the fiscal 1980 budget that would go to Congress in January.

> Almost immediately, the Ad Hoc Low Income Housing Coalition sent a letter to Carter, signed by representatives of seventy-five groups, demanding that the [housing] starts be increased to 400,000 [instead of 315,765]. "We realize that you are concerned with curbing inflation and with lowering the federal deficit," the letter said, "but we urge you to find other ways to do this than to cut back on an already inadequate program level of housing assistance for lower-income people."

Timothy B. Clark, "The $30 Billion Deficit — An Elusive Goal," *National Journal* (Nov. 25, 1978), 10:1905.

Consider two presidential examples. In Chapter 8 we noted that in the Postal Reform Act of 1962 President Kennedy won a pay increase for five hundred thousand postal workers to go into effect just before the fall elections. The increase in postage rates to pay for the higher salaries would not take effect until seven weeks after the election, too late for any kind of voter protest in November.

Ten years later Democratic Congressman William Anderson of Tennessee charged the Nixon administration with timing fiscal 1972 expenditures in just the right way to influence the 1972 elections. Anderson contended that the administration was spending at a 20 percent rate in the nonelection half of the fiscal year (late 1971) and would unleash 80 percent of the appropriations in the first half of 1972.[72] A year and a half later consumer advocate Ralph Nader reported that Anderson's charges had been borne out, at least in the Nixon agriculture program.

> Nader said that in late 1971, Agriculture Secretary Earl L. Butz launched a $600 million subsidy increase to reduce the 1972 feed grain crops "in order to prop up the incomes of corn belt voters in time for the 1972 elections.
>
> "The plan succeeded in garnering 67–70% of the farm vote for President Nixon. . . . Some frauds are so large that no one notices them," Nader said.[73]

One can see the force of politics at work in the legerdemain involved in the unified cash budget adopted during the Johnson administration and in the full employment budget of the Nixon administration. In different ways, both were designed to minimize or hide politically unpopular deficits in the regular federal funds budget. The unified budget did it by counterbalancing administrative budget deficits with trust fund surpluses, totaled together in this new format. For example, in fiscal 1969, the only year in fourteen to show a balance ($3.3 billion), there was a $5.5 billion deficit in the federal funds budget.

The full employment budget discussed earlier justifies spending up to the (imaginary) revenues present tax rates would generate if the nation were at full employment. On this basis, Nixon's 1974 budget indicated a balanced (full employment) budget for four out of the seven years, 1969–1975, when in fact the federal funds budget was unbalanced during all seven years, as was the unified budget during six out of the seven years.[74]

Some Rules of the Game

We need to take a fresh look at McCamy's vector analysis presented in Chapter 9 as we devise a strategy for proposing a budget that meets the test of political soundness (see Figure 13.3). The vectors illustrate both of McCamy's categories — personal and expersonal. Pressured by them all, the budget maker

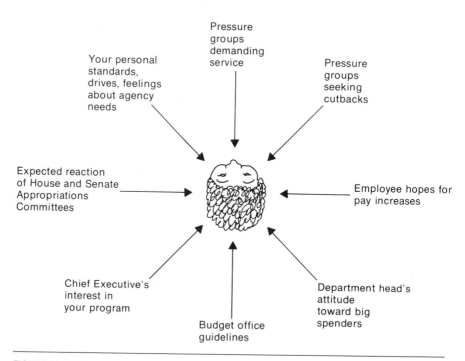

FIGURE 13.3 POLITICAL VECTORS IN BUDGETING

must present requests that will *satisfice** — keep things in balance, make some progress toward agency and group goals, and still enable him to live with himself.

Some suggestions for that survival course have been offered in Aaron Wildavsky's *The Politics of the Budgetary Process*.[75] For example, incrementalism may add to the possibilities of getting the budget over its various hurdles by minimizing change, following the old maxim that "The moving target catches the eye." Where the increases are not large, they may go unnoticed.

Strategists need to develop a feel for their agency's *fair share* of the department's budget and work within self-imposed limits. Asking for the sky marks you as a dreamer upstairs, and the departmental budget officer is happy to give you bad dreams with his cutting tool.[76]

Sensing the inevitability of the cut, some administrators pad, adding extra items here and there that amount to boondoggling, and an extra percentage here and there that is fat to protect the muscle. The practice is widespread but invites discovery and retaliation by reviewing officers and Congress.

Probably the best handling of OMB is through careful preparation and cogent reasoning. Then the examiners come to have confidence in your budget staff and documentation, taking some of the heat out of the September hearings. It is true that "If you can't lick 'em, join 'em" might be tried by attempting a transfer of one of your best people to OMB, but in fact this would be almost impossible to engineer.

Planning end runs around OMB and the president to your outside trumps in Congress is a strategy only the most sacred cows can risk, the Corps of Engineers being the archetype in the federal government. The ploy may gain you some extra money in the current budget, but you are also likely to get burned when you go before OMB the next year.

The calculations budgeteers need to make as they contemplate their climb to Capitol Hill will be treated in the next chapter on Congress. Suffice it to say here that such calculations are a necessary part of the politics of budgeting and help assure that the best-laid plans of managers have to touch earth at least annually.

SUMMARY

We call budgeting the allocation of scarce dollars to public programs. It is no longer the simple, straightforward deciding of how many people to hire, how much gasoline to buy, and how many offices to rent. Because governments now consume about one third of the gross national product, their budgets have come to have far-flung implications.

---

* Recall from Chapter 9 that "satisfice" is Herbert Simon's word for the decision maker's going along with suboptimal or less than perfect solutions.

We use budgets to influence the economy through fiscal policy, to manage enterprises by feeding and starving programs and measuring efficiency, to plan the future, and to provide a base for accountability and control.

As purposes have changed, so have budget systems, from the old object classification budgets to control the minutiae, through performance budgeting to strengthen management, and on to planning-programming-budgeting and zero-base systems for systematic analysis of goals and alternative programs. The demise of PPBS at the federal level was noted here, with the hope expressed that the good in it would live on, in particular cost/benefit analysis and multiyear planning horizons.

PPBS turned out to be exhausting to those who like the simpler approach called incrementalism — base year plus some percent. That kind of budgeting generates fewer waves, less conflict, and far less creative thinking about the soundness of how agencies are currently being run.

The arguments for and against segregated capital budgets were briefly examined, and a model budget system for the federal government was laid out in pursuit of the fiscal policy, management, and planning goals.

Finally, we returned to an old theme as we looked at the politics of budgeting, the element in the system that somehow forces all the discounting, all the benefit/cost analyses, and all the bookkeeping to come periodically back to the heart of things — how this budget will *affect people.*

KEY CONCEPTS

fiscal policy	object budget
gross national product equation	performance budget
cash budget	planning program budget (PPB)
administrative budget	zero-base budget (ZBB)
unified budget	cost benefit analysis
program control	discounting
cost accounting	non-quantifiable benefits
opportunity cost	program mix
Taft Commission on Economy and Efficiency	decision packages
	capital budget
General Accounting Office	fairshare

DISCUSSION QUESTIONS

1. Discuss the various purposes of budgeting. To what extent do you feel these purposes are fully accomplished?

2. What additional information (to the budget reader) does a performance budget provide that an object budget does not? What are the advantages and disadvantages of having this additional information?

3. Discuss PPBS. What were its requirements? What benefits, in terms of helping to meet one or more of the four major purposes, did it provide?

4. Discuss the criticisms of PPBS found on page 344. Looking back on the experience with PPBS, do you feel the disadvantages have outweighed the advantages?

5. The budget type that is closest to an incremental budget is an object budget. Compare an object budget with ZBB. In what ways is ZBB the antithesis?

PROJECT

Choose an agency budget from your local government. Interview the agency head or budget officer, with the goal of examining the extent to which the budget aids management and planning for that agency.

Notes

1. Figures are from the *Economic Reports of the President* and *Economic Indicators* (Washington, D.C.: Government Printing Office, annual and monthly, through January 1979).
2. The cartoon appeared in 1973 to pillory similar budget choices by Richard Nixon in his first post-Vietnam budget.
3. See the *U.S. Budget in Brief, 1980* (Washington, D.C.: Government Printing Office, 1979).
4. See Lewis H. Kimmel, *Federal Budget and Fiscal Policy* (Washington, D.C.: Brookings Institution, 1959), for the historical background.
5. Data from the *Economic Report of the President, 1979* (Washington, D.C.: Government Printing Office, 1979), p. 183.
6. P.L. 79-304; 60 Stat. 24.
7. See the *Budget of the United States for 1943* (Washington, D.C.: Government Printing Office, 1942), pp. 1115–1118. A clearer presentation of the cash budget appeared a year later in the *Budget for 1944* (Washington, D.C.: Government Printing Office, 1943), p. xxiv.
8. For comparisons of the various budgets, see U.S. Senate Committee on Government Operations, *Improving Congressional Control over the Budget* (93d Cong., 1st Sess.) (Washington, D.C.: Government Printing Office, 1973), p. 577.
9. Senate Report 88-396 (Washington, D.C.: Government Printing Office, 1963).
10. *Fiscal and Monetary Policy for High Employment* (New York: Committee for Economic Development, 1961), pp. 25–28.
11. *U.S. Budget in Brief, 1972* (Washington, D.C.: Government Printing Office, 1971), pp. 5–7.
12. Joseph Pechman, ed., *Setting National Priorities: The 1979 Budget* (Washington, D.C.: Brookings Institution, 1978), chs. 1 and 2; and *U.S. Budget in Brief, 1979* (Washington, D.C.: Government Printing Office, 1978), part II.
13. Turn back to an old classic from one of the great directors of the Bureau of the Budget, Harold Smith, "The Budget as an Instrument of Legislative Control and Executive Management," *Public Administration Review* (Summer 1944) 4:181–188.

14. These are the kinds of policy issues that underlay two of Jimmy Carter's most significant decisions on the defense budget — scrapping the B-1 bomber in July 1977 and vetoing funds for an additional nuclear aircraft carrier in August 1978.

15. The planning focus in budgeting is clearly discernible in the seminars conducted by the Senate Budget Committee during its first year of existence. The committee called in specialists during February 1975 to discuss the critical choices ahead in the country's physical resources, human resources, defense posture, energy needs, and credit markets. See the Senate Budget Committee, *Seminars: Macroeconomic Issues and the Fiscal Year 1976 Budget* (committee print) (Washington, D.C.: Government Printing Office, 1975).

16. The budgetary dilemmas of the Carter administration are clearly laid out by Joseph Pechman in *Setting National Priorities, 1979,* pp. 1–8.

17. The House and Senate appropriations committees, which had provided some degree of a consolidated legislative approach to agency funding, lost their exclusive jurisdiction over departmental budgets to the functional standing committees in 1885 and did not regain control until 1920.

18. See Vincent J. Brown, *The Control of the Public Budget* (Washington, D.C.: Public Affairs Press, 1949).

19. U.S. President's Commission on Economy and Efficiency, *The Need for a National Budget* (Washington, D.C.: Government Printing Office, 1912).

20. See Arthur MacMahon, "Woodrow Wilson: Political Leader and Administrator," in Earl Latham, ed., *The Philosophy and Policies of Woodrow Wilson* (Chicago: University of Chicago Press, 1958), pp. 120–122.

21. 42 Stat. 20.

22. Fortunately, Dawes found time to relate the opening chapters of the era in *The First Year of the Budget of the United States* (New York: Harper, 1923).

23. Part of a symposium on PPBS in the *Public Administration Review* (Dec. 1966) 26:243–258. We shall rather closely follow the major outline of Schick's article in the portrayal of budgeting systems that follows.

24. The latter concept emerged in works like David Novick, ed., *Program Budgeting* (Cambridge, Mass.: Harvard University Press, 1965).

25. A clear how-to-do-it manual on performance budgeting was George Terhune's *An Administrative Case Study of Performance Budgeting in the City of Los Angeles, California* (Chicago: Municipal Finance Officers Association, 1954); see also the companion study, *Performance Budgeting and Unit Cost Accounting for Governmental Units* (Chicago: Municipal Finance Officers Association, 1954).

26. U.S. Commission on Organization of the Executive Branch of the Government, *Budgeting and Accounting* (Washington, D.C.: Government Printing Office, 1949), pp. 8–12.

27. 64 Stat. 832.

28. U.S. Office of Management and Budget, Circular A-11 (June 12, 1972) (Washington, D.C.: Government Printing Office, 1972), p. 25.

29. See, for example, U.S. Office of Management and Budget, *Special Analyses of the Budget, 1979* (Washington, D.C.: Government Printing Office, 1978), part 3.

30. Allen Schick, "A Death in the Bureaucracy: The Demise of Federal PPB," *Public Administration Review* (Mar.–Apr. 1973) 33:153.

31. One of the Rand pioneers, David Novick, puts the real beginning of program budgeting back to 1942 and the Controlled Materials Plan of the War Production Board. See David Novick, *Origin and History of Program Budgeting* (Santa Monica, Calif.: Rand Corporation, 1966).

32. See G. M. Taylor, "Designing the Program Structure," in Harley Hinrichs and G. M.

Taylor, *Program Budgeting and Benefit/Cost Analysis* (Pacific Palisades, Calif.: Good-year, 1969), pp. 32–47, especially pp. 40–47.

33. See, for example, the Office of Management and Budget's A-11 Circular (June 12, 1972), p. 26.

34. Schick, "A Death in the Bureaucracy," p. 149.

35. Just as Carter was launching his summer drive for the presidency, the House Budget Committee, with commendable prescience, decided to take a look at zero-base budgeting. See their *Hearings on Zero-Base Budget Legislation* (94th Cong., 2d Sess.) (Washington, D.C.: Government Printing Office, 1976).

36. For the application of systems analysis to defense budgeting, see Charles J. Hitch and Roland N. McKean, *The Economics of Defense in the Nuclear Age* (Cambridge, Mass.: Harvard University Press, 1960); and the later study of Alain Enthoven and K. W. Smith, *How Much Is Enough?* (New York: Harper & Row, 1971).

37. U.S. Joint Economic Committee, *Innovations in Planning, Programming and Budgeting in State and Local Governments* (91st Cong., 1st Sess.) (Washington, D.C.: Government Printing Office, 1969).

38. See Jack Carlson's in-depth treatment in "The Current Status of the Planning-Programming-Budgeting System," vol. 2 of the U.S. Joint Economic Committee, *The Analysis and Evaluation of Public Expenditures: The PPB System* (91st Cong., 1st Sess.) (Washington, D.C.: Government Printing Office, 1969), pp. 613–798.

39. Observers differ, of course, on the distinguishing features of PPBS. Merewitz and Sosnick listed these five: program accounting, multiyear costing, detailed description of activities, zero-base budgeting, and quantitative evaluation of alternatives or cost/benefit analysis. *The Budget's New Clothes* (Chicago: Markham, 1971), p. 273.

40. For an introductory article, see Harley Hinrichs, "Government Decision-Making and the Theory of Benefit-Cost Analysis: A Primer," in Hinrichs and Taylor, *Program Budgeting*, pp. 9–20. For a detailed treatise, see Otto Eckstein, "A Survey of the Theory of Public Expenditure Criteria," in National Bureau of Economic Research, *Public Finances: Needs, Sources and Utilization* (Princeton, N.J.: Princeton University Press, 1961), pp. 439–494.

41. As a start, see State-Local Finances Project (Selma Mushkin, director), "The Role and Nature of Cost Analysis in a PPB System," Note 6 in *Planning, Programming, Budgeting for City, State and County Objectives* (Washington, D.C.: George Washington University, 1967).

42. See William J. Baumol, "On the Appropriate Discount Rate for Evaluation of Public Projects," in Hinrichs and Taylor, *Program Budgeting*, pp. 202–212.

43. See Gene Fisher, "The Role of Cost-Utility Analysis in Program Budgeting," in Novick, *Program Budgeting*, ch. 3.

44. For a statement of the doubts, see Merewitz and Sosnick, *The Budget's New Clothes*, ch. 11.

45. Representative of the critical literature are the following: "Planning-Programming-Budgeting System Reexamined — A Symposium," *Public Administration Review* (Mar.–Apr. 1969) 29:111–202; Merewitz and Sosnick, *The Budget's New Clothes;* and Aaron Wildavsky, *The Politics of the Budgetary Process* (Boston: Little, Brown, 1964), especially ch. 4. The Schick appraisal will be found in his "A Death in the Bureaucracy."

46. The issue was thoughtfully analyzed by Dr. Alice R. Rivlin, later head of the Congressional Budget Office, in "What Does the Most Good?" in her *Systematic Thinking for Social Action* (Washington, D.C.: Brookings Institution, 1971), pp. 46–62.

47. One gets a feeling of the complexity in a chart portraying the budgetary process under PPBS in the Defense Department. See Daniel Seligman, "McNamara's Management Revolution," *Fortune* (July 1965) 72, 118–119.

48. What George Shultz would not do, Allen Schick did in his 1973 *Public Administration Review* obituary (previously cited), "A Death in the Bureaucracy: The Demise of Federal PPB."

49. Legislative Reorganization Act of 1970, P.L. 91-510, 84 Stat. 1140, Title II, at p. 1167ff.

50. As related by Kenneth Howard in Howard and Gloria Grizzle, eds., *What Happened to State Budgeting?* (Lexington, Ky.: Council of State Governments, 1972), p. 46.

51. See O. A. Davis, M. A. Dempster, and Aaron Wildavsky, "A Theory of the Budgetary Process," *American Political Science Review,* (Sept. 1966) 60:529–547; and Aaron Wildavsky, "Toward a Radical Incrementalism," in Cornelius P. Cotter et al., *Twelve Studies of the Organization of Congress* (Washington, D.C.: American Enterprise Institute, 1966).

52. See John Wanat, "Bases of Budgetary Incrementalism," *American Political Science Review* (Sept. 1974) 68:1221–1228.

53. Peter Natchez and Irvin Bupp have warned of the descriptive inaccuracies in the incremental theory of budgeting. What it overlooks is the intense interbureau rivalry and gamesmanship that fundamentally affect the changing shares of successful and unsuccessful program managers. "Policy and Priority in the Budgetary Process," *American Political Science Review* (Sept. 1973) 67:951–963.

54. Peter A. Pyhrr, "Zero-Base Budgeting," *Harvard Business Review* (Nov.–Dec. 1970) 48:111–121; "The Zero-Base Approach to Government Budgeting," *Public Administration Review* (Jan.–Feb. 1977) 37:1–8; and Pyhrr's monograph on the subject, *Zero-Base Budgeting: A Practical Management Tool for Evaluating Expenses* (New York: Wiley, 1973).

55. A clear-cut presentation of zero-base budgeting can be found in Graeme M. Taylor, "New Management Approach to Federal Budgeting," *Civil Service Journal* (July–Sept. 1977) 18:13–19.

56. G. S. Minmier and R. H. Hermanson, "A Look at Zero-Base Budgeting — The Georgia Experience," *Atlanta Economic Review* (July–Aug. 1976), p. 6.

57. Minmier and Hermanson, "A Look at Zero-Base Budgeting," p. 9.

58. Pyhrr, "The Zero-Base Approach," p. 8.

59. Minmier and Hermanson, "A Look at Zero-Base Budgeting," p. 7.

60. For a comparative view in other states, see U.S. Senate Committee on Government Operations, *Compendium of Materials on Zero-Base Budgeting in the States* (S. Doc. 95-52) (Washington, D.C.: Government Printing Office, 1977).

61. Office of Management and Budget Bulletin 77-9, April 19, 1977. See also G. M. Taylor, "New Management Approach"; Joseph A. Pechman, ed., *Setting National Priorities: The 1978 Budget* (Washington, D.C.: Brookings Institution, 1977), pp. 379–385; and *The Budget of the United States Government, Fiscal Year 1980* (Washington, D.C.: Government Printing Office, 1979), pp. 27–28.

62. Pechman, *Setting National Priorities, 1978,* pp. 382–385; see also "Z BB Revisited," a forum issue of *The Bureaucrat* (Spring 1978) vol. 7, no. 1.

63. For some earlier insights on the multiyear projection matter, see Allen Schick, "The Road to PPB," p. 254.

64. See Office of Management and Budget Bulletin 78-7 of January 16, 1978, and Robert W. Hartman, "Multiyear Budget Planning," in Pechman, ed., *Setting National Priorities: The 1979 Budget,* App. B.

65. One of the early classical statements of the problem was Richard Musgrave, "The Nature of Budgetary Balance and the Case for the Capital Budget," *American Economic Review* (June 1939) 29:260–271.

66. The first Hoover Commission, for example, endorsed capital budgeting for the federal government. *Budgeting and Accounting.*

67. For an analysis of capital budgeting at the federal level, see the *Special Analyses* volume of the fiscal 1979 budget, section D (Washington, D.C.: Government Printing Office, 1978).

68. The present system is described in *U.S. Budget in Brief, 1980* (Washington, D.C.: Government Printing Office, 1979), pp. 65–68.

69. Ceilings imposed on the agencies at budget preparation time date, in the U.S., from 1948. Though dropped later, they have always seemed to this author to be a vitally important budgetary tool, locking the budget's doors before the horses escaped with runaway requests. One of the earlier descriptions of the ceiling process is still revealing, the testimony of Truman's budget director, Frank Pace, before the U.S. Joint Economic Committee, *Hearings on the 1950 Economic Report* (81st Cong., 2d Sess.) (Washington, D.C.: Government Printing Office, 1950), pp. 97–99.

70. See James W. Davis, ed., *Politics, Programs and Budgets* (Englewood Cliffs, N.J.: Prentice-Hall, 1969); and Aaron Wildavsky, *The Politics of the Budgetary Process,* 3d ed. (Boston: Little, Brown, 1979).

71. See L. L. Ecker-Racz, *The Politics and Economics of State-Local Finance* (Englewood Cliffs, N.J.: Prentice-Hall, 1970).

72. *Congressional Record* (January 19, 1972) 118:H99–101.

73. *Salt Lake City Deseret News* (July 17, 1973), p. 12A.

74. See U.S. Office of Management and Budget, *Budget Highlights, 1974* (Washington, D.C.: Government Printing Office, 1973), p. 13.

75. See Aaron Wildavsky, *The Politics of the Budgetary Process,* 3d ed. (Boston: Little, Brown, 1979), ch. 3; and Robert N. Anthony and Regina Herzlinger, *Management Control in Nonprofit Organizations* (Homewood, Ill.: Richard Irwin, 1975), pp. 248–258.

76. A gentle rebuke the author received from his dean is too much to the point to omit. The memo read: "Enclosed find a copy of the budget which I sent forward for your Institute. It reflects pay increases in accordance with our earlier discussions. It does not, sad to say, respond to your request for a massive increase in support. While I am aware that you had legitimate expansionist aims, to the extent that the budget controls matter you will have to package your activities in light of the constraints. In this respect, of course, you are in no different a position from any other individual managing a budget for the coming year."

Chapter 14
Appropriating, Spending, and Controlling

THE BUDGET AND THE LEGISLATURE

How to Put a Smile on a Bureaucrat

The U.S. Constitution says that "Congress shall have power to lay and collect taxes . . . to pay the debts and provide for the common defense and general welfare of the United States . . ." (article I, section 8). Thus, it is with that body, state legislatures, and city councils that spenders in executive branches at all levels of government must come to terms.

Coming to terms with these deeply political bodies is one of the most dramatic interfaces in government. The president is still committed to foreign aid, but a powerful group in the Senate Foreign Relations Committee no longer is — collision. The surgeon general marks tobacco as a carcinogen, but southerners dominate the committee chairmanships in Congress and insist on continuing the subsidies for tobacco growers — collision. A Republican president prefers business stimulants to public works as the way to reduce unemployment and a Democratic Congress disagrees — collision. The president, determined to curtail a host of social welfare programs, impounds appropriated funds, and the House and Senate erupt in anger — collision.

Some bureaucrats will see that battering and conclude that the legislature is an impassable coral reef, with hundreds of sharp edges to tear their budgets apart. Others will understand that for very fundamental reasons about democracy, budgets must be adapted to the political contours of that reef if openings are to be found into the calmer waters of congressional support.

As we said in Chapter 8, the judgments of experts in the executive branch are subjected to political appraisals in Congress as one of the best ways of keeping bureaucracy humble, responsible, approachable, and responsive. That is what a democratic system is all about. The experts are on tap, not on top; the people's representatives are in the saddle; and politicians, counting votes and effecting compromises, make the whole arrangement work.[1] From the origins of lawmaking power in the British Parliament on, a better way has never been found to make bureaucrats smile than to require them to ask politicians for money.[2]

The Political Milieu of Appropriations

It is important to understand the political forces at work when a legislature faces up to its fiscal chores. An important one in the behavioral world of these *elected* officials is a concern for *constituent interests* back home. There are roads to be built, jobs to be created, crops to be supported, school districts that need help, a National Guard armory awaiting construction, a national park to be expanded, and a post office begging for my name on the bronze plaque. In part, one's reelection next year is contingent on his track record in financing these home state needs.[3]

One of the surest things we know about the appropriation process is that budgets will be tested against this home base criterion. Making proper allowance for those needs — and for their advocates who sit on the appropriations subcommittee — is a practical place to begin.

That is precisely what novitiate Jimmy Carter failed to do during his first month in the presidency when he announced his opposition in February 1977 to eighteen water projects Congress had endorsed.[4] With home district needs uppermost in their minds, congressmen quickly restored to the Public Works Appropriation Act (for fiscal 1978) nine of the projects on Carter's "hit list." Then, adding insult to injury, in 1978 the House and Senate provided funding for seven of the remaining projects on the original list Carter thought he had permanently killed the year before.

Sheer sloppiness characterized the actions of the House Public Works Committee in passing the authorization measure for fiscal 1979:

In some cases they violated their own committee rule requiring localities to share in project costs.

They declared "benefit/cost ratios to be favorable for some projects *even if costs exceeded benefits* or if no benefit/cost study had been done [emphasis added]."

They didn't even show a dollar figure for eight of the approved projects.

They approved thirty-seven out of fifty-one projects in violation of the rule requiring a Corps of Engineers review of proposed projects prior to congressional approval.[5]

It would seem that when water projects are coming down the congressional pipeline, not even a veto can turn off the spigot.

Beyond the constituent ties are other kinds of preferences legislators exhibit:

The joint appropriations committee in the state legislature is down on big-city schools that bring well-known "radicals" on campus.

The chairman of appropriations places retarded children programs high on his list.

The chairman of the Military Appropriations Subcommittee loved planes and boats as a kid and loves them even more now.

The majority leader knows that deficit financing is a tool of the devil.

The *philosophical set* is a part of the coral reef that needs to be understood.

Realizing that the requests of all claimant agencies are not mutually compatible and cannot all be financed is a third point to understand about the appropriation process. Balancing, compromising, and rejecting competing claims will certainly take place. And you can repose some confidence in the collective judgment of a committee when a project you hope to have funded seems about to be caught in a pincer movement of rival parochial interests.[6]

Then there is a special legislative syndrome that flows in part from the checks-and-balances concept in American government — "Our job is to oversee the executive." It leads to a focus in appropriation hearings that is called *preauditing* the department, or controlling, through the appropriations process, the most minute aspects of agency administration.[7] Similarly, the same concept generates the additional role perceptions of budget cutter, economizer, and protector of the public purse.[8]

In the pluralistic world of Congress, fortunately, there are some countervailing drives to that of preauditing the executive. Many members in both chambers are far more concerned with macrojudgments than with microstrings. Conservatives of this stamp will be trying to strengthen the private sector, cut social welfare programs, balance the budget, and bring about tax reform to encourage business investment and dividend distribution. Liberals will be trying to open the financial pipelines to reduce unemployment, rebuild the cities, and assist the elderly through medical and other crises.

What all that means in practical terms is that for every ten budget cutters your agency will face in Congress there should be four or five who are staunch champions of your bureau. The fundamental reason is that you are doing important things for their constituents (and that equals voters, and voters talk).

Another factor in congressional handling of the budget is *small-group interaction*, influencing norms and role behavior in the appropriations committees,[9] putting together regional blocs without regard to party lines, and in other ways generating reaction patterns when agencies come knocking for money and a president wants to increase the debt limit.

Lobbies represent still another vector in the congressional scene. Some work for your budget — if you are in the Department of Agriculture, the Farm Bureau, the food processors, or the spokesman for one of the various commodity associations; and if you are in a foreign aid agency, an export industry or an agent of recipient countries (e.g., the "Korean connection"). Some lobbies work against you: Medicare (in its formative days) brings out the American Medical Association (AMA), Reclamation the environmentalists, and the Defense Department the peace groups. Realpolitik would suggest lining up some effective lobbies on your side.

As a final influence we should note the force of powerful *institutional factors* in Congress: the Senate and House budget committees, the two appropriations committees,[10] the chairman of each one, and the two majority leaders. All are significant power brokers in the legislative process.

At the state level, there are other kinds of institutional influences that vitally affect the appropriation process. A number of the states have only part-time legislatures, and many of those experience high-level turnover after every election. Add to that the widespread problem of poor committee staffing, and one can quickly understand why agency heads hold their breaths as their budgets begin to run the gauntlet of the lay legislature.

$550 Billion = Excedrin Headache

Empathy is probably the first step to understanding, and we ought to emphathize with the monstrous congressional headache the budget and related matters generate.

Let's face it: the budget annually produces an enormous headache for Congress. It is presented to Congress in late January. In the late 1970s, it required congressional judgments on over $550 billion worth of federal projects. Only about 25 percent of the annual total can even be controlled by Congress (civilian agencies and national defense). And they have eight months to get the various appropriation acts through both houses of Congress before the new fiscal year begins on October 1, which represents more than a pain in the pocketbook.

In state government, one of the comparable problems is called *earmarking*, committing certain revenues to specified programs without any annual legislative judgment. Two familiar examples dramatize the power of lobbies in the appropriation process: the highway lobby (the trucking industry, warehousers, and so on) manages to get through constitutional amendments or statutes that earmark all gasoline taxes to road building; the outdoor sportsmen win an automatic plowback of fish and game license revenues into programs for their play.

At the federal level, earmarking is only one of a number of reasons why 75 percent of the budget is relatively uncontrollable. In Table 14.1, we examine the proposals for fiscal 1979 as a case in point. The problem is accentuated, of course, in the unified budget because of the inclusion of the earmarked social security program along with the federal funds for the regular government agencies. (The social security item by itself represents 30 percent of the uncontrollable funds.)

What Table 14.1 reveals is a variety of forms of backdoor, or mandatory, spending.[11] Some of the items represent *permanent appropriations,* such as interest on the public debt and social security funds. Others consist of *borrowing authority* whereby programs are financed by loans either from the public or from the Treasury Department instead of by appropriations (guaranteeing student loans, rural electrification, etc.). A third type of backdoor spending is occasioned by *contract authority* granted in past years with bills now coming due that Congress must provide for. Such authority makes it possible for federal agencies to undertake projects that have long lead times, such as the Water Pollution Control Act of 1972. But as Allen Schick says: "Contract authority exacts a high price in its fragmentation of the appropriations process, in the difficulty of maintaining a lid on overall spending, and in the uncontrollability of current outlays."[12]

Beyond the sheer size of the task, the eight-month deadline, and the uncontrollability factor, there is the additional headache posed by the intricacies of many of the federal programs seeking funding. Many questions must be asked: What will we have to pay enlisted men in an all-volunteer army in order to recruit enough of them? Are there ancillary benefits to justify irrigation projects that flunk a straight cost/benefit test? How will foreign aid expenditures affect our international balance of payments and the value of the dollar abroad? What will the impact of a bold new public investment program (such as mass transit for America's ten most congested cities) be on the capital goods market, interest rates, economic expansion, and inflation? These are enormously tough policy problems, and their very complexity adds greatly to the burdens involved in the annual congressional appropriations cycle.

New Tools to Cope with the Headache

From 1798 until 1865, tax and spending measures were considered by the same House and Senate standing committees, the ideal arrangement for fiscal policy purposes. During 1865–1867, the appropriations committees were broken off and separately established. More fracturing occurred in 1885 when some of the other standing committees were given funding responsibilities for the agencies they oversaw. Not until 1920 and the coming of a national budget system was the authority over all the spending measures restored to the appropriations committees.

TABLE 14.1   UNCONTROLLABILITY OF THE FEDERAL BUDGET, FISCAL 1979

	$ Billions	$ Billions	Percent
Relatively controllable items		130.5	26.1
Civilian programs	56.7		
National defense	73.8		
Relatively uncontrollable items		374.8	74.9
Social security and RR retirement	108.0		
Federal employees retirement	22.3		
Unemployment compensation	12.6		
Veterans benefits	12.6		
Medicare and Medicaid	42.1		
Housing payments	4.3		
Public assistance	22.0		
Interest	39.9		
Revenue sharing	6.9		
Farm price supports	4.5		
Prior year obligations and miscellaneous	89.5		
Other open-ended programs	10.1		
Miscellaneous adjustments		−5.1	
		$500.2	

Source: Adapted from *The Budget of the U.S. Government, 1979* (Washington, D.C.: Government Printing Office, 1978) pp. 470–471.

Nevertheless, the congressional handling of the budget until 1975 presented a picture of dispersion at its worst. A budget representing an integrated fiscal policy, whether sound or unsound, would come up every January from the president and would then be disassembled into thirteen separate authorization and appropriations bills. The program committees (Armed Services, Interior and Insular Affairs, Foreign Relations, and so on) would process the authorization measures, while thirteen appropriations subcommittees would be probing agency spending requests, playing the game of legislative preaudit. The expenditure totals would be arrived at inductively, one appropriation bill added to another, with congressional fiscal policy emerging only after the last act was passed — and that one frequently as late as three months into the new fiscal year for which the act was providing money.

Tax changes were coming down different pipelines — the the House Ways and Means Committee and Senate Finance Committee. Their leadership and that of the appropriations committees did not report to a common head in any meaningful way. What it meant was that congressional fiscal policy grew like wild weeds, one bill at a time; there was little chance that the macroconsequences would make much sense.

The process did not make much sense, and many congressmen knew it. That recognition kept the reform of their fiscal procedures on the congressional agenda from the post–World War II period on.

A significant milestone was achieved in the adoption of the *legislative budget* concept in the Legislative Reorganization Act of 1946.[13] That proposal called for a huge joint committee, consisting of the representatives and senators on appropriations and tax committees (about one hundred in all) to deliberate and recommend a budget ceiling by February 15 of each year. The first attempt in 1947 resulted in House-Senate disagreement on the total. The second, in 1948, resulted in the adoption of a $26.6 billion ceiling, which the same Congress then ignored by appropriating $32 billion. In 1949, the Joint Budget Committee didn't even convene, and the reform faded away for awhile.

A second reform was attempted in 1950 when the House Appropriations Committee packaged all the spending bills into one huge *omnibus appropriation act*. That device held promise for fiscal policy analysis, since one could see the proposed total of government outlays for once, but it again minimized the control role (how could a congressman effectively cope with such a massive document?) and antagonized the Senate Appropriations Committee by making the committee wait endlessly for the House to complete its action on the big bill.[14]

In 1969 and in the two following years, Congress imposed a spending ceiling on itself, violating it significantly only in 1970. But more important, the concept of the legislative budget would be revived in the 1974 reforms, which we'll describe shortly. (It seemed like a classic case of Justice Frankfurter's description of legislative gestation: agitation, incubation, education, and then legislation.)

The next major step in the search for congressional reform came in title II of the Legislative Reorganization Act of 1970.[15] Broadly conceived and well aimed, that legislation called for:

cost/benefit program analyses to be undertaken by the GAO as an aid to congressional appraisals of agency budgets

price tags on all new legislative measures requiring public expenditures, projected over five years

early hearings by the appropriations committees on macrobudget implications

greater use of annual appropriations (rather than multiyear)

June 1 updating by OMB of the revenue and expenditure estimates contained in the preceding January's budget

Controller General Elmer Staats subsequently reported that the GAO had developed a program analysis capability but implied that Congress was not fully utilizing his agency's help.[16]

The proposal to require standing committees to estimate and publish the cost of proposed legislation is an essential one if Congress is to be aware at all of the budgetary implications of what it is approving week by week, simultaneously with its handling of the appropriation acts.[17]

Early hearings on the large questions of budgetary policy represent a partial return to the 1946 idea of developing a legislative budget, with ceilings to be observed in later actions by the appropriations committees. The concept was reaffirmed in 1973 when the Joint Study Committee on Budget Control called for a mechanism in Congress that would determine the proper level of expenditures in terms of fiscal policy considerations and then translate the total into ceilings on budget authority to be granted.[18]

The call for annual, rather than multiyear, appropriations has both supporting logic and foes. The logic holds that it is the long-term spending authority, mortgaging the future, that makes it impossible for Congress to be its own fiscal master. Remember that currently, Congress can manipulate only 25 percent of the enormous federal budget.

Others take a different view. Aaron Wildavsky thinks that Congress ought to pass permanent spending authority, forget the annual appropriations rat race, and follow the exception principle of looking only at proposed changes in an agency's spending (plus conducting periodic program reviews).[19] A somewhat similar idea is the three-year proposal of a recent Brookings Institution study.[20] The common thread here is that Congress can no longer hope to cope intelligently with the maze of federal agencies and their fiscal needs in eight months' time every year.

The final requirement of the 1970 act for a June 1 updating of revenue and spending estimates is designed, of course, to improve the informational base on which Congress acts (and reminds one of the executive budget cycle where the president gets a fresh set of economic predictions from the Council of Economic Advisers in the fall as he makes his final decisions on fiscal policy).

The major reform of the congressional budget process came in the historic Congressional Budget and Impoundment Control Act of 1974,[21] the most significant legislation in the field since the Budget and Accounting Act of 1921. The new statute was the product of very intensive study during 1973 by House and Senate committees.[22]

The act provided for Senate and House budget committees, ultimately to be composed of sixteen and twenty-five members, respectively. In the House, five were to hold joint appointments on the Ways and Means Committee and five on the Appropriations Committee. Receiving preliminary recommendations from the program committees and from the appropriations committees, plus analyses from an impressive new Congressional Budget Office (CBO), the budget committees would formulate a legislative budget for preliminary congressional action by May 15 and for binding action by September 15. Now, at long last, the vehicle had been fashioned for the intelligent shaping of a congressional fiscal policy and a macrolook at the budget pie — what shares there are for the major functional areas in the budget. See Table 14.2 for a picture of the budget time-table laid down by the 1974 act. To see how it all worked out in the first full year of the reform (1976, for fiscal 1977), see Table 14.3.

The recommendation to increase the outlays and the deficit above President Ford's figure was heavily laced with Keynesian economic analysis.[23] The Senate Budget Committee, dissatisfied with Ford's projected growth rate of 3 to 4 percent, wanted a 6 percent rate, which they hoped to generate with more public service jobs and $3 billion more in pump priming. Thus, they proposed a total of $17.5 billion more in outlays than Ford did and a $6.2 billion higher deficit. With these changes, the Senate Budget Committee hoped to reduce unemployment from 8 to 6.5 percent, with an inflation rate not to exceed 5.5 percent.*

TABLE 14.2 THE NEW TIMETABLE IN CONGRESSIONAL BUDGETING

November 10	President submits a Current Services Budget to Congress, providing an update on current levels of expenditures which may influence the base-line in Congressional appropriations for the next fiscal year
January 18–20	President submits the proposed budget for the new fiscal year
January–February	Hearings and analyses under way by the House and Senate Budget Committees, Appropriations Committees, program committees, and the CBO
March 15	Appropriations and program committees make recommendations to the Budget Committees on spending allocations[a]
April 15	Budget Committees report the first concurrent resolution to the House and Senate, proposing (a) ceilings on budget authority and appropriations, overall and by program areas; (b) desired revenues; (c) surplus or deficit; and (d) size of the federal debt[b]
May 15	Deadline for the introduction of all authorization measures from the program committees and for Congressional adoption of the first concurrent resolution[c]
Week after Labor Day	Completion of Congressional action on all appropriations bills
September 15	Passage of the second (and final) concurrent resolution on the budget, setting binding ceilings on spending
September 25	Reconciliation to be completed by Congress on any differences between appropriations acts and the totals in the second resolution
October 1	New fiscal year begins

[a] See, for example, Senate Appropriations Committee, *Report to the Committee on the Budget on the Views of the Committee on Appropriations on the Budget Proposed for FY1976* (Committee print March 15, 1975).

[b] In the 94th Congress (1976), it was Senate Report 94-731 and Senate Concurrent Resolution 109.

[c] For the results of the first concurrent resolution, see *Congressional Quarterly Weekly Report* (May 15, 1976), 34: 1166.

* Economic analysis would suggest that a 3 to 4 percent growth rate would, in fact, be deflationary. We need 1 percentage point in growth for every 1 percentage point reduction we want to achieve in the unemployment rate (thus, 3 percent to bring unemployment down from 8 to 5 percent); we need 1.5 percent to compensate for the annual improvement in the nation's productivity; and we need 2 percent to absorb the rising population of the labor force. Thus, we need about a 6.5 percent rise in real GNP to reduce unemployment to less severe levels and to employ our growing work force.

TABLE 14.3   COMPARISON OF THE FORD AND CONGRESSIONAL BUDGETS FOR FISCAL 1977
($ billions)

	President's budget (1/76)	First concurrent resolution	President's summer revision (7/76)	Second concurrent resolution
Total outlays	$394.2	413.3	400.0	413.1
Budget authority	433.4	454.2	431.4	451.5
Total revenues	351.3	362.5	352.5	362.5
Deficit	−43.0	−50.8	−47.5	−50.6
Public debt	710.4	713.1	712.7	700.0

Source: Adapted from *Congressional Quarterly Weekly Report*, September 18, 1976, pp. 2516–2517. Copyright 1976, Congressional Quarterly, Inc. Reprinted by permission.

In addition to these macrodifferences, the Senate Budget Committee also altered some of the president's program allocations as well as cutting $30 billion from the figures recommended by the other Senate standing committees. Defense outlays were reduced $200 million (only a fraction, in fact, below the president's request), but funds for social welfare programs were increased by $11 billion.

There was some interplay between the budget committees and the two tax-writing committees concerning the formers' more sanguine estimate of a $2 billion revenue increase from prospective taxes. But on September 9, in one of the convincing moments of the whole new process, the new tax bill was reported back from the conference committee, calling for an extra $1.6 billion in fiscal 1977, the exact amount asked for in the second concurrent budget resolution. Left and right hands had effected a handshake.

Appraising the Budget's New Clothes*

First, the key events (Table 14.2) took place on time. Second, budgetary decisions in Congress were made with the most sophisticated economic analysis that had ever been provided.[24] Third, as House Budget Chairman Brock Adams observed on passage of the second concurrent resolution, "it contains the budget *of the Congress* and not that of the President [emphasis added]."[25]

Furthermore, some important tactical victories had been won in early skirmishes with other standing committees. In the preceding trial year, members of the Senate Budget Committee on August 1, 1975, successfully persuaded the Senate to reject a conference report brought in by the powerful John Stennis of the Armed Services Committee that proposed a total for military procurement above that recommended by the first concurrent resolution for fiscal 1976.

* The phrase is Merewitz and Sosnick's.

Later that fall, the House Post Office and Civil Service Committee brought in a retirement pension bill that threatened the adopted budget ceiling. The budget chairman persuaded the chairman of the program committee to withdraw it, killing it for the year.[26]

Two similar victories of great import were won in 1976. The Senate Interior Committee, four months after the May deadline, brought in a bill for the Young Adult Conservation Corps and asked for a waiver to allow its consideration. The Senate turned them down.

On September 13, 1976, Congress passed the Defense Appropriations Act for 1977, at $104.3 billion in outlays, $3.5 billion above the first concurrent resolution ceiling. Three days later Congress approved the second resolution, providing only $100.65 billion for the Defense Department. According to Ford's budget, the following January Defense received $100.075 billion for fiscal 1977, the figure provided in the second resolution.

But overshadowing everything else, the emergence of a legislative budget meant that the mechanisms and the will had now emerged to join together that which had been disparate and to lift the congressional line of sight from pre-auditing the executive branch to the largest questions of fiscal policy and program balancing (defense versus health and welfare, etc.). Without too much modesty, the Senate Budget Committee noted in August 1976 that:

> Had it been forced to rely on the fragmented procedures of the past, the Congress would not have moved so decisively in dealing with the recession. Neither would Congress have exercised sufficient restraint on the growth of permanent programs.

> The Congressional budget for fiscal 1976 brought unemployment down from 8.7% in the second quarter of 1975 to 7.4% a year later while employment increased by 2.4 million. . . . Inflation fell from a 12% annual rate at the end of 1974 to less than 5% in July of this year [1976].[27]

Thus, Congress had fashioned for itself a most useful tool for containing expenditures or expanding parsimonious ones, the legislative budget. Clearly, it has taken a leading position among the legislative implements for reshaping executive budgets.

In the Carter administration, the reforms of 1974 were still at work. The first and second concurrent resolutions were adopted (although the second was adopted a week late in 1978); appropriation acts were brought into line; and Congress put its imprimatur on the budget. The moment of drama in September 1978 centered on the insistence of the Senate Budget Committee not to fund any new public works as an anti-inflationary measure. (The ultimate compromise between the House and Senate conferees was one of the most laughable on record — see the box below.)[28] Congress had effected a $9 billion cut in outlays below the president's revised figure and had brought the contemplated deficit below $40 billion for the first time since fiscal 1974 (see Table 14.4).

TABLE 14.4 COMPARISON OF THE REVISED CARTER BUDGET AND FINAL CONGRESSIONAL
BUDGET FOR FISCAL 1979 ($ billions)

	President's budget (1/78)	First concurrent resolution	President's summer revision (7/78)	Second concurrent resolution
Total outlays	500.2	498.8	496.6	487.5
Total revenues	439.6	447.9	448.1	448.7
Deficit	−60.6	−50.9	−48.5	−38.8

Source: Adapted from *Congressional Quarterly Weekly Report* (September 23, 1978) 36:2584. Copyright 1978, Congressional Quarterly, Inc. Reprinted by permission.

Legislative Cutlery

Over time, Congress has developed a number of other scalpels for removing epidermis, fat, or muscle from agency budgets they think need trimming. The cutlery ranges from fine laser beams to reduce an office from ten positions to six (via restrictive language in the appropriation act) on to meat axes to lop off aircraft carriers and foreign aid programs.

The most-used instrument in reducing those budgets is the *program-by-program* cut. Thus, the House Appropriations Subcommittee on HEW works through the National Institutes of Health budget, raising the cancer program $750,000, while cutting ear and lung research $1 million, dental research by $75,000, arthritis by $1.2 million, and so on.

Percentage cuts across the board more closely resemble the meat ax. "The Coast Guard request is 15 percent too high; simply cut each of its programs by that much." (Note how readily the practice of cutting an agency by 7 percent each year would invite budget padding by 7 percent each year.)

Then there are some *restrictive riders* that seek to excise funds by tying the hands of administrators in managing their agencies. One was the Whitten amendment of the 1950s to curb grade escalation. It required that a civil servant be in grade (e.g., at GS-12) for eighteen months before being promoted. But what if a civil servant were a brilliant woman chemist in the National Bureau of Standards, toying with the idea of quitting to accept a job with Union Carbide? Congressman Jamie Whitten of Mississippi made your personnel decision for you: you couldn't woo her with a promotion.

Another was the Jensen rider of the same period that allowed administrators to fill only three-fourths of their vacancies in a given fiscal year, thus forcing a cutback of 25 percent of whatever their turnover rate happened to be. Imagine the disaster that awaited the agency that moved a regional office and had forty people quit. No matter, Representative Ben Jensen of Iowa had lopped off ten jobs when you relocated, whether you could spare them or not. These are nonsensical ways of achieving economy in government.

Another technique for budget cutting is the coward's way out. It advocates

---

The House Can Look at It One Way, and the Senate the Other

The House and Senate conferees on the second budget resolution in September 1978 were miles apart on public works spending and disaster relief. The House wanted to authorize $2 billion for public works, the Senate none. They were also far apart in their estimates of what disaster relief would cost in fiscal 1979; the House said $430 million, the Senate said $1.2 billion. To get the resolution passed, Senator Muskie fashioned this double-vision compromise:

> The conference, he said, could accept the Senate combined figure for public works and disaster relief [$1.2 billion]. The Senate could interpret that to mean there were no funds for public works and that there was $1.2 billion for disaster relief. The House could interpret it to mean that there was $700 million for public works and only $430 million for disaster relief.

And that is what the conferees adopted — one combined figure for public works and disaster relief that each chamber could interpret as it saw fit. Intentional double vision had saved the day.

Congressional Quarterly Weekly Report (Sept. 23, 1978) 36:2585.

---

passing all the appropriations congressmen desire and then authorizing *presidential excision* to bring the total outlays down to a figure Congress really regards as prudent. With the reforms of 1974 behind them, congressmen are not likely to have to resort to this abdication tool very often.

Against that choice of weaponry, how can administrators develop a tactical plan to see their budgets through Congress relatively unscathed?

The Art of Getting Your Budget Through

Sizing up the significant others on the House and Senate appropriations subcommittees who are waiting to greet you is a must. The chairman and ranking minority member must be analyzed and appropriately handled. The suggestions made in Chapter 8 on the art of managing politicians are germane here. The politics of the situation — the Appropriations Subcommittee vis-à-vis the agency — will demand some compromises in the proposals you will have to include in your budget in order to meet the constituent needs and special hang-ups of these legislative power brokers. To be specific, if the subcommittee chairman in question wants a post office in a certain town in his district, that may be the price you have to pay for his support on the rest of your budget.

(Dirty politics, you say? Remember, the citizens who will receive better postal service pay taxes — and vote.)[29]

A statement attributed to Senator Frank Church, a Democrat from the water-hungry state of Idaho, is instructive. He once had the temerity to admit that "My most important vote this entire session was for Mike Kirwan's fishbowl." Mike Kirwan's fishbowl was an aquarium project in the District of Columbia, dear to the heart of this powerful chairman of the House Civil Works Appropriations Subcommittee through which all measures had to go for funding water projects in Idaho. The name of the game, for administrators as well as for fellow lawmakers, is still quid pro quo.

The care and feeding of subcommittee staffs is almost equally important. Meeting their information needs promptly and honestly and soliciting their advice on matters of presentation and emphasis are the ways you can win staffs and influence congressmen.

As we noted earlier, lining up some outside trumps, powerful pressure groups who depend on your appropriations, is sometimes resorted to. They are often in a position to marshal support to help change congressional minds about the legitimacy of your budget requests. One way to get these satellite groups hopping mad is to cut popular programs affecting their interests. Then comes the trick of directing their ire toward Congress and away from you.

In some forty-two states where governors possess item veto authority to kill or reduce specific appropriations of which they disapprove, agency heads have to think twice about legislative tactics to increase their budgets over the figure recommended by the governor. The ultimate embarrassment in budgeting, we surmise, is to score with the legislature and then be chopped down by an item veto of your own governor.[30]

When the hour arrives for your appearance before the House Appropriations Subcommittee, some of Wildavsky's techniques for putting your case may come in handy.[31] He colorfully describes the art of rounding your requests (always up); pointing to the increased work load; suggesting how small the changes are; linking up "If we do this, then we'll need that"; and advancing one of the real oldies of all: "This project will pay for itself."

After you have given them the business, then the subcommittee members proceed to give you the treatment in a closed-door session to mark up the appropriation bill and prepare it for final action by the full House Appropriations Committee before being sent back to the House of Representatives.

Now the question before the House is: "How shall we shape that bill?"

Give 'Em the Dough or Tie Their Hands?

Where a legislative body is content with its large cuts of the revenue pie — so much for industrial development, so much for public safety, and so much for natural resources — and has general confidence in administrators in the executive branch, the appropriation will often be given in *lump sum,* by agency, as shown in Table 14.5.

What the city council omits when it adopts a generalized budget like that shown in Table 14.5 is the breakdown of activities within each of the departments. For example, the appropriation act will not direct the city health chief to spend her $1.2 million in some fashion such as this:

By object		*By activity*	
01. Personnel	$700,000	01. Administration	$100,000
02. Equipment	120,000	02. Epidemiology	180,000
03. Rent, heat, and light	90,000	03. Home nursing	200,000
04. Supplies	280,000	04. General sanitation	150,000
05. Transportation	10,000	05. School nursing	500,000
Total	$1,200,000	06. Veneral disease control	70,000
		Total	$1,200,000

The freewheeling breadth of lump sum appropriations can be narrowed in at least two ways: by restrictive language in the acts themselves (e.g., imposing limits on car purchases, entertainment, and travel); and by the expression of Appropriations Committee sentiments ("thou shalt nots") in the committee reports filed with the bills. The enforcement behind the second is simple: "We expect to see you back up here next year."

Now contrast lump sum grants with *line-item* appropriation acts, the familiar form in state and local government funding. An example would look like this:

Item 43. Development Services Administration: $182,500

Administration	$58,000
Hearings	12,500
Travel	42,000
Interstate programs	10,000
Transportation Council	1,000
Industrial agents	31,700
Nuclear Energy Commission	25,300
Salary adjustment	2,000

Here the legislature has preaudited the development services administration to a fare-thee-well, even down to a $1,000 item representing barely 0.5 percent of the department's budget.

In addition to broad versus narrow spending authority, there is the additional complexity concerning the right of agencies to spend money (appropriations or outlays) versus their right to incur bills requiring later outlays (contract authority).[32] It is the budget authority provided in preceding years whose bills are now coming due that constitutes one of the factors reducing congressional control of this year's budget to about 25 percent of total outlays. The message is clear.

TABLE 14.5   LUMP SUM CITY BUDGET ($ millions)

General administration	0.9
Fire protection	0.8
Health	1.2
Parks and recreation	2.0
Police	2.8
Courts and corrections	0.7
Streets	1.8
Water	1.5
Debt retirement	0.7
Capital improvements	1.5
Total city budget	$13.9

Controlling the budget does not begin at the appropriation stage but a year or more before at the point where Congress authorized a program and the running up of agency bills. (In private life the translation usually is, "When you want to get out of debt, cancel your charge accounts.")

Appraising the Appropriators

How well does Congress perform under the current system in accomplishing the goals we talked about at the outset — of providing for their districts, overseeing the executive, and financing the public good? It is clear that congressmen with clout (having seniority, holding important committee posts, and having other kinds of influence) probably do exceptionally well in taking care of the folks back home. But for the junior members, some congressmen are more equal than others.

Preauditing the executive, a debatable goal, seems to be well provided for. The eyeball-to-eyeball hearings in both chambers, the ease of writing in restrictions in the appropriation acts afford congressmen the chance to get agencies to walk tiptoe when the legislators are so inclined.

Making enlightened judgments about both budget allocations and fiscal policy must now also be given very high marks. As we have seen, the 1974 reforms at long last gave the spending and taxing committees a coordinating panel, the Senate and House budget committees, plus the backup staffs for analysis as good as that available to the president.

Two additional reforms would seem to be a logical extension of the 1974 changes: abolition of the two appropriations committees, transferring the detailed analysis of agency requests to the standing program committees (e.g. interior, public works, armed services, and so on) that already supervise each agency, thus permitting the merger of authorization and appropriation measures into a single bill for each agency.

The fiscal record of Congress during the 1970s left much to be desired. During the raging inflation of the early 1970s, Congress made no effort to stem the excessive demand by bringing the unified budget into balance, which would thus soak up private funds. They continued to subsidize tobacco production with one arm while driving cigarette commercials off the television screens with the other. They watched quarter after quarter as exports fell behind imports until the dollar ultimately collapsed abroad without making an effort to curtail government expenditures overseas (for military bases, etc.).

Conversely, depending upon your value judgments, Congress has accomplished some impressive things with our money during the past two decades. They financed the exploration of the moon President Kennedy asked for; their poverty programs contributed to the reduction of Americans living in poverty from 22 to 12 percent of the population in ten years' time; and they belatedly provided financing for a synthetic fuels program to reduce our dependence on foreign oil, among other notable achievements.

With that, we conclude our examination of the appropriation process and return again to the executive branch to see how the money Congress has provided is spent and how postappropriation controls function.

POSTAPPROPRIATION CONTROLS ON SPENDING

To all of you who suffer (like the author) from the old problem of too much month left at the end of your money, would the kind of system shown in Table 14.6 be of any help? "Rent had to be paid at the beginning of the month, but we've been a bit heavy on food — we're now down to less than two dollars a day for the next fifteen days. The old car has behaved and we're looking good there. It looks like a lot of TV time and a couple of malts for the next two weeks' entertainment (unless we can get by with no more lab breakage this month and then tap my old friend, Miss Elainey, for eight dollars for some more playtime). Savings I can't touch — that's the plane ticket home for Christmas break."

If that thirty-day budget and sixteenth-day accounting report make any sense, then you're a third of the way home in understanding postappropriation controls used in government.

Keeping a Rein on the Feds

When the president signs the appropriations act, the money (budget authority to incur and pay bills) lies momentarily unencumbered on Treasury Department books. Agencies quickly return an Office of Management and Budget form, "Request for Apportionment of Funds." That step stems from the old Antideficiency Acts of 1905 and 1906[33] that Congress passed to force agencies to stretch their appropriations over the twelve months of the fiscal year (in most

TABLE 14.6   STRETCHING $200 OVER THIRTY DAYS (16th day of the month report)

	Obligated	Spent	Unexpended balance
Board and room	$120	$95	$25
Car	30	12	18
Entertainment	20	16	4
Laundry	10	4	6
Miscellaneous	10	2	8
Savings	10	10	0
Monthly total	$200	$139	$61
% gone: 52% month 69% money			

cases through the device of quarterly apportionments, where the Treasury would release only one fourth of their appropriations from July through September, etc.). It is ordinarily at the stage of approving the proposed apportionments that OMB and its predecessor, the Bureau of the Budget, would set up reserves by impounding appropriated funds the agencies could not spend.

At this stage, two sets of accounting records are set up: detailed accounts in the agencies and summary accounts in the Treasury Department. In microcosm, the books look something like that one-month personal budget we just discussed. Paying close attention to restrictive language and amounts specified in the relevant congressional committee reports and in the appropriation act itself, the agencies will lay out their accounts by program and object (defined in Chapter 13), following guidelines issued by the GAO.

Obligating the various programs and objects is an important step. It means committing or mortgaging a stated amount of money for specified items of expenditure (e.g., $100 million for forest road construction, $20,000 for new tennis courts, $1,800 for supplies). It's the bookkeeper's version of the marked jars that contain the proceeds from the widow's social security check (for food, rent, grandchildren, church, etc.). The obligations represent the checkpoints or restrainers on agency spending. With the computer keeping daily tab on the ebb and flow of agency funds, it is possible to make the bells clang and the whistles blow (translation: your phone rings with your in-house auditor on the line) whenever you butt up against the spending limit on any of your objects of expenditure.

With an eye on those controls, you're more than ready to begin spending money. The typical pattern goes like this:

Your buildings and grounds unit initiates a *purchase requisition* to acquire a backhoe for $25,000.

The requisition goes to the finance office where your in-house auditor *pre-audits* the request, checking to see if you have an equipment object with

Don't Ever Underspend Your Budget

Stretching your budget to last twelve months is one half of the problem; not ending with a surplus is the other (lest Congress should cut you by the unspent amount next year). That fear then gives rise in the summer months to a disorderly scene of many federal agencies simply opening the spending floodgates to use up their appropriations before the end of the fiscal year on September 30. What happened to Winter Park, Florida, probably was a case in point:

City Scrambles for Ways to Spend Federal Windfall

WINTER PARK, Fla. (AP) — City officials asked the federal government for $883,500 to build a new library, but the government has approved an allocation of $2.65 million.

Now city officials and planning consultants are busy designing and estimating costs on some 20 projects to ensure that they can take advantage of the windfall.

This fashionable central Florida community of 23,000 got word a few weeks ago that the Economic Development Administration had allocated the grant based on unemployment statistics for the area.

But the EDA won't give final approval to the grant unless the town produces by July 13 a list of projects on which to spend the money.

Commissioner Harold Roberts suggested the city refuse to accept the money to show patriotism. But later he said he was just being "philosophical."

Among projects under study are the library, a second floor to the police station, a parking lot for the fire department, tennis courts, a bike path, a $400,00 grandstand at the city's baseball field, $200,000 worth of repairs to the sewage treatment plant and paving and drainage of various streets.

Stars and Stripes (June 24, 1977), p. 4.

unspent funds available and if the purchase is consistent with the appropriation act for the agency.

She approves, and the purchasing agent is then authorized to draw up performance specifications and call for *competitive bids.*

A *purchase order* is issued to the winning bidder, who then delivers the backhoe and submits an *invoice* to your finance office.

The buildings and grounds unit *inspects* the equipment and indicates acceptance to the finance office.

The finance office issues a *voucher* authorizing the preparation of a check to pay the invoice.

A *check* is then mailed, your equipment account is debited, and your unspent balance is reduced by $25,000 (the accounting step).

In essence, that is how governments buy goods and services and pay their bills: through the preaudit, or control in advance, of proposed expenditures; and then accounting for the transactions in accrual accounting, for bills being incurred.

The controls just described are designed to achieve two of those major purposes of budgeting talked about in the last chapter — management and accountability:

payments for purposes intended by the legislature

by authorized personnel

at proper rates

to lawful recipients

In larger compass, these postappropriation controls are there to see that the will of the legislature that authorized the money is carried out and to provide managers with important financial data and checks on possible corruption.[34]

The accounting field has been a fertile one for reform the last quarter century. Against the backdrop of steady presidential complaints against GAO interference in executive affairs, the comptroller-general joined the Treasury and Budget Bureau in 1948 to launch the Joint Financial Management Improvement Program.[35] Aided and abetted by two Hoover Commissions and a cooperative Congress, within eight years these three agencies changed the whole landscape of keeping the federal accounts:

Accounting and preauditing became executive branch prerogatives, with the GAO setting standards and checking on agency compliance.

A cost accounting base for performance budgeting was developed.

Budgeting and accounting classifications were harmonized.

The wasteful shipment of tons of agency vouchers to the GAO was stopped when the GAO received authorization in 1950 to conduct onsite audits (going to the agencies rather than vice versa).

Establishing accountability after the fact is the *postaudit.* One of the clearest principles of public administration is that postauditors are to be absolutely independent of the spenders in the executive branch. That independence is to be achieved through such devices as direct election, as in state and local governments; appointment for long terms; and/or location in the legislative branch, as in the federal arrangement.

On occasion one encounters strange reversals of these arrangements. An independently elected city auditor prepares the city budget and performs the preaudit, both strictly executive functions that should not be independently

---

You'd Have to Call It Grand Theft

In a 1978 report to Congress the comptroller-general of the United States added up the costs of embezzlement in the government's economic assistance programs:

> The extent of fraud in Government programs cannot be taken lightly. Even a low-side estimate of fraud, such as 1 percent, would amount to *$2.5 billion annually*. While substantial in itself, this amount is more significant when considered in terms of the goods and services it could provide at current funding levels — enough to (a) fund the school lunch program for over 1 year; (b) increase the number of jobs provided under the Comprehensive Employment and Training Act (CETA) programs; (c) increase nearly five-fold the grants for cancer research; or (d) increase nearly 20-fold the grants for air pollution control.

U.S. Comptroller General, *Federal Agencies Can, and Should, Do More to Combat Fraud in Government Programs* (Washington, D.C.: General Accounting Office, 1978), p. 12.

---

controlled; and the city fathers hire a certified public accounting firm to conduct the postaudit, which should never be conducted by the hired agents of the spenders.

Those kinds of mismatches have now been straightened out at the federal level, thanks to the Budget and Accounting Procedures Act of 1950.[36] The GAO, located in the legislative branch, is the independent postauditor, reporting to Congress about executive branch compliance with legislative mandates. Equally important, the GAO is now even more concerned with audits of managerial effectiveness than simply with misapplication of funds.[37]

We need to turn now to a tough postappropriation control, impounding of funds by the executive, only briefly considered up to this point.

Item Vetoing the Congress Without an Item Veto

Unlike the charters of forty-two of the states, the U.S. Constitution gave the president no authority to veto *parts* of appropriation acts. His is a take-it-or-leave-it authority, which leaves him at the mercy of whatever outlandish project may be added to an appropriation measure, which measure taken by itself, he approves.

While the Constitution is clear on that, it is vague on another matter that never would have occurred to the Founding Fathers: are appropriation acts *mandates* to spend, or do they constitute *permission* to spend? Modern-day presidents have taken the latter view, interposing their judgment to that of Congress on *how much* of an appropriation ought to be obligated.

Third, the Constitution also created a separation of powers that recognized the independence and equality of the presidency vis-à-vis the Congress and imposed on him the duty "to see that the laws are faithfully executed." Against that background, what is a president supposed to do when Congress tells him to avoid deficits, stay under a debt ceiling, control inflation, protect the environment, and then gives him the money for vast public works that will break through the debt ceiling, generate inflation, and impair the beauty of canyons and countryside? When faced with that kind of conflict of laws, recent presidents have impounded offensive appropriations right and left (see Table 14.7).

The first impoundment on record was an action of the third president, Thomas Jefferson, in 1803. On October 17, he reported in his annual message to Congress that he had set aside $50,000 Congress had appropriated for acquiring gunboats for the Mississippi River. Presaging in an exact way the course later presidents would take, Jefferson gave two reasons for ignoring the will of Congress: (a) conditions had changed (we have acquired the territory and pacified the river); and (b) he didn't want to waste money on outmoded gunboats when better ones were being designed. A year later he reported that he had allowed the expenditure to begin.[38]

Modern-day impoundments, however, rest more on legislative enactments than on distant presidential precedents. The basic statutes have already been noted, the Antideficiency Acts of 1905 and 1906.[39] They required department heads to apportion funds in such a way (ordinarily by calendar quarters) as to make them last to the end of the fiscal year and to provide for contingencies. Apportionment means reserving funds for later expenditure, and that underlies at least part of the idea of impoundment (the part not covered is where impoundment is used to kill a project Congress has authorized).

On numerous occasions since 1906, Congress has added additional authority for executive action to cut appropriations. The Economy Acts of 1932 and 1933 authorized Presidents Hoover and Roosevelt to cut salaries and eliminate unneeded offices.[40] The Omnibus Appropriation Act of 1950 vindicated innovations in impounding during World War II (to be discussed below) by providing

TABLE 14.7   IMPOUNDING OF FUNDS, EISENHOWER TO FORD, SELECTED YEARS (billions)

Fiscal year	Total unified budget outlays	Dollars impounded	% of outlays
1960	$ 92.2	8.0	8.7
1963	111.3	4.5	4.0
1968	178.8	9.9	5.5
1972	231.9	10.6	4.6
1976	366.5	12.1	3.3

Source: Report of OMB Director Roy Ash to the Senate and House, February 5, 1973 (Senate Document 93-4); and report of OMB Director James T. Lynn, June 9, 1976 (House Document 94-524).

in section 1211 that reserves could be established "to provide for contingencies or to effect savings" where changed requirements or improved efficiency made them possible. The act stated that apportionments and, by implication, reserves could be set up according to months, quarters, functions, projects, or objects.[41] The statute went on to instruct President Truman to do what Congress had not had the courage to do — to cut an additional $550 million out of the amounts appropriated in the same act "through the apportionment procedure provided in Section 1211" (section 1214). In the light of later troubles, it is instructive to recall this 1950 era when Congress endorsed and relied on executive impoundment of appropriated funds.

Add to all of that the Employment Act of 1946[42] that obligated both branches of government to fight inflation and recession, the Environmental Quality Improvement Act of 1970,[43] and the Economic Stabilization Act of 1970,[44] and you quickly sense the statutory authority a president can claim when he feels the need to impound some part of an appropriation that strikes him as inflationary; threatening to the environment; or, like Jefferson, untimely. In defending Nixon's impoundments to the Ninety-third Congress, OMB Director Roy Ash cited thirteen separate authorities.[45]

The seminal period for modern-day impoundments was World War II. Emboldened by suggestions from his Budget Bureau on how to stop pork-barrel projects for the duration of the war, President Roosevelt ordered substantial amounts for dams and highways to be placed in frozen reserves, unavailable for expenditure. FDR had concocted a reasonable facsimile of an item veto.*[46]

In the wake of the World War II impoundments came many others: Truman's to keep the air force at forty-eight groups (instead of the fifty-eight Congress provided for), and other presidents' to halt water projects, aircraft carriers and B-70 bombers, highway expansion, and rural aid programs, among many others.[47]

Any given instance of impounding has to step on some congressional toes as pet projects are stopped. But during the Nixon administration the cries of pain reached decibel levels not heard before.

The Nixon impoundings of 1970–1973 reflected the same philosophy as the budget he submitted in January 1973: cut back on the Great Society programs. That philosophy was expressed in presidential actions to shut down the poverty agency (Office of Economic Opportunity), sending its functions elsewhere; to restrict health grants, public housing, rent subsidies, and highway construction; to close down Model Cities and urban renewal; to curtail the Rural Environmental Assistance Program; and to impound $6 billion from the Muskie grant-in-aid program for municipal sewage treatment, among a number of others. (In the last instance, the impoundment came right in the teeth of one of the few suc-

---

* Only two senators, Pat McCarran (D. Nev.), and Kenneth McKellar (D. Tenn.) were able to get funds unfrozen for their pet projects, while the Bureau of the Budget successfully stopped $500 million worth of public works.

cessful overridings of a Nixon veto the Ninety-second Congress had been able to muster.) Taken together, these impoundments represented the bold face of Nixon's conservative revolution: to do by executive action what he could not persuade the Democratic Congress to do.

Reprisal and reversal came quickly, both from the Congress and the courts. The Senate Judiciary Committee held extensive hearings in March 1971 on executive impoundment of appropriated funds.[48] That exposure led in turn to Hubert Humphrey's successful move in 1972 to secure passage of the Federal Impoundment and Information Act,[49] which required periodic reporting of both the amounts of, and justification for, all executive impoundments; and then Senator Ervin's bill (S. 373), which paved the way for Title X of the Congressional Budget and Impoundment Control Act of 1974.

The deep antipathy of Congress to the Nixon impoundments can be felt as well in some of the retaliatory moves of the Ninety-third Congress. Knowing of OMB's rejection of a Veterans Administration request for $10 million to air-condition eight VA hospitals, Democratic Senator Alan Cranston of California moved not only to provide the money but also to cut off the air-conditioning in the Executive Office of the President (which houses OMB) if the funds should be impounded (that's called sweat for swat). The Senate agreed by voice vote to cut off money for salaries and expenses of agencies administering community development and housing subsidy programs unless all of the new money and that previously impounded were spent.

For the first time in American history, the courts got into the act. In rapid succession, U.S. district courts held that Nixon impoundments of funds for the poverty program, highways, and water pollution violated the will of Congress. The judges were unimpressed with the president's reasoning that his actions were required to fulfill other statutes (to prevent inflation, etc.), following instead the traditional canon that the most recent enactment of the legislature takes precedence over earlier statutes.[50]

Supreme Court review finally came in late 1974, after the impounder had already been removed to San Clemente.[51] As we have noted, Congress had passed the Federal Water Pollution Control Act of 1972, providing federal grants for municipal sewage systems, over Nixon's veto. Thirty days later, the president instructed Russell Train, the EPA administrator, to allot $6 billion in grants less than the act authorized, primarily as an anti-inflationary move.

The city of New York, always in danger of sewage it can't handle, sued and won a summary judgment from the U.S. district court requiring Train to stop braking and start unloading the federal dollars needed for New York's sewage system.

In his opinion for a unanimous Supreme Court, Byron R. White, associate justice of the Court, focused on a narrow issue of statutory interpretation (as a strict constructionist would) and did not address the broader issue of presidential authority to balance a congressional order to spend with his other statutory duties, such as stabilizing the economy (e.g., under the Employment Act of 1946). Reading the statute and its legislative history, plus taking a side glance at the Impoundment Control Act passed five months earlier, Justice White concluded that it was the clear intent of the Congress "to provide a firm commitment of substantial sums within a relatively limited period of time" to solve an urgent problem. He did not say it, but the president is bound by Article II to see that the laws are faithfully executed; and he may not accomplish by impoundment what he tried unsuccessfully to do by veto.

Victorious in the courts, and on the threshold of removing from office the president who impounded with one hand and covered up burglaries with the other, Congress in the summer of impeachment undertook to establish once and for all its authority in forcing the executive to spend appropriated moneys.

Title X of the Impoundment Control Act of July 12, 1974, distinguished between *deferrals* and *rescissions* of appropriations, subjecting the former to a one-house veto and the latter to the toughest legislative check yet invented, the two-house affirmative action technique.

The new act narrowed the grounds of any future impoundment of funds to (a) provide for contingencies, or (b) effect savings. Under the first, a president might theoretically hold up dam construction (a deferral) in the face of derogatory engineering reports; under the second, he could require the return to the Treasury of $1.5 million should the dam be finished that much below its authorized amount (a rescission).

Section 1013 of the Control Act now requires the president to notify the Congress about the pertinent facts surrounding the impoundment (amounts involved, agency, time period, reasons, and likely impact).[52] Impoundments may not last beyond the fiscal year, and the funds must be released if *either house* passes a disapproving resolution.

In the case of rescissions, where the president seeks to cancel outright budget authority passed by Congress, he must follow the same reporting requirements for deferrals and must release the budget authority for obligation if both houses of Congress fail to enact a rescission bill endorsing what he has proposed. To repeat: Congress as a whole must *act affirmatively* to permit the president's negative action to stand.

The act's muscle was quickly demonstrated. In the spring of 1975, President Ford announced the impoundment of $9.1 billion in highway construction funds in an effort to curtail federal spending. Hoping for a reduction in unemployment from the countercyclical effect of spending the money, the Senate voted 77 to 7 for a disapproving resolution that forced Ford to release the funds.[53]

In the early phase of the Carter administration, covering the first half of fiscal 1978, OMB Director James McIntyre indicated that President Carter had proposed rescinding $698 million (net) in appropriated funds. Congress resisted him on the funds for missile procurement, forcing the expenditure of $105 million, but they let his other cuts stand. The president had also deferred $3.7 billion (net), of which Congress overturned only $39 million.[54]

Sanctions to Keep the Spenders Honest

Remembering well James Madison's warning that we wouldn't be governed by angels, we have hemmed in the spenders in government with budgets, statutes, controls, and auditors; and yet FBI chiefs still furbish their private homes with agency funds, mayors receive kickbacks from contractors, and on occasion decisions from antitrust to zoning still are sold to the highest bidder.[55]

Recognizing, then, the fallibility of administrators, we must conclude our examination of fiscal management by listing the *sanctions* that have been developed to encourage fiduciary trust in public officials:

warranty bonds to be sacrificed when losses occur because of misfeasance or malfeasance in office

suits at law to recover losses

criminal complaints to deal with embezzlement and bribery

removal from office through judicial or legislative impeachment

legislative retaliation by cutting off an agency's funds

SUMMARY

It is in the interface we call the appropriation process that managerial dreams are measured up (and sometimes cut down) to constituent realities. Now comes the baptism by fire, when the ten-year budget director faces a veteran of twenty years on the Appropriations Committee who knows the budget director's agency inside and out — a John Taber, a Clarence Cannon, a George Mahon, or a Kenneth McKellar. In that confrontation, the seemingly anesthetized budget of the executive branch becomes the thoroughly politicized appropriations act of the legislative branch.

Congress not only transforms the budget in political directions but uses it as well to preaudit the executive branch and control the details of administration. For many years prior to 1974, congressmen seemed far less interested in the large policy questions of the proper allocations to the major components of government, such as health, welfare, defense, and the like; their whole approach was inductive rather than deductive, incremental rather than global.

Then came two and a half decades of experimentation and reform — legislative budgets, omnibus appropriation acts, reporting of impoundments, and so on. The culmination came in the Congressional Budget and Impoundment Control Act of 1974, which finally enabled the Congress to focus on fiscal policy, take a macrolook at the whole budgetary pie, and bring its disparate taxing and spending arms together.

Postappropriation controls are designed to carry out the will of the legislature and to enable managers to keep on top of their operations effectively.

These controls are the stock-in-trade of the accounting and auditing professions: obligating funds before expenditure, apportioning funds, keeping current books, preauditing, and postauditing. The last quarter century has been a period of truly significant progress in federal fiscal management, highlighted by the GAO's withdrawal from preauditing, going to site auditing with emphasis on managerial performance rather than narrow legalisms, and the computerization of agency accounts.

Impoundment of funds by the executive developed as a substitute for an item veto authority the Constitution withheld from the president. Although often reaffirmed by congressional statutes, the practice of freezing parts of appropriation acts always ran the risk of stepping on too many toes. Ignoring the political realities led the Nixon administration in the 1970s to unwise use of the tool and resulted in a statutory check on the practice in the 1974 Impoundment Control Act through which Congress reestablished its authority to force the spending of funds it appropriates.

Like Diogenes, we continue the search for honest men and women in government to handle our funds. We threaten them with picking up their warranty bonds, suing them for losses, and imprisoning them for embezzlement. Yet we know that dozens of such controls can never be a substitute for generating in public officials an ethical sense that public spending is a public trust.

KEY CONCEPTS

home base criterion
preauditing the department
earmarking
permanent appropriations
borrowing authority
contract authority
legislative budget
omnibus appropriation act

Legislative Reorganization Act of 1970
Congressional Budget and
    Impoundment Control Act
    of 1974
program-by-program cut
percentage across-the-board cut
restrictive riders
lump sum appropriations

DISCUSSION QUESTIONS

1. How does politics affect the appropriations process? What other factors add to the complexity of the process?

2. Since 1970, reforms have been introduced to help strengthen the role of Congress in the federal appropriations process. Identify the major reforms and assess their impact. What benefits have occurred? For what reasons might one argue that the impact has been limited?

3. For what reasons would a legislature choose to make line-item appropriations rather than lump sum appropriations?

4. Discuss the process by which the Treasury Department controls the spending of appropriated money. What are the purposes of these controls? How effective do you think they are?

5. Briefly trace the history of impoundment powers, emphasizing the experience of President Nixon. Do you think the 1974 Impoundment Control Act has placed too many restrictions on presidential powers?

Notes

1. No one ever said it better than C. C. Maxey, "A Plea for the Politician," *Western Political Quarterly* (Sept. 1948) 1:272–279.

2. How it worked with the military some time back was related by Elias Huzar, *The Purse and the Sword* (Ithaca, N.Y.: Cornell University Press, 1950).

3. No one ever portrayed this better than Maxwell Anderson in his insightful drama, *Both Your Houses* (1933).

4. The 1977 round of the Carter water fight with Congress can be found in the *Congressional Quarterly Almanac, 1977* (Washington, D.C.: Congressional Quarterly, 1978) 33:650–659.

5. *Congressional Quarterly Weekly Report* (Aug. 12, 1978) 36:2150.

6. Dramatically evidenced in the formative years of the Budget Bureau's impounding of funds to control unwanted projects in World War II. Senators' home state interests had been stepped on by the impoundings, but the bureau found a powerful ally in the collective judgment of the House Appropriations Committee. See this author's *Impounding of Funds by the Bureau of the Budget* (ICP case series #28) (University, Ala.: University of Alabama Press, 1955). Hereafter cited as *Impounding of Funds.*

7. Still one of our favorite examples of the preauditing syndrome is the colloquy many years ago between Democratic Representative Preston of Georgia and Mr. Marvel, a spokesman for a State Department office, the International Claims Commission. "What about this figure here of $60,930 for six people in the Office of the Commissioners? What are their salaries?" When it developed that three of the six were secretaries, each getting over $5,000 per annum (vintage 1952, remember), the congressman pressed on: "What are these people, female secretaries?" Marvel answered, "Female secretaries." The congressman then let loose on paying such high salaries to secretaries. There was no concern about foreign affairs versus national defense versus welfare; no concern about agency efficiency or cost/benefit — simply this overweening drive for Congress to call the shots on tiny details of how an agency spends its money. The exchange can be found in U.S. House Appropriations Committee, *Hearings on the Department of State Appropriations for 1953* (82d Congress, 2d session) (Washington, D.C.: Government Printing Office, 1952), part 1:173.

8. See Aaron Wildavsky, *The Politics of the Budgetary Process* (Boston: Little, Brown, 1964), pp. 47–48.

9. In his perceptive and carefully documented behavioral study of the appropriations committees, Richard Fenno provides abundant information on the small group at work. He quotes one House Appropriations Committee member as saying, "This is one committee where you will find no partisan politics. We carry on the hearings and we mark up the bill and we compromise our differences. We bring a bill to the floor of the House each year with the unanimous approval of the committee members." (The allusions were to a subcommittee of House Appropriations.) *The Power of the Purse* (Boston: Little, Brown, 1966), p. 200 and ch. 5.

10. Consider the fact that from 1947 to 1962 the House followed the recommendations of

its Appropriations Committee 90 percent of the time. See Fenno, *The Power of the Purse*, p. 450.

11. We follow here the helpful discussion in U.S. Senate Committee on Government Operations, *Improving Congressional Control over the Budget — A Compendium of Materials* (committee print, 93d Cong., 1st sess.) (Washington, D.C.: Government Printing Office, 1973), pp. 181–182. (Hereafter cited as *Improving Congressional Control.*)

12. Allen Schick, "Backdoor Spending Authority," in *Improving Congressional Control*, p. 295.

13. P.L. 79-601; 60 Stat. 24, section 138. The history of the 1946 experiment has been recounted by Louis Fisher in "Experience with a Legislative Budget, 1947–1949," *Improving Congressional Control*, pp. 249–251.

14. See Dalmas Nelson, "The Omnibus Appropriations Act of 1950," *Journal of Politics* (May 1953) 15:274–288. This 1950 statute was also memorable in confirming the Bureau of the Budget's impounding of funds and in authorizing President Truman to use his impounding authority to cut spending below the total appropriated in the act.

15. P.L. 91-510; 84 Stat. 1140 at 1167ff.

16. Statement before the Joint Study Committee on Budget Control (Mar. 7, 1973), in *Improving Congressional Control*, p. 215.

17. Budget expert Allen Schick's judgment three years after the statute was that the price-tagging feature had not made a substantive difference. Telephone conversation, Aug. 1973.

18. See *Improving Congressional Control*, p. 176.

19. He calls it radical incrementalism. Reprinted in *Improving Congressional Control*, pp. 422–473, especially pp. 455–456.

20. Charles L. Schultze, et al., *Setting National Priorities* (Washington, D.C.: Brookings Institution, 1972).

21. P.L. 93-344 of July 12, 1974; 88 Stat. 297.

22. See *Improving Congressional Control* and House Report 93-688 and Senate Report 93-579.

23. Two dissenters on the Senate Budget Committee, James Buckley and James McClure, took sharp issue with the Keynesian foundations of the analysis: "Much of the advice we have seen presented to the Budget Committee in the last two years unfortunately is based on the economic theory generated by Lord Keynes 40 years ago. [We have had better theories validated since then.] But this has not deterred the old-style theoreticians from wasting our time and the Nation's resources in an attempt to prove the validity of the Keynesian theory. . . . In summary, the economic theory which underpins the Committee's recommendation has little to recommend it." Senate Report 94-1204, pp. 63–64.

24. It's fascinating to read, for example, the colloquy between two very bright people, the laissez-faire senator from New York, James Buckley, and the Keynesian staff director of the CBO, Dr. Alice Rivlin, on August 26, 1976, during the Senate Budget Committee hearings on the *Second Concurrent Resolution on the Budget, FY 1977* (Senate Report 94–1204), pp. 16–17.

25. *Congressional Quarterly Weekly Report* (Sept. 11, 1976) 34:2455.

26. Eileen Shanahan, "The Budget Watchdogs are Watching," *New York Times* (Oct. 19, 1975), sec. 4.

27. Senate Budget Committee, *Second Concurrent Resolution on the Budget, FY 1977*, pp. 4–5, 8. The claims are a bit excessive, of course. They seem to leave no room for any job creation by the private economy. And they raise the question, then, of who must share in the blame when unemployment shot back up to 8 percent in the fall of 1976.

28. *Congressional Quarterly Weekly Report* (Sept. 16, 1978) 36:2455–56; and (Sept. 23, 1978) 36:2584–85.

29. Forgive the repetition, but *Both Your Houses* said this so well.

30. See Dale E. Carter, "The Governor and the Budget: The Case of Mental Hygiene," in Richard J. Stillman, *Public Administration: Concepts and Cases* (Boston: Houghton Mifflin, 1976), pp. 256–263.

31. Wildavsky, *Politics of the Budgetary Process,* pp. 111–123.

32. See the *U.S. Budget in Brief. 1979* (Washington, D.C.: Government Printing Office, 1978), p. 71, for visual portrayal of the problem.

33. 33 Stat. 1257 and 34 Stat. 48; 31 USC 665.

34. As the troika of federal financial management (Treasury, Budget Bureau, and GAO) said in *Fifteen Years of Progress,* "Today, managerial accounting is the goal. This means fashioning accounting systems to develop accrual, cost and fund information that meets the operating needs of responsible officials at the various levels of management." Joint Financial Management Improvement Program (Washington, D.C.: Government Printing Office, 1963), p. 19.

35. See *Fifteen Years of Progress.*

36. P.L. 81-946; 64 Stat. 832.

37. See Wysong, "Accounting Systems in the Civil Agencies: Could They Serve Management Better?" *General Accounting Office Review* (Winter 1973), pp. 52–58.

38. Recounted by Professor Joseph Cooper in the *Congressional Record* (Mar. 8, 1973) 119:7065. We disagree with the conclusions which Professor Cooper draws from the events.

39. See 33 Stat. 1257 and 34 Stat. 48; 31 USC 665.

40. 47 Stat. 382 and 48 Stat. 8.

41. 64 Stat. 595.

42. 60 Stat. 24.

43. P.L. 91-224; 84 Stat. 114.

44. P.L. 379; 84 Stat. 799.

45. Senate Document 93-4, pp. 3–5.

46. See the author's *Impounding of Funds.*

47. The story has been effectively told by Louis Fisher, "The Politics of Impounded Funds," *Administrative Science Quarterly* (Sept. 1970) 15:361–377.

48. Senate Judiciary Committee, *Hearings on Executive Impoundment of Appropriated Funds* (92d Congress, 1st Session) (Washington, D.C.: Government Printing Office, 1971).

49. P.L. 92-599.

50. See, for example, the opinion of the Eighth Circuit Court in *State Highway Commission* v. *Volpe,* 479 F. 2d 1099 (Apr. 2, 1973), requiring the release of impounded federal highway funds.

51. *Train* v. *City of New York,* 95 S.Ct. 839 (1975); 420 U.S. 35 (1975).

52. Congressional reaction to the reports that were filed during 1974 can be found in the hearings of the Senate Appropriations Committee on *Budget Rescissions and Deferrals, 1975* (94th Cong.); and in the Senate Budget Committee's report, *Analysis of Executive Impoundment Reports* (committee print, 94th Cong., 1st Sess.) (Washington, D.C.: Government Printing Office, 1975).

53. For a detailed picture of Ford's rescissions and deferrals, and the subsequent actions of Congress in forcing the release of $3.6 billion of the $12 billion impounded, see House Document 94-524.

54. Director, Office of Management and Budget, *Cumulative Report on Rescissions and Deferrals, April 1978* (H. Doc. 95-319), pp. 2–3.

55. For two graphic portrayals, see Robert Heilbroner, *In the Name of Profit* (New York: Warner Books, 1973), pp. 59–95; and Zeigler and Olexa, "The Energy Issue: Oil and the Emergency Energy Act of 1973–74," in Robert L. Peabody, *Cases in American Politics* (New York: Praeger, 1976), pp. 159–205.

Part IV
PERSONNEL ADMINISTRATION

Chapter 15
Patronage, Merit, or Muscle?

PERSONNEL ADMINISTRATION:
A TRIANGULAR TUG OF WAR

Chapter 13 suggested in monetary terms what a big enterprise government has become. Now let us look at it in human terms, government as the giant employer in America (in 1978):

 2.8 million federal civilian workers

 3.5 million state employees

 9.2 million local government and school employees

15.5 million total government employees*

They constitute 15 percent of our entire labor force. Finding, hiring, and motivating them are the tasks of public management. Test design, job ranking, salary surveys, and performance rating are all complicated aspects of it. But the dramatic aspects of personnel administration lie elsewhere, chiefly in the tug-of-war that continually bedevils personnel administration. It is a three-way pull involving: (a) elected officials and party people, who want a responsive bureaucracy, secured through political appointments (patronage); (b) administrators,

---

* Between 1950 and 1977, public employment rose 140 percent, while private sector employment was rising by 55 percent. The federal sector grew by 35 percent, and the state and local sector rose by 200 percent.

who want people of talent, not party hacks, on their staff (the merit system advocates); and (c) public employees, who are turning increasingly to unions to protect their interests vis-à-vis management (through collective bargaining).

Put yourself in the middle of that tug-of-war: What kind of a personnel operation are you going to have when every move has to be balanced against the demands of the White House Personnel Office (WHPO) for more jobs, the demands of your division chiefs for people of ability, and the demands of the union for a straight seniority ladder and promotion from within? We begin with the political dimension.

Political Claims on the Civil Service[1]

One of the chief musclemen of the Nixon administration, Fred Malek, put the issue bluntly:

> In our constitutional form of Government, the Executive Branch is, and always will be, a political institution. This is not to say that the application of good management practices, sound policy formulations, and the highest caliber of program implementation are not of vital importance. The best politics is still good Government. BUT YOU CANNOT ACHIEVE MANAGEMENT, POLICY OR PROGRAM CONTROL UNLESS YOU HAVE ESTABLISHED POLITICAL CONTROL. The record is quite replete with instances of the failures of program, policy and management goals because of sabotage by employees of the Executive Branch who engage in the frustration of those efforts because of their political persuasion and their loyalty to the majority party of Congress rather than the executive that supervises them. And yet, in their own eyes, they are sincere and loyal to their Government [emphasis in original].[2]

From Washington's day to the present, presidents have counted on political appointments as their best means of capturing the loyalty of the executive branch and turning it promptly in the direction of the administration's goals. Patronage meant *responsiveness.* The first president laid down the principle:

> I shall not, whilst I have the honor to administer the government, bring a man into any office, of consequence knowingly, *whose political tenets are adverse* to the measures which the general government are pursuing; for this, in my opinion would be a sort of political suicide; that it would embarrass its movements is most certain. But of two men equally well affected to the true interests of their country, of equal abilities and equally disposed to lend their support, it is the part of prudence to give a preference to him, against whom the least clamour can be excited; for such a one my inquiries have been made and are still making; how far I shall succeed is at this moment problematical [emphasis added].[3]

Washington's proffer of the post of secretary of state to anti-Federalist Patrick Henry indicated that some other uses of patronage may have to be balanced with loyalty and responsiveness — co-opting a potential source of trouble by bringing him aboard ("can't lick 'em, join 'em," as we said in Chapter 8). Henry declined the offer, which some, including Secretary of State Jefferson, thought was insincere on Washington's part to begin with.[4]

Coalition building has been one of patronage's most important purposes. For example, groups in the body politic may be brought into a political coalition through judicious distribution of jobs to representatives of such groups: maintaining a Catholic-Jewish-Protestant balance on the court of appeals, appointing a black woman as urban affairs secretary, naming persons of Greek and Japanese descent to the alcohol board of control, and having a prominent attorney from the Italian community on the board of regents. Such appointments not only woo group support at future elections but may also generate smoother compliance with agency demands. ("We'll go along — one of our boys is running the show.")

Some have pointed to patronage as a useful lever in dealing with the legislature. "Congressman, your law partner gets the judgeship if we have your vote for strip-mining controls" seems pretty crass; but on occasion a government post may have greater exchange value than the appointee's intrinsic merit in the post.

Government jobs constitute other kinds of political currency, such as *payoffs for faithful service* during election time. The appointment of Jimmy Carter's principal campaign aides from the 1976 election to major posts in the White House, Justice Department, and OMB followed a time-honored practice.

Another time-honored but not honorable practice that developed in patronage systems was the collection of *political tithing* from the appointees to office. Local parties often came to rely on monthly assessments of 1 or 2 percent on patronage holders' salaries to keep party headquarters open and build a kitty for the next election.

The hoary argument for patronage always was its contribution to governmental efficiency: the fresh viewpoint, appointments without tenure to keep the civil servant on the ball, motivation to do a good job in order to get my boss reelected (and me reappointed!). Andrew Jackson's was the classic statement:

> The duties of all public officers are, or at least admit of being made, so plain and simple that men of intelligence may readily qualify themselves for their performance; and I cannot but believe that more is lost by the long, long continuance of men in office than is generally to be gained by their experience. I submit, therefore, to your consideration whether the efficiency of the Government would not be promoted and official industry and integrity better secured by a general extension of the law which limits appointments to four years.

> In a country where offices are created solely for the benefit of the people, no one man has any more intrinsic right to official station than another. Offices were not established to give support to particular men at the public expense. No individual wrong is, therefore, done by removal, since neither appointment to nor continuance in office is a matter of right. The incumbent became an officer with a view to public benefits, and when these require his removal they are not to be sacrificed to private interests. It is the people, and they alone, who have the right to complain when a bad officer is substituted for a good one. He who is removed has the same means of obtaining a living that are enjoyed by the millions who never held office. The proposed limitation would destroy the idea of property now so generally connected with official station,

and although individual distress may be sometimes produced, it would, by promoting that rotation which constitutes a leading principle in the republican creed, give healthful action to the system.[5]

From our point of view, the argument for patronage that makes the best sense is the first one. In order to turn the government in new directions, an administration needs to be able to bring its partisans into policymaking offices. Washington needed Alexander Hamilton in the Treasury to formulate a Federalist political economy; Andrew Johnson did not need Edwin M. Stanton as secretary of war to frustrate moderate reconstruction of the South; FDR needed a "Ma Perkins" as labor secretary to help mother a New Deal for the working class; and Jack Kennedy needed a free hand in sending Adlai Stevenson to the United Nations (although Kennedy royally misused him there) and Chester Bowles to India. Somehow all of these political appointments (except Stanton's) helped presidents immeasurably in setting the tone of their terms in office.

The Case Against Patronage

Building coalitions or multiplying enemies?   Anyone who has seen ten applications on the state party chairman's desk, all seeking the same post with a new state administration, can well understand the truth of the statement that "Every political appointment brings one friend and nine enemies."

The very nature of patronage appointment compounds the frustration of the nine disappointed office seekers. With patronage, influence counts heavily, and there are no objective measures like tests to indicate why one person succeeded and the others lost out. Embittered, they can only conclude that they just don't count.

Big demands and short memories   A patronage dispenser hopes that his appointees and the groups they represent will show some signs of gratitude beyond the first month on the payroll. But human nature, shifting alliances, and short memories being what they are, the patronage dispenser may soon find that loyalty and a sense of obligation are a will-o'-the-wisp.

Efficient hacks?   Patronage may not be synonymous with hackery, but it almost always entails slipshod recruitment. Inevitably, whom you know counts far more than what you know in landing a plum. That is a poor way to run a destroyer, a computer, a hospital, or an urban redevelopment office in this day and age.

Patronage is antiefficiency in another sense as well. It portends rather widespread removal of people already trained in their jobs. If, for example, it takes a year and a half to train a new crew of assistant attorneys general, patronage has brought about inefficiency, not efficiency, in a state's legal department when the newcomers replace the old.

One chortles at the efficiency claims of patronage in watching what goes on during a change of state administrations. How ludicrous it is to see party hacks begin to eye the post of state planner, held by a superbly trained holdover from the previous administration. (It reminds one of the egalitarian Jacksonian spirit in William Jennings Bryan's statement to Senator Carter Glass after the senator's exhausting experience in writing the Federal Reserve Act: "Why Senator, anyone can write a banking act.")

Patronage and Gresham's Law   The nearly inevitable result of bringing the political appointee into professional operations of government is to drive away the qualified employees. The whole tone of the agency changes; hopes for a career are dashed when political pull is substituted for competence in filling top jobs; and the hacks don't even talk your language. As case in point, the author recalls one of the few patronage appointees in his old agency, the Library of Congress. This man ran the football pool, sold Irish sweepstake tickets, and operated a numbers racket. On being refused a bet one day, he said, "I see you plan to work for the rest of your life."

Corruption in government   Fairly or unfairly, in the American mind patronage has come to be regarded as the twin of corruption, if not the mother. The stereotype is of course unfair, given the instances of corruption within the permanent civil service as well.

But there is no question that the roots of corruption find rich soil in patronage systems. Patronage employees' salaries are fair game for political dues; employees may be drafted on agency time to help with campaign chores; and since favoritism got them their jobs, political appointees may play favorites in dealing with their clientele.

During the 1950s the state government of Massachusetts became riddled with corruption, involving an ex-governor, a half-dozen legislative leaders, and more than a dozen agency officials (all told, indictments were returned against fifty-two individuals and fifteen corporations). The report of the blue-ribbon Massachusetts Crime Commission, created in 1962 to clean out the stables, had some trenchant things to say about patronage and corruption:

> There is a direct connection between corruption in government at state levels and the presence of poor morale and political influences in the classified civil service system. Employees in a department or division with poor morale knowing of corrupt activities often look the other way to avoid involvement. Political influences not only create poor morale; they afford means of circumventing or using loopholes in the civil service laws to place persons amenable to corrupt activities in positions in which opposition to corruption would otherwise be encountered.

> Poor morale and decay in the civil service system have been due to excessive patronage, political interference and deficiences in the system itself, which should have been remedied long ago. The primary cause has been the attitude of legislators and influ-

> ential officials who have protected and increased patronage in defiance of the principles of civil service and the best interests of the state.
>
> The Governor's office has customarily made substantial patronage demands.
>
> The Legislature has passed statutes freezing employees into position.
>
> Examinations have been rigged for favored candidates, and provisional "temporary appointments" for long periods have been used to reward the faithful.
>
> All of these practices depress the morale of the civil service. Some of them afford the opportunities needed by corrupt officials to surround themselves with persons who will not interfere with improper actions.[6]

Against these dangers, proven real from the Grant administration to the present, patronage defenders are still heard, unaware of, or unimpressed by, the voices of history. But maybe they will be forced to listen to a new voice that entered the debate in 1976, the Supreme Court of the United States. In a rather dramatic development growing out of the patronage dismissals of some Republican holdovers in the sheriff's office in Cook County, Illinois, the Supreme Court held that dismissals of civil servants from non-policy-making positions because of their political affiliations deprived them of their rights of belief and association protected against state encroachment by the First and Fourteenth Amendments. In those lower-level positions, the Court was now holding patronage removal to be unconstitutional.[7]

In the governing opinion of the deeply divided Court (3-2-3), Justice William J. Brennan, Jr., rejected the notion that patronage promotes efficiency in government. Instead, Justice Brennan held that trained people are replaced by the untrained, whose primary claim to office was "party service, not job capability." There are ample means under merit systems, Brennan observed, to motivate and discipline inefficient workers without the wholesale encroachment on First Amendment rights that occurs under patronage removals because incumbent civil servants have not paid homage to the victorious political party.

The case of *Elrod* v. *Burns* seemed to be saying that "To the victor belong the spoils, but not while this Court sits!"

But what about the merit system that Justice Brennan had so much regard for? What is it, and does it deserve his kind of confidence?

THE MERIT SYSTEM[8]

Know-how Rather than Pull

The philosophy of merit in public personnel administration says that personnel decisions ought to be based on what applicants and employees know, not whom they know.

Its basic premises are these: (a) tasks to be performed and abilities to perform them can be rationally determined and compared; (b) the public interest and an agency's interest are better promoted by enlarging, rather than narrowing, the field of applicants; and (c) the public interest and the agency's interest are better served by the rising experience of a *tenured* civil service than by rotation in office.

Four features almost universally characterize merit systems:

competitive examinations at entry for most jobs (aiming at the twin objectives of demonstrated ability and equality of opportunity)

tenure (or permanent appointments) for able employees and removal only for cause (inefficiency, malfeasance, etc.), not for politics' sake

willingness of civil servants to serve administrations of either political party (an essential concomitant of the tenure principle; if civil servants are to be permanent, they must be loyal to whichever party is in power)

protection against political exploitation such as the performance of mandatory political chores, compulsory payment of political dues, etc.[9]

The merit system contemplates, then, public personnel management that bases personnel decisions — from appointment through promotion to dismissal — on demonstrated ability and seeks to enhance the quality of the public service by building careers open to the talented. In a sense, the fundamental spirit of the merit system was expressed long ago in ancient Islam: "A ruler who appoints any man to an office when there is in his dominions another man better qualified for it, sins against God and against the state."

Laments About the Merit System

The first lament was noted at the outset of this chapter: the feeling that permanent civil servants are *not responsive* to the policies of a new administration. The civil servants in the Departments of Agriculture, Commerce, Transportation, and so on have operated the programs of those departments for years. In expertise, they can outgun any new political appointees who take over the assistant secretary posts. How, then, does one begin turning those old-line employees away from the policies they have helped shape over the last eight or more years around to the new philosophies of the incoming administration?

There is the even more familiar complaint that civil servants *won't work at all* and you can't fire them. Secure against dismissal, they begin to view their posts as personal preserves and feel that their performance does not matter.[10]

Like most generalizations, this one describes some bureaucrats we've all known and slanders many others. It is an unrecognizable portrait of government employees like Lewis and Clark and their teams who mapped the Northwest; of the engineers of the Panama Canal; of the Public Health Service teams who, with others, eliminated smallpox and polio as significant health threats; of the employees of the U.S. Civil Service Commission who helped to register a million new blacks following the Voting Rights Act of 1965; or of the men and women of the Park and Forest Services and the Bureau of Land Management who bring modern resource management to public lands, among many others who make their careers in government.

The stereotype is false in another sense. Public personnel administration has a range of motivators (from incentive awards through performance ratings to discipline) to keep the tenured civil servant from petrifying before retirement. To correct an old misconception that government workers don't get fired—some seventeen thousand were fired by the federal government in 1976 alone.

The critics then ask if *qualifications are measurable.* How valid are personnel tests? Does one need to test those who already have shown their stuff (acquired a college degree, passed the bar, or finished a medical residency)? "Q.E.D., she must be qualified."

But some engineers (and some lawyers, nurses, and so on) are better than others. Is a letter of endorsement from a precinct captain or state senator a rational basis on which to decide which of five engineers is better than the others? Or would it be better to undertake a careful review of training and experience in similar lines of work?

As a final lament, merit systems clearly violate an important phase of Parkinson's Law: *people make work for each other.* As soon as you pull personnel functions away from the line agencies into a centralized merit system, the personnel technicians become rabbits and multiply. Recruiters have to be classified and the classifiers have to be rated; the raters have to be tested and the tests have to be validated; the test experts have to be counseled and the counselors have to have incentive awards. Meanwhile, someone is supposed to be performing the major functions for which the agency was established.

"Furthermore, we line operators know the kind of people who can do our work a whole lot better than those rabbits from personnel. They don't talk our language, they waste our time, and they strangle us in forms and regulations. Rule of Three? Humbug! That means hire whom they want and don't hire whom we want." In some such fashion, the merit system and personnel people become shuttlecocks in the battle between line and staff.

Pitted against the claimed benefits of competitive recruitment, systematic selection, and the mounting proficiency of a career service under the merit system are these objections about unresponsiveness and inefficiency, tests that claim too much, irremovability, empire building, and interference.

Federal Adoption of the Merit System[11]

Historically, the debate was not a standoff. The corruption of the Grant administration (1869–1876), the exploitation of civil servants in raising campaign funds during the 1870s, and the assassination of President James A. Garfield in 1881 by a frustrated patronage seeker moved personnel reform onto the national agenda and led to the passage in 1883 of the Pendleton Act, creating a federal merit system. For just over a decade, events moved like a riptide (see Table 15.1).

What emerged was a Civil Service Act sponsored by an Ohio Democrat, George H. Pendleton, which passed primarily with Republican votes (recall that Republicans had controlled the federal bureaucracy since 1861 and would benefit from having all of their employees now covered under the new merit system).

Two excerpts from the *Congressional Record* of December 1882 give something of the hopes and the partisan forebodings that surrounded the bill:

SENATOR PENDLETON: . . . This subject, in all its ramifications, was submitted to the people of the United States at the fall elections, and they have spoken in no low or uncertain tone. . . . I do say that the civil service is inefficient; that it is expensive; that it is extravagant; that it is in many cases and in some sense corrupt; that it has welded the whole body of its employees into a great political machine; that it has converted them into an army of officers and men, veterans in political warfare, disciplined and trained, whose salaries, whose time, whose exertions at least twice within a very short period in the history of our country have robbed the people of the fair results of Presidential elections.

Mr. Jefferson was right. The experience of eighty years has shown it. The man best fitted should be the man placed in office, especially if the appointment is made by the servants of the people. It is as true as truth can be that fidelity, capacity, honesty are essential elements of fitness, and that the man who is most capable and most faithful and most honest is the man who is the most fit, and he should be appointed to office. . . .

TABLE 15.1   THE CHRONOLOGY OF REFORM, 1869–1883

1869–76	Corruption of the Grant administration
1871–73	Grant's Civil Service Commission
1876	Law prohibiting political assessments on lower-grade federal officers (widely violated in the 1878 election year)
1877	New York Civil Service Reform Association formed
1877	President Hayes's executive order barring federal officers from political activity (a Hatch Act forerunner)
1877–80	Hayes's cleanup of the New York Customs Bureau and Post Office
1880	Introduction of a civil service bill by Ohio Democratic Senator George Pendleton
1881	National Civil Service Reform League organized
1881	President Garfield's assassination by Charles Guiteau, a disappointed office seeker
1882	Republican setbacks in the congressional elections; they then moved quickly in the lame-duck session to protect their federal officeholders
1883	Passage of the Pendleton Act establishing a federal merit system and the U.S. Civil Service Commission
1883	Establishment of the New York State Civil Service Commission

[Under the bill] . . . the President shall, with the concurrence of the best advice which he can obtain, form a plan, a scheme of examination free for all, open to all, which shall secure the very best talent and the very best capacity attainable for the civil offices of the Government. The method adopted in the bill is by competitive examination.

SENATOR JONAS: . . . I deal with this bill in good faith, Mr. President. I am not voting against it as a politician or a party man. I beleive that the civil service of this country is to a large extent incompetent, if not corrupt, and I will favor any measure which proposes an examination into the competency and character of the persons who fill the positions under it. But this is to be denied to us. All of the people who are in office are to remain. They are to constitute a privileged class, if they are not to be submitted to the same competition or the same examination which is proposed for candidates for appointment. Well, sir, I do not believe that the people wish this sort of civil service reform. . . . By the passage of this bill we are creating the people who now hold the offices of this country into a permanent organization of officers into whose sacred precincts new blood may intrude only when vacancies occur and new candidates are presented for examination.

Following the Senate adoption, Senator Brown, a Democrat, proposed that the title of the bill be amended:

I think the title ought to conform to some extent to the body of the bill. I move to strike out the words, "A bill to regulate and improve the civil service of the United States" and insert the words "A bill to perpetuate in office the Republicans who now control the patronage of the government" (Laughter).[12]

The tarnished spoilsman from New York, Chester A. Arthur, then president of the United States, signed the Pendleton Act into law on January 16, 1883.[13]

The statute set up a three-person bipartisan U.S. Civil Service Commission, who would serve at the pleasure of the president.* Its mission was threefold: to conduct investigations, promulgate needed personnel rules, and prepare and administer examinations for federal job applicants.

The Pendleton Act covered only about 10 percent of the federal civil service at the time. But the president was given authority to extend the "classified list" (those positions subject to examination) by executive order.

In the strongest language, the Pendleton Act prohibited any coercion of federal civil servants either to make political contributions or to serve in politics. The law forbade any solicitation for political purposes of officers or employees of any branch of the government by the officers or employees of any branch, or political solicitation by any private persons on government premises. Moreover, the law banned all money exchanges for political purposes between federal officers (including congressmen) and clerks. The act said nothing about off-the-job political rights of civil servants (those were deprived later in the Hatch Acts of 1939 and 1940); rather, it placed a shield around government employees in their job-related setting and declared them off limits to politicians. It is that

---

* A 1956 amendment added six-year terms but didn't change the fact that the commissioners are subject to the will of the president.

part of the statute that has always suggested to this observer that its drafters sought political neutrals on the job rather than political eunuchs off the job. The later Hatch Act eliminated this important distinction.

There was a strange omission in the law; there was no provision that employees with tenure could be removed only for cause. A thirty-year wait transpired before that gap was filled by the Lloyd–La Follette Act of 1912.

Armed with the Pendleton Act, the Civil Service Commission began its work with a veritable minefield before it from then until now, involving inadequate funds, presidents who would bend the commission's back (and ethics) with their demands for patronage, interagency rivalry (especially with the Bureau of Efficiency during the 1920s and the OMB in later years), and the heavy burdens of staffing the government during times of war.

At major junctures, Congress and the presidents have intervened with new mandates or restrictions for the Civil Service Commission to carry out (see Table 15.2).

Some major themes that emerge from the legal roster given in Table 15.2 include: (a) the increasing professionalization of the merit system (job classification, training, incentive awards); (b) the impact of politics (Hatch Acts and Truman's loyalty-security program); (c) the emergence of unions as a major force in personnel administration; (d) the development of important fringe benefits (health care, vacations, insurance, and retirement); and (e) the requirement that the federal merit system accept a twin goal of equal employment opportunity.

The expansion of the merit system has fulfilled Franklin Roosevelt's famous phrase "upward, outward and downward," with 92 percent of all federal employees under the merit system by the late 1970s (see Table 15.3).

Thus, the domain of patronage has significantly shriveled over time. The sound and fury of reform may have been supplied by reformers like Carl Schurz, George Curtis, Senator George Pendleton, and Teddy Roosevelt, but the big guns against patronage have been the fundamental changes in the political processes of the nation: the increasing complexity of governmental services (what ward heeler ever wrote a clean air regulation?); a growing demand for knowledge in civil servants, not influence; the rising costs of political campaigns that reduced political tithing collected from officeholders to chicken feed; and the ability of some political parties to recruit workers through ideological and psychological rewards rather than through the promise of jobs. Some of the forces that have eroded patronage include the highly persuasive federal requirement that states must use merit systems if they want grants-in-aid for health, welfare, and education; the federalizing of welfare programs, which has undermined the local political boss;[15] the increasing competition for workers posed by private business, forcing governments to improve their climate of work; and the scandals that have so frequently erupted in patronage systems.[16]

TABLE 15.2   MAJOR DEVELOPMENTS IN FEDERAL PERSONNEL LAW

1883	Pendleton Act creating the federal merit system
1912	Lloyd–La Follette Act granting federal postal employees the right to join employee organizations and stating that dismissals could be made only if they promoted the good of the service (thus, for cause only)
1923	Classification Act, prescribing for the ranking of jobs by qualifications, duties, and level of responsibility
1938	FDR's Executive Order 7916 requiring all federal agencies to set up personnel offices
1939	Social Security Act amendment requiring that state agencies handling federal grants be placed under merit systems (for many states the beginning of their merit systems)
1939–40	The Hatch Acts, barring federal and state employees hired under federal grants from off-the-job partisan political activity[14]
1944	The Veterans Preference Act
1947	Truman's Executive Order 9380 delineating the responsibilities of the Civil Service Commission and delegating significant responsibilities for personnel management to the respective agencies
1947	Truman's Executive Order 9847 instituting the federal government's loyalty-security program
1949	Classification Act
1950	Performance Rating Act
1953	Eisenhower administration's creation of schedule C for political appointees
1954	Incentive Awards Act
1954	Group Life Insurance Act
1957	Health Benefits Act

Taking the Merit Out of Merit Systems?

While these very powerful forces were undermining patronage as a way of staffing government, merit systems also experienced troubles, and a rising number of critics in some places.

In the early 1970s, E. S. Savas and S. G. Ginsburg took a close look at New York City's civil service with some four hundred thousand employees and found it to be a meritless system on many counts, including:

unvalidated examinations, which do not predict which applicants are likely to be proficient employees

long delays in filling jobs after exams have been given, with the result that high scorers take other jobs and the city ends up hiring the dregs

widespread exclusion of outsiders from competition for upper-level positions

automatic pay increases unrelated to performance

increasing union domination of merit system administration[17]

1958	Government Employees Training Act
1962	Salary Reform Act, committing federal pay to a level of comparability with the private sector
1962	Kennedy's Executive Order 10988 regularizing collective bargaining within the federal civil service and granting recognition for the first time to employee unions
1967	Johnson's Executive Order 11246 initiating affirmative action toward equal employment opportunity within the federal service
1967	Creation of the executive assignment system to provide staffing for the supergrades (GS-16 to GS-18)
1969	Nixon's Executive Order 11491, spelling out collective bargaining procedures and impasse resolution
1970	Reorganization Plan No. 2, expanding the personnel role of OMB (at the Civil Service Commission's expense)
1970	Intergovernmental Personnel Act, providing federal assistance for strengthening state and local merit systems
1970	Job Evaluation Policy Act, adopting the point system in federal position classification
1970	Federal Pay Comparability Act, bringing unions into an advisory role in establishing General Schedule (GS) salaries
1972	Equal Employment Opportunity Act, bringing federal and state governments under the requirements of the 1964 Civil Rights Act
1978	Carter's reorganization of the civil service, creating the Office of Personnel Management and the Merit Systems Protection Board in place of the U.S. Civil Service Commission, providing statutory provision for collective bargaining in the federal service, and so on

Chief among the critics are major officeholders at all levels of government who yearn for a freer hand in picking their deputies.

Merit systems, like virtue, spend much of their time on defense, as politicians and administrators probe for ways upward, outward, and downward to appoint and promote whom they want without regard to merit system procedures. Bernard Rosen has catalogued some of the techniques of personnel realpolitik:

> Tailoring a job description and job requirements to a particular candidate's experience; soliciting declinations in order to reach a favorite candidate; writing an overblown job description to raise the grade; establishing duties in the job description that will justify excepting the position from the competitive service even though the designated duties will not be performed; making temporary appointments to continuing positions so the appointees can acquire additional qualifying experience in hopes of achieving preferred status for permanent appointments; making temporary appointments to continuing positions in order to stay within the ceiling for permanent employees; using inadequate evaluation methods which may result in selections being made inadvertently from those not best qualified, or intentionally facilitating the selection of favorite candidates.[18]

TABLE 15.3   FEDERAL PERSONNEL STRUCTURE, 1976

Employed under merit		2,650,963	92%
In the "Competitive Service" (jurisdiction of the U.S. CSC)	1,749,660		
Under special agency merit systems (e.g., TVA, FBI)	901,303		
Employees excepted from the competitive system[a]		230,519	8%
Schedule A (not subject to examination)	75,000		
Schedule B (noncompetitive exams)	3,000		
Schedule C (policy-making and confidential posts)	1,000		
Noncareer Executive Assignments (NEA's)	580		
Foreign nationals outside the U.S.	65,800		
Veterans readjustment appointments	22,900		
Temporaries	62,239		
Total federal civilian employment		2,881,482	100%

Source: U.S. Civil Service Commission, *Federal Career Service at Your Service* (Washington, D.C.: Government Printing Office, 1977), pp. 3 and 6; and *Federal Civilian Manpower Statistics* (Washington, D.C.: Government Printing Office, November, 1976), p. 15 (adjusted).

[a] Relatively few of these are available for patronage.

But even these dodges do not begin to convey the contempt in which some administrations hold the merit system and the intensity of their efforts to subvert it. The volume that best tells that story is the fifteen-hundred-page final report of the House Post Office and Civil Service Committee on the *Violations and Abuses of Merit Principles in Federal Employment* by the Nixon administration.

Coming on the heels of eight Democratic years, the Nixon administration began its takeover of the government with the establishment of the White House Personnel Office, which instituted a "must" referral and tracking system to see that White House-approved people were moved into jobs quickly. That may have been fairly standard practice. But it hardly prepared anyone for the Machiavellian attack on the merit system that was undertaken by the second Nixon administration after the Watergate election of 1972.

Resignations of those previously appointed by Nixon were demanded en masse to make way for the White House insiders who had proved their toughness and loyalty to the Nixon ethic (although that seems like a contradiction in terms).

Fred Malek was then assigned to write a *Federal Political Personnel Manual*, sarcastically dedicated to the U.S. Civil Service Commission, instructing the new Nixon appointees on how to warp civil service rules, to purge an agency of unwanted employees and complete the takeover of lower and lower levels of the government.[19]

Here is a glimpse of Malek's advice on how to get rid of such employees:

Use a frontal assault. Call them in, tell them they are no longer wanted, and take their duties away ("There should be no witnesses in the room at the time").

Transfer the "employee victim" (Malek's phrase) to some godforsaken post, which will force that employee to resign instead.

Put him on the road away from his family, criss-crossing the country from hamlet to hamlet ("hopefully with the worst accommodations possible").[20]

Those techniques would begin to create vacancies, but what about replacements? Controlling that would require controlling the protector of the merit system, the U.S. Civil Service Commission.

The commission's chairman, Robert Hampton, went along with the demands made on him. In the subsequent investigation it was found that, among other things, he had made a political referral to the General Services Administration and had advised Nixon aides on how to decentralize political personnel management to the agencies in order to leave the WHPO free to handle high-level political clearances.[21] In addition, the commission was pink-tagging the files of White House nominees for speedy processing and hiring.

In the face of mounting complaints over the rape of the merit system, the Civil Service Commission undertook an investigation. On January 7, 1974, they recommended disciplinary action (from thirty-day suspensions through removal) against nineteen GSA personnel for their complicity in political referrals and other violations of civil service hiring procedures.[22]

There is some humor here. The ultimate body that would hear the appeals was the Civil Service Commission, all three of whom had written referral letters to GSA. The cases were dismissed "on technical grounds."[23]

The House subcommittee concluded that "these events paint a dim portrait of the personnel activities of both the Civil Service Commission and General Services Administration, leaving, in the final analysis, both agencies severely tarnished."[24] The subcommittee then went on to say:

[We believe] that the cumulative effect of improper use of personnel authorities and official misconduct documented in this report seriously damaged the fabric, if not the foundation, of the civil service merit system. [The] manipulation was an accepted practice by Executive departments and agencies, indeed aided and abetted by the Civil Service Commission.[25]

What was the Civil Service Commission's response to the charge of having itself participated in the Nixon administration's rape of the merit system? Guilty as charged. In the April 1976 issue of the *Civil Service Journal,* the commission published the findings of its own review team and then added its own mea culpa: ". . . there can be no question that things happened which should not have happened and that there were errors of omission as well as commission."[26]

The commission then committed itself to a wide range of reforms that its review team had recommended. Among them were: (a) ban any future referrals of applicants to agencies other than through the regular certification process; (b) scrutinize "unassembled examination" procedures (including a review of the candidates' application and supporting documents) that had been used for clearing pink-tagged individuals for appointment; and (c) develop a means to discover and correct political manipulations of the merit system as they occur "rather than depending almost entirely on after-the-fact reviews."[27]

It may be that this horrible sellout to the machinations of the Nixon administration constituted the nadir in the entire history of the U.S. Civil Service Commission.[28] Certainly the capitulation dramatized the conflicting roles (and resulting schizophrenia) that had been imposed on the commission — simultaneously to serve as the president's personnel arm and to function as protector of the merit system.[29]

To rectify the problem, the Carter administration decided that surgery was the answer to the role conflict.[30] With the support of the Ninety-fifth Congress, Carter then took scalpels in hand (Reorganization Plan No. 2 of 1978 and P.L. 95-454) to separate the ninety-five-year-old Civil Service Commission into (a) the Office of Personnel Management (OPM) to oversee recruiting, examining, job classification, pay, and the like, and (b) the Merit Systems Protection Board (MSPB) to investigate and prosecute political abuses of the merit system and to handle employee appeals. The OPM would be headed by a director and the MSPB by a three-member bipartisan board appointed for six years.

Other features of the Carter reform included the establishment of the Senior Executive Service (SES), the institution of incentive pay for mid-level and senior managers, a reduced burden of proof for firing unsatisfactory employees, and the codification of federal rules governing labor-management relations. (We will deal with each reform at the appropriate point hereafter.)

Now we need to turn to another force that is also making demands on public personnel administration — the unions.

COLLECTIVE BARGAINING IN THE PUBLIC SECTOR

At the beginning of this chapter, we spoke of a triangular tug of war for the control of public personnel administration. Having taken a look at the patronage and merit system advocates, we now turn to the third corner of the triangle, public employee unions. Their startling rise in membership during the 1960s, with increases of over 250 percent, while government employment was rising by only 70 percent, clearly matched the equal rights movement as the dominant new development in managing government employees.

In this section we are going to examine the public unions' meteoric rise, the issues posed by collective bargaining in the public sector, and some emerging patterns as we move from agency-dominated to bilateral management of personnel.

Public Unions Are Older than You Think[31]

Some of the earliest unions in the country, dating from the early nineteenth century, were organized at government installations, in particular at navy shipyards and army arsenals. In both cases, industrial workers were involved. By 1835, the first work stoppage by government employees was recorded at the Philadelphia Navy Yard to obtain a ten-hour day! Two things are worth noting about that protest: workers were being exploited by their government employer, and the strike was efficacious. In 1840, President Martin Van Buren lowered the hours ceiling for all federal employees to ten a day. It would be dropped to eight hours in 1888, with no loss of pay.

Under more pressure from Navy Yard employees, the Congress adopted the comparability principle in wage administration in 1861 in establishing the prevailing wage rate in vicinities surrounding naval yards as the criterion for navy workers' pay. (In 1962, one hundred years later, Congress adopted the comparability principle for the whole federal work force.)

New milestones followed, as indicated in Table 15.4. With significant beachheads thus established at federal, state, and municipal levels by 1961, the public unions put their organizers to work and within a decade occupied a significant share of the territory of public employment. By 1973, public unions and employee associations (the distinction between them having rapidly diminished during the 1970s) covered one third of all government employees in the country, whereas only a fourth of the employees in the private sector were unionized.

By 1977, 58 percent of all federal employees outside the U.S. Postal Service were represented by unions, and 88 percent of the postal workers, for a combined total of 1.8 million federal workers represented by recognized unions, or 66 percent of total civilian employment.[32] Some 670,000 are represented by the American Federation of Government Employees, the union with the largest percentage gain in numbers (362 percent) between 1960 and 1970 of all private sector and public unions. The second two big percentage gainers were also public unions: the teachers (AFT), with a 265 percent gain (embracing now more than 400,000);* and state, county, and municipal employees (AFSCME) with 112 percent. AFSCME reached the 700,000 mark of dues-paying members in 1973, with contracts representing 1 million public employees (out of 10 million employed by state and local governments).

Not only are the public unions growing, but in some instances they are also merging with former rivals. One begins to sense the clout, for example, of teachers in New York State in the merger of their teacher associations and

---

* It should also be noted that the National Education Association has 1.5 million members.

TABLE 15.4   MILESTONES IN PUBLIC SECTOR UNIONISM, 1889–1978

1889	The letter carriers and the postal clerks form national unions
1912	The Lloyd–La Follette Act grants federal postal employees the right to join unions
1916	The AFL, itself created in 1886, charters the American Federation of Teachers
1917	The AFL charters the National Federation of Federal Employees (NFFE), an unusual AFL union at that time because of no craft restriction
1924	Kiess Act accepts collective bargaining over wages and other matters at the Government Printing Office
1931	The NFFE leaves the AFL, the latter then chartering a rival public union, the American Federation of Government Employees (AFGE) for federal workers
1936	The AFL charters the American Federation of State, County and Municipal Employees (AFSCME)
1958	Mayor Robert Wagner of New York City grants a measure of collective bargaining to city employees
1959	Wisconsin becomes the first state to recognize the right of state employees to organize and bargain collectively
1961	President Kennedy issues Executive Order 10988 providing for agency recognition of unions and setting up bilateral collective bargaining procedures
1969	President Nixon's Executive Order 11491 sets up a multilateral collective bargaining system
1978	The principles of Executive Order 11491 are codified in law as Title VII of Carter's civil service reorganization, P.L. 95-454

unions, with a resulting membership of 200,000. (If that combined teachers union were able to produce an almost monolithic bloc vote, note how close it would come to Jimmy Carter's slim margin of 276,000 votes in New York in 1976.)

Some of the reasons underlying this rapid growth of unionized public employees seem clear: more rapidly rising wages in the unionized private sector than enjoyed by government workers in the early 1960s;* richer private fringe benefits, especially in medical and dental care; and a desire for a much stronger voice in such matters as promotion, layoffs, and grievances than employees enjoyed under monocratic agency management.

Have Membership, Will Strike!

The rise in public service union membership was matched by a rising union militancy. Although strikes by government employees were prohibited by the federal government and all the states, the number of strikes by public employees rose from 15 in 1958 to 142 in 1966 and to 259 in 1968. In the latter year, the strikes involved 202,000 workers and caused the loss of a half-million man-days.

* Consider, for example, that New York City's sanitation workers, with the right to strike, had pushed wages above $13,000 a year, while U.S. postal employees in 1970 were making about $7,000.

There were 378 strikes by government employees in 1976, the lowest number since 1972.

Note who the strikers are in local government: fire fighters in Kansas City, police officers in Baltimore and New York, sanitation workers in New York and Memphis,[33] plumbers and electricians in San Francisco, prison guards in Ohio, and teachers everywhere (e.g., in the fall of 1978 there were 58 teachers' strikes in fifteen states).

At the federal level, the no-strike ban has been equally ineffective, with strikes or slowdowns by TVA workers; air traffic controllers; letter carriers and postal clerks;[34] nurses and teachers in the District of Columbia; and IRS employees in Detroit and elsewhere. Somewhere along the line, Calvin Coolidge's dictum that "There is no right to strike against the state" got lost in a union board room.*

The 1970 postal strike of 200,000 letter carriers and postal clerks was precedent setting for the national government. Disenchanted with their union leaders' efforts in Washington to obtain satisfactory pay increases and a reduction in the twenty-one years required to climb their twelve-step ladder from $6,176 to $8,442, the letter carriers in New York violated their no-strike affidavits and federal law and walked off the job. The strike traveled a lot faster than a special delivery letter, quickly reaching post offices in California.

After Nixon ordered army units into the postal breach and a U.S. district court threatened the unions with stiff fines, collective bargaining began. The agreement called for a reorganization of the Post Office Department, a two-step wage increase, a commitment to future collective bargaining (including wages), and a shortening of the salary ladder to eight years.[35]

Congress passed the necessary legislation and Nixon signed it in less than three weeks. No penalties were imposed on the strikers, and they won essentially everything they asked for. It must have represented one of the great union victories in the whole history of collective bargaining, public or private. However, there is a sad sequel to the story: the mails have moved slower ever since.

The muscle demonstrated in these strikes, at the polls, and in lobbying scored some other impressive victories for the public unions. By 1976, the federal government, the District of Columbia, and forty states had granted bargaining rights to the unions that win secret ballot elections among public employees. Almost everywhere in the public sector, unilateral personnel management was dead.

The Large Issues

Public collective bargaining and its backup authority, the right to strike against government agencies, has far-reaching significance for citizens, employees,

---

* Or perhaps in an annual convention like that of the AFGE, whose delegates in Las Vegas in September 1976 voted to strike if Congress did not provide significant salary increases. In that same month, the NFFE deleted the no-strike pledge from their 1917 constitution.

agency managers, and legislators. For employees like the postal workers, it says, "You ignored us once too often"; for citizens, it may mean stinking garbage and striking cops who look the other way while you're accosted by toughs as you leave Yankee Stadium; for managers, it may mean a frustrating time trying to initiate Theory Y when the union representatives impassively reply, "You've gotta deal through us now."

For employees, public collective bargaining may spell a new day and a new deal. In 1978, mail carriers found their union-negotiated salaries at $15,000 a year (starting level, PS-5), while their GS-4 counterparts, who may not as yet negotiate their wages, were receiving $9,391 — a $5,600 tribute to the power of collective bargaining.

No longer on rainy days will white supervisors in the Memphis public works department send the black garbagemen home with half-day earnings while keeping the white crews on the job to pick up a full day's pay. Try it, and tomorrow AFSCME Local 1733 will leave you without garbagemen.

For other employees, the union presence in their agency may have negative implications. To these nonjoiners, the union demand for a union shop, which every employee must join after thirty days on the job, is a direct threat to their right to *not affiliate* unless they so choose.

Public collective bargaining also has implications for the public weal. What happens to public safety when police, firemen, garbage collectors, and air traffic controllers are on strike? How do schoolchildren make up for the missed learning of a lost September when their teachers take a walk? And if the disgruntled pressmen who destroyed the presses of the *Washington Post* had been the employees of a nuclear power plant, what would the cost be of a little union violence? What are the implications for pluralism and the public good in Alaska when the nation's largest union, the Teamsters, unionized the police department in Alaskan cities after organizing the major sectors of the Alaskan economy? Who then will respond to some violence in a Teamster picket line at an Anchorage trucking company? ("Cops are not only our friends — they're our brothers!")

What happens to the public interest when the labor dispute is a fight among three rival unions for the right to represent some state workers (the old-fashioned jurisdictional strike transferred to the public sector)? That occurred in Pennsylvania in 1970–1971, in a rough-and-tumble encounter between the AFSCME and a coalition of rival AFL-CIO unions (of service employees, laborers, and the operating engineers). The AFSCME finally won the battle to represent seventy thousand state employees, but the AFL-CIO Executive Council condemned all the rivals for employing unfair tactics.

Consider the implications for agency managers when a union wins exclusive bargaining rights from the employees. That happy preserve of management prerogative has now shrunk considerably. Instead, a whole array of personnel problems is now on the table for *labor-management resolution:* distribution of shifts and overtime work, promotion plans, physical working conditions, coffee breaks, some kinds of employee benefits, the handling of grievances, and in some jurisdictions the negotiation of wages.

The Civil Service Commission staff described the change well:

> Decisions regarding personnel policies and working conditions may no longer be made unilaterally by top management. At a minimum, management must consult with the union. Often it must negotiate. No longer can top management alone make such decisions; not even if it bases a decision on what it thinks the workers want or on what it thinks is best for the workers. Bilateralism means an end to such paternalism, however well-intentioned. Workers, through their exclusive labor representatives, now have a right to share in decision-making.[36]

Yet if something is lost to managers, something else is often gained: an uninhibited expression of employee needs, without which management plans in the dark. It is not surprising, then, that a 1976 field study by the Civil Service Commission found their agency field managers generally viewing union relationships "as making a constructive contribution to the total management process."[37]

Collective bargaining may also pose a considerable obstacle to the Theory Y endeavors of management. Exclusive bargaining status means that management is to act *through the union* on many personnel matters, not directly with individual employees (important exceptions to that include assigning them duties, disciplining them, etc.). It is conceivable that an aggressive union might respond with considerable hostility to attitude surveys taken by management to measure the intervening variables, an open-door policy for employee complaints, and participatory discussion groups on the ground that the *union is to be the sole interpreter* of employee feelings and their only voice with management on needed changes.

Furthermore, the historical opposition of organized labor to job enlargement is well known, and union officials frequently regard it as a form of exploitation of workers. Hopefully, the kinds of strikes that hit General Motors at their Lordstown plant in the early 1970s (boredom over massive routinization of work—"installing right windows in Vegas all day long") may have opened union eyes to the necessity of job redesign.

In our view, it would be of critical importance to write into a labor-management agreement a joint commitment to support efforts that make jobs more meaningful and that give all employees more opportunity to be heard on agency issues affecting them.[38] To the extent that unions prefer to monopolize that kind of communication, *individual employee powerlessness* has once again been increased rather than decreased, and everyone is a loser for that.

Collective Bargaining and the Merit System

What kind of impact does public collective bargaining have on merit system principles?[39] Historically, the answer was encouraging. Unions were vigorous champions of the merit idea and defenders of the system against patronage abuse. But some points in collective bargaining are inimical to the ideas of appointment through competitive exams, promotion based on demonstrated skill, and the like. Those points include the hiring hall (where the union is actually the recruiter-appointer) and the traditional insistence on seniority as the governing principle in promotion and retention matters.

To minimize any public union threat to merit principles, a collective bargaining statute for government employees must plainly indicate that systemwide merit principles and practices are nonnegotiable and may not be breached by labor-management agreements.

One of the merit system areas that may be the hardest to preserve in the face of collective bargaining will be job classification and its related pay scales. There is the likelihood everywhere that unionized employees, such as police and firemen, will find their salaries moving ahead of nonunionized workers, regardless of what the classification system may say their respective jobs are worth.

But there is also some hope for reciprocation and a continuation of public unionism's traditional stance in defense of merit. Even on the matter of seniority, the unions are not immovable. In Boulder, Colorado, for example, the labor-management agreement allows job performance, not seniority, to determine layoffs.

In short, then, the union presence in public personnel management has far-reaching implications, not only for the public service, but for the public interest as well.

Developing Guidelines for Public Sector Collective Bargaining

The possibility of escaping unions in an agency now seems long gone. In the public sector, collective bargaining has clearly come to stay. That fact would seem to require: (a) a positive attitude toward the good things that can come from this strengthened employee voice in agency affairs;[40] (b) a well-drawn law defining the territory of collective bargaining; and (c) training programs to prepare key agency personnel for the critical role they will have to play as agency negotiators in collective bargaining with their opposite numbers in the union.

A well-drawn statute ought to require that collective bargaining take place *within the boundaries of the merit system;* define management, union, employee rights and obligations, and unfair practices; clearly delineate subjects excluded from collective bargaining; provide for secret ballot elections; and set up grievance and impasse resolution procedures.

At the federal level, the guiding rules are laid down in Carter's reform of the merit system, P.L. 95-454, passed in 1978.[41] The law marks out the broad territory exempt from collective bargaining, the most important of which is pay! (Recall that GPO printers and postal workers have won the right to negotiate their pay.) Other exceptions are agency mission, budget, and directing or disciplining employees.

The governing statute will also have to come to grips with the truly vexing issue of the right of public employees to strike. The Taft-Hartley Act still forbids it at the national level (providing penalties of a year in prison and a $1,000 fine for its violation); and as of 1978 thirty-eight states also prohibited it. The case seems very strong for denying that right to employees who render services absolutely essential to the public's health and safety: those involving water-works and police and fire departments to name the rock-bottom three.

But beyond these, the prohibition becomes less defensible. Freedom ought to include the right not to work under unsatisfactory conditions; collective bar-gaining too frequently becomes collective chatting without it; and as the 1970 postal strike indicates, the prohibition seems to have been irrevocably breached — and the strike resulted in rewards rather than penalties.[42]

Bargaining in Good Faith

The most hopeful answer to strike avoidance lies in good-faith collective bar-gaining and a managerial system that provides challenging work and treats people with dignity (the message of Chapters 6 and 7).

The collective bargaining sequence is represented in Table 15.5. Essentially every agreement will provide for the handling of grievances. They cover a wide range of complaints: an improper assignment, a prejudiced performance rating, being passed over for promotion, disciplinary actions in violation of agency rules, and so on.

In the federal sector, careful provision has been made for the handling of grievances bargainers are unable to resolve. The machinery is depicted in Fig-ure 15.1. The case load statistics reveal something about the functioning of the Federal Service Impasses Panel (FSIP). The panel is the alternative to strikes in the federal system. But between 1970 and 1978, it received 440 cases, less than 50 cases per year, indicating that most conflicts were being resolved at the primary collective bargaining stage, the agency level.

TABLE 15.5 COLLECTIVE BARGAINING SEQUENCE

Union organizing among agency's employees

Secret ballot election

Union receives exclusive bargaining rights to represent all agency employees (union and nonunion)

Call for negotiation (initiated by either side)

Submission of union demands; management analysis

Bargaining stage: negotiation—resistance — counteroffer — compromise or impasse

Impasse resolution: further negotiation, a strike to coerce a settlement, or third-party intervention — fact-finding, mediation, or arbitration

Completion of the labor-management agreement

Contract administration stage

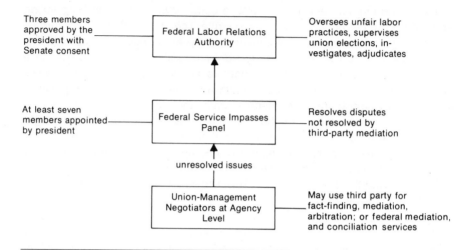

FIGURE 15.1 FEDERAL LABOR RELATIONS ORGANIZATIONS AND APPEALS PROCEDURE

In that fashion, collective bargaining has come to the federal government.[43] Unions represent 71 percent of all governmental units; rule-making machinery now exists; conflicts are being resolved; and a wide array of grievances is being resolved. There is no right to strike at the federal level, nor are wages of most civil servants subject to collective bargaining. But there have been no full-scale strikes of federal workers since 1970. The record since then looks encouraging.

SUMMARY

Control of personnel management is a much-sought-after thing in government. Presidents and parties want patronage to assure a civil service responsive to their directives. Agency managers want merit in their employees, and unions want a significant piece of the action in matters affecting employees.

Parties have many reasons for wanting control of government jobs: to build coalitions, influence legislators, reward faithful service, and provide a source for much-needed funds.

But in a technological age, an effective government cannot be staffed on the principle of whom you know when what you know is so important. For that reason, and to remove one cause of corruption, the government ultimately turned to the merit system for hiring, rewarding, and removing personnel.

The Pendleton Act of 1883 created the U.S. Civil Service Commission and called for examinations for a competitive, permanent civil service. With that statute, it was to be neutral on the job; with the Hatch Acts (1939–1940), neutered off the job as well.

Merit systems are not without critics, who point to the lack of responsiveness in tenured employees and the red tape involved in handling personnel.

Over time, merit systems have become less the guardian against the spoilsman and much more the positive personnel manager, by means of advanced selection techniques, incentives management, salaries that are increasingly competitive with those in the private sector, and increased training consciousness.

In recent times, the merit system has faced two new demands: equal employment opportunity and collective bargaining. With 15 percent of the labor force, governments could not remain immune to unionization. The 1960s constituted the takeover decade and saw the provision of machinery to handle collective bargaining at the federal level and within some of the states.

Public unionism has wide implications for orderly government, the costs of government, management practices, and employee protection. But collective bargaining is now the reality, rounding out the tug-of-war for control of personnel that for so long involved the two other contestants, parties and managers.

In Chapter 16, we turn to two critical aspects of public personnel management, job classification and pay.

KEY CONCEPTS

patronage	The postal strike of 1970
the merit system	E. O. 11491
The Pendleton Act	impasse resolution
personnel realpolitik	Federal Labor Relations Council
The "Malek Manual"	Civil Service Reform Act. 1978

DISCUSSION QUESTIONS

1. Present the case for and against patronage. Which view is the most viable?

2. To what extent does the present day merit system achieve the purposes for which it is intended? What arguments could be made to support a patronage system rather than a merit system?

3. Should all public sector employees have the right to strike? Or should only certain groups? Which?

4. Discuss the pros and cons of public sector unionism. What is the future of labor relations in the public sector? Will unions have a beneficial or detrimental effect?

PROJECT

Talk to a political party official and attempt to obtain information on the nature of the patronage system in your locality or state.

Notes

1. See Martin and Susan Tolchin, *To the Victor* (New York: Random House, 1971), for an overview.

2. U.S. House of Representatives, Post Office and Civil Service Committee, *Final Report on Violations and Abuses of Merit Principles in Federal Employment* (Committee print 94-28) (Washington, D.C.: Government Printing Office, 1976), p. 577. Called hereafter *94-28*.

   The Nixon administration's frustration with the federal merit system was somewhat understandable. They found only 47 positions available to them out of 115,000 jobs in Health, Education, and Welfare, and only 2 out of 52,000 in the Social Security Administration (*94-28*, p. 579).

3. Letter to the acting secretary of state, Sept. 27, 1795, in *Writings of George Washington*, Fitzpatric ed. (Washington, D.C.: Government Printing Office, 1940) 34:315–316.

4. Leonard White, *The Federalists* (New York: Macmillan, 1948), p. 264n.

5. Annual message to Congress, Dec. 8, 1829, as quoted in James D. Richardson, *A Compilation of the Messages and Papers of the Presidents* (New York: Bureau of National Literature, 1897) 3:1011–1012.

6. Massachusetts Crime Commission, "Official Report," *Boston Globe* (May 18, 1965), p. 7.

7. *Elrod* v. *Burns*, June 28, 1976, 96 S.Ct. 2673.

8. As a start, see the memoirs of one of the great practitioners of the federal merit system in this century, John Macy, *Public Service: The Human Side of Government* (New York: Harper and Row, 1971).

9. We commend to your attention the explication of merit principles in the Intergovernmental Personnel Act (1970) and in Bernard Rosen, *The Merit System in the U.S. Civil Service* (Committee print 94-10 of the House Committee on Post Office and Civil Service) (Washington, D.C.: Government Printing Office, 1975), pp. 7–8, 72. (Hereafter cited as *94-10*.)

10. The portrait we prefer was painted by Stephen K. Bailey in "The Excitement of the Public Service," *Civil Service Journal* (July–Sept. 1963) 4:5–9.

11. History buffs will be greatly rewarded by Paul Van Riper's thorough study, *History of the United States Civil Service* (Evanston, Ill.: Row, Peterson, 1958); and the House Post Office and Civil Service Committee, *History of Civil Service Merit Systems of the U.S. and Selected Foreign Countries* (Committee print 94-29) (Washington, D.C.: Government Printing Office, 1976).

12. *Congressional Record* 14:204–207, 659.

13. 22 Stat. 403.

14. The constitutionality of these statutes was first upheld in *United Public Workers* v. *Mitchell* 303 U.S. 75. In 1974, Congress lifted the restrictions imposed by the Hatch Act (1940) on state and local employees hired under federal grants-in-aid. The Ninety-fourth Congress, in 1976, then voted to repeal the federal Hatch Act (1939) while leaving protections against political exploitation of federal employees. The repeal was vetoed by President Ford.

   For a reasoned defense of the Hatch Acts, see Bernard Rosen, *94-10*, p. 34. As a rejoinder, consider Justice William O. Douglas's dissent in *Broaderick* v. *Oklahoma*,

413 U.S. 619 (1973): "A bureaucracy that is alert, vigilant, and alive is more efficient than one that is quiet and submissive. It is the First Amendment that makes them alert, vigilant, and alive. It is suppression of First Amendment rights that creates faceless, nameless bureaucrats who are inert in their localities and submissive to some master's voice. High values ride on today's decision in this case and in Letter Carriers. I would not allow the bureaucracy in the State or Federal Government to be deprived of First Amendment rights. Their exercise certainly is as important in the public sector as it is in the private sector. Those who work for Government have no watered-down constitutional rights. So far as the First Amendment goes, I would keep them on the same plane with all other people."

Also see J. C. Rinehart and E. L. Bernick, "Political Attitudes and Behavior Patterns of Federal Civil Servants," *Public Administration Review* (Nov.–Dec. 1975) 35:603–611.

15. See Edwin O'Connor, *The Last Hurrah* (Boston: Little, Brown, 1956), pp. 374–375.

16. Frank Sorauf, "The Silent Revolution in Patronage," *Public Administration Review* (Winter 1960) 20:28–34.

17. Savas and Ginsburg, "The Civil Service: A Meritless System?" *The Public Interest* (Summer 1973) 32:70–85.

18. Rosen, *94-10*, p. 25.

19. The infamous "Malek Manual" is reproduced in *94-28*, beginning at p. 573. Much of its authorship is attributed to a Malek associate, Alan May.

20. From p. 103 of the "Malek Manual," in *94-28*, at p. 677, paraphrased in part and quoted in part (as shown).

21. *94-28*, p. 140. Hampton was relieved as civil service chairman by the incoming Carter administration on Jan. 20, 1977, and the other two holdovers were replaced shortly thereafter.

22. *94-28*, p. 242.

23. *94-28*, p. 243.

24. *94-28*, p. 244.

25. *94-28*, pp. xiii and 2.

26. "CSC Carries Out Merit Team Recommendations," *Civil Service Journal* (Apr.–June 1976) 16:8.

27. "CSC Carries Out . . . ," pp. 10–12.

28. For a commentary, see Robert G. Vaughn, *The Spoiled System: A Call for Civil Service Reform* (New York: Charterhouse, 1975). A wideranging reform bill to correct many of the weaknesses in the federal civil service was introduced by Representative David Henderson, chairman of the House Post Office and Civil Service Committee in 1976, but got nowhere. Politics would suggest that the year before a possible change of administrations may not be the best time to tinker with the government's personnel system (the Pendleton Act of 1883 to the contrary notwithstanding). For the proposed reforms, see "The Civil Service Amendments of 1976," *Civil Service Journal* (Apr.–June 1976) 16:14–17.

29. Federal Personnel Management Project, *Final Staff Report* (Washington, D.C.: Government Printing Office, Dec. 1977) 1, sec. 11.

30. See the *Civil Service Journal* (Oct.–Dec. 1978) 19: inside cover; and the *Congressional Quarterly Weekly Report* (Sept. 14, 1978) 36:2458–2462, and (Oct. 14, 1978) 36:2945–2951.

31. In sketching this history, we are indebted to the excellent work of the U.S. Civil Service Commission's staff in Labor Relations Training for their *Collective Bargaining for Public Managers (State and Local)* (Washington, D.C.: Government Printing Office, 1975).

32. Useful source books include the U.S. Civil Service Commission's *Collective Bargaining in the Federal Sector* (Washington, D.C.: Government Printing Office, 1975), U.S. Labor Department's *Register of Federal Employee Unions* (Washington, D.C.: Government Printing Office), and the (private) Bureau of National Affairs, *Government Employee Relations Report (circulated monthly).*

33. See Ray Marshall and A. A. Adams, "The Garbagemen's Strike That Led to Dr. Martin Luther King's Assassination," in R. J. Stillman, *Public Administration: Concepts and Cases* (Boston: Houghton Mifflin, 1976), pp. 86–100.

34. Joseph Loewenberg, "The Post Office Strike of 1970," in Loewenberg and Moskow, *Collective Bargaining in Government* (1972), and reprinted in Stillman, *Public Administration,* pp. 302–310.

35. Stillman, *Public Administration,* p. 308.

36. *Collective Bargaining for Public Managers,* RN 1-4, p. 2.

37. U.S. Civil Service Commission, *Administrator's Alert* (Apr. 1977) 7(no. 10):2.

38. See Sam Zagoria, "Bargaining and Productivity in the Public Sector," in Gerald Somers, ed., *Collective Bargaining and Productivity* (Madison, Wis.: Industrial Relations Research Association, 1975), pp. 63–82.

39. See the discussion in *Collective Bargaining for Public Managers,* RN 1-8, pp. 1–4.

40. Madison Philips, "Developing Healthy Attitudes for Dealing with a Union," *Personnel* (Sept.–Oct. 1977) 54:68–71.

41. See the helpful summary in the *Congressional Quarterly Weekly Report* (Oct. 14, 1978) 36:2950.

42. It is interesting to watch the case law unfold in public sector strikes and related techniques. For example, in September 1976, U.S. District Court Judge Gerhard A. Gesell upheld the right of the National Treasury Employees Union (NTEU) to picket two IRS offices on their own time in the wake of an impasse in negotiations. The judge indicated that a rule dealing with picketing must clearly advance an important government interest, and with minimum interference with First Amendment rights. *National Treasury Employees Union* v. *Fasser et al.,* 428 F. Supp. 295 (1976).

43. See Anthony Ingrassia, "Status Report on Federal Labor Management Relations," *Civil Service Journal* (July–Sept. 1977) 18:38–43.

Chapter 16
What's A Person Worth These Days?

JOB CLASSIFICATION

Those Overpaid Lab Technicians

On her first day on the job at County General Hospital, the new personnel director was less than amused that the office had nicknamed one of the clerks "The Undertaker." But it was fitting; he spent his entire time processing the resignations of departing employees.

The resignation count the personnel director asked for revealed a turnover rate of 48 percent of the hospital's nursing, technician, and custodial staff, an attrition rate two or three times what it should have been. No one had ever bothered to ask the quitters why they were leaving. (Some said you didn't have to ask; you just needed to listen to the wailing during coffee breaks.) But the personnel director established an exit questionnaire before her second day was over, and within a few weeks the picture began to emerge:

"I've had to shrivel my brains to get inside the Mickey Mouse job they put me in."

"Why should the lab technicians get paid more than the obstetrical nurses?"

"I'm burned up that the sister of the chief of pediatrics gets paid more than the other women in her division!"

"I've slaved here for twelve long years. Had to grovel for all the crummy pay raises I've had in that time. This time I've had it!"

And so on — *miserable!*

Beyond the normal complaints about the unpleasantness of hospital work, the exit survey showed that the big contributors to the excessive quit rate were meaningless job assignments, jealousies over unequal pay for comparable work, favoritism in salary administration, and the total lack of any plan for regular advancement of the staff. I'd quit too, the director thought. But she didn't quit. In less than a month on the job, she faced up to the challenge of the 48 percent turnover rate by resorting to that cumbersome but critical personnel tool, job classification.*

Why Pigeonholes?

Think of the chaos that would occur in the personnel programs (e.g., recruiting, paying, promoting) of agencies like the U.S. Department of Health, Education, and Welfare (150,000 employees) or your state highway department if every job had to be treated individually. Organizations, like the human mind, have to categorize and simplify if they are going to be able to cope.

Job classification is just that — the categorizing of the myriad positions in an agency into series, classes, and grades so that large numbers of similar positions can be treated alike for personnel and other purposes (see Figure 16.1).

A *series* of positions is a vertical cut down through the agency dividing employees into their occupational specialties (e.g., accountants, clerk-typists, engineers, and economists). *Grades* are a horizontal cut through the salary system, embracing many different positions in different series but related as to level of difficulty (duties, responsibilities, and qualifications) and therefore receiving similar rates of pay (grade 4s, wage board 8s, GS-14s, to suggest the designations given grades in different governmental jurisdictions).

A *class* of positions brings together jobs that are highly similar in terms of occupational specialty (i.e., all in the same series) and in levels of difficulty (i.e., at the same grade) and denotes comparable levels of pay. Thus, one might find in a local police department some classes of positions like these:

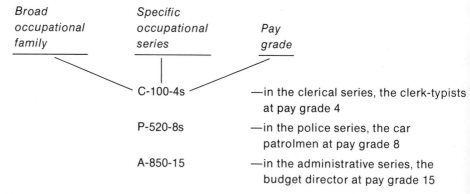

Broad occupational family	Specific occupational series	Pay grade	
	C-100-4s		—in the clerical series, the clerk-typists at pay grade 4
	P-520-8s		—in the police series, the car patrolmen at pay grade 8
	A-850-15		—in the administrative series, the budget director at pay grade 15

---

* In the jargon of industry, "job evaluation," not to be confused with "performance rating," which measures the employee rather than the position.

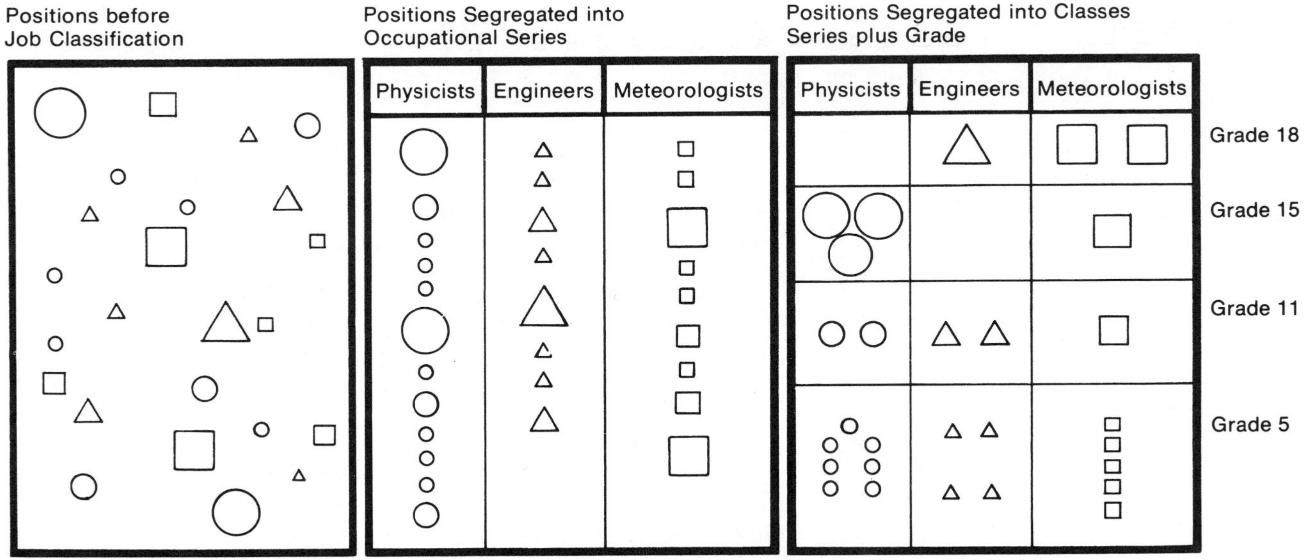

FIGURE 16.1 SYMBOLIC REPRESENTATION OF THE CLASSIFICATION PROCESS

Adapted from U.S. Civil Service Commission, *Basic Training Course*, part 1:10–17 (Washington, D.C.: Government Printing Office, 1961).

What kind of a tool have we got once these categories are laid out and related positions are brought together? If handled properly, a critically important one (see Figure 16.2). Some of the specific contributions job classification has to make are these:[1]

To motivation of workers: realizing that with the design of jobs, we deal with the most important motivator of all, *the job itself.*

To organization planning: using standard terminology for positions; proper relating of jobs so as to expose overlapping duties.

To recruitment, testing, and placement: carefully spelling out in the duties and qualifications statements of the job description the kind of person best qualified for each position (the five-sided peg for the five-sided hole).

To performance rating: providing a list of duties against which to measure the work of each employee.

To training: identifying those duties that require additional preparation of the employee.

To career planning: establishing occupational ladders of related positions by grades of difficulty, a critical element in promotion systems.

To budgeting: consolidating positions into manageable categories for projecting personnel costs.

To salary administration: providing a series of grades for the steps of a salary schedule, affording equal pay for equal work.

To morale: eliminating salary jealousy by securing equal pay for equal work.

To equal treatment: assuring that pay differences between occupations that are currently sex cast (nurses, firemen, typists, etc.) are based on actual job worth and not on sexual or racial differences.

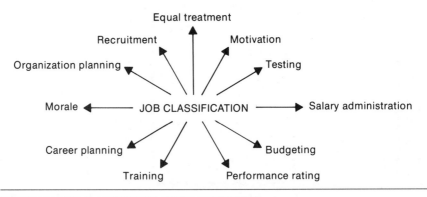

FIGURE 16.2 JOB CLASSIFICATION AND ITS DEPENDENTS

No wonder job classification occupies the central position it does in personnel administration; many other phases of administration would be helpless without it.

The Long History of the Job Classification

In the very seedtime of the patronage system, a Senate resolution of 1838 required federal department heads to classify employees "in reference to the character of the labor to be performed, the care and responsibility imposed, the qualifications required, and the relative value to the public of the services of each class as compared with the others."[2] But the seed did not take root at the time. Another effort was made during 1853–1854 when Congress required five departments to arrange their clerks into four defined classes, with a specified salary for each class.

However, the federal government's "system" remained a jungle of unrelated positions and unmeshed salaries for decades. Congress either passed lump sum appropriations, leaving salary matters without guidelines in the hands of department officials, or went to the other extreme and listed fixed salaries for each position in an agency.

A new impetus came in the 1880s from industrial engineering. Urging managers to find the science of every job, Frederick Taylor and his scientific management disciples were responsible for making industry, and later government, position conscious. That public personnel administration should one day have a deep analytical interest in individual positions is in large part attributable to Taylor's influence.

Then, with the Pendleton Act (discussed in Chapter 15) forty years old, Congress passed the historic Classification Act of 1923.[3] Taking as its goal equal pay for equal work, the act required that positions in the federal service be classified according to their duties, responsibilities, and qualifications. Administration of the classification plan was not vested in the line agencies or in the Civil Service Commission but in a new auxiliary agency, the Personnel Classification Board (whose function was subsequently transferred to the Civil Service Commission).

Later statutes altered the compensation of federal employees and enabled the president to bring new positions within the classified service by executive order. But the significant change in classification procedure came in the wake of the first Hoover Commission's criticism that federal personnel management was far too centralized.[4] What the commission was faulting was the classification of virtually all federal positions by the Civil Service Commission rather than by the agencies themselves.

Responding to the Hoover Commission suggestions, Congress drastically amended the parent statute in passing the Classification Act of 1949.[5] Under this new law, the line departments were to classify their own positions (section

502), with the Civil Service Commission writing the classification standards. In addition, the CSC would decide appeals from departmental decisions, oversee departmental classification systems, and revoke a department's delegated authority to classify jobs when necessary. The change in roles represented a logical extension of the decentralization of federal personnel management that began during World War II. The 1949 act also created three new supergrades (GS-16, GS-17, GS-18) that enabled the government to compete more effectively with private enterprise in the search for high-level administrative and scientific personnel.

Following what now seems to be a twenty-year cycle, Congress stepped in again in 1970, bluntly telling the U.S. Civil Service Commission that it had not been innovative enough in exploring improved methods of job classification or in bringing effective order to the ranking of federal jobs.[6] The Job Evaluation Policy Act instructed the commission to develop a coordinated job evaluation system throughout the federal service.

After extensive field testing and lengthy consultation with agency officials, professional associations, and employee unions (which initially opposed the reform), the commission adopted the new factor evaluation system (FES) on December 17, 1975. Its installation marked a significant shift away from the old cumbersome narrative classification system to the cleaner point system used in industry (described in a later section in this chapter).[7]

In 1978, the Carter administration persuaded the Ninety-fifth Congress in its massive overhaul of the federal civil service to create the long-discussed Senior Executive Service (SES). The SES would be a new classification category of top-level managers where pay would be significantly based on outstanding performance and the possibilities increased of forced retirement if the managers didn't deliver.[8]

Classification — The High Stakes

What fits in small pigeonholes?   Small pigeons, of course. And if line managers and job classifiers design positions with a Frederick Taylor mind set of reducing every job to tasks so simple that simpletons can perform them, think about who will be conducting the people's business in no time at all.

Job classification deals with that element of work life Frederick Herzberg has shown to be the most critical of all for morale — the job itself. In an important degree, then, the élan and motivation of the whole agency ride on how well or poorly classifiers do their job. If managers and classifiers design meaningless jobs, they are going to bore workers to death; if they build challenge and significance into jobs, they have a fair chance of propelling many employees toward self-actualization.[9] Robert Townsend has underscored the dangers:

> *Job descriptions — Straitjackets.* Great for key-punch operators and other jobs where the turnover is high and the work is largely repetitive. Insane for jobs that pay $150 a

week or more. Judgment jobs are constantly changing in nature and the good people should be allowed to use their jobs to see how good they are.

At best a job description freezes the job as the writer understood it at a particular instant in the past. At worst, they're prepared by personnel people who can't write and don't understand the jobs. Then they're not only expensive to prepare and revise regularly, but they're important morale-sappers.[10]

The classifier is a spook   Years ago some specialists in the Indian Service had a plan for raising Navaho farm income by reducing the size of sheep herds to a level the range could more adequately sustain. But the plan was full of sheep droppings because the Anglos forgot one thing: in Navaho culture, the size of the herd is a primary status symbol. The Navaho would prefer a head count of his sheep to a dollar count any day.[11]

So it is with civil servants when the job classifiers from the personnel office appear on the scene. When the classifiers say "relax," everyone is spooked because they all intuitively seem to understand that it is the "size of their herd," their grade and pocketbook, that may be at stake. Why, the rush down the Maslow ladder past self-esteem to insecurity would put a stampeding herd of sheep to shame.

If this psychological threat to individuals is not well handled, the classifiers soon find that the primary work groups and individuals have built a wall of resistance against any tampering with their jobs. When this happens, not even a passport from the chairman of the Office of Personnel Management could get a classifier over the "Berlin Wall" that now confronts him. It should be clearly understood that this is the normal way for employees to react. Their own psyches are much more powerful influences of behavior than the lofty (and threatening) standards of a job classification system. As Max Weber observed a long time ago:

> Numerous quite conspicuous uniformities in the course of social behavior are not based at all on the orientation toward some "valid" norm or usage; rather on the fact that the corresponding type of social behavior is, in the nature of the case, best adapted to the normal interests of the individuals involved as they themselves perceive them to be.[12]

Two to tango   In addition to the employees, two other groups are vitally concerned with job classification: line management and the personnel office. A division or section chief, for example, has two important stakes to protect: the right to run her own shop ("We know our positions and how they should be graded a lot better than the personnel office") and her need for generous job classifications, with correspondingly higher salaries, to attract better workers. As seen by the line manager, the position classifier from the personnel office may be a threat to both. No wonder, then, that the classifier sometimes feels as welcome in a line office as a Dodger scout in the Giants' dugout.

Conversely, the personnel office has a real stake here too. Charged by top management with maintaining an effective classification system and resisting grade creep, the personnel people feel a responsibility to restrain the line's attempts to withhold information and pad job descriptions. Moreover, the classifiers are as much subject to the expert's disease as any other profession: "We know how to classify and you don't." Thus, they find their prerogative to classify in frontal conflict with line management's right to manage.

These, then, are some of the stakes involved in job classification: employee motivation and morale, the line's ability to recruit talented people into higher-paying jobs, and top management's concern about restraining runaway salaries and maintaining some sense of equity throughout the agency. Trouble may arise at every one of those points. Thus, there is a critical need for a minimax strategy that will minimize the harmful potential of job classification and maximize the great good it can do when handled properly.

Reducing Employee Resistance to Classification

The central thesis of this book is that involvement leads to commitment and that organizations based on trust and valid sharing of information have a problem-solving capability way ahead of their opposites. Those principles of management reappear here, as primary points of reliance in reducing friction in job classification.

Making jobs — and job classification — amount to something   The beginning point in winning employee and management cooperation with job classification is the end result — providing more meaningful jobs than existed before. The clue to success, of course, is to use job classification as the midwife of job enrichment through effectively designed jobs.

We need to review here what was said in Chapter 6 about making work worthwhile. Workers are alienated and therefore less productive in jobs involving:

monotonous, repetitive tasks

tasks involving the simplest motor skills that demand nothing of their minds

tasks that are performed in isolation from other workers

subassemblies with no opportunity for workers to see the completion of whole units or products

little worker control over the way the job is to be handled

dead ends

The job classifier needs to begin his work, then, with an understanding of those alienators in the work place. His task ought no longer to be merely a *describer* of what this or that employee is doing; rather, in partnership with the line manager, his task is to be a *job designer* who knows how to bring the best in behavioral science to bear on the redesign of work.

Here are some approaches classifiers can employ to that end:[13]

1. In boring jobs, plug in a *variety* of duties. Move the switchboard operator during certain hours of the day to the receptionist's desk; move the mail room clerk into the files and the duplicating room on a rotating schedule. Employ the modular assignment system in which time modules are used of perhaps two or three hours on each task rather than eight hours a day in pure drudgery.

2. Add some *mental activity* to the motor skills called for in the job description: the responsibility to analyze one's work, choose appropriate means to accomplish it, and develop new approaches (a la the Lincoln Electric format).[14]

3. Develop job descriptions that enhance *cooperation and relationships* with others rather than solo performances (think in terms of the women in the Hawthorne relay assembly test room and of the production workers at General Foods).[15]

4. Design jobs to enable workers to see things through to conclusion, to *see things whole:* social workers, typists, and file clerks tied together around the social workers' case loads; computer programmers with job descriptions involving them with analysts using the computer printouts, and so on.

5. Build both *responsibility and autonomy* into positions by having workers become responsible for their own quality control. Eliminate the next higher supervisory level over the typists, and then hold them accountable for their finished products.[16]

6. Through the appropriate linkage of job descriptions, *build promotion ladders* that require improved performance but not vacancies for advancement: (a) apprentice, journeyman, master carpenter; (b) social science analyst, economist, senior macroeconomist, and so on.

When job classification is put to those uses and the word gets around, employees will see that only high rollers are playing in the game, and for the highest stakes of all — jobs that matter, jobs that motivate, jobs that are worth doing forty hours a week instead of jobs that lead to goofing off whenever possible. At last sensing that "there really is something in this for me," the employee will hopefully pull in his antennas and buckle down willingly to the classifier's questions.

Employee involvement in the classification process The next approach in winning employee commitment to job classification is involving them in discussion groups (which we discussed in Chapters 6 and 12). The rap sessions provide the arena where the need for a classification survey can be set forth and employee reactions and anxieties can be expressed and dealt with.

A third technique, employed in some cities, is to create a classification review board that includes employee representatives chosen by employees or their unions, some designees of management, and someone from personnel. These boards would classify positions, assigning the grade level to each one. Having employee representatives as members can help reduce some of the anguish of classification.

A fourth step is aimed directly at the alleviation of the fear of pay loss that can derail the entire effort if it is not handled properly. The politics of administration is clear on this point: management assures present employees of no pay cut resulting from the survey as a quid pro quo for employee cooperation in the review. Where jobs are found to have been classified too high, rectification must wait until the positions in question have been vacated or until some grace period has expired.[17]

A fifth way to reduce employee resistance is to invite workers to come up with their own job descriptions or to amend ones already in existence. This procedure provides a meaningful way for the wearer of the shoes to indicate where the shoe pinches. And it might not be a bad idea to periodically ask employees what they wish their jobs might look like — a normative job description pointing the way to job enlargement.

Sixth, employees should not be kept in the dark about their job descriptions and classifications. A study among Utah State employees some years ago points up the problem. Some 29 percent of the sample did not know if there was a job description for their position; another 35 percent said they had not seen theirs; 31 percent did not know or were not sure of their classifications. Half of the state employees were dissatisfied with, or had doubts about, the fairness of their classification.[18] Meaningful communication can go a long way toward letting some light into the cellars of doubt these figures portray.

Seventh, the role of the front-line supervisor in the classification process is of critical importance in overcoming employee resistance. The supervisor's endorsement of the survey is likely to be far more important to his workers than endorsement by top management. In addition, his going to bat for his team over disputed classifications, where warranted, helps to build group solidarity, which is so important for productivity, and to obtain for his workers better salaries and the prestige that goes with higher classifications.

Resolving the Line-Staff Conflict

Two techniques loom large as therapies for line-staff conflicts in job classification: (a) heavy involvement of line officials in classification decisions and (b) the linking-pin principle for bridging the gap between the line and the personnel office.

By means of healthy delegations of classification authority to line officials, top management can literally and psychologically reduce the threat that middle managers otherwise see in the classification roles played by personnel officials. In particular, line officers should be consulted in the writing of classification standards and have a large voice in determing qualifications for positions. So substantially involved, line officials could begin to think of the program as their own, not as one imposed from outside.

What would such a delegation leave for the personnel office (or, on a broader plane, for a civil service commission) to do in job classification? The office or commission would have a final voice on standards, the right to review agency classification actions (including the power to revoke improper allocations), the power to initiate audits of agency systems, and the authority to hear appeals.

This division of responsibility is essentially that in use at the federal level since the Classification Act of 1949. As noted earlier, section 502 of the statute vested authority to classify jobs in the agencies themselves, not in the Civil Service Commission, as before. It should be noted that the delegation of authority comes at a price. A CSC study in 1978 of agency classification decisions revealed that 10 percent (136,000 positions) of the General Schedule jobs were overgraded; 3 percent were undergraded; and 440 were otherwise misclassified.[19]

The involvement of line officials in addition to the personnel officers can go far to bridge the line-staff gap through application of Likert's linking-pin principle. That calls for their joint membership on top-level committees that advise the agency's chief policymakers. Here line and personnel officers have a chance to visualize themselves as partners in the same enterprise rather than as rivals. Seeing clearly the overall needs of the agency from the vantage point of these bridging committees, the line manager may be less apt to pad job descriptions and withhold information. In the same atmosphere, the personnel man may shed his "policeman" complex. The left hand begins to understand what the right hand is doing.

Achieving human relations that are soundly based and group feelings that are harmonized are essential aspects of any ultimate success of the classification effort. Much rides on these aspects of the undertaking: employee morale, management's ability to retain good workers, and the personnel office's influence on line affairs far beyond the classification field.

Alternative Classification Systems[20]

In job classification, analysts are attempting to measure *job worth.* Among the kinds of scales available for such weighing are the ranking, the narrative class, the point system, factor evaluation systems, and combinations of these. A quite different approach based on rank in the person rather than rank in the job is known as the *skills-based classification* system.

The ranking system In this approach to job classification, the positions in an office are arranged from most to least important. Similar evaluations are made in the other units of the agency, and rankings are then matched up for the entire agency.

If this system were applied to a university, for example, we might find the following ranking (from most down to least important):

Head Football Coach

Alumni Secretary

President of the University

Football Coach, Offense

Football Coach, Defense

Provost or Academic Vice-President

Basketball Coach

Academic Deans

Director of Public Relations

Academic Department Heads

Superintendent of Buildings and Grounds

Dean of Students

Squash Coach

Professors, Associate Professors, Assistant Professors

Instructors

Residence Halls Supervisors and House Mothers

TAs (Teaching Assistants)

The ranking system gives a vertical distribution but without providing any way of really measuring between-grade differentials.

The narrative class system A much more cumbersome system, called the narrative class system, was employed for many decades by the U.S. Civil Service Commission (before FES, the factor evaluation system).

Its heart and soul were the endless notebooks in which classes of positions within each occupational series were described in paragraph form. For example, in the classification manual dealing with the stenotypist series, there were hair-splitting distinctions to differentiate the novitiate clerk-typist (GS-2), the pool typist (GS-3), the stenotypist (GS-4), the secretary (GS-5), and on up to the executive secretary (GS-7 or GS-9).

The class specifications (specs) covering duties, qualifications, and levels of responsibilities would then be used by a classifier as the benchmark against which to measure a job description awaiting a grade.

No Classification Big Enough for This Job

A description of duties and responsibilities:

> Without direct or intermediate supervision and with a broad latitude for independent judgment and discretion, the incumbent directs, controls, and regulates the movement of interstate commerce, representing a cross section of the wealth of the American economy.
>
> On the basis of personal judgment founded on past experience, conditioned by erudition and disciplined by mental intransigence, the incumbent integrates the variable factors in an evolving situation and on the basis of simultaneous cogitation formulates a binding decision relative to the priority of flow in interstate and intrastate commerce, both animate and inanimate. These decisions are irreversible and are not subject to appellate review by a higher authority, nor can they be reversed by the legal determination of any echelon of our judicial complex.
>
> The decisions of the incumbent are important since they affect with great finality the movement of agricultural products, forest products, minerals, manufacturers' goods, machine tools, construction equipment, military personnel, defense materials, raw materials, and products, finished goods, semi-finished products, small business, large business, public utilities, and government agencies.
>
> In effective implementation of these responsibilities, the incumbent must exercise initiative, ingenuity, imagination, intelligence, industry and/or discerning versatility. The incumbent must be able to deal effectively with all types of personalities and all levels of education from college president and industrial tycoon to truck driver. Above all, the incumbent must possess decisiveness and the ability to implement motivation on the part of others consistent with the decision the incumbent has indicated. An erroneous judgment or the failure to properly appraise the nuances of an unfolding development could create a complex obfuscation of personnel and equipment generating an untold loss of mental equilibrium on the parts of innumerable personnel of American industry who are responsible for the formulation of day-to-day policy and guidance implementation of the conveyances of transportation, both intrastate and interstate.
>
> In short, at highway construction projects where only one-way traffic is possible, this character waves a red flag and tells which car to go first.

Skill with words was the long suit of the adroit classifier, and adjectives were perhaps the most important weapon of all:

"a working knowledge of a specialized field"

"expert knowledge of a specialized field"

TABLE 16.1   JOB FACTORS AND THE FEDERAL POINT SYSTEM

Factors	1	2	3	4	Max.
1. Knowledge required	50	200	350	550	1850
2. Supervisory controls	25	125	275	450	650
3. Guidelines	25	125	275	450	650
4. Complexity	25	75	150	225	450
5. Scope and effect	25	75	150	225	450
6. Personal contacts	10	25	60	110	110
7. Purpose of contacts	20	50	120	220	220
8. Physical demands	5	20	50	. . .	50
9. Work environment	5	20	50	. . .	50

Source: U.S. Civil Service Commission, *The Factor Evaluation System* (mimeo), (Washington, D.C.: Civil Service Commission, Jan. 1976), Appendix A.

"a specialist, capable of expanding knowledge in a technical field"

"directs an operation of average size and complexity"

"an organization of above-average complexity"

"a moderately large and complex organization"

There was considerable difficulty in measuring the words in the *job description* against the words in the *specs*. In such a verbal roundhouse where it was so hard to corner a classification, the classifier often yearned for the exactness and commensurability of the point system.

The point system[21]   A mathematical system, as its name implies, the point system evaluates positions in terms of key job factors (e.g., education, supervision, physical demands) and degrees for each factor that are given points (e.g., if the educational side of a job requires a high school diploma, 15 points; two years of business college, 20 points; four years of college, 80 points; a master's degree, 135 points; a doctor's degree, 200 points). (See Table 16.1.)

As with the narrative class system, the point system requires a definition of standards. It lists all the factors, the degrees into which each factor is divided, and their point values. In addition, the standard will also provide a conversion table, indicating the range of points for each pay grade (Table 16.2, where the GS grades denote salary levels).

Now let's see the point system at work, in this case, determining the grade level for a football coach at a small midwestern college (Table 16.3). (The weight and point spreads in Tables 16.1 and 16.2 are *not* involved here.) The total points allocated to the coach's position, 863, are then located on the point spread for the various grades. This position is classified as a grade 6 job.

The point system, the favorite in industrial classification, is often heralded for its exactness and freedom from value judgments. Bunkum! When the U.S. Office of Personnel Management (formally the CSC) decides that the knowledge

TABLE 16.2 GRADE CONVERSION TABLE IN THE FEDERAL POINT SYSTEM

GS grades	Range of points	GS grades	Range of points
1	190–250	9	1855–2100
2	255–450	10	2105–2350
3	455–650	11	2355–2750
4	655–850	12	2755–3150
5	855–1100	13	3155–3600
6	1105–1350	14	3605–4050
7	1355–1600	15	4055–up
8	1605–1850		

Source: U.S. Civil Service Commission, *The Factor Evaluation System* (mimeo), (Washington, D.C.: Civil Service Commission, Jan. 1976), p. 32.

component of a job is worth up to 1850 points, while lousy working conditions (facing the postman in winter) are worth only 50 points, it is wallowing in value judgments.

Admittedly, there is a certain kind of fascination to this numbers game approach to classification: evaluate the job against the degrees shown in the standard, add up the points, and bingo, you've got the grade level!

Two hookers in the system are finding point differentials that actually mark off less important from more important jobs (janitor adds up to 302; section chief to 900) and then matching the whole point structure to wage patterns in the labor market.

TABLE 16.3 CLASSIFYING THE FOOTBALL COACH UNDER THE POINT SYSTEM

Factors	Weights	Coach's points	Grade	Conversion Table Point range
Education	339	280	1	200–299
Experience	190	55[a]	2	300–399
Responsibility	248	248[b]	3	400–499
Relationships	120	100	4	500–649
Mental application	120	40[c]	5	650–749
Physical application	70	65	6	750–899
Working environment	60	60[d]	7	900–999
Supervision	55	15[e]	8	1000–1099
			9	1100–1149
			10	1150–1202
	1202	863		

[a] Small industrial arts college; has to take football coaches at the beginning of their careers.

[b] Keeping the chamber of commerce, the legislature, the student body, the alumni, the president, the team, and the crowds all happy is a terrifically responsible job!

[c] This is just a straight T conference; no I formations or anything like that.

[d] The last half of the season is always played in snow.

[e] Coach functions as a bench quarterback, with the college president suggesting plays from the president's box by walkie-talkie.

Factor Evaluation System   FES, the name of the new federal classification system, is basically the point system with some refinements. Agency personnel shops will have three standards to go by in classifying positions:

the primary standard (illustrated in Table 16.1) that spells out the nine job factors and factor levels for the entire civil service

the factor-level descriptions and points for each occupational series (e.g., fiscal, engineering, medical, custodial, etc.)

benchmark jobs described and point-rated for each occupational series and grade level as an extra point of comparison for the classifier

In many point systems, only the primary standard (Table 16.1) would be used, keeping the standard book very brief. But with the addition of the benchmarks and factor-level descriptions in all the occupational series, it appears that the federal civil service is going to lose one of the great blessings of the point system — brevity. (As harbinger, the first instruction manual dated January 1976, ran fifty-two pages, for example.)[22]

Skills-based classification system   Departing dramatically from the traditional classification fix on a limited number of duties is a very new approach to job classification that would delight Abraham Maslow: classifying the person in terms of how many different tasks she has mastered. In that approach, the climb to self-actualization is actually built into the job classification system.

One of the current pioneers in skills-based classification is the General Foods plant at Topeka, Kansas. An employee moves to the second pay level when five tasks have been mastered. The top grade is achieved when the employee can perform all the production tasks in the plant. The work groups certify when a worker has effectively mastered a new task. In these ways, General Foods is building an omnicompetent work force, flexibly trained and motivated toward personal growth through the skills-based classification plan.[23]

Classification Procedure

Let's assume that an agency is starting from scratch to develop a job evaluation system. At an early stage, a jurisdictional classification will have to be arrived at to pinpoint the few jobs that will not be classified. Usually found in the *unclassified* service are elected officials, department heads, undersecretaries, and assistant secretaries, who are ordinarily exempted from classification by law. All other positions fall in the *classified* service, whether filled by competitive examination or not (note the difference between the "classified service" and the "competitive service" in federal government terminology, with many more positions being embraced in the former than in the latter).

Then the question must be answered: Will classification be based upon the job or the person in the job? Military organizations, among some others, prefer rank in the person to rank in the job. Under rank in the person, the classification attaches to the employee — to a second lieutenant who wears his gold bars whether performing at a sergeant's level at Fort Meade, Maryland, or at a first lieutenant's level in Heidelberg (although the practice is, of course, to assign lieutenants to lieutenants' work). Most other classification systems are based on rank in the job.

Where rank in the job is adopted, the individual position is the item for analysis — the *duties* that are regularly assigned to it, the *responsibility* entrusted to it, plus the necessary *qualifications* a person occupying the position must have to fill it. Although human beings are not the center of attraction in this system, they quite obviously have an impact on the positions they hold. The extremely able secretary (GS-5) invites such confidence from her boss that her position really grows into that of an administrative assistant (GS-9). When this happens, the job has clearly changed and should be reclassified. But at any one point in time, the classifier is to analyze *positions* as she finds them, not what they were nor what they are becoming (although some allowance may be made for projected duties). Specifically, the classifier is not doing a *performance rating* on the incumbent.

The next step in the classification process is the *continuous* one of maintaining good human relations. As noted earlier, this process primarily entails employee involvement from the outset, good communication, and assurances that no incumbent will suffer a salary cut as a result of the survey.

The observable beginning of the survey itself comes with fact gathering on the individual positions. Principal techniques include the employee questionnaire, interviews with the incumbents and their supervisors, and analysis of organization charts.

The next step is writing the job description. As noted earlier, many benefits may accrue from having employees do the first drafts themselves, even though they may require extensive translation, because of inflation, gobbledygook, or reticence (see Table 16.4).

When the fact-gathering and descriptive steps are completed, the position is ready to be classified. On a day-to-day basis, this key step is ordinarily done by the trained staff in the personnel office (subject to negotiation and appeal). Where an entire office has been resurveyed, the classification of many positions may be done by a representative committee, as described earlier.

When done well, the classification process works with amazing speed, and often by phone. In a new unit, the director answers a classifier's questions about her proposed secretary, waits a minute or two while the classifier checks the job points against the conversion table, and then receives the word that the position will be a grade 6.

Classification Follow-through

Handling appeals There's nothing quite so dead as the second-place club the day after the Pirates have clinched the pennant — unless it's a classification

TABLE 16.4 JOB DESCRIPTION, BEFORE AND AFTER

Original draft: *maintenance engineer*	*Translation:* *janitor*
1. With great latitude, makes important decisions as to work priorities	1. Decides which of ten stalls to clean first in the men's room
2. Oversees the activities of everyone else in the agency	2. Watches for foot marks of employees as he scrubs the hall
3. Applies a knowledge of a substantial array of chemicals to his daily task	3. Knows the difference between floor cleaners and soap for the washbasin dispensers
4. Exercises great diplomacy in relationships of a very delicate character	4. Chooses slack periods to ask women to leave their washroom while he cleans it

plan with no provision for change. Sometimes they may move with the speed of glaciers, but human beings, jobs, and organizations do change; and classifications, to be both fair and meaningful, must change too.

One method of handling the reclassification employees will request is a regularized appeals procedure. There may have been errors in the original classification; additional duties may have been added; or the incumbent may be just plain dissatisfied. Whatever the reason, she wants a new look taken at her job classification. A possible line of review is first to her boss, from there to the classification office in personnel, and then to the Merit Systems Protection Board.

Keeping current In addition to employees' initiating their own appeals, classification reviews can and should be instituted in other ways. Before a vacancy is filled, line and personnel people should take a fresh look at the classification to see if it still measures the job accurately.

More ambitious are the large-scale classification surveys that may be launched by line or personnel officials. These surveys present the opportunity to uncover misclassified positions and violations of standards and to review an agency's classification network and procedures.

Beyond all of this, someone needs to be asking continually, "Does your whole classification scheme make sense?" That question can be answered in part through close observation of the turnover rate, exit interviews, and questionnaires, and through consultation with management and employees.

Handling these phases of the continual follow-through clearly requires available staff, principally classification specialists in the agency personnel office. Classification plans do not automatically update themselves; they need tending — and renewal.

SALARY ADMINISTRATION

Money: Way Ahead of Whatever Is Second?

The studies measuring the importance of money as a factor in morale really leave one wondering. As noted in Chapter 2, Harold Sheppard and N. Q. Herrick found blue-collar workers listing money last among the conditions of work needing improvement.[24]

In the 1972 strike at General Motors' ultraefficient Lordstown plant, highly paid auto workers were griping about boredom, not inadequate pay.[25] And Herzberg's research relegated money to the ranks of dissatisfier rather than motivator.[26]

In your own experience, you must have found plenty of evidence to verify the scripture, "Man shall not live by bread alone": the lost love of your life, who could not be wooed back at any price; the leukemia that took a friend's life; the jobs you wouldn't consider at any price — carrying bedpans in the county hospital, participating in a CIA drug project on unsuspecting victims, or helping Don Segretti in the 1972 dirty tricks campaign in the Florida Democratic primary.

Yet the evidence is everywhere that if money is not the most important thing in life, it comes far ahead of whatever comes second.[27] Almost all major labor disputes are primarily over paychecks (Lordstown was a modern-day exception).[28] Price gouging by oil companies in 1979 painfully reminded us that the ethic of capitalism is still to "make a buck as fast as you can." Your lawyer even tantalizes you: "J.D., you can't imagine how much fun it is to make money."

Research is plentiful that suggests how important paychecks (and bonuses) are to most people. Particularly significant were Edward Lawler's findings among highly paid managers.[29] Although ranking just below autonomy and achievement, money was perceived as highly important by these executives. Even at their levels, money had not yet evidenced diminishing returns.

At low-income levels, the relationship between pay and job dissatisfaction seems clear, as revealed in the data from the Survey Research Center compiled by Neal Herrick (see Table 16.5).

Pay is important up and down the Maslow scale. Dollars buy food and pleasure, reduce some kinds of insecurity, help build self-esteem (who has the Rabbit, who has the Mercedes on your street?), and may provide the take-off point for self-actualization and achievement for many (going to Harvard Law instead of to West Chestnut Law School, for those who have the tuition).

A perennial fact of life is that few of us ever have enough money. So the hunger and yearning are there, opening up the possibility of getting people to work their tails off if pay and productivity are intelligently linked together.

To the disbelievers we can put it simply: pay is very important to almost all of us.

TABLE 16.5   WORKER DISSATISFACTION BY PAY LEVELS

	Percentage dissatisfied with work	
Variable	Income below $5,000	Income above $10,000
Age:		
29 and under	27	10
30 to 44	20	9
45 and older	16	7
Occupational group:		
Blue collar	22	11
White collar	18	7
Marital status:		
Married	20	8
Unmarried	21	8
Education:		
High school or less	19	8
Some college or more	28	9

Source: From University of Michigan Survey Resource Center, "Survey of Working Conditions," compiled by Neal Q. Herrick, W.E. Upjohn Institute for Employment Research, Washington, D.C., in Levitan and Johnston, *Work Is Here to Stay, Alas*, p. 78. Copyright © 1973 by Olympus Publishing Company. Reprinted by permission of Neal Herrick.

The Juggling Act Called Pay Setting

It would be appropriate here to recall James McCamy's vector analysis that we discussed in Chapter 9, for the contesting forces in the field of pay setting are both numerous and intense. We are going to look at seven of the most important of them.

Job worth   First, what is the job worth? We get answers to that question through the job classification techniques described in the first part of this chapter, comparing positions in terms of the duties, the levels of responsibility, and the qualifications that are required. Culture has a lot to say about job worth as well; for example, our culture says that executive suite jobs involving decision making affecting many people are worth a lot more than backbreaking jobs installing gaslines and maintaining roads, which also affect many.

Having salaries reflect job worth is called the *alignment principle* (lining up positions of equivalent responsibility and paying at the same rate). Its application contributes to equitable distribution of monetary rewards in an agency: "equal pay for equal work."

Employee worth   Second, what is the employee worth? That question is especially relevant where an agency pursues rank-in-the-person rather than rank-in-the-job classification or has very broad, professional-type job descriptions. Highly significant in attracting and keeping top people and motivating stars on the job, this principle of recognizing *employee worth* clearly modifies *job worth.* Thus, the great scholar in your academic department may receive $5,000 to $8,000 more a year than another full professor who is sleeping his way into retirement.

In most pay systems another individual employee factor, worker seniority, is given considerable weight (which may have little to do with employee worth). The easy logic is that the longer a worker is on the job, the more he has mastered, even if ten years' seniority turns out in fact to be one year of experience repeated nine times.

Salaries as motivators   Third, a salary system ought to motivate better performance. The old piece-rate system (e.g., paying the census taker for every home visited) was designed to do just that — have pay tied to output. But the rates were sometimes subject to so much manipulation by authoritarian managers that they alienated workers on all sides.

Edward Lawler has reminded us that pay plans to motivate operate on three levels: that of the individual worker, the work group, and the whole organizational unit.[30] For example, the one-shot cash payment in the federal service known as the Sustained Superior Performance Award is given to individual workers for service beyond expected levels over a period of time.

Federal cash payments for cost-saving suggestions may illustrate group awards. Three mechanics at an air base who discover how to salvage the faulty wings of a costly aircraft may receive a $15,000 payment (based on a percentage of the savings they have effected) for their innovation. In fiscal 1977, 150,000 federal employees were recognized for cost-saving suggestions that saved the government $318 million.

The Scanlon plan is perhaps the best-known incentive pay arrangement based on whole-company performance.[31] Basically it pays back to all employees a percentage of improved sales or profits above a base rate. Its inner strengths are welding employees around a common goal, eliminating person-to-person competition, and giving employees a personal stake in the success of the enterprise.

For a pay system to be a motivator, these features seem to be critical: (a) there should be significant pay differentials between superior and average workers (what the employee is worth); (b) the existence of the differential must be plainly visible as a come-on; and (c) pay changes should promptly follow the demonstration of superior performance.

Note how governments can incorporate those features into their pay systems. In addition to the one-shot cash bonus (Sustained Superior Performance Award) already alluded to, the federal service may also grant "quality step increases" to specifically recommended employees with outstanding performance ratings.[32] The procedure involves boosting a staff member to the next in-grade pay level (see Table 16.6) without waiting for the anniversary of his

TABLE 16.6 THE GENERAL SCHEDULE SALARY TABLE, 1978

	1	2	3	4	5	6	7	8	9	10
GS-1	$ 6,561	$ 6,780	$ 6,999	$ 7,218	$ 7,437	$ 7,656	$ 7,875	$ 8,094	$ 8,313	$ 8,532
2	7,422	7,669	7,916	8,163	8,410	8,657	8,904	9,151	9,398	9,645
3	8,366	8,645	8,924	9,203	9,482	9,761	10,040	10,319	10,598	10,877
4	9,391	9,704	10,017	10,330	10,643	10,956	11,269	11,582	11,895	12,208
5	10,507	10,857	11,207	11,557	11,907	12,257	12,607	12,957	13,307	13,657
6	11,712	12,102	12,492	12,882	13,272	13,662	14,052	14,442	14,832	15,222
7	13,014	13,448	13,882	14,316	14,750	15,184	15,618	16,052	16,486	16,920
8	14,414	14,894	15,374	15,854	16,334	16,814	17,294	17,774	18,254	18,734
9	15,920	16,451	16,982	17,513	18,044	18,575	19,106	19,637	20,168	20,699
10	17,532	18,116	18,700	19,284	19,868	20,452	21,036	21,620	22,204	22,788
11	19,263	19,905	20,547	21,189	21,831	22,473	23,115	23,757	24,399	25,041
12	23,087	23,857	24,627	25,397	26,167	26,937	27,707	28,477	29,247	30,017
13	27,453	28,368	29,283	30,198	31,113	32,028	32,943	33,858	34,773	35,688
14	32,442	33,523	34,604	35,685	36,766	37,847	38,928	40,009	41,090	42,171
15	38,160	39,432	40,704	41,976	43,248	44,520	45,792	47,064	48,336*	49,608*
16	44,756	46,248	47,740*	49,232*	50,724*	52,216*	53,708*	55,200*	56,692*	
17	52,429*	54,177*	55,925*	57,673*	59,421*					
18	61,449*									

*Basic pay is limited by Section 5308 of Title 5 of the United States Code to the rate for level V of the Executive Schedule. In addition, pursuant to Section 304 of the Legislative Branch Appropriation Act, 1979, funds are not available to pay a salary in this schedule at a rate which exceeds the rate for level V of the Executive Schedule in effect on September 30, 1978, which is $47,500.

appointment to roll around (the normal time to receive in-grade raises). When that anniversary arrives, this hotshot employee steps up another pay notch, possibly enjoying a double jump in one fiscal year (and that means that the benefits continue to roll pay period after pay period).

An even more dramatic application of the incentive pay principle is the payment of large cash awards under the Incentive Awards Act of 1954.[33] Ordinarily not to exceed $5,000 either for individuals or for groups of workers, under unusual circumstances these handsome stipends may reach $25,000, in addition to the civil servant's salary!

Some years ago, the navy scientist who invented the Sidewinder missile, which homes in on enemy aircraft via heat waves from their engines, received the bundle. In 1977, another navy researcher, Lawrence Guzick, received $25,000 for inventing a metering device to reduce steam loss from steam pressure systems. In a short period of time, Guzick's innovation saved the navy 875,000 barrels of oil and $10.5 million.

In short, private industry has no monopoly on the use of money to stimulate better performance.

Salaries as recruitment and retention devices   The fourth factor in salary administration is the pegging of salaries at the right levels to attract and hold able employees. The seniors among you know the point: Should you work for state government at $9,000 right after graduation, for the federal government at $11,500, or starve your way through law school in the hope of making $25,000 three and a half years from now?

That kind of weighing is called opportunity cost analysis, and potential employees as well as ones already on the job both engage in it. When you lose an excellent secretary because the Bureau of Land Management can pay her $1,000 more than the university, you suddenly realize how much her opportunity can cost you.

Comparing how green the money is elsewhere can be deeply upsetting to a work force where government salaries have fallen behind. In 1969–1970, postal workers could look at New York City garbage collectors making $1,500 more than they were and then suffer the additional pain of realizing that it required postal employees twenty-one years to climb the twelve steps between $6,176 and $8,442![34]

Since 1962, the federal government has been committed to maintaining comparability between public sector and private sector salaries for their wage-board (blue-collar) and General Schedule (white-collar) employees.[35] Data published by the 1976 Quadrennial Salary Commission suggest how tough a goal that has been. Figure 16.3 shows that civil servants were about 4 percent behind the growth rate in private nonfarm wage earnings over the seven-year period. Although the supergrade federal managers were only 3 percent behind the *growth* in executive salaries in the private sector, the Civil Service Commission esti-

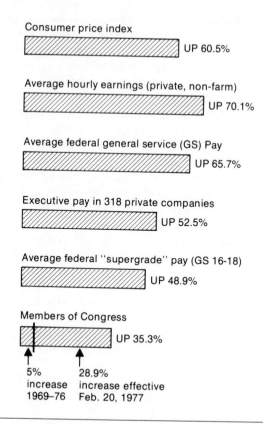

Consumer price index
UP 60.5%

Average hourly earnings (private, non-farm)
UP 70.1%

Average federal general service (GS) Pay
UP 65.7%

Executive pay in 318 private companies
UP 52.5%

Average federal "supergrade" pay (GS 16-18)
UP 48.9%

Members of Congress
UP 35.3%

5%   28.9%
increase   increase effective
1969–76   Feb. 20, 1977

FIGURE 16.3   INCREASE IN FEDERAL AND PRIVATE PAY, 1969–1976
Congressional Quarterly Weekly Report (February 12, 1977), p. 269.

mated in 1974 that the salaries for GS-16 to GS-18 federal executives were 30 percent behind their corporate counterparts.[36] The Congressional Budget Office has provided some interesting examples of the gap:

Salaries as of 1976

Private sector		*Public sector*	
legal vice-president of a large corporation	$ 89,000	General counsel of HEW	$39,900
financial vice-president	104,000	Controller of the Defense Department	39,900
vice-president for industrial relations	69,000	Chairman of the Civil Service Commission	42,000[37]

The gap was reduced appreciably by the pay increases approved in 1977 for the federal executive schedule.

While it's well known that nonfinancial perquisites greatly beef up the attractability of these high-ranking government posts and help to soften the salary deficit somewhat, nevertheless the salary gap is generating a significant brain drain from the federal sector to the private.

About 20 percent of all eligible federal employees retired in 1973–1974, but 30 percent of the federal executives whose salaries had been frozen at $39,600 since 1969 quit (the next year saw early retirement jump to 46.6 percent).

The National Labor Relations Board lost fifteen administrative law judges in 1975.

From 1973 through 1976, four of the eleven National Institutes of Health were without directors for over a year, with eighty-five out of eighty-seven applicants declining to serve because of inadequate pay.[38]

The Quadrennial Commission estimated that these departing federal professionals were experiencing salary increases of more than 84 percent by moving to the private sector.

In facing this kind of turnover, salary managers have to ask themselves which will cost more: a pay increase that will keep their staff or no pay increase and rising resignations with a loss of all that has been invested in their training, plus the cost of replacement.

Although it's hard to tie down the magnitudes involved for all kinds of American workers, it seems conservative to suggest that when an agency loses a valued employee, the cost must typically approach $1,500 or more, $1,000 in training and experience (investment cost) and at least $500 to go through the recruitment, selection and hiring of a replacement. That kind of figure may begin to make any lesser amount that might be granted in a salary increase look like a very good deal: a $1,000 raise to avoid losing $1,500.

When salaries begin to fall behind, something beyond opportunity cost begins to eat at your staff and threatens more resignations: inflation and the erosion of a living wage. Recall that Figure 16.3 indicates that most federal workers stayed about 5 percent ahead of inflation from 1969 to 1976. But from 1976 through 1979, they fell significantly *behind* inflation.

	Inflation rate (%)	Federal pay increases (%)	Pay-inflation gap
1976	5.7	4.83	− .8
1977	6.5	7.05	+ .5
1978	10.0	5.5	− 4.5
1979	13.0	7.0	− 6.0
		net	−10.8

Many thousands of state and local workers and school teachers found themselves in even worse shape.

At first blush, the living wage concept seems about as vague as the concept of the public interest. But it is not quite so indistinct. For some years the Bureau of Labor Statistics has computed not only the poverty level but also what a family of four must make in various American cities in order to enjoy a "moderate standard of living." In the postal strike of 1970, postal workers didn't have to be told that their average salary of $7,000 was $4,000 below what a family of four needed in New York City ($11,236 in 1970) to get by on. They knew.[39] (The disparity was softened, of course, in those postal worker families where there were two wage earners.)

Others were getting the message as well. Democratic Congressman William Clay of Missouri was certainly one. He had some important questions to ask during the 1976 hearings on the blue-collar wage system of the federal government, where wages are set through local market surveys rather than nationally (as is the case for the General Schedule employees). He wondered if the government might not be paying poverty wages if they were set comparably to the low wages of a distressed area:

> You don't believe then that this government has a responsibility over and beyond the principle of comparability in areas where it is obvious that labor is being exploited; we ought to just go in and continue the exploitation of labor?

> Well, take Puerto Rico, for instance, where people are being paid less than what it costs them to live. Do you think this government has a responsibility over and above just following what the prevailing wages are in an area like that, or do we have a responsibility to pay these people a living wage?[40]

Have you ever thought about what workers think about on the job when they receive less than a living wage? Watch out.

Union demands With the rapid rise of public sector unions that we charted in Chapter 15, a tough new vector has entered the salary scene in many governments across the country: collective bargaining by public employees. With it has come an increased willingness to strike if wage demands are ignored, regardless of what federal or state law may have to say about it.

One successful strike seems to build on another. As a spokesman for the letter carriers in New York put it as they began their walkout in March 1970:

> Everybody else strikes and gets a big pay increase. The teachers, sanitation men and transit workers all struck in violation of the law and got big increases. Why shouldn't we? We've been nice guys too long.[41]

Look at what that first major illegal strike in the history of the federal government achieved: (a) an 8 percent pay raise, (b) a compression of the pay steps into eight years instead of twenty-one, (c) the right to bargain collectively over postal wages (denied to other federal employees), (d) binding arbitration in any future labor disputes but with no right to strike, and (e) no reparations imposed for their collective violation of the no-strike prohibition of federal law.[42] That postal workers' victory emboldened other public unions across the country to become increasingly militant in dealing with governmental employers. And in communities where perhaps only the police, fire fighters, and schoolteachers are organized, their clout came to have implications not only for their own salaries but for other city employees as well. As the mayor said in Centerville, "Al, if we raise police wages, the firemen will want a raise, and then the clerks."[43] Everybody wants on the gravy train that union negotiators start rolling each year.

So in salary setting, we measure not only the incumbent's worth and the importance of her job but also the biceps of the union official standing behind her — all pitted against the agency manager's own posture of encouragement or resistance to the wage demands.

All that is done with one eye cocked on another dimension: How much will the legislature provide for salaries?

Budgetary restraints   A legislature can tie you down really well if it desires and leave you with little room to manage employee compensation:

appropriate by line item with a fixed amount for salaries

statutorily prescribe the salary for each grade

prohibit more than one promotion per employee per year

fail to provide any funds for incentive awards, among many others

Thus, all that we have said about job worth, employee worth, pay as a motivator, and so forth has to be modified by the political reality: What restrictions has the legislature imposed? How much money have they provided for salaries? How well has the agency described its needs?

An example of a legislative restriction with a serious effect on salary administration is the congressional requirement that no GS position may be paid a salary exceeding the bottom rung of the Executive Schedule (level V), the schedule embracing cabinet members (level I), on down through assistant secretaries and bureau chiefs. Until 1976, level V executives' pay of about $37,800 imposed a ceiling on some two thousand supergrade employees between the seventh step of GS-15 and GS-18, who should have been paid $5,300 to $14,800 more per year than they were receiving because of the salary compression. In February 1977, Congress approved major salary increases for high-ranking officials in all three branches, raising executive level V to $47,500. That eliminated the salary compression for almost all the supergrades except those above step 6 of GS-17.

The politics of pay   That brings us to the final vector in salary setting: Will the proposed increases float politically, with the citizenry, the taxpayers' associations, the media, and the legislature?

Taking It out of Employee Hides

Operating under the cloud of Proposition 13, the 1979 state legislature in Utah decided to cut costs by suspending for one year any merit increases (in-grade raises for satisfactory performance) for state employees. The appropriators voted a 5.25 percent across the board cost-of-living increase to cover the 10 percent rate then prevailing.

The Utah Public Employees Association responded:

This is a bitter pill to swallow. . . . Taxpayers should be called upon to be involved by either providing sufficient taxes, user fees, etc., or [accepting] reduced services. It is totally unfair for the taxpayers to expect full service at self-service prices. State employees, as taxpayers, too, desire responsible tax relief, but not at their expense.

Salt Lake Tribune (July 22, 1979).

The outcry during February 1977 that greeted the departed President Ford's recommendations for huge increases for congressmen, judges, and high-level executives suggests how politically sensitive these matters are. *Editorial Research Reports* reported that "Tax payers [are] outraged at salary increases" averaging 28 percent.[44] Few taxpayers were willing to focus on the fact that the cost of living had risen 60 percent during the past seven years, while federal elected officeholders had received only a 5 percent increase during that period. What seemed unthinkable was that congressional salaries were to rise $12,900, or 28.9 percent, to reach $57,500. Had those salaries moved incrementally with inflation year by year rather than in one fell 28.9 percent swoop, the public reaction might have been less hostile.

The politics of the situation was evident in the legerdemain that avoided a House vote on their own pay increases. Under a 1967 law, the president's recommendations for salary increases for Congress and others go into effect thirty days after submission if not overridden by either house of Congress (one-house veto).[45] As the thirtieth day approached on Ford's proposals, the issue was still in commmittee, sparing House members from a vote that might have prevented each one of them from receiving a pay increase of $12,900. (Also note that the action was taken in February of the odd-numbered year, months away from the time when they would have to face the voters in November 1978 to answer for the unvoted pay increase.)

The preceding quadrennial adjustments of congressional salaries also revealed the politics of compensation, particularly congressional sensitivity to election-year increases of their own salaries. The first Quadrennial Commission under the 1967 act reported in 1968, recommending salary increases for Congress in 1969, a nonelection year — they went through. The second commission got its recommendations to the president late, in June 1973, and Nixon didn't pass them on to Congress until 1974, an election year — they were vetoed by Congress.

As noted, the third quadrennial review was acted upon in 1977, a nonelection year, and the raises went through.[46]

What emerges from this review are these conclusions:

1. Public officials must be adequately paid by the public, or private interests lure them away.

2. The statistical review of changes in the cost of living and salaries of comparable private jobs, plus the recommendation of pay increases, should come from sources independent of the recipient of the salary increases.

3. Alterations should be made annually ("small changes don't excite").

These, then, seem to be the great influences in salary setting: job worth, employee worth, a way to motivate workers, a magnet to attract and hold good people, union demands, budget and other legislative restrictions, and political constraints.

Three Policy Questions

How much flexibility in the pay system?   When one begins building a salary system tied to job worth with some consideration for performance ratings and time on the job, is the system undermined by introducing elements of flexibility into its operation? We think, for example, of granting recruiters permission to offer sought-after recruits starting salaries two or three steps up in the grade for the vacancy rather than the beginning salary. A bit further removed, perhaps, is the question of allowing employees time off later on for overtime work (compensatory time) rather than paying them time and a half in dollars.

If we keep in mind that the system is a means, not an end, dilemmas like these are resolvable. Recruiters ought to have some flexibility to meet the competition in their recruiting efforts; and with many applicants, money talks.

As to compensatory time off, management should welcome that also. It gives an employee a sense of autonomy to be able to call the shots on matters like her work schedule; that psychic need may be worth a lot more to her than 150 percent of her regular hourly rate when she works overtime.

Other kinds of flexibility include part-day or part-year employment, which may be important in attracting women into agency work. Another useful pay device is WAE (when actually employed) compensation for consultants. The compensation system is there to serve the agency mission, not vice versa, and that means that the flexibility must be in the tail, not the dog.

Secrecy or openness about salaries?   In most civil service jurisdictions, essentially everyone in an office or small agency knows each other's grade, and thus approximately the salaries of co-workers. Go beyond those jurisdictions to the private sector and *wage secrecy* becomes the order of the day.

Secrecy must seem so much easier to the boss. It's a perfect adjunct to his authoritarian rule: "The boss gives, the boss takes away; blessed (?) be the name of the boss." He's not faced with defending his pay decisions, because comparisons are hard to make in ignorance. Too, secrecy may have removed one possible source of jealousy and contention.

But Edward Lawler has suggested some important arguments for *openness* and shared knowledge about pay. First, it may alleviate some gross misperceptions about others' pay that have affected one's morale. Second, appropriate sharing of salary information clearly buttresses the element of trust so badly needed in organizations (Argyris). Third, we need feedback about our work. When others received well-justified merit pay increases of 12 percent and I got 6 percent, the medium was the message.[47]

A beginning step in opening up pay data would be the publication of ranges and averages for each pay grade. This would certainly provide enough information for the feedback purposes just alluded to. To get maximum mileage out of incentive awards, the granting of them, as we said earlier, ought to be done with some fanfare, partly to say "Well done," and partly to say to others, "Go for it this coming year yourselves."

An employee voice in salary determination?   In a way there has always been a tiny voice: "Boss, I need a raise." With the appearance of unions in the public sector, the whisper has become a roar.

Even in those areas where public employee unions are barred from negotiating wages, ways have been found to give them a voice. At the federal level, for example, five union officials sit with five federal agency personnel directors on the Prevailing Rate Advisory Committee (PRAC) to formulate recommendations concerning blue-collar rates of pay. Five representatives of employee unions constitute the Federal Employees Pay Council, advising the president's agents (OPM chairman and OMB director) on white-collar pay.

Going far beyond union-negotiated wage settlements are some participatory schemes being tried by Theory Y managements such as those of General Foods, the Friedman-Jacobs Company, and others.[48]

All the arguments for participative management reoccur here. Allowing employees a meaningful voice in pay setting greatly enhances the flow of information to them, reducing doubt and suspicion and building trust; gives the employees a greater feeling of control in the organization rather than that of being merely pawns; and quite clearly advances involvement leading to commitment. Edward Lawler has diagramed it well (see Figure 16.4). Do employees ask for the moon when they are allowed to set their own pay rates? Summarizing extensive field research, Lawler concludes no:

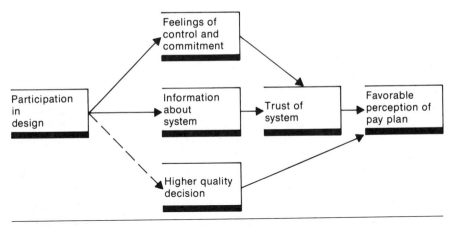

FIGURE 16.4 IMPACT OF EMPLOYEE PAY SETTING ON THE INTERVENING VARIABLES

From Edward E. Lawler, "Reward Systems" in Hackman and Suttle, eds., *Improving Life at Work*, p. 214. Copyright © 1977 by Goodyear Publ. Co. Reprinted by permission.

Thus it seems that when employees are given the responsibility for decisions about something important like pay, they often behave responsibly. This is, of course, in contrast to the kinds of demands employees make when they are placed in an adversary relationship, such as most union-management negotiations. Here large demands are the norm. The crucial difference seems to be that in negotiations the workers are bargaining for salaries, not setting salaries.[49]

Despite that kind of record, it is likely to be a very long time before there is much direct employee involvement in government wage setting. (Remember that outside the postal unions, federal employee unions may not yet even talk about wages.)

Pretty clearly what is happening in pay setting is another indication of the contingency theory of Morse and Lorsch at work (see Chapter 6). Theory X settings exhibit narrow job descriptions and pay systems imposed from above; Theory Y firms more often reveal professional-type job descriptions, if not rank in the person, and peer-negotiated salaries, including peer reviews.[50]

The Federal Pay Mechanisms

Although we don't perceive it as a model, the federal pay system needs to be briefly reviewed here. There are basically five component pay plans (see Table 16.7). Salaries for the General Schedule civil servants are currently governed by the Federal Pay Comparability Act of 1970, which carried forward reforms first legislated in 1962:[51]

1.   The GS salaries should provide equal pay for equal work (the alignment principle, rooted in job classification).

TABLE 16.7 FEDERAL PAY SYSTEMS

Pay System	% of Federal Employ- ment	Range, 1977	Salary Determination
A. *General Schedule (GS)* for most white-collar civil servants	49%	GS-1, $5,810– GS-18, $47,500	*National* pay scales set by president and Congress, employing alignment and comparability principles, providing for in-grade raises based on performance and longevity
B. *Wage Systems* for blue-collar workers	19	Wage laborer, leader, and supervisor $8,840– $25,681	Based on *local* wage market surveys to assure comparability
C. *Postal Service*	24	PS-1, $11,419– PS-11, $17,885	Nationally set, through collective bargaining
D. *Executive Levels* (cabinet heads — asst. secs., etc.) approximately 865	(less than .03)	Level V, $47,500– Level I, $66,000	Quadrennial Commission, presidential determination, congressional veto
E. *Miscellaneous* Foreign Service, VA, TVA, etc.	8	(E.g.) Foreign Service: FSO-8, $11,523– FSO-1, $51,226	Linked by the OPM to the General Schedules TVA set by collective bargaining

Source: Adapted from U.S. House Committee on Post Office and Civil Service, *Current Salary Schedules* (Committee print 95-3) (Washington, D.C.: Government Printing Office, 1977).

2. Pay distinctions should reflect differences in duties and performance.

3. Salary levels should be comparable to salaries for similar positions in the private sector (the comparability principle).*

4. Proper interrelationships among the various federal pay systems should be maintained.

To assure comparability and meet inflation, the president, after receiving reports, promulgates the new General Schedule to take effect each October 1, unless he concludes that economic conditions preclude the adjustment.† As noted earlier, the president's action is subject to a one-house congressional veto. The mechanism to do all that has grown like Topsy (Figure 16.5).

In the early 1970s, an ad hoc panel on federal compensation had some recommendations to make about General Schedule pay. The panel proposed to

---

* The government relies on an arm of the Bureau of Labor Statistics, the National Survey of Professional, Administrative, Technical and Clerical Pay (PATC), for the delineation of benchmark jobs and pay in the private sector.

† As case in point, President Carter approved only a 5.5 percent salary increase in the General Schedule in October 1978, when inflation was averaging 10 percent for the year. He said the federal government must set the example in the fight against inflation.

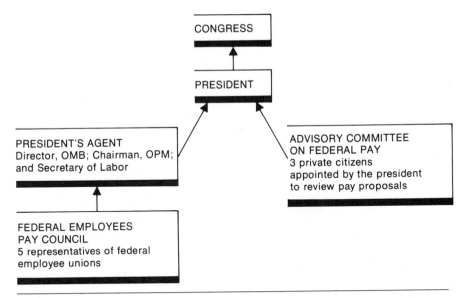

FIGURE 16.5 THE PAY-SETTING HIERARCHY FOR FEDERAL WHITE-COLLAR WORKERS

President Ford that the General Schedule be broken up into a Professional, Administrative, Executive Service with nationally set salaries, and a Clerical, Technical Service with locally set salaries (like those of the blue-collar workers).

Equally significant was the recommendation to cease granting annual in-grade raises to the professional ranks, based on longevity and satisfactory performance ratings, which 98 percent of the GS employees receive. In their place, the Compensation Panel called for a true *merit-earned salary plan* that hopefully would strengthen the incentive feature of federal pay.

The pay-setting mechanism for 500,000 federal blue-collar workers is depicted in Figure 16.6. Thus, unlike the General Schedule, which is nationally set, the federal wage system has locally determined rates for carpenters, plumbers, electricians, and the like, set to match the prevailing wage for each trade in the area.

For salaries of top executives in the government as well as congressional and judicial salaries, there is the Quadrennial Review Commission (established in 1967), followed by what amounts to salary setting by presidential decree (as described above).[52]

The newest development of all is the incentive pay plan incorporated in title IV of President Carter's 1978 civil service reform law. As noted earlier, it provided for the long-discussed Senior Executive Service (SES), embracing major administrators above GS-15. Five percent of the SES will be eligible for annual incentive bonuses of $10,000; another 1 percent may be designated as "distin-

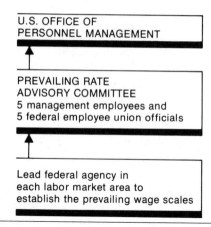

FIGURE 16.6 PAY MECHANISM FOR THE FEDERAL WAGE (blue-collar) SYSTEM

guished executives,'' eligible to receive $20,000 bonuses on top of their base salary of between $45,000 and $53,000.

Overall, substantial progress has been made since 1962 in closing the gap between federal and private sector salaries and providing some protection for Federal workers against inflation. The stereotype says it: the federal service is well paid today.

SUMMARY

The carrot of compensation can too frequently become the stick of alienation. For that reason and many others, governments have spent considerable energy in finding ways to measure job worth. The basic technique for doing that in the public sector is job classification, with important spin-offs for motivation, morale, recruitment, testing, and organization planning.

Job classification has some significant implications for human behavior and motivation: the damage that can be done to employees when Mickey Mouse jobs are concocted and classified versus the self-actualization that can develop when job classification is used to build ''the job itself'' (a la Herzberg) as a primary motivator.

Theory Y techniques can help reduce employee resistance to job classification — from individuals drafting their own job descriptions to group meetings and employee representation on classification boards.

A number of alternative classification systems are available: ranking, narrative class systems, point, factor evaluation, and skills-based systems. The bias here has supported the point system for its brevity, relative simplicity, and the speed with which classifiers can use it in classifying jobs.

The classification sequence stretches all the way from preparing the employees, through surveys, writing the standards, and on to the final allocation of a position to its class. Continuous follow-up and the handling of appeals are critical to the success of any classification system.

After reviewing many sides of the debate about the alleged significance or insignificance of money as a factor in employee morale, we simply concluded that it's plenty important — and had better be handled right.

Salary administration is an extension of the juggler's art, as the manager tries to balance seven hot potatoes in the air: "What is the job worth?" "What is the employee worth?" "What kind of a pay system will really motivate a staff?" "How do we peg salaries to attract able people and then meet the outside opportunities beckoning our employees so that we don't lose our investment in them?" "What are the unions asking for?" "What legislative limitations, including the budget, must be observed?" "Can I live with the political repercussions that are sure to follow my salary decisions?"

Salary administration is going to reflect a contingency theory, shaped by understanding of the managerial philosophy, the size of the work force, and the nature of the work and the workers. A variety of conditions will influence secrecy or openness about salaries as well as the degree of employee involvement in the process.

At the federal level, great stress has been placed both on the alignment principle, or internal equity (equal pay for equal work, as measured by job classification), and on the comparability principle, or external equity (as measured by labor market surveys to find salaries of positions in the private sector similar to those in the public).

A fair degree of automaticity has now been achieved in keeping the pay of both federal white-collar and blue-collar workers current with the marketplace.

The top executive salaries, ranging up to $66,000 (plus power and prestige) certainly emit enough magnetic pull to attract able men and women into government service.

Among some remaining questions is the perplexing one of how to relate performance and pay more meaningfully in the federal sector. And for hard-pressed states and local governments, the great question is almost always how to maintain comparability with the private sector so that able citizens are attracted to the people's business.

KEY CONCEPTS

series
grades
class
The Classification Act of 1923

class specifications
the point system
factor evaluation system
alignment principle

The Classification Act of 1949   comparability principle
Classification Review Board   federal pay systems
ranking system   the general schedule

DISCUSSION QUESTIONS

1.   What are the major purposes of job classification? Which is the most crucial for a healthy organization?

2.   To successfully create a job classification system, a classifier must first overcome employee resistance to such an effort. Discuss the various ways in which this resistance can be overcome.

3.   Discuss the various classification systems. What are the advantages and disadvantages of each?

4.   A classification system is meant to be a system that is dynamic and continuously adaptable to change. In presenting the various classification procedures and follow through, note those aspects that are the most flexible.

5.   If a pay system is going to be an effective motivator, what factors have to be present?

6.   Salary setting in the public sector would seem to be very difficult with union demands, taxpayer protests, and highly qualified personnel taking better paying jobs in the private sector. Is there any way to end what seems to be a natural tendency toward conflict?

PROJECT

Have each class member interview ten employees, each in a different government agency. Ask employees to rank the key features of the "perfect job." How important is pay? The job itself?

Notes

1. See also Paul A. Katz, "Standards and Tests," *Civil Service Journal* (Jan.–Mar. 1975), 15:28.

2. Quoted in the U.S. Civil Service Commission, *Basic Training Course in Position Classification* (Washington, D.C.: Government Printing Office, 1961), part 1:35–36.

3. 42 Stat. 1488.

4. U.S. Commission on Organization of the Executive Branch of the Government (I Hoover Commission), *Personnel Management* (Washington, D.C.: Government Printing Office, 1949), pp. 3, 9.

5. P.L. 81-429: 63 Stat. 954.

6. Job Evaluation Policy Act of 1970, P.L. 91-216; 84 Stat. 72.

7. The transition was described in Arch Ramsay, "The New Factor Evaluation System of Position Classification," *Civil Service Journal* (Jan.–Mar. 1976) 16:15–19.

8. See *Congressional Quarterly Weekly Report* (Oct. 14, 1978) 36:2948–2949.

9. See U.S. Department of Health, Education, and Welfare, *Work in America* (Cambridge, Mass.: MIT Press, 1973), pp. 10–23; and Jay Shafritz, *Position Classification: A Behavioral Analysis for the Public Service* (New York: Praeger, 1973).

10. Robert Townsend, *Up the Organization* (New York: Knopf, 1970), p. 91.

11. Clyde Kluckhohn and Dorothea Leighton, *The Navaho* (Garden City, N.Y.: Doubleday, 1962), pp. 74–76.

12. Max Weber, *Basic Concepts in Sociology* (New York: Citadel Press, 1913, 1962), p. 68.

13. See *Work in America,* ch. 4, an outstanding contribution to the literature on job redesign. See also L. E. Davis, et al., *The Quality of Working Life* (New York: Free Press, 1975) 2:270–346, and Frederick Herzberg, "One More Time: How do You Motivate Employees?" *Harvard Business Review* (Jan.–Feb. 1968) 46:53–62.

14. J. D. Hershauer and W. A. Ruch, "Worker Productivity Model and Its Use at Lincoln Electric," *Interfaces* (May 1978) 8:80–90. A key part of Lincoln Electric's famed incentive system is the responsibility placed on each worker for job innovation.

15. B. A. Duval and R. S. Courtney, "Upward Mobility: The General Foods Way of Opening Employee Advancement Opportunities," *Personnel* (May 1978) 55:43–53.

16. This elimination of a supervisory level was a major part of the reform undertaken by Bankers Trust Company in New York to beef up the jobs of the women typing stock transfers. HEW, *Work in America*, pp. 99–100.

17. As a case in point, title VIII of Carter's reorganization of the civil service, P.L. 95-454, provided a two-year grace period during which employees could not be reduced in grade as a result of a reclassification survey.

18. Oakley Gordon, et al., *Personnel Management in Utah State Government* (Salt Lake City, Utah: University of Utah Press, 1962), pp. 76–77.

19. *Administrator's Alert* (May 1978), 8:1.

20. Lee G. Craver, "Survey of Job Evaluation Practices in State and County Governments," *Public Personnel Management* (Mar. 1977) 6:121–131.

21. A brief, exceptionally clear portrayal of the point system and its linkage with the wage scale can be found in E. C. Snyder, "Equitable Wage and Salary Structuring," *Personnel Journal* (May 1977) 56:240–244.

22. U.S. Civil Service Commission, *The Factor Evaluation System of Position Classification: Introduction* (mimeo, Jan., 1976), 52 pp. Our friends in the OPM rejoin, however, that a primary standard with accompanying instructions totaling 52 pages and covering 1.3 million positions may not be excessively long after all.

23. See Edward E. Lawler III, "Reward Systems," in J. R. Hackman and J. L. Suttle, *Improving Life at Work* (Santa Monica, Calif.: Goodyear, 1977), pp. 183–186.

24. Harold L. Sheppard and N. Q. Herrick, *Where Have All the Robots Gone?* (New York: Free Press, 1972), p. 181.

25. HEW, *Work in America*, p. 19.

26. Frederick Herzberg, *Work and the Nature of Man* (Cleveland: World Publishers, 1966), pp. 73–74.

27. See especially Levitan and Johnston, "Is Money Still Important?" *Work Is Here to Stay, Alas* (Salt Lake City, Utah: Olympus Research 1973), pp. 75–80.

28. As a graphic example, look at the economic issues involved in the postal strike of 1970. See J. J. Loewenberg, "The Post Office Strike of 1970," in R. J. Stillman, *Public Administration: Concepts and Cases* (Boston: Houghton Mifflin, 1976), pp. 302–310.

29. Edward E. Lawler, "How Much Money Do Executives Want?" *Transaction* (Jan.–Feb. 1967), pp. 23–24.

30. Lawler, "Reward Systems," pp. 193–197.

31. For a brief description and evaluation see "Reward Systems," pp. 203–207.

32. The quality step increases were authorized by the Salary Reform Act of 1962; P.L. 87-973; 76 Stat. 841.

33. P.L. 83-763; 68 Stat. 1112. For the incentive pay features of President Carter's reform of the civil service, see Titles IV and V of P.L. 95-454 (1978).

34. Loewenberg, in Stillman, *Public Administration*, p. 304.

35. Federal Salary Reform Act of 1962 (see note 32).

36. U.S. Congress, Congressional Budget Office, *Executive Compensation in the Federal Government* (95th Cong., 1st sess.) (Washington, D.C.: Government Printing Office, 1977), p. 19.

37. *Executive Compensation,* p. 21.

38. U.S. Commission on Executive, Legislative, and Judicial Salaries, (the Quadrennial Commission) *Report* (Washington, D.C.: Government Printing Office, 1976), pp. 19–20.

39. Loewenberg, in Stillman, *Public Administration*, p. 304.

40. House Post Office and Civil Service Committee, *Hearings on the Federal Wage System* (ser. 94-63) (Washington, D.C.: Government Printing Office, 1975), p. 15.

41. Loewenberg, in Stillman, *Public Administration,* p. 309.

42. Loewenberg, in Stillman, *Public Administration,* p. 308.

43. Shades of Steve Bailey, "Harpsichord and Kazoo," *Public Administration Review* (Summer 1954) 14:202.

44. Reprinted in the *Salt Lake City Deseret News* (Feb. 16, 1977), p. A3.

45. P.L. 90-206, section 225 (1967).

46. The history is related in U.S. House Committee on Post Office and Civil Service, *Current Salary Schedules of Federal Officers and Employees, together with a History of Salary and Retirement Annuity Adjustments* (95th Cong., 1st sess.) (Washington, D.C.: Government Printing Office, 1977), pp. 21–26.

47. Lawler, "Reward Systems," p. 209.

48. Lawler, "Reward Systems," pp. 212–219.

49. Lawler, "Reward Systems," p. 217.

50. We acknowledge the sound things which Nancy Bauman had to say in her unpublished research paper, "Situational Approach to Compensation Design," in Management 789, University of Utah, Dec. 1976,

51. P.L. 91-656; 84 Stat. 1946; 5 U.S.C. 5301.

52. P.L. 90-206; 81 Stat. 642.

Chapter 17
Recruitment and Selection in the Public Service

THE SEARCH FOR ABLE PEOPLE[1]

When we begin to think about how governments go about finding good people, some haunting questions arise:

How is it possible that in an otherwise professional research agency, a character could slip through the screening process who ultimately runs the numbers racket in the agency and can get you anything from an Irish sweepstake ticket to a pass to the Army-Navy game?

In a time of recession when you advertise to fill five janitorial positions and two hundred applicants show up, how do you decide who will get the job?

As chief of police, when you begin to realize that your white cops are totally ineffective in black neighborhoods, you wonder where your lily-white staffing ideas ever came from.

When a delegation of angry women's liberationists enters the provost's office and threatens to strangle you, you suddenly realize how strange it is that a 1,000-man faculty really means 995 men and 5 women.

The questions come down to the overriding challenge of how governments are going to recruit and select able people, abide by the merit system, and still contribute toward the nation's goal of 1 = 1. Those are some of the great tasks and growing worries that confront recruitment and selection in the public service. The key steps in the process are shown in Figure 17.1.

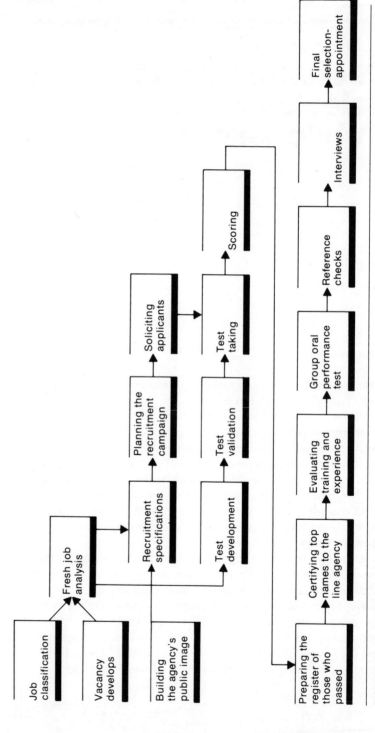

FIGURE 17.1 RECRUITMENT AND SELECTION

Recruitment Is Some Task

Management begins with people, and they come into government through the recruitment - selection doors. Getting able people, as the preceding chart suggests, is a job that stretches all the way back to building the reputation of the agency and to job classification, and on to the hustling of talent and the measurement of applicants. The key factor agency recruiters should bear in mind is the painful truth that if they produce only lemons, the whole agency will suffer.

Consider the magnitude of recruiting people for the federal government. With an overall turnover rate each year of just under 10 percent, the Office of Personnel Management offices throughout the country receive 2.5 million job applications each year, administer sixty different tests some sixty-seven thousand times for 1.9 million applicants, 1.3 million of whom are referred to agencies, of whom 220,000 are hired.[2] Considering the Professional, Administrative Career Examination (PACE) alone (the main portal of entry for social scientists into the U.S. civil service), we might note that 166,000 took the exam in fiscal 1978, with only 7,500 hired from its registers. (Registers are the lists of those who pass an exam, in rank order of their scores.)

Recruitment Goals

Two overriding objectives have come to dominate government recruiting and selection: to attract able people and to serve as a model in eliminating racism and sexism for the private sector to emulate. As to the first, no political hack belongs in the Federal Aviation Administration (FAA) control tower at Kennedy Airport in New York, nursing down a supersonic Concorde; nor in the Food and Drug Administration (FDA) labs measuring the cancer danger of saccharin; nor in the Outer Continental Shelf Office of Interior, determining the propriety of an oil lease to the Union Oil Company off the Santa Barbara coast.

As to the second goal, the constitutional mandate to government is to provide equal protection of the law. So long as the pattern of a 2 to 1 unemployment ratio of blacks compared with whites prevails, with many other minorities also shunted aside, it is imperative that the public sector demonstrate for all to see how to build an interracial work force as we begin to provide equal protection at the personnel office door.

Over time, personnel recruiters have come to believe that the way to accomplish the twin goals of finding good people and assuring equality of opportunity to all is through a system that includes these features:

effective publicity about available jobs

attractive salaries

realistic selection factors

appraisal methods that are free of racial and sex bias

ranking on the basis of ability

Some Recruiting Dilemmas

Standards like those listed do not resolve all the problems, however. One that we explore below is whether a merit system can pursue the goal of equal employment opportunity without sacrificing something in its search for ability.

A second dilemma involves the question of hiring people for immediate jobs or for careers. If the line office is absolutely certain (and at least fairly correct) that they want typists who never rise to supervisor or do anything but type, then recruitment/selection can give applicants a typing test and forget about aptitude and vocational interest tests.

But when an agency has developed well-thought-out training programs and a promotion policy, it may see the duchess in every flower girl it hires, and recruiters ought to go looking accordingly. The implications concerning self-actualization discussed in Chapters 2 and 6 strongly argue for recruitment for careers rather than for dead-end jobs.

Closely related is the question of recruitment for what level: entry at the beginning professional level only, feeding into a *closed* career system, or entry at upper levels as well in an *open* career system (see Figure 17.2).

The historical model of closed career systems has been the British administrative class. Recruitment sought the brightest, most liberally trained graduates of Oxford and Cambridge. What counted was not a set of existing skills but enormous growth potential that could carry these young men of letters up the ministerial ladder to the level of permanent undersecretary in twenty-five years. On this side of the Atlantic, career systems essentially closed are to be found in the military and in such highly professional civilian agencies as the Park Service and the Forest Service.

Prevailing opinion, however, seems to be against systems that recruit only at entry grades and fill upper levels exclusively by recruitment from within (promotions). There are the risks of stagnation — no new ideas, too little challenge. There is the worry about incompatibility between a kind of elite caste system in government and the larger society that seeks openness and equality. Suffice it to say, recruiters need to know if they are to look for plain typists or for typists-plus.

Still another problem is how to attract able executive talent into all levels of government. The city managers have a professional association that is a ready-made source for a city needing a manager. Associations of people in public health, public accounting, and law enforcement are recruiting sources in those specialties. But visualize what is involved in keeping seven thousand positions in the supergrades of the federal civil service (GS-16 to GS-18) filled with truly able policy developers for posts in environmental protection and program man-

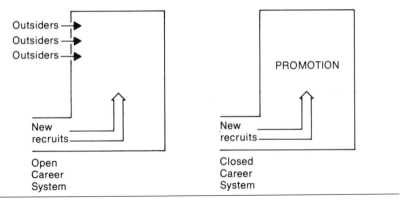

FIGURE 17.2   THE CONTRAST BETWEEN OPEN AND CLOSED CAREER SYSTEMS

agers for everything from urban mass transit to supplementary security income for the retired poor. Compounding the problem is the readiness of special-interest groups to provide executives for government service for the clear purpose of shaping agency policy to benefit their own groups.[3]

With those problems in mind, we turn now to some of the major techniques used in government recruiting.

Building the Agency's Image

Would you consider a career with the state tax commission, the county recreation department, the city streets department, the Internal Revenue Service, the CIA or FBI, or the Peace Corps? Your reaction to each one immediately suggests the impact that agency image has on agency recruiting. Some of the agencies listed may leave you cold — those with dreary missions, questionable ethics, or unpleasant duties to perform. Others would have you packing if a job offer came, enlisting you in a cause you deeply believe in or the administration of an essential program.

What the foregoing suggests is the responsibility of agencies to build their public image as a means of attracting capable people. The aura that has traditionally surrounded the city government of Cincinnati, the state government of California, the old U.S. Bureau of the Budget, the Peace Corps, and the Apollo program suggests what can be done by professionally run institutions of government. Achieving that kind of repute involves a combination of strongly actualized staffs, effective leadership, innovative programs, and highly effective public relations.

One public relations asset that should not be overlooked is the testimony of an agency's best employees. On-the-job briefings should encourage them to talk with friends off the job about their work. Their views can be effectively presented on recruiting missions either by taking them along or through the printed word in recruitment pamphlets.[4]

Occasions when employees are honored for outstanding service is the time for press releases and taped interviews to let the employees' hometowns and alma maters hear the good word about their progeny. What they also hear is the good word about the agency that hired one of their own. These self-actualized workers then become the recruiters' best allies in finding new employees who are like themselves.

One of the best image makers the public service has is the high school civics teacher.[5] She transmits her favorable view of government work to undisillusioned high school students, and that promising personnel source needs cultivating. Among other things that can be done, this calls for presentations by civil service recruiters in high school classes and during career day programs.

Building the government's image is the long-range, unending task of agency heads, recruiters, and many others. But recruitment also involves some immediate kinds of things if skilled people are to be brought on board. Knowing the position to be filled is one of the first.

Job Analysis

Having a sound, updated job classification plan (see Chapter 16) is the necessary foundation for effective recruiting: What kind of a job is to be filled? What kind of a person should we look for? In getting answers to those questions, recruiters cannot rely on old job descriptions; fresh job analysis is called for before the search begins (see the top left-hand corner of Figure 17.1). The courts have held that valid selection procedures (absent discrimination) must begin with a carefully done job analysis.[6]

Initial responsibility for the job specifications rests with the line unit where the vacancy exists. They are the ones who need to define:

the duties to be performed

the specialized knowledge or skills that may be required

the kind of mental ability desired (retentive memory, analytical insight, heuristic problem-solving capabilities)

personal traits that would help (the outward-going receptionist, the "Marine sergeant" security guard, the persuasive EEO officer)

The Office of Personnel Management has nicknamed these the KSAOs (knowledge, skills, abilities, and other requisites needed to perform a job). The ones of particular importance for recruiting and selecting are the job elements that: (a) clearly demarcate superior and mediocre workers (e.g., a manuscript typist in contrast to a correspondence typist); (b) cause trouble if ignored in an appointee (misuse of the telephone, male chauvinism, inability to complete a project); and (c) are practical (portraying neither Superman nor Miss Universe but actual people in your labor supply).[7] They represent the most important threads in the recruiters' net.

Planning the Approach

Let's say the FAA needs radar technicians. To save a lot of time and dollars, its recruiting needs a laser beam, not a floodlight. (The floodlight is for clerk-typists.) Intelligent recruiting begins, then, with a plan based on the job analysis already made.[8] That plan should include a careful projection of individual agency needs (based on turnover rates for different jobs, etc.), publicity built around those needs and beamed to likely sources of supply, diversion of applicants away from surplus registers, and a computerized skills bank.[9]

Places to Search

One of the marks of a sound plan will be the sources of possible workers it points to. Inside recruiting will be greatly aided by the existence of an agency skills roster, just alluded to. For example, at a major air base we're familiar with, to fill a vacancy the personnel office plugs the needed KSAOs into its computer, quickly obtains a printout of eligible people on base, and has the computer print notices to those identified, requesting their application, if interested. That is pinpointed recruitment from within.

Outside, the basic rule echoes Meredith Willson's: you have to know the territory. To whom do we turn in the black community to generate applicants for the police department? Would that Chicano newsletter net us some Spanish-Americans? Which industrial arts school is turning out the kind of people we need for this specialized heating system? Where did our best employees come from? Are others like them coming through those same pipelines? Is a nearby company or agency folding (a Boeing plant closing down in Seattle) with able people to fill job slots in our agency?

Smart recruiters will be exploring all those avenues as well as making the general announcements a merit system requires.

Communications and Recruitment

The basic point is simple enough: no one will apply if vacancies are not advertised (except during times of severe unemployment, when job seekers camp out in personnel office waiting rooms). Thus, it is imperative for recruitment people to master the art of communication.

All the concepts discussed in Chapter 12 arise here. Can recruitment surmount the abstraction ladder and semantic problems in getting across to applicants *what is actually expected* in a certain job? Can recruitment/selection effectively perceive what makes the finalists tick?

Beyond these conceptual problems is the broadcasting problem in recruitment — getting the proper word to the most likely sources of talent so as to assure the hiring agency a number of highly qualified applicants to choose from. The traditional methods called for advertisements in the help wanted columns of the newspaper and bulletin board announcements in the local post office.

But today, an aggressive recruitment staff looks upon the bulletin board posting as the foghorn of last resort. Contacting black ministers to apprise their congregations, putting up notices in inner-city grocery stores and recreation centers, making team visits to colleges with walk-in exams (involving no advance applications and immediate offers to the high scorers), and waiving written tests for students with outstanding grades — these are the kinds of techniques hustling recruiters now employ.[10] They may go armed with authority to start recruits at salaries two or three notches higher than the first step in the grade and to pay moving expenses.

Recruitment literature in many jurisdictions has taken on a professional air. Often printed on glossy paper, replete with action scenes from agency life, and concluding with a personal come-on from the department head herself, many agency brochures herald the new hard sell of government recruitment. The use of mailing lists of secretarial schools and college placement officers has become a standard practice for government recruiters. In some jurisdictions, imaginative use is made of radio (e.g., catching commuter traffic around San Francisco) to publicize available jobs.

Two other recruiting devices are worth noting. One is the use of a "jobs trailer" that can be brought into Chicano neighborhoods, onto the campus of a business college, and so on, with recruiting teams representing federal, state, county, and municipal governments (a kind of cooperative federalism on wheels). The other is the storefront recruiting office (think Marines!) represented by the Job Information Centers the U.S. Civil Service Commission opened in many large cities between 1972 and 1974.

Some Obstacles to Overcome

The phony sell One of the no-nos to be observed in putting the hard sell together is to avoid the oversell.[11] It is the abstraction ladder again: when a recruitment pitch grossly exaggerates the nature of a job, the agency will only be inviting morale problems when the young social scientist comes on board to find that the position of assembling a history of the State Department really means running a clipping service on the daily press. Warren Bennis, looking back on his troubled years at the State University of New York at Buffalo, pointed to mistakes that had been made in recruiting a bright new team at that university. The recruiters had overpromised the space that would be available, the permanency of the positions, and the opportunity to innovate. The failure to deliver sapped morale, leading Bennis to observe: "Recruit with scrupulous honesty."[12]

Prejudices of hiring officials   The recruitment field is greatly restricted when the line officer has a hidden agenda that says "Women are file clerks and blacks are for someone else." When cities expect to hire a local man as city manager, when they require that all city employees live within the city boundaries, and when administrators assume people are too young under twenty-five and over the hill after forty, they place heavy strictures on finding talented applicants.

The economic barriers   If the salary scale for GS-3 clerk-typists slips $75 per month behind the going community rate, some agency typing pools will begin to run dry. If a bureau lacks funds to bring its best prospects to regional head-quarters for interviewing, recruitment may be impossible. And an inability to pay moving expenses may mean the loss of a prize prospect from the recruiter's net.

The recruitment program must be designed to overcome all of those obsta-cles — to discover talent, to uncover *potential talent* (among the disadvan-taged), to lure future employees away from competitors and into active pursuit of posts in government.

Is Our Recruitment Any Good?

A favorable image, job analysis, career planning, effective communications, and flexibility to meet prevailing conditions are among the central pillars of person-nel recruiting. Any agency that wants to stay in business needs to find out if those pillars are in place, and that means asking, "Are we getting qualified people on our staff?"

Performance ratings and the skills ratio will tell part of the story. The turnover rate and answers to exit questionnaires will reveal still more about the kind of people that have been recruited and why the agency is losing them. Attitude surveys among the staff may help uncover weaknesses going all the way back to poor recruitment.

When those weaknesses become apparent, there are some critical points worth reviewing:

Is there any real reason why bright, dedicated people would want to work for us?

Can we promise new recruits meaningful careers?

Do we know where to look for talent?

Is our communication effective (as to target, format, and impact)?

One Administrator Who Said "No"

The frustrations many administrators feel in dealing with the products of a merit system found expression in the fall of 1978 in a statement made by Dr. Tony Mitchell, head of Utah's largest state agency, the Department of Social Services: "A large percentage of state employees are deadwood who are not pulling their own weight."

When rapped by the state employees' organization for the slur, Mitchell indicated that his remarks "were intended to be a criticism of the state merit system, not of individuals who work for the state."

The Utah Public Employee (Nov. 1978) 19:1–3.

Are our salaries attractive?

Have we minimized the delays between application, examination, and job offer?[13]

How do we treat new employees during the first few days and the first few weeks on the job?

Have we ended up with the same old agency — white male professionals, female clerical workers, and black custodians?

For the moment, let us assume that the recruiters have done their job. Ninety applicants with above-minimum qualifications for the position of radar technician have appeared for a vacancy in the FAA. The problem now is how to pick the winner. That conundrum takes us to selection, the twin of recruitment.

SELECTION[14]

Making the choice is no simple matter, a step made all the more difficult by the kinds of vectors at work here: the line agency wants the best of the lot; a powerful senator wants his son-in-law appointed; Congress has mandated a nondiscriminatory hiring process;[15] the courts have required selection devices of proven validity (tests that truly predict who the best workers will be);[16] the local chapter of the National Organization for Women (NOW) insists the appointee be a woman, the NAACP wants it to be a black, and SOCIO (the Spanish speaking organization) pressures for a Chicano. Whom do we appoint?

Fortunately, there are some sieves for sifting the applicants. As Figure 17.3 suggests, the selection process involves a *battery* of devices to weed out the less fit and identify the best fit for a vacant position. We say a battery of devices

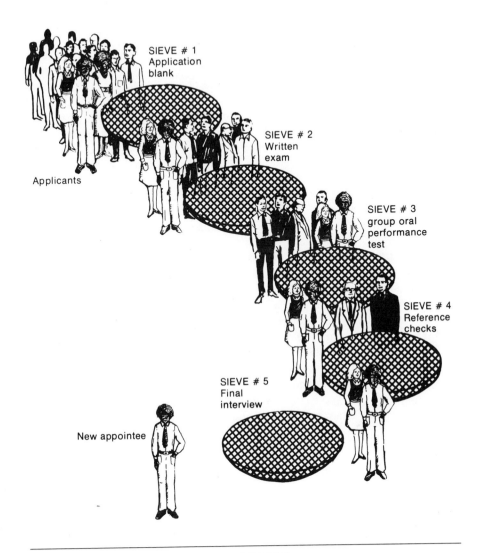

SIEVE # 1
Application
blank

Applicants

SIEVE # 2
Written
exam

SIEVE # 3
group oral
performance
test

SIEVE # 4
Reference
checks

SIEVE # 5
Final
interview

New appointee

FIGURE 17.3   SEPARATING THE SHEEP FROM THE GOATS

because of the realization that written exams cannot possibly tell an employer all he needs to know about applicants and because the one-to-one interview is notoriously unreliable. The evidence is compelling that an intelligent combination of selection instruments can produce far better results than selection by chance. That evidence is to be found in the selection successes chalked up in NASA's astronaut program and in the Peace Corps.[17]

Preselection

There is a good opportunity to apply the exception principle in personnel selection. It simply involves specifying the desired qualifications and asking those lacking the qualifications not to apply. Some potential applicants then screen themselves out at the outset.

The *application blank* is a key instrument in the preselection process. It should require adequate information for appraisal and avoid excessive length and irrelevancies. In addition to calling for basic personal data (residence, age, address, social security number, etc.), the application should probe for education and experience, honors, special skills, conviction record, drug and alcohol usage, and a list of references.[18] As a result of EEO, there are some questions that may no longer be asked: hair and eye color, number of children, credit standing, submission of a photograph, arrests (in contradistinction to *convictions,* which may be asked for). They have nothing to do with job performance but a lot to do with feeding the prejudices of appointing officers.

Like all other selection devices, the application blank should be subjected to validation analysis. One possibly fruitful procedure would be to review the application blanks of the employees who have subsequently been fired or who have quit. Did the application blank provide any clue to the subsequent "malfunction"? Might it have provided one if designed differently?

The completed application blank lies at the heart of one kind of selection procedure called the *unassembled exam.* The term signifies a careful scrutiny of education and experience as reported on the application (backed up by transcripts, degrees, and so on) and a thorough check of applicants' references. The unassembled exam may be part of a competitive or noncompetitive selection process.

Tests in the Selection Process

The keystone of the merit system is the *competitive examination,* paper-and-pencil tests given to assembled groups of applicants. Those with passing scores are listed on a *register,* from which the top scorers are referred to the line office having a vacancy. Additional selection techniques are then applied to these finalists, ultimately leading to the appointment of one of them.

The goals of the process are to assure equality of opportunity (the exam should play no favorites) and appointments based on merit, not on pull. The underlying hope is reasonable enough: a competitive examination can identify the stronger applicants who deserve further evaluation. With the passage of time, however, critics have appeared to challenge every vulnerable point in the theory and practice of civil service examinations:[19]

> Unvalidated tests are used, leaving agencies in the dark as to what high scores may be predicting.

Untrained personnel misinterpret test results (especially on personality inventories) and don't know that they don't know what they are doing.

Tests that were supposed to be the great equalizers may be loaded with cultural bias against those with good job skills but inadequate language ability.

Tests may be poorly constructed.

Some kinds of tests invade privacy, particularly the personality tests.[20]

Tests of personality have been particularly troublesome. But other kinds of civil service examinations have had a better track record:

tests of general mental ability to discover potential employees who are equipped to handle written materials and analytic processes

tests of specific cognitive abilities — words, space, visual speed, numbers, symbols

tests of dexterity and coordination, when physical movements are important

fields of knowledge and skills tests for hiring librarians, dietitians, meteorologists, typists, stenographers, keypunch operators, and so on

A central emphasis in test development in the last decade has been *job element* testing. It calls either for performing duties typical of the position being sought (taking a typing test, servicing a carburetor, etc.) or taking a written test whose questions pertain directly to the duties of the position. Consider the job of mine inspector, for example. Ernest Primoff has suggested a job element test for that post, including:[21]

Job element	*Test*
Ability to prepare inspection reports	Arrangement of four-sentence sets in causal order
Ability to interpret mine drawings and observations	Presentation of report of mine accident and sketches, with multiple-choice questions
Knowledge of first aid and mine rescue	Questions probing for rescue and treatment procedures

Job element tests have two principal virtues — reduction of cultural bias and improved validity — both of which are important to the courts if the testing procedure is challenged. With regard to cultural bias, for example, consider the difference between asking applicants for a position of reading meters to demonstrate their ability to do so versus giving them a general knowledge test measuring what they learned in high school. In the actual registering of what the meters say, applicants with minimal language skills are not going to be at a disadvantage in the test.[22]

Oral examinations Many jurisdictions in the country supplement paper-and-pencil tests with oral examinations. There are two variations:

the group interview, with one applicant facing a panel of questioners

the group oral performance test, where a number of applicants are placed together in a problem-solving situation observed by an evaluation team

The rather frightening quiz session with a State Department panel that greets an applicant who survives the assembled Foreign Service exam illustrates the group interview. The group oral that federal management intern applicants had to go through (e.g., acting out a school board dealing with a racial crisis) illustrates the second.

Two virtues commend the group interview in preference to the one-to-one interview. The interrogation may be more searching, as the product of more than one mind; and biased judgments of one interviewer can be checked by the other panel members.

The group oral performance test provides an opportunity for evaluation of many facets of the applicants' qualifications and shortcomings: intellectual sharpness, language ability, ability to defend and modify points of view, interpersonal skills, leadership ability, and other qualities. On the other hand, the method may give a false picture of some applicants, whose only shortcoming may be reticence. Furthermore, the *competitive* milieu of the group oral may provide a kind of cutthroat introduction to the agency that may disturb able applicants.

Test preparation The basic requirements the courts have laid down for test design include the following:[23]

thorough job analysis to determine what knowledge, skills, and abilities (KSAOs) will be required

design of the test items by professionally qualified people*[24]

weighting of sections of the exam to match job elements (e.g., heavy weighting on verbal skills in a police examination might be a factor in disallowing that exam)

determination of the passing score to enhance the predictive validity of the exam

validation of the exam by methods approved by the psychology profession, including criterion-related, construct, and content validity measures

elimination of racial bias from the exam (see the section below on equal employment opportunity)

---

* As case in point, a U.S. district court judge in *Kirkland* v. *N.Y. Department of Corrections* 520 F.2d 420 (1974) denied the qualifications of all six people who had prepared a sergeant's promotional exam, three from the corrections department and three from the state civil service commission staff.

Test preparation, like recruitment, begins with job analysis to determine the duties (job elements) to be performed and the KSAOs required (knowledge, skills, abilities, and other requirements). Then the test developer, ordinarily a psychologist, determines what kinds of evidence of knowledge and ability will most clearly separate the able from the marginal applicants and makes a preliminary decision on the test format — performance, multiple choice, essay, oral, and so on. Where the number of applicants is large and they are widely dispersed, a machine-readable, multiple-choice exam is almost always indicated. The draft exam is then field-tested to correct the bugs (poorly worded questions, questions that give away the answers to other questions, etc.), to determine if there is cultural bias, and to find other flaws.

Then the test is ready for the critical validation step: Will it really predict which applicants are likely to become able employees?

Validation   Two factors compel the expenditure of time and money to determine whether the test is valid. First, it's a waste of everybody's time if the test is not a good predictor; second, since *Griggs* v. *Duke Power Company* (1971), the courts have insisted on tests being validated for the *jobs being filled* from a given test's results.[25]

The concept of validity is rather easily portrayed by what I like to call the cigar diagram (see Figure 17.4). The valid test (on the left) shows the "cigar" covering much of areas A and C, little of areas B and D (the two quadrants of misses — poor prediction). That suggests that a high proportion of those who do well on the test will do well on the job and that a similar proportion of low scorers would, if hired, do poorly on the job.

But with the invalid exam, the bloated "cigar" suggests many poor scorers would do well on the job (area B), while many high scorers would do poorly on the job (area D).[26] (Note the areas of hits and misses can be affected by where the pass line on the exam is set and where the satisfactory performance line is set.)

There are at least three different ways of measuring the validity of exams:[27]

1. *Content validity (or face validity):* Do the questions asked clearly pertain to what the job will require? In *Bridgeport Guardians, Inc.* v. *Bridgeport Civil Service Commission,* for example, a federal circuit court rejected a municipal police exam because of irrelevant test items.[28] The central concern about content validity is the lack of empirical proof that it provides any basis for predicting success on the job.

2. *Construct validity:* Do the questions accurately measure the underlying knowledge, skills, and psychological predispositions required on the job (e.g., the visual acuity needed in an air traffic controller, the mathematical competence required in a computer programmer, the cool-under-fire disposition of a cop, etc.)?

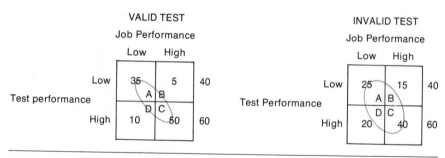

FIGURE 17.4 HOW GOOD ARE OUR TESTS?

3. *Predictive (or criterion) validity:* How will the test scores compare with the criterion of job performance (e.g., actual performance ratings), either of people hired from the test in the past whom the validators have tracked (longitudinal validation), or of current employees with known performance ratings who have been given the test as guinea pigs (concurrent validation)?

All three validation methods pose problems: (a) frequently the lack of any predictive linkage between test scores and job performance in the case of content (job element) tests and the construct tests (doing a concurrent validation study would help meet this problem); (b) the fact that lower scorers are usually not hired, thus skewing the sample upward of people actually hired whose performance ratings are to be used in arriving at correlations later on between test scores and performance ratings; (c) the costs involved, particularly in the longitudinal studies; and (d) the widely held doubts about performance ratings as adequate measures of job success.*[29]

Despite these weaknesses, the 1978 federal selection standards authorized all three approaches to validation under appropriate conditions and professional administration.[30] The general reputation of nationally developed tests, however, will not be accepted as a substitute for in situ validation. The only leeway permitted by the regulations is use of examinations validated elsewhere by others in directly related job categories.[31]

A word about correlation analysis The statistical measuring device to determine the regularity with which two variables move together (in our present discussion, test scores and performance ratings on the job) is the Pearson Coefficient of Correlation.[32] Coefficients of correlation are not percentages or

---

* Inadequacies in Scott Paper's performance ratings led a U.S. circuit court in 1976 to reject the exams being used by that company on the ground they had not been properly validated. See *Watkins* v. *Scott Paper,* 530 F. 2d 1159 (1976).

proportions; they are rates of occurrence between two variables, measured on a scale from -1.0 (where the two variables are moving in exactly opposite directions — the high test scorers are the first to leave the job, the low test scorers stay with the job) through 0 correlation (where there is no relationship at all between the two variables), on to $+1.0$ (where there is absolute concurrence between the two variables — the high scorers are the outstanding performers on the job). G. G. McClung's description of the correlation coefficients (Table 17.1) is a helpful one to bear in mind.

Reliability of examinations   In addition to their predictive value, we need to know how reliable and believable the examinations are. Reliability looks at the question of how much chance enters into examination results. How quixotic are the scores? If I took that same exam next week, would I perform far differently than I did when I took it yesterday? Was my score on the multiple-choice section completely unrelated to my showing on the essay question?

There are a number of measures for testing reliability. One of them is a rigorous check called the split-half method that compares the scores of the applicants on one half of the examination with their scores on the second half.

TABLE 17.1   INTERPRETING THE COEFFICIENTS OF CORRELATION BETWEEN TEST SCORES AND LATER JOB PERFORMANCE

	Correlation coefficients	Interpretation
A. High scorers perform better on the job than low scorers	1.00	Perfect prediction (never occurs)
	.75	Very strong relationship (rarely occurs)
	.50	Substantial correlation (most you can hope for)
	.25	Small but definite correlation (typical occurrence)
B. Low scorers perform better on the job than high scorers	$-.25$	Small but definite correlation (typical occurrence)
	$-.50$	Strong negative correlation
	$-.75$	Essentially certain that low scorers will be the high performers on the job
	-1.00	Perfect prediction of negative correlation (never occurs)

Source: G.G. McClung, "Statistical Techniques in Testing," in J.J. Donovan, *Recruitment and Selection in the Public Service* (Chicago: Public Personnel Association, 1968), p. 340. Reprinted by permission of the International Personnel Management Association.

The second method is to repeat the examination (without forewarning the guinea pigs so as to prevent their boning up for the second round) and then compare the scores from the two exposures.

Standardization of exams   Personnel people also need to have a clear picture of the level of difficulty of test questions (items) and of whole test batteries. There is really only one way to measure the level of difficulty, and that is to keep meticulous records of correct and incorrect answers to each test question.

Visualize a filing cabinet alongside the desk of a test designer. Each drawer contains a tray of examination questions, one per card, with the pass-fail records carefully noted. Using a coding system, the examiner has designated the level of difficulty of each question. In a tight labor market, the request may come for a relatively easy exam. The line agency must fill its vacancies and will take almost any applicant who can sign his name. Thanks to standardization of exam items, the examiner can put together a patsy of a quiz. Conversely, when there is a flood of applicants, she can design a rigorous go-around that only the Phi Beta Kappas can survive.

The time element   The testing sequence must meet one additional criterion: the speed with which examinations can be scheduled, scored, registers prepared, and results announced so that hot prospects do not take other jobs while an agency is waiting for the test results. In the mid-1970s the U.S. Civil Service Commission, deeply conscious of this problem, established a national test center at Macon, Georgia, with optical scanning equipment and the capacity to provide one-week service to the commission's area offices, instead of the six to eight weeks formerly required. In 1977, the commission launched an experiment allowing selected agencies with unique technical occupations to do their own testing and preparation of registers. Small may be not only beautiful but faster!

Getting Certified

Passing a civil service exam will place you somewhere on a register, where the applicants are ranked from high down to passing scores. It is at this point that we encounter for the first time veteran's preference in public personnel administration. Depending on the rules of the Office of Personnel Management, the length of military service, and the type of disability, the veteran who achieves *a passing score on the exam* will have points added to his earned score, thus lifting his position on the register. A tougher form of veteran's preference reserves some kinds of positions exclusively for veterans (ordinarily in the non-professional category).*

* There are right and wrong ways for a nation to repay its debt to its veterans. The GI Bill, enhancing the educational level of the whole nation, was a superbly right way to do it; subverting the idea of merit in personnel selection is demonstrably the wrong way, in this author's opinion.

With the register ready, how are some test takers hired? Preparing for summer, let's say, the state fish and game department notifies the state personnel office that it intends to hire game management trainees and requests that the names of eligibles be certified for departmental selection. With a highly specialized game management examination and register to draw from, the personnel office refers the top names on the pass list to the line agency.

The traditional rule called for the certification of the top three names (the "Rule of Three"), plus some extra names in case of nonavailability of some of the top three. But since the first Hoover Commission, doubts have increased about so limiting the choices of the hiring official.[33] Modifications of the Rule of Three have thus appeared, such as the Rule of Three Scores, which permits referral of all the names receiving the top three whole numbers (including ties and ignoring decimal points). The Rule of Five also broadens the line's field of choice.

Another technique that enables the appointing officer to get from the register the specific kinds of people she needs is selective certification — referring those names from a register who have the job skills for the vacancies at hand and bypassing others who may have higher scores but who lack the particular skills required. This procedure seems especially appropriate where the examination measures broad fields (such as engineers, social science analysts, and the like) rather than specialties (such as hydraulic engineers, civil engineers, historians, and statisticians). Problems posed by lengthy registers for selective certification can be readily handled by a computer: from a generalist register we want the five top scorers who majored in economics and have B's or better in at least two statistics courses; properly programmed, a computer could have a printout of those five young economists in seconds.

But selective certification also poses some risks — hanky-panky between the line officer who wants to reach a certain person some notches down on the register, and a friend at the Office of Personnel Management. Here selective certification may hop and skip down the register to assure that Dolly Varden makes the certified list, thoroughly vitiating the idea of a merit system.

The Final Sieves

Up to this point in the selection process, the personnel office has done the lion's share of the work; the principal input from the line has been *job analysis* to guide both recruitment and examining. Now, with names from the register in hand and a vacancy to be filled, the line office undertakes the final stages of the selection process.

Appraising training and experience The unassembled exam procedure discussed earlier is the first sieve to be used after names have been certified from the register. This appraisal of candidates' applications and supporting documents is no rote exercise of counting up years of schooling, giving so many points for this degree or that many years of work.

Qualitative questions must be asked. What is the reputation of the college this woman attended? How tough was her major? Were her grades going downhill or uphill during her last two years? How much responsibility did this other applicant shoulder in his most recent employment? How many promotions did he have in the last five years?

Reference checks This sieve of reviewing the candidates' backgrounds narrows the field still further. The reference checks on the remaining applicants may then produce the semifinalists. The candidates have listed people on the application blank who they believe will praise them, not appraise them. But the selection officer needs an appraisal. For key positions the employer may want to probe an applicant to find individuals known to both, so that the employer can judge the reference (his candor, judgment, and so on) who is going to judge the applicant. Names of former employers also need to be checked out. The information they can provide is likely to be more job related than that provided by neighbor, pastor, and family physician of the applicant.

Many factors may dictate the use of a reference form to be transmitted by mail — distance, number of applicants to be considered, and so on. The form may call for open-ended answers on particular job qualities the agency is looking for (as in the case of the Peace Corps reference form); or it may utilize a graphic rating scale with job qualities listed down one side and a five-point scale to the right to be checked by the reference (see Table 17.2).

For key positions, the telephone or face-to-face interview is far superior to the reference form. Probing into weak points, noting where the reference is holding back, measuring his or her enthusiasm about the applicant are all facilitated by voice contact.

In addition to the questions shown in Table 17.2, there are some others an employer ought to resolve about an applicant:

Did she apply herself without prodding?

Was she a goof-off, the "queen of the coffee break"?

Were there quirks to her personality that made you relieved to have her quit — was she an endless talker, a constant complainer, cold and aloof, hypercritical of others, full of racial or religious prejudice, often late and an abuser of sick leave?

Through this kind of probing, one may be able to screen out some genius who was in the 97th percentile on the exam but who would be a lemon on the job.

Interview If the sieves have functioned well, the field should now be reduced to a couple of finalists. The interview, one of the most relied on and least reliable of all the selection devices, now awaits them.[34]

TABLE 17.2 REFERENCE FORM (graphic rating scale)

Applicant qualities	Your appraisal of the applicant		
	Nonexistent	Average	Superb
1. Motivation and hustle			
	1 2 3 4 5		
2. Creativity and new ideas			
	1 2 3 4 5		
3. Perception of and dedication to the public interest			
	1 2 3 4 5		
4. Harmonious relationships with co-workers			
	1 2 3 4 5		
5. Honesty and integrity			
	1 2 3 4 5		
6. Willingness to make decisions and accept responsibility			
	1 2 3 4 5		

7. Would you want this applicant in an important post in your organization? Please comment:

8. What are the applicant's chief shortcomings?

The pitfalls in the one-to-one interview are many. The candidate freezes and rapport is never established; the candidate is glib and snows the interviewer; the candidate is gorgeous and wows the interviewer; the candidate is black and the interviewer is not color-blind; a reviewable record is not kept; the interviewer ends up wallowing in value judgments and being hypnotized by halos.

Those kinds of traps have led some agencies to employ a group interview of an applicant (discussed earlier). Here the panel of questioners can compare notes after the interviews are completed and look for consensus on critical traits and weaknesses. As noted previously, the extra observations provide a check on the biases of one.

Final selection The decision to hire can be made after determining and validating the weights for the various selection devices and the scores on each one that the finalists earned. Consider a hypothetical case (see Table 17.3). Candidate 2 emerges with the most points in this quantitative appraisal, the largest margin of difference having arisen during the final interview (but with a weight of only one, note). The final decision isn't going to be based on a numbers game; but in a sense the selection table presents a nomination, like a null hypothesis, to be challenged.

With a choice finally made, a job offer is tendered. When accepted, the

TABLE 17.3 SELECTION TABLE

		Candidate 1		Candidate 2	
Selection factor	Weight[a]	× Raw score (100 poss.)	Total	× Raw score (100 poss.)	Total
Education and experience	4	90	360	93	372
Written examination	3	95	285	91	273
Group oral performance test	2	80	160	88	176
References	4	95	380	95	380
Final interview	1	70	70	90	90
Total weighted points			1255		1291

[a]Must be validated.

appointment papers are initiated by the line office, reviewed by the personnel office for compliance with merit system standards, and a new employee prepares to come on board.

The selection process itself, however, culminates only after successful completion of the *probationary period.* This trial of six months to a year provides the ultimate validation (or flunking) of the whole recruitment-selection effort. How does the new appointee turn out on the job? During this time, the novitiate has few job rights (although she may not be dismissed for reasons of sex, race, religion, or political beliefs). Near the end of her probationary service, she receives a supervisory rating and recommendation for separation (dismissal or transfer) or for tenure (career appointment with job rights).

Taking the Measure of Recruitment and Selection

As with all personnel procedures, the feedback question must be asked of recruitment and selection: "How are we doing?" Norman Sharpless has suggested some specifics to look for:

1. How do the line officials feel about the employees the personnel office has provided?

2. What kind of turnover rate are we experiencing with employees during their first three years on the job (those who could not hack it, bright ones who were recruited away)?

3. What kinds of promotions and honors have come to the employees we have recruited and hired (do our methods uncover any stars)?

4. How much bypassing of the merit system goes on in recruitment and selection in our agency, and how do the "provisionals" who get sneaked in compare with employees who are hired through our regular procedures?[35]

A management information system to provide data on those questions is a must.

Then there is another must that confronts public recruitment and selection: staffing units of government without racist or sexist discrimination, demonstrating to all employers what equality of opportunity means.

EQUAL EMPLOYMENT OPPORTUNITY

The Very Large Stakes

Consider what an anachronism it is that this far into American history, the governments of the United States and its subdivisions are predominantly white and male in the professional ranks, female in the clerical, with heavy concentrations of minorities in the blue-collar jobs.

To be specific, in 1977 women (who constitute 51 percent of the population) held 77 percent of the GS-1 through GS-4 jobs in federal civil service, only 5 percent of the GS-14 to GS-15 grades, and only 3 percent of the supergrades. Minorities in 1977 (13 percent of the population) constituted 29 percent of the GS-1 to GS-4 ranks, 6 percent of the GS-14 to GS-15, and 5 percent of the GS-16 to GS-18 supergrades.[36]

Table 17.4 tells the story of declining expectations for both groups (focus on the two percentage columns). The picture presented in the table of unequal opportunity in the public service has some far-flung implications:

clearly the loss of talent by excluding women and minorities from positions they might otherwise be filling*

further frustration of the legitimate hopes for recognition on the part of important subgroups in the body politic

a public service far from representative of the people it serves[37]

That picture becomes all the more significant when seen against the backdrop of other social indicators of our day:

median black families whose income never reaches 65 percent of median white families

twenty-eight percent of our black people living in poverty, in contrast to 7 percent of our whites

the unemployment rate always running at least 2 to 1 against blacks and engulfing over 40 percent of black teenagers in many cities during the 1970s

women, on the average, earning about 60 percent of what men make[38]

---

* As a painful case in point, one thinks of Philadelphia's unwillingness to hire blacks as city bus drivers during the labor shortage of World War II.

TABLE 17.4 FEMALE AND MINORITY SHARES OF THE GENERAL SCHEDULE FEDERAL JOBS IN 1977

GS grades	Total employees	Women	Their % share	Minorities	Their % share
1–4	291,450	224,649	77.1	85,409	29.3
5–8	435,468	267,554	61.4	99,609	22.9
9–11	339,493	93,608	27.6	45,652	13.4
12–13	265,161	24,667	9.3	21,737	8.2
14–15	90,769	4,313	4.8	5,591	6.2
16–18	6,829	230	3.4	337	4.9
Totals	1,429,170	615,021	43.0	258,335	18.1

Source: U.S. Civil Service Commission, *Civil Service News*, Aug. 23, 1978, pp. 4–5.

Taken together, these aspects of our national life dramatically underscore how important it has become for governments to be the *model employers* in this country. In some special way the title deeds to "all men are created equal" and the equal protection clause of the Fourteenth Amendment seem to have come to rest on the shoulders of public personnel systems.

Changing Attitudes and the Law

The awareness of how long we had slept without noting the racism around us began to develop after World War II. A feisty president named Harry Truman commissioned a study of major import in 1947, *To Secure These Rights,* and then followed up on the spirit of that report by integrating the Armed Forces in 1948.

The judiciary was a tower of strength in effecting change in the treatment of racial minorities in the 1950s and 1960s. The beginning point came in May 1954 with the Warren Court's historic decision, *Brown* v. *Board of Education,* unanimously striking down school segregation. What Chief Justice Warren was accomplishing on the bench, Martin Luther King, Jr., was hastening in the streets — desegregation of buses in Montgomery and access to lunch counters in Birmingham, Alabama, and better treatment of black sanitation workers in Memphis, Tennessee (where King was killed).

For public personnel management, the culminating event of this civil rights revolution was clearly the 1964 Civil Rights Act.[39] Its Title VII (section 703) mandated an end to discrimination in employment because of an individual's race, color, religion, sex, or national origin.

Section 703(h) of title VII permitted different standards of compensation, appointments under merit systems, and the use of professionally developed tests of ability so long as there is no intent in any of these areas to discriminate on the basis of race, color, religion, sex, or national origin.

The 1964 Commitment to Equal Employment Opportunity

Section 703(a) of the 1964 Civil Rights Act reads:

SEC. 703. (a) It shall be an unlawful employment practice for an employer —
(1) to fail or refuse to hire or to discharge any individual, or otherwise to discriminate against any individual with respect to his compensation, terms, conditions, or privileges of employment, because of such individual's race, color, religion, sex, or national origin; or

(2) to limit, segregate, or classify his employees in any way which would deprive or tend to deprive any individual of employment opportunities or otherwise adversely affect his status as an employee, because of such individual's race, color, religion, sex, or national origin.

P.L. 88-352; 78 Stat. 241 (July 2, 1964).

In section 703(j) the act mildly rejected reverse discrimination. It provided that nothing in title VII should be interpreted as requiring any employer to grant preferential treatment to any individual or group because of race, color, religion, sex, or national origin to correct an imbalance that might exist with respect to the total number or percentage of persons employed in comparison to the base percentage of that group in the surrounding community or state.

President Johnson launched the federal government's affirmative action program in 1967 with Executive Order 11246. Five years later, Congress extended the coverage of the 1964 Civil Rights Act to all levels of government in the Equal Opportunity Act of 1972.[40]

Enter the Courts[41]

The dramatic entry of the courts into personnel management came in a private sector case in 1971, *Griggs* v. *Duke Power Company* (a North Carolina public utility).[42] Prior to the 1964 Civil Rights Act, this utility had openly discriminated against blacks, relegating them to the company's labor department. With the advent of the new law, Duke Power required that employees desiring to transfer out of the labor department complete high school and achieve a satisfactory score on the Wonderlic General Intelligence test and the Bennett Mechanical Comprehension test. The requirements significantly blocked the advancement of blacks in the company.

The Supreme Court's rulings in the case were significant:

1. Where a test is found to have an adverse impact on minorities, the burden of proof then shifts to the employer to demonstrate the "business

necessity" of the test: "The [Civil Rights] Act proscribes not only overt discrimination but also practices that are fair in form but discriminatory in operation. The touchstone is business necessity.* If an employment practice which operates to exclude Negroes cannot be shown to be related to job performance, the practice is prohibited."[43]

2. Tests must be validated for the positions being filled. In the instant case, the requirement of the high school diploma and the tests being used represented excessive and invalid hurdles for the kinds of jobs being filled: "any test used must measure the person for the job and not the person in the abstract."[44]

3. Discriminatory intent need not be proved; racially discriminatory results will establish a violation of equal employment opportunity.

The *Griggs* case was like a lightning bolt, flashing warnings to personnel managers in the private and public sectors as well that the day of sloppy selection devices with discriminatory results was over, that the time to validate tests had arrived. By 1977, a U.S. circuit court would tell the city of Chicago that the burden of proof that its tests were valid predictors of on-the-job success for whites and minorities rested on the city. Only then would the court tolerate a higher flunk rate for minorities, indicating a relative lack of qualifications on their part.[45]

The matter of bad intent as an element in proving unlawful discrimination would confront the Supreme Court again. In the *Griggs* case, intent was irrelevant. But the Court reached a different conclusion five years later when two blacks charged the Washington, D.C., police force with racial discrimination in *Washington* v. *Davis.*[46]

A higher percentage of blacks — four times the percentage of whites — had failed a written test of verbal skills administered to police officer applicants. But the Supreme Court rejected the charge of discrimination on two grounds: (a) intent to discriminate was clearly absent in this police department, as evidenced by its affirmative action recruitment effort, the rising number of blacks in the recruit classes, and other factors; and (b) validity was demonstrated in studies showing a correlation between the written test and success in a training program dealing with verbal skills for new police officers, which the Court was willing to accept in lieu of a validation study looking at on-the-job performance. Clearly, the good intent of the police department to promote equal employment opportunity prevented a finding of racial discrimination in this case.†

Increasingly the courts seem to be relying on two barometers of employment

---

* Chief Justice Burger's term, "business necessity," seems singularly inapt. The whole thrust of his thought points instead to how valid the exams are.

† That the issue of having to prove bad intent is not settled is indicated by cases since *Washington* v. *Davis.* A federal circuit court held in 1977 that bad intent need not be proved in showing that a test is discriminatory in *Richardson* v. *Pennsylvania Department of Health,* 561 F. 2d 489 (1977).

discrimination: (a) wide disparity between the racial composition of a government agency and the racial makeup of the surrounding community; and (b) a clearly adverse impact on minorities taking civil service examinations. In those circumstances, personnel officers will have to carry the burden of proof in establishing the validity of the exams for positions being filled.[47]

Faulty recruitment methods have also been dealt with by the courts. In *Boston Chapter, NAACP* v. *Beecher* (1974), the U.S. district court for Massachusetts struck down word of mouth recruiting for the Boston fire department (then 90 percent white) and the use of a written test measuring general intelligence and basic fire fighting. Face validity was not enough, the court said, to validate the exams.

The remedies imposed were tough: the department was ordered to validate its exams and then follow a hiring ratio favoring blacks until their numbers on the force were proportionate to their percentage of the black population of Boston.[48]

Quotas and Reverse Discrimination

The courts have found themselves between a rock and a hard place in dealing with agencies exhibiting gross underrepresentation of minorities. The rock was section 703(j) of title VII of the 1964 Civil Rights Act, noted earlier, which proscribed preferential treatment based on race, sex, and so on, and the hard place was the lily-white employers who have made a mockery out of the 1964 act's mandate for equal employment opportunity.

In a number of instances, registers from unvalidated examinations have been suspended, and minority hiring quotas have been imposed to correct the imbalances of past discrimination. For example, a U.S. district court in *Officers for Justice* v. *Civil Service Commission* (1973) required that 60 percent of those hired in a local police department be minorities until their percentage in the department reached 30 percent.[49] In *NAACP* v. *Allen* (1974), the lower federal courts were asked to develop a remedy for the state highway patrol of Alabama, which in thirty-seven prior years had never hired a black trooper. The district court required that one black highway trooper be hired for each white one employed until the force was approximately 25 percent black.[50]

In the later 1970s, however, there have been a number of cases moving against quotas and reverse discrimination. For example, a U.S. circuit court in *Chance* v. *The Board of Examiners* in 1976 voided preferential treatment for a black in New York that required that a senior white employee stand aside and lose his seniority.[51] And in *Hiatt* v. *City of Berkeley,* a California court struck down a city affirmative action program that required racial quotas in all city departments matching the population makeup of the city. The quotas violated Title VII of the 1964 Civil Rights Act and the equal protection clause of the Fourteenth Amendment.[52]

The litmus test of the Supreme Court's attitude on these racial issues came in the summer of 1978 in *Regents of the University of California* v. *Bakke*.[53] While not a public employment case, the *Bakke* case raised the directly related question of how far a public institution (a state medical school) may go in using racial quotas to build a racially diversified student body and, beyond graduation, a racially diversified corps of doctors.

The faculty of the medical school at the University of California at Davis had reserved sixteen places out of one hundred in each new entering class for minority students (the term "disadvantaged" was window dressing for a minority affirmative action program).[54] That meant that racial minorities could compete for all one hundred seats, with sixteen reserved for them, while white applicants could compete for only eighty-four. During a four-year period, sixty-three minority students were admitted at Davis under the special admissions program and forty-four under the general admissions program.

In two years of trying, a white applicant named Allan Bakke, with combined scores higher than those admitted under the special program, was rejected. He charged racial discrimination by a state agency, the university, in violation of title VI of the Civil Rights Act of 1964, which forbids such discrimination in any federally assisted program; he also charged the university with violation of the equal protection clause of the Fourteenth Amendment.

The case was full of drama, with the adversaries a university, with good motives, adopting a quota system on its own to do something affirmatively about racial discrimination in the medical field, and a white male, charging that that system had subjected him to racial discrimination.

The Supreme Court could not have been more divided. Four justices held that the quota system was proper and that Bakke's exclusion was permissible (the two liberals, Justices Brennan and Marshall, with two conservatives, Justices White and Blackmun); four other justices held to the contrary and called for Bakke's admission (the conservatives, Chief Justice Burger and Justices Stevens, Rehnquist, and Stewart). The ultimate decision of the Court thus rode on the swing man, Justice Powell. Allied with the first group of justices, Lewis Powell held that race may be taken into account along with other factors in determining school admissions. Allied with the second group, he held that the university's quota system was on its face discriminatory and violative of federal law.* By a 5 to 4 vote, the Court ordered Bakke admitted, held that quotas in the fashion used were unlawful, and permitted public institutions to consider race among other selection factors.

While the Court's willingness to allow universities to take race into account gave some hope for affirmative action programs, some of Justice Powell's language clearly undercut the spirit of affirmative action:

---

* "The guarantee of equal protection cannot mean one thing when applied to one individual and something else when applied to a person of another color. If both are not accorded the same protection, then it is not equal." J. Powell, 98 S. Ct. 2733, 2748. In reply, one recalls the maxim that "The greatest inequality of all is the equal treatment of unequals."

It is far too late to argue that the guarantee of equal protection to *all* persons permits the recognition of special wards entitled to a degree of protection greater than that accorded others.[55]

[We have allowed preferential treatment only where there have been authoritative findings of past discrimination. The university] is in no position to make such findings. Its broad mission is education, not the formulation of any legislative policy or the adjudication of particular claims of illegality.... Isolated segments of our vast governmental structures are not competent to make those decisions, at least not in the absence of legislative mandates and legislatively determined criteria.[56]

I find the second statement especially galling. The nondiscrimination policy of the 1964 Civil Rights Act was applied to the states and to the University of California at Davis by the Equal Employment Opportunity Act of 1972 (a legislative mandate for governments to get going on removing the barriers to racial equality in America). The university caught the spirit of that mandate, devised a program to give the medical school a multiracial student body — and then the Supreme Court spanked the institution as "not competent to make those decisions." In reply, we paraphrase a scripture which suggests that "It is not meet that man should be commanded in all things, but of his own free agency should bring to pass much righteousness." In fine, the *Bakke* case tells government officials that they may be race conscious in recruitment and selection but that quotas are out.

One year later, in June 1979, the Court (with Mr. Justice Powell not participating), removed a fair part of the sting of *Bakke.* They had under consideration in *United Steelworkers of America* v. *Weber* a joint labor-management affirmative action effort in Louisiana to prepare more blacks for skilled craft positions. (At the time Weber brought suit in 1974, 15 percent of the workers in the Louisiana plant were black, but only 2 percent of the craft workers were — five employees out of 273. The local work force was 39 percent black.) Kaiser Aluminum, in conjunction with the Steelworkers Union, instituted a training program to correct that imbalance, with a 50 percent black and 50 percent white enrollment.

Weber, a white worker, was not admitted to the training program, and brought suit under Title VII of the 1964 Civil Rights Act. The relevant language of Title VII (sec. 703[d]) prohibits a joint labor-management committee controlling an on-the-job training program from discriminating "against any individual because of his race, color, religion, sex, or national origin in admission to, or employment in, any [training] program."

Focusing on the broad purposes of Civil Rights Act rather than the specific prohibitions in sec. 703 (d), the Court (through Mr. Justice Brennan) upheld Kaiser's voluntary effort to promote equal employment opportunity and "eliminate traditional patterns of racial segregation." In so doing, the Court provided broad judicial underpinning for race-conscious affirmative action programs in both the private and public sectors. The vote was 5 to 2 (with Justices Powell and Stevens not participating).[57]

The Shape of Affirmative Action

An important preliminary step toward EEO in the public service is *improving community conditions* that may militate against the program, particularly discriminatory housing and inadequate education and public transportation.

Given the traditional Hatch Act stance of political neutrality imposed on the civil service, the EEO directives of the U.S. Civil Service Commission during 1967–1969 were almost revolutionary in character in instructing federal managers to plunge into community affairs to bring about changes in conditions.[58] A graphic case in point is that of Robert H. Terry, manager of the large IRS Western Service Center in Ogden, Utah. Finding housing discrimination a barrier to talented blacks transferring from IRS posts in California and elsewhere, Terry spearheaded a community effort to open up housing opportunities for his integrated work force.

Job classification (discussed in Chapter 16) has an important role to play in EEO. Consider the federal civil service program known as MUST (Maximum Utilization of Skills and Training). The underlying concept of MUST was simple. By redesigning GS-4 jobs that may require post–high school training, job classifiers can peel off the GS-2 and GS-3 duties that are included in those GS-4 classifications and then create new positions at the lower levels that high school dropouts can fill satisfactorily.

At the *recruiting stage,* the EEO philosophy may thoroughly reshape the way governments find workers. A partnership springs up between the city personnel office and neighborhood development centers, the latter funneling job applicants to the former. The state employment security agency hires a minorities specialist who originates a skills roster of the disadvantaged. Jobs trailers begin moving into black and brown neighborhoods, bringing current job opportunities and testing facilities right to the doorsteps of the disadvantaged. Black ministers and Catholic priests serving in Chicano parishes are enlisted to publicize government careers in their church bulletins. Recruiters no longer bypass black junior colleges and universities.

The *selection stage* is equally subject to EEO reform. Earlier in this chapter we looked at the problem of cultural bias in written examinations. Among the solutions that have been proposed are:

> greater reliance on performance tests and less reliance on tests of verbal skills, which may have little to do with job success in many positions
>
> development of culture-free or culture-fair tests, probing for more talents than our WASP culture usually acknowledges
>
> offering training sessions on test taking for those with minimal experience in the ordeal that most of us have grown up with[59]

The final selection stage also clearly needs to be scrutinized under the EEO magnifying glass. Operating within, let's say, the Rule of Three, do the hiring officers ever choose the woman, the black, the Chicano, or the Indian over the white male finalists? Without using a quota system, the personnel office should begin to disallow appointment recommendations for whites from line units that consistently pass over women and minority finalists. One doesn't have to wait until all attitudes are reformed; one can change behavior (in this case, through tough personnel vetoes) and swing attitudes around.[60]

Now we are faced with the government version of "Look who's coming to dinner" or "Look who's joining our staff." *Getting ready for the arrival* of the new nonwhite employee often calls for some thoughtful efforts on behalf of front-line supervisors in changing attitudes in the work groups. The starting point is certainly the significant others in these groups. Some can be converted to the gospel of integration by exposure to the legal mandates (presidential orders, OPM directives, agency policy statements, etc.); others through the carrot of individual or group awards; and still others through involvement leading to commitment, where these significant others are given the problem of preparing for integration to work out some solutions.

Affirmative action, then, calls for a review of the whole gamut of personnel administration — classifying, testing, recruiting, selecting, and training — if the public service is to become the employer of first resort, the model employer in this country. What is at stake for thousands of Americans is the chance to earn a livelihood on which the "inalienable right to life" itself depends. The question, therefore, must be asked of government, as of us all: "If not you, then who? If not now, when?"

Equal Employment Opportunity versus Merit

In asking public personnel administration to provide equal employment opportunity and to correct years of discrimination and neglect with vigorous affirmative action, are we inviting the destruction of the merit system? My own view is clearly no. If recruiters could not find blacks and women of ability, then any kind of preferential hiring of blacks and women would contradict the merit principle. But the assumption is of course phony. What begins to happen, then, with affirmative action programs is a wider search for merit than has taken place heretofore — to find *talented* women, blacks, Chicanos, white males, and others — without the blinders of sexism and racism narrowing the search. So viewed, we have a marriage of merit and equality of opportunity rather than a duel.

Or one may look at the issue historically. As we saw in Chapter 15, the merit system was developed to select employees without regard to *party;* merit *cum* EEO seeks to select them without regard to *race* or *sex*. The historical continuity is clear: a public service, open to the talented, and assuring equality of opportunity.

The data clearly suggest that a determined government can begin to change its complexion over time. Between 1969 and 1977, employment of minorities by the federal government rose 37 percent, in comparison with a 5 percent increase in the number of whites. The minorities' share of federal jobs rose from 14 percent in the earlier year to 21 percent in 1977.[61] The remaining challenge is to give women and minorities an equal shot at upper-level positions and a wider choice of occupations.

The merit system can certainly survive this accommodation to EEO and will be better for it — in exactly the same way baseball was enhanced when Dodger manager Branch Rickey brought Jackie Robinson into his club in 1947, the first black athlete to play in the major leagues. Down this kind of road lies a society free of male chauvinism, of white supremacy, of black power, of the brown and red revolts. In their places, hopefully we can create the beautiful world of seven-year-old Brad Baird. Son of a white Ph.D. candidate at the University of North Carolina a few years ago, Brad attended a North Carolina public school during the first years of integration in that state. Soon after school started, Brad was asked by his father at dinner one night, "Any black kids in your school-room?" Brad's elegant answer: "I'll look tomorrow."

Helping to build that kind of world is a special challenge of recruitment and selection in government today.

SUMMARY

The portal of entry for new employees is that marginal point that can make or shake an agency, and the reason is painfully simple: the agency is no better than its personnel.

But hiring able people starts a long way back — having a job classification plan to guide the search, building an image that attracts talent, purging recruitment and selection of all phony prejudices based on race and sex, and keeping salaries and other come-ons attractive. Central to recruitment success is the communication phase: knowing where able people are to be found and then getting the word to them to apply.

Separating the sheep from the goats calls for the sophisticated application of a battery of selection devices. They include appraisal of education and experience, reference checks, competitive examinations (among them written, oral, and performance tests), interviews, and on-the-job trials (probationary periods). The great hope underlying these techniques is to reduce as much as possible the chance of misfits being hired.

All the selection devices must themselves be tested. Are they shot through with cultural bias? On their face, do they relate to duties to be performed? In fact, is there solid evidence to show that test scores validly predict on-the-job performance?

Examinations can tell line officials only part of what they need to know about applicants. Consequently, three or more names will be certified from the examination register to the line people for further appraisal. Final selection belongs to the line officers who must live with the appointees.

In this day and age, recruitment and selection by government must meet the additional test of assuring equal opportunities to women and minorities. A case has been made here for enough modification in the merit system philosophy to make room for the EEO objective, for government to be the employer of *first resort*. That demands a whole set of innovations in every phase of recruitment and selection.

Finally, management information systems must be set up to monitor the recruitment-selection effort: Is the agency hiring misfits, close fits, or stars? Do the new recruits stay and grow in public service? Are the line officials pleased with their new staffers?

Those are some of the continuing questions surrounding that critical *margin* in personnel administration: How good will the *next person* be whom we bring on board? In the concluding chapter that follows, we turn to the question of how to translate "good" into "ethical" in the conduct of the people's business.

KEY CONCEPTS

open career system	validity and reliability
closed career system	certification
job analysis	rule of three
unassembled exam	equal employment opportunity
competitive examination	1964 Civil Rights Act
register	*Griggs* v. *Duke Power Co.*
job element testing	*Regents* v. *Bakke*
oral examinations	

DISCUSSION QUESTIONS

1. What should be the goals of a recruitment program? Identify those factors which impede the achievement of those goals.

2. Discuss the essentials of a good recruitment program: building agency image, job analysis, places to work, and so on. Which part of the program is the most important?

3. Discuss the various testing procedures commonly found in the selection process. Which is the best?

4. Explain test validation. How do you know if a test is valid or not?

5. Assess the reference form (page 481). Does it omit any factors that might be crucial to know? Could an applicant who has scored highly on the examination and also had a superb appraisal on the reference form still perform poorly once hired?

6. Are EEO and a merit system compatible?

PROJECT

Investigate the nature of affirmative action in a public or private organization in your community. If possible, assess the nature of the affirmative action plan. Learn about the past accomplishments of the program and the future efforts it hopes to make.

Notes

1. A wise book on the subject is J. J. Donovan, ed., *Recruitment and Selection in the Public Service* (Chicago: Public Personnel Association, 1968).

2. U.S. House of Representatives, Committee on Post Office and Civil Service, *Final Report on Violations and Abuses of Merit Principles in Federal Employment* (94th Cong., 2d sess.) (Washington, D.C.: Government Printing Office, 1976), p. 2.

3. For example, note the attempt of the oil industry to staff key positions in the Federal Energy Administration during the "oil shortage" crisis of the Nixon administration. See Harmon Zeigler and Joseph Olexa, "The Energy Issue," in Robert L. Peabody, *Cases in American Politics* (New York: Praeger, 1976), pp. 176 and 182.

4. The potentialities of these techniques can be clearly seen in the testimonials of some former civil servants: Steven K. Bailey, "The Excitement of the Public Service," *Civil Service Journal* (July–Sept. 1963) 4:5–9; and Delia and Ferdinand Kuhn, eds., *Adventures in Public Service* (New York: Vanguard Press, 1963). See also Alan K. Campbell, "What's Right with Federal Employees," *Civil Service Journal* (Apr.–June 1978) 18:6–12.

5. Noted a long time ago in a Brookings Institution study by Franklin P. Kilpatrick, M. C. Cummings, and M. K. Jennings, *The Image of the Federal Service* (Washington, D.C.: Brookings Institution, 1964).

6. See, for example, *Kirkland v. N.Y. State Department of Correctional Services,* 374 F. Supp. 1361 (1974). See also Roscoe W. Wisner, "The Kirkland Case — Its Implications for Personnel Selection," *Public Personnel Management* (July–Aug. 1975) 4:265–266.

7. U.S. Civil Service Commission (Ernest S. Primoff), *How to Prepare and Conduct Job Element Examinations* (Washington, D.C.: Government Printing Office, 1975), pp. 11–14.

8. See U.S. Civil Service Commission, *Federal Recruiting, 1976–1977* (Washington, D.C.: Government Printing Office, 1977), for a summary of federal agency recruiting programs.

9. Arch J. Ramsay, "Toward a Modernized Federal Examining System," *Civil Service Journal* (Oct.–Dec. 1976) 17:17–20.

10. W. A. Ward, "How the Government Is Going on Campus," *Civil Service Journal* (July–Sept. 1978) 19:22–23.

11. See N. M. Gallas in Donovan, *Recruitment and Selection,* p. 39.

12. Warren Bennis, "Who Sank the Yellow Submarine?" *Psychology Today* (Nov. 1972) 6:114.

13. These processing delays constitute a real enemy of the merit system. As E. S. Savas and S. G. Ginsburg documented in their study of the New York City merit system, delays of many months between application and job offer meant that the top candidates on the registers chose other jobs, leaving less able people available for hire by

the city. Savas and Ginsburg, "The Civil Service: A Meritless System," *Public Interest* (Summer 1973) 32:70–85.

14. In addition to the fine work by Donovan et al., *Recruitment and Selection,* we recommend Robert Ebel et al., *Improving Public Personnel Selection* (Chicago: Public Personnel Association, 1963).

15. The Equal Opportunity Act of 1972 (P.L. 92-261) applied the anti-discrimination provisions of the 1964 Civil Rights Act to all levels of government.

16. *Griggs* v. *Duke Power Company,* 401 U.S. 424 (1971).

17. E. R. Henry, "What Business Can Learn from Peace Corps Selection and Training," *Personnel* (July–Aug. 1968) 42:17–25.

18. See Arch Ramsay, "A New Look in Federal Job Applications," *Civil Service Journal* (Apr.–June 1977) 17:19–21.

19. See Martin L. Gross, *The Brain Watchers* (New York: Random House, 1962); Banesh Hoffman, *Tyranny of Testing* (New York: Crowell-Collier, 1962); William H. Whyte, *The Organization Man* (New York: Simon and Schuster, 1957), appendix.

20. See Norman Sharpless in Donovan et al., *Recruitment and Selection,* pp. 16–20.

21. U.S. Civil Service Commission, *How to Prepare,* p. 73.

22. U.S. Civil Service Commission, *How to Prepare,* p. 33.

23. The governing federal standards for test design were promulgated on August 25, 1978, as the *Uniform Guidelines on Employee Selection Procedures* and may be found in a special supplement to the *Government Employee Relations Report* (*GERR*) (Aug. 28, 1978), no. 774.

24. Congress felt that professional preparation of tests was important enough to be required by statute in Title VII of the 1964 Civil Rights Act, section 703(h).

25. 401 U.S. 424 at 436 (1971).

26. Brian O'Leary, "The Case for Written Tests in Federal Employment," *Civil Service Journal* (July–Sept. 1976) 16:29–31.

27. See David Rosenbloom and Carole Obuchowski, "Public Personnel Examinations and the Constitution: Emergent Trends," *Public Administration Review* (Jan.–Feb. 1977) 37:10–11.

28. 482 F. 2d 1333, 1338 (1973). The courts continue to be tough about content validity, unless based on rigorous job analysis. In *Allen* v. *City of Mobile,* a U.S. district court rejected a police officer's promotional exam that had a disparate impact on black and white candidates. Applying the new federal *Uniform Guidelines on Employee Selection Procedures,* the court held that Mobile's content validity study was inadequate, and consequently so was the exam. 464 F. Supp. 433 (1978).

29. We have followed the Rosenbloom-Obuchowski article closely in these comments on validity.

30. Cited in note 23. See section VII of the *Guidelines.*

31. *Guidelines,* I 7(b)(2).

32. For the exact statistical procedure in measuring the correlation between test scores and performance ratings, see G. G. McClung in Donovan, *Recruitment and Selection,* pp. 340–341.

33. For a portrayal of an unbelievable "Rule of One" and the shenanigans that can go on in a merit system, see an early case study by Chester and Valerie Earle, *The Promotion of Lem Merrill* (Indianapolis: Bobbs-Merrill, 1960 rev.).

34. C. W. Downs, "What Does the Selection Interview Accomplish?" *Personnel Administration* (No. 3, 1968) 31:8–14.

35. See Donovan, *Recruitment and Selection,* pp. 384–388.

36. U.S. Civil Service Commission, *Civil Service News* (Aug. 23, 1978), p. 5.

37. Rosenbloom and Obuchowski, "Public Personnel Examinations," pp. 11–13.

38. See the helpful study by the U.S. Commission on Civil Rights, *Social Indicators of Equality for Minorities and Women* (Washington, D.C.: Government Printing Office, Aug. 1978). For a succinct history of the struggle to win equal rights for women in the federal service, see Janice Mendenhall, "Roots of the Federal Women's Program," *Civil Service Journal* (July–Sept. 1977) 18:21–24.

39. P.L. 88-352; 78 Stat. 241; 42 U.S.C.A. 2000e.

40. P.L. 92-261 (1972); 88 Stat. 109.

41. See the useful compendium by the U.S. Civil Service Commission, *Equal Employment Opportunity Cases* (Washington, D.C.: Government Printing Office, 1976).

42. Previously cited in note 16.

43. 401 U.S. 424, 431.

44. 401 U.S. 436.

45. *U.S.* v. *City of Chicago,* 549 F. 2d 415 (1977).

46. 426 U.S. 229 (1976).

47. Rosenbloom and Obuchowski, "Public Personnel Examinations," p. 14.

48. 371 F. Supp. 507 (1974).

49. 371 F. Supp. 1328 (1973).

50. 493 F. 2d 6111 (1974).

51. 534 F. 2d 993 (1976).

52. 149 Cal. R. 155 (1978).

53. 98 S.Ct. 2733 (1978).

54. See note 14 in Justice Powell's opinion for the Court in 98 S.Ct. 2743, and also 2748.

55. 98 S.Ct. 2751.

56. 98 S.Ct. 2758-2759.

57. *United Steelworkers of America* v. *Weber,* 99 S.Ct. 2721 (1979).

58. See especially the attachment to the *Federal Personnel Manual* 713-3, section 713.203(d) (1969).

59. See discussion in Wallace, Kissinger, and Reynolds, "Testing of Minority Group Applicants for Employment," U.S. Equal Employment Opportunity Commission, *Personnel Testing and Equal Employment Opportunity* (Washington, D.C.: Government Printing Office, 1970), p. 5.

60. Earl Rabb (ed.), *American Race Relations Today* (Garden City, N.Y.: Doubleday, 1962), pp. 35–43.

61. *Civil Service Journal* (Jan.–Mar. 1978) 18:2; and *Administrator's Alert* (June 1978) 8:2. The figure of 21 percent is based on total federal jobs, blue collar as well as white collar, whereas the 18.1 percent figure for minorities shown in Table 16.1 is based only on white-collar (GS) jobs.

Part V
ADMINISTRATIVE ETHICS

Chapter 18
The Ethics of Management

THE ETHICAL DILEMMAS THAT MAKE IT ALL WORTH DOING

It's above the timberline, Steve Bailey once wrote, where the ethical winds blow the fiercest — and that's exactly where the person with backbone wants to be.[1] For some, corporate law practice can't hold a gavel to a post in the Antitrust Division of the Justice Department, where the successful prosecution of an oil oligopoly would benefit the whole country. For others, being a private sector engineer couldn't hold a transit to writing an environmental impact statement that will queer a coal-fired power plant whose smoke would cover three national parks. The interests of millions of people ride on the vision and courage of public decision makers who wrestle with the dilemmas of public policy that make the job of governing so worth doing.

The dilemmas frequently, although not always, raise ethical questions, sometimes of a pecuniary sort, sometimes of a more fundamental kind. Notice the range:

President Taft's interior secretary, Richard A. Ballinger, wondered where the public interest lay as his business cronies in the Northwest pressured him for easy access to Alaska's coal and lumber resources.[2]

Ballinger's deputy, Louis Glavis, pondered the safe course of keeping silent versus speaking out on Ballinger's deals in Alaska.[3]

A later interior secretary, Harold Ickes, under pressure from the State Department to let Hitler have U.S. helium, began searching for the public interest in the international arena.*

FDR weighed General John L. De Witt's recommendation to intern seventy-five thousand Japanese-American citizens following the Japanese attack on Pearl Harbor.[4]

Dr. J. Robert Oppenheimer, consultant to the Atomic Energy Commission, faced the dilemma of expressing to the AEC his deep doubts about building a hydrogen bomb versus simply confirming their yen for a bigger bang.[5]

An official of the Agency for International Development (AID) contemplated junking the controversial satellite aid program to Poland and Yugoslavia so as not to jeopardize the whole foreign aid program when it went to Congress.

A woman colonel of the U.S. Marine Corps received a request from two of Senator Joseph McCarthy's investigators to quiz her platoon on anticommunism, which she weighed against the constitutional standard of the separation of powers.

An FBI agent contemplated tapping the phone conversations of government employee Judith Coplon, who had been feeding Justice Department secrets to her Russian boyfriend; the FBI planned the arrest of escaped communist Robert Thompson, in a Yosemite mountain cabin, without benefit of search or arrest warrants.[6]

A NASA research director began to think about padding his job descriptions for physicists and engineers so that he could recruit the team to beat the Russians to the moon.

The deputy director of the CIA, Gen. Robert C. Cushman, wondered whether he should obey the law or a White House order from John Ehrlichman to provide masks and cameras to the plumbers unit for the break-in on Dr. Lewis Fielding, the psychiatrist of Dr. Daniel Ellsberg.[7]

Richard Nixon, confronted with the news about the Watergate burglary, weighed his obligations to execute the law against his desire to hang on to his job.[8]

A governor gets ready to direct his environmental protection council to proceed against a polluting copper mill and then worries about the consequences for this biggest payer of state and local taxes and one of his primary campaign contributors.

---

* Ickes's answer to Hitler was "No!" As his eulogist, Mike Strauss, put it: "Ickes was a flop at appeasement." See Harold L. Ickes, *The Inside Struggle,* vol. II of *The Secret Diary of Harold L. Ickes* (New York: Simon and Schuster, 1953), pp. 143, 325, 344, 346, 373, 391–393, 396–399, and 418. Secretary of State Cordell Hull tells his side of the story in the *Memoirs of Cordell Hull* (New York: Macmillan, 1948) 1:597–598.

The county purchasing agent ponders (but not for long) the issuance of a purchase order for a $40,000 bit paver (road equipment), for which he and his outside crony originally paid only $18,000.

A perusal of this list rather quickly reveals that the ethics of management raise far more complex issues than the problem of good old-fashioned corruption in government.[9] To the contrary, it has at least three dimensions: the ethic of means and ends, the ethic of private gain at public expense, and the ethic of how to define and secure the *public interest.* We begin with the age-old question of what kind of means to attain what kind of ends.

THE ETHIC OF MEANS AND ENDS

In 1513, Niccolò Machiavelli held up a mirror in Florence to enable Giuliano de Medici to see what he would have to be like to rule successfully. Machiavelli suggested that he should be part fox and part lion, part trickery and part strength:

> Everybody sees what you appear to be, few feel what you are, and those few will not dare to oppose themselves to the many, who have the majesty of the state to defend them; and in the actions of men, and especially of princes, from which there is no appeal, *the end justifies the means* [emphasis added].[10]

The French put a label on the doctrine: *raison d'état.* or reason of state[11] — whatever advances the glory of Florence, or the First Republic, or the Third Reich is sanctified by the end itself. Its corollary, *reason of agency.* naturally followed in later years. The logic is clear: "I'm assigned a vital part of the national interest to secure in this agency; therefore, whatever strengthens or protects this agency is justified by the ends we're pursuing."

Notice how the rule resolves some of the dilemmas referred to in the previous list:

Roosevelt concluded that national security was so critical that it justified incarcerating Japanese-Americans without a trial.

The AID official didn't want to jeopardize the whole foreign aid program, so he junked the controversial satellite aid proposals.

In order quickly to get the Communists and fellow travelers behind bars, the FBI tapped Ms. Coplon's telephone conversations with her lawyer and arrested Robert Thompson, cabin owner Shirley Kremen, and others without warrants.

The NASA research director not only inflated his job descriptions but padded his budget requests as well to enable him to recruit the talent that would enable him to beat the Russians to the moon.

When Mr. Justice Black Sanctioned Ignoble Means

It came as a real shock to turn back the pages of the *U.S. Reports* to discover that the great civil libertarian, Mr. Justice Hugo Black, had written the opinion for the Supreme Court in *Korematsu* v. *U.S.* in 1944 sanctioning the removal to relocation centers without a trial, two years earlier, of 75,000 American citizens of Japanese descent:

> We uphold the exclusion order as of the time it was made and when the petitioner violated it. . . . In doing so, we are not unmindful of the hardships imposed by it upon a large group of American citizens. . . . But hardships are part of war, and war is an aggregation of hardships. All citizens alike, both in and out of uniform, feel the impact of war in greater or lesser measure. Citizenship has its responsibilities as well as its privileges, and in time of war the burden is always heavier. Compulsory exclusion of large groups of citizens from their homes, except under circumstances of direst emergency and peril, is inconsistent with our basic governmental institution. But when under conditions of modern warfare our shores are threatened by hostile forces, the power to protect must be commensurate with the threatened danger. . . .

Korematsu v. *U.S.*, 323 U.S. 214 (1944).

In each instance, the administrator could say that the end was so vital that any means were justified in attaining it.* Using that logic, some government officials proceed to violate both ethics and the law.

The Range of Unethical Techniques

The lawyer's classification of improper means is a useful one in seeing the full range of techniques employed by unethical administrators: *misfeasance*, involving improper performance of lawful duties; *malfeasance*, engaging in prohibited activities; and *nonfeasance*, failing to perform required duties.

Misfeasance   Although the boundary line between misfeasance and malfeasance is a bit thin, note some examples of improper means being employed in government:

A Georgia sheriff, Claude Screws, arrested a black named Robert Hall for stealing tires and beat him to death on the way to jail.[12]

---

* As a case in point, consider how Assistant Secretary of War John J. McCloy responded to Attorney General Francis Biddle's question, a la 1942, concerning the constitutionality of incarcerating all Japanese-American citizens on the West Coast: "You are putting a Wall Street lawyer in a helluva box, but if it is a question of the safety of the country [and] the Constitution . . . why, the Constitution is just a scrap of paper to me." Noted in Roger Daniels, *Concentration Camps, USA*, (New York: Holt, Rinehart and Winston, 1971), pp. 55–56.

In a grizzly rape-murder case in Illinois in 1955, a state prosecutor used a pair of bloody men's shorts to convict Floyd Miller, knowing all the time that the stains were paint, not blood.[13]

The Chicago police, purportedly attempting to control the crowd around the Democratic National Convention in 1968, engaged in a wholesale police riot against innocent bystanders as well as antiwar demonstrators.[14]

In 1968 an Alabama election judge secretly deleted the names of six black candidates from the ballot while preparing the ballot for the printer.[15]

In 1971, Attorney General John Mitchell justified the use of domestic wiretapping without warrants against radical student groups.[16]

One of the clearest areas of misfeasance (and sometimes nonfeasance) at the federal level concerns the independent regulatory commissions, such as the Interstate Commerce Commission, the Securities and Exchange Commission, and the Civil Aeronautics Board, among others. Their responsibility is to *regulate* designated industries in the public interest, not to be co-opted by those industries. But after a searching review during 1975–1976, the Moss subcommittee of the House Interstate and Foreign Commerce Commission found that substantial misrepresentation of the public interest had taken place instead:

> Although we firmly believe that reform must proceed agency-by-agency, we have nonetheless identified certain common failings in the agencies studied.
>
> All suffer from a critical defect, an insufficient response to the public they were created to serve. Our studies confirm earlier observations that the actions of regulatory agencies reflect more than anything else their primary attention to the special interests of the regulated industry and lack of sufficient concern for underrepresented interests. Given the frequent communication between regulated industry and regulatory agencies, and given the cohesive structure of regulated industry, this finding should not be surprising.[17]

The Moss subcommittee then drew up some measuring rods to appraise the independent commissions: "Fidelity to the public protection mandate defined by Congress; quantity and quality of agency activity; effectiveness of agency enforcement programs; and quality of public participation."[18] Under these criteria, the Securities and Exchange Commission received the top ranking from the House subcommittee, and the Federal Power Commission the lowest:

> The Federal Power Commission takes the cellar position because of its overt disregard of its congressional mandate. Specifically it has refused to maintain a program of "just and reasonable" natural gas prices consistent with its governing statutes and applicable court decisions. It has acted without sound evidence. It has not enforced the delivery of natural gas supplies to consumers. The Federal Power Commission has displayed a conscious indifference to the public beyond comparison with any other regulatory agency. The Subcommittee believes that this agency is in line for a major overhaul by the Congress.*[19]

---

* That is exactly what happened. The FPC was scrapped by an act of Congress on August 4, 1977, to be replaced by the Federal Energy Regulatory Commission in the Department of Energy.

Far more shocking than these sins of the independent regulatory commissions has been the sad tale of misfeasance by the FBI over many years. From FDR at least through Lyndon Johnson, the agency played voyeur on the sex lives of political opponents of the presidents, the findings to be used either for titillation (as in the case of LBJ) or as possible levers to manipulate presidential critics. Longtime aide to J. Edgar Hoover, C. J. DeLoach, told a Senate committee in 1975 that he couldn't recall an instance of the FBI turning down a request from the White House for surveillance on some "enemy."[20]

Surveillance and apprehension of those committing federal crimes are the lawful mission of the FBI; but disclosing their findings to congressional committees, rather than grand juries, is not. But no less an authority than Senator Karl Mundt let the strategy out of the bag when he disclosed the hanky-panky between the FBI and congressional investigating committees as a way of getting around the Fifth Amendment's grand jury requirement for the prosecution of federal crimes:

> These probes are a valuable supplement to the investigative work of the FBI. The FBI may compile much evidence on Communist infiltration, but not enough to justify indictments. Often in such cases, said the Senator, the FBI will tip off a Congressional committee as to a situation where it is convinced American security is endangered. The committee's inquiry makes it possible to bring the case into the open and, with the suspected Communist spy usually taking refuge in the Fifth Amendment's protection against incriminating himself, it is possible to eliminate that particular threat.[21]

What is the explanation for these kinds of deeds by the FBI? In the sex surveillance activity, the misfeasance was attributable in part to the politics of administration (do the president's bidding in order to maintain presidential support of the FBI), and in part to the Adolf Eichmann syndrome (transferring your ethical judgments upstairs): the chief executive ordered it and that settled any doubts about impropriety.

In ignoring the constitutional requirement for a grand jury indictment, the FBI opted for a Machiavellian success ethic rather than for obeying the law. They reasoned that these Communists were a menace to the Constitution; thus, they would expose them even if they had to employ unconstitutional means.

Malfeasance   The record of governments doing things they are forbidden to do by the Constitution, law, or ethics is discouragingly long. Note some episodes:

Dwight Eisenhower significantly moved us toward the Vietnam War when he derailed the 1956 referendum in Vietnam.

The CIA committed crimes against humanity with its MK-Ultra project of the 1960s, involving drug expermentation (with LSD and others) on unsuspecting human beings, leading to at least one suicide.[22]

Richard Nixon almost cornered the market on presidential malfeasance:

1. In exchange for some $682,500 in campaign contributions from the American Milk Producers Institute (AMPI), Nixon overrode his agriculture secretary and raised the federal milk price-support level to give the dairy industry a "milkfall" of over $300 million.[23]

2. He kept an "Enemies List" in the White House and pressured the IRS to harass some who were on that list with discriminatory tax audits.

3. He obstructed justice by withholding information from investigatory bodies, by having the CIA throw an FBI investigation of Watergate off course, by approving the bribery of the burglars to obtain their silence, and by interfering with the trial in progress of Dr. Ellsberg by proffering to the sitting judge an important post in his administration.

4. He maintained a White House "plumbers unit" to engage in burglary against American citizens, among many others.[24]

It's a tragedy, but the sick ethic of employing improper means to accomplish agency goals is most clearly demonstrated by the FBI, the agency set up to deter lawbreaking by others. Its record of malfeasance includes:

wiretapping communications between a defendant and her lawyer (the Coplon case previously mentioned)

breaking and entering without search warrants over two hundred times between 1948 and 1960 and continuing at least until 1973 (called burglary in the Criminal Code, these surreptitious entries were known as "black bag jobs" within the FBI)[25]

carrying out the COINTELPRO (Counterintelligence Program) against anti–Vietnam War demonstrators, civil rights groups, the Ku Klux Klan, and others, despite J. Edgar Hoover's often repeated statement that the FBI was an investigative unit only, not a national police force.*

sending a note to Dr. Martin Luther King, Jr., suggesting suicide in the face of evidence the FBI had on his extramarital encounters (a copy of their eavesdropping tape was included with the note)[26]

providing J. Edgar Hoover with an incredible array of personal services (carpentry, interior design work, etc.) at his private residence at FBI expense[27]

Clearly, this once prestigious agency had lost its soul. Somewhere along the line, the agency heads stopped asking the critical question: "Is what we're doing right?" Here is Assistant Director William Sullivan's mea culpa before Senator Frank Church's investigating committee:

---

* The tactics included sending anonymous letters to wives about sexual misconduct of their husbands whose politics the FBI disapproved of, generating internecine battles among black groups over phony issues trumped up by the FBI, and undermining college chapters of the Young Democrats by alleging to state Democratic leaders that the YDs had been infiltrated by socialists.

. . . never once did I hear anybody, including myself, raise the question, is this course of action which we have agreed upon lawful, is it legal, is it ethical or moral? We never gave any thought to this realm of reasoning, because we were just naturally pragmatists. The one thing we were concerned about [was] will this course of action work, will it get us what we want, will we reach the objective that we desire to reach?

As far as legality is concerned, morality or ethics, [the question] was never raised by myself or anybody else. . . . I think that this suggests really in government we are amoral.[28]

We need to understand that loss of soul, for the sickness that permeated the FBI can so easily afflict other agencies. The first factor was the *hero worship* of J. Edgar Hoover, which apparently generated blind obedience among many FBI agents. A second was their *fear* of the man, a fear, for example, of how easily he could transfer anyone to Timbuktu if he got out of line. That fear also intimidated generations of congressmen, who somehow never got around to nailing Hoover during the annual FBI appropriations hearings.

The third factor was the apparent wide acceptance throughout the FBI of the *Machiavellian ethic* that the end justifies any means. The FBI's targets were Communists, Weathermen, the Ku Klux Klan, assassins, and spies; thus, it was easy to develop the rationale that although the FBI tactics were illegal, "they represent an invaluable technique in combatting subversive activities . . . aimed directly at undermining and destroying our nation."[29] As the Church committee wryly observed ten years later, "In other words, breaking the law was seen as useful in combatting those who threatened the legal fabric of society."[30]

Thus, Plato would return to haunt us: "Glaucon," he said, "we must make the guardians gentle toward the citizens but fierce toward the enemy. If not, the guardians will have defeated the enemy by destroying the city from within."[31]

Nonfeasance This third category of unethical means to promote ends is a kind of no means — standing pat when the situation desperately calls for action.

Under its Mine Safety Act, Illinois State officials had ample authority to close dangerous mines. But in the face of World War II (and corporate) pressure to get the coal out, the officials of the Department of Mines and Minerals ignored the blunt reports of their mine inspector at the Centralia Mine, and on March 25, 1947, the mine blew up, killing 111 men.*[32]

New York had a bevy of statutes requiring nondiscriminatory hiring on public works projects. But a study by a blue-ribbon committee documented that the

---

* Evidence suggests that we rarely learn. Congress passed the Coal Mine Health and Safety Act in 1969 after a 1968 explosion at Farmington, West Virginia, the year before which claimed the lives of 78 miners. During the first year of the statute mine deaths rose a third (260 fatalities), and a GAO report on the conditions in Appalachian mines indicated that "fewer than one third of the 1969 requirements for safety inspections" had been met. Lieberman, *How the Government Breaks the Law* (Baltimore, Md.: Penguin Books, 1973), p. 195.

It Did Happen Here

The Senate Select Committee on Intelligence Activities concluded its investigation of the CIA and FBI in 1976 on this ominous note:

> We have seen segments of our government, in their attitudes and action, adopt tactics unworthy of a democracy, and occasionally reminiscent of the tactics of totalitarian regimes. We have seen a consistent pattern in which programs initiated with limited goals, such as preventing criminal violence or identifying foreign spies, were expanded to what witnesses characterized as "vacuum cleaners," sweeping in information about lawful activities of American citizens.

U.S. Senate, Select Committee on Intelligence Activities, *Intelligence Activities and the Rights of Americans* (Senate Report 94-755) (Washington, D.C.: Government Printing Office, 1976) II:3.

---

responsible state agencies had done essentially nothing to compel contractors to hire minorities as a condition of landing state contracts.[33]

In 1961, Governor John Patterson of Alabama failed to provide any protection for the Freedom Riders, a group of whites and blacks who were traveling on interstate buses to challenge segregated facilities in the southern states. Alabama mobs fire-bombed the buses and attacked the church where the Freedom Riders and their supporters had gathered. The Alabama police did nothing, and that state's worst racial conflagration then took place.[34]

In Alabama, the police chief in Birmingham promised the Ku Klux Klan fifteen minutes without police interruption during which the Klan could attack the Freedom Riders.[35]

Under direct pressure from Richard Nixon, the Justice Department in 1971 suspended the prosecution of International Telephone and Telegraph for its acquisition of the Hartford Fire Insurance Company, backing off shortly after ITT had offered the Republican party $400,000 for its 1972 nominating convention.[36]

For years, the good work of the Food and Drug Administration has been seriously marred by some extraordinary slipups:

1. permitting the marketing of nitrofurans for animal feed, which can produce tumors and cancer

2. failing to examine defective cardiac pacemakers recalled by manufacturers

3. allowing chymopapain on the market for the relief of back pain when it caused a significant incidence of paraplegia (paralysis) and death and exposed fifteen thousand users to needless danger[37]

4. licensing MER-29 (a Merrill Pharmaceutical product for heart disease) in the face of laboratory warnings and reports that it frequently resulted in eye infections and the loss of both hair and sex drive among its users[38]

Nonfeasance is a product of many things: cowardice on the part of the decision makers; co-optation by the interests they serve (the FDA and the pharmaceutical industry) and the culture that surrounds them (Governor Patterson and white racists); bribery (ITT and Nixon); ignorance of, or indifference to, events (coal dust in mines, cracks in reclamation dams, etc.).

Taken together, the techniques of misfeasance, malfeasance, and nonfeasance suggest the kinds of responses administrators are capable of when a certain goal is very important to them. The goal then subsumes the means. During the time when a goal seems attainable through normal activity, the typical administrator will often be found on the side of the angels, pursuing conventional morality. But when goal accomplishment is in jeopardy and the administrator is staring failure in the face, the expected response is a resort to Machiavellian ethics. *Fear of failure*, then, is a central influence, we think, in resorting to unethical means.

With ethics pushed aside, the administrator proceeds to his tasks, hoping either that success in accomplishing the agency's ends will stifle his critics (the J. Edgar Hoover syndrome) or that he won't get caught (the Richard Nixon syndrome). But there's another way to go — and some good arguments for it.

The Ethic of Right Means to Secure Right Ends

In his first inaugural address, George Washington expressed the hope that the new federal government would "win the affections of its citizens and command the respect of the world." To do so, he thought, would require governmental conduct that reflected principles of private morality, "since there is no truth more thoroughly established than that there exists in the economy and course of nature an indissoluble union between virtue and happiness [and] between duty and advantage."[39]

Will what duty requires also be advantageous? Conversely, can one expect trouble when he acts unethically? Our opening dilemmas may cast some light:

The AID official watched in dismay as congressmen started cutting up the whole foreign aid program, emboldened by their having killed the satellite proposals without firing a shot.

The FBI, after winning in the district courts in the Coplon and Kremen-Thompson cases, found the convictions reversed in the circuit courts because the FBI had violated the Fourth Amendment's guarantee against unreasonable searches and seizures in the Kremen case and the Sixth Amendment's right to counsel (without eavesdropping) in the Coplon case.

The NASA research director watched his able physicists and engineers begin to quit almost a year later as a result of the jealousies stemming from the pay jungle he had created in tampering with the agency's classification plan.

Richard Nixon and Spiro Agnew lost only Massachusetts and the District of Columbia in 1972; but in eleven months, Agnew was gone, and in eighteen months Richard Nixon was gone.

In short, using unethical means runs the high risk of contaminating or preventing the accomplishment of the very ends we had in view.

Perhaps even more convincing of what happens when unethical means are employed is the deterioration that takes place in an office where skewed ethics are the order of the day. Let's say our antihero here is the section chief, whose conduct includes the following: he has made no effort to recruit blacks or promote women; he pads his travel expenses; he uses sick leave for his golf games; he drifts in late; and he takes care of his home needs from the office supply cabinet.

Through it all he sings an old Scotch ballad: "You take the high road, and I'll take the low road," but to his amazement, the staff is humming a different tune: "Where you lead me, I will follow." And the chief sits back dumfounded as he watches an epidemic of tardiness, a rash of petty thievery, abuse of leave, and the surfacing of hostile sexist and racist attitudes.

Somehow he never learned about how values are transmitted in human groups. We talked about the socialization process in Chapter 2. Newcomers size up the conduct of the significant others in their work group (role taking). Then, having figured out the cues, and wanting the acceptance of the significant others, the newcomers begin copying what they see others doing (role playing); fairly soon, many of the staff are walking the low road with the boss. The prudent administrator understands this and is going to ask himself before resorting to unethical means, "Can I handle it when my employees begin to follow my bad example?"

As Wayne Broehl of the Tuck School at Dartmouth once observed:

> It is remarkable how quickly and intuitively subordinates can sense a man's ethics. Over the long run, humility, kindness, trustworthiness cannot be projected unless they are genuine. And firm and lasting human relations can be effected only through the application of principles within an ethical framework. A man who turns his human relations "principles" on and off at will is usually found lacking in the long run.[40]

We would add: he soon finds himself surrounded by people just as unpredictable as he himself has become.

Some Remedies for the Means-Ends Problem

We are never going to be governed by saints; and so instead of waiting for the "saints to come marching in" to conduct the people's business, we need some

approaches to deter ethical shortcuts and to cope promptly with their consequences when they occur. Some standards to judge means may be useful;
structural reforms may help somewhat; legislative oversight can undo some
wrongs and ward off others; and prosecution of unlawful activities by those in
government may have a deterrent effect.

A management code of means and ends[41]   A careful review of some of the
administrative tragedies noted in this chapter suggests some shoulds and
oughts about the kinds of means to secure agency ends:

1. Good ends frequently become unattainable or undesirable through the
    use of unethical means to achieve them (our failure to overthrow Castro
    through the Bay of Pigs invasion).

2. Treat every person as an end and no one simply as a means (Immanuel
    Kant). (Note our treatment of blacks for three hundred years that led to
    the whirlwind of Watts, Detroit, and Memphis in the civil rights revolution
    of the 1960s.) The on-the-job application of this precept is the develop-
    ment of the competence of employees as ends in themselves; then watch
    what happens to their self-actualization and to the spirit of the agency.

3. Take as your standard of conduct that which you are prepared to let
    everyone else take (Kant) (not so much how I want to be treated as,
    "What would the whole world be like if it followed my example?").

4. Take as your overriding objective the promotion of the *public interest* as
    against any subordinate interest.

5. Let your service to the public be friendly and courteous, they are the
    reason for your job in government.*

6. Let no favoritism influence your decisions: in personnel matters, long-
    range merit; in procurement, maximum quality at least cost to the gov-
    ernment. Whenever possible, look for the guiding principle that will
    advance the general good.

7. Never transfer your moral judgments to someone else. Instead of Adolf
    Eichmann finding justification for burning Jews in the orders of his
    superiors, or James McCord's reliance on Attorney General John Mitch-
    ell for the Watergate burglary, take a page from Martin Luther or Abra-
    ham Lincoln:

---

* As an example, consider the attitude of an Omaha doctor who commuted during summer months by
private plane between Omaha, Nebraska, and Estes Park, Colorado. "When I call the FAA for flight
information, does their field man at Estes give me the bureaucratic treatment? Hell, no," the doctor
says. "Come on in, Doc, and we'll check things out in Omaha." "So he gets on the teletype and Omaha
says if I can land by 6:15, I'll just beat a storm front. So I hop in my plane, take off, and as I taxi into the
Omaha hangar, all hell breaks loose. Now that's the federal government to me," the doctor says.
(Conversation with the author a few years ago.) Thus the FAA employee, realizing that the doctor's
safety was "the whole ball game" at that point in time, won for the civil service the gratitude of a
member of the profession often among its chief critics, the doctors.

Luther before the Diet at Worms: "Here I take my stand. I could not do otherwise. God help me."

Lincoln: "I desire to so conduct the affairs of this administration that if, at the end, when I come to lay down the reins of power, I have lost every other friend on earth, I shall have at least one friend left, and that friend shall be down inside of me."[42]

8.   Follow the rule of law, not because the law is always wise, but because law is the fundamental bulwark of a civilized society, the antithesis of government by whim and caprice.

Like the Ten Commandments, a management code, even if one could be agreed upon, is never self-enforcing. Its only possible utility lies in the hands of those of you who a decade from now will be powers in city hall, state government, and the federal service. The hope of any country is the promise of renewal that comes with the changing of the guard of one generation with its mistakes to a new one *that has been watching.*

There are other approaches for developing an improved ethic of means and ends.

Structural and procedural reforms   We noted earlier some ethical slippage in the conduct of the independent regulatory commissions. The Moss subcommittee of the House Interstate and Foreign Commerce Committee offered a number of useful reforms to strengthen their performance:

creation of an agency for consumer protection to help counteract the industry bias of the commissions (a suggestion employing an old Madisonian idea of having "ambition counteract ambition")

improved congressional oversight

increased openness in agency proceedings

new independence from executive pressures

recruitment and selection of commissioners with a clear public interest rather than an industry commitment

broadened opportunities for citizens' class action suits[43]

What about heading off future Watergates, the epitome of unethical means to advance an administration's ends? The Watergate Prosecution Task Force recommended a number of steps that should be taken to reduce the likelihood of another Watergate someday (to the right, we have noted what has happened to each recommendation):[44]

A constitutional amendment to subject a president to criminal indictment for malfeasance in office	Not implemented

Increased congressional oversight of intelligence activities	Permanent oversight committees created by the Ninety-fourth Congress; plus the dramatic revelations of the Senate's Select Committee on Intelligence Activities (the Church committee) of the same Congress
Tightened standards for wiretapping and other forms of surveillance in both foreign and domestic security cases	Set forth in President Carter's Executive Order No. 12036 of January 24, 1978, Section 2-202; and in the Foreign Intelligence Surveillance Act of October 25, 1978, P.L. 95-511
Exclusion of the president's campaign aides from posts in the Justice Department	Section 603 of the Ethics in Government Act of 1978 requiring the attorney general to promulgate rules for the exclusion of any Justice Department employee from any matter which would pose, among other conflicts, a *political* conflict of interest
Creation of a new unit in the Justice Department to prosecute official misconduct	Authorization of the Office of Special Prosecutor on an as-needed basis to prosecute crimes by the president or vice-president or other high government officials (Ethics in Government Act of 1978, section 601); new emphasis on the work of the public integrity section of the Justice Department's Criminal Division to prosecute crimes committed by other public officials

Congressional oversight   In addition to strengthening ombudsmanlike agencies in the executive branch, Congress can apply a mighty corrective in fulfilling its own oversight role. How we wish that J. Edgar Hoover had had to confront a tough House Appropriations Subcommittee and a Senate Committee on Government Operations twice a year to answer detailed questions about the number of, and reason for, wiretaps, FBI black bag jobs, and COINTELPRO plots. But it didn't happen; ambition didn't counteract ambition; Hoover walked all over spineless congressmen and senators for four decades.[45]

The epitaph was written by Senator Frank Church, after the Senate resuscitated its power of investigation over the intelligence community:

> The root cause of the excesses which our record amply demonstrates has been failure to apply the wisdom of the constitutional system of checks and balances to intelligence activities. . . . The founding fathers foresaw excess as the inevitable

consequence of granting any part of government unchecked power. This has been demonstrated in the intelligence field where, too often, constitutional principles were subordinated to a *pragmatic course of permitting desired ends to dictate and justify improper means* [emphasis added].[46]

The Church committee then recommended, and the Senate agreed, that a permanent intelligence oversight committee be established.

The oversight role is especially vital in other policy areas. Former Federal Power Commissioner Lee White testified to its efficacy in getting an independent commission to sit upright: "The most important period while I was at the Commission was preparing for the two oversight hearings we had, and we did more shaping up . . . in preparation for those than for anything else."[47]

Translating ethics into law[48]   Perhaps even more telling than the threat of a congressional investigation is the passage of new laws prohibiting unethical means that agencies have been resorting to. The Ninety-fifth Congress, for example, passed legislation restricting the wiretapping authority of the FBI and the scope of the covert operations the CIA could engage in.[49] As the Ninety-sixth Congress opened in 1979, a major battle loomed over further delimitation of FBI activities.[50] Picking up on a central recommendation of Senator Church's 1976 committee, Senator Edward Kennedy, new chairman of the Senate Judiciary Committee, introduced legislation in the form of an *agency charter* to rein in the FBI, to spell out specifically what it is authorized to do and specifically what it may not do. Kennedy's hope was to end forever the idea that the bureau had any inherent power to do anything it desired to protect national security.

While the boundary drawing would certainly divide agency defenders and civil libertarians, there apparently was agreement on the basic need for a charter. As FBI Director William Webster put it: existing law doesn't provide

> sufficient benchmarks to permit our agents to act or refuse to act with certainty that their conduct is correct. History tells us that reliance on inherent authority has been a major contributor to some of the sad events that have been fully chronicled.[51]

Then ethics become something more than platitudes; as Woodrow Wilson once said, "*Mala prohibita*" — *things wrong because they are prohibited.*[52]

Ombudsmen as a check   A number of governments around the world have turned to independent officials called ombudsmen to help check the abuse of power. Like the tribunes in ancient Rome, they stand as protectors of citizens against oppressive governments; they may conduct investigations, issue subpoenas, and publish findings that may then lead to action in the courts.[53] The establishment of inspectors general (the IGs) in the major federal departments during the Carter administration seemed to reflect the ombudsman idea whose time had come.

Prosecute the manipulators   A final remedy for public miscreants, as for private criminals, is to sue or prosecute them:

Interior Secretary Albert Fall for his complicity in the Teapot Dome scandal

dozens of congressmen for exacting kickbacks from their staffs

Attorney General John Mitchell and White House aides John Ehrlichman and Robert Haldeman for obstruction of justice

CIA Director Richard Helms for perjury before a congressional committee

FBI Director Patrick Gray and deputies Mark Felt and Edward Miller for authorizing illegal break-ins by FBI agents[54]

the FBI for instituting mail covers on citizens vaguely suspected of subversive activities*

It's a painful but dramatic way to remind other civil servants that some means to ends are intolerable in a government under law.

A Summary View About Means and Ends

Without even requiring a magnifying glass, we find widespread resort by public servants to means that cannot stand ethical scrutiny. The tactics cover the range from misfeasance through malfeasance to nonfeasance.

A multitude of forces may lead administrators to walk the low ethical road in pursuit of their goals: the Machiavellian rationalization that the ends are so important that any means are justified; the gnawing fear of failure that can transform a good person into a schemer overnight; beyond that, general fear and cowardice, which may drive some spineless wonders to shrink from their ethical duty; the politics of administration, which may lead underlings to curry favor in questionable ways; hero worship and the abdication of one's ethical judgments to the hero; co-optation; bribery; and many others.

The consequences of employing unethical means may be somewhat contradictory. Sometimes there is a short-run gain: a prosecutor wins a conviction with tainted evidence and doesn't get caught; ITT escapes an antitrust prosecution. But we are convinced of the much greater risk of bad means either preventing the accomplishment of good ends or so badly contaminating them that they are no longer worth pursuing (Watergate and the fall of Richard Nixon). Moreover, the use of bad means is contagious. Observing your example,

---

* Mail covers involve the recording of persons and organizations who correspond with someone under government surveillance. A U.S. district court held that an FBI mail cover of a high school student who sought information from the Socialist Workers party was unconstitutional. *Paton* v. *LaPrade,* 469 F. Supp. 773 (November, 1978). Within a few weeks, however, the Supreme Court refused to overturn a U.S. circuit court decision that allowed a Post Office Department mail cover in behalf of the Bureau of Customs in a tax evasion case. *U.S.* v. *Choate,* 576 F. 2d 165 (March 1978). The courts are apparently willing to tolerate mail covers, *without search warrants,* in cases involving the location of fugitives and obtaining evidence of the commission of a crime.

others get the message and rather quickly a whole staff may be walking the low road. When ethics disappear, so does the predictability of government.

There are no permanent solutions to the means-ends problem. The constant threat of failure is the assurance of recurring ethical end runs back to success. But there are some remedies, of unequal efficacy to be sure, which seem worth trying in curbing Machiavellian behavior in government: (a) codes of ethics and clear specification of standards as demarcations of what kinds of conduct will and will not be tolerated; (b) structural and procedural reforms (inspectors general in all departments, open meeting laws, etc.); (c) much more intensive legislative oversight of high-risk agencies such as the FBI and CIA; (d) new legal prohibitions on unethical conduct (e.g., prohibiting wiretapping and mail covers without warrants); and (e) a willingness to prosecute miscreants in government, from the U.S. attorney general on down, who behave as if the ends justify any means. But no single safeguard will ever be a panacea.

THE ETHIC OF PRIVATE GAIN AT PUBLIC EXPENSE

Good Old-fashioned Corruption in Government

Rivaling prostitution as the oldest game in town has to be making a buck at the public's expense. Hope of private gain galvanizes people to think about it; and if the price (payoff) is right, they'll do it.

A quick romp down the seamy side of American history tells the story:

Spiro Agnew, who began taking money under the table while executive of Baltimore County, Maryland, from engineering firms who wanted county business, remained on the take as vice-president of the country.

Bobby Baker, secretary to the Senate majority in Lyndon Johnson's day, made a bundle peddling influence on Capitol Hill and in the executive branch.

Navy Secretary Fred Korth, fired by President Jack Kennedy for indiscretion, used Navy Department letterhead to solicit business for a bank he had an interest in.

Sherman Adams, chief of staff under President Eisenhower, was fired for "down-field blocking" at the FTC in behalf of one Bernard Goldfine (with vicuña coats as the symbol of the era).

In the Truman administration, there was a whole bevy of corrupt officials: Merl Young, a Reconstruction Finance Corporation loan examiner who approved a multi-million-dollar loan for the Lustron Corporation and shortly thereafter accepted a vice presidency with that firm; T. Lamar Caudle, an assistant attorney general, and Daniel Bolich, the deputy commissioner of the IRS, who were both fired for improper conduct; over one hundred IRS officials fired in the single year 1951 for accepting payoffs from taxpayers, with the pastel mink coats and deep freezers as the symbols of the times.[55]

The Teapot Dome scandal of the 1920s involved Sinclair Oil Company bribes to Interior Secretary Albert Fall to obtain access to naval oil reserves, which led to the imprisonment of Fall, the removal of Attorney General Harry M. Daugherty, and the thorough disgrace of the Harding administration.[56]

The Crédit Mobilier scandal of the Grant administration involving gifts of stock to high-placed government officials and congressmen in exchange for their support of corporations building the transcontinental railroad.

Vast corruption plagued military procurement during the Civil War.[57]

The list goes back to the beginning of the Republic. True, the saga of corruption has brought some fascinating characters across the stage of American history, but the misuse of public office for private gain has clearly left a stench.

Corruption Techniques

Conflicts of interest   The Bible identified (but perhaps misdiagnosed) the conflict-of-interest problem a long time ago: "No man can serve two masters, for either he will hate the one and love the other, or he will hold to one and despise the other. You cannot serve God and mammon."[58] In conflict-of-interest situations, the culprit's left hand knows exactly what his right one is doing, and he has them working in tandem to serve one master — his pocketbook:

A city engineering inspector moonlights on a sewer construction project at night and then inspects the same project in his official capacity during the day.

A county commissioner arranges to lease space for county offices in a building he privately owns.

A state purchasing agent channels procurement contracts to an office supply house he and a partner own.

The president of General Motors is appointed secretary of defense, then divests himself of his GM holdings as required by law but still retains fond memories of what great tanks GM can build for the Pentagon.

The scope of the problem is vast. Common Cause reported in 1976 that it had identified 518 employees in eleven agencies with financial conflicts of interest. They included 279 out of 429 senior employees with the Nuclear Regulatory Commission and 22 out of 42 commissioners of the various regulatory commissions who came from the industries they were about to regulate. Of 36 retiring regulatory commissioners, 17 returned to the companies or law firms they had been regulating.[59]

Bribes and other inducements From *cumshah* in the Orient to *baksheesh* in the Middle East, to greasing the mayor's palm in Jersey City, bribes have been the hidden persuaders from time immemorial to induce public officials to sell their souls — and decision making to outside profiteers. Antitrust prosecution of ITT is lifted during 1971–1972 for a proffered $400,000; the dairy interests obtain a milk price-support increase for $682,500; the McDonald's fast-food chain wins permission to raise its prices (during price control) for a $250,000 contribution to the Nixon kitty; and the carpet industry succeeds in having flammability restrictions lifted for a similar contribution to Maurice Stans, secretary of commerce under Nixon, who was responsible for the flammability regulations and at the same time chairman of the Finance Committee to Reelect Nixon.[60]

The bicentennial year, 1976, was tarnished when the SEC began calling the roll of major American corporations that had been using bribes all over the world to sell airplanes, obtain oil, ease export taxes, and so forth, including Lockheed, Boeing, Northrup, Grumman, United Brands, Ashland Oil, Gulf and Exxon, Merck Pharmaceutical, and other firms.[61] The spectacle was an ugly one in which American bribes toppled Japanese ministers, embarrassed Italian prime ministers and disgraced the ruling prince of the Netherlands. Only here and there was there anything to laugh about: while Gulf Oil was dishing out $4 million in bribes to Korean officials, a Korean lobbyist, Tongsun Park, was passing out $750,000 to some thirty congressmen on rice deals. One wondered if the bilateral bribing might have affected the exchange rate!

Some twenty-six companies were charged with making illegal domestic contributions, and in substantial amounts: Ashland Oil, $850,000 in bribes during a five-year period; Gulf Oil, $1.4 million over twelve years; the 3M Company, $500,000 over nine; and Phillips Petroleum, $585,000 over eight years, involving illegal campaign contributions, doctored books, and executive suite culpability for the bribes.[62]

In contrast to Tongsun Park's envelopes full of dollar bills, a fairly subtle way to lay a little cash on congressmen is by means of carefully orchestrated, well-paid speaking engagements. The 1976 financial disclosures required of senators revealed, for example, that Herman Talmadge, chairman of the Senate Agriculture Committee, had received $25,000 in honorariums, the maximum allowed, for speeches delivered primarily to farm groups. Jewish groups had booked newly elected Senator Patrick Moynihan twenty times and paid him $72,750 for his efforts, well above the $57,500 he would earn during his first year as a senator.[63]

The temptation is far greater, of course, where the public salaries are much lower; then the marginal value of a bribe can look enormous to a government employee. That explains why city police are so often on the take and why so many businesses are around to provide it. Since the early 1950s, four major city police departments have gone belly up in corruption — those of Washington,

D.C.; Chicago; Denver; and New York City (in the last case, a detective named Frank Serpico ultimately proved that the NYPD was not "the city's finest"). Bribes from drug dealers, madams, gambling houses, construction firms, and hotels had effectively diverted New York City's law enforcement;[64] and that, unfortunately, is also public administration.

There are, of course, more innocent-looking ways than bribes to establish a community of interest between government officials and private firms with whom the officials have to deal. Take hunting lodges, for example. Almost as if they were providing the script for C. Wright Mills's military-industrial-political complex, major defense suppliers like Martin Marietta Corporation, Northrup, Rockwell International, Raytheon, and others built hunting lodges in eastern Maryland and elsewhere. Key senators and congressmen, Pentagon brass and high-ranking civilians were invited to the lodges as guests; in those convivial surroundings it was easy for the defense contractors to establish a mood of shake the hand that feeds you. In 1975, Rockwell was the tenth largest defense supplier; Northrup, the thirteenth.

For a decade the Pentagon drafted prohibitions and rapped knuckles to little avail. A Defense Department code of 1967 forbade its employees to accept any favor or gift from any corporation doing business with the department but left a loophole for gifts stemming from personal or family relationships. In November 1975, under pressure from the U.S. Civil Service Commission, the Pentagon closed the personal friendship exemption to ban all favors between their procurement people and the defense contractors.[65]

A few months later, Senator Proxmire embarrassed a Defense Department witness with a list of sixty new names of Pentagon officials on the guest lists at Rockwell's and Raytheon's lodges. Adding insult to injury, the senator revealed that *Northrup was billing the Pentagon for expenses incurred in wining and dining the Pentagon officials.*[66] That makes lobbying both fun and inexpensive! By the early spring of 1976, it began to appear as if the revised code, congressional, and Department of Defense investigations had at last begun to alter the hunting lodge nexus of the military-industrial complex.[67] (But let's not count our ducks until they're clean.)

Protecting private gain by boring from within   One of the most effective tactics for turning public administration into private aggrandizement is to have your people take over the agency. The rationale offered to the public always seems so reasonable: "We can't regulate the oil industry without having oil specialists on board."

Take the oil crisis of 1972–1973 as case in point. The American Petroleum Institute not only asked the Nixon administration for exemption from the antitrust laws while they did a little joint planning on how to end the oil shortage (and raise prices) but also proffered 250 oil executives to staff the fuel allocation programs of the federal government.[68] That kindly offer brought back memories of oilmen in charge of the navy's oil reserves during the Truman administration, which led an old curmudgeon, Harold Ickes, to resign in disgust as secretary of the interior.

A natural target for corporate takeovers of government, of course, is the independent regulatory commissions. The Moss subcommittee of the House Commerce Committee drew a statistical map in 1976 of the infiltration that had taken place for a quarter of a century (1951–1975) in that sector of the government. Less than 10 percent of the commission appointees had reflected any clear sensitivity to consumer interests, and some 35 percent came directly or indirectly from the regulated industries.[69]

The problem never ends. Jimmy Carter loudly declaimed against oil lobby domination of Congress in the late fall of 1977 and then appointed a Texan, Bob Strauss, as his trade ambassador, and Lynn Coleman, an oil lawyer, as chief counsel of the U.S. Energy Department.[70] It would certainly seem that oil stocks would be a prudent investment for awhile longer, if you're interested in private gain.

A little in-house embezzlement and burglary   At the grubbiest level of corruption are the inside thieves. Their negative impact on the public interest is a thousand times less than a co-opted Energy Research and Development Administration (ERDA) official giving the oil industry a break, but crooked cops and civil servants can also do damage. In 1961, a burglary ring involving at least fifty-two policemen was finally broken in the Denver Police Department. In the late 1960s, over fifty agents of the Federal Bureau of Narcotics and Dangerous Drugs were indicted for selling drugs or accepting bribes.[71]

In 1977, a federal employee named William Sibert of the Urban Mass Transit Agency demonstrated how to steal on a grand scale. In three months' time he hoodwinked his superior with vouchers made out to himself that generated checks worth $850,000. (Bear that figure in mind when we talk shortly about "the reward for doing it.")

In 1978, revelations of corruption began to surface concerning the government's giant purchaser, warehouser, and motor fleet operator, the General Services Administration (GSA). Estimates of losses due to fraud ranged from $66 million to $200 million per year.

The fun and games employed by GSA employees to make a buck at the public's expense constituted as comprehensive a catalogue of how-to-do-it techniques as we have ever seen:

A GSA store manager approves payment of, say, $10,000 to a pencil manufacturer for pencils that were never delivered and then receives a kickback from the manufacturer.

A GSA contracting officer authorizes payment to a firm for painting 20,000 square feet of walls in a building that had only 15,000 square feet — with another kickback for his kindness.

A third GSA employee trades a GSA credit card for a reserved parking space, with $80,000 subsequently charged to that card (to show how sweet the scales of justice are, this employee received, in order, a suspended sentence and a promotion!).[72]

The GSA pays a firm $1.5 million for unusable steel lockers and then orders replacements from the same firm — ninety thousand too many.[73]

Behind these practices lay not only the crassest cupidity but also a shocking lack of competitive bidding procedures, quality control checks, internal audits, adequate managerial supervision, and discipline. Apparently one of the contributing factors (discussed in Chapter 15) was the old problem of patronage: the GSA had become a dumping ground for political castoffs.

To clean up the mess, a Justice Department strike force was set up and obtained indictments against thirty-two persons, twenty-four of whom pleaded guilty.* The first case that went to trial resulted in the conviction of a GSA store manager who accepted a Bermuda vacation and $5,000 from a Maryland supplier.

Exploring the Causes of Corruption in Government

We need to get a handle on the sources of corruption, even though the inquiry may lead us to James Madison's position about giant pressure groups: we can't do much about the causes; we'll have to control the effects.[74]

A little lower than the angels   One speculation goes to the inherent moral weakness of humankind. "God created man a little lower than the angels," the Book of Psalms observed, and you look at the bribers and bribe takers we've been describing and probably conclude, "a whole lot lower in an instance or two."

It may well have been that kind of moral deficiency that led to Madison's observation in *The Federalist* (paraphrased) that if men were angels, we would have no need of government; if we were governed by angels, we would have no worries; but since neither proposition is true, we need government . . . and we need to watch it with great care.[75]

The thing that makes it tough for the civil servant, though, is trying to figure out when the angel wings of upstanding businessmen, like the executives of ITT, Gulf, and Rockwell, are really a cover-up for corporate manipulators. An old St. Louis prosecutor, Joseph W. Folk, passed on the warning to Lincoln Steffens: "It is good businessmen that are corrupting our bad politicians; it is good business that causes bad government."[76]

For the record, we ought to note that sometimes the causation is the other way around, with corrupt politicians standing like gatekeepers until business-

---

* Those thirty-two were only a fraction of the ninety-one persons indicted in the Chicago area during a similar period for unemployment compensation theft involving a different agency.

men pay their toll to pass through. A graphic example involved a bribe which Colonial Pipeline Company had to pay local politicians in Woodbridge, New Jersey, for a critical favor. A costly interstate oil line was to deadhead in the town, requiring an oil tank farm to receive the flow. The town's zoning laws gave the mayor the leverage to hold up Colonial for $110,000 for a building permit for the tank farm. *Public sector grand larceny* was clearly the initiator here.[77]

The invitation to sin[78]   A better explanation for that kind of cupidity lies in a more telling episode in Steffens's *Autobiography*. Steffens was a leading muck-raker in the early decades of this century, studying the linkage between the city machine and the businesses it served for a price. On one occasion Steffens was asked by an Episcopal minister who was familiar with his studies of municipal corruption, "Who started it?"

"Well, I know whom you boys blame it on — you blame it on Adam. And I know whom he blamed it on (that old chauvinist!) — Eve. And I know whom she blamed it on," Steffens said, "the serpent. But my research leads me to believe that the origin of evil was the apple — the reward for doing it" (paraphrased).[79]

When linked with the corporate profit motive, that explanation goes a long way toward explaining the constancy of corruption in government. Paint the government as apple orchard; hundreds of apple trees stand there behind a protective fence, with dollar signs on every apple: procurement contracts, Lock-heed loans, subsidies to small business, unemployment compensation, taxes and rebates, exemptions from the antitrust laws,* price supports to dairymen, tariffs on steel, charters, certificates of public convenience and necessity, TV and radio licenses.† The Steffens doctrine says: expect businessmen to come over and under the fence in unethical ways to pluck those apples because the rewards will be worth the risks. (Recall that the 0.5 percent increase in the milk price-support levels in 1971 that the American Milk Producers Institute got from Nixon for an estimated $682,500 was worth more than $300 million to the dairy interests. Ergo, if the rewards are grand enough, one can *expect bribery*.)

The principle applies at the local level as well. In 1973 the National Advisory Commission on Criminal Justice laid bare the endemic pattern of bribery by contractors in New York City. The construction of a new building may require forty different licenses or building permits. A delay on any one of them might cost far more than the bribe demanded by a corrupt city official to speed things up. The commission's estimate was that bribes to local officials constitute about 5 percent of construction costs in New York City (perhaps $75 million annually).[80]

---

* Remember, this one was worth $400,000 to ITT in 1971.

† The allocation of TV channel 10 in the Miami area in the mid-1950s (1954–1957) involved thousands of dollars in payments to FCC Commissioner Richard Mack from a National Airlines lobbyist named Thurman Whiteside. The bribes cost National its bid for channel 10 and Commissioner Mack his job. Reported in Victor Rosenblum, "How to Get into TV," in Alan F. Weston (ed.), *The Uses of Power* (New York: Harcourt, Brace, 1962), pp. 173–228.

A bribe to the county assessor may save hundreds of thousands of dollars at property tax time (and what assessor comes that high-priced?). A favorable zoning decision allowing a gas station in a residential area may add thousands to the value of a piece of property. As Steffens suggested, if $10,000 will bring in annual revenues of $100,000, some will be highly tempted to pursue private gain at the public's expense.

There are other contributing factors as well. We live in an *age of mass persuasion*, which seems to say, "We can make the public believe anything." So we get suckered by a safety razor commercial on TV that shows a razor smoothly shaving a piece of sandpaper; months later, the FTC reveals there was a pane of glass between the blade and the sandpaper. Viewers get the message subliminally: "Make a buck and don't worry about how you make it." The private sector has taught us a lesson that can be transferred to our dealings with the public sector.

Administrators are sometimes afflicted by a strange malady called a *lack of a sense of history*, or the short-nose syndrome. The symptoms are clear: "I retire in three years; then someone else can come in and clean up the mess." A good example of this was the case of a U.S. district attorney who got caught up in the Bert Lance affair, the "Spiro Agnew case" of the Carter administration. The U.S. attorney, John W. Stokes, was investigating banker Lance's overdrafts in his 1974 campaign for governor. Stokes dropped the matter on December 2, 1976, after Lance was nominated as OMB director in the incoming Carter administration. Stokes's explanation was honest enough: he wasn't going to make waves about the president-elect's right-hand man and jeopardize the civil service pension he would be eligible for in November 1977.[81]

Contrast that view with Woodrow Wilson's sense of history. When a young acting secretary of the navy, Franklin D. Roosevelt, proposed to Wilson in 1917 that the time had come to prepare the navy for war against German U-boats, Wilson turned him down.

> I do not want the United States to do anything in a military way, by way of war preparations, that would allow the definitive historian in later days to say that the United States had committed an unfriendly act against the central powers. . . . I do not want to do anything that would lead [that historian] to misjudge our American attitude sixty or seventy years from now.[82]

That kind of vision and sense of history automatically exclude a good deal of unethical conduct.

Some final explanations of corruption would have to include government secrecy (you're tempted to try to do what you can get away with unnoticed); Andrew Jackson's warning about a stale bureaucracy (one more concerned with feathering its own nest than with protecting the public's interest); and the failure of an occasional president and some department heads to set the right example. What that long list of causes adds up to is the pessimistic conclusion that corruption in government will be a *continuous* headache in public administration. There will be no weed killer for this grab-grass.

The Consequences

Benjamin Franklin expressed the underlying principle best of all:

> Much of the strength and efficiency of any government in procuring and securing happiness to the people depends on opinion, on the general opinion of the goodness of the government, as well as of the wisdom and integrity of the governors.[83]

Corruption eats at those roots. An IRS in trouble (vintage 1951) finds a tide of dishonest tax returns flowing in; influence peddling begets influence buying; and citizen disrespect for the law mounts.

Something else goes wrong. A government once thought to be by and for the people becomes a government by the fixers for the cronies and the special interests.[84]

In addition, something also happens to the public servants who are on the take — the Albert Falls and the Spiro Agnews of this world. As the Old Testament says: "Thou shalt take no gift, for the gift blindeth the wise and perverteth the words of the righteous." When the oil lobbyists, defense contractors, and Korean bagmen come marching in, the saints go marching out.

Some Possible Antidotes to Governmental Corruption

The National Advisory Commission on Criminal Justice (1973) concluded that no single approach to government corruption would be adequate. When the causes are so diverse clearly no single cure can begin to do the job. Some broad-band antidotes are called for: improved recruitment standards, prohibitions on conflicts of interest, criminal law extensions, codes of ethics, enforcement mechanisms, financial disclosure requirements, and a host of others.[85]

The quality of people we're recruiting   A place to begin in shoring up agency defenses against corruption is the recruitment office door. What do we really know about the people we are hiring? The question points back to the reference checks that are conducted on job applicants. It suggests new kinds of queries civil service investigators ought to be asking college professors about their former students: "Williams, you say this student was Phi Beta Kappa? Did she do her own term papers, or did she get them from the national term paper rental service? You say this former student had a straight A average. Did he exhibit 'wandering gaze trouble' during examinations?" In short, can we find any reliable predictors of the ethics of new people we intend to bring on board from their past conduct?

Conflicts-of-interest statutes and codes of ethics[86] The next line of resort against those who seek to turn public service into private gain is the conflict-of-interest statute. Its purpose is to prohibit official involvement in any governmental matters that will redound to the official's private financial benefit. The kind of conduct these statutes intend to proscribe includes:

> the new county commissioner who rents his private office building to the county for office space

> the mayor who engineers a change in the zoning law so that a building he owns can be turned into a tavern

> the insurance men in the legislature who rewrite the state's insurance laws to lift the deductible on home insurance (glass damage, etc.) to $50, grossly reducing the claims their companies will have to pay

> the Small Business Administration's loan examiner who approves a multi-million-dollar loan for a manufacturing company that shortly thereafter hires him as a vice-president

What the conflict-of-interest laws seek to prevent, then, is the right hand of the public interest from being bent out of shape by the left hand of private interest.

President Johnson's Executive Order 11222 of 1965 was representative of the codes in this field. It directed federal employees to avoid using public office for private gain and forbade their soliciting or accepting any gift, directly or indirectly, from any person or corporation that might be affected by the employees' official decisions. Employees were barred from having any direct or indirect private financial interest that would conflict with their official responsibilities. The use of inside information for private gain was also prohibited, as was making any governmental decision outside official channels.

The executive order then turned to a technique now widely used by the states to help expose conflicts of interest, the *public disclosure* by government officials of their private holdings and associations. The disclosure statements "shall list such other financial information as the appointing department or agency shall decide is relevant in the light of the duties the appointee is to perform."[87]

In addition to making such disclosures, public officeholders are frequently required to divest themselves of investments in companies that might profit from their official decisions. Furthermore, the Ethics in Government Act of 1978 imposed strict limitations on postemployment contacts between former high-ranking agency employees and the agencies that they had left behind for the private sector (e.g., army procurement officials retiring to high-salaried posts with General Motors). Title V of the 1978 act placed a lifetime ban on these ex-wheels if they should attempt to influence any matter in their old agency on which they exercised decision-making responsibility while in government; a *two-year ban* on influencing any matter that had been pending under their jurisdiction while in government; and a *one-year ban* on influencing any policy matter that had been before their agency during their employment. The penalties were stiff: a $10,000 fine or two-year imprisonment or both; and a five-year ban on any representation of a private interest before their old agency.[88]

The disclosure statutes are not without drawbacks, however. One of them is poor enforcement. During the first three years of the New Jersey Financial Disclosure Act of 1971, for example, only 8 percent of the financial statements were properly prepared. In Michigan, a code covering sixty thousand state employees was supervised by a state board of ethics in 1975 with a budget of only $10,000.[89] At the federal level, enforcement of Johnson's Executive Order 11222 was entrusted to a single lawyer and a part-time secretary by the U.S. Civil Service Commission.[90] In 1975, the General Accounting Office found forty-nine apparent violations of law by employees of the Geological Survey alone (in the Interior Department) involving conflicts of interest with the private sector that the Geological Survey had not dealt with.[91]

A second problem has been the *unevenness* of the requirement to disclose financial holdings and liabilities. For example, not until Congress passed the Ethics in Government Act in 1978 were the president and vice president or the Supreme Court justices bound by the financial reporting requirements that applied to their high-ranking subordinates.

Another drawback is turning away from public office able people who are unwilling to disclose their holdings. Mayor Thomas Allen of Olympia, Washington, said, "I don't want everybody to know how poor I am." Others have an embarrassment of riches. But having to play show and tell may be too high a price to pay, as in the town of Spangle, Washington, where the mayor and council all resigned rather than comply with Washington's Initiative 276 of 1972.[92]

In the first year of Alaska's 1974 disclosure statute, thirty-three state commissioners resigned, decimating at least six regulatory boards. An Alabama report suggested that some three hundred local officials chose to fold rather than file.[93]

Despite these losses, states are making increasing use of codes of ethics. The strategy behind them seems to be at least threefold:

to improve employee conduct by clearly laying out the metes and bounds of what is acceptable behavior[94]

to provide due notice and warning for possible disciplinary action

to improve the public image of an agency by taking a "we're trying" posture

But whatever the strategy may be, we are left with Moses' dilemma: Will verbal lightning bolts from on high (the legislature, the chief executive, the merit council, the ethics commission, or the department head) ever change behavior?[95] As a starting point, ask yourself: In the absence of sanctions, has the definition of things prohibited significantly deterred you so far in life?

Some states have taken significant steps on the enforcement front. In Alabama, for example, the ethics commission may take the following actions:

transmit findings about legislators with conflicts of interest to the officers of the House or Senate

notify the attorney general or a district attorney if a crime has been committed

inform the department head of an offending civil servant and of code violations that may be grounds for disciplinary action

make public disclosure if an elected official or lobbyist has violated the code[96]

These sanctions begin to take an ethics code beyond the "thou shalt nots" to "we'll go after you if you do." But it should also be noted that the work of the ethics commissions is not entirely ex post or negative. In rendering advisory opinions to public servants who face real dilemmas in the handling of their jobs, the commissions may solve a lot of problems ex ante.

Doing just that was a major hope of the Johnson administration in requiring the appointment of ethics counselors in each agency. Their job was to advise employees confronted with ethical dilemmas, police the financial disclosure system, and monitor conflict-of-interest situations that might arise.[97]

The Carter administration went still further in obtaining congressional approval for an Office of Government Ethics (OGE) within the U.S. Office of Personnel Management. To be headed by a director requiring Senate confirmation, the OGE would have government-wide responsibilities in these areas:

promulgating and interpreting rules covering conflicts of interest and other ethical problems

monitoring compliance with the financial disclosure requirements of the 1978 Ethics Act

consulting with ethics counselors in the agencies

rendering formal advisory opinions

directing corrective actions to be taken by agencies and employees

reporting violations to the attorney general for prosecution

promoting wide understanding of ethical standards throughout the executive branch[98]

In short, the born-again Jimmy Carter had created a Moses corps within the federal bureaucracy.

Special prosecutors In states and communities with a long record of corruption — Massachusetts in the 1960s, Jersey City and Baltimore much of the time — special strike forces are undoubtedly called for to provide the independence for investigation, the legal prowess for prosecution, and the continuity to outlast the bribers and influence peddlers.[99] One example was the creation of the special prosecutor's office in the Justice Department to prosecute the Watergate crimes.[100] But long before the Archibald Coxes and Leon Jaworskis were the Ferdinand Pecoras and Thomas Deweys whose early claim to fame lay in their cleanups of stock market manipulation and local corruption.

The key things to be observed in providing for these special prosecutors are: (a) continuous standby authority provided by the legislature to create the office, (b) an appropriate triggering mechanism (perhaps the governor if he is not involved in the mess, the attorney general, or a panel of state district court judges) to set up the office, (c) a ready source of funds to finance the operation, and (d) adequate authority to investigate, including subpoena power, and to prosecute.

Carter's 1978 Ethics Act provided for the Office of Special Prosecutor to investigate crimes charged to the president, vice-president, high-level employees of the Executive Office of the President or the Justice Department, or officers of the national committees who sought the election of the president.[101]

The special prosecutor would be appointed by a panel of the Circuit Court of Appeals for the District of Columbia. The prosecutor would enjoy all the investigative and prosecutorial powers of the attorney general except the power to authorize wiretaps. The prosecutor could be removed by the attorney general "only for extraordinary impropriety, physical disability, mental incapacity," or other conditions impairing the performance of duty. The removal power would be circumscribed by the requirement of a prompt report from the attorney general both to the circuit court and to the House and Senate judiciary committees and by the possibility of a civil suit and restoration to office by the court of appeals that appointed the special prosecutor.

In providing for this office, Congress rejected a proposal to create a division within the Justice Department to be known as the Office of Government Crimes. The congressional view was that it made better sense to leave the continuing oversight role in that area to the Criminal Division of the Justice Department.

The "Inspector General" inside government agencies   The IG in the military is a tough, frightening unit. Its staff are the eyes and ears of the base commander, with additional reporting lines directly to the inspector general in the Pentagon. The IG's mission, among other things, is to keep a close watch on unethical conduct within the ranks.

Since the late 1950s, civilian departments have begun to make increasing use of the inspector general idea: the Treasury Department a number of years ago, HEW (by act of Congress in 1976), and the Federal Energy Agency in 1977, to name but three. The FEA administrator indicated that his IG would conduct "scheduled and unscheduled inspections and audits" of both headquarters and regional offices.[102] Among the reports that triggered the action were those concerning oil company gratuities to agency employees and the representation of private interests before the FEA by its own former employees.

With the GSA scandal staring them in the face, Congress directed all major federal agencies in October 1978 to create the office of inspector general to direct in-house efforts against fraud and corruption.[103] The president then designated the Office of Management and Budget as the focal point in the executive branch for implementing the Inspector General Act.

Fiscal controls   Another internal check on corruption lies in the proper design and administration of the preaudit and postaudit controls discussed in Chapter 14. The internal auditors are in a position to determine if bidding procedures have been followed, expenditure ceilings observed, and vouchers issued only for authorized objects of expenditure.

But these controls are not foolproof. Clever schemes may elude them where line officers collect checks for phantom employees and money passes under the table for negotiated contracts; and the auditors themselves may occasionally be on the take (who then watches the watchdog?). The watcher of the watchdog is the General Accounting Office, peering down on auditors in the executive branch from its vantage point in the legislative branch. In 1978 the controller general, Elmer Staats, created a special GAO task force to help prevent fraud in the government.[104] Its mission included assessing the vulnerability of high-risk programs to influence peddling, following up on the prosecution of known instances of fraud, and suggesting to Congress and the agencies new approaches to reduce corruption. As an initial step, the task force set up a hotline telephone number in Washington for whistle blowers to use in passing on tips about misconduct they have observed. With the new protection afforded them against agency reprisal by title I of Carter's Civil Service Reform Act, and a phone in their hands, the whistle blowers may be the fastest-rising fraternity in Washington. (One note of sadness, however: a government of informants is an unlovely sight.)

Providing policy guidelines in areas of administrative discretion   One of the troubled agencies of the Truman administration was the Reconstruction Finance Corporation (RFC) with large apples to distribute. One loan examiner, Merl Young, approved a multi-million-dollar loan to the Lustron Corporation and then joined the corporation as a high-paid vice-president about six months later. Another loan examiner approved a loan to the Saxony Hotel in Florida and then enjoyed a Florida vacation as guest of the hotel.

The Senate investigating committee began to wonder if there were any RFC loan examiners who had any standards. Then one appeared before them: "What will you, and what will you not, accept from clients with whom you're conducting RFC business?" a senator asked. "Senators," the examiner replied, "a twelve-pound ham. Anything more than that and I've been had."[105] And so a new maxim appeared in the ethics field: "I won't accept anything from the public that I can't consume in twenty-four hours."

What those episodes highlight is the need in many agencies for more objective guidelines on discretionary authority: criteria to judge creditworthiness of potential borrowers, performance standards for contractors bidding on government jobs, explicit zoning guidelines for the issuance of building permits, and so on.

As the National Advisory Commission on Criminal Justice observed:

> The greatest single cause of corruption in these three areas of government operation (zoning, licensing, and tax assessment) is the availability of excessive discretion involving significant sums of money. Vague and improperly-stated decision guidelines invite attempts at manipulation and fraud and are, at a minimum, indicative of sloppy management.[106]

Beset with the possibility that inside and outside chiselers are stealing some $25 billion annually from federal programs, late in 1978 the Justice Department developed a new approach employing the guidelines technique. Borrowing a page from environmental legislation, the Justice Department proposed to Congress that a "fraud impact statement" (FIS) be required for each new piece of legislation. The FISs would attempt to identify aspects of the program particularly vulnerable to fraud and then recommend specific safeguards to be built into the administration of each program.[107]

Outside checks   The New Testament says that "everyone who does evil hates the light and shuns the light, lest his deeds should be reproved." There are some powerful beacons outside government agencies that can let the light shine in: annually called grand juries, ethics commissions (noted earlier), legislative investigating committees, and the pitiless publicity of the press.

The annually called grand jury is a hallmark feature of California's local government: citizen bodies looking for inefficiency and corruption in public agencies. The work of congressional investigating committees has become legendary: the Committee on the Conduct of the (Civil) War, the Walsh committee probing the Teapot Dome scandal, the Truman War Investigating Committee, and the later oversight investigations into the Commodity Credit Corporation, the FCC, the FPC, and the corporate bribery scandals of the 1970s.

Nor should we overlook the work of the investigative reporters in pinpointing private gain at the public's expense: Jack Anderson's revelation of the Dita Beard memo that revealed the ITT payment to the Nixon administration;[108] the reporters' consortium that moved in to expose Arizona's corruption after the bombing death of investigative reporter Don Bolles in 1977; and the *St. Louis Post Dispatch*'s revelations of coal mine operators' payments to Illinois Governor Dwight Green, payments that co-opted that state's department of mines and led to the Centralia mine disaster.[109]

On a broader scale, the United States can never repay its debt to Bob Woodward and Carl Bernstein of the *Washington Post* for their dogging the tracks of "all the president's men" until the Watergate felonies were fully exposed. The First Amendment is still some kind of shield against the money changers and power brokers in the temple.

What leaders can do   The ancient proverb, "Where there is no vision, the people perish," might well be retranslated today to read, "Where there is no vision, the people may perish because the bureaucrats are taking such good care of themselves." Conversely, where there is vision and leadership, significant things can happen to agencies. Gifted leaders can transform plodding, lackadaisical, corrupt institutions into agencies with both purpose and ethics. Our governmental history has seen dozens of them do just that: Carl Schurz and the Interior Department, Gifford Pinchot and the Forest Service, Harold Ickes and the Public Works Administration, Henry Stimson and George Marshall in the War Department during World War II, and Sargent Shriver in Jack Kennedy's Peace Corps, among many others.

Leaders of that caliber have the capacity to transform jobs into crusades, to lift the whole level of perception of their staffs from "How little I can get by with today?" to "What can I do for my country?"

One could feel the impact of such leadership in the applause of the Justice Department employees, as Attorney General Elliot Richardson bade farewell to them after getting the ax in Nixon's Saturday Night Massacre (October 20, 1973) — somebody reviving their belief in themselves and in the almost lost sense of an agency ethic that the John Mitchells, the Richard Kleindiensts, the J. Edgar Hoovers, and their kind had come so close to destroying.

My own view is that first-class leadership — from front-line supervisors to division chiefs, department heads, and presidents — may hold the greatest promise of all as an antidote to corruption in government. If leaders can give their people a vision of the promised land, they may have to spend a lot less time chipping out the "ten commandments" on what ought not to be done while the folks are getting there.

THE ETHIC OF SECURING THE PUBLIC INTEREST

The largest ethical questions of all involve defining and securing the *public interest*. No longer is the quest some wrenching concern over questionable means, or self-serving calculations on how to profit at the public's expense. What now confronts the public servant in this third ethical area are the very reasons for the government's existence: What will promote the good life for our people? What will enhance freedom, equality, justice, the beauty of life, and economic well-being? What is it that the government should really be about?

An old English quatrain best sets this issue apart from the earlier ones concerning means and ends and sheer cupidity:

> The law locks up both man and woman
> Who steal the goose from off the Common
> But lets the larger felon loose
> Who steals the Common and leaves the goose.

We mean to suggest that the greatest unethic of all is allowing the Common to be stolen through the inattention, ignorance, cowardice, or co-optation of those who might have prevented it. Consider how often this happens at every level of government:

> federal, state, and local officials who seemed to have no awareness before Watts in 1965 that we had a black problem of enormous proportions in this country (black writer James Baldwin said it best: "Nobody knows my name")
>
> local health officials in Birmingham, Alabama, who allowed U.S. Steel to pollute the air with impunity and cause lung disease in 30 percent of those living downwind from the steel plant[110]
>
> city planners who busily mark maps where subdivisions are going in and then fail to get property easements for extending the freeways to serve those subdivisions; five years later $70,000 homes have to be condemned as the price of the oversight
>
> a state air pollution control board that bows to "progress," grants variances for polluting industries, and watches an irreversible degradation of pristine air take place over choice recreation land
>
> a state legislature that strips the public service commission of critical authority and staff, leaving natural gas consumers hapless in their fight with the utilities' drive for profits
>
> the Congress that promotes cancer by subsidizing tobacco production
>
> a U.S. attorney general and his Antitrust Division that allowed forty-three hundred retail gas stations to be snuffed out of existence during the "oil shortage of 1973" without firing a shot under the Sherman Act

The list could go on and on.

What is ethical government in this largest public interest sense? First, hear Graham Wallas, English political scientist:

> Governments have come to be engaged not merely in preventing wrong things from being done, but in bringing it about that right things shall be done. A negative government only requires courage and consistency in its officials; but a positive government requires a constant supply of invention and suggestion.[111]

Then consider Carl Friedrich:

> Too often it is taken for granted that as long as we can keep the government from doing wrong, we have made it responsible. What is more important is to insure effec-

tive action of any sort. To stimulate initiative, even at the risk of mistakes, must now-adays never be lost sight of as a task in making the government's services responsible. An official should be as responsible for inaction as for wrong action; certainly the average voter will criticize the government as severely for one as for the other.[112]

Instead of nonfeasance, then, this largest ethical concern is asking of those who serve in government, "When we needed your vision, wise planning, and above all, your timely action, *were you there?* If you weren't, then you fractured the most important ethical precept of responsible government: you violated the public trust."

What Is the Public Interest?[113]

A simple evasion of an answer is: "the thing pressure groups and parties are constantly fighting about." That definition contains a grain of truth, that the defining of the public good is the very heart of the political struggle. In fact, the definition reflects one conception of politics as "the system whereby any society *defines its ends* and acquires the means to achieve them."

But the debate is sharp over the utility — or the vacuity — of the concept of the public interest. Here are some contrasting views:

In drawing up a list of phrases "which never would be missed," Frank Sorauf would begin with "the public interest."[114]

"In spite of operational dilemmas," Steve Bailey believes that the public interest "is the central concept of a civilized polity."[115]

The public interest is what we're fighting for and our enemies would like defeated — the concept of most lobbyists.

The public interest exhibits the same flaw as all theories of value — value judgments cannot be proved by science or logic; they are mere noises — no-sense, nonsense — the logical positivists.[116]

The public interest is "what men would choose if they saw clearly, thought rationally, acted disinterestedly and benevolently" — Walter Lippmann.[117]

A review of political theory suggests a number of differing notions about the public interest, some focusing on process, some on end results (matching in part the distinction constitutional law scholars draw between *procedural* due process of law and *substantive* due process).

1. For Rousseau, the public interest was defined by the general will — we can count heads and find it*[118] — thus, a British referendum on joining the Common Market.

2. For Edmund Burke the public (or national) interest emerges from the legislative debates of rational members of Parliament who are committed to its discovery.[119]

---

* Rousseau also offered some "uncountable" versions of the general will as well.

3.   For Jeremy Bentham, it is the greatest good of the greatest number.[120]

4.   For many, it is that which emerges from right procedures — the democratic process for a Jefferson,[121] procedural due process for a Justice Black.[122]

5.   For others, the public interest is a normative conception about the great goals of public policy — freedom, justice, equality, economic progress, and so on.*[123]

6.   The public interest is that which emerges from the pressure group struggle and legislative compromise.†

Frank Sorauf summarized the debate on the public interest in this way:

> Generally it has come to mean some criterion or desideratum by which public policy may be measured, some goal which policy ought ideally to pursue and attain. But just *whose* standard it is to be remains the problem. It may variously be an ethical imperative (such as the natural law), some superior standard of rational and "right" political wisdom, or the goals or consensus of a large portion of the electorate. Or it may be some amalgam, some almost mystical balance of narrower interests in which the final product appears to be considerably greater than the sum of its "selfish" parts.[124]

He went on to suggest the kinds of contributions the ethical and able public servant can make in weighing rival approaches to the public good:

> The practitioners of politics, just as the academic political scientists, need phrases and concepts which will clarify competing interests, separate the "is" from the "ought," shield the debate from undue moralism, and frame practicable and specific policy alternatives. Above all, they need intellectual tools for discussing the morality and wisdom of political policy, not in vague moralizations and rationalizations, but in terms of identifiable results and consequences and in terms related to policy itself.[125]

In brief, sharpening the tools of policy analysis, delineating costs and benefits, and raising the level of rational decision making may be the great things public servants can bring to the discovery of the public good.

Portrait of the Ethical Public Servant

In my view, there must be a few other dimensions to the deeply ethical public servant who fully meets the test in this third area we have been discussing. It is *conscience;* it is *commitment* to matters beyond one's own welfare; it is a kind of love affair with those concerns that drove you (in Chapter 1) to run for governor: *res publica, pro bono publico, salus populi suprema lex esto.* As George Washington wrote long ago, "For such a one my inquiries have been

---

* One thinks, for example, of Ernest Griffith's prescriptions for the public interest: (a) public policy should favor consumers rather than producers; (b) long-term goals should take priority over short-term goals; (c) freedom is preferable to coercion; and (d) policies should be predicated on the equality of all. "The Ethical Foundations of the Public Interest," in Carl J. Friedrich, *The Public Interest* (New York: Atherton, 1962), pp. 22–23.

†See David B. Truman, *The Governmental Process* (New York: Knopf, 1951).

made and are still making; how far I shall succeed is at this moment problematical."[126]

At this juncture in our history, this standard suggests that we need a government recruiting program that is looking for people with a kind of binocular vision and a mountain climber's determination: the binoculars to see the public interest range and the climber's determination to scale every peak before retirement. But it's some range:

creating an atmosphere for labor-management relations that will not overlook the public's interest

wise husbanding and development of America's water resources

achieving for our black citizens, other minority groups, and women full enjoyment of civil rights and equality of opportunity

restoring the beauty of the land, air, and water of the United States

adjusting our energy demands to the equally legitimate needs of succeeding generations

fostering the enjoyment of liberty and adequate standards of living wherever we can appropriately help

That's no agenda for the Frederick Jackson Turners, who "closed the frontier" in 1893. Rather, it calls for the kind of public servants John F. Kennedy had in mind when he beckoned us all to a new frontier:

Today our concern with man's environment ranges from the ocean floor to the stars. Since there are virtually no limits to the physical dimensions of the tasks set for us, we must identify and unshackle limitless creativity in the government's career service. In every phase of government operations, we must be certain that we provide today's solution to today's problem.[127]

And to tomorrow's, and the day after tomorrow's as well, we would add.

In one of the most important pieces ever written about ethics in government, Steve Bailey drew a picture of the "ethical public servant" from an important model in his life, Dean Paul Appleby. Bailey argued that the ethical person would exhibit three mental traits and three moral qualities. The mental traits were these:

a recognition of the moral ambiguity of all people and of all public policies

a recognition of the contextual forces that condition moral priorities in the public service

a recognition of the paradoxes of procedures[128]

As to the recognition of moral ambiguity:

Gerald Ford could pardon Richard Nixon, who had already lost what meant most in life to him, power and glory.

Making Allowance for Moral Ambiguity and Contextual Circumstance

The pardoning of Richard M. Nixon by President Gerald Ford, September 8, 1974:

> . . . I have . . . searched my own conscience with special diligence to determine the right thing for me to do with respect to my predecessor in this place, Richard Nixon, and his loyal wife and family. Theirs is an American tragedy in which we all have played a part. It could go on and on and on, or someone must write "The End" to it. I have concluded that only I can do that. And if I can, I must.

> [Nixon] would be cruelly and excessively penalized either in preserving the presumption of his innocence or in obtaining a speedy determination of his guilt in order to repay a legal debt to society. During this long period of delay and potential litigation, ugly passions would again be aroused, and our people would again be polarized in their opinions, and the credibility of our free institutions of government would again be challenged at home and abroad. . . .

> But it is not the ultimate fate of Richard Nixon that most concerns me — though surely it deeply troubles every decent and every compassionate person. My concern is the immediate future of this great country. . . . As President, my primary concern must always be the greatest good of all the people of the United States, whose servant I am.

> As a man, my first consideration is to be true to my own convictions and my own conscience. . . .

> Finally, I feel that Richard Nixon and his loved ones have suffered enough, and will continue to suffer no matter what I do, no matter what we as a great and good nation can do together to make this goal of peace come true. . . .

> Now, therefore, I, Gerald Ford, President of the United States . . . do grant a full, free, and absolute pardon unto Richard Nixon for all offenses against the United States which he . . . has committed or may have committed or taken part in during the period from January 20, 1969, through August 9, 1974.

Congressional Quarterly Weekly Report (Sept. 14, 1974) 32:2455.

Another president experienced no pain in putting a Senate coalition together for an energy bill that included senators who would later fight him on foreign aid and fighter aircraft for Saudi Arabia and Israel.

A bureau chief could keep in proper perspective the great strengths of a deputy whose momentary slip with the press had just caused the chief considerable embarrassment.

As Theodore White once stated, these kinds of administrators have an eight-octave view of the people around them, not a one-octave view. That kind of perception is the starting point for the ethical treatment of co-workers and citizens.

The appreciation of contextual forces adds another ethical perspective to the conduct of administration:

Judge Matt Byrne could end the trial of Dr. Daniel Ellsberg for the unlawful disclosure of the Pentagon Papers after White House aide John Ehrlichman offered the judge the directorship of the FBI (the contextual forces spelled "bribe").

Secretary of War Henry L. Stimson could look at Japanese lives that would be snuffed out if we dropped an atom bomb in August 1945 and balance them against American lives that would be saved through not having to invade Japan, and Japanese lives and cities that would not be destroyed if the bomb quickly ended the war.[129]

Daniel Webster, who had promised earlier never to vote for slavery, could speak eloquently for the Compromise of 1850 because a new factor in the equation raised a larger question for him now — the preservation of the Union.[130]

Thomas Jefferson could (with enormous pain) delete his philippic against the slave trade from the draft of the Declaration of Independence because he saw the winning of southern support for independence as a hundred times more important than retaining a paragraph of his prose.[131]

Bailey put it eloquently: "If value priorities are never adjusted, the saints come marching in and viable democratic politics goes marching out."[132]

As to understanding the paradoxes of procedures and how that capability enhances ethical decision making, consider the following:

the police chief who, instead of bucking *Miranda* v. *Arizona* (and its required warnings to suspects in custody), meticulously trains his staff to comply, knowing that "liberty lies in the interstices of due process" (as Felix Frankfurter once wrote)

a National Park Service director who will not budge on an application for a coal-fired power plant until a critical procedural step has been completed, the environmental impact statement

a state merit system director who will not approve a new psychological test until it has been validated

Add to those mental qualities Bailey's suggested *moral* qualities:

Optimism: FDR and Senator George Norris believed that the Tennessee River could be tamed, Jack Kennedy that we could reach the moon, and Lyndon Johnson that the franchise could be successfully extended to blacks.

Optimism in a Wheel Chair

Robert Sherwood recounts Roosevelt's morning routine in the White House that sustained all their spirits during the depths of World War II:

> The signal bells announced the President's approach to his office and we stood by the French windows leading out to the colonnade and watched him go by in his armless, cushionless, uncomfortable wheelchair, pushed by his Negro valet, Chief Petty Officer Arthur Prettyman. Accompanying him was the detail of Secret Service men, some of them carrying the large, overflowing wire baskets of papers on which he had been working the night before and the dispatches that had come in that morning. When Fala came abreast of the wheelchair as it rolled along, Roosevelt would reach down and scratch his neck. This progress to the day's work by a crippled man was a sight to stir the most torpid imagination; for here was a clear glimpse of the Roosevelt that the people believed him to be — the chin up, the cigarette holder tilted at what was always described as "a jaunty angle," and the air of irrepressible confidence that whatever problems the day might bring, he would find a way to handle them. The fact that this confidence was not always justified made it none the less authentic and reassuring.

Robert E. Sherwood, *Roosevelt and Hopkins* (New York: Harper, 1948), pp. 215–216.

Courage: Jack Kennedy bulldozed Khrushchev into removing missiles from Cuba. Jimmy Carter announced his plans for pardoning Vietnam draft dodgers before the annual convention of the American Legion.

Fairness tempered by charity: an agriculture secretary, in a time of great adversity for farmers, turned his department upside down for every bit of legal authority and money he could marshal to ease their plight; a division chief realized how male and lilly-white his division had become and then got going on affirmative action in behalf of those who have waited so long for equal opportunity — minorities and women.

To those moral qualities, others can and should be added: plain honesty, concern for scarce resources, commitment to the general good ahead of narrow interests, and so on.

A Smithsonian scholar, Anders Richter, has added to the list some ethical dimensions for the public administrator that have emerged from existentialism, which teaches that the essence of being is the result of choice — the choices we make as responsible persons without external dictation.[133] Those qualities include a readiness to decide and to act (some existentialists must have loved Harry Truman!), a sense of objectivity, a willingness to accept responsibility for one's acts, authenticity as a person, and a commitment to the freedom of others.[134]

Now the rub: as we look to the future of public administration and caring for the people's business, can anything very useful be done about producing people for government with those kinds of qualities?[135] A postmortem on Watergate by the National Academy of Public Administration pointed up the tragedy of getting people in government who lacked these qualities:

> Almost none [of the Watergate participants who testified] mentioned any special considerations of *public* service for the *public* interest apart from the President's interest. They had not learned in secondary school or in college or in law school that there is something special and different about public office and public responsibility.[136]

The Cloning* of the Ethical Public Servant

Start early!   Amorality begins early in life. Your five-year-old swipes candy bars at the drugstore when you're not looking; your ten-year-old plagiarizes a school report from the *Encyclopaedia Britannica;* at college, he gets his term papers from the national term paper rental service. By the time he reaches Harvard Law School, he views the world "essentially in cost-benefit terms — prudence rather than ethics," as a *Wall Street Journal* survey revealed in 1974.[137]

Ethics begin at home. Children can learn to live comfortably with the moral ambiguity of people. ("The family next door belongs to another church, but they're the kindest people on the street.") They can begin to get a feel for contextual circumstances — why the ambulance is permitted to run red lights. And they can certainly begin to appreciate at an early age the importance of procedures (skate boards never left on the stairs, bikes never laid behind dad's car, etc.).

Existentialist values can also be inculcated in youngsters on the part of parents by:

providing early opportunities for children to make choices

allowing natural consequences to follow their choices (except where life and limb are at stake)

exhibiting standards of right and wrong

being role models of objectivity (free of racial and religious prejudice) and of good citizenship (standing up and being heard on important causes)

challenging children to develop their own moral sensitivities

generating a climate in family affairs that stresses freedom, individuality, and creativity

With that kind of rearing we have a fair chance of cloning future public servants who closely resemble Bailey's and Richter's portraits.

---

* "Cloning" is a term that came into vogue during 1978 suggesting test-tube creation and duplication of living things.

The high school civics course as a cloner[138] Look back a couple of years to your dinner conversations after a school day at old Sawtooth High: there was probably a fair amount of, "Dad, can I have twenty bucks for the junior prom?" or "Do you mind if I join a secret fraternity at school?"

But how often did you blow your parents' minds with "I didn't know we had a bowling alley in this town that wouldn't let blacks bowl before eleven o'clock at night" or "Why hasn't anyone ever taken on that copper mill for what it's doing to our air and lungs?" In one question parents sense the radicalization of their son or daughter. All of a sudden the realization is that "They're really beginning to talk about American problems in the American Problems course at that high school."

If that is *not* happening, and you, your peers, and your siblings are receiving high school diplomas without any deep and lasting concern about the real windmills that need tilting at in this life, then where are we going to find the Don Quixotes a few years later to staff the government?

The high school social science curriculum and the quality of teaching that goes on there are enormously important in the cloning of the ethical public servant. What might be studied in a high school course on ethics (without bringing a lot of your parents and half the ordained ministers in town down on the principal)? As a starter:

1. How do we arrange our priorities in life? What values are revealed in the list? What are some possible consequences?

2. What are the predictable consequences of using unethical means to achieve our goals?

3. How would our behavior change if we sought to treat every individual as an end and not simply as a means?

4. How useful is the rule that "I will take as my standard of conduct that which I'm prepared to let everyone else take"? What if hundreds began to follow my current example?

5. When should my personal interests ever bow to larger interests?

6. How should governments treat people?

8. Under what circumstances should I ever allow another person to make my moral judgments for me?

9. How do I define the good life, and what obstacles exist in this community for the enjoyment of the good life by all our citizens? ("Some people see things as they are and ask 'Why?' Others see things that never have been, and ask 'Why not?' " How recently have I asked the "why not?" question about this town, this state, my country?).

That sounds like a fun course to take and a great course to teach.

The recruitment net again Agency recruitment needs to be fine-tuned to identify job applicants who possess the binocular vision and the public interest sense we've been discussing. I sit waiting for Office of Personnel Management investigators doing reference checks on my former students to begin asking some new kinds of questions:

> "Do you ever remember this student resigning the presidency of her sorority because the national organization wouldn't let them pledge anyone but white Christians?"

> "Do you ever remember this student cutting class to picket a bowling alley that wouldn't let blacks bowl before eleven o'clock at night?"

When those kinds of questions begin to be asked, it will be clear that government recruiters are at long last looking for the kind of people — *pro bono* people — whom we so badly need at all levels of government.

Training as a cloning device   Smart agencies not only do the kind of recruiting just described but also work overtime in developing the human beings once hired. While training new employees as aquatic biologists or computer programmers, why shouldn't agencies also spend some training dollars on developing ethical perceptions in all their recruits? Some sessions built around Adolf Eichmann's buck-passing, how Spiro Agnew became a household word, Steve Bailey's portrait of the ethical public servant, and the Glavis-Ballinger dispute — these and other cases might have a useful impact on that novitiate biologist or programmer.

Among other suggestions that have been made for developing a heightened sense of the public interest in the people serving in government are these:[139]

> special care in appointing civil servants to the new Senior Executive Service who not only know public health, civil rights, or antitrust law, but who also — all of them — are models of ethical behavior at its best: the Louis Glavises, Billy Mitchells, Harold Ickeses, William Jumps, Elliot Richardsons, and William Ruckelshauses wherever we can find them; the advancement of these types to the elite corps of the civil service would translate a loud message that ethical conduct pays

> continuous legislative oversight of agency activities that have notably advanced the public good (e.g., the Public Health Service, the Forest Service) or have badly abused it (the FBI of COINTELPRO days, the CIA and drug experiments, the GSA for grand theft and waste)

> a willingness of the new Merit Systems Protection Board to act as an administrative court for enforcing the ethics codes, thus giving power to precept

With what purpose in mind, once again? To staff the governments of the United States and its subdivisions with people at every level who will see to it that the "Common" shall be protected for ourselves and succeeding generations. If we are at all successful in this endeavor, then perhaps we will have lifted American government closer to the ethical plane Louis Brandeis described in his closing argument in the Glavis-Ballinger case in 1910:

> With this great government building up, ever creating new functions, getting an ever-increasing number of employees who are attending to the people's business, the one thing we need is men in subordinate places who will think for themselves and who will think and act in full recognition of their obligations as a part of the governing body. . . . We want men to think. We want every man in the service, of the three or four hundred thousand who are there, to recognize that he is part of the governing body, and that on him rests responsibility within the limits of his employment just as much as upon the one on top. They cannot escape such responsibility. . . . They cannot be worthy of the respect and admiration of the people unless they add to the virtue of obedience some other virtues — the virtues of manliness, of truth, of courage, of willingness to risk positions, of the willingness to risk criticisms, of the willingness to risk the misunderstandings that so often come when people do the heroic thing.[140]

How we rear our children, how we prepare them for effective citizenship, how we recruit and train employees as they enter government service can contribute significantly to expanding the supply curve of people in public service with the ethical qualities Brandeis was describing. Therein may lie our best hope of producing men and women who can do the heroic thing in administering the people's business.

SUMMARY

In this final chapter, we have assayed the ethical dilemmas that frequently make the job of the public administrator so difficult and at the same time so worth doing: (a) what kinds of means to achieve what kinds of ends, (b) private gain at the public's expense, and (c) how to define and secure the *public interest*.

The Machiavellian standard of ends justifying any means surfaces frequently in public administration, and predictably so when administrators stare failure in the face. Consequently, misfeasance, malfeasance, and nonfeasance appear all too frequently in the management of the people's business.

Resort to unethical means, however, is something of a roller coaster ride. If such means carry a J. Edgar Hoover to the heights of power for a period of time, they portend a terrible fall from grace for his agency once the misdeeds are exposed. The risk is clear: unethical means may either prevent the accomplishment of good ends or thoroughly contaminate them in the process. A further worry is the contagious quality of unethical conduct, as subordinates sense and then emulate the ethics of significant others in an agency.

A wide array of remedies is available to help resolve some of the means-ends dilemmas: codes of ethics and statutory changes to define impermissible conduct more specifically; structural and procedural reforms, from special prosecutors to open meeting laws; rigorous legislative oversight of agency conduct; ombudsmen; and prosecution of those whose choice of means is incompatible with a government under law.

Equally prevalent as an ethical problem in public administration is the pursuit of private gain at the people's expense. From county purchasing agents to secretaries of defense, left hands frequently know exactly what right hands are doing in conflict-of-interest situations. Corporate bribery scandals, Korean pay-offs, police corruption, and zoning payments have provided dismaying evidence of the numbers in government who are on the take.

The most telling explanation for this kind of good old-fashioned corruption in government is Lincoln Steffens's observation that there are *rewards* for doing it. Other causes were explored: deficiencies in our moral makeup, bad examples set in the private sector and in government by occasional presidents and depart-ment heads, a short-nose syndrome of some administrators ("I retire in three years — someone else can come in and clean up the mess"), and government secrecy, among others.

Private gain at the public's expense has serious implications not only for the government official who is involved in corruption (Spiro Agnew became a household word!) but for broader issues as well: jeopardizing the people's faith in their government and thus undermining compliance with that government's laws; and greatly enhancing the influence in policymaking of special-interest groups that have the resources to stroke the governmental hands that feed them.

Although the prognosis is zero for completely eradicating the problem, some remedies may be helpful: greater care in the recruitment of those who work for government (reference checks, etc.); statutory prohibitions on conflicts of inter-est, bribes, and gifts; codes of ethics; public disclosure of the personal assets of government officials; internal auditors and inspectors general within agen-cies; special prosecutors; more detailed policy guidelines for the awarding of government contracts and loans; and outside checks such as annually called grand juries, legislative investigations, and rigorous scrutiny by the press. One of the most hopeful antidotes to corruption lies in the hands of gifted leaders who are able to set a tone of excellence for their employees to follow.

Finally, we canvassed the vaguest and most difficult problem of the three — the ethic of defining and securing the public interest. The question was posed for everyone in government: "When we needed your vision, wise planning, and timely action, were you there?"

Ethics now takes on the larger meaning of invention and suggestion, of initiative, of responsibility for inaction as for wrong action; and it requires the binocular vision to clearly perceive the public good and a willingness to wear oneself out in its pursuit. It is the ethic of the *new frontier*, the unfinished agenda of America's continuing revolution.

To generate an adequate flow of civil servants who can meet these chal-lenges and exhibit ethics in its highest form (creative, responsible service to the public) calls for action on many fronts — inculcating ethical values in the very young at home; generating a public conscience in students in high school civics classes, some of whom may later enter the public service; searching with care at the recruitment stage for people who have already exhibited this public interest sense; utilizing in-service training to lift the ethical perceptions of an agency's staff; developing role models of high-level ethical civil servants; congressional spotlighting of administrators who choose to walk the low road; and enforcing of ethical codes by administrative bodies.

In such ways as these we may be able to generate significant new numbers of civil servants who possess "the virtues of truth, courage, and the willingness to risk position" as they attend to the people's business.

KEY CONCEPTS

ethic of means and ends
ethic of private gain
the public interest ethic
reason of agency
misfeasance
malfeasance
nonfeasance

codes of ethics
special prosecutors
Inspector-general
Ethics in Government Act, 1978
cloning of ethical public
   servants

DISCUSSION QUESTIONS

1. Why do agencies engage in Machiavellian ethics, whether the mis-, mal-, or non-feasance type? Do important ends sometimes justify questionable means?

2. Discuss the management code of ethics. What problems would a public manager have in adhering to this code? Would you support activity that represents exceptions to this code?

3. Describe the various ways corruption operates in government. What are its causes? How can it be stopped?

4. What is the public interest? How do you know when a public official is acting in the best interests of the public and when she is not?

5. Discuss Bailey's ethical public servant. What values, morals, and mental capabilities should this person hold? How can such a person be cloned?

Notes

1. Stephen K. Bailey, "Ethics and the Public Service," *Public Administration Review* (Dec. 1964) 24:238.

2. Harold Stein, ed., *Public Administration and Policy Development* (New York: Harcourt, Brace, 1952), pp. 80–81.

3. Stein, *Public Administration*, pp. 81–84.

4. Roger Daniels, *Concentration Camps, USA: Japanese Americans and World War II* (New York: Holt, Rinehart and Winston, 1971), ch. 3, esp. pp. 70–73.

5. Philip M. Stern, *The Oppenheimer Case* (New York: Harper and Row, 1969), ch. 5.

6. *Coplon* v. *U.S.*, 191 F. 2d 749 (D.C. Cir., 1951) and 185 F. 2d 626 (2d Cir., 1950). See J. K. Lieberman, *How the Government Breaks the Law* (Baltimore: Penguin Books, 1973), pp. 87–88.

7. New York Times, *The Watergate Hearings* (New York: Bantam Books, 1973), pp. 608–611.

8. "The Nixon Transcripts," in Peter Woll, *American Government: Readings and Cases* (6th ed.) (Boston: Little, Brown, 1975), p. 391.

9. For a portrayal of the corruption problem with a comparative government perspective, see Caiden and Caiden, "Administrative Corruption," *Public Administration Review* (Mar.–June 1977) 37:301–308.

10. Niccolo Machiavelli, *The Prince* (New York: Modern Library, 1940), p. 66.

11. For a brief discussion of reason of state and its ethical implications, see Dwight Waldo, "Reflections on Public Morality," *Administration and Society* (Nov. 1974) 6:274.

12. *Screws* v. *U.S.*, 325 U.S. 91 (1945).

13. *Miller* v. *Pate*, 386 U.S. 1 (1967), where the U.S. Supreme Court ten and a half years after the violation of due process reversed Miller's conviction.

14. Daniel Walker, *Rights in Conflict* (New York: Bantam Books, 1968), p. 5.

15. J. K. Lieberman, *How the Government*, p. 135. The Supreme Court later called for a new election, and the once-deleted black candidates all won. Judge Herndon was found guilty and fined $5,700 for his misfeasance.

16. Rebuked and reversed in *U.S.* v. *U.S. District Court*, 407 U.S. 297 (1972). See also Lieberman, *How the Government*, pp. 91–92; and *Facts on File* (Apr. 1971) 31:315 c2.

17. U.S. House Committee on Interstate and Foreign Commerce, *Federal Regulation and Regulatory Reform* (Committee print, 94th Cong. 2d sess.) (Washington, D.C.: Government Printing Office, 1976), p. 3. (Cited hereafter as *Federal Regulation*.)

18. *Federal Regulation*, p. 11.

19. *Federal Regulation*, p. 13.

20. *Congressional Quarterly Weekly Report* (Dec. 6, 1976) 34:2643.

21. *Salt Lake City Tribune* (Nov. 22, 1953), p. A12; reprinted in *I. F. Stone's Weekly* (March 29, 1954), p. 4. When challenged, Mundt denied making the statement; the reporter denied the denial.

22. U.S. Senate Select Committee . . . on Intelligence Activities, *Intelligence Activities and the Rights of Americans* (94th Cong., 2d sess.) (Washington, D.C.: Government Printing Office, 1976), bk. II: 57–58. (Hereafter cited as *Intelligence Activities*.)

23. Herbert E. Alexander, *Financing Politics* (Washington, D.C.: Congressional Quarterly, 1976), pp. 118–120.

24. See, among other sources, the Articles of Impeachment of Richard Nixon, reported by the House Judiciary Committee in its final report to the House of Representatives, *Impeachment of Richard M. Nixon, President of the United States* (House Report 93-1305, 93d Cong., 2d sess.) (Washington, D.C.: Government Printing Office, 1974), pp. 1–4ff.

25. *Intelligence Activities*, bk. II: 61–62, 185.

26. *Intelligence Activities*, bk. II: 220–221.

27. *New York Times*, (Jan. 11, 1978), p. 8.

28. Testimony of FBI Assistant Director William Sullivan before the Church committee. *Intelligence Activities,* bk. II: 14, 141. See also William C. Sullivan, *The Bureau: My Thirty Years in Hoover's FBI* (New York: Norton, 1979).

29. Internal memorandum from Assistant Director William Sullivan to Hoover aide, C. D. DeLoach, July 17, 1966; reproduced in *Intelligence Activities,* bk. II: 142.

30. *Intelligence Activities,* bk. II: 142.

31. The Plato quotation paraphrased here can be found in *The Republic* (A. D. Lindsay trans., Everyman's Library) (New York: E. P. Dutton, 1950), bk. II, sec. 375, p. 55.

32. John B. Martin, "The Blast in Centralia No. 5," in Richard J. Stillman, *Public Administration: Concepts and Cases* (New York: Houghton Mifflin, 1976), pp. 19–34.

33. T. L. Becker and V. G. Murray, *Government Lawlessness in America* (New York: Oxford University Press, 1971), pp. 231–238.

34. Becker and Murray, *Government Lawlessness,* pp. 302–305.

35. Testimony of FBI agent Gary Rowe before the Senate Select Committee on Intelligence Activities, Dec. 2, 1975, *Congressional Quarterly Weekly Report* (Dec. 6, 1975) 33:2645.

36. The story is related in Lieberman, *How the Government,* pp. 208–211. Attorney General Richard Kleindienst admitted Nixon's pressure in a statement to the press in January 1978. See *San Francisco Chronicle* (Jan. 23, 1978), p. 11.

37. *Federal Regulation,* pp. 281, 471.

38. Sanford J. Ungar, "Get Away with What You Can," in Robert Heilbroner, ed., *In the Name of Profit* (New York: Warner, 1973), pp. 97–114.

39. James D. Richardson, *Compilation of the Messages and Papers of the Presidents, 1789–1897* (New York: Bureau of National Literature, 1897) 1:52–53.

40. Wayne G. Broehl, "Ethics and the Executive," *Dun's Review* (May 1957) 69:124.

41. See the thoughtful code suggested by George Graham in "Ethical Guidelines for Public Administrators," *Public Administration Review* (Jan.–Feb. 1974) 34:90–92.

42. Carl Sandburg, *Abraham Lincoln: The Prairie Years and the War Years* (New York: Harcourt, Brace, 1954), p. 427.

43. *Federal Regulation,* ch. 17.

44. Final report of the Watergate Prosecution Force, Oct. 16, 1975, in the *Congressional Quarterly Weekly Report* (1975) 33:2214, and the *Congressional Quarterly Almanac 1975* (Washington, D.C.: Congressional Quarterly, 1976) 31:519–520.

45. *Intelligence Activities,* bk. II:277–281. The account of congressional failures recorded in these pages by the Church committee is astounding, must reading, we think, for any student of contemporary legislative-executive relations.

46. *Intelligence Activities,* bk. II:iii.

47. *Federal Regulation,* p. 446. As another case in point, see U.S. House Judiciary Committee, *Hearings on Congressional Review of Administrative Rulemaking* (94th Cong., 1st sess.) (Washington, D.C.: Government Printing Office, 1975). The committee reviewed proposals for a congressional veto on regulations promulgated by executive agencies (pp. 253–260).

48. A recent book that casts the problem of ethics largely in terms of constitutional law is John Rohr, *Ethics for Bureaucrats* (New York: Marcel Dekker, 1978).

49. See *Congressional Quarterly Weekly Report* (Apr. 1, 1978) 36:795–796; and the Foreign Intelligence Surveillance Act of 1978, P.L. 95-511.

50. "Battle over Restrictions Is Expected When Congress Seeks to Write FBI Charter," in *Congressional Quarterly Weekly Report* (Dec. 16, 1978) 36:3436–3440.

51. *Congressional Quarterly Weekly Report* (Dec. 16, 1978) 36:3440.

52. Woodrow Wilson, *The State* (Boston: Heath, 1889), pp. 84–85.

53. Donald C. Rowat, *The Ombudsman Plan* (Toronto: McClelland and Stewart, 1973); and "Note: The Office of Public Counsel: Institutionalizing Public Interest in State Government," *Georgetown Law Journal* (Mar. 1976) 64:895–923.

54. See the *New York Times* for Apr. 11, 1978, p. 1, for the indictments of top FBI leaders under Richard Nixon.

55. See Louis W. Koenig, *The Truman Administration* (New York: New York University Press, 1956), pp. 72–75; and Booth Mooney, *The Politicians, 1945–1960* (Philadelphia: Lippincott, 1970), pp. 123–125.

56. For the scandals of the Harding administration, see S. H. Adams, *Incredible Era: The Life and Times of Warren Gamaliel Harding* (Boston: Houghton Mifflin, 1939).

57. Carl Sandburg, *Abraham Lincoln*, ch. 42.

58. Gospel according to Matthew.

59. U.S. House Committee on Interstate and Foreign Commerce, *Joint Hearings on Regulatory Reform — Quality of Regulators* (ser. 94-80) (Washington, D.C.: Government Printing Office, 1975) 1:46–51.

60. See Herbert E. Alexander, *Financing Politics*, pp. 120, 125.

61. U.S. Senate Committee on Banking and Housing, *Report of the Securities and Exchange Commission on Questionable Corporate Payments* (94th Cong., 2d sess.) (Washington, D.C.: Government Printing Office, 1976).

62. *Report on Questionable Corporate Payments*, pp. 39–40.

63. *Congressional Quarterly Weekly Report* (July 23, 1977) 35:1507–1517.

64. Lieberman, *How the Government*, pp. 213–216.

65. "Members Defend Contacts with Defense Firms," *Congressional Quarterly Weekly Report* (Feb. 14, 1976) 34:344–347.

66. "Proxmire Charges Pentagon Lacks Zeal in Investigating Favors by Contractors," *Wall Street Journal* (Feb. 4, 1976), p. 4.

67. "End of the Free Lunch? Pentagon and Contractors Grow Cautious after Disclosures of Wining and Dining," *Wall Street Journal* (Apr. 8, 1976), p. 40.

68. Harmon Zeigler and J. S. Olexa, "The Energy Issue," in Robert L. Peabody, *Cases in American Politics* (New York: Praeger, 1976), p. 182.

69. *Federal Regulation*, p. 451.

70. See Jack Anderson, "President's Attack on Oil Barons Only Rhetoric," *Salt Lake City Deseret News* (Feb. 16, 1978), p. A-3. For the subsequent developments flowing from these events see also Jack Anderson, "Dollar-a-Gallon Gas Is Carter's Gift to Big Oil Companies," *Salt Lake City Deseret News* (Mar. 22, 1979), p. A-3.

71. Lieberman, *How the Government*, p. 214.

72. "GSA Corruption Outlined at Senate Hearing," *Congressional Quarterly Weekly Report* (Sept. 23, 1978) 36:2578.

73. "Scandals of the GSA," *Newsweek* (Sept. 11, 1978), p. 29.

74. Tenth *Federalist Paper*.

75. Fifty-first *Federalist Paper*.

76. Lincoln Steffens, *Autobiography* (New York: Harcourt, Brace 1931), p. 371.

77. Morton Mintz, "A Colonial Heritage," in Robert Heilbroner (ed.), *In the Name of Profit*, pp. 59–95.

78. For a highly sophisticated economic analysis of corruption in the public and private sectors, see Susan Rose-Ackerman, *Corruption: A Study in Political Economy* (New York: Academic Press, 1978).

79. Steffens, *Autobiography,* p. 574.

80. U.S. National Advisory Commission on Criminal Justice Standards and Goals, *A National Strategy to Reduce Crime* (Washington, D.C.: Government Printing Office, 1973), p. 100.

81. Paraphrased from the *Congressional Quarterly Weekly Report* (Sept. 17, 1977) 35:1944.

82. Quoted in Donald Day, ed., *Franklin D. Roosevelt's Own Story* (Boston: Little, Brown, 1951), pp. 38–39.

83. Franklin's final speech to the Constitutional Convention, Sept. 17, 1787, in Winton U. Solberg, ed., *The Federal Convention and the Formation of the Union of the American States* (New York: Liberal Arts Press, 1958), p. 340.

84. Walter D. Burnham, "The Coming Crisis in American Political Legitimacy," *Society* (Nov.–Dec. 1972) 10:24–31.

85. National Advisory Commission on Criminal Justice Standards and Goals, *A National Strategy,* p. 98. See also U.S. Department of Justice, Law Enforcement Assistance Administration, *Maintaining Municipal Integrity* (Washington, D.C.: University Research Corporation, 1978); and, same author, *Prevention, Detection and Correction of Corruption in Local Government* (Washington, D.C.: Government Printing Office, 1978).

86. Council of State Governments, *Ethics: State Conflict of Interest/Financial Disclosure Legislation, 1972–75* (Lexington, Ky.: Council of State Governments, 1975), pp. 15ff. (Cited hereafter as Council *Ethics.*)

87. Executive Order 11222 (May 8, 1965), sections 306 and 401.

88. Ethics in Government Act of 1978, P.L. 95-521, title V.

89. Council *Ethics,* p. 30.

90. See Senate Report 95–170, p. 30.

91. U.S. General Accounting Office, *Action Needed to Make the Executive Branch Financial Disclosure System Effective* (FPCD 77-23) (Washington, D.C.: Government Printing Office, 1977).

92. Clayton Fox, "Taking the Initiative in Washington," in Citizens' Conference on State Legislatures, *Ethics: A Special Report on Conflict of Interest Legislation. . . .* (Kansas City: Citizens' Conference on State Legislatures, 1975), p. 40.

93. M. A. Kunstel, "Alabama's Ethics Law," in Citizens' Conference on State Legislatures, p. 8.

94. See George Graham, "Ethical Guidelines for Public Administrators," *Public Administration Review* (Jan.–Feb. 1974) 34:91.

95. There is some humor (very slight, however!) in discovering an old code of ethics of the General Services Administration dated Sept. 6, 1950 (Administrative Order 49) forbidding all the corrupt things that a group of GSA employees were engaged in some twenty-five years later. The echo to "Thou shalt not" seemed to ring back, "Oh, yes we shall."

96. Coleman B. Ransone, *Ethics in Alabama State Government* (University, Ala.: Bureau of Public Administration, 1972), pp. 47–49.

97. For the Civil Service Commission regulations pertaining to the ethics counselors, see 5 CFR 735.105 (a). For the kind of guidance these agency counselors received from the home office in the CSC, see "Ethics in Action — Memorandum No. 1," issued by the commission's general counsel, Carl Goodman, on May 18, 1976.

98. Ethics in Government Act of 1978, title IV. To observe the early moves of the Office of Government Ethics in implementing the financial reporting requirements of the act, see *U.S. Civil Service Commission Bulletin* 735-3 (Dec. 28, 1978).

99. National Advisory Commission on Criminal Justice, *A National Strategy,* p. 101.

100. For a brief history on special prosecutors in the federal government, see Senate Report 95-170, pp. 2–3, or the *U.S. Code Congressional and Administrative News* (St. Paul, Minn.: West Publishing, 1978) 11A:5968–69.

101. Ethics in Government Act of 1978, sec. 601.

102. *Stars and Stripes*, July 30, 1977, p. 1.

103. Inspector General Act, P.L. 95-452, Oct. 12, 1978.

104. See the Joint Financial Management Improvement Program (JFMIP), *News Bulletin* (Jan. 1979), p. 6. The entire issue was devoted to President Carter's "war on fraud and waste."

105. Statement of Frank Prince before the 1950–1951 investigation of the RFC by the Senate Banking and Currency Committee, *Study of the Reconstruction Finance Corporation* (82d Cong., 1st, sess.) (Washington, D.C.: Government Printing Office, 1951). Or see *Facts on File* (Sept. 14–20, 1951), p. 300.

106. National Advisory Commission on Criminal Justice, *A National Strategy*, p. 100.

107. "Federal Fraud Stirs Action," *Salt Lake City Tribune* (Dec. 11, 1978), p. A-5.

108. Lieberman, *How the Government*, pp. 208–211.

109. Martin, "The Blast in Centralia No. 5," in Stillman, *Public Administration*, pp. 30–31.

110. Patrick J. Sloyan, "The Day They Shut Down Birmingham," in Stillman, *Public Administration*, pp. 52–53.

111. Source not known.

112. Carl J. Friedrich, "Public Policy and the Nature of Administrative Responsibility," *Public Policy, 1940* (Cambridge, Mass.: Harvard Graduate School of Public Administration, 1940), p. 3.

113. As a start, see Carl J. Friedrich, ed., *The Public Interest* (Nomos V) (New York: Atherton Press, 1962); Virginia Held, *The Public Interest and Individual Interests* (New York: Basic Books, 1970); and John Guinther, *Moralists and Managers: Public Interest Movements in America* (Garden City, N.Y.: Anchor Books, 1976).

114. Friedrich, *The Public Interest*, p. 190.

115. Friedrich, *The Public Interest*, p. 106.

116. A. J. Ayer, *Language, Truth and Logic* (London: Gollancz, 1950), esp. p. 108.

117. Quoted in Susan Wakefield, "Ethics and the Public Service," *Public Administration Review* (Nov.–Dec. 1976) 36:664.

118. J. J. Rousseau, *The Social Contract* (Baltimore, Md.: Penguin Books, 1975).

119. Edmund Burke, "Letter to the Bristol Constituents," (1774) in J. M. Swarthout and E. R. Bartley, *Materials on American National Government* (New York: Oxford University Press, 1952), pp. 254–255.

120. Jeremy Bentham, *A Fragment on Government and Introduction to the Principles of Morals and Legislation*.

121. Thomas Jefferson, *The Declaration of Independence;* and Carl Becker, *The Declaration of Independence* (New York: Knopf, 1942).

122. See, for example, Justice Black's opinion in *Chambers* v. *Florida*, 309 U.S. 227 (1940).

123. See, for example, Christian Bay, "The Cheerful Science of Dismal Politics," in Theodore Roszak (ed.), *The Dissenting Academy* (1968), pp. 208–229.

124. Sorauf, in Friedrich, *The Public Interest*, p. 184.

125. Sorauf, in Friedrich, *The Public Interest*, pp. 189–190.

126. *Writings of George Washington*, Fitzpatric ed. (Washington, D.C.: Government Printing Office, 1940) 34:316.

127. President John F. Kennedy to the career service, *Civil Service Journal* (Jan.–Mar. 1962) 2, no. 3:1.

128. Stephen K. Bailey, "Ethics and the Public Service," p. 235.

129. See the case study, "Decision to Use the Atomic Bomb," by Henry L. Stimson in Stillman, *Public Administration,* pp. 167–168.

130. See John F. Kennedy, *Profiles in Courage,* memorial ed. (New York: Harper and Row, 1964), pp. 59–71.

131. Carl Becker, *Declaration of Independence,* pp. 212–215.

132. Bailey, "Ethics and the Public Service," p. 238.

133. Anders Richter, "The Existentialist Executive," *Public Administration Review* (July–Aug., 1970) 30:415–422.

134. Building on the existentialist notion of personal accountability, the American Society for Public Administration published in 1979 a checklist for administrators, *Professional Standards and Ethics,* to generate "meaningful self-evaluation." In a few brief pages, the pamphlet raises many of the toughest questions ethical administrators must answer.

135. Susan Wakefield provided a highly useful compendium of ideas for instilling ethical concerns in those headed for the public service in "Ethics and the Public Service: A Case for Individual Responsibility," esp. pp. 665–666.

136. Quoted in Wakefield, "Ethics and the Public Service," from the National Academy of Public Administration, *Watergate: Implications for Responsible Government* (New York: Basic Books, 1974), pp. 12–13.

137. Quoted in Wakefield, "Ethics and the Public Service," pp. 663–664.

138. Wakefield addressed herself in a thoughtful way to the possible contributions our schools can make to the cloning of ethical administrators in "Ethics and the Public Service," pp. 665–666. See also William J. Bennett and Edwin L. Delattre, "Moral Education in the Schools," *Public Interest* (Winter, 1978), 50:81–98.

139. Wakefield, "Ethics and the Public Service," p. 663.

140. U.S. Senate Committee of Investigation of the Interior Department and Bureau of Forestry, *Hearings* (S. Doc. 179, 61st Cong. 3d sess. (Washington, D.C.: Government Printing Office, 1910) 9:4922–23.

Bibliography

ARTICLES

"Acheson Says Luck Saved JFK on Cuba," *Washington Post* (Jan. 19, 1969), pp. B1–B4.

"Admiral Cites Pressures on Military Buyers," *Washington Post* (Feb. 19, 1952), p. 2.

Argyris, Chris. "The CEO's Behavior: Key to Organizational Development," *Harvard Business Review* (Mar.–Apr. 1973) 51:55–64.

———. "Some Limits of Rational Man Organizational Theory," *Public Administration Review* (May–June 1973) 33:253–266.

———. "We Must Make Work Worthwhile," *Life* (May 5, 1967) 62:56–68.

Bailey, Stephen K. "Ethics and the Public Service," *Public Administration Review* (Dec. 1964) 24:234–243.

———. "The Excitement of the Public Service," *Civil Service Journal* (July–Sept. 1963) 4:5–9.

———. "A Structured Interaction Pattern for Harpsichord and Kazoo," *Public Administration Review* (Summer 1954) 14:202–204.

Barton, Weldon. "Administrative Reorganization by Presidential Plan, 1939–1968," *Rocky Mountain Social Science Journal* (Apr. 1970) 7:120–123.

Bavelas, Alex, and Barrett, Dermott. "An Experimental Approach to Organizational Communication," *Personnel* (Mar. 1951) 27:366–371.

Benne, Kenneth, and Sheats, P. "Functional Roles of Group Members," *Journal of Social Issues* (Spring 1948) 4:41–49.

Bennis, Warren. "Who Sank the Yellow Submarine?" *Psychology Today* (Nov. 1972) 6:112–120.

Bonafede, Dan. "President Nixon's Executive Reorganization Plans Prompt Praise and Criticism," *National Journal* (Mar. 10, 1973), pp. 329–340.

Bonjean, Charles, and Vance, Gary. "A Short Form Measure of Self-Actualization," *Journal of Applied Behavioral Science* (July–Sept. 1968) 4:299–312.

Bowers, David G., and Seashore, Stanley E. "Predicting Organizational Effectiveness With a Four-Factor Theory of Leadership," *Administrative Science Quarterly* (Sept. 1966) 11:238–263.

Brady, Rodney. "Computers in Top-level Decision-Making," *Harvard Business Review* (July–Aug. 1967) 45:67–76.

————. "MBO Goes to Work in the Public Sector," *Harvard Business Review* (Mar.–Apr. 1973) 51:65–74.

"Breaching the Chinese Wall," *New Republic* (Mar. 10, 1973) 168:7–8.

Broehl, Wayne G. "Ethics and the Executive," *Dun's Review* (May 1957) 69:45, 122–124.

Brown, Louise. "The I.R.S.: Taxation with Misrepresentation," *The Progressive* (Oct. 1973) 37:27–31.

Bucklow, Maxine. "A New Role for the Work Group," *Administrative Science Quarterly* (Mar. 1969) 14:73–84.

Bureau of National Affairs. *Government Employee Relations Report.* Washington: Bureau of National Affairs, monthly.

Burnham, Walter D. "The Coming Crisis in American Political Legitimacy," *Society* (Nov.–Dec. 1972) 10:24–31.

Caiden, G. E., and Caiden, N. J. "Administrative Corruption," *Public Administration Review* (May–June 1977) 37:301–309.

Calvin, A. D., et al. "The Effect of Intelligence and Social Atmosphere in Group Problem-Solving Behavior," *Journal of Social Psychology* (Feb. 1957) 45:61–74.

"Collaboration in Work Settings," *Journal of Applied Behavioral Science* (July–Sept. 1977) 13:261–464.

Craver, Lee G. "Survey of Job Evaluation Practices in State and County Governments," *Public Personnel Management* (Mar. 1977) 6:121–131.

Cronin, Thomas E. "The Swelling of the Presidency," *Saturday Review of the Society* (Feb. 1973) 1:30–36.

Davis, O. A., Dempter, M. A., and Wildowsky, Aaron. "A Theory of the Budgetary Process," *American Political Science Review* (Sept. 1966) 60:529–547.

Derber, Milton. "Crosscurrents in Workers' Participation," *Industrial Relations* (Feb. 1970) 9:123–136.

Detteback, W. W., and Kraft, Philip. "Organization Change Through Job Enrichment," *Training and Development Journal* (Aug. 1971) 25:2–6.

Divine, William R. "The Second Hoover Commission Reports," *Public Administration Review* (Oct. 1955) 15:263–269.

Downey, H. K., et al. "The Path-Goal Theory of Leadership: A Longitudinal Analysis," *Organizational Behavior and Human Performance* (June, 1976) 16:156–176.

Downs, C. W. "What Does the Selection Interview Accomplish?" *Personnel Administration* (Nov. 3, 1968) 31:8–14.

Drucker, Peter. "The Effective Decision," *Harvard Business Review* (Jan.–Feb. 1967) 45:92–98.

Duval, B. A., and Courtney, R. S. "Upward Mobility: The General Foods Way of Opening Employee Advancement Opportunities," *Personnel* (May 1978) 55:43–53.

Eckardt, W. V. "The Hoover Reports," *New Leader* (July 11, 1955) 38:3–6.

"Eisenhower vs. Congress," *U. S. News and World Report* (May 28, 1954) 36:105–109.

"Elite Committee Forms Economic Policy," *Congressional Quarterly* (Feb. 28, 1976), pp. 475–476.

Emery, F. E., and Trist, E. L. "The Causal Texture of Organizational Environments," *Human Relations* (Feb. 1965) 18:21–32.

Etzioni, Amitai. "Mixed Scanning: A 'Third Approach' to Decision-Making," *Public Administration Review* (Dec. 1967) 27:385–392.

"Famous Notations from History Translated into Officialese," *Army Digest* (May 1967).

Feild, H. S., and Holley, W. H. "Performance Appraisal — An Analysis of State-wide Practices," *Public Personnel Management* (May–June 1975) 4:145–150.

Fiedler, Fred. "Engineer the Job to Fit the Manager," *Harvard Business Review* (Sept.–Oct. 1965) 43:115–122.

Fisher, Louis. "The Politics of Impounded Funds," *Administrative Science Quarterly* (Sept. 1970) 15:361–377.

Ford, Guy B. "Why Doesn't Everyone Love the Personnel Man?" *Personnel* (Jan.–Feb. 1963) 40:49–52.

Franke, Richard H., and Kaul, James D. "The Hawthorne Experiments: First Statistical Interpretation," *American Sociological Review* (Oct. 1978) 43:623–643.

Frankel, Max. "Air Raid on Missile Sites Was Weighed," *New York Times* (Oct. 30, 1962), pp. 1, 3.

Gibson, F. K., and Teasley, C. E. "The Humanistic Model of Organizational Motivation: A Review of Research Support," *Public Administration Review* (Jan.–Feb. 1973) 33:89–96.

Golembiewski, Robert T. "Civil Service and Managing Work," *American Political Science Review* (Dec. 1962) 56:961–973.

———. "Specialist or Generalist: Structure as a Crucial Factor," *Public Administration Review* (June 1965) 25:135–141.

———. "Three Styles of Leadership and Their Uses," *Personnel* (July–Aug. 1961) 38:34–45.

Graham, George. "Ethical Guidelines for Public Administrators," *Public Administration Review* (Jan.–Feb. 1974) 34:90–92.

Greene, Charles. "The Satisfaction-Performance Controversy," *Business Horizons* (Oct. 1972) 15:31–41.

Greiner, Larry. "What Managers Think of Participative Leadership," *Harvard Business Review* (Mar.–Apr. 1973) 51:111–117.

Halal, William. "Toward a General Theory of Leadership," *Human Relations* (Apr. 1974) 27:401–416.

Hall, Douglas, and Nougaim, Khalil E. "An Examination of Maslow's Need Hierarchy in an Organizational Setting," *Organizational Behavior and Human Performance* (Feb. 1968) 3:12–35.

Hammond, Paul Y. "The National Security Council as a Device for Interdepartmental Coordination," *American Political Science Review* (Dec. 1960) 54:899–910.

Hemphill, J. A., and Westie, C. M. "The Measurement of Group Dimensions," *Journal of Psychology* (Apr. 1950) 29:325–342.

Henry, E. R. "What Business Can Learn from Peace Corps Selection and Training," *Personnel* (July–Aug. 1968) 42:17–25.

Hershauer, J. C., and Ruch, W. A. "Worker Productivity Model and Its Use at Lincoln Electric," *Interfaces* (May 1978) 8:80–90.

Herzberg, Frederick. "One More Time: How Do You Motivate Employees?" *Harvard Business Review* (Jan.–Feb., 1968) 46:53–62.

Hicks, John A., and Stone, J. B. "The Identification of Traits Related to Managerial Success," *Journal of Applied Psychology*, (Dec. 1962) 46:428–432.

Hinkle, C. L., and Kuehn, A. A. "Heuristic Models: Mapping the Maze for Management," *California Management Review* (Fall 1967) 10:59–68.

Hoos, Ida R. "Systems Techniques for Managing Society: A Critique," *Public Administration Review* (Mar.–Apr. 1973) 33:157–164.

Hoover, Herbert. "The Government Is Too Big," *U. S. News and World Report* (Aug. 5, 1955) 39:48–52.

"How to Move a Staff 2400 Miles by Use of PR Techniques," *Public Relations Journal* (Nov. 1968) 24:12–14.

Hyde, A. C., and Shafritz, Jay. "HRIS: Introduction to Tomorrow's System for Managing Human Resources," *Public Personnel Management* (Mar.–Apr. 1977) 6:70–77.

Ickes, Harold. "Not Guilty! Richard A. Ballinger, an American Dreyfuss," *Saturday Evening Post* (May 25, 1940) 212:9–11ff.

James, Lawrence R., and Jones, Allan P. "Organizational Structure: A Review of Structural Dimensions and Their Conceptual Relationships with Individual Attitudes and Behavior," *Organizational Behavior and Human Performance* (June 1976) 16:74–113.

"The Job Blahs: Who Wants to Work?" *Newsweek* (Mar. 26, 1973), pp. 79–89.

Jun, Jong, ed. "Management by Objectives in the Public Sector," *Public Administration Review* (Jan.–Feb. 1976) 36:1–45.

Kaplan, H. R., and Tausky, Curt. "Humanism in Organizations: A Critical Appraisal," *Public Administration Review* (Mar.–Apr. 1977) 37:171–180.

Kerr, Steven, et al. "Toward a Contingency Theory of Leadership Based Upon the Consideration and Initiating Structure Literature," *Organizational Behavior and Human Performance* (Aug. 1974) 12:68–82.

Kirschten, David. "The Coal Industry's Rude Awakening to the Realities of Regulation," *National Journal* (Feb. 3, 1979), pp. 178–182.

Kraut, Allen I. "Predicting Turnover of Employees from Measured Job Attitudes," *Organizational Behavior and Human Performance* (Apr. 1975) 13:233–243.

Kuhn, David, et al. "Does Job Performance Affect Employee Satisfaction?" *Personnel Journal* (June 1971) 50:455–459ff.

Lawler, Edward E. "How Much Money Do Executives Want?" *Transaction* (Jan.–Feb. 1967) 4:23–29.

Lear, John. "To Restore Adventure to American Democracy," *Saturday Review of Literature* (Sept. 7, 1963) 46:39–42.

Levinson, Harry. "Asinine Attitudes Toward Motivation," *Harvard Business Review* (Jan.–Feb. 1973) 51:70–76

———. "Reciprocation: The Relationship Between Man and Organization," *Administrative Science Quarterly* (March 1965) 9:370–390.

Lindblom, Charles E. "The Science of Muddling Through," *Public Administration Review* (Spring 1959) 19:79–88

Lott, A. J., and Lott, B. E. "Group Cohesiveness as Interpersonal Attraction: Consequences of Liking," *Psychological Bulletin* (Oct. 1965) 64:259–302.

McCamy, James. "Analysis of the Process of Decision-Making," *Public Administration Review* (Winter 1947) 7:41–48.

"McNamara's Human Problem," *Life* (Sept. 20, 1963) 55:4.

Mann, Dean E. "The Selection of Federal Political Executives," *American Political Science Review* (Mar. 1964) 48:81–99.

Mansfield, Harvey C. "Federal Executive Reorganization: Thirty Years of Experience," *Public Administration Review* (July–Aug. 1969) 29:332–345.

Marsh, J. J. "Personnel Employees' Perceptions of a State Merit System," *Public Personnel Management* (Mar.–Apr. 1977) 6:93–97.

Maslow, Abraham. "A Dynamic Theory of Human Motivation," *Psychological Journal* (1943) 50:370–396.

Maxey, C. C. "A Plea for the Politician," *Western Political Quarterly* (Sept. 1948) 1:272–279.

Mechanic, David. "The Power to Resist Change among Low-Ranking Personnel," *Personnel Administration* (July–Aug. 1963) 26:5–11.

Medalia, N. Z. "Authoritarianism, Leader Acceptance, and Group Cohesion," *Journal of Abnormal and Social Psychology* (Sept. 1955) 51:207–213.

Minmier, G. S., and Hermanson, R. H. "A Look at Zero-Base Budgeting — The Georgia Experience," *Atlanta Economic Review* (July–Aug. 1976) 26:5–12.

Mintzberg, Henry, et al. "The Structure of 'Unstructured' Decision Processes," *Administrative Science Quarterly* (June 1976) 21:246–275.

Mire, J. "European Workers' Participation in Management," *Monthly Labor Review* (Feb. 1973) 96:9–15.

Mirvis, P. H., and Lawler, Edward E. "Measuring the Financial Impact of Employee Attitudes," *Journal of Applied Psychology* (Feb. 1977) 62:1–8.

Morano, R. A. "Down the Performance Appraisals," *Supervisory Management* (1974) 19:18–22.

Morse, John, and Lorsch, Jay. "Beyond Theory Y," *Harvard Business Review* (May–June 1970), pp. 61–68.

Moynihan, Daniel P., and Wilson, James Q. "Patronage in New York State, 1955–1959," *American Political Science Review* (June 1964) 58:286–301.

Musgrave, Richard. "The Nature of Budgetary Balance and the Case for the Capital Budget," *American Economic Review* (June 1939) 29:260–271.

Natchez, Peter, and Bupp, Irwin. "Policy and Priority in the Budgetary Process," *American Political Science Review* (Sept. 1973) 67:951–963.

Nelson, Dalmas. "The Omnibus Appropriation Act," *Journal of Politics* (May 1953) 15:274–288.

Neustadt, Richard E. "Presidency and Legislation: The Growth of Central Clearance," *American Political Science Review* (Sept. 1954) 48:641–671.

Newland, Chester, ed. "Management by Objectives in the Federal Government," *The Bureaucrat* (1973), vol. 2, no. 4.

Oberg, Winston. "Make Performance Appraisal Relevant," *Harvard Business Review* (Jan.–Feb. 1972) 50:61–67.

Padover, Saul K. "Ickes: Memoir of a Man without Fear," *The Reporter* (Mar. 4, 1952), pp. 36–38.

Patchen, Martin. "Supervisory Methods and Group Performance Norms," *Administrative Science Quarterly* (Dec. 1962) 7:275–290.

Pelz, Donald. "Influence: A Key to Effective Leadership in the First-Line Supervisor," *Personnel* (Nov. 1952) 29:209–217.

Philips, Madison. "Developing Healthy Attitudes for Dealing With a Union," *Personnel* (Sept.–Oct. 1977) 54:68–71.

"Planning-Programming — Budgeting System Reexamined — A Symposium," *Public Administration Review* (Mar.–Apr. 1969) 29:111–202.

Powell, Reed M., and Schlachter, John L. "Participative Management, A Panacea?" *Academy of Management Journal* (June 1971) 14:165–173.

Pye, Lucian. "China and the United States: A New Phase," *Annals* (July 1972) 402:97–106.

Pyhrr, Peter A. "The Zero-Base Approach to Government Budgeting," *Public Administration Review* (Jan.–Feb. 1977) 37:1–8.

———. "Zero-Base Budgeting," *Harvard Business Review* (Nov.–Dec. 1970) 48:111–121.

Richter, Anders. "The Existentialist Executive," *Public Administration Review* (July–Aug. 1970) 30:415–422.

Rinehart, J. C., and Bernick, E. L. "Political Attitudes and Behavior Patterns of Federal Civil Servants," *Public Administration Review* (Nov.–Dec. 1975) 35:603–611.

Roche, John P. "The Founding Fathers: A Reform Caucus in Action," *American Political Science Review* (Dec. 1961) 55:799–816.

Roe, Richard. "Implementation and Evaporation: The Record of MBO," *Public Administration Review* (Jan.–Feb. 1977) 37:64–71.

Rogers, Carl K., and Roethlisberger, F. J. "Barriers and Gateways to Communication," *Harvard Business Review* (July–Aug. 1952) 30:47–52.

Rosenbloom, David, and Obuchowski, Carole. "Public Personnel Examinations and the Constitution: Emergent Trends," *Public Administration Review* (Jan.–Feb. 1977) 37:9–18.

Rowan, T. C. "Systems Analysis in Society," *Industrial Research* (Aug. 1966) 8:63–66.

Rus, Veljko. "Influence Structure in Yugoslav Enterprise," *Industrial Relations* (Feb. 1970) 9:148–160.

Saunders, George B., and Stanton, John T. "Personality as an Influencing Factor in Decision-Making," *Organizational Behavior and Human Performance* (Apr. 1976) 15:241–257.

Savas, E. S., and Ginsburg, S. G. "The Civil Service: A Meritless System," *Public Interest* (Summer 1973) 32:70–85.

Schick, Allen. "The Budget Bureau That Was," *Law and Contemporary Problems* (Summer 1970), pp. 519–539.

———. "A Death in the Bureaucracy: The Demise of Federal PPB," *Public Administration Review* (Mar.–Apr. 1973) 33:146–156.

———. "The Road to PPB: The Stages of Budget Reform," *Public Administration Review* (Dec. 1966) 26:243–268.

Schlesinger, Arthur M. "Our Presidents: A Rating by Seventy-five Historians," *N. Y. Times Magazine* (July 29, 1962), pp. 12–13ff.

Schriescheim, Chester, House, Robert, and Kerr, Steven. "Leader Initiating Structure," *Organizational Behavior and Human Performance* (Apr. 1976) 15:297–321.

Seligman, Daniel. "McNamara's Management Revolution," *Fortune* (July 1965) 72:117–120ff.

Shepard, Herbert A. "Innovation-Resisting and Innovation-Producing Organizations," *Journal of Business* (Oct. 1967) 40:470–477.

Simon, Herbert. "Applying Information Technology to Organization Design," *Public Administration Review* (May–June 1973) 33:268–278.

———. "Organizational Man: Rational or Self-Actualizing?" *Public Administration Review* (July–Aug. 1973) 33:346–353.

———. "Proverbs of Administration," *Public Administration Review* (Winter 1946) 6:58–71.

Smith, Harold. "The Budget as an Instrument of Legislative Control and Executive Management," *Public Administration Review* (Summer 1944) 4:181–188.

Somit, Albert. "Bureaucratic Realpolitik and Teaching of Administration," *Public Administration Review* (Autumn 1956) 16:292–295.

Sorauf, Frank. "The Silent Revolution in Patronage," *Public Administration Review* (Winter 1960) 20:28–34.

Spitzer, M. E., and McNamara, W. J. "Managerial Selection Study," *Personnel Psychology* (Spring 1964) 17:19–40.

Stahl, O. Glenn. "The Network of Authority," *Public Administration Review* (Winter 1958) 18:ii–iv.

Stanfield, Rochelle L. "The Best Laid Reorganization Plans Sometimes Go Astray," *National Journal* (Jan. 20, 1979) 11:84–89.

"Stonewalling Plant Democracy," *Business Week* (Mar. 28, 1977), pp. 78–82.

Straus, Michael W. "The Old Curmudgeon," *Washington Post* (Feb. 4, 1952), p. A1ff.

A Symposium: Workers Participation in Management — An International Comparison," *Industrial Relations* (Feb. 1970) 9:117–214.

Synder, E. C. "Equitable Wage and Salary Structuring," *Personnel Journal* (May 1977) 56:240–244.

Taylor, Vernon R. "You Just Can't Get Through to Whitey," *Public Personnel Review* (Oct. 1969) 30:199–204.

Thompson, Arthur A. "Employee Participation in Decision Making: The TVA Experience," *Public Personnel Review* (Apr. 1967) 28:82–88.

Thompson, James C. "Dragon under Glass: Time for a New China Policy," *Atlantic* (Oct. 1967) 220:55–61.

Thurber, James. "File and Forget," *New Yorker* (Jan. 8, 1949) 24:24–28.

Tressidder, A. J. "On Gobbledygook," *Military Review* (Apr. 1974), pp. 16–24.

Udell, John. "An Empirical Test of Hypotheses Relating to Span of Control," *Administrative Science Quarterly* (Dec. 1967) 12:420–439.

Valentine, Raymond. "The Pitfalls of Informal Organization," *Management Review* (Jan. 1968) 57:38–46.

Vogel, Donald B. "Analysis of Informal Organization Patterns," *Public Administration Review* (Sept.–Oct. 1968) 28:431–436.

Wahba, M. A., and Bridwell, L. G. "Maslow Reconsidered: A Review of Research on the Need Hierarchy Theory, *Organizational Behavior and Human Performance* (1976) 15:212–240.

Wakefield, Susan. "Ethics and the Public Service: A Case for Responsibility," *Public Administration Review* (Nov.–Dec. 1976) 36:661–666.

Waldman, Raymond J. "The Domestic Council: Innovation in Presidential Government," *Public Administration Review* (May–June 1976) 36:260–268.

Waldo, Dwight. "Organization for the Future." *Public Administration Review* (July–Aug. 1973) 33:299–335.

———. "Reflections on Public Morality," *Administration and Society* (Nov. 1974) 6:267–282.

Walker, C. R., and Guest, R. H. "The Man on the Assembly Line," *Harvard Business Review* (May–June 1952) 30:71–83.

Walton, R. E., and Dutton, J. M. "The Management of Interdepartmental Conflict: A Model and Review," *Administrative Science Quarterly* (Mar. 1969) 14:73–84.

———. "Work Innovations at Topeka: After Six Years," *Journal of Applied Behavioral Science* (July–Sept. 1977) 13:422–433.

Wanat, John. "Bases of Budgetary Incrementalism," *American Political Science Review* (Sept. 1974) 68:1221–1228.

Weaver, Charles M. "What Workers Want from Their Jobs," *Personnel* (May–June 1976) 54:48–54.

West, George. "Bureaupathology and the Failure of MBO," *Human Resource Management* (Summer 1977) 16:33–40.

"Where Being Nice to Workers Didn't Work," *Business Week* (Jan. 20, 1973), pp. 98–100ff.

Wilcox, Herbert G. "Hierarchy, Human Nature, and the Participative Panacea," *Public Administration Review* (Jan.–Feb. 1969) 29:53–64.

Wisner, Roscoe W. "The Kirkland Case — Its Implications for Personnel Selection," *Public Personnel Management* (July–Aug. 1975) 4:263–267.

Worthy, James C. "Organizational Structure and Employee Morale," *American Sociological Review* (Apr. 1950) 15:169–179.

Yourman, Julius. "Following Up on Your Terminations," *Personnel* (July–Aug. 1965) 42:51–55.

"ZBB Revisited," *The Bureaucrat* (Spring 1978), vol. 7, no. 1.

BOOKS

Acheson, Dean. *Morning and Noon.* Boston: Houghton Mifflin, 1965.

Ackoff, Russell L., and Riveti, Patrick. *A Manager's Guide to Operations Research.* New York: Wiley, 1963.

Adams, Samuel H. *Incredible Era: The Life and Times of Warren Gamaliel Harding.* Boston: Houghton Mifflin, 1939.

Adler, Bill. *The Kennedy Wit.* New York: Bantam Books, 1964.

Alexander, Herbert. *Financing Politics.* Washington: Congressional Quarterly Press, 1976.

Alexander, K. C. *Participative Management: The Indian Experience.* New Delhi, India: Shri Ram Centre, 1972.

American Assembly. *The Secretary of State.* Englewood Cliffs, N.J.: Prentice-Hall, 1960.

American Society for Public Administration, Professional Standards and Ethics Committee. *Professional Standards and Ethics: A Workbook for Public Administrators.* Washington, D.C.: American Society for Public Administration, 1979.

Anderson, James E. *Politics and the Economy.* Boston: Little, Brown, 1966.

Anthony, Robert N., and Herzlinger, Regina. *Management Control in Nonprofit Organizations.* Homewood, Ill.: Richard Irwin, 1975.

Argyris, Chris. *Integrating the Individual and the Organization.* New York: Wiley, 1964.

———. *Intervention Theory and Method.* Reading, Mass.: Addison–Wesley, 1970.

———. *Personality and Organization.* New York: Harper & Row, 1957.

———. *Understanding Organizational Behavior.* Homewood, Ill.: Dorsey, 1960.

Aristotle. *Politics.* New York: Modern Library, 1943.

Ayer, A. J. *Language, Truth and Logic.* London: Gollancz, 1950.

Bailey, Stephen K. *Congress Makes a Law.* New York: Columbia University Press, 1950.

Bailey, Thomas A. *Presidential Greatness.* New York: Appleton-Century-Crofts, 1966.

Barber, James D. *The Presidential Character.* 2nd ed. Englewood Cliffs, N.J.: Prentice-Hall, 1977.

Barnard, Chester. *Functions of the Executive.* Cambridge, Mass.: Harvard University Press, 1938.

Barnlund, Dean. *Interpersonal Communication.* Boston: Houghton Mifflin, 1968.

Barth, Alan. *The Loyalty of Free Man.* New York: Viking, 1951.

Becker, Carl. *The Declaration of Independence.* New York: Knopf, 1942.

Becker, Theodore, and Murray, Vernon D. *Government Lawlessness in America.* New York: Oxford University Press, 1971.

Bennis, Warren. *Beyond Bureaucracy.* New York: McGraw-Hill, 1973.

———. *Organization Development.* Reading, Mass.: Addison-Wesley, 1969.

Bennis, Warren, Benne, Kenneth, and Chin, Robert. *The Planning of Change.* New York: Holt, Rinehart & Winston, 1969.

Bentham, Jeramy. *A Fragment on Government and an Introduction to the Principles of Morals and Legislation.* New York: Macmillan, 1948.

Bentley, Arthur. *The Process of Government.* Chicago: University of Chicago Press, 1908.

Berne, Eric. *Games People Play.* New York: Grove, 1964.

Bernstein, Carl, and Woodward, Bob. *All the President's Men.* New York: Warner, 1975.

Bigelow, Page E. *Ethics in Government: Selected Statutes and Reports.* New York: National Municipal League, 1973.

Blake, Robert R., and Mouton, Jane. *The Mangerial Grid.* Houston, Texas: Gulf, 1964.

Blau, Peter, and Scott, Richard W. *Formal Organizations.* San Francisco: Chandler, 1962.

Bolling, Richard. *House out of Order.* New York: Dutton, 1965.

Brandeis, Louis D. *The Curse of Bigness.* O. K. Fraenkel, ed. New York: Viking, 1934.

Brinton, Crane. *Anatomy of Revolution.* New York: Vintage Books, 1956.

Brown, Vincent J. *The Control of the Public Budget.* Washington, D.C.: Public Affairs, 1949.

Brundage, Percival F. *The Bureau of the Budget.* New York: Praeger, 1970.

Burdick, Eugene, and Lederer, William J. *The Ugly American.* New York: Norton, 1958.

Burtenshaw, Claude. *"The State: Cooperation or Contest."* Ph.D. dissertation, University of Utah, 1955.

Cartwright, Dorwin C., and Zander, Alvin, eds. *Group Dynamics.* Evanston, Ill.: Row, Peterson, 1960.

Chester, Lewis, et al. *Watergate: The Full Inside Story.* New York: Ballantine Books, 1973.

Citizens Conference on State Legislatures. *Ethics: A Special Report.* Kansas City: Citizens Conference on State Legislatures, 1975.

Clark, Joseph S. *Congress: The Sapless Branch.* New York: Harper & Row, 1964.

Cleland, David, and King, William. *Systems Analysis and Project Management.* New York: McGraw-Hill, 1975

Committee for Economic Development. *Fiscal and Monetary Policy for High Employment.* New York: Committee for Economic Development, 1961.

————. *Improving Productivity in State and Local Government.* New York: Committee for Economic Development, 1976.

Common Cause. *Serving Two Masters: A Common Cause Study of Conflicts of Interest in the Executive Branch.* Washington, D.C.: Common Cause, 1976.

Conference Board. *Job Design for Motivation.* New York: Conference Board, 1971.

Congressional Quarterly. *Congress and the Nation.* Washington, D.C.: Congressional Quarterly, 1976.

Corson, John J., and Paul, R. S. *Men Near the Top.* Baltimore, Md.: Johns Hopkins University Press, 1966.

Cotter, Cornelius P., et al. *Twelve Studies of the Organization of Congress.* Washington, D.C.: American Enterprise Institute, 1966.

Council of State Governments. *Ethics: State Conflict of Interest/Financial Disclosure Legislation, 1972–75.* Lexington, Ky.: Council of State Governments, 1975.

Cronin, Thomas E. *Presidential Advisory Commissions.* New York: Harper & Row, 1969.

Cummings, L. L., and Scott, W. E. *Readings in Organizational Behavior and Human Performance.* Homewood, Ill.: Irwin, 1969.

Dalton, Melville. *Men Who Manage.* New York: McGraw-Hill, 1967.

Daniels, Roger. *Concentration Camp USA: Japanese Americans and World War II.* New York: Holt, Rinehart & Winston, 1976.

Davis, Elmer. *But We Were Born Free.* Indianapolis: Bobbs-Merrill, 1954.

Davis, James W. *Politics, Programs and Budgets.* Englewood Cliffs, N.J.: Prentice-Hall, 1969.

Davis, Keith. *Human Relations at Work.* New York: McGraw-Hill, 1962.

Davis, Louis E., Cherns, A. B., et al. *The Quality of Working Life.* 2 vols. New York: Free Press, 1975

Dawes, Charles G. *The First Year of the Budget of the United States.* New York: Harper & Row, 1923.

Day, Donald. *Franklin P. Roosevelt's Own Story.* Boston: Little, Brown, 1951.

Destler, I. M. *President, Bureaucrats and Foreign Policy: The Politics of Organizational Reform.* Princeton, N.J.: Princeton University Press, 1972.

Dewey, John. *Democracy and Education.* New York: Macmillan, 1916, 1961.

Dimock, Marshall. *The Executive in Action.* New York: Harper & Row, 1945.

Domhoff, G. William. *Fat Cats and Democrats.* Englewood Cliffs, N.J.: Prentice-Hall, 1972.

————. *The Higher Circles.* New York: Random House, 1970.

————. *Who Rules America?* Englewood Cliffs, N.J.: Prentice-Hall, 1967.

Donovan, J. J. *Recruitment and Selection in the Public Service.* Chicago: Public Personnel Association, 1968.

Downs, Anthony. *Inside Bureaucracy.* Boston: Little, Brown, 1967.

Drucker, Peter. *The Effective Executive.* New York: Harper & Row, 1967.

————. *The Practice of Management.* New York: Harper & Row, 1954.

Drury, Horace. *Scientific Management.* New York: Columbia University Press, 1915.

Dubin, Robert, et al. *Leadership and Productivity.* San Francisco: Chandler, 1965.

Dye, Thomas R. *Policy Analysis.* University, Ala.: University of Alabama Press, 1976.

Earle, C. B., and V. A. *The Promotion of Lem Merrill.* (Interuniversity case program No. 20) University, Ala.: University of Alabama Press, 1953.

Ebel, Robert, et al. *Improving Public Personnel Selection.* (Personnel Report No. 635) Chicago: Public Personnel Association, 1963.

Eccles, Marriner. *Beckoning Frontiers.* New York: Knopf, 1951.

Ecker-Racz, L. L. *The Politics and Economics of State-Local Finance.* Englewood Cliffs, N.J.: Prentice-Hall, 1970.

Engels, Friedrich. "Socialism: Utopian and Scientific," in *Essential Works of Marxism.* Edited by Arthur P. Mendel. New York: Bantam Books, 1961.

Enthoven, Alain, and Smith, K. W. *How Much Is Enough?* New York: Harper & Row, 1971.

Etzioni, Amitai, ed. *Complex Organizations.* New York: Holt, Rinehart & Winston, 1961.

Feis, Herbert. *The Atomic Bomb and the End of World War II.* Princeton, N.J.: Princeton University Press, 1966.

Fenno, Richard. *The Power of the Purse.* Boston: Little, Brown, 1966.

Ferkiss, Victor C. *Technological Man.* New York: Braziller, 1969.

Fesler, James W. *Area and Administration.* University, Ala.: University of Alabama Press, 1949.

Feuer, Lewis S. *Marx and Engels.* N.Y.: Doubleday, 1959.

Fiedler, Fred E. *A Theory of Leadership Effectiveness.* New York: McGraw-Hill, 1967.

Finer, Herman. *The Road to Reaction.* Boston: Little, Brown, 1945.

Flash, Edward S. *Economic Advice and Presidential Leadership: The Council of Economic Advisers.* New York: Columbia University Press, 1965.

Fleishman, Edwin A., Harris, Edwin F., and Burtt, H. E. *Leadership and Supervision in Industry.* Columbus, Ohio: Ohio State University Press, 1955.

Follett, Mary Parker. *Dynamic Administration.* Metcalf and Urwick, eds. New York: Harper & Row, 1942.

Ford, Robert N. *Motivation through the Work Itself.* New York: American Management Association, 1969.

Foulkes, Fred. *Creating More Meaningful Work.* New York: American Management Association, 1969.

Fried, Robert C. *Performance in American Bureaucracy.* Boston: Little, Brown, 1976.

Friedrich, Carl J., ed. *The Public Interest.* (Nomos V.) New York: Atherton, 1962.

————. *Public Policy, 1940.* Cambridge, Mass.: Harvard Graduate School of Public Administration, 1940.

Gawthrop, Louis C. *Bureaucratic Behavior in the Executive Branch.* New York: Free Press, 1969.

Gerth, Hans, and Mills, C. Wright. *From Max Weber: Essays in Sociology.* New York: Oxford University Press, 1958.

Ghiselli, Edwin E. *The Validity of Occupational Aptitude Tests.* New York: Wiley, 1966.

Golembiewski, Robert T. *Approaches to Planned Change.* 2 vols. New York: Dekker, 1979.

————. *Behavior and Organization.* Chicago: Rand McNally, 1962.

————. *Renewing Organizations.* Itasca, Ill.: Peacock, 1972.

————, and Blumberg, Arthur, eds. *Sensitivity Training and the Laboratory Approach.* Itasca, Ill.: Peacock, 1973.

Gordon, Oakley, Richardson, Reed, and Williams, J. D. *Personnel Management in Utah State Government.* Salt Lake City: University of Utah Press, 1962.

Gore, William, and Dyson, J. W., eds. *The Making of Decisions.* New York: Free Press, 1964.

Goulden, Joseph C. *The Super Lawyers.* New York: Weybright and Talley, 1972.

Gross, Bertram. *The Managing of Organizations.* 2 vols. Glencoe, Ill.: Free Press, 1964.

———. *Organizations and Their Managing.* New York: Free Press, 1968.

Gross, Martin L. *The Brain Watchers.* New York: Random House, 1962.

Gross, Neal, Mason W., and McEachern, A. *Explorations in Role Analysis.* New York: Wiley, 1958.

Guest, Robert H. *Organizational Change: The Effect of Successful Leadership.* Homewood, Ill.: Dorsey, 1962.

Guinther, John. *Moralists and Managers: Public Interest Movements in America.* Garden City, New York: Anchor Books, 1976.

Gulick, Luther H., and Urwick, Lyndall, eds. *Papers on the Science of Administration.* New York: Institute of Public Administration, 1937. Reprinted, Fairfield, N.J.: Kelley, 1979.

Hackman, J. Richard, and Suttle, J. L. *Improving Life at Work.* Santa Monica, Calif.: Goodyear, 1977.

Haire, Mason. *Modern Organization Theory.* New York: Wiley, 1959.

Halberstam, David. *The Best and the Brightest.* New York: Random House, 1972.

Harper, Alan. *The Politics of Loyalty.* Westport, Conn.: Greenwood, 1969.

Harris, Thomas A. *I'm O.K., You're O.K.* New York: Harper & Row, 1969.

Harvey, Donald R. *The Civil Service Commission.* New York: Praeger, 1970.

Harvey, Ray., ed. *The Politics of This War.* New York: Harper & Row, 1943.

Hayakawa, S. I. *Language in Thought and Action.* New York: Harcourt, Brace, 1964.

Hayman, Donald, and Stahl, O. Glenn. *Political Activity Restrictions: An Analysis with Recommendations.* (Personnel Report No. 636.) Chicago: Public Personnel Association, 1963.

Heggen, Thomas, and Logan, Joshua. *"Mr. Roberts,"* New York: Random House, 1948.

Heidenheimer, Arnold J. *Political Corruption.* New York: Holt, Rinehart & Winston, 1970.

Heilbroner, Robert, et al. *In the Name of Profit.* New York: Warner, 1973.

Held, Virginia. *The Public Interest and Individual Interests.* New York: Basic Books, 1970.

Herzberg, Frederick. *The Managerial Choice.* Homewood, Ill.: Dow, Jones, Irwin, 1976.

———. *Work and the Nature of Man.* Cleveland, Ohio: World Publishers, 1966.

Hess, Stephen. *Organizing the Presidency.* Washington, D.C.: Brookings Institution, 1976.

Hinrichs, Harley H., and Taylor, G. M. *Program Budgeting and Benefit/Cost Analysis.* Pacific Palisades, Calif.: Goodyear, 1969.

Hinton, Bernard L., and Reitz, H. J. *Groups and Organizations.* Belmont, Mass.: Wadsworth, 1971.

Hitch, Charles J., and McKean, Roland N. *The Economics of Defense in the Nuclear Age.* Cambridge, Mass.: Harvard University Press, 1960.

Hobbes, Thomas. *Leviathan.* New York: Liberal Arts Press, 1958.

Hoffmann, Banesh. *Tyranny of Testing.* New York: Crowell-Collier, 1962.

Hofstadter, Richard. *The Progressive Movement, 1900–1915.* Englewood Cliffs, N.J.: Prentice-Hall, 1963.

Howard, S. Kenneth. *Changing State Budgeting.* Lexington, Ky.: Council of State Governments, 1973.

———, and Grizzle, Gloria, eds. *What Happened to State Budgeting?* Lexington, Ky.: Council of State Governments, 1972.

Hull, Cordell. *The Memoirs of Cordell Hull.* New York: Macmillan, 1948.

Huzar, Elias. *The Purse and the Sword.* Ithaca, N.Y.: Cornell University Press, 1950.

Ickes, Harold, L. *The Secret Diary of Harold L. Ickes.* New York: Simon & Schuster, 1953.

Jun, Jong, and Storm, William B. *Tomorrow's Organizations: Challenges and Strategies.* Glenview, Ill.: Scott, Foresman, 1973.

Jungk, Robert. *Brighter Than a Thousand Suns.* New York: Harcourt, Brace, 1958.

Kant, Immanuel. *Fundamental Principles of the Metaphysic of Morals.* Indianapolis: Bobbs-Merrill, 1949.

Keller, Helen. *The Story of My Life.* New York: Doubleday, 1954.
Kennedy, John F. *Profiles in Courage.* Memorial ed. New York: Harper & Row, 1964.
Kennedy, Robert. *Thirteen Days.* New York: Norton, 1971.
Kilpatrick, Franklin P., Cummings, M. C., and Jennings, M. K. *The Image of the Federal Service.* Washington, D.C.: Brookings Institution, 1964.
Kimmel, Lewis H. *Federal Budget and Fiscal Policy.* Washington, D.C.: Brookings Institution, 1959.
Koenig, Lowis W. *The Truman Administration.* New York: New York University Press, 1956.
Kluckholn, Clyde, and Leighton, Dorothea. *The Navaho.* New York: Doubleday, 1962
Kuhn, Delia, and Ferdinand, eds. *Adventures in Public Service.* New York: Vanguard, 1963.
Lasswell, Harold D. *Power and Personality.* New York: Norton, 1948.
Latham, Earl, ed. *The Philosophy and Policies of Woodrow Wilson.* Chicago: University of Chicago Press, 1958.
Lawler, Edward E. *Motivation in Work Organizations.* Monterey, Calif.: Brooks Cole, 1973.
Lawrence, Paul R., and Lorsch, Jay W. *Developing Organizations: Diagnosis and Action.* Reading, Mass.: Addison-Wesley, 1969.
Leavitt, Harold J. *Managerial Psychology.* Chicago: University of Chicago Press, 1972.
Lerner, Daniel, and Laswell, Harold, eds. *The Policy Sciences.* Stanford, Calif.: Stanford University Press, 1951.
Levin, Richard, and Kirkpatrick, C. A. *Planning and Control with PERT/CPM.* New York: McGraw-Hill, 1966.
Levitan, Sar, and Johnston, W. B. *Work Is Here to Stay, Alas.* Salt Lake City: Olympus Research, 1973.
Lewin, Kurt. *Field Theory in Social Science.* New York: Harper, 1951.
Lieberman, Jethro K. *How the Government Breaks the Law.* Baltimore, Md.: Penguin Books, 1973.
Likert, Resis. *The Human Organization.* New York: McGraw-Hill, 1967.
———. *New Patterns of Management.* New York: McGraw-Hill, 1961.
Lincoln, James F. *Incentive Management.* Cleveland, Ohio: Lincoln Electric, 1951.
———. *Lincoln's Incentive System.* New York: McGraw-Hill, 1946.
Lindblom, Charles. *The Policy-Making Process.* Englewood Cliffs, N.J.: Prentice-Hall, 1968.
Link, Arthur. *Woodrow Wilson and the Progressive Era.* New York: Harper & Row, 1954.
Lippitt, Ronald, et al. *The Dynamics of Planned Change.* New York: Harcourt, Brace, 1958.
Lipsett, Laurence, et al. *Personnel Selection and Recruitment.* New York: Allyn & Bacon, 1964.
Lipset, Seymour M., Trow, M. A., and Coleman, J. S. *Union Democracy.* Glencoe, Ill.: Free Press, 1956.
Loeber, Thomas S. *Foreign Aid: Our Tragic Experiment.* New York: Norton, 1961.
Loewenberg, J. Joseph, and Moskow, M. H. *Collective Bargaining in Government.* Englewood Cliffs, N.J.: Prentice-Hall, 1972.
MacArthur, Douglas. *Reminiscences.* New York: McGraw-Hill, 1964.
MacFarland, Dalton E. *Cooperation and Conflict in Personnel Administration.* New York: American Foundation for Management Research, 1962.
McGregor, Douglas. *The Human Side of Enterprise.* New York: McGraw-Hill, 1960.
Machiavelli, Nicolo. *The Prince.* New York: Modern Library, 1940.
McLuhan, Marshall. *Understanding the Media: The Extensions of Man.* New York: McGraw-Hill, 1964.
Macy, John W., Jr. *Public Service: The Human Side of Government.* New York: Harper & Row, 1971.
March, James G., ed. *Handbook of Organizations.* Chicago: Rand McNally, 1965.
———, and Simon, Herbert A. *Organizations.* New York: Wiley, 1958.
Marrow, Alfred J., Bowers, David G., and Seashore, Stanley E. *Management by Participation.* New York: Harper & Row, 1967.
Marx, Fritz Morstein. *Elements of Public Administration.* Englewood Cliffs, N.J.: Prentice-Hall, 1946.

Marx, Karl. "Communist Manifesto," in Arthur P. Mendel. *Essential Works of Marxism.* New York: Bantam Books, 1961

———. "Critique of Political Economy" in *Selected Works.* Moscow: Progress Publishers, 1969.

Maslow, Abraham H. *Eupsychian Management.* Homewood, Ill.: Irwin, 1965.

———. *Motivation and Personality.* New York: Harper's Magazine Press, 1954.

———. *New Knowledge in Human Values.* New York: Harper & Row, 1959.

Mayer, J. P. *Max Weber and German Politics.* London: Faber, 1944.

Mayo, Elton. *The Human Problems of an Industrial Civilization.* New York: Viking, 1933, 1960.

Mead, George H. *Mind, Self, and Society.* Chicago: University of Chicago Press, 1934.

Merewitz, Leonard, and Sosnick, Stephen. *The Budget's New Clothes.* Chicago: Markham, 1971.

Merton, Robert K. *Social Theory and Social Structure.* Glencoe, Ill.: Free Press, 1957.

Michels, Robert. *Political Parties.* New York: Free Press, 1911, 1962.

Mill, John Stuart. *Considerations on Representative Government.* New York: Liberal Arts Press, 1958.

Miller, David, and Starr, Martin. *Executive Decisions and Operations Research.* Englewood Cliffs, N.J.: Prentice-Hall, 1969.

Millett, John D. *The Process and Organization of Government Planning.* New York: Columbia University Press, 1947.

Millikan, Max F. *Income Stabilization for a Developing Democracy.* New Haven, Conn.: Yale University Press, 1953.

Mills, C. Wright. *The Power Elite.* New York: Oxford University Press, 1956.

Mishan, E. J. *Economics for Social Decisions: Elements of Cost/Benefit Analysis.* New York: Praeger, 1973.

Mooney, Booth. *The Politicians.* Philadelphia: Lippincott, 1970.

Morrow, William L. *Public Administration: Politics and the Political System.* New York: Random House, 1975.

Mosher, Frederick C., ed. *Governmental Reorganizations.* Indianapolis: Bobbs-Merrill, 1967.

Mouzelis, Nicos P. *Organization and Bureaucracy.* Chicago: Aldine, 1973.

Mushkin, Selma, ed. *Planning, Programming, Budgeting for City, State and County Objectives.* Washington, D.C.: George Washington University Press, 1967.

Nash, Allan L., and Carroll, Stephen J. *The Management of Compensation.* Monterey, Calif.: Brooks Cole, 1975.

Nathan, Richard P. *The Plot That Failed: Nixon and the Administrative Presidency.* New York: Wiley, 1975.

National Academy of Public Administration. *Watergate: Implications for Responsible Government.* New York: Basic Books, 1974.

National Bureau of Economic Research. *Public Finances: Needs, Services and Utilization.* Princeton, N.J.: Princeton University Press, 1961.

New York Times Staff. *The Watergate Hearings.* New York: Bantam Books, 1973.

Neustadt, Richard E. *Presidential Power.* New York: Wiley, 1960.

Nourse, Edwin G. *Economics in the Public Service.* New York: Harcourt, Brace, 1953.

Novick, David. *Origin and History of Program Budgeting.* Santa Monica, Calif.: Rand Corporation, 1966.

———, ed. *Program Budgeting.* Cambridge, Mass.: Harvard University Press, 1965.

O'Connor, Edwin. *The Last Hurrah.* Boston: Little, Brown, 1956.

Odiorne, George. *Management by Objectives.* New York: Pitman, 1973.

Olmstead, Michael. *The Small Group.* New York: Random House, 1959.

Padover, Saul, ed. *Thomas Jefferson on Democracy.* New York: Mentor, 1954.

Parkinson, C. Northcote. *Parkinson's Law.* Boston: Houghton Mifflin, 1957.

Parsons, Talcott. *Sociological Theory and Modern Society.* New York: Free Press, 1967.

Peabody, Robert L. *Cases in American Politics.* New York: Praeger, 1976.

Pechman, Joseph, ed. *Setting National Priorities: The 1979 Budget.* Washington, D.C.: Brookings Institution, 1978.

Perrow, Charles. *Complex Organizations.* Glenview, Ill.: Scott, Foresman, 1972.

Plato. *Republic*. A. D. Lindsay, trans. New York: Dutton, 1950.

Polenberg, Richard. *Reorganizing Roosevelt's Government*. Cambridge, Mass.: Harvard University Press, 1966.

Popper, Karl. *The Open Society and Its Enemies*. 2 vols. New York: Harper & Row, 1962.

Porter, Lyman. *Managerial Attitudes and Performance*. Homewood, Ill.: Irwin, 1968.

Powell, Theodore. *Democracy in Action*. New York: Macmillan, 1962.

Presthus, Robert. *The Organizational Society*, rev. ed., New York: St. Martin's Press, 1978.

Probst, John B. *Measuring and Rating Employee Value*. New York: Ronald Press, 1947.

Pyhrr, Peter A. *Zero-Base Budgeting*. New York: Wiley, 1973.

Raab, Earl, ed. *American Race Relations Today*. New York: Doubleday, 1962.

Ransone, Coleman B. *Ethics in Alabama State Government*. University, Ala.: Bureau of Public Administration, 1972.

Rehfuss, John. *Public Administration as Political Process*. New York: Scribner's 1973

Reich, Charles. *The Greening of America*. New York: Random House, 1970.

Richardson, James D. *Compilation of the Messages and Papers of the Presidents*. New York: Bureau of National Literature, 1897.

Riesman, David. *The Lonely Crowd*. New Haven, Conn.: Yale University Press, 1950.

Rivlin, Alice M. *Systematic Thinking for Social Action*. Washington, D.C.: Brookings Institution, 1971.

Roberts, Ernie. *Workers' Control*. London: Allen & Unwin, 1973.

Roethlisberger, F. J. *Men-in-Organization*. Cambridge, Mass.: Harvard University Press, 1968.

———, and Dickson, W. J. *Management and the Worker*. Cambridge, Mass.: Harvard University Press, 1939.

Rohr, John. *Ethics for Bureaucrats*. New York: Dekker, 1978.

Rose-Ackerman, Susan. *Corruption: A Study in Political Economy*. New York: Academic Press, 1978.

Roszak, Theodore. *The Dissenting Academy*. New York: Pantheon Books, 1968.

Rouseau, Jean Jacques. *Social Contract*. Baltimore, Md.: Penguin Books, 1975.

Rowat, Donald C. *The Ombudsman Plan*. Toronto, Canada: McClelland & Stewart, 1973.

Rubenstein, Alvin Z., and Thumm, G. W. *The Challenge of Politics*, 3d ed. Englewood Cliffs, N.J.: Prentice-Hall, 1970.

Rubenstein, Max, ed. *Max Weber on Law in Economy and Society*. New York: Simon & Schuster, 1967.

Ruhl, Eleanor. *Public Relations for Government Employees*. Chicago: Civil Service Assembly, 1952.

Rush, Harold. *Job Design for Motivation*. New York: Conference Board, 1971.

Sandburg, Carl. *Abraham Lincoln: The Prairie Years and the War Years*. New York: Harcourt, Brace, 1954.

Sapir, Edward. *Culture, Language and Personality*. Berkeley, Calif.: University of California Press, 1956.

———. *Selected Writings*. Berkeley, Calif.: University of California Press, 1949.

du Sautoy, Peter. *The Civil Service*. London: Oxford University Press, 1957.

Sayre, Wallace S., ed. *The Federal Government Service*, 2d ed. Englewood Cliffs, N.J.: Prentice-Hall, 1965.

Schlesinger, Arthur M., Jr. *A Thousand Days*. Boston: Houghton Mifflin, 1965.

Schoderbek, Peter, and Reif, W. E. *Job Enlargement: Key to Improved Performance*. Ann Arbor, Mich.: University of Michigan Press, 1969.

Scholz, William. *Communication in the Business Organization*. Englewood Cliffs, N.J.: Prentice-Hall, 1962.

Schultze, Charles L., et al. *Setting National Priorities*. Washington, D.C.: Brookings Institution, 1972.

Scott, William G., and Mitchell, Terence R. *Organization Theory: A Structural and Behavioral Analysis*. Homewood, Ill.: Irwin, 1972.

Selznick, Philip. *Leadership in Administration*. New York: Harper & Row, 1957.

Shafritz, Jay M. *Position Classification: A Behavioral Analysis for the Public Service*. New York: Praeger, 1973.

———, et al. *Personnel Management in Government*. New York: Dekker, 1978.

————, and Hyde, Albert C., eds. *Classics of Public Administration.* Oak Park, Ill.: Moore, 1978.

Sharkansky, Ira, ed. *Policy Analysis in Political Science.* Chicago: Markham, 1970.

Sheppard, Harold L., and Herrick, N. Q. *Where Have All the Robots Gone?* New York: Free Press, 1972.

Sherwood, Robert E. *Roosevelt & Hopkins.* New York: Harper & Row, 1948.

Shibutani, Tamotsu. *Society and Personality.* Englewood Cliffs, N.J.: Prentice-Hall, 1961.

Shirer, William L. *The Rise and Fall of the Third Reich.* New York: Simon & Schuster, 1960.

Silverman, Corinne. *The President's Economic Advisers.* (Interuniversity Case Program No. 48.) University, Ala.: University of Alabama Press, 1959.

Simon, Herbert. *Administrative Behavior,* 3d ed. New York: Free Press, 1976.

————. *The New Science of Management Decision.* New York: Harper & Row, 1960.

Skinner, B. F. *Beyond Freedom and Dignity.* New York: Bantam Books, 1972.

Smith, Michael P., ed. *American Politics and Public Policy.* New York: Random House, 1973.

Solberg, Winton U., ed. *The Federal Convention and the Formation of the Union of American States.* New York: Liberal Arts Press, 1958.

Somers, Gerald, ed. *Collective Bargaining and Productivity.* Madison, Wisc.: Industrial Relations Research Association, 1975.

Sorensen, Theodore. *Decision-Making in the White House.* New York: Columbia University Press, 1963.

————. *Kennedy.* New York: Harper & Row, 1965.

Stahl, O. Glenn. *Public Personnel Administration,* 7th ed. New York: Harper and Row, 1976.

Stanley, David, Mann, Dean, and Doig, J. W. *Men Who Govern.* Washington, D.C.: Brookings Institution, 1967.

Steffens, Lincoln. *Autobiography.* New York: Harcourt, Brace, 1931.

Stein, Harold, ed. *Public Administration and Policy Development.* New York: Harcourt, Brace, 1952.

Stern, Phillip. *Oppenheimer Case.* New York: Harper & Row, 1969.

Stillman III, Richard J., ed. *Public Administration: Concepts and Cases.* Boston: Houghton Mifflin, 1976.

Struening, Elmer L., and Guttentag, Marcia. *Handbook of Evaluation Research.* Beverly Hills, Calif.: Sage, 1975.

Sutermeister, Robert A. *People and Productivity,* 2d ed. New York: McGraw-Hill, 1969.

Swarthout, J. M., and Bartley, E. R. *Materials on American National Government.* New York: Oxford University Press, 1952.

Tannenbaum, Robert, Weschler, J. R., and Massarik, Fred. *Leadership and Organization.* New York: McGraw-Hill, 1961.

Taylor, Frederick A. *Scientific Management.* New York: Harper & Row, 1911, 1947.

Terhune, George. *An Administrative Case Study of Performance Budgeting in the City of Los Angeles, California.* Chicago: Municipal Finance Officers Association, 1954.

————. *Performance Budgeting and Unit Cost Accounting for Governmental Units.* Chicago: Municipal Finance Officers Association, 1954.

Thompson, James D. *Organizations in Action.* New York: McGraw-Hill, 1967.

Thompson, Victor A. *Bureaucracy and the Modern World.* Morristown, N.J.: General Learning Press, 1976.

————. *Modern Organization.* New York: Knopf, 1961.

Toffler, Alvin. *Future Shock.* New York: Random House, 1970.

Tolchin, Martin and Susan. *To the Victor.* New York: Random House, 1971.

Tonge, Fred M. *Summary of a Heuristic Line-Balancing Procedure.* (P-1799.) Santa Monica, Calif.: Rand Corporation, 1959.

Townsend, Robert. *Up the Organization.* New York: Knopf, 1970.

Truman, Harry S. *Memoirs.* New York: Doubleday, 1955.

Tullock, Gordon. *The Politics of Democracy.* Washington, D.C.: Public Affairs Press, 1965.

Van Riper, Paul. *History of the United States Civil Service.* Evanston, Ill.: Row, Peterson, 1958.

Vaughn, Robert G. *The Spoiled System.* New York: Charterhouse, 1975.

Verba, Sidney. *Small Groups and Political Behavior.* Princeton, N.J.: Princeton University Press, 1961.

Vosloo, William. *Collective Bargaining in the U.S. Federal Civil Service.* Chicago: Public Personnel Association, 1967.

Vroom, Victor H. *Work and Motivation.* New York: Wiley, 1964.

Walker, Daniel. *Rights in Conflict.* New York: Bantam Books, 1968.

Weber, Max. *Basic Concepts in Sociology.* New York: Citadel Press, 1962.

————. *The Theory of Social and Economic Organization.* Glencoe, Ill.: Free Press, 1947.

————. *Wirtschaft and Gesellschaft.* Translated by Talcott Parsons and A. M. Henderson. New York: Oxford University Press, 1947.

Westin, Alan F. *The Uses of Power.* New York: Harcourt, Brace & World, 1962.

Wexley, K. N., and Yukl, G. A. *Organizational Behavior and Industrial Psychology.* New York: Oxford University Press, 1975.

Whisler, Thomas L. and Harper, Shirley F. *Performance Appraisal: Research and Practice.* New York: Holt, Rinehart & Winston, 1962.

White, Leonard D. *Introduction to the Study of Public Administration,* 3d ed. New York: Macmillan, 1948.

————. *The Federalists.* New York: Macmillan, 1948.

Whitehead, Clay T. *Uses and Limitations of Systems Analysis.* Santa Monica, Calif.: Rand Corporation, 1967.

Whitehead, T. N. *The Industrial Worker.* Cambridge, Mass.: Harvard University Press, 1938.

Whitman, Walt. *Democratic Vistas,* in Malcolm Cowley, ed. *The Works of Walt Whitman.* New York: Minerva Press, 1948.

Whorf, Benjamin L. *Language, Thought and Reality.* New York: Wiley, 1956.

Whyte, William F. *Men at Work.* New York: Irwin-Dorsey, 1961.

Whyte, William H. *The Organization Man.* New York: Simon & Schuster, 1957.

Wildavsky, Aaron. *The Politics of the Budgetary Process,* 3d ed. Boston: Little, Brown. 1979.

Williams, J. D. *Defeat of Home Rule in Salt Lake City.* New York: Holt, Rinehart, & Winston, 1970.

————. *Impounding of Funds by the Bureau of the Budget.* (I.C.P. case series No. 28.) University, Ala.: University of Alabama Press, 1955.

Wilson, Woodrow. *The State,* rev. ed. Boston: Heath, 1898.

Wise, David. *The Politics of Lying.* New York: Random House, 1973.

Wolanin, Thomas R. *Presidential Advisory Commissions.* Madison, Wisc.: University of Wisconsin Press, 1975.

Woll, Peter. *America Government: Readings and Cases,* 5th ed. Boston: Little, Brown, 1975.

GOVERNMENT PUBLICATIONS

Campbell, Alan K. "What's Right with Federal Employees," *Civil Service Journal* (Apr.–June 1978) 18:6–12.

"Civil Service Commission Carries Out Merit Team Recommendations," *Civil Service Journal* (Apr.–June 1976) 16:8–12.

Donaldson, William. "Tapping Municipal Employees' Creative Talents," *Civil Service Journal* (Jan.–Mar. 1971), pp. 16–17.

Gardner, John. "The Luckiest People," *Civil Service Journal* (Apr.–June 1967) 7:6–8.

Ingrassia, Anthony F. "Status Report on Federal Labor-Management Relations," *Civil Service Journal* (July–Sept. 1977) 18:38–43.

Kator, Irving. "When Federal Employees Complain," *Civil Service Journal* (Jan.–Mar. 1969) 9:16–19.

Katz, Paul A. "Standards and Tests," *Civil Service Journal* (Jan.–Mar. 1975) 15:28.

Kimsey, Ada R. "Civil Service and the Nation's Progress," *Civil Service Journal* (Jan.–Mar. 1977) 16:21–25.

Mendenhall, Janice. "Roots of the Federal Women's Program," *Civil Service Journal* (July–Sept. 1977) 18:21–24.

O'Hayre, John. *Gobbledygook Has Gotta Go.* Washington, D.C.: Government Printing Office, 1966.

O'Leary, Brian. "The Case for Written Tests in Federal Employment," *Civil Service Journal* (July–Sept. 1976) 16:29–31.

Ramsay, Arch J. "The New Factor Evaluation System of Position Classification," *Civil Service Journal* (Jan–Mar. 1976) 16:15–19.

———. "A New Look in Federal Job Applications," *Civil Service Journal* (Apr.–June 1977) 17:19–21.

———. "Toward a Modernized Federal Examining System," *Civil Service Journal* (Oct.–Dec. 1976) 17:17–20.

Taylor, Graeme M. "New Management Approach to Federal Budgeting," *Civil Service Journal* (July–Sept. 1977) 18:13–19.

Ward, W. A. "How the Government is Going on Campus," *Civil Service Journal* (July–Sept. 1978) 19:22–23.

Washington, George. *Writings of George Washington.* Fitzpatrick, ed. Washington, D.C.: Government Printing Office, 1940.

U. S. Bureau of the Budget. *Production Planning and Control in Office Operations.* Washington, D.C.: Government Printing Office, 1949.

———. *Supervisor's Guide to the Process Chart.* Washington, D.C.: Government Printing Office, 1953.

———. *The United States at War.* Washington, D.C.: Government Printing Office, 1946.

U. S. Civil Service Commission. *Basic Training Course in Position Classification* (Personnel Methods Series No. 3). Washington, D.C.: Government Printing Office, 1961.

———. *Building Better Promotion Programs* (Personnel Management Series No. 2). Washington, D.C.: Government Printing Office, 1958.

———. *Classification Principles and Policies* (Personnel Management Series No. 16). Washington, D.C.: Government Printing Office, 1963.

———. *Collective Bargaining in the Federal Sector.* Washington, D.C.: Government Printing Office, 1975.

———. *Collective Bargaining for Public Managers (State and Local).* Washington, D.C.: Government Printing Office, 1975.

———. *Equal Employment Opportunity Cases* (BIPP 152-46). Washington, D.C.: Civil Service Commission, 1976.

———. *The Factor Evaluation System of Position Classification (Introduction).* Washington, D.C.: Civil Service Commission, mimeo, 1976.

———. *The Federal Career Service at Your Service.* Washington, D.C.: Government Printing Office, 1977.

———. *Federal Recruiting, 1976–1977.* Washington, D.C.: Government Printing Office, 1977.

———. *A Guide for Executive Selection* (Personnel Methods Series No. 13). Washington, D.C.: Government Printing Office, 1961.

———. *How to Prepare and Conduct Job Element Examinations* (Technical Study 75-1 Bureau of Policies and Standards, by Ernest S. Primoff). Washington, D.C.: Government Printing Office, 1975.

———. *An Instrument for Progress.* Washington, D.C.: Government Printing Office, 1965.

———. *Merit Promotion Plans.* Washington, D.C.: Government Printing Office, 1958.

———. *The Skills Survey: What It Is and How It Works.* Washington, D.C.: Government Printing Office, 1977.

———. *The Training of Federal Employees* (Personnel Methods Series No. 7). Washington, D.C.: Government Printing Office, 1958.

———, Federal Personnel Management Project. *Final Staff Report.* Washington, D.C.: Government Printing Office, 1977.

U. S. Commission on Civil Rights. *Federal Civil Rights Enforcement Effort.* Washington, D.C.: Government Printing Office, 1971.

————. *For All the People . . . By All the People.* Washington, D.C.: Government Printing Office, 1969.

————. *Social Indicators of Equality for Minorities and Women.* Washington, D.C.: Government Printing Office, 1978.

U. S. Commission on Executive, Legislative, and Judicial Salaries (Quadrennial Commission III). *Report.* Washington, D.C.: Government Printing Office, 1976.

U. S. Commission on Organization of the Executive Branch of the Government (I Hoover Commission). *Budgeting and Accounting.* Washington, D.C.: Government Printing Office, 1949.

————. *Concluding Report.* Washington, D.C.: Government Printing Office, 1949.

————. *Personnel Management.* Washington, D.C.: Government Printing Office, 1949.

————, Natural Resources Task Force. *Organization and Policy in the Field of Natural Resources.* Washington, D.C.: Government Printing Office, 1949.

U. S. Congress
Congressional Budget Office. *Executive Compensation in the Federal Government.* (Background Paper No. 18.) Washington, D.C.: Government Printing Office, 1977.

House of Representatives
Committee on the Budget. *Hearings on Zero-Base Budget Legislation.* (94th Congress, 2d Sess.) Washington, D.C.: Government Printing Office, 1976.

Committee on Government Operations. *Reorganization by Plan and by Statute* (Committee print, 88th Congress, 1st Sess.). Washington, D.C.: Government Printing Office, 1963.

————. *Summary of the Objectives, Operations, and Results of the Commissions on Organization of the Executive Branch of the Government* (Committee print, 88th Congress, 1st sess.). Washington, D.C.: Government Printing Office, 1963.

Committee on Interstate and Foreign Commerce. *Federal Regulation and Regulatory Reform* (Subcommittee print, 94th Congress, 2d sess.). Washington, D.C.: Government Printing Office, 1976.

————. *Joint Hearings on Regulatory Reform — Quality of Regulators.* (Ser. 94–80.) Washington, D.C.: Government Printing Office, 1975.

Committee on the Judiciary. *Hearings on Congressional Review of Administrative Rulemaking* (94th Congress, 1st Sess.). Washington, D.C.: Government Printing Office, 1975.

————. *Impeachment of Richard M. Nixon, President of the United States* (House Report 93-1305, 93d Congress, 2nd Sess.). Washington, D.C.: Government Printing Office, 1974.

————. *Transcripts of Eight Recorded Presidential Conversations* (93d Congress, 2d Sess.). Washington, D.C.: Government Printing Office, 1974.

Committee on Labor. *Taylor and Other Systems of Shop Management* (House Report 63-403). Washington, D.C.: Government Printing Office, 1913.

————. *Taylor System of Shop Management* (House Report 62-52). Washington, D.C.: Government Printing Office, 1911.

Committee on Post Office and Civil Service. *Current Salary Schedule of Federal Officers and Employees, Together with a History of Salary and Retirement Annuity Adjustments* (Committee print 95-3). Washington, D.C.: Government Printing Office, 1977.

————. *Current Salary Schedules of Federal Officers and Employees* (Committee print 95-21, 95th Congress, 2d Sess.). Washington, D.C.: Government Printing Office, 1978.

————. *Final Report on Violations and Abuses of Merit Principles in Federal Government* (94th Congress, 2d Sess.). Washington, D.C.: Government Printing Office, 1976.

————. *Hearings on the Federal Wage System* (Serial 94-63, 94th Congress, 2d Sess.). Washington, D.C.: Government Printing Office, 1976.

————. *History of Civil Service Merit Systems of the U. S. and Selected Foreign Countries* (Committee print 94-29, 94th Congress, 2d Sess.). Washington, D.C.: Government Printing Office, 1976.

————. *The Merit System in the U. S. Civil Service* (by Bernard Rosen), (Committee print 94-10, 94th Congress, 1st Sess.). Washington, D.C.: Government Printing Office, 1975.

Joint Committee on the Economic Report. *Monetary Policy and the Management of the*

Public Debt (82d Congress, 2d Sess.). Washington, D.C.: Government Printing Office, 1952.

Joint Economic Committee. *The Analysis and Evaluation of Public Expenditures: The PPB System* (91st Congress, 1st Sess.). Washington, D.C.: Government Printing Office, 1969.

————. *The Federal Budget as an Economic Document* (Senate Report 88-396.). Washington, D.C.: Government Printing Office, 1963.

————. *Hearings on National Priorities and the Budgetary Process* (93d Congress, 1st Sess.). Washington, D.C.: Government Printing Office, 1974.

————. *Innovations in Planning, Programming and Budgeting in State and Local Governments* (Committee print, 91st Congress, 1st Sess.). Washington, D.C.: Government Printing Office, 1969.

Senate

Appropriations Committee. *Hearings on Budget Rescissions and Deferrals, 1975* (94th Congress, 1st Sess.). Washington, D.C.: Government Printing Office, 1975.

————. *Report to the Committee on the Budget on [Our] Views on the Budget Prepared for FY 1976.* (Committee print, March 15, 1975.) Washington, D.C.: Government Printing Office, 1975.

Committee on Banking and Currency. *Study of the Reconstruction Finance Corporation* (82d Congress, 1st Sess.). Washington, D.C.: Government Printing Office, 1951.

Committee on Banking, Housing, and Urban Affairs. *Report of the Securities and Exchange Commission on Questionable Corporate Payments* (Committee print, 94th Congress, 2d Sess.). Washington, D.C.: Government Printing Office, 1976.

Committee on the Budget. *Analysis of Executive Impoundment Reports* (Committee print, 94th Congress, 1st Sess.). Washington, D.C.: Government Printing Office, 1975.

————. *Seminars: Macroeconomic Issues and the Fiscal Year 1976 Budget* (Committee print, 94th Congress, 1st Sess.). 2 vols. Washington, D.C.: Government Printing Office, 1975.

Committee on Government Operations. *Compendium of Materials on Zero-Base Budgeting in the States* (Senate Doc. 95-52.). Washington, D.C.: Government Printing Office, 1977.

————. *Improving Congressional Control over the Budget (with a Compendium of Materials)* (93d Congress, 1st Sess.). Washington, D.C.: Government Printing Office, 1973.

Committee on the Judiciary. *Hearings on Executive Impoundment of Appropriated Funds* (92d Congress, 1st Sess.). Washington, D.C.: Government Printing Office, 1971.

Select Committee on Presidential Campaign Activities. *Hearings* 93d Congress, 2d Sess.). Washington, D.C.: Government Printing Office, 1974.

Select Committee to Study Government Operations with Respect to Intelligence Activities. *Alleged Assassination Plots Involving Foreign Labors* (94th Congress, 1st Sess.). Washington, D.C.: Government Printing Office, 1975.

————. *Covert Action in Chile, 1963–1973* (94th Congress, 1st Sess.). Washington, D.C.: Government Printing Office, 1975.

————. *Intelligence Activities and the Rights of Americans* (94th Congress, 2nd Sess.). Washington, D.C.: Government Printing Office, 1976.

U.S. Department of Health, Education and Welfare. *Motor Vehicle Injury Prevention Program.* Washington, D.C.: Government Printing Office, 1966.

————. *Work in America.* Cambridge, Mass.: MIT Press, 1973.

U.S. Department of Labor. *Register of Federal Employee Unions.* Washington, D.C.: Government Printing Office, annual.

U. S. Department of Labor, Women's Bureau. *Underutilization of Women Workers.* Washington, D.C.: Government Printing Office, 1971.

U.S. Equal Employment Opportunity Commission. *Personnel Testing and Equal Employment Opportunity.* Washington, D.C.: Government Printing Office, 1970

————. "Uniform Guidelines on Employee Selection Procedures," *Government Employee Relations Report* (Aug. 28, 1978), no. 774.

U.S. Federal Aviation Administration. *The Putt-Putt Air Force* (GA-20-84, by Patricia Strickland). Washington, D.C.: Government Printing Office, 1970.

U.S. General Accounting Office. *Action Needed to Make the Executive Financial Disclosure System Effective* (FPCD 77-23). Washington, D.C.: Government Printing Office, 1977.

———. *Federal Agencies Can, and Should Do More to Combat Fraud in Government Programs.* Washington, D.C.: Government Printing Office, 1978.

U.S. Joint Financial Management Improvement Program (G.A.O., O.M.B., and Treasury). *Annual Report, 1971.* Washington, D.C.: Government Printing Office, 1971.

———. *Fifteen Years of Progress.* Washington, D.C.: Government Printing Office, 1963.

———. "President Declares War on Fraud and Waste," *News Bulletin* (Jan. 1976), pp. 1–6.

U. S. Legislative Reference Service. *A Compilation of Basic Information on the Reorganization of the Executive Branch of the Government of the United States, 1912–1947.* Washington, D.C.: Library of Congress, 1947.

U. S. National Advisory Commission on Criminal Justice Standards and Goals. *A National Strategy to Reduce Crime.* Washington, D.C.: Government Printing Office, 1973.

U. S. National Center for Productivity and Quality of Working Life. *Guide to Productivity Improvement Projects,* 3d ed. Washington, D.C.: Government Printing Office, 1976.

U. S. Office of Management and Budget. *Budget in Brief.* Washington, D.C.: Government Printing Office, annual.

———. *Budget of the United States.* Washington, D.C.: Government Printing Office, annual.

———. *Papers Relating to the President's Departmental Reorganization Program.* Washington, D.C.: Government Printing Office, 1972.

———. *Special Analyses of the Budget.* Washington, D.C.: Government Printing Office, annual.

U. S. President. *Economic Report.* Washington, D.C.: Government Printing Office, annual.

———. *Executive Reorganization* (House Doc. 92-75.). Washington, D.C.: Government Printing Office, 1971.

———. *Submission of Recorded Presidential Conversations to the (House) Judiciary Committee* Washington, D.C.: Government Printing Office, April 30, 1974.

U. S. President, Commission on Economy and Efficiency. *The Need for a National Budget.* Washington, D.C.: Government Printing Office, 1912.

———, Commission on National Goals. *Goals for Americans.* Washington, D.C.: Government Printing Office, 1960.

———, Committee on Administrative Management. *Report with Special Studies.* Washington, D.C.: Government Printing Office, 1937.

———, Committee on Civil Rights. *To Secure These Rights.* Washington, D.C.: Government Printing Office, 1947.

———, Materials Policy Commission. *Resources for Freedom.* Washington, D.C.: Government Printing Office, 1952.

U. S. Veterans' Administration, Dept. of Medicine. *Training for Individual and Group Effectiveness and Resourcefulness: A Handbook for Trainers.* Washington, D.C.: Government Printing Office, 1977.

Index